*Human Rights in
Cross-Cultural Perspectives*

University of Pennsylvania Press
PENNSYLVANIA STUDIES IN HUMAN RIGHTS

Bert B. Lockwood, Jr., Series Editor
Professor and Director, Urban Morgan Institute for Human Rights,
University of Cincinnati College of Law

Advisory Board

Marjorie Agosin
Philip Alston
Kevin Boyle
Richard P. Claude
David Weissbrodt

Ian Guest. *Behind the Disappearances: Argentina's Dirty War Against Human Rights and the United Nations.* 1990.
Thomas B. Jabine and Richard P. Claude, editors. *Human Rights and Statistics: Getting the Record Straight.* 1991.
Abdullahi Ahmed An-Na'im, editor. *Human Rights in Cross-Cultural Perspectives: A Quest for Consensus.* 1991.

Human Rights in Cross-Cultural Perspectives

A Quest for Consensus

Edited by
Abdullahi Ahmed An-Naᶜim

University of Pennsylvania Press
Philadelphia

*Publication of this book has been aided by a grant from the College of Law,
University of Saskatchewan.*

Library of Congress Cataloging-in-Publication Data
Human rights in cross-cultural perspectives: a quest for consensus / edited by Abdullahi
    Ahmed An-Na'im.
        p.   cm. — (Pennsylvania studies in human rights)
    Includes bibliographical references and index.
    ISBN 0-8122-3104-X
    1. Human rights.   I. Na'im, 'Abd Allāh Ahmad, 1946–   .   II. Series.
K3240.6.H8767   1991
323—dc20   91-29297
                                                                        CIP

Contents

Acknowledgments   ix

Introduction
Abdullahi A. An-Na‘im   1

**Section I. General Issues of a Cross-Cultural
Approach to Human Rights**

1. Toward a Cross-Cultural Approach to Defining
International Standards of Human Rights: The Meaning
of Cruel, Inhuman, or Degrading Treatment or Punishment
Abdullahi A. An-Na‘im   19

2. Cultural Foundations for the International Protection
of Human Rights
Richard Falk   44

3. Making a Goddess of Democracy from Loose Sand:
Thoughts on Human Rights in the People's Republic
of China
William P. Alford   65

4. Dignity, Community, and Human Rights
Rhoda E. Howard   81

**Section II. Problems and Prospects of Alternative
Cultural Interpretation**

5. Postliberal Strands in Western Human Rights Theory:
Personalist-Communitarian Perspectives
Virginia A. Leary   105

6. Should Communities Have Rights? Reflections on
Liberal Individualism
Michael McDonald   133

7. A Marxian Approach to Human Rights
Richard Nordahl   162

**Section III. Regional and Indigenous Cultural
Perspectives on Human Rights**

8. North American Indian Perspectives on Human Rights
James W. Zion   191

9. Aboriginal Communities, Aboriginal Rights, and the
Human Rights System in Canada
Allan McChesney   221

10. Political Culture and Gross Human Rights Violations
in Latin America
Hugo Fruhling   253

11. Custom Is Not a Thing, It Is a Path: Reflections on the
Brazilian Indian Case
Manuela Carneiro da Cunha   276

12. Cultural Legitimacy in the Formulation and
Implementation of Human Rights Law and Policy
in Australia
Patricia Hyndman   295

13. Considering Gender: Are Human Rights for Women,
Too? An Australian Case
Diane Bell   339

14. Right to Self-Determination: A Basic Human Right
Concerning Cultural Survival. The Case of the Sami
and the Scandinavian State
Tom G. Svensson   363

**Section IV. Prospects for a Cross-Cultural Approach
to Human Rights**

15. Prospects for Research on the Cultural Legitimacy of
Human Rights: The Cases of Liberalism and Marxism
Tore Lindholm   387

Conclusion
Abdullahi A. An-Na'im   427

Bibliography   437
Contributors   463
Index   469

Acknowledgments

The conference (Human Rights in Cross-Cultural Perspectives) at which the first drafts of almost all the essays contained in this book were presented and discussed was organized under the auspices of the College of Law, University of Saskatchewan, Canada, in October 1989. I was able to organize the conference and undertake the revision and editing of these essays while holding the Ariel F. Sallows Chair in Human Rights at the College of Law. Funding for the conference was provided by the College of Law Endowment Fund, University of Saskatchewan, the Department of Justice Canada, the Social Science and Research Council of Canada, and the City of Saskatoon. We are most grateful to these sponsors for their financial support.

I am deeply grateful to the Faculty of the College of Law and Trustees of the Sallows Fund for graciously granting me the honor and privilege of holding the Sallows Chair for three years. In particular, I wish to express my profound gratitude to Dean Peter MacKinnon and Professor Ken Norman for their extraordinary support and courtesy throughout the duration of my term. Without their moral support and intellectual contribution, neither the conference nor the publication of this book would have been possible.

My deep appreciation and respect go to Marie McMunn and Deanna Hunter, who undertook all the logistical aspects of the conference with exceptional competence and courtesy, and to Ms. Hunter in particular for typing countless versions of these papers and preparing the final manuscript. I am indebted to Ms. Hunter for her professionalism and unfailing courtesy throughout the duration of my term at the College of Law.

I also wish to gratefully acknowledge the editorial assistance of my colleagues Kate Sutherland and Shelley-Anne Cooper-Stephenson. My special appreciation goes to Mary Adede, my research assistant, for her valuable, cheerful, and enthusiastic help in preparing the final manuscript.

Abdullahi Ahmed An-Naᶜim

Introduction

More than forty years after the adoption of the Universal Declaration of Human Rights in 1948, persistent and gross violations of fundamental human rights continue to occur in most parts of the world. It would therefore be appropriate to celebrate the achievements of the past four decades by reaffirming genuine global commitment to the ideal of the universality of human rights, and by seeking a deeper understanding of the underlying causes of the continuing discrepancy between the theory and practice of these rights. This endeavor should enhance the credibility of national and international human rights standards by developing more effective approaches to promoting and implementing those rights.

Both the ideal of universality and the objective of greater efficacy for international human rights practice require a dynamic process of constantly refining the concepts of recognized human rights, as well as developing new rights and mechanisms for enforcing and implementing them. This vision is hampered by the limitations of traditional international law and the cultural biases of various nations. In particular, competing cultural perspectives tend to undermine each other's priorities and, in the process, to diminish the prospects of developing truly universal standards of human rights and more effective mechanisms for achieving them.

An international conference was convened in Saskatoon, Canada, by the College of Law, University of Saskatchewan, on October 12–14, 1989, to examine these issues and concerns. Speakers were invited to reflect on the implications of global cultural diversity for the legitimacy and efficacy of international standards of human rights, and to consider, inter alia: To what extent is there cultural support and/or antagonism to human rights standards and what does that mean? How can the discrepancy between the theory and practice of these standards be understood? How can the credibility of these standards be enhanced at the national and international levels and strategies be identified to promote and implement them more effectively? The first drafts of almost all the chapters in this volume were presented and discussed at the conference (Tom Svensson participated in the conference but wrote his chapter subsequently). The authors then revised their drafts in the light of other contributions and discussions at the conference.

The authors were also invited to consider the prospects of overcoming difficulties they perceive regarding the cultural legitimacy of international standards of human rights through reinterpretation and reconstruction. This is the central idea behind what I call a cross-cultural approach to the universal cultural legitimacy of human rights, which I shall explain further. While most authors responded to this issue in one way or another, some chose to do so by presenting specific cultural perspectives. These latter chapters fit the cross-cultural theme of this book because they represent minority human rights cultural perspectives and priorities in relation to those of the majority or dominant cultures in their respective parts of the world. Not all contributors to this volume, however, accept the underlying premise of this approach. Rhoda E. Howard, for example, is skeptical about the possibility of locating transcultural foundations for human rights.

Although some chapters in this book explain and discuss the cross-cultural approach and its implications and difficulties in greater detail, I shall introduce it briefly here. The following, of course, represents my own thinking on the subject and may not necessarily reflect the views of other contributors to this volume.

Toward a Cross-Cultural Approach

Without underestimating the value of other possible approaches to the issues and concerns mentioned previously, a cross-cultural approach may be helpful in deepening our understanding of the underlying causes of the continuing discrepancy between the theory and practice of human rights, and in addressing those causes more effectively. Clearly, the credibility and practical efficacy of national and international human rights standards would be enhanced by increasing their legitimacy in the widest possible range of cultural traditions. Current and foreseeable new human rights cannot be seen as truly universal unless they are conceived and articulated within the widest possible range of cultural traditions.

The term *culture* is used here in its broadest sense as the "totality of values, institutions and forms of behavior transmitted within a society . . .

this wide conception of culture covers *Weltanschauung* [world view], ideologies and cognitive behavior." In this sense, liberalism and Marxism, for example, are part of, or ideological manifestations of, the culture of some societies. As normative propositions, human rights are much more credible and thereby stand a better chance of implementation if they are perceived to be legitimate within the various cultural traditions of the world.

Some scholars and political leaders have argued that the current international standards of human rights, together with the machinery for promoting and implementing them, may not be sufficiently universal because they lack legitimacy in major cultural traditions. Others argue that these standards and machinery are universal because the vast majority of governments have either participated in the formulation process or subsequently ratified the relevant international instruments. They also warn against the dangers of claiming cultural relativity as a pretext for justifying human rights violations. While appreciating that the first position might be adopted cynically to justify human rights violations, and that the second position might reflect undue formalism or naive idealism, I suggest that a constructive approach can draw on the element of truth in each position in order to enhance the credibility and efficacy of international human rights standards.

As will be shown in several chapters of this book, it is not realistic to deny the real or apparent insufficiency of cultural legitimacy of some human rights standards. Because there are obvious areas of conflict and tension between the current international standards of human rights and major cultural traditions, relativist arguments often seem plausible. Nevertheless, the dangers of extreme relativism should not be underestimated. My view, therefore, is that scholars and activists should neither underestimate the challenge of cultural relativism to the universality of human rights nor concede too much to its claims. Rather, it is preferable to adopt a constructive approach that recognizes the problems and addresses them in the context of each cultural tradition, as well as across cultural boundaries.

The proposed approach seeks to explore the possibilities of cultural reinterpretation and reconstruction through *internal cultural discourse and cross-cultural dialogue,* as a means to enhancing the universal legitimacy of human rights.[1] This approach does not assume that sufficient cultural support for the full range of human rights is either already present or completely lacking in any given cultural tradition. Rather, more realistically prevailing interpretations and perceptions of each cultural tradition can be expected to support some human rights while disagreeing with or even completely rejecting other existing human rights. For example, while fully supportive of civil and political rights, adherents of the Western liberal tradition may find it difficult to accept certain collective or communal rights, such as a right to development, as human rights. In contrast, the Chinese and Soviet Marxist-Leninist perspective(s) may have problems incorporating individual civil and political rights.[2] Moreover, one would expect most "traditional" cultural perspectives to disagree with the status and rights of women as formulated in international instruments.

Since cultural norms and attitudes influence individual and collective or institutional human behavior, one may reasonably expect cultural antagonism toward some human rights standards to diminish the efficacy of these standards in a particular society. Although such antagonism may reflect the prevailing or dominant view of the cultural position, it may not necessarily be the only available view. There may therefore be room for changing a cultural position from within, through *internal discourse* about the fundamental values of the culture and the rationale for these values. In view of the fact that such discourse is always taking place in relation to moral, political, and social issues, it should not be difficult to focus attention on the human rights implications of those issues. This public awareness can be achieved through intellectual and scholarly debate, artistic and literary expression of alternative views on those issues, and political and social action furthering those views. It is imperative, however, that the proponents of alternative cultural positions on human rights issues should seek to achieve a broad and effective acceptance of their interpretation of cultural norms and institutions by showing the authenticity and legitimacy of that interpretation within the framework of their own culture. Even when the very nature and substance of the culture make it unlikely for human rights advocates to achieve complete success, I believe that they can achieve significant improvements through this approach.[3]

Furthermore, since cultures are constantly changing and evolving internally, as well as through interaction with other cultures, it may be possible to influence the direction of that change and evolution from outside through *cross-cultural dialogue*. Again, in view of the fact that cross-cultural interaction and mutual influence is always occurring, it should not be difficult to introduce into it some elements of a human rights agenda. There are already human rights implications to the processes of intercultural relations, but these tend to be incidental and somewhat arbitrary. The proposed approach to the cross-cultural legitimacy of universal human rights recommends that the processes of intercultural relations should be more deliberately and effectively utilized to overcome cultural antagonism to human rights norms that are problematic in a given context. Once again, however, this process must be both mutual between cultures and sensitive to the needs of internal authenticity and legitimacy. Those of one cultural tradition who wish to induce a change in attitudes within another culture must be open to a corresponding inducement in relation to their own attitudes and must also be respectful of the integrity of the other culture. They must never even appear to be imposing external values in support of the human rights standards they seek to legitimize within the framework of the other culture.

This approach, however, does not seek to repudiate the existing international standards of human rights. On the contrary, it maintains that there are compelling reasons for accepting and working with these standards. Despite problems with the cultural legitimacy and practical efficacy of existing standards, we may never regain the ground gained by the international human rights movement thus far if these standards are repudiated today. Moreover, the processes of internal cultural discourse and cross-cultural dialogue advocated by this approach need the existing standards for at least two reasons. First, it is useful to have the framework and the specific provisions of the existing standards as a point of reference—that is to say, as something to debate and agree or disagree with or modify—in an effort to perfect the concept and better to articulate standards of *genuinely universal* human rights. Second, as Richard Falk explains and illustrates in Chapter 2, scholars and activists can derive some protection from the existing standards and machinery in their efforts to develop and implement more culturally legitimate standards within their respective societies, and in sharing their insights with others. Thus, for example, I need the framework of the existing standards in working for the cultural legitimacy of universal human rights within my own Islamic tradition. Moreover, and speaking from personal experience, I need the protection of these standards because my efforts challenge certain powerful interest groups that might wish to prevent me from expressing my views.

Nevertheless, the logic of this approach makes it possible that cross-cultural analysis might lead to revisions and/or reformulations of the existing international standards. Although I would not lightly recommend such revisions or reformulation, I must concede that the pursuit of genuine universal cultural legitimacy for human rights may lead to that conclusion if a sufficiently strong case is made for it. In other words, I propose a *process of retroactive legitimation* of the existing international human rights standards, which involves the possibility, however slight, that revisions and/or reformulations may be necessary. It is precisely my personal belief in the universality of human rights that leads me to suggest that we must seek to verify and substantiate the genuine universality of the existing standards. This exercise will not be credible, however, if we are not open to the possibility of revisions and/or reformulations should the need arise.

As I indicated earlier, these are my own views on this subject, which may not necessarily represent the views of the other contributors to this volume. In addition, my own views are tentative and open to change in light of further research and thinking on these issues. I believe in the utility of the dynamic and scholarly process that this approach will hopefully initiate, and expect the human rights movement to benefit from its outcome.

Objectives and Scope of this Book

It must first be noted that this *exploratory* book does not purport to present an ultimate thesis about the cross-cultural legitimacy of human rights, or the final resolution of real or perceived conflicts and tensions between the ideal of their universality and the reality of cultural diversity. Despite some efforts I shall mention briefly, which are more extensively considered in some of the chapters in this volume, this theme has not yet received sufficient scholarly attention to make it possible to present such a thesis or resolution at this stage. Moreover, as indicated in the last section of this book, more work needs to be done on the methodology of internal and cross-cultural analysis, as applied to human rights issues, before a credible ultimate thesis or resolution of the issues can be proposed.

Some degree of concern with cultural legitimacy and genuine universality has clearly been present from the beginning of the modern international human rights movement. For example, UNESCO has conducted various surveys and seminars on the subject. Some human rights scholars have also discussed similar questions in articles and chapters in edited volumes of essays. Most of these works, however, are not particularly helpful for establishing *universal* cultural legitimacy for human rights. Some of them tend to be apologetic and highly selective surveys of cultural traditions in support of human rights, which ignore problematic aspects of the same traditions. Others assert a militant relativistic position without addressing the implications of that position for the universality of human rights. A third group of essays tends to be critical from an exclusively liberal perspective, identifying the problems without proposing any solutions. Even efforts that seek to provide a *universal moral* justification and foundation for human rights tend to do so solely from a Western perspective.

Concern with cultural integrity is also evident in the provisions of some international human rights instruments. For example, Article 27 of the Universal Declaration of Human Rights of 1948 provides for "the right freely to participate in the cultural life of the community, to enjoy the arts and to share in scientific advancement and its benefits." The meaning and objectives of this right, however, as reiterated in Article 15 of the International Covenant on Economic, Social and Cultural Rights of 1966, appear to be based on a narrow conception of culture. A broader conception of culture is probably envisaged by the right of ethnic, religious or linguistic minorities to enjoy their own culture, and so forth, under Article 27 of the International Covenant on Civil and Political Rights of 1966. Yet, as I see it, the article is carefully worded in order to ensure the subordination of minority culture(s) to that of the majority by providing for a limited enjoyment of the former within the framework of the latter.[4] This stipulation is not surprising, because one would not expect the dominant culture (which controls the machinery of the state, and therefore its representation in international negotiations to develop these "universal" human rights) to undermine its own supremacy by granting minority culture(s) a status equal to its own.

In any case, in my view, these provisions do not purport to establish the legitimacy of human rights in the diverse cultural traditions of the world. The rights of individuals to "take part in cultural life" or of communities to "enjoy their own culture" are merely one of the individual (and possibly collective) human rights, not the foundation of, or the source of the legitimacy of, these rights. The way in which these articles reflect sensitivity to cultural integrity is probably helpful in arguing for the importance of universal cultural legitimacy for international human rights. These provisions, however, are not directly applicable to the cross-cultural approach explained earlier and discussed in several chapters in this book. This approach seeks to initiate a global process of internal discourse and cross-cultural dialogue to promote the universal legitimacy of human rights. That is to say, it approaches universal legitimacy from "the bottom up," by broadening and deepening global consensus on human rights.

Although this volume does not claim to cover all regions of the world comprehensively, a brief explanation of its geographical scope is in order. In particular, one may query whether there is too much emphasis on so-called Western perspectives in a volume purporting to deal with the universality of human rights. First, comprehensive geographical coverage is not possible in a single book if one wishes to avoid unsubstantiated sweeping generalizations and platitudes. Second, this volume contains essays on a substantial part of the world, namely, North and South America, Australia, China, and Northern Europe. It does not contain any chapter specifically on Africa because that part of the world was covered in the volume *Human Rights in Africa: Cross-Cultural Perspectives*, cited earlier. Moreover, several of the essays in the present collection present and discuss perspectives other than those of the dominant cultures in their respective parts of the world. Third, the Islamic perspective discussed in the first chapter is relevant to the Middle East and to significant parts of South and Southeast Asia. Fourth, it is proper to give so much space to Western theories, not only because of their formative impact on the human rights field, but also because liberalism and Marxism are, and will continue to be, relevant and highly influential in many parts of the world. It should be emphasized that one of the objectives of the project is to promote interaction and dialogue between Western and non-Western cultural perspectives, not to replace the former by the latter as the foundation of the universal legitimacy of human rights.

Organization and Content

The collection of essays in this book is organized into four sections. General issues and fundamental problems of the proposed approach are discussed in the chapters of Section 1. These include Howard's chapter, which challenges the underlying assumption of the approach itself, and Alford's chapter, which questions its feasibility. The chapters in Section 2 explore the prospects and problems of cultural reconstruction within the liberal and Marxist traditions. These chapters highlight the apparent antagonism of prevailing interpretations of these traditions toward some of the presently recognized human rights. They also seek reconciliation or accommodation of these rights through an alternative interpretation of the primary sources of these traditions and/or reexamination of their philosophical and moral underpinnings. In part of Chapter 15 (in Section 4),

Tore Lindholm also discusses the prospects of reconstructive efforts within both the liberal and the Marxist traditions. The case studies in Section 3 present a range of perspectives and issues raised by the cross-cultural approach in relation to certain regions and countries. Tore Lindholm's chapter and my Conclusion in the final section discuss the theoretical and practical implications of the proposed approach, and suggest topics and issues for further reflection and research in this field.

In Chapter 1, I attempt to explain the proposed cross-cultural approach, with reference to notions of relativity and universality of human rights. I also address the most serious challenge facing the proposed approach, namely, what should happen when a cultural tradition insists on maintaining a practice that others deem to be a violation of established standards of human rights? To illustrate the nature and magnitude of this challenge in a Muslim context, I raise the question whether religiously sanctioned punishments, such as amputation of the hand from the wrist for theft, constitute cruel, inhuman, and degrading treatment or punishment.

In Chapter 2, Richard Falk rejects an all-or-nothing view of the relevance of culture to human rights, be it universalist or relativist, and suggests an intermediating relevance for both international human rights (standards, procedures, and implementation) and cultural hermeneutics. While appreciating the need to mediate international human rights through the web of cultural circumstances, he argues that the latter must be tested against the norms of the former to avoid a regressive disposition toward the retention of cruel, brutal, and exploitative aspects of religious and cultural tradition. He also addresses several pertinent questions, including whether human rights discourse should take precedence over contrary cultural practices; issues of rethinking human rights, including a rethinking of culture itself and the need to implement human rights in the tendons of civil society, and international power relations.

The two remaining chapters in the first section raise reservations in different ways. In Chapter 3, William Alford appears to accept the rationale of universal cultural legitimacy for human rights in principle, but uses recent experience with the so-called pro-democracy movement and its suppression in China to illustrate the complexity and ambiguity of the situation. On the one hand, he argues that this movement may not have been as committed to universal human rights for all segments of the Chinese population and other peoples as its supporters outside China, primarily in the West, may have assumed. He seeks the guidance of the historical and intellectual context in understanding the apparent contradictions of the movement. On the other hand, he maintains that the dichotomy between the universality and cultural relativity of human rights is often overstated. Advocates of universality, he concludes, must build on and take account of Chinese circumstances, aspirations, and historical experience.

In Chapter 4, Rhoda Howard raises a more fundamental objection to the enterprise of surveying world cultures in order to establish a consensus on human rights. She argues that human rights are a modern concept, now universally applicable in principle, because of the social evolution of the entire world toward state societies. The concept of human rights, according to Howard, springs from modern human thought about the nature of justice in state societies, not from an anthropologically based consensus about the values, needs, or desires of human beings. Ideologically rights-based (liberal and/or social democratic) societies, then, hold particular conceptions of human dignity and social justice that are in principle universally applicable, although not universal in origin. She also perceives that there is potential incompatibility between human and collective rights. Since collective rights give precedence to the collectivity (nation, people, community or family), Howard argues, they are radically at odds with the idea of human (individual) rights.

Virginia Leary discusses the prospects of internal cultural reconstruction through an examination of personalist-communitarian perspectives within the liberal tradition in Chapter 5. The basic premise of her chapter is that the concept of "rights," even within the same tradition, is an evolving paradigm. She finds in the perspectives of a number of Western scholars (especially Emmanuel Mounier, Jacques Maritain, and Roberto Unger) an openness to evolution, within the Western cultural traditions, to accommodate economic, social, and group or collective rights while retaining the importance of individual rights. She highlights the shared perspectives of their scholars and examines their implications for human rights. This approach, Leary concludes, has more in common with non-Western approaches to rights and is more fully in harmony with the present international human rights instruments than are traditional liberalist interpretations.

In Chapter 6, Michael McDonald also considers, from the theoretical or normative point of view, whether communal rights are possible in the context of liberalism. He starts with a conceptualization of collective rights and liberalism, then proceeds to explore the positions liberals can take on collective rights. Collective rights, according to McDonald, can be seen as a story within a story or shared understanding within another larger or more encompassing shared understanding: the first makes disparate individuals into a group, and the second is that in which that group stands as a right-holder vis-à-vis others. Liberalism is conceptualized as centering on individuals at three levels of theses: political, justificatory, and contextual. He then scans a spectrum of liberal attitudes toward collective rights, ranging from outright hostility to all group rights, through moderate skepticism about the need for them to sympathetic though guarded endorsement of at least some group rights.

Richard Nordahl's rationale in Chapter 7 is to see what can be learned about human rights from the Marxist theoretical tradition as derived from Marx's philosophy and political and economic sociology. Nordahl argues that it makes sense, from a Marxist perspective, to try to construct an international standard of human rights which can be used to evaluate all societies. He distinguishes between this Marxist approach to human rights and some of the specific answers Marx himself comes to regarding certain questions, such as those concerning economic development. According to Nordahl, one could reject or amend some of these specific answers, for empirical or ethical reasons, and still adhere to the Marxist approach presented in this chapter. Nevertheless, although he sees them as an important part of the empirical and theoretical work needed to be done in order to develop an adequate Marxist theory of human rights, Nordahl is not concerned here with historical developments since Marx's time, including the experiences of the so-called Marxist states.

The seven chapters in Section 3 deal with aspects of the theme of this book in relation to specific countries or regions of the world. In Chapter 8, James Zion focuses on the situation of Native Americans in general, primarily in Canada and the United States. After briefly surveying some contemporary aspects of the predicaments of the original inhabitants of North America, he proceeds to argue that the formulation of human rights laws and policies that nourish, rather than destroy, Indian culture depends upon the acceptance of Indian views on the matter. He considers the implications of this argument for the concept of human rights, the social conditions of Indians and their demands. Zion maintains that despite the great cultural diversity of hundreds of Indian tribes, bands and groups, there are some common base values, which he identifies in relation to the collectivity (family, clan, group, and pan-Indianism), the individual, religion, and so on. He argues that the Anglo world must open up lines of communication and hear Indian views on their substantive human rights demands, as derived from their cultural values.

A similar but more specialized analysis is provided in Chapter 9 by Allan McChesney, who discusses the human rights situation of Aborigines in Canada. He examines the practical utility, from an aboriginal point of view, of the mechanisms established in Canada to combat discrimination and promote equal opportunity within the system, including the relevance and importance of international human rights law in this respect. This includes the implications of affirmative action policies on traditional aboriginal livelihoods, and the questions of collective and individual rights. In an effort to apply aboriginal perspectives on human rights concretely, the chapter concludes with some speculations as to the form human rights protective systems might take within self-determined, self-governed aboriginal jurisdictions associated with Canada.

In Chapter 10, Hugo Fruhling discusses the relationship between Latin American culture, and political violence and human rights in general. He deals with the impact of an authoritarian political culture and the role of the social process in producing massive violations of human rights throughout the continent. His analysis suggests to him that gross human rights violations are perhaps due more to the internal dynamics of the recurrence of episodes of political violence, leading to further violence, than to the hegemony of a particular authoritarian tradition. He notes, however, that it is good that liberal legalism and democratic values have remained a part of Latin American culture and continue to set standards of legitimacy for governments, even though their application has not been successful. Fruhling is also encouraged by certain recent developments, such as the emergence of a network of Latin American nongovernmental groups and organizations dedicated to denouncing human rights violations, and the growing positive role of the Inter-American System for the protection of human rights.

Manuela Carneiro da Cunha then examines in Chapter 11 the human rights situation of Brazilian Indians against the background of historical and current serious governmental and other encroachments that threaten the very survival of these people. After explaining the nature and magnitude of these encroachments and their rationale, she discusses Indian rights under the new Constitution of Brazil and the prospects of reconciling local culture and customary law with universal human rights standards. She perceives the fundamental issue as one of acknowledging a people's "authority" or control over the ever-changing content of their culture and customary law. According to da Cunha, this content is changing in response to a variety of factors and forces, including responses to the need to enlist the support of domestic and international public opinion. Brazilian Indian leaders, she maintains, are aware of the conflict and trying to redress it. The point is that their authority to do so must be recognized.

Chapter 12, by Patricia Hyndman, and Chapter 13, by Diane Bell, deal with Australia, the first from a broader point of view, and the second from a specific perspective. Hyndman presents an extensive treatment of the central theme of cultural legitimacy, in the formulation and implementation of human rights law and policy in Australia. She deals, first, with the issues in relation to the Anglo-Celtic English-speaking majority; second, with respect to Aboriginal-majority relations; and finally discusses the yet-tentative and embryonic attempts to deal with human rights issues relevant to communities that have immigrated to the country more recently. In the final section of her study, Hyndman introduces the wider regional perspective of the draft Pacific Charter of Human Rights. She concludes that some progress, albeit hesitant and inadequate, has been made over the last few years: some legislation resulting from Australia's ratification of international human rights instruments, the adoption of a federal policy of multiculturalism; public commitment to the need for real reconciliation between Aboriginal people and the dominant community, and so on.

In contrast, Diane Bell is more critical of the Australian human rights record from a feminist anthropological point of view, with special reference to the plight of indigenous peoples. To her, much of the literature dealing with human rights focuses on the texts, rather than the contexts. It thereby fails to offer a systematic analysis of the power relations in which the law, and attempts to use it to restructure relations within society, are embedded. She argues, for example, that in the Aboriginal struggle for a measure of self-determination, the rights of Aboriginal women have been submerged. Bell also confronts the implications of diverse and often contradictory notions of what it is to be human, and what it is to enjoy rights in the heterogeneous Australian society; she raises issues of gender, on the one hand, and of culture, race, the state, and law and power, on the other. In her view, the promulgation of international instruments is a necessary but insufficient step in the attainment of human rights. Law cannot restructure relations between the state and the individual because it is not applied in a cultural vacuum.

Finally, in this third section, Tom Svensson demonstrates the close connection between self-determination and cultural survival for the Sami of Scandinavia, especially in Norway and Sweden, in Chapter 14. His primary purpose in this chapter is to explore the ethnopolitical goal of cultural survival, with some reference to human rights issues as such. He deals with the concept of human rights in cultural terms, presenting Sami perspectives on self-determination, political and cultural autonomy, and land concerns, and examining in detail their strategic use of human rights standards in domestic litigation.

The two chapters in Section 4 are concerned with the future prospects of the cultural legitimacy of human rights. In Chapter 15, Tore Lindholm presents an extensive examination of programmatic and methodological issues, in order to develop a set of conceptual and methodological proposals in relation to the notion of cultural legitimacy and conception of human rights. Here Lindholm argues for a definite conception of human rights against which, he proposes, cultural items as well as further developments and elaborations of the existing system may be tested. In the third section of the chapter he explores in detail the possibilities of the reconstructive approach to the legitimacy of human rights in liberalism and Marxism. Lindholm's purpose is to set the framework and agenda for empirical studies of political systems and processes in order to supplement the conceptual study of doctrines along the lines he suggests.

In my short, somewhat personal Conclusion, I attempt to clarify my own position on the subject and to emphasize the need for further research and examination of the concrete empirical dimension of the rationale of universal cultural legitimacy for human rights. As in the case of the substantive views I expressed earlier in this Introduction, the reflections and remarks I offer in Chapter 16 are my own and do not necessarily represent the position of any of the contributors to this book. Both sets of views, however, naturally are open to change or modification in light of further research and thinking on the subject.

This volume seeks to advance the case for the universal legitimacy of human rights by addressing some of the difficulties facing cross-cultural analysis and by examining some of its specific implications. To the extent that the search for universal legitimacy of human rights through cross-cultural analysis and reinterpretation is accepted as a useful approach to enhancing the credibility and efficacy of international standards, the remaining challenge is to develop the appropriate methodology for identifying and pursuing the goals indicated. This and other outstanding issues will be addressed in the Conclusion. It is hoped that this project will succeed in persuading human rights scholars and activists to take cultural differences seriously, appreciating the potential utility of cross-cultural analysis and dialogue, and providing viable proposals for research and action within the various cultural traditions of the world.

Notes

1. *See* Abdullahi Ahmed An-Naᶜim, "Problems of Universal Cultural Legitimacy for Human Rights," in *Human Rights in Africa: Cross-Cultural Perspectives,* ed. A. An-Naᶜim and F. Deng. (Washington, D.C.: Brookings Institution, 1990), 331–67.

2. This statement may appear to be somewhat dated in view of the recent liberal trends in Eastern Europe and the Soviet Union. It is too early to say whether these trends will last, however; if they do it is still too soon to know how they will find ideological expression, whether through modifying Marxist-Leninist theory or totally rejecting it.

3. For example, feminists may not succeed in repudiating patriarchy altogether, but they can at least modify its negative impact on the status and rights of women in a particular society through internal discourse.

4. The full text of this article reads as follows: "In those States in which ethnic, religious or linguistic minorities exist, persons belonging to such minorities shall not be denied the right, in community with the other members of their group, to enjoy their own culture, to profess and practise their own religion, or to use their own language." G.A. res. 2200 A(XXI), 21 U.N. GAOP Supp. (No. 16) at 52. U.N. Doc. A/6316 (1966), 999 U.N.T.S. 171, entered into force March 23, 1976. For the full text of this covenant, *see Basic Documents on Human Rights,* ed. Ian Brownlie, 2nd ed. (Oxford: Clarendon Press, 1981), 128.

Section I

General Issues of a
Cross-Cultural Approach
to Human Rights

Abdullahi Ahmed An-Naʿim [1]

1. Toward a Cross-Cultural Approach to Defining International Standards of Human Rights

The Meaning of Cruel, Inhuman, or Degrading Treatment or Punishment

An intelligent strategy to protect and promote human rights must address the underlying causes of violations of these rights. These violations are caused by a wide and complex variety of factors and forces, including economic conditions, structural social factors, and political expediency. For the most part, however, human rights violations are due to human action or inaction—they occur because individual persons act or fail to act in certain ways. They can be the overlapping and interacting, intended or unintended, consequences of action. People may be driven by selfish motives of greed for wealth and power, or by a misguided perception of the public good. Even when motivated by selfish ends, human rights violators normally seek to rationalize their behavior as consistent with, or conducive to, some morally sanctioned purpose. Although their bid to gain or maintain public support may be purely cynical, such an attempt is unlikely unless they have reason to believe that their claim of moral sanction is plausible to their constituency.

It is not possible in this limited space to discuss the multitude of factors and forces that contribute to the underlying causes of human rights violations in general. I maintain that the lack or insufficiency of cultural legitimacy of human rights standards is one of the main underlying causes of violations of those standards. In this chapter, I argue that internal and cross-cultural legitimacy for human rights standards needs to be developed, while I advance some tentative ideas to implement this approach. The focus of my supporting examples will be the right not to be subjected to cruel, inhuman, or degrading treatment or punishment. Insiders may perceive certain types of punishment, for example, as dictated or at least sanctioned by the norms of a particular cultural tradition, whereas to outsiders to that culture, such measures constitute cruel, inhuman, or degrading treatment. Which position should be taken as setting the standards for this human right? How can the cooperation of the proponents of the counter-position be secured in implementing the chosen standards?

My thesis does not assume that all individuals or groups within a society hold identical views on the meaning and implications of cultural values and norms, or that they would therefore share the same evaluation of the legitimacy of human rights standards. On the contrary, I assume and rely on the fact that there are either actual or potential differences in perceptions and interpretations of cultural values and norms. Dominant groups or classes within a society normally maintain perceptions and interpretations of cultural values and norms that are supportive of their own interests, proclaiming them to be the only valid view of that culture. Dominated groups or classes may hold, or at least be open to, different perceptions and interpretations that are helpful to their struggle to achieve justice for themselves. This, however, is an *internal* struggle for control over the cultural sources and symbols of power within that society. Even though outsiders may sympathize with and wish to support the dominated and oppressed groups or classes, their claiming to know what is the valid view of the culture of that society will not accomplish this effectively. Such a claim would not help the groups the outsiders wish to support because it portrays them as agents of an alien culture, thereby frustrating their efforts to attain legitimacy for their view of the values and norms of their society.

Cross-Cultural Perspectives on Human Rights

The general thesis of my approach is that, since people are more likely to observe normative propositions if they believe them to be sanctioned by their own cultural traditions, observance of human rights standards can be improved through the enhancement of the cultural legitimacy of those standards.[2] The claim that all the existing human rights standards already enjoy universal cultural legitimacy may be weak from a historical point of view in the sense that many cultural traditions in the world have had little say in the formulation of those standards. Nevertheless, I believe not only that universal cultural legitimacy is necessary, but also that it is possible to develop it retrospectively in relation to fundamental human rights through enlightened interpretations of cultural norms.

Given the extreme cultural diversity of the world community, it can be argued that human rights should be founded on the existing least common denominator among these cultural traditions. On the other hand, restricting international human rights to those accepted by prevailing perceptions of the values and norms of the major cultural traditions of the world would not only limit these rights and reduce their scope, but also exclude extremely vital rights. Therefore, expanding the area and quality of agreement among the cultural traditions of the world may be necessary to provide the foundation for the widest possible range and scope of human rights. I believe that this can be accomplished through the proposed approach to universal cultural legitimacy of human rights.

The cultural legitimacy thesis accepts the existing international standards while seeking to enhance their cultural legitimacy within the major traditions of the world through internal dialogue and struggle to establish enlightened perceptions and interpretations of cultural values and norms. Having achieved an adequate level of legitimacy *within* each tradition, through this internal stage, human rights scholars and advocates should work for *cross-cultural* legitimacy, so that peoples of diverse cultural traditions can agree on the meaning, scope, and methods of implementing these rights. Instead of being content with the existing least common denominator, I propose to broaden and deepen universal consensus on the formulation and implementation of human rights through internal reinterpretation of, and cross-cultural dialogue about, the meaning and implications of basic human values and norms.

This approach is based on the belief that, despite their apparent peculiarities and diversity, human beings and societies share certain fundamental interests, concerns, qualities, traits, and values that can be identified and articulated as the framework for a common "culture" of universal human rights. It would be premature in this exploratory essay to attempt to identify and articulate these interests, concerns, and so on, with certainty. Major theoretical and methodological issues must first be discussed and resolved so that the common culture of universal human rights may be founded on solid conceptual and empirical grounds. At this stage, I am concerned with making the case for internal and cross-cultural discourse on the subject, raising some of the questions and difficulties that must be faced and generally describing the process that should be undertaken. Neither concrete results nor guarantees of success can be offered here, only a promising approach to resolving a real and serious issue.

Concern with the implications of cultural diversity has been present since the earliest stages of the modern international human rights movement. In 1947, UNESCO carried out an inquiry into the theoretical problems raised by the Universal Declaration of Human Rights. This was accomplished by inviting the views of various thinkers and writers from member states,[3] and organizing subsequent conferences and seminars on this theme. Other organizations have also taken the initiative in drawing attention to the dangers of ethnocentricity and the need for sensitivity to cultural diversity in the drafting of international human rights instruments.[4] Individual authors, too, have addressed these concerns.

My approach draws upon these earlier efforts and supplements them with insights from non-Western perspectives. Some Western writers have highlighted conflicts between international human rights standards and certain non-Western cultural traditions, without suggesting ways of reconciling them.[5] Despite their claims or wishes to present a cross-cultural approach, other Western writers have tended to confine their analysis to Western perspectives. For example, one author emphasizes the challenge of cultural diversity, saying that it would "be useful to try to rethink the normative foundations of human rights and consider which rights have the strongest normative support."[6] Yet, the philosophical perspectives he actually covers in his discussion are exclusively Western. Another author calls for taking cultural diversity seriously, yet presents arguments based exclusively on Western philosophy and political theory.[7]

Alison Renteln is one of the few human rights scholars sensitive to issues of cultural legitimacy. She suggests a cross-cultural understanding that will shed light on a common core of acceptable rights.[8] Her approach seems to be content with the existing least common denominator, however, a standard I find inadequate to assure sufficient human rights throughout the world. In my view, a constructive element is needed to broaden and deepen cross-cultural consensus on a "common core of human rights." I believe that this can be accomplished through the internal discourse and cross-cultural dialogue advocated here.

CULTURAL RELATIVITY AND HUMAN RIGHTS
Culture is defined in a variety of ways in different contexts.[9] A wide array of definitions is available in the social sciences.[10] In this chapter, culture is

taken in its widest meaning—that of the "totality of values, institutions and forms of behavior transmitted within a society, as well as the material goods produced by man [and woman] . . . this wide concept of culture covers *Weltanschauung* [world view], ideologies and cognitive behavior."[11] It can also be defined as "an historically transmitted pattern of meanings in symbols, a system of inherited conceptions expressed in symbolic form by means of which men [and women] communicate, perpetuate and develop their knowledge and attitudes towards life."[12]

Culture is therefore the source of the individual and communal world view: it provides both the individual and the community with the values and interests to be pursued in life, as well as the legitimate means for pursuing them. It stipulates the norms and values that contribute to people's perception of their self-interest and the goals and methods of individual and collective struggles for power within a society and between societies. As such, culture is a primary force in the socialization of individuals and a major determinant of the consciousness and experience of the community. The impact of culture on human behavior is often underestimated precisely because it is so powerful and deeply embedded in our self-identity and consciousness.

Our culture is so much a part of our personality that we normally take for granted that our behavior patterns and relationships to other persons and to society become the ideal norm. The subtlety of the impact of culture on personality and character may be explained by the analogy of the eye: we tend to take the world to be what our eyes convey to us without "seeing" the eye and appreciating its role.[13] In this case, the information conveyed by the eye is filtered and interpreted by the mind without the individual's conscious awareness of this fact. Culture influences, first, the way we see the world and, further, how we interpret and react to the information we receive.

This analogy may also explain our ethnocentricity, the tendency to regard one's own race or social group as the model of human experience. Ethnocentricity does not mean there is no conflict and tension between a person and his or her own culture, or between various classes and groups within a society. It rather incorporates such conflict and tension in the ideal model, leading us to perceive the conflict and tension we have within our own culture as part of the norm. For example, some feminists in one cultural tradition may assume that women in other cultures have (or ought to have) the same conflicts and tensions with their societies and are seeking (or ought to seek) the same answers.

A degree of ethnocentricity is unavoidable, indeed indispensable. It is the basis of our acceptance of the validity of the norms and institutions of our culture, an acceptance that ultimately is a matter of material and psychological survival.[14] Even the most radical "dissidents" rely on their culture for survival. In fact, their dissent itself is meaningful to them only as the antithesis of existing cultural norms and institutions. Rigid ethnocentricity, however, breeds intolerance and hostility to societies and persons that do not conform to our models and expectations. Whether operating as initial justification or as subsequent rationalization, the tendency to dehumanize "different" societies and persons underlies much of the exploitation and oppression of one society by another, or of other classes within a society by one class of persons in the same society.

The appreciation of our own ethnocentricity should lead us to respect the ethnocentricity of others. Enlightened ethnocentricity would therefore concede the right of others to be "different," whether as members of another society or as individuals within the same society. This perspective would uphold the equal human value and dignity of members of other societies and of dissidents within society. In sociological terms, this orientation is commonly known as cultural relativism, that is to say, the acknowledgment of equal validity of diverse patterns of life.[15] It stresses "the dignity inherent in every body of custom, and . . . the need for tolerance of conventions though they may differ from one's own."[16]

Cultural relativism has been charged with neutralizing moral judgment and thereby impairing action against injustice.[17] According to one author, "[It] has these objectionable consequences: namely, that by limiting critical assessment of human works it disarms us, dehumanises us, leaves us unable to enter into communicative interaction; that is to say, unable to criticize cross-culturally, cross-sub-culturally; intimately, relativism leaves no room for criticism at all . . . behind relativism nihilism looms."[18] Some writers on human rights are suspicious of a cultural relativism that denies to individuals the moral right to make comparisons and to insist on universal standards of right and wrong.[19]

As John Ladd notes, however, relativism is identified with nihilism because it is defined by its opponents in absolute terms.[20] I tend to agree with Clifford Geertz that the relativism/antirelativism discourse in anthropology should be seen as an exchange of warnings rather than as an analytical debate. Whereas the relativists maintain that "the world being so full of a number of things, rushing to judgment is more than a mistake, it's a crime," the antirelativists are concerned "that if something isn't anchored everywhere nothing can be anchored anywhere."[21] I also agree with Geertz's conclusion:

> The objection to anti-relativism is not that it rejects an it's-all-how-you-look-at-it approach to knowledge or a when-in-Rome approach to morality, but that it imagines that they [these approaches] can only be defeated by placing morality beyond culture and knowledge beyond both. This . . . is no longer possible. If we wanted home truths, we should have stayed at home.[22]

In my view, the merits of a reasonable degree of cultural relativism are obvious, especially when compared to claims of universalism that are in fact based on the claimant's rigid and exclusive ethnocentricity. The charge that it may breed tolerance of injustice is a serious one, however. Melville J. Herskovits, one of the main proponents of cultural relativism, has sought to answer this charge by distinguishing between absolutes and universals:

> To say that there is no absolute [not admitted to have variations] criterion of value or morals . . . does not mean that such criteria, in differing *forms*, do not comprise universals [least common denominators to be extracted from the range of variations] in human culture. Morality is a universal, and so is enjoyment of beauty, and some standard of truth. The many forms these concepts take are but products of the particular historical experience of the societies that manifest them. In each, criteria are subject to continuous questioning, continuous change. But the basic conceptions remain, to channel thought and direct conduct, to give purpose to living.[23]

Although this statement is true, it does not fully answer the charge. Morality may be universal in the sense that all cultures have it, but that does not in any way indicate the *content* of that morality, or provide criteria for judgment or for action by members of that culture or other cultures. The least common denominator of the universality of morality must include some of its basic precepts and not be confined to the mere existence of some form of morality. Moreover, in accordance with the logic of cultural relativism, the shared moral values must be authentic and not imposed from the outside. As indicated earlier, the existing least common denominator may not be enough to accommodate certain vital human rights. This fact would suggest the need to broaden and deepen common values to support these human rights. This process, however, must be culturally legitimate with reference to the norms and mechanisms of change within a particular culture.

Another author has sought to respond to the charge that cultural relativism impairs moral judgment and action by saying that, although it is appropriate to distinguish between criticism corresponding to standards internal to the culture and that corresponding to external ones, the theory of cultural relativism does not block either.[24] This observation holds true of a reasonable degree of cultural relativism but not of its extreme form.[25] Moreover, we should not only distinguish between criticism corresponding to standards internal to a culture and that corresponding to external ones, but also stress that the former is likely to be more effective than the latter.

I would emphasize that, in this age of self-determination, sensitivity to cultural relativity is vital for the international protection and promotion of human rights. This point does not preclude cross-cultural moral judgment and action, but it prescribes the best ways of formulating and expressing judgment and of undertaking action. As Geertz states, morality and knowledge cannot be placed beyond culture. In intercultural relations, morality and knowledge cannot be the exclusive product of some cultures but not of others. The validity of cross-cultural moral judgment increases with the degree of universality of the values upon which it is based; further, the efficacy of action increases with the degree of the actor's sensitivity to the internal logic and frame of reference of other cultures.

Cultural Universality and Human Rights

Although human rights require action within each country for their implementation, the present international human rights regime has been conceived and is intended to operate within the framework of international relations. The implications of culture for international relations have long been recognized. For example, as Edmund Burke has said:

> In the intercourse between two nations, we are apt to rely too much on the instrumental part. We lay too much weight on the formality of treaties and compacts. . . . Men [and women] are not tied to one another by paper and seals. They are led to associate by resemblances, by conformities, by sympathies. It is with nations as with individuals. Nothing is so strong a tie of amity between nation and nation as correspondence in laws, customs, manners and habits of life. They are obligations written in the heart. They approximate men [and women] to one another without their knowledge and sometimes against their intentions. The secret, unseen, but irrefragable bond of habitual intercourse holds them together even when their perverse and litigious nature sets them to equivocate, scuffle, and fight about the terms of their written obligations.[26]

This bonding through similarities does not mean, in my view, that international peace and cooperation are not possible without total global cultural unity. It does mean that they are more easily achieved if there is a certain minimum cultural consensus on goals and methods. As applied to cooperation in the protection and promotion of human rights, this view means that developing cross-cultural consensus in support of treaties and compacts is desirable. Cultural diversity, however, is unavoidable as the product of significant past and present economic, social, and environmental differences. It is also desirable as the expression of the right to self-determination and as the manifestation of distinctive self-identity. Nevertheless, I believe that a sufficient degree of cultural consensus regarding the goals and methods of cooperation in the protection and promotion of human rights can be achieved through internal cultural discourse and cross-cultural dialogue. Internal discourse relates to the struggle to establish enlightened perceptions and interpretations of cultural values and norms. Cross-cultural dialogue should be aimed at broadening and deepening international (or rather intercultural) consensus. This direction may include support for the proponents of enlightened perceptions and interpretations within a culture. This effort, however, must be sensitive to the internal nature of the struggle, endeavoring to emphasize internal values and norms rather than external ones.

One of the apparent paradoxes of culture is the way it combines stability with dynamic continuous change.[27] Change is induced by internal adjustments as well as external influences. Both types of change, however, must be justified through culturally approved mechanisms and adapted to preexisting norms and institutions. Otherwise, the culture would lose the coherence and stability that are vital for its socializing and other functions.

Another feature of the dynamism of culture is that it normally offers its members a range of options or is willing to accommodate varying individual responses to its norms. As Herskovits observes, "culture is flexible and holds many possibilities of choice within its framework . . . to recognize the values held by a given people in no wise implies that these values are a constant factor in the lives of succeeding generations of the same group."[28] Nevertheless, the degree of flexibility permitted by a culture, and the possibilities of choice it offers its members, are controlled by the culture's internal criteria of legitimacy.

A third and more significant feature of cultural dynamism is the ambivalence of cultural norms and their susceptibility to different interpretations. In the normal course of events, powerful individuals and groups tend to monopolize the interpretation of cultural norms and manipulate them to their own advantage. Given the extreme importance of cultural legitimacy, it is vital for disadvantaged individuals and groups to challenge this monopoly and manipulation. They should use internal cultural discourse to offer alternative interpretations in support of their own interests. This internal discourse can utilize intellectual, artistic, and scholarly work as well as various available forms of political action.

Internal cultural discourse should also support cross-cultural dialogue and set its terms of reference. It should encourage good will, mutual respect, and equality with other cultural traditions. This positive relationship can be fostered, for example, by enlisting the support of what I would call the principle of reciprocity, that is to say, the rule that one should treat others in the same way that he or she would like to be treated. Although this is a universal rule, most traditions tend to restrict its applications to "others" from the same or selected traditions rather than all human beings and societies. Internal discourse should propagate a broader and more enlightened interpretation of the principle of reciprocity to include all human beings.

It is vital for cross-cultural dialogue that internal cultural discourse along these lines be undertaken simultaneously in all cultural traditions. As a matter of principle, it should be admitted that every cultural tradition has problems with some human rights and needs to enhance the internal cultural legitimacy of those rights. From a tactical point of view, undertaking internal cultural discourse in relation to the problems one tradition has with certain human rights is necessary for encouraging other traditions to undertake similar discourse in relation to the problematic aspects of their own culture.

The object of internal discourse and cross-cultural dialogue is to agree on a body of beliefs to guide action in support of human rights in spite of disagreement on the justification of those beliefs. Jacques Maritain, a French philosopher, explained this idea more than forty years ago:

> To understand this, it is only necessary to make the appropriate distinction between the rational justifications involved in the spiritual dynamism of philosophic doctrine or religious faith [that is to say, in culture], and the practical conclusions which, although justified in different ways by different persons, are principles of action with a common ground of similarity for everyone. I am quite certain that my way of justifying belief in the rights of man and the ideal of liberty, equality and fraternity is the only way with a

firm foundation in truth. This does not prevent me from being in agreement on these practical convictions with people who are certain that their way of justifying them, entirely different from mine or opposed to mine, in its theoretical dynamism, is equally the only way founded upon truth.[29]

Total agreement on the interpretation and application of those practical conclusions may not be possible, however, because disagreement about their justification will probably be reflected in the way they are interpreted and applied. We should therefore be realistic in our expectations and pursue the maximum possible degree of agreement at whatever level it can be achieved. This approach can be illustrated by the following case study of the meaning of the human right "not to be subjected to cruel, inhuman or degrading treatment or punishment."

Cruel, Inhuman, or Degrading Treatment or Punishment

Some international human rights instruments stipulate that "no one shall be subjected to torture or to cruel, inhuman or degrading treatment or punishment."[30] There is obvious overlap between the two main parts of this right, that is to say, between protection against torture and protection against inhuman or degrading treatment or punishment. For example, torture has been described as constituting "an aggravated and deliberate form of cruel, inhuman or degrading treatment or punishment."[31] Nevertheless, there are differences between the two parts of the right. According to the definition of torture adopted in United Nations instruments, it "does not include pain or suffering arising only from, inherent in or incidental to lawful sanctions."[32] As explained below, this qualification is not supposed to apply to the second part of the right. In other words, lawful sanctions can constitute "cruel, inhuman or degrading treatment or punishment."

The following discussion will focus on the meaning of the second part of the right, that is to say, the meaning of the right not to be subjected to cruel, inhuman or degrading treatment or punishment. In particular, I will address the question of how to identify the criteria by which lawful sanctions can be held to violate the prohibition of cruel, inhuman or degrading treatment or punishment. The case of the Islamic punishments will be used to illustrate the application of the cross-cultural perspective to this question.

The Meaning of the Clause in United Nations Sources

Cruel or inhuman treatment or punishment is prohibited by regional instruments, such as the European Convention for the Protection of Human Rights and Fundamental Freedoms, as well as under the international system of the United Nations. While regional jurisprudence is applicable in the regional context, and may be persuasive in some other parts of the world, it may not be useful in all parts of the world. For example, the jurisprudence developed by the European Commission and Court of Human Rights under Article 3 of the European Convention would be directly applicable in defining this clause from a European point of view, and may be persuasive in North America. It may not be useful, however, when discussing non-Western perspectives on cruel, inhuman, or degrading treatment or punishment. The following survey will therefore focus on U.N. sources because they are at least supposed to reflect international perspectives.

The early history of what is now Article 7 of the Covenant on Civil and Political Rights indicates that drafters and delegates were particularly concerned with preventing the recurrence of atrocities such as those committed in concentration camps during World War II.[33] Thus, the Commission on Human Rights proposed in 1952 that the Article should read: "No one shall be subjected to torture or to cruel, inhuman or degrading treatment or punishment. In particular, no one shall be subjected without his free consent to medical or scientific experimentation involving risk, where such is not required by his state of physical or mental health."[34] At the 13th Session of the Third Committee in 1958, however, most discussion centered on the second sentence. Some delegates felt that the sentence was unnecessary and also weakened the Article in that it directed attention to only one of the many forms of cruel, inhuman, or degrading treatment, thereby lessening the importance of the general prohibition laid down in the first sentence. Others insisted on retaining the second sentence as complementing the first sentence rather than being superfluous.[35] Although several suggestions were made to meet the objection that the second part of the Article was emphasized at the expense of the first, the second sentence was retained and eventually adopted, as amended, by the General Assembly.[36]

Whether because of preoccupation with this issue or due to the belief that the first sentence of the Article was self-explanatory, there is little guidance from the history of the Article on the meaning of "cruel, inhuman or degrading treatment or punishment." It was generally agreed early in the drafting process that the word "treatment" was broader in scope than the word "punishment." It was also observed that the word "treatment" should not apply to degrading situations that might be due to general economic and social factors.[37] In 1952, the Philippines suggested before the Third Committee that the word "unusual" should be inserted between the words "inhuman" and "or degrading." Some delegates supported the addition of the word "unusual" because it might apply to certain actual practices that, although not intentionally cruel, inhuman, or degrading, nevertheless affected the physical or moral integrity of the human person. Others opposed the term "unusual" as being vague: what was "unusual" in one country, it was said, might not be so in other countries. The proposal was withdrawn.[38]

It is remarkable that the criticism of vagueness should be seen as applying to the word "unusual" and not as applying to the words "cruel, inhuman or degrading." Surely, what may be seen as "cruel, inhuman or degrading" in one culture may not be seen in the same light in another culture. Do other U.N. sources provide guidance on the meaning of this clause and criteria for resolving possible conflicts between one culture and another regarding what is "cruel, inhuman or degrading treatment or punishment?"

A commentary on Article 5 of the U.N. Code of Conduct for Law Enforcement Officials of 1979 states: "The term 'cruel, inhuman or degrading treatment or punishment' has not been defined by the General Assembly, but it should be interpreted so as to extend the widest possible protection against abuses, whether physical or mental."[39] Decisions of the Human Rights Committee under the Optional Protocol provide examples of treatment or punishment held to be in violation of Article 7 of the covenant by an official organ of the U.N.[40] Although these examples may be useful in indicating the sort of treatment or punishment that is likely to be held in violation of this human right, they do not provide an authoritative criteria of general application.[41]

When the Human Rights Committee attempted to provide some general criteria, the result was both controversial and not particularly helpful. For example, the committee said of the scope of the protection against cruel, inhuman, or degrading treatment or punishment:

[It] goes far beyond torture as normally understood. It may not be necessary to make sharp distinctions between various forms of treatment and punishment. These distinctions depend on the kind, purpose and severity of the particular treatment . . . the prohibition must extend to corporal punishment, including excessive chastisement as an educational and disciplinary measure.[42]

This statement is not particularly helpful in determining whether a certain treatment or punishment is cruel, inhuman, or degrading; and the example it cites is controversial. In the majority of human societies today, corporal punishment is not regarded as necessarily cruel, inhuman, or degrading. It may be even more debatable whether this characterization applies to what might be considered by some as excessive chastisement but which is routinely used for educational and disciplinary purposes in many parts of the world. This example clearly shows the dangers and difficulty of providing generally accepted criteria for defining the concept. Nevertheless, such criteria are necessary to implement this human right. Would a cross-cultural approach be helpful in this regard?

Again, this discussion focuses on the question of how lawful sanctions can be held to violate the prohibition of cruel, inhuman, or degrading treatment or punishment. It is important to address this question because such sanctions have been excluded from the definition of torture under Article 1 of the Convention Against Torture and Other Cruel, Inhuman or Degrading Treatment or Punishment of 1984. Does this give the state a free hand to enforce whatever treatment or punishment it deems fit, so long as it is enacted as the lawful sanction for any conduct the state chooses to penalize? Does the international community have the right to object to any lawful sanction as amounting to cruel, inhuman, or degrading treatment or punishment?

Article 16 of the 1984 Convention provides for the obligation to prevent "other acts of cruel, inhuman or degrading treatment or punishment which do not amount to torture." Unlike Article 1, however, which defines torture in detail, Article 16 neither defines the clause "cruel, inhuman or degrading treatment or punishment," nor excludes pain or suffering arising only from, inherent in, or incidental to lawful sanctions. This phrasing means that States Parties to the Convention may not enforce lawful sanctions which constitute cruel, inhuman, or degrading treatment or punishment. But this obligation cannot be implemented or enforced in accordance with provisions of the Convention unless there is agreement on the definition of this clause.

Cross-Cultural Perspectives on the Concept

Some predominantly Muslim countries, such as Afghanistan and Egypt, have already ratified the 1984 Convention; others may wish to do so in the future. The meaning of cruel, inhuman, or degrading treatment or punishment in Islamic cultures, however, may be significantly, if not radically, different from perceptions of the meaning of this clause in other parts of the world.

Islamic law, commonly know as Shariᶜa, is based on the Qurᵓan, which Muslims believe to be the literal and final word of God, and on Sunna, or traditions of the Prophet Muhammad. Using these sources, as well as pre-Islamic customary practices of the Middle East which were not explicitly repudiated by Qurᵓan and Sunna, Muslim jurists developed Shariᶜa as a comprehensive ethical and legal system between the seventh and ninth centuries A.D. To Muslim communities, however, the Qurᵓan and Sunna were always believed to be absolutely binding as a matter of faith and were applied in individual and communal practice from the very beginning. Shariᶜa codes were never formally enacted, but the jurists systematized and rationalized what was already accepted as the will of God, and developed techniques for interpreting divine sources and for supplementing their provisions where they were silent.[43]

Due to the religious nature of Shariᶜa, Muslim jurists did not distinguish among devotional, ethical, social, and legal aspects of the law, let alone among various types of legal norms. The equivalent of penal or criminal law would therefore have to be extracted from a wide range of primary sources. For the purposes of this discussion, Islamic criminal law may be briefly explained as follows.[44] Criminal offenses are classified into three main categories: *hudud, jinayat,* and *taᶜzir. Hudud* are a very limited group of offenses which are strictly defined and punished by the express terms of the Qurᵓan and/or Sunna. These include *sariqa,* or theft, which is punishable by the amputation of the right hand, and *zina,* or fornication, which is punishable by whipping of one hundred lashes for an unmarried offender and stoning to death for a married offender. *Jinayat* are homicide and causing bodily harm, which are punishable by *qisas,* or exact retribution (an eye for an eye) or payment of monetary compensation. The term *taᶜzir* means to reform and rectify. *Taᶜzir* offenses are those created and punished by the ruler in exercising his power to protect private and public interests.

It is important to emphasize that the following discussion addresses this question in a purely theoretical sense and should not be taken to condone the application of these punishments by any government in the Muslim world today. The question being raised is: Are Muslims likely to accept the repudiation of these punishments *as a matter of Islamic law* on the ground that they are cruel, inhuman, or degrading? This question should not be confused with the very important but distinct issue of whether these punishments have been or are being applied legitimately and in accordance with all the general and specific requirements of Islamic law.

Islamic law requires the state to fulfill its obligation to secure social and economic justice and to ensure decent standards of living for all its citizens *before* it can enforce these punishments. The law also provides for very narrow definitions of these offenses, makes an extensive range of defenses against the charge available to the accused person, and requires strict standards of proof. Moreover, Islamic law demands total fairness and equality in law enforcement. In my view, the prerequisite conditions for the enforcement of these punishments are extremely difficult to satisfy in practice and are certainly unlikely to materialize in any Muslim country in the foreseeable future. Nevertheless, the question remains, can these punishments be abolished as a matter of Islamic law?

Shari'a criminal law has been displaced by secular criminal law in most Muslim countries. Countries like Saudi Arabia, however, have always maintained Shari'a as their official criminal law. Other countries, such as Iran, Pakistan, and the Sudan, have recently reintroduced Shari'a criminal law. There is much controversy over many aspects of the criminal law of Shari'a that raise human rights concerns, including issues of religious discrimination in the application of Shari'a criminal law to non-Muslims.[45] To the vast majority of Muslims, however, Shari'a criminal law is binding and should be enforced today. Muslim political leaders and scholars may debate whether general social, economic, and political conditions are appropriate for the immediate application of Shari'a, or whether there should be a preparatory stage before the reintroduction of Shari'a where it has been displaced by secular law. None of them would dispute, at least openly and publicly, that the application of Shari'a criminal law should be a high priority, if not an immediate reality.

Although these are important matters, they should not be confused with what is being discussed here. For the sake of argument, the issue should be isolated from other possible sources of controversy. In particular, I wish to emphasize that I believe that the Qur'anic punishments should *not* apply to non-Muslims because they are essentially religious in nature. In the following discussion, I will use the example of amputation of the right hand for theft when committed by a Muslim who does not need to steal in order to survive, and who has been properly tried and convicted by a competent court of law. This punishment is prescribed by the clear and definite text of verse 38 in chapter 5 of the Qur'an. Can this punishment, when imposed under these circumstances, be condemned as cruel, inhuman, or degrading?

The basic question here is one of interpretation and application of a universally accepted human right. In terms of the principle Maritain suggests—agreement on "practical conclusions" in spite of disagreement on their justification—Muslims would accept the human right not to be subjected to cruel, inhuman, or degrading treatment or punishment. Their Islamic culture may indicate to them a different interpretation of this human right, however.

From a secular or humanist point of view, inflicting such a severe permanent punishment for any offense, especially for theft, is obviously cruel and inhuman, and probably also degrading. This may well be the private intuitive reaction of many educated modernized Muslims. However, to the vast majority of Muslims, the matter is settled by the categorical will of God as expressed in the Qur'an and, as such, is not open to question by human beings. Even the educated modernized Muslim, who may be privately repelled by this punishment, cannot risk the consequences of openly questioning the will of God. In addition to the danger of losing his or her faith and the probability of severe social chastisement, a Muslim who disputes the binding authority of the Qur'an is liable to the death penalty for apostasy (heresy) under Shari'a.

Thus, in all Muslim societies, the possibility of human judgment regarding the appropriateness or cruelty of a punishment decreed by God is simply out of the question. Furthermore, this belief is supported by what Muslims accept as rational arguments.[46] From the religious point of view, human life does not end at death, but extends beyond that to the next life. In fact, religious sources strongly emphasize that the next life is the true and ultimate reality, to which this life is merely a prelude. In the next *eternal* life, every human being will stand judgment and suffer the consequences of his or her actions in this life. A religiously sanctioned punishment, however, will absolve an offender from punishment in the next life because God does not punish twice for the same offense. Accordingly, a thief who suffers the religiously sanctioned punishment of amputation of the right hand in this life will not be liable to the much harsher punishment in the next life. To people who hold this belief, however severe the Qur'anic punishment may appear to be, it is in fact extremely lenient and merciful in comparison to what the offender will suffer in the next life should the religious punishment not be enforced in this life.

Other arguments are advanced about the benefits of this punishment to both the individual offender and society. It is said that this seemingly harsh punishment is in fact necessary to reform and rehabilitate the thief, as well as to safeguard the interests of other persons and of society at large, by deterring other potential offenders.[47] The ultimately *religious* rationale of these arguments must always be emphasized, however. The punishment is believed to achieve these individual and social benefits because God said so. To the vast majority of Muslims, scientific research is welcome to confirm the empirical validity of these arguments, but it cannot be accepted as a basis for repudiating them, thereby challenging the appropriateness of the punishment. Moreover, the religious frame of reference is also integral to evaluating empirical data. Reform of the offender is not confined to his or her experience in this life, but includes the next life, too.

Neither internal Islamic reinterpretation nor cross-cultural dialogue is likely to lead to the total abolition of this punishment as a matter of Islamic law. Much can be done, however, to restrict its implementation in practice. For example, there is room for developing stronger general social and economic prerequisites and stricter procedural requirements for the enforcement of the punishment. Islamic religious texts emphasize extreme caution in inflicting any criminal punishment. The Prophet said that if there is any doubt (*shubha*), the Qurʾanic punishments should not be imposed. He also said that it is better to err on the side of refraining from imposing the punishment than to err on the side of imposing it in a doubtful case. Although these directives have already been incorporated into definitions of the offenses and the applicable rules of evidence and procedure, it is still possible to develop a broader concept of *shubha* to include, for example, psychological disorders as a defense against criminal responsibility. For instance, kleptomania may be taken as *shubha* barring punishment for theft. Economic need may also be a defense against a charge of theft.

Cross-cultural dialogue may also be helpful in this regard. In the Jewish tradition, for instance, jurists have sought to restrict the practical application of equally harsh punishment by stipulating strict procedural and other requirements.[48] This theoretical Jewish jurisprudence may be useful to Muslim jurists and leaders seeking to restrict the practical application of Qurʾanic punishments. It is difficult to assess its practical viability and impact, however, because it has not been applied for nearly two thousand years. Moreover, the current atmosphere of mutual Jewish-Muslim antagonism and mistrust does not make cross-cultural dialogue likely between these two traditions. Still, this has not always been the case in the past and need not be so in the future. In fact, the jurisprudence of each tradition has borrowed heavily from the other in the past and may do so in the future once the present conflict is resolved.

I believe that in the final analysis, the interpretation and practical application of the protection against cruel, inhuman, or degrading treatment or punishment in the context of a particular society should be determined by the moral standards of that society. I also believe that there are many legitimate ways of influencing and informing the moral standards of a society. To dictate to a society is both unacceptable as a matter of principle and unlikely to succeed in practice. Cross-cultural dialogue and mutual influence, however, is acceptable in principle and continuously occurring in practice. To harness the power of cultural legitimacy in support of human rights, we need to develop techniques for internal cultural discourse and cross-cultural dialogue, and to work toward establishing general conditions conducive to constructive discourse and dialogue.

It should be recalled that this approach assumes and relies on the existence of internal struggle for cultural power within society. Certain dominant classes or groups would normally hold the cultural advantage and proclaim their view of the culture as valid, while others would challenge this view, or at least wish to be able to do so. In relation to Islamic punishments, questions about the legitimate application of these punishments—whether the state has fulfilled its obligations first and is acting in accordance with the general and specific conditions referred to earlier—are matters for internal struggle. This internal struggle cannot and should not be settled by outsiders; but they may support one side or the other, provided they do so with sufficient sensitivity and due consideration for the legitimacy of the objectives and methods of the struggle within the framework of the particular culture.

Conclusion: Toward a Cross-Cultural Approach

I have deliberately chosen the question of whether lawful sanctions can be condemned as cruel, inhuman, or degrading punishment or treatment in order to illustrate both the need for a cross-cultural approach to defining human rights standards and the difficulty of implementing this approach. The question presents human rights advocates with a serious dilemma. On the one hand, it is necessary to safeguard the personal integrity and human dignity of the individual against excessive or harsh punishments. The fundamental objective of the modern human rights movement is to protect citizens from the brutality and excesses of their own governments. On the other hand, it is extremely important to be sensitive to the dangers of cultural imperialism, whether it is a product of colonialism, a tool of international economic exploitation and political subjugation, or simply a product of extreme ethnocentricity. Since we would not accept others' imposing their moral standards on us, we should not impose our own moral standards on them. In any case, external imposition is normally counterproductive and unlikely to succeed in changing the practice in question. External imposition is not the only option available to human rights advocates, however. Greater consensus on international standards for the protection of the individual against cruel, inhuman, or degrading treatment or punishment can be achieved through internal cultural discourse and cross-cultural dialogue.

It is unrealistic to expect this approach to achieve total agreement on the interpretation and application of standards, whether of treatment or punishment or any other human right. This expectation presupposes the existence of the interpretation to be agreed upon. If one reflects on the interpretation she or he would like to make the norm, it will probably be the one set by the person's culture. Further reflection on how one would feel about the interpretation set by another culture should illustrate the untenability of this position. For example, a North American may think that a short term of imprisonment is the appropriate punishment for theft, and wish that to be the universal punishment for this offense. A Muslim, on the other hand, may feel that the amputation of the hand is appropriate under certain conditions and after satisfying strict safeguards. It would be instructive for the North American to consider how she or he would feel if the Muslim punishment were made the norm. Most Western human rights advocates are likely to have a lingering feeling that there is simply no comparison between these two punishments because the Islamic punishment is "obviously" cruel and inhuman and should never compete with imprisonment as a possible punishment for this offense. A Muslim might respond by saying that this feeling is a product of Western ethnocentricity. I am not suggesting that we should make the Islamic or any other particular punishment the universal norm. I merely wish to point out that agreeing on a universal standard may not be as simple as we may think or wish it to be.

In accordance with the proposed approach, the standard itself should be the product of internal discourse and cross-cultural dialogue. Moreover, genuine total agreement requires equal commitment to internal discourse and equally effective participation in cross-cultural dialogue by the adherents or members of different cultural traditions of the world. In view of significant social and political differences and disparities in levels of economic development, some cultural traditions are unlikely to engage in internal discourse as much as other cultural traditions and are unable to participate in cross-cultural dialogue as effectively as others. These processes require a certain degree of political liberty, stability, and social maturity, as well as technological capabilities that are lacking in some parts of the world.

The cross-cultural approach, however, is not an all-or-nothing proposition. While total agreement on the standard and mechanisms for its implementation is unrealistic in some cases, significant agreement can be achieved and ought to be pursued as much as possible. For example, in relation to cruel, inhuman, or degrading treatment or punishment, there is room for agreement on a wide range of substantive and procedural matters even in relation to an apparently inflexible position, such as the Islamic position on Qurʾanic punishments. Provided such agreement is sought with sufficient sensitivity, the general status of human rights will be improved, and wider agreement can be achieved in relation to other human rights. We must be clear, however, on what can be achieved and how to achieve it in any given case. An appreciation of the impossibility of the total abolition of the Qurʾanic punishment for theft is necessary for restricting its practice in Muslim societies as well as for establishing common standards, for instance, in relation to punishments that are, from the Islamic point of view, the product of human legislation.

Notes

1. I am grateful to Prof. Wanda Wiegers and Dr. Tore Lindholm for their helpful comments and suggestions on an earlier draft of this chapter. I am also grateful to Shelley-Anne Cooper-Stephenson for editorial assistance with the final draft.

2. *See generally* Abdullahi Ahmed An-Naʿim, "Problems and Prospects of Universal Cultural Legitimacy for Human Rights," in *Human Rights in Africa: Cross-Cultural Perspectives,* ed. A. An-Naʿim and F. Deng (Washington, D.C.: Brookings Institution, 1990), 331–67.

3. For the results of this questionnaire *see* UNESCO, *Human Rights: Comments and Interpretations* (London: Allan Wingate, 1949), Appendix I.

4. *See, for example,* Executive Board of the American Anthropological Association, "Statement on Human Rights," *American Anthropologist* 49 (1947): 539.

5. *See, for example,* Jack Donnelly, "Human Rights and Human Dignity: An Analytic Critique of Non-Western Conceptions of Human Rights," *American Political Science Review* 76 (1982): 303; Rhoda Howard and Jack Donnelly, "Human Dignity, Human Rights and Political Regimes," *American Political Science Review* 80 (1986): 801.

6. James W. Nickel, "Cultural Diversity and Human Rights," in *International Human Rights: Contemporary Issues,* ed. Jack L. Nelson and Vera M. Green (Stanfordville, N.Y.: Human Rights Publishing Group, 1980), 43.

7. A.J.M. Milne, *Human Rights and Human Diversity: An Essay in the Philosophy of Human Rights* (Albany, N.Y.: State University of New York Press, 1986).

8. Alison D. Renteln, "The Unanswered Challenge of Relativism and the Consequences for Human Rights," *Human Rights Quarterly* 7 (1985): 514–40; and "A Cross-Cultural Approach to Validating International Human Rights: The Case of Retribution Tied to Proportionality," in *Human Rights Theory and Measurements,* ed. D. L. Cingranelli (Basingstoke, Hampshire, and London: Macmillan, 1988), 7. *See generally* her recent book, *International Human Rights: Universalism Versus Relativism* (Newbury Park, Calif., London, and New Delhi: Sage Publications, 1990).

9. *See, for example,* T. S. Eliot, *Notes Toward the Definition of Culture* (London: Faber and Faber, 1948); Raymond Williams, *Keywords: A Vocabulary of Culture and Society* (New York: Oxford University Press, 1976), 76–82.

10. *See generally, for example,* A. L. Kroeber and C. Kluckhohn, eds., *Culture: A Critical Review of Concepts and Definitions* (New York: Vintage Books, 1963).

11. Roy Preiswerk, "The Place of Intercultural Relations in the Study of International Relations," *The Year Book of World Affairs* 32 (1978): 251.

12. Clifford Geertz, *Interpretation of Culture* (New York: Basic Books, 1973), 89.

13. I am grateful to Tore Lindholm for suggesting this useful analogy.

14. Melville J. Herskovits, *Cultural Dynamics* (New York: Knopf, 1964), 54.

15. *See generally,* Ruth Benedict, *Patterns of Culture* (Boston: Houghton Mifflin, 1959) and Herskovits, *Cultural Dynamics,* chap. 4.

16. Melville Herskovits, *Man and His Works* (New York: Knopf, 1950), 76.

17. Elvin Hatch, *Culture and Morality: The Relativity of Values in Anthropology* (New York: Columbia University Press, 1983), 12.

18. I. C. Jarvie, "Rationalism and Relativism," *British Journal of Sociology* 34 (1983): 46.

19. Rhoda E. Howard and Jack Donnelly, "Introduction," in *International Handbook of Human Rights,* ed. R.E. Howard and J. Donnelly (Westport, Conn. Greenwood Press, 1988), 20.

20. John Ladd, "The Poverty of Absolutism," *Acta Philosophica Fennica* (Helsinki) 34 (1982): 158, 161.

21. Clifford Geertz, "Distinguished Lecture: Anti Anti-Relativism," *American Anthropologist* 86 (1984): 265.

22. *Ibid.* at 276.

23. Herskovits, *supra* note 14, at 62.

24. Alison D. Renteln, "Relativism and the Search for Human Rights," *American Anthropologist* 90 (1988): 64.

25. I find Jack Donnelly's classification of radical relativism and universalism as extreme positions in a continuum, with varying mixes of (strong or weak) relativism and universalism in between, useful in this connection. While a radical (extreme) relativist would hold that culture is the sole source of validity of a moral right or rule, a radical universalist would hold that culture is irrelevant to the validity of moral rights or rules that are universally valid. *See* his article "Cultural Relativism and Universal Human Rights," *Human Rights Quarterly* 6 (1984): 400–401. He argues that "weak" cultural relativism is acceptable and even necessary for the implementation of human rights.

For a critique of Donnelly's position *see* Renteln, "The Unanswered Challenge of Relativism," *supra* note 8, at 529–31.

26. Edmund Burke as quoted in R. J. Vincent, "The Factor of Culture in the Global International Order," *Year Book of World Affairs* 34 (1980): 256.

27. Herskovits, *supra* note 14, at 4 and 6.

28. *Ibid.* at 49–50.

29. In his Introduction to UNESCO, *supra* note 3, at 10–11.

30. Article 5 of the Universal Declaration of Human Rights of 1948 and Article 7 of the International Covenant on Civil and Political Rights of 1966. The latter adds that "In particular, no one shall be subjected without his free consent to medical or scientific experimentation." For the texts of these instruments *see Basic Documents on Human Rights,* ed. Ian Brownlie, 2nd ed. (Oxford: Clarendon Press, 1981), 21 and 128, respectively.

31. Article 1.2 of the Declaration on the Protection of All Persons From Being Subjected to Torture and Other Cruel, Inhuman or Degrading Treatment or Punishment of 1975. United Nations General Assembly Resolution 3452 (XXX), 30 U.N. GAOR, Supp. (No. 34) 91, U.N. Doc. A/100 (1975).

32. *Ibid.,* Article 1.1 and Article 1 of the Convention Against Torture and Other Cruel, Inhuman or Degrading Treatment or Punishment. United Nations General Assembly Resolution 3946 (1984). This convention came into force in June 1987. For the text of the convention, *see International Commission of Jurists Review* 39 (1987): 51.

It is interesting to note that whereas the 1975 Declaration requires such pain and suffering to be consistent with the United Nations Standard Minimum Rules for the Treatment of Prisoners, the 1984 Convention omitted this requirement. This was probably done in order to encourage countries that do not comply with the Minimum Rules for the Treatment of Prisoners to ratify the Convention.

33. M. J. Bossuyt, *Guide to the "Travaux Preparatoires" of the International Covenant on Civil and Political Rights* [hereinafter cited as Bossuyt, *Guide*] (Dordrecht: Martinus Nijhoff, 1987), 151. *See* the review of early work of the Drafting

Committee, 1947–48, *ibid.* at 147–49; and discussions at meetings of the Commission on Human Rights, 1949–52, *ibid.* at 151–54.

34. U.N. Doc. E/CN.4/SR.312, 13.

35. Bossuyt, *supra* note 33, at 155.

36. *Ibid.* at 155–58. In its final version, the sentence ends with the word "experimentation," and does not include the phrase "involving risk."

37. The 5th and 6th Sessions of the Commission on Human Rights, 1949 and 1950. *Ibid.* at 150.

38. *Ibid.* at 151.

39. United Nations General Assembly Resolution 3469 (1979), cited in Amnesty International, *Human Rights: Selected International Standards* (London: Amnesty International Publications, 1985), 27.

40. By virtue of Article 1 of the Optional Protocol to the International Covenant of Civil and Political Rights of 1966, a State Party to the Covenant may recognize the competence of the Human Rights Committee established under the Covenant to receive and consider communications from individuals subject to the state's jurisdiction who claim to be victims of a violation by that state. The protocol provides for the admissibility and processing of such communications, which may culminate in the communication of the committee's views to the state party concerned and to the individual and the inclusion of those views in the annual report of the committee. Thus this procedure may bring moral and political pressure to bear on a state which elected to ratify the Optional Protocol by publicizing its human rights violations, but it does not provide for direct enforcement.

For the text of the protocol *see* Brownlie, *Basic Documents on Human Rights, supra* note 30, at 146.

41. In the context of the Optional Protocol, the Human Rights Committee is restricted by its terms of reference to making specific findings on the case rather than stating general principles and guidelines. *See* CCPR/C/OP/1, *International Covenant on Civil and Political Rights: Human Rights Committee, Selected Decisions under the Optional Protocol (Second to Sixteenth Sessions)* (New York: United Nations, 1985), for examples of the sort of treatment which, according to the committee, constituted violations of Article 7 of the Covenant, *see* 40, 45, 49, 57, 72, 132, and 136. All the communications relating to Article 7 published in this report involve very similar situations in a single country, Uruguay, over a short period of time, between 1976 and 1980. It would have been more helpful if the report had covered a wider variety of situations from more countries.

42. U.N. Doc. A/3740, at 94–95 (1982).

43. On the sources and development of Shariʿa *see generally*, Abdullahi A. An-Naʿim, *Toward an Islamic Reformation: Civil Liberties, Human Rights and International Law* (Syracuse: Syracuse University Press, 1990), chap. 2.

44. For fuller explanations see, generally, *ibid.*, chapter 5; Mohamed S. El-Awa, *Punishment in Islamic Law* (Indianapolis: American Trust Publications, 1982); and Safia M. Safwat, "Offenses and Penalties in Islamic Law," *Islamic Quarterly,* 26 (1982): 149.

45. An-Naʿim, *supra* note 43, at 114–18 and 131–33.

46. Rationality is also relative to the belief system or frame of reference.

What may be accepted as rational to a believer may not be accepted as such by an unbeliever, and vice versa.

47. Mahmoud Mohamed Taha, *The Second Message of Islam,* trans. Abdullahi A. An-Naʿim (Syracuse: Syracuse University Press, 1987), 74–75.

48. *Encyclopedia Judaica* (Jerusalem: Keter 1971), vol. 5, 142–47; vol. 6, 991–93.

Richard Falk

2. Cultural Foundations for the International Protection of Human Rights

It may be helpful to overgeneralize at the outset in approaching this diffi-cult, yet challenging and vital, topic. Until recently, most human rights specialists have taken an all-or-nothing view of the relevance of culture; some ignore culture in favor of some sort of universalism, while others regard cultural specificity as the supreme guide to moral behavior. Those who would disregard culture come from various backgrounds, sometimes overlapping, sometimes not. There are, first of all, jurisprudential schools associated with positivism or naturalism. The positivists consider the con-tent of human rights to be determined by the texts agreed upon by states and embodied in valid treaties, or determined by obligatory state practice attaining the status of binding international custom. The naturalists, on the other hand, regard the content of human rights as principally based upon immutable values that endow standards and norms with a universal validity. In neither jurisprudential instance does culture enter into the de-liberative process of interpreting the meaning, justifying the applicability, and working for the implementation of human rights.

Additionally, there are secularists of many stripes who believe that a universal normative order based on the dignity of the human individual is the only acceptable basis for political governance. The following words are used by Myres S. McDougal, Harold D. Lasswell, and Lung-chu Chen to identify their method of presenting the international law of human rights:

> The conception of human rights which we recommend . . . can be made to transcend all differences in the subjectivities and practices of peoples, not merely across national-state lines, but as between the different arenas of the larger community.[1]

These images of the human rights enterprise have been principally generated in the West, evolving over time from the Enlightenment mind-set,
including a confidence in the possibility of a rational social and political
order based on individual rights that, over time, could facilitate progress
and happiness for humankind as a whole.[2] Underlying such convictions is
a belief in the sufficiency of human reason, especially as it is manifested in
science and technology, and a vestigial distaste for any intrusion on the
terrain of human rights by recourse to religion, tradition, and emotion.
The ideological foundations of this secularist approach are often implicit.
Nevertheless, it tended to generate a cult of modernization that has for
several centuries occupied center stage in the West. One result has been a
dualism between progress and backwardness that has been damaging to
nonmodernizing peoples.

On the other side of the debate, keeping in mind that these orienting
observations are deliberate oversimplifications, one finds cultural relativists
who take their cues from societal tradition, specific religious teachings,
and the primacy of cultural settings. Such a position, often oblivious to
plural and incompatible elements in cultural precept and practice, leads to
an endorsement of the view that cultural attitudes automatically deserve
deference and anything inconsistent that claims to derive from the international law of human rights has been either misinterpreted or can be
disregarded. This position may also be accompanied by the ideological
counterpoint in non-Western societies that alleged human rights standards
are more properly understood to be disguised hegemonic claims by the
West that, in a postcolonial era, are no longer entitled to respect and
should more properly be repudiated.

As will be explained, both of these polar positions on the relevance of
culture should be rejected. If the field of the protection of human rights
continues to be controlled by these two interpretive perspectives in their
various forms, the most probable result is a demeaning encounter between
two forms of fundamentalism, the pitting of relentless secularists against
hardened traditionalists.

The position taken here is that, without mediating international human rights through the web of cultural circumstances, it will be impossible
for human rights norms and practices to take deep hold in non-Western
societies except to the partial, and often distorting, degree that these societies—or, more likely, their governing elites—have been to some extent
Westernized. At the same time, without cultural practices and traditions

being tested against the norms of international human rights, there will be a regressive disposition toward the retention of cruel, brutal, and exploitative aspects of religious and cultural tradition. One objective of normative standards is the protection of vulnerable individuals and groups from harsh forms of local prejudice that have hardened over time into custom and tradition and thereby achieved a kind of provincial legitimacy.

These two standpoints taken together suggest an intermediating relevance for both international law (standards, procedures, implementation) and for cultural hermeneutics, above all seeking to reconcile cultural and global sources of authority by reference to a core concern for the minimum decencies of individual and group existence. An emphasis on suffering and victimization provides indispensable guidance both in relation to gaps in international legal protection and to the task of distinguishing acceptable cultural orientations from unacceptable ones.[3] Of course, the whole undertaking is complicated and contingent as different observers and experts will often disagree. What is sought, and must be relied upon in the end, is a dialogue about appropriate behavioral standards in an atmosphere of growing toleration for divergency arising from varying cultural identities.[4]

One important consequence of the globalization of social, political, and economic life which often goes unnoticed is cultural penetration and overlapping, the coexistence in a given social space of several cultural traditions, as well as the more vivid interpenetration of cultural experience and practice as a consequence of media and transportation technologies, travel and tourism, cross-cultural education, and a logarithmic increase in human interaction of all varieties. Such a reality posits its own distinctive and opposing social demands: respect for *difference* (culture; to sustain diversity), acknowledgment of *sameness* (international law of human rights; to reestablish normative authority). The emergence and the implementation of international human rights embody both the opportunities and obstacles arising from this always-shifting interplay between the valuing of difference and the quest for sameness.

Such an interplay presupposes various interpreters and interpretations and, as such, has either produced controversy or led to the repression of one or more lines of interpreters and interpretations by the other on the basis of its greater power. A theme of this chapter is a bias in favor of controversy—conversation or dialogue—that expresses itself in political and social terms as a commitment to maximum political democracy. A vibrant society, on a global scale, is needed to ensure that democracy both engages the issues that affect lives and feelings and takes account of inter-dependencies.[5] In effect, human rights and political democracy are symbiotically bonded.

It would be helpful to illustrate concretely the working out of this intermediation of culture and international law, and the reason why it seems a necessary and desirable enterprise. Consider what happens when intermediation is not undertaken. The neglect of the displacement and destruction of indigenous peoples reveals both a glaring oversight in the protection offered by the international law of human rights and the degree to which this corpus of authoritative law dedicated to the protection of all humans has itself been distorted by a modernization bias. The neglect of indigenous peoples is what might be described as an area of "normative blindness." It does not improve matters to contend that governments in non-Western cultural space have given their assent to the human rights framework embodied in an international law that is deficient in its treatment of indigenous peoples.[6] First of all, virtually every government of a sovereign state, north or south, has adopted a modernization outlook that regards premodern culture as a form of backwardness to be overcome for the sake of the indigenous. Proceeding on this basis, the preferred normative response to the existence of indigenous peoples is not deference to their cultural autonomy, but rather their orderly and equitable assimilation into the more benevolent and promising cultural space of the modernizing ethos.[7] To the extent that international law offers any protection at all to indigenous peoples, it does so in an oblique and obscure manner that ineffectually purports to prohibit discrimination against individuals belonging to indigenous peoples and otherwise aims to remove those obstacles that prevent assimilation.[8]

Such a deficiency in the protective framework, admittedly now being nominally challenged by recent initiatives,[9] adds a dimension to this analysis—namely, that for governments inhabiting non-Western cultural space there exists an important overlay derived from the reception of Western ideas and influence about statecraft and progress. In the name of development, indigenous peoples have been and are being destroyed and displaced in many parts of the Third World. Of course, such a process of displacement was virtually completed in the West by the middle of the last century. Such a deficiency in normative protection has been contested by countertraditions of thought within Western culture from the time of initial settlement in "the era of discovery," but with little success. The attempt to extend human rights protection to all individuals and groups within the orbit of sovereign authority, however, has been endorsed uncritically and universally. Even the cult of modernization has now been somewhat tempered and qualified to take account of the evident wish by many indigenous peoples to retain their autonomous cultural space as enclaves within the states that *resist* rather than *aspire* to assimilation into the encompassing cultural habitat of modernization.[10]

This example of the fate of indigenous peoples as a subordinate culture victimized by a dominant culture suggests the relevance of exclusion and inclusion in evaluating the normative adequacy of human rights as a protective framework at a given time and place. Those *excluded* from rights-creating processes are only likely to be taken into account, if at all, in a partial and paternalistic manner. The achievement of more attention and understanding will depend on organized acts of defiance and resistance by those victimized peoples. This approach has hitherto been ignored by specialists in rights.

Exclusion from the rights-forming process is itself a denial of human rights, and is at best likely to produce unsatisfactory substantive results. The observation here is structural; to the extent that the international law of human rights is an exclusive result of the states system, it cannot hope to take account of the values and needs of peoples that are not adequately represented in that system or even constituted to qualify for membership. One factor that confirms this failure of coverage is the greater extension of concern as a state system has evolved in ways that have at least provided weak forms of representation for nonstate actors such as indigenous peoples. Indigenous peoples are an extreme instance, but the struggle of women, gays, children, ethnic minorities, and the poor for normative acknowledgment has also been agonizingly slow despite the pretensions of the West to uphold the dignity of the individual and to honor liberty of choice.[11] Until pressed by agitation and movements from below, these vulnerable groups have only rarely, and then insufficiently, enjoyed legal protection from abuse. Neither the abstract promise of the cultural myth of toleration nor that of the positive legal order is sufficient. One role of a robust civil society is to overcome both normative and cultural blindness to human suffering. This raising of awareness requires deliberate efforts to counteract the vulnerability of previously excluded groups; lessening vulnerability in turn depends on developing inclusive forms of decentralized participatory democracy. As asserted earlier, democratization is both a vital precondition and a crucial ingredient of human rights protection.[12]

Suppose, however, that contested cultural practices are democratically endorsed as beneficial. For instance, the Hindu practice of suttee may seem cruel to outsiders (and even to many insiders), but it is alleged by some to be a functionally necessary way to uphold the integrity of Indian family life. The cultural endorsement of suttee within Hinduism, however, is by now local and restricted and should not be exaggerated. Hinduism is rich in contradictory understandings of precept and traditions, and various Hindu evaluations of the status and duties of widows are tenable. Also, all cultures evolve in relation to experience, being influenced partly by intra-cultural and intercultural interaction, as well as through their participation and reflection upon wider normative frameworks, including that of human rights itself. In this regard, Hindu contact with the West, including its commitment to gender equality, alters Hinduism as a comprehensive be-lief system. These cultural revisionings flow in the reverse direction as well and have influenced the West's normative discourse on materialist values and relations with animals and nature. Cultural influence can also be re-gressive, as seen in the case of Eastern societies in relation to the environ-mental effects of an uncritical adoption of the cult of modernization.

Does human rights discourse take precedence over contrary cultural practices? I believe, together with many interpreters of the social and po-litical scene, that taking suffering seriously is the Archimedes point for intermediation between the universal claim and the particular practice when it comes to resolving antagonisms between widely endorsed human rights norms and culturally ordained patterns of behavior. R.B.J. Walker has aptly expressed this ethical disposition in the course of a more general examination of international relations: "The primary ground for ethical reflection no doubt remains a capacity to identify the intolerable."[13] To be effective at local and community levels, the imposition of the universal must be by way of an opening in the culture itself, not by external impo-sition on the culture. Therefore, it is of great importance to nurture cul-tural rethinking, reinterpretation, and internal dialogue, an approach that is so powerfully and creatively embodied in the work of Abdullahi A. An-Na'im.[14]

Can we ground this process of normative assessment on realities be-yond the arbitrary and subjective? Is there a core enterprise of protection that relates to the individual and group experience of the species at a given stage of its biological evolution? One starting point for response is to set forth an enumerated list of practices that strike observers as "intolerable."

Rhoda Howard has recalled Barrington Moore's recital of "universal causes" of human misery as a way of validating core human rights claims:

- torture, or slaughter by a cruel enemy;
- starvation and illness;
- the exaction of labor by ruthless authorities in an exploitative manner;
- loss of beloved persons by the hostile action of others;
- rotting in prison, being burned at the stake, or losing means of subsistence as a result of expressing heretical or unpopular beliefs.[15]

Such an enumeration identifies the territory of human suffering while leaving considerable latitude for interpretation, discussion, and even controversy. Walker offers an even more complex sense of the elements he associates with the intolerable:

- the devotion of resources to the extermination of the human species in whole or part;
- forms of economic development that bring extreme wealth to some while threatening the very survival of others;
- rapacious destruction of the planet for progress or profit;
- flagrant abuse of established human rights.

Walker cavalierly contends: "From the South Bronx to Beirut, from the proliferation of refugee camps to the persistence of apartheid, the intolerable is always visible to those who would nevertheless celebrate the achievements of the modern world."[16]

I doubt whether Walker's sense of the intolerable is as widely noticed or as visible as he supposes. His far-reaching contention goes beyond Moore's more intuitive enumeration in that much of what he would have us call "intolerable" is a hidden consequence of an essentially capitalist orientation toward nature and society that rests on the whole idea of modernity so central to the identity of and dominance by the West. In the language of this chapter, Walker is closely associating "the intolerable" with the historical negative consequences of what has been earlier referred to here as "the cult of modernization." The broader point being made here is not that this or that conception of the intolerable ought to be favored, but that a series of discourses on the nature of the intolerable as a method of deepening and extending discussion of human rights priorities and cultural obstacles can make a vital contribution to cultural intermediation and internal dialogue.[17]

Such discourses may be of primary and most immediate benefit to activists, those animated to take action by conscience and compassion, engaged elements in civil society, that are seeking to promote reforms or safeguard vulnerable individuals or groups. The implementation of human rights is dependent on such interpretative work by activists but precisely where such efforts are most needed, their undertaking can be dangerous for the practitioners of interpretive work.

An-Na'im refers to the 1985 execution of his mentor, *Ustadh* Mahmoud Mohammed Taha, in Khartoum in reaction to his exegetical work of normative reconstruction in relation to Islamic cultural practices and traditions.[18] What Taha was doing cast doubt upon those elements of Islamic religious law, Shari'a, that are, in An-Na'im's, words "morally indefensible and practically impossible to maintain." What is proposed as corrective is liberating, and for that reason, threatening to the normative pretensions of those defending the status quo:

> The author submits, as a Muslim, that God communicates through the social and physical environment as well as through the Qur'an, His literal and final word, and through the Sunna, traditions of His final prophet, Mohammed Ibn Abdillah. This Article contends that God's instructions must be understood and applied in light of all social and material phenomena.[19]

An-Na'im's insistence that "a legitimate and lasting" solution "must develop from within Islam"[20] places great responsibility on the scholarly capacity to interpret and persuade. As he acknowledges, the obstacles in real world circumstances are formidable: "Most Muslim scholars are either silent, in exile, or in prison."[21] Elsewhere he confronts an even more difficult question as to whether authoritative cultural practices that inflict "intolerable" results and are more or less resistant to techniques of interpretative softening, can be overcome, or at least restricted in their application, by relying upon cross-cultural and intracultural reinterpretation.[22]

Other efforts to find an interpretative foundation upon which to rest the basic quest for human rights deserve mention. These efforts, as with those of An-Na'im, often draw upon an enlarged and an enriched conception of culture and tradition, as well as try to bring religious energy directly to bear in a constructive manner. A recent document issued by a group of self-styled Third World Christians under the title "The Road to Damascus: Kairos and Conversion" is a fascinating contribution to this direction of human rights thinking, even though it is not so designated. I quote a passage that conveys the tenor of the whole:

> God is on the side of the poor, the oppressed, the persecuted. When this faith is proclaimed and lived in a situation of political conflict between the rich and the poor, and when the rich and the powerful reject this faith and condemn it as heresy, we can read the signs and discern something more than a crisis. We are faced with a *Kairos,* a moment of truth, a time for decision, a time for grace, a God-given opportunity for conversion and hope.[23]

This extension of liberation theology anchors human rights in the struggle against those forms of oppression afflicting especially the poor, and it entrusts the poor with a critical role as agents of their own liberation. It does not, in any sense, scorn political rights related to elections and representative democracy, nor does it rest its hopes on the fulfilling of economic rights conceived of as distinct claims, but rather it responds to an oppressive structure by issuing its own mandate to engage in collective resistance and transformative struggle, in effect suggesting that without a transformed social structure human rights will not be realized by the great majority of Third World peoples.

In introducing the very important collection of essays published recently under the title *Rethinking Human Rights,* editors Smitu Kothari and Harsh Sethi emphasize the critical importance they attach to moving beyond legalist and statist conceptions of human rights. They call for "a relevant *politics* of human rights," as well stressing the importance of "a human rights consciousness" which they believe is inhibited in Hindu India as a consequence of a lamentably passive attitude toward suffering, pain and death.[24] Kothari and Sethi speculate:

> Maybe we have lived with too much of them for too long. Mass death and suffering, we, as a society are keen to exorcise quickly. How else do we explain the near absence of a civic and humanitarian response to either the Bhopal disaster, or the subsequent governmental callousness? Nor are we, for that matter, very bothered about the thousands of hungry who swarm around us as beggars.[25]

They conclude, "None of this augurs well for human rights consciousness." In passing, it should be noted that cultural callousness is present in the West as well—it does not take long to learn that in public places in the United States it is best to avert one's eyes from the often horrific spectacle of homelessness. By averting our eyes, we are keeping "the intolerable" at a safe distance; this usually results in societal indifference. Significant, here, is the enlargement of our understanding of "culture" to incorporate prevalent attitudes toward various forms of suffering, including the efforts of repressive, dominant, and exploitative elites to hide the costs of existing structures or to numb the sensitivities of the citizenry.

What I want to stress here is the recentering of the quest to implement human rights in the sinews of civil society. As such, cultural outlook becomes of transcending importance to the realization of human rights. It is less the crystalized abuses of state power that are of primary concern than the specific character of human suffering regardless of its source, and, as in the *kairos* document of Third World Christians, Kothari and Sethi call for "a social praxis, rooted in the need of the most oppressed communities, that seeks to create shared norms of civilized existence."[26] Part of such rethinking involves the realization that waiting for the state and waiting for the United Nations are not nearly enough, even in situations in which one has a favorable view of those institutions.

The rethinking of human rights here proposed also entails a rethinking of culture itself. Reverting once more to Kothari and Sethi's approach, they note that India's cultural achievements, including the sustaining of democracy and her formal acceptance of human rights covenants as an ingredient of constitutionalism, are not enough, nor even is its leadership role in "the international struggle against colonialism, imperialism and racism," nor even its great fight to bring to the world "the message of 'nonviolence'":

> Rarely do many of us realize, that underneath this impressive veneer and national pride about our 3000 year old civilizational legacy, lies a history of systematic violation of basic civil, democratic, and human rights of large sections of our population.[27]

India's cultural traditions, they argue, generate and are responsible, in various respects, for a significant portion of this oppressiveness; but the same culture, as they remind us, is also diverse enough to generate liberatory ethical and political possibilities. As with An-Na'im's approach to Islam, this Indian effort emphasizes a root cultural/religious possibility of working within the Hindu framework for peace and justice, a possibility given historical plausibility by Gandhi's extraordinary exemplification of what Hinduism, reconstructed, could mean for all forms of social relations in the modern world. While An-Na'im emphasizes mainly doctrinal perspectives as a foundation for action, Kothari and Sethi (and their collaborators) call for social praxis, struggle, taking suffering seriously at the grassroots level of local and communal circumstances. The two standpoints are complementary, although their degrees of usefulness will depend on the context. India's social decentralization and severe communal tensions, together with the failure of the central state structure to exert influence on the tradition-bound countryside, commends an emphasis on activism. Islam's reliance on dogmatic applications of doctrine commends an emphasis on exegesis. *Scriptural explanation*

Kothari and Sethi believe that the international protection of human rights comes about through the activation of civil society. The most effective type of activation depends on the circumstances of time and place. As developments of recent years in Eastern Europe, especially Poland, suggest, the promotion of human rights there became almost exclusively a project of nonviolent movements of opposition and resistance, remarkably courageous jand sustained movements directed toward the nonviolent, yet militant, transformation of state power.[28] Again, a legalistic understanding of the international protection of human rights could not provide much insight, especially as oppressor governments had previously mechanically and unproblematically accepted international human rights covenants, presumably believing that their firm domination of societal behavior by party and state made the commitment to uphold such standards of conduct irrelevant to the stability of internal control of the populations living in these countries.

At another level, these acknowledgments of legal obligation became important, although unwittingly, as they called the attention of the citizenry to the gap between rhetoric and performance that underscored and objectified the illegitimacy of these governments on their own terms, and the corresponding legitimacy of popular struggle for reform. In the end, it was the cultural resources which survived totalitarian assault, gave decisive strength and direction to these movements of resistance, and provided support and guidelines on a day-to-day basis. This was especially true of the religious institutions and traditions that acted as main legitimating sources of inspiration.[29] Often, as in Poland, these elements of cultural heritage could themselves be historically associated with oppressiveness; the point, however, is that virtually any cultural heritage is morally rich enough that it can, if appropriately construed, under some circumstances make inspirational contributions to the struggle for human rights, democracy, and social justice. The international protection of human rights cannot proceed very far without liberating the culture itself to serve these ends.

The protection of human rights is hindered by the prevailing structure and organizational features of international society, especially the persisting predominance of a sovereign state. A built-in tension exists between the structure of international society and the effective implementation of international standards of human rights. True, governments representing states and their population to varying degrees have accepted human rights standards directly or indirectly, but many governments also violate these norms, often in systematic and extreme ways. Of course, even nominal adherence to human rights standards reduces the weight of purely sovereignty-oriented arguments, thus giving international public opinion, including diplomatic interchange, a platform to stand on.[30] Even here, it is less the state structure than the array of transnational voluntary associations (NGOs) that have exposed human rights failures. Most states, even when avowedly concerned about human rights, often lack capability and credibility, having too much to hide themselves and generally subordinating and eroding the credibility of their human rights concerns by according priority to geopolitics. Such selectivity in protest activity introduces an element of hypocrisy and manipulativeness into most statist (and even international institutional) approaches to human rights. There are some notable exceptions, for instance, the Scandinavian group: countries that have a decent record on human rights at home and take pains to keep their international concerns about human rights distinct from their geopolitical position and outlook.[31]

World order thinkers have long noted that the state is both too big and too small—it is too big in the sense that it can wield world-disruptive military power externally and that it loses ability to sustain a political community internally; it is too small in the sense that it cannot extend its authority far or effectively enough to control the flow of entropic forces in the world or to fashion suitable regimes for handling global scale problems. Human rights thinkers might well conclude that the state is both too strong and too weak in relation to the protective enterprise—it is too strong in the crucial respect that if it is the source of gross violations, it becomes exceedingly difficult, if not impossible, to organize effective opposition, at least in the short run; it is too weak in the equally crucial respect that, even when disposed to implement human rights standards internally, it can only rarely and marginally overcome contrary cultural practices, especially if these are deeply ingrained and widely dispersed. The irony can be expressed as a paradox: only a totalitarian state could hope to realize human rights fully in a fundamentalist culture, but by being totalitarian it would stake out an identity that would necessarily be antagonistic to basic human rights. In contrast, several, but by no means all, human rights NGOs have achieved a measure of influence because of their single-minded dedication to human rights without regard to the ideological identity and political alignment of the state accused of violating human rights. Their information on human rights abuses is difficult to refute or dismiss on the grounds of bias or partisan politics.

Yet another element must enter into consideration: political power tends to be distributed territorially. An oppressive state, while possibly even the object of intense censure, generally remains master of its domestic scene until challenged from below and within—that is, by aroused societal forces that, though they may invoke international law as their justification, are mainly motivated by values and experiences associated with domestic, cultural, and political reality. Of course, arenas external to the state can participate and contribute, as the anti-apartheid campaign so well illustrates. Still, such external pressure has marked limits, enabling a tiny and isolated Albania, for example, to disregard international pressure for decades. Bypassing the state can be extraordinarily important to counteract domestic oppression. The reorientation of cultural consciousness, such as Gandhi attempted so heroically in India, can directly challenge oppression at its communal and behavioral roots. Whether Gandhi's link between justice and nonviolence is indispensable in this process of cultural renovation is far from evident and undoubtedly depends on the specific context, it is true. At the same time, it is certainly notable that widely disparate popular struggles for human rights and democracy during the 1980s have rejected violence as a means, or at least as a principal means, for pursuing their ends. One thinks immediately of democratization initiatives in Eastern Europe and the Soviet Union, but also of the "people power" in the Philippines that drove Ferdinand Marcos into exile, of the Chinese student movement so brutally crushed in June of 1989 on Tiananmen Square, and of the Palestinian *intifada*.[32]

In the end, the protection of human rights is not distinguishable from the struggle for democracy and decency in the world, and may not long be separable from the repudiation of the cult of modernization in the West.[33] The Greens (and those who are working to reexpress the religious affirmation of feminine sacred energy as pervading earthliness) are bringing back into the cradle of Western civilization a normative questioning that is itself subversive of the supposed cultural mainstream. It is not surprising that Matthew Fox, a Dominican theologian who reinterprets the Christian message under the sway of ecofeminism, has been silenced for a year by Cardinal Joseph Ratzinger, the chief Vatican guardian of orthodoxy.[34]

My conclusion is that the prospects for human rights are linked to the prospects for cultural reconstruction and that these prospects depend upon an open process of communication, free from dogmatic interferences. It is only from within the spiritual and humanistic core of civil society that restorative energies can emerge to redress cultural imbalances. History may move, but global circumstances are exceedingly uneven. The core of human rights is one thing for the Kairos group, another for Solidarity in Poland, still another for Indians beset by menacing communal violence, another for those seeking to perpetuate and protect the cultural forms of indigenous peoples, and still another for the ecologically threatened West. It is ironically appropriate that the birthplace of modernity should also be most audibly in its death throes in this period. Europe 1992 is a continuation of the cult of modernization in a more efficient form of larger aggregations of capital; but it is also a stimulus to ecological consciousness, proceeding by way of reorienting territorially based geopolitics. The electoral success of the Greens in Europe is, above all, an indication of deep cultural ferment, including a very different fix on what upholding human rights entails from the orientation implied in the Enlightenment.

My closing self-indulgence is to offer a few comments on the affair of Salman Rushdie that follow from the preceding analysis. Let me stake a small personal claim. I am probably one of a very small number of wanderers on this planet that has had the experience of a personal meeting with both Rushdie and his now deceased adversary, Khomeini. Reduced to essentials, the turmoil generated by the publication of *The Satanic Verses* cries out for careful reflection from many distinct angles. To begin with, Khomeini's reaction was grounded in a widespread Islamic sense that Rushdie's novel exceeded the boundaries of literary convention, that it was deliberately provocative by scandalizing the Prophet Muhammad and his associates.[35] I have discussed the book with several friends living in various Islamic countries who are not themselves religious yet found the book deeply offensive to their Muslim identity, leading them to regard Rushdie's literary exploits as an almost pathological expression of creative talent.[36] Of course, the glory of Western liberty is based on protecting precisely those forms of expression thus castigated at the time of their utterance; but such an achievement itself depends on what might be called "cultural preparation," which is definitely not present at this time in the Muslim world. Put differently, human rights enshrined in international law, and largely embodied in Western cultural practice, cannot be effectively protected in some cultural settings. Indeed, their attempted implementation may produce a devastating breakdown of social order as well as a heightening of influence for restrictive or fundamentalist cultural tendencies.

Rushdie's novel also illuminates the problematics surrounding the territorial organization of the contemporary world. Although published in the West, the book (and its outlook) quickly penetrated the Muslim world. Indeed, there were riots in India, Pakistan, and elsewhere in reaction to the book weeks before Khomeini issued his infamous death sentence (which was backed up by a huge monetary reward for the prospective assassin). At the same time, Khomeini by his own decree effectively "killed" Rushdie as a normally functioning citizen in a democratic society; nothing the West could do by way of territorial law or moral protest has enabled Rushdie to continue fully with his life as a public man of letters, someone who had previously played an active role in English political and literary life, giving readings around the world and taking controversial stands on policy issues. Even after Khomeini's death, Rushdie remains in deep hiding, possibly condemned to live underground for the rest of his life, or, at best, to live more openly but in a certain indeterminate jeopardy. Who can know the extent of risk that Rushdie would face if he emerged from hiding? The modern state, despite its military and police prowess, can be penetrated in many ways; it can no more give Rushdie protection against this onslaught of Islamic fundamentalism than it can insulate its borders against the influx of drugs, illegal immigrants, acid rain, the vagaries of financial markets, or "alien" ideas.

But there is another facet of *The Satanic Verses* that bears on my main theme. Insulating the sensitivities of Islamic society against such provocations is not necessarily oppressive at the present time, and may well represent a prudent intervention by a ruler faced with the likelihood of riots. To condemn such governments by invoking international law and piously insisting upon unrestricted freedom of expression is to fall into the trap of secular fundamentalism, which can in its own way be as repressive of human dignity as Islamic (or otherwise religiously grounded) forms of fundamentalism.[37] The Enlightenment conception of virtue is not necessarily prescriptive for non-Western peoples, although it has been largely entrenched in the positive law of human rights.[38]

In addition, perhaps unrestricted artistic expression may even not yet be thoroughly grounded in the lifeworld of the West.[39] Martin Scorsese's film *The Last Temptation of Christ,* offensive to many Catholics, exhilarating to many others (including Catholics), induced boycotts and bomb scares at theaters.[40] One can only speculate about what violence might have ensued had the Pope encouraged Catholics to take all means to prevent the showing of the film and backed the injunction with huge financial rewards. From the perspective of democratic values, it would invariably seem desirable to open up a culture as far as imaginable to enable diverse viewpoints to be freely expressed and debated. Of course, the option of a culture to minimize outside influence and intrusion cannot be always ruled out. Assessment depends on context. Small tribal peoples, for example, might opt for insulation in a spirit that outsiders should generally respect, especially if the tribes' cultural practices did not involve deliberate cruelty or universally condemned abuses such as torture.

Toleration is the positive reverse side of orthodoxy and fundamentalism, but the problems of repressiveness should not be superciliously posited in non-Western cultures such as Islam, whose interests can then be ignored as unworthy of concern.[41] Also, the abuse of artistic freedom to deride vulnerable peoples, or worse, to stimulate harm against them, is culturally problematic and ambiguous even from a human rights standpoint. For instance, literature or films that evoke hatred of minorities or vulnerable groups, and which might lead to abuse and violence, present difficult choices for leaders. Only secular fundamentalist attitudes toward human rights can resolve such issues at the abstract level of human rights standards. As such, the one-sidedness of the reaction to Rushdie's plight in the liberal West must be understood, in part, as a continuing expression of what Edward Said has so convincingly portrayed as "Orientalism," the negative stereotyping in the West of Islam leading to dreadful consequences for the Palestinians and others.[42] Many of those who were most "outraged" by Khomeini's response to *The Satanic Verses* have also been outspoken opponents of justice for the Palestinians.

In the end, I think, we can most successfully uphold human rights by struggling against "the intolerable" in all its forms. We must make full use of our ingenuity and democratic opportunities to discuss what is intolerable, trusting in freedom of communication to be itself clarifying and hence liberating. As such, *human rights, cultural renewal,* and *participatory democracy* are implicated, for better or worse, in a common destiny.

But suppose there is no democratic possibility? As recent decades have shown, authoritarian repression of media, intellectual life, and cultural expression drives freedom of communication underground, although it cannot abolish it. Whether by *samizdat,* satire, or humor, the voices of dissent manage eventually to find arenas and forums, although not without risk, often with the help of religious institutions that under other circumstances have themselves exerted their influence to restrict the dissemination of dangerous knowledge. Even in Iran, it was the mosque that mainly kept alive the possibility of democratic questioning of the Shah's repressive political order during the twenty-five years of dynastic rule.[43] It is not plausible to imagine the triumph of Solidarity and democratization in Poland without the earlier inspirational support given by the Catholic Church, an institution so notable in Polish history for playing the opposite role. There are no fixed points of normative reference, so that we are all responsible for the discovery and protection of human rights, and must establish such a process of inquiry as to be itself an expression of the integrity of any given cultural identity.

Notes

1. Myres S. McDougal, Harold D. Lasswell, and Lung-chu Chen, *Human Rights and World Public Order* (New Haven, Conn.: Yale University Press, 1980), xvii. Their emphasis on "respect" does move this understanding of human rights away from ethnocentrism, however, and toward dialogue, communication, and reciprocal patterns of toleration.

2. But account should also be taken of K. P. Saksena's important comment as a complement to the textual attribution of human rights *positive law* to the Western initiative and heritage: "There is an incredibly widespread assumption that 'human rights' is a Western concept, meant for a certain group of people and not for all human beings, universally. This is sheer political propaganda perpetuated by Third World leaders with vested interests. In fact, the genesis of the concept of human rights could be traced back to the dawn of civilization, when man first started living in groups. With the passage of time these 'rights,' or established customs and understandings, including the relationship between ruler and the ruled, were brought together in different forms, in various parts of the world. They found expression, for instance, in the Confucian system in China and the 'Panchayat' system in India." K. P. Saksena, "Foreword," in *Human Rights and Development: International Views,* ed. David P. Forsythe (London: Macmillan, 1989), ix–x.

3. For an illuminating and wide-ranging inquiry that links human rights to victimization, *see* Robert T. Elias, *The Politics of Victimization* (New York: Oxford University Press, 1986).

4. *Cf.* Jürgen Habermas, *The Theory of Communicative Action: Lifeworld and System* (Boston: Beacon Press, 1989).

5. Ralf Dahrendorf suggestively locates hope for the future in the emergence of what he calls "World Civil Society," oriented toward the fulfillment of human rights for all persons: "The next step toward a World Civil Society is the recognition of universal rights of all men and women by the body of international law." Ralf Dahrendorf, *The Modern Social Conflict* (London: Weidenfeld and Nicolson, 1988), 181.

6. For an illuminating discussion of the clash of Fourth World (indigenous peoples) perspectives with those of the Third World, *see* Roxanne Ortiz, *Indians of the Americas: Human Rights and Self-Determination* (London: Zed Press, 1984). *See also* the account of Indonesia's exterminist policy toward the East Timorese over an extended period reaching back to 1975, if not further, in José Ramos-Horta, *FUNU: The Unfinished Saga of East Timor* (Trenton, N.J.: Red Sea Press, 1987); *cf. also* an excellent essay on "Brazil's aboriginal peoples," Paulo Suess, "Evangelization and the Tribal Cultures of Brazil," *Cross Currents* 39 (1989): 161–80.

7. When a government rejects modernization as part of a repudiation of the West, as has been the case with Iran since the Islamic Revolution of 1979, the normative ideology has been narrow and intolerant, denigrating all other cultural traditions represented within the sovereign territory. It should be remembered that one positive feature of Westernization as it has evolved since the Enlightenment is a principled toleration of diverse views, not so much as reflected in group membership but as indirectly validated by including within individual rights discretion as to group identity and cultural affiliation.

8. ILO Convention No. 107; *see* the more sensitive approach to these concerns contained in ILO Convention No. 169, June 27, 1989; a more satisfactory effort has been undertaken under the auspices of the U.N. Sub-Commission on Prevention of Discrimination and Protection of Minorities. *Cf.* especially, Report of the Sub-Commission, 40th Session, August 8–September 2, 1988, containing the interesting preliminary document: "Universal Declaration on Indigenous Rights: A Set of Draft Perambular Paragraphs and Principles," E/CN.4/1989/3, E/CN.4/Sub.2/1988/45, 25 October 1988.

9. The annual sessions of the Working Group on Indigenous Populations, which meets in Geneva, have been especially important.

10. This ambivalence modifying the cult of modernization is a consequence of several factors: the resurgent activism of indigenous peoples, a loss of confidence in the positive effects of continuing along the path of modernization, and an appreciation of ecological approaches that correspond more closely to the mindset of many indigenous peoples than they do to that of post-Enlightenment outlooks.

11. Jane Rule, a leading Canadian writer, explained her association with a controversial gay magazine called *Body Politic* in a manner that illustrates this grassroots approach to human rights: "I felt I had to support the *Body Politic* because gay people have been silenced for so long . . . . I think what writing requires us to do is to address the problems of minorities who are being silenced." Quoted in the *Toronto Globe and Mail,* October 12, 1989, at A14.

12. This argument is based on the evaluation of the legitimacy of the inter-

national law of human rights through an assessment of the representativeness of its law-forming processes; in this regard, representation provides an alternative, and possibly complementary, set of criteria to that provided by various naturalist or neo-naturalist orientations, including that of the New Haven approach associated with McDougal, Lasswell, and their many collaborators. Representation is, of course, also a way of entrenching democracy in social reality, and its realization advances the prospects of decentralization.

13. "Ethics, Modernity, and the Theory of IR" (unpublished manuscript), 5. Also revealing is the dedication page of a powerful set of responses to Sandinista Nicaragua produced by the Amanecida Collective of United States women: "We dedicate this book to everyone who responds with courage and compassion to suffering—and to all who suffer today the violence wrought by our own nation." *Revolutionary Progressiveness* (Mary Knoll, N.Y.: Orbis, 1987).

14. *Cf.* his Chapter 1 in this volume.

15. As presented in Rhoda Howard, "Is There an African Concept of Human Rights?" in *Foreign Policy and Human Rights,* ed. R. J. Vincent (Cambridge: Cambridge University Press, 1986), 12–13.

16. Walker, *supra* note 13, at 5.

17. One aspect of this dialogue is the moral ambiguity associated with certain forms of voluntary suffering. Some religious beliefs endow human suffering with a positive value, even associating suffering with prospects for salvation.

18. Abdullahi A. An-Na'im, "Islamic Law, International Relations, and Human Rights: Challenge and Response," *Cornell International Law Journal* 20, no. 2 (1987): 335.

19. *Ibid.* at 318.

20. *Ibid.* at 333; *see also* 333–35.

21. *Ibid.* at 334.

22. *Cf.* again his Chapter 1 in this volume, especially the discussion of "cruel and inhuman punishment." I am not yet persuaded that so little room for interpretive maneuvering exists. Is not one additional method to obtain more "acceptable" results, a resort to metaphorical styles of interpretation that deliteralize Qur'anic directives, however clear their language may intuitively appear to be? Although not a student of Islam, I have the impression that exploring such metaphorical lines of interpretation might be helpful, even if problems remain after such an exploration.

23. (London: Catholic Institute for IR, 1989), 13; *cf. also* Lester Edwin J. Ruiz, "Towards a Theology of Politics," *Tugon* 6 (1986): 1–44.

24. Suffering and poverty are often positively valued, especially in religious traditions, but not if imposed; also, the struggle to overcome suffering is usually valued even within these traditions.

25. *Rethinking Human Rights* (Delhi: Lokoyan, 1989), 9.

26. *Ibid.* at 9; *cf. also* the contributions of R. Kothari and U. Baxi to the same volume, 19–30, 101–118, 151–166.

27. *Ibid.* at 1.

28. *Cf.* Adam Michnik, *Letters from Prison* (Berkeley, Calif.: University of

California Press, 1985); George Konrad, *Anti-Politics* (New York: Harcourt Brace Jovanovich, 1984); Mary Kaldor, Gerard Holden, and Richard Falk, eds., *The New Detente* (London: Verso, 1989).

29. Of course, casual inferences are notoriously difficult to make. The situation in Eastern Europe was also deeply influenced by the changed role of Soviet hegemony as a result of Gorbachev's "new thinking" in foreign policy.

30. Of course, adherence need not be explicit, or by way of a formal acceptance of international agreements; it is generally accepted by international law experts that most of the standards contained in the Universal Declaration and two covenants are part of general international law binding on all states.

31. To the extent that a state distances itself from geopolitics while still participating on the normative side of international relations, it possesses greater credibility on human rights issues. Sweden is an important positive case, although it is arguable how far it has truly withdrawn from geopolitics.

32. I share the view that up until the time of this writing, October 1989, the *intifada* has waged its struggle against Israeli occupying authorities by a reliance on "relative nonviolence" of a generally principled character, typified both by the ratio of casualties and by the use of stones as symbols of defiance (more than weaponry) against Israeli occupying authorities armed with the latest versions of automatic weaponry.

33. This repudiation is directed only at the excesses of modernization and is not meant to imply a wholesale rejection of efforts to use science and technology for human benefit. On the contrary, preserving these positive aspects of modernization at this time in history requires a more careful and critical application of Enlightenment ideas, possibly restructured around principles of wholeness and planetary vulnerability.

34. *See* Matthew Fox, *The Cosmic Christ* (New York: Harper and Row, 1988); *cf. also* Matthew Fox, "Is the Catholic Church Today a Dysfunctional Family? A Pastoral Letter to Cardinal Ratzinger and the Whole Church," *Creation* 4 (1988): 23–28.

35. For one balanced, insightful assessment *see* Shiraz Dassa, "What Rushdie Knew," *Cross Currents* 39 (1989): 204–12.

36. Such an assessment would not have led them personally to favor any kind of restrictions on the distribution of Rushdie's book; but it did lead them to a more sympathetic understanding of the ruler's dilemma in such countries as Egypt, Pakistan, Malaysia, and even India. *Cf.* the statement on the Rushdie incident that was signed by more than seven hundred writers, including many of the most celebrated, published on the front page of the *Times Literary Supplement,* March 3–8, 1989. Rushdie's own view of Islam is evidently consistent with that proposed here of conceiving of much space for intracultural dialogue and reconstruction. *See* Rushdie, "An End to the Nightmare" [published prior to *The Satanic Verses* and relating to Zia's fundamentalism in Pakistan] *Seminar* (Delhi, India), 351 (1988): 14–15.

37. Tentatively, there appears to be an analogy to feminist efforts to prohibit the publication of pornography on grounds of its abusive portrayal of women.

Can we assert dogmatically that such an inroad on liberty of expression is per se undesirable? Of course, to banish pornography places some representative of government in the role of censor; and that is a delicate matter, as modern society has discovered. If the sensibility of some members of society is too highly privileged, then the sensibility of certain other marginalized members may be diminished. Such has been the case in relation to mainstream homophobic efforts to withdraw federal support for artistic work that exhibits gay forms of romantic love.

38. The discourse of international human rights laws also requires the temporizing effects of intermediation, that is, the interplay between cultural circumstances and prescriptive mandate. As I understand it, such intermediation is a discourse distinct from either the intracultural reconstruction or the intercultural dialogue and interaction that An-Na'im relies upon so effectively.

39. *Cf. supra* note 35.

40. It is interesting to observe that both Rushdie and Scorsese evidently conceive of their irreverence as falling well within a show of respect for hallowed cultural tradition. Scorsese regards himself as a believing Catholic, and Rushdie expressed support for a moderate variant of Islam well before his book provoked such a storm. *Cf. supra* note 36.

41. The treatment of Japanese citizens during World War II or of those suspected of Communist leanings during the Cold War should be chastening to those who suppose that toleration of unpopular views is safely instilled in the political culture of the United States.

42. *Cf.* Edward Said, *Orientalism* (New York: Pantheon, 1978).

43. Despite the Shah's Westernness, such Western classics as Shakespeare's *Macbeth* and *King Lear* were suppressed.

William P. Alford

3. Making A Goddess of Democracy from Loose Sand
Thoughts on Human Rights in the People's Republic of China

> China has always been called a loose sheet of sand. . . . [Absent the Communist Party] China will retrogress into divisions and confusion and will then be unable to accomplish modernization.
>
> —Deng Xiaoping in 1980

The Beijing Spring[1] of 1989 poses all too sharply the issue that lies at the core of this volume of essays and of the work of many of its contributors: To what extent are conceptions of human rights universal? Advocates of universality can point to those Chinese students, workers, and other citizens who at great sacrifice sought fundamental freedoms of assembly and of the press while demanding that their voices be heard. Conversely, scholars espousing the view that human rights are culturally specific or relative can argue that the Chinese leadership's brutal crushing of the pro-democracy movement and the seeming acquiescence of the larger populace therein demonstrate how foreign the ideas of human rights expressed in major international conventions concerned with civil and political rights[2] are to Chinese civilization.

This chapter suggests that just as the mid-May portrayals of the triumph of democracy in the People's Republic of China (PRC) and mid-June characterizations of the inevitability of authoritarianism there were overdrawn, so too, the dichotomy between universality and cultural specificity in the area of human rights is often overstated. The first part, "The Pro-Democracy Movement and the Universality of Human Rights," examines the rhetoric and actions of the PRC's pro-democracy movement in an effort to identify respects in which it may or may not affirm notions of universality. The second part, "The Historical Context," casts the seeming and actual contradictions of the movement in a broader context. The final part, "Reflections on the Universality and Relativity of Human Rights," returns to the question of universality versus specificity or relativity, offering modest suggestions as to steps toward a realization of greater civil and political rights for that quarter of humanity that is Chinese.

The Pro-Democracy Movement
and the Universality of Human Rights

If the Chinese populace suffers from the propagandistic nature of the PRC's state-run press, the North American public is also ill-served by the superficial coverage of the PRC that most United States media provide. So it was that safari-jacket–clad American journalists equated the student leaders of the PRC's pro-democracy movement with the founders of the American revolution while solemnly intoning that the democratic genie was forever out of its bottle. The truth is a good deal more complex.[3]

To be sure, the PRC's pro-democracy movement has been deeply influenced by and is in several important respects seriously committed to many of the key civil and political rights recognized in international law. Throughout the 1980s, PRC citizens experienced an unprecedented, if still curtailed, measure of freedom and openness to the outside world.[4] Both were seen by the leadership as necessary to engage a disenchanted intelligentsia[5] and to enlist foreign technology and capital in rebuilding an economy ravaged by the Great Proletarian Cultural Revolution and earlier times of turmoil.[6] That relatively greater freedom[7] made it possible for bolder souls to question the feasibility of attaining economic modernization in the absence of political reform.[8] Simultaneously, the PRC's "open door" policy provided examples of other nations, East and West, that were perceived by Chinese intellectuals as offering their citizenry much more in the way of human rights.[9]

Both before and after the PRC government's declaration of martial law on May 19, 1989, the pro-democracy movement provided confirmation for those who espouse the universality of human rights. Individuals such as Wei Jinsheng,[10] Ren Wending,[11] and Fang Lizhi[12] who, in their different ways, were to provide major inspiration for the movement, argued that the PRC could not move forward without far greater respect for what they saw as fundamental human rights. These views were perhaps most forcefully articulated by the celebrated astrophysicist Fang, who, in essence, declared that just as worldwide there was but one physics, so, too, could there be but a single democracy encompassing the types of civil and political liberties set forth in the Universal Declaration of Human Rights.[13] Although the students who formed the vanguard of the pro-democracy movement chose not to echo Fang directly, from its inception the "Autonomous Student Union of Beijing" called for freedom of the press,[14] while also endeavoring to constitute itself democratically.[15] And as in the days prior to martial law the movement came to include rapidly increasing number of teachers, journalists, bureaucrats, workers, and other citizens, calls for "democracy and science"—in which were blended what were perceived to be the essence of international human rights—became ever more abundant.[16]

Responses by demonstrators and others, prior to June 3, 1989, to the declaration of martial law, drew even more heavily upon the language and themes of international human rights. Students who had previously directed their energies toward sincere, if unworkable, demands for televised "dialogue" with the leadership now spoke of thoroughgoing democratization of China's political processes.[17] A full third of the members of the Standing Committee of the PRC's National People's Congress sought to deal with the crisis by petitioning for a special meeting of the Committee to review the legality of the martial law declaration.[18] And notwithstanding the government's reimposition of tight controls over the media, calls for increased human rights continued.[19]

The brutality of the leadership's efforts to suppress the pro-democracy movement from June 3, 1989, evidenced the futility of moral appeals to the leadership and consequently had a radicalizing effect upon many involved with or sympathetic to the movement. This, not surprisingly, led some to shift their focus from goals to tactics, including calls for the use of violence against both symbols of the Chinese leadership and foreigners viewed as collaborating with the authorities.[20] Nonetheless, for many more, the slaughter perpetrated by the ironically named People's Liberation Army and the subsequent widespread purges have reaffirmed how important it is that China move in a direction of greater respect for legality and for what are understood to be international human rights.[21]

To move beyond the monolithic picture of the forces espousing greater democratization presented in the United States media and to portray its features inconsistent with international human rights is not to denigrate that movement. Instead, it is to take seriously what the movement had to say, rather than merely hearing one's own voice in its words.[22]

Ironically, in equating the pro-democracy movement with the beginnings of the American Revolution, the American media failed to appreciate that many leaders of the movement echoed not only Thomas Jefferson and James Madison's call for greater democracy, but also the American Founders' constricted view of who was entitled to enjoy the full benefits of democracy. Just as the American Founders had scant room in their definition of democracy for blacks, women, and those at the bottom of society,[23] the students who comprised the core of the PRC's pro-democracy movement had little interest in the provision of democratic rights to ethnic minorities, women, or the PRC's vast peasantry and proletariat. Students from the campuses that were in the forefront of the Beijing Spring attacked African students resident in the PRC months earlier,[24] and raised no objection either to the imposition of martial law in Lhasa or to the slaughter of Tibetan activists by the People's Liberation Army in March of 1989 that presaged their own experience.[25] Nor had any appreciable number among them objected to the pervasive gender discrimination that permeates Chinese universities and intellectual circles.[26] And, at least in its early rhetoric, the movement did little to suggest that the right of suffrage, which was being sought primarily for intellectuals, should be extended to workers and farmers.[27] Indeed, the movement seemed almost as concerned with the possibility that peasants were free to make a great deal more money than newly minted university graduates as it was with enfranchising the PRC's unwashed.[28] Much as was the case with U.S. students of the 1960s and 1970s, whose demonstrations against the Vietnam War were shaped by both moral outrage against their government's perceived transgressions and their own desire to avoid an all-expenses-paid trip to Southeast Asia courtesy of Uncle Sam, the student movers of the pro-democracy forces in China were motivated by a mixture of idealism and self-interest.

The less than total affirmation of the principles of international human rights expressed in the pro-democracy movement's definition of those persons entitled to participate in governance is mirrored in other areas. Particularly before the government's brutality drove the movement to seek more comprehensive reform, its demands encompassed a relatively limited spectrum of what are typically seen as fundamental civil and political rights. With its early emphasis on dialogue between its elite membership and the state's governing elders, an end to corruption, and a more open press, the movement hardly spoke to, let alone challenged, the array of ways in which the Chinese government has routinely contravened a number of internationally recognized freedoms. These include freedom of movement,[29] freedom of emigration,[30] freedom of religion,[31] freedom to form independent trade unions,[32] the right to enter into marriage "only with the free and full consent of the intending spouse,"[33] the right to found a family,[34] freedom from arbitrary detention,[35] and the right to be presumed innocent.[36] Although it may be argued that the movement kept its demands to a minimum at the outset both to attain consensus and so as not to seem threatening to the government, there is little evidence to suggest that these other rights were of particular concern either before or after the evacuation of Tiananmen Square.[37] In any event, even the movement's more modest demands proved to be too much for the PRC leadership.

The Historical Context

Central to any determination of the degree to which contemporary notions of human rights are universal or culturally specific is the question of what it is to be human.[38] As Rhoda E. Howard, Manuela Carneiro da Cunha, and other contributors to this volume remind us, culture—and with it, definitions of humanity—are hardly static or monolithic within any given society.[39] To the contrary, culture varies over time and according to one's relative position and power. The artificiality of efforts to set forth the central features of any society's culture is heightened in the case of China, given that it has the world's longest continuously documented history and that it has for long been the most populous nation. Nonetheless, there is a value in endeavoring to portray the core of Chinese culture, even in the limited space permitted by this short chapter, lest one fail to heed Abdullahi An-Na'im's injunction against lightly presuming universality.[40] And so, in this spirit and being mindful of the ancient Chinese admonition about the folly of "viewing flowers on horseback" (*zuo ma kan hua*) I attempt here, albeit too simplistically, to sketch Chinese thinking as to what it means to be human.

As with so much else in the PRC, to understand current definitions of humanity it is necessary first to appreciate traditional Chinese ideas concerning it—not because the latter have been unchanging, but because a failure to take them into consideration will diminish our ability to discern the impact that the domestic changes of the past four decades, increasing international contact, and other forces have had upon them.

Although it would be erroneous to reduce traditional Chinese thinking about the essence of humanity to a single set of ideas, it would be no less misleading to ignore the centrality in Chinese society of the notion that individuals derived meaning in life through their membership in an intricate web of social relationships, rather than chiefly on their own or in a solitary nexus with a higher authority.[41] Especially in classical Confucian thought, civilization was defined through adherence to a paradigmatic set of relationships, each bearing reciprocal although not necessarily equal responsibilities and expectations which the parties involved were morally bound to meet.[42] Adherence to the most important of these—between ruler and subject, husband and wife, father and son—on the part of all involved was thought necessary if social harmony was to flourish.[43]

To note the importance of this holistic view is not to endorse stereotypic portrayals either of the Chinese as lacking in individuality or of the imperial Chinese state as an unrelieved autocracy. To be sure, values such as autonomy and mobility were not prized as ends in themselves in the way that they are in contemporary Western democracies. Nonetheless, individuals from the humblest female subject on up were seen both as having expectations that others would treat them in accord with the relationships of which they were a part, as well as concomitant obligations to discharge the responsibilities that flowed from their own role in those established relationships.[44]

Chinese government and law throughout much of the imperial era (221 B.C.–A.D. 1912) mirrored the vision previously described. Rather than being conceived of as a state, the imperial Chinese polity was more typically understood, at least in theory, as an extended family. In it, the ruler, as parent, had fiduciary obligations to provide for both the physical and spiritual well-being of the populace, who, in turn, were to be loyal and productive.[45] Law, which was to be resorted to only if more desirable instruments of social ordering, such as morality, failed,[46] reinforced the metaphor of family by providing for differential punishments according to the relationship of the individuals involved.[47] As befits a family, however, there was no formal legal recourse against the ruler should moral suasion fail to lead him to discharge his duties properly, although particular officials could be punished for failing to carry out their imperially charged responsibilities.[48]

Not surprisingly, initial contact between imperial China and post-Enlightenment Europe did not proceed smoothly, given their fundamentally different definitions of humanity and society. Although the Chinese accorded these "hairy barbarians,"[49] who they did not see as fully human, extraordinary privileges,[50] by the mid-eighteenth century the Europeans were distressed with what they construed as an absence in Chinese justice of respect for fundamental human dignity.[51] These differing visions came to a head in the Opium War (1839–43)[52] and the treaties flowing therefrom, pursuant to which the British—and later the United States and other so-called Treaty Powers—provided that foreign nationals committing offenses against Chinese in China would be tried by foreign officials pursuant to foreign law.[53] So it was that, in the name of humanity and legality, Britain fought a brutal war on behalf of opium sales that resulted in the semicolonial imposition of a legal system that in many respects replicated what was supposedly most deficient in the Chinese system.[54]

Defeat in the Opium War and the imposition of a system of extraterritoriality shocked Chinese thinkers, raising fundamental questions as to how China might restore its earlier power and independence. Initially, Chinese "self-strengtheners" assumed that the issue was simply one of acquiring Western armaments and other items of advanced technology.[55] When these early efforts proved incapable of appreciably altering the balance of power vis-à-vis the West, a second wave of intellectuals argued that while society should essentially be preserved as it was, China needed to emulate certain of the institutions and forms of the West.[56] Some called for the adoption of representative government and equality before the law, but not as ends. Instead, these foreign ideas were seen as having been instrumental in the West's rise to power and, as such, capable of strengthening China by enhancing the bond between ruler and people.[57]

The failure of such instruments—which the Qing dynasty (A.D. 1644–1912) adopted only grudgingly and in limited form in its last years[58]—persuaded yet other late nineteenth- and early twentieth-century thinkers that more was needed if the challenges of the day were to be met. China could only be saved as a state and, indeed, as a civilization, it was felt, if the very core of traditional Chinese ways of thinking was revised to take serious account of "modern" ideas of rights and democracy. While advocates of these views did not necessarily address the definition of an individual as such, implicit in the reordering for which they called was a different notion of what it meant to be human. Eager to transcend the hierarchical and other bonds imposed by Confucianism while preserving its more worthy features, they spoke increasingly of equality as an objective, rather than merely an instrument. Most prominent among them was Sun Yat-sen, who argued that only adoption of a hybrid system of government that blended together what he saw as the best of East and West could keep the "loose sand" that was China from falling into disorder.[59] And yet even Sun—and other proponents of such reform—evidenced something less than complete faith in their fellow Chinese, as they advocated withholding the franchise from China's largely rural and uneducated populace until it had undergone a period of "tutelage."

The popularity that the ideas of Sun and others of like mind gained among Westernized intellectuals and foreign sympathizers masks their relative ineffectuality.[60] The models that they sought to emulate presumed conditions that did not—and still do not—obtain in Chinese society, such as political stability, an independent press, a professional bench and bar, and, perhaps most tellingly, a leadership ultimately willing to share its power with the populace.[61] Even had these conditions obtained, it is unclear what effect the ideas in question might have had, given the degree to which they ran counter to so many fundamental dimensions of Chinese thought[62]—including its definition of what it meant to be human.

What is clear is that another Western import—albeit in such highly sinicized form that its pregenitors[63] and advocates outside of China[64] would hardly have recognized it—did carry the day. As it swept to power, Chinese Communism spoke of redefining and enhancing the humanity of a wide range of persons essentially at the bottom of traditional Chinese society. Both theoretically and concretely, Chinese Communism addressed itself to the situation of the vast rural underclass, a much smaller urban proletariat, and Chinese women in general. In theory, the new state was said to be led by an alliance of peasants, workers, and others who had historically been deemed unworthy of ruling.[65] More concretely, the People's Republic in its early years engaged in social engineering on a scale heretofore unknown, redistributing land,[66] liberating women from imposed wedlock,[67] tackling illiteracy and disease,[68] and confronting other enduring social problems.[69]

Nonetheless, for all its differences in rhetoric and advances in material conditions, Chinese Communism not only bore the imprint of many elements of earlier Chinese ideologies regarding what it means to be human, but also may well have been successful because its mass appeal was cast in such terms. Although rejecting Confucianism, Chinese Communism shared with it—at least relative to Western liberalism—an emphasis upon collective welfare and a sense that a morally superior elite was uniquely positioned to prevent China's "loose sand . . . from retrogress[ing] into divisions and confusion," as Deng Xiaoping put it in 1980, consciously borrowing Sun Yat-sen's words.[70] The "rights" of which the PRC Constitutions spoke were neither inherent nor inalienable by virtue of one's humanity.[71] Instead, as with Confucian relational bonds, they were a product of one's status in society (with class replacing family)[72] meant to be exercised with that end in mind and available, ultimately, for the purpose of fostering collective welfare.[73] And as with Confucianism, moral suasion, rather than formal legality, was to be the means of prompting wayward leaders properly to discharge their responsibilities to the populace—as evidenced by the absence in each PRC Constitution of any clear legal remedy for unconstitutional acts.[74]

Given this heritage and context, it may be appropriate to understand the pro-democracy movement of 1989 as much as an echo of the Chinese past as a clarion call to a new future. In using a rhetoric of rights and legality borrowed from abroad to try to coax a recalcitrant ruler to abandon its corrupt ways and fulfill its responsibilities to the collective, the student elite of 1989 bears more than a faint resemblance to the self-strengtheners of the late nineteenth century, the eclectic reformers of the early twentieth century and, for that matter, the Communist Party itself. And even now the pro-democracy movement—for all its heroism—in general seems more concerned with the acquisition of proper use of power to attain the collective good than it does with the value of rights for individuals in and of themselves, apart from any instrumental function. In short, as distinct as they may seem to be, these different Chinese schools of thinking may be closer to one another in their definition of humanity and concomitant conception of what fosters human dignity than they are to the assumptions that undergird those portions of the principal international conventions devoted to civil and political rights.

Reflections on the Universality and Relativity of Human Rights

Efforts to suggest paths for bringing definitions of human rights articulated in the principal international instruments and Chinese values closer must commence with a candid acknowledgment of their differences. It is true that both the Western liberal tradition and the Chinese schools of thought previously discussed are concerned with promoting human dignity, but their respective ways of fostering it and their sense of its purpose are different in important regards. That they are different need not entail an absolute endorsement of one and total rejection of the other, nor a valueless and mindless relativism equating the two. Put concretely, while both the PRC government's massacre of predominantly unarmed civilian demonstrators and the British government's refusal of the right of abode to its Hong Kong Chinese subjects on racial grounds[75] are repugnant from an international human rights viewpoint, these actions neither wholly condemn the traditions from which they flow nor are problematic in the same way or to the same degree.

The commonalities and differences are evident in the PRC's so-called one-child policy.[76] Clearly, certain extralegal steps taken by the citizenry in reaction to the policy—such as female infanticide[77] and coerced abortion and sterilization[78] are abhorrent from the standpoint of human rights as expressed in the international instruments, and warrant far stronger approbation than the PRC government has provided.[79] The government ought not to escape responsibility for the fact that its principal rural economic policies work at cross-purposes with its population control policy.[80] But the more difficult question lies in assessing the one-child policy as the PRC government intends it to work. An argument can be made that even when functioning as intended, the policy violates Article 16 of the Universal Declaration of Human Rights. After all, if mature adults are not free to have a family when they choose, is that not a violation of that portion of Article 16 providing that "men and women of full age . . . have the right to . . . found a family"? But one may argue in response that a basic and broadly shared precept underlying human rights is that of the fundamental human "dignity" spoken of in Article I of the Declaration and reflected throughout the whole body of international human rights documents.[81] Given the best demographic and agricultural projections, there is currently little doubt that mass malnutrition and even starvation—and a concomitant loss of human dignity—would ensue early in the next century if all Chinese were free to bear children whenever they chose.[82]

Confronted with what is arguably the PRC's most compelling challenge to human rights, the Universal Declaration and the other major international human rights documents—which, after all, were drafted predominantly by Western men having little direct interest in or experience with the type of population pressures confronting nations such as China—provide faint, if any, guidance. Indeed, they are of no help with respect to the question of the prevention or termination even of a single pregnancy, be it in the PRC or elsewhere. In this void, the Chinese have, in a manner redolent of the definition of humanity described in the previous section of this chapter, at least in theory chosen to emphasize collective welfare and to rely upon the familiar mechanism of the small group employing moral suasion as the chief means of attaining that end.[83]

The dilemma of the one-child policy underscores the complexity of bringing Chinese values and international human rights into closer alignment. Touching though it may be, the faith exhibited in Tore Lindholm's chapter in this volume, that current international standards of human rights should and will prevail universally, is deeply troubling in its ethnocentricity. The chapter fails to heed seriously the critique of those who choose to place less emphasis than does the contemporary West on the atomized autonomous individual. It discounts the importance of participation by persons outside of the West in the formation of international standards. And it ignores the contribution other cultures might make to our own understanding of what it is to be human. If Lindholm is too quick to see that understanding emanating from the West as universal, Richard Falk may well be too ready to abandon it in favor of the culturally specific.[84] As the Chinese case amply illustrates, contrary to Falk's romanticization of the agrarian past, "cultural foundations" do not necessarily provide a distinct "civil society," let alone strong affirmations of egalitarianism, democracy, and tolerance for diversity. Nor, as the Chinese case also reveals, is modernization necessarily synonymous with Westernization.

To the extent that Chinese or foreign observers would advocate further Chinese movement toward the civil and political rights standards articulated in the international documents, it would seem that their efforts would be enhanced to the degree that they seek to build on and take account of Chinese circumstances. Appeals to adopt international standards for their own sake or because their advocates believe that these standards enhance individual freedom as an end in itself are less likely to be successful than those that endeavor to portray the instrumental value of human rights in the process of building the state, and thereby securing the collective good.[85] Although purists might recoil, the more that one can show the relationship between those features of foreign societies that are most desired by the Chinese—such as the West's technological prowess—and fundamental human rights, as embodied in the Universal Declaration of Human Rights,[86] the more likely it is that one will generate support for such rights. So, too, the more mindful one is of the manner in which a century and a half of foreigners have denounced Chinese standards as inferior, the better is one's chance of being heard.

In advocating that the Chinese move further toward internationally recognized civil and political rights, one nevertheless ought not to ignore the impact of such movement upon that which may be most admirable in the Chinese tradition. The very conditions that are likely over time to generate more support for international ideas of civil and political rights—such as industrialization, urbanization, and internationalization—also work to erode the sense of the community and of the collective that provides much of what has been respectful of human dignity in Chinese civilization.[87] Witness, for example, recent developments with regard to the one-child policy, as wealth, rather than community consensus, is increasingly becoming the practical determinant of who shall have second children.[88] In this, as with so many other aspects of Chinese life, the challenge will be to ascertain how best to preserve worthy dimensions of a long and rich history while expanding opportunities for the Chinese people to partake more fully in the panoply of internationally recognized human rights. Only then will the PRC's "loose sand" form a genuinely Chinese Goddess of Democracy.

Notes

1. I use this term to refer to the events arising in the People's Republic of China (PRC) between the death of former Chinese Communist Party General Secretary Hu Yaobang on April 15, 1989, and the installation of Jiang Zemin as Party General Secretary late in June 1989. It encompasses the so-called pro-democracy movement, the PRC Army's attack on the occupiers of Tiananmen Square and similar assaults launched elsewhere on June 3–4, and the trials and purges conducted since that time of persons understood by the Chinese government to be connected with that movement.

2. Here for example, I refer to the United Nations Charter, the Universal Declaration of Human Rights, and the International Covenant on Civil and Political Rights. The PRC, although a member of the United Nations, has yet to endorse the Declaration or ratify the Covenant.

3. See William P. Alford, "'Seek Truth from Facts'—Especially When They Are Unpleasant: America's Understanding of China's Efforts at Law Reform," *UCLA Pacific Basin Law Journal* 8 (1990): 177.

4. J. K. Fairbank, *The Great Chinese Revolution: 1800–1985* (New York: Harper and Row, 1986), 342–68.

5. On the experience of the intelligentsia in modern times, *see* A. Thurston, *Enemies of the People: The Ordeal of the Intellectuals in China's Great Cultural Revolution* (Cambridge, Mass.: Harvard University Press, 1988), *passim.*

6. *Ibid.*

7. For a survey of the many restraints throughout even the best of these times, *see* Y. L. Wu, F. Michael, J. Copper, T. L. Lee, M. H. Chang, and A. J. Gregor, *Human Rights in the People's Republic of China* (Boulder Colo.: Westview Press, 1988).

8. *See* the example of Wei Jingsheng, who argued that the four modernizations advocated by the Chinese state (of industry, agriculture, technology and the military) would be possible only if joined with a "fifth" (that is, political) modernization. In 1979, Wei was convicted of "writing counterrevolutionary articles and editing a counterrevolutionary magazine" (as well as passing materials to a foreigner about China's war in Vietnam) and sentenced to fifteen years' imprisonment. Timothy Gelatt, "The Bounds of Free Expression in China," *Asian Wall Street Journal* (December 18, 1979), 6. For more on Wei, *see* Amnesty International, *Violations of Human Rights: Prisoners of Conscience and the Death Penalty in the People's Republic of China* (London, 1984), 24–27.

9. Orville Schell, "An Act of Defiance," *New York Times,* April 16, 1989, 27. The PRC government has been slow to provide its people with news of the changes underway in Eastern Europe.

10. *See supra* note 8. In the winter and spring of 1989 Chinese intellectuals petitioned the government to release Wei. *Ibid.*

11. *See* the materials from Ren in *Seeds of Fire, Chinese Voices of Conscience,* ed. G. Barme and J. Minford (Hong Kong: Far Eastern Economic Review, 1986).

12. Fang Lizhi, *Women zhengzai xieli shi* (Taipei: Taipei Reprint, 1987).

13. *See* the essays of Fang in O. Schell, *Discoes and Democracy: China in the Throes of Reform* (New York: Pantheon, 1988). *Also see* William P. Alford and Fang Lizhi, "The Image and the (Overrated) Influence," *Chicago Tribune,* September 21, 1990, 21.

14. "Students Present Demands," Agence France Presse, May 2, 1989, 1.

15. For example, the students sought to assure representation from all major Beijing institutions of higher learning. For a comprehensive compilation of the views of those taking part in the spring 1989 demonstrations, *see* Han Minzhu, ed., *Cries for Democracy* (Princeton, N.J.: Princeton University Press, 1990).

16. "The Shattered Dream," *Los Angeles Times,* June 25, 1989, part I-A.

17. *Ibid.*

18. The issue of the legality of martial law was raised, for example, in an open letter by PRC students in the United States to Wan Li, Chair of the National People's Congress. Zhongguo liu Mei xueren (Chinese Scholars in North America), "Zi Wan Li de gongkai xin" (An Open Letter to Wan Li), reprinted in *Minyun zhuanzhi* [*The Quest*], no. 66 (June 1989): 26–27.

19. *See supra* note 16.

20. "Return of the Leftist Line," *Asiaweek* (August 4, 1989): 25; Cheung Po-ling, "Clandestine Hit Squads Reportedly Forming," *Hong Kong Standard,* July 19, 1989, 6; "The Hopes of China," *Mother Jones* (December 1989), 52.

21. Roderick MacFarquhar, "Outside Agitators for Democracy," *U.S. News & World Report* (August 7, 1989), 34.

22. William P. Alford, "On the Limits of 'Grand Theory' in Comparative Law," *Washington Law Review* 61 (1986): 945.

23. *See, for example,* Thomas Jefferson, *Notes on the State of Virginia* (New York: Norton, 1972).

24. Helena Kolenda and Yvonne Chan, "Outsiders in China," *Boston Globe,* January 31, 1989, 32.

25. Both the attack by the People's Liberation Army upon essentially unarmed (if angry) civilians and the martial law imposed on Beijing had precedents in Tibet. Indeed, the martial law decrees are, in their most important provisions, virtually identical.

26. *See, for example,* E. Honig and G. Hershatter, *Personal Voices: Chinese Women in the 1980s* (Stanford, Calif.: Stanford University Press, 1988), 323–25.

27. Alford, *supra* note 3.

28. Sarah Lubman, "The Myth of Tiananmen Square: The Students Talked of Democracy But They Didn't Practice It," *Washington Post,* July 30, 1989, C5.

29. *See* Article 13 of the Universal Declaration of Human Rights.

30. *Ibid.*

31. *Ibid.,* Art. 18.

32. *Ibid.,* Art. 23. The PRC has trade unions, but they are state-controlled—which was a key objection of workers who participated in the pro-democracy movement.

33. *Ibid.,* Art. 16.

34. *Ibid.*

35. *Ibid.,* Art. 9.

36. *Ibid.,* Art. 11.

37. These problems are discussed in Wu et al., *supra* note 7.

38. This basic idea was presented by James Feinerman in a talk on human rights in China at Harvard Law School (April 1989).

39. *See* Rhoda E. Howard's Chapter 4 and Manuela Carneiro da Cunha's Chapter 11 in this volume.

40. *See* Abdullahi A. An-Na'im's Chapter 1 in this volume. *See also* William P. Alford, "The Inscrutable Occidental: Roberto Unger's Uses and Abuses of the Chinese Past," *Texas Law Review* 64 (1986): 915.

41. Alford, *ibid., passim.*

42. *Ibid.*

43. *Ibid.*

44. *Ibid.*

45. *Ibid.*

46. *Ibid.*

47. *Ibid.* Thus, for example, a son striking a father would be punished more severely than a father striking a son. *See* "The Case of Hsü Chüng-wei," in William P. Alford, Chinese Law (unpublished course materials, 1989, section 2), 113.

48. *Ibid.* Indeed as the case of Hsü Chüng-wei demonstrates, officials were, in theory, to be punished for misfeasance, as well as malfeasance.

49. Edwards, "Ch'ing Legal Jurisdiction Over Foreigners," in *Essays on China's Legal Tradition,* ed. J. Cohen, R. Edwards and F. Chang Chen (Princeton, N.J.: Princeton University Press, 1980), 222.

50. *Ibid.*

51. *Ibid.*

52. Opium was virtually the only commodity the British were able to sell to balance their earlier huge trading deficit with China. Although there was opium usage in China prior to British sales, it was relatively modest.

53. G. Keeton, *The Development of Extraterritoriality in China* (New York reprint, 1969), 137–99.

54. W. Fischel, *The End of Extraterritoriality in China* (Berkeley and Los Angeles: University of California Press, 1952). The consular legal system established by the United Kingdom, the United States, and other Treaty Powers could be faulted on the very grounds on which the West believed Chinese justice to be deficient. Executive and judicial authority resided with a single official, who typically had no legal training. The laws were in a foreign language and frequently inaccessible. And the procedures pursuant to which trials were to be conducted were unfamiliar and ill-designed to produce a just result.

55. Fairbank, *supra* note 4, at 100–21.

56. M. Wright, *The Last Stand of Chinese Conservatism* (Stanford, Calif.: Stanford University Press, 1957).

57. *Ibid.*

58. A. Nathan, *Chinese Democracy* (Berkeley and Los Angeles: University of California Press, 1985).

59. Sun Yat-sen, *San Min Chu I: The Three Principles of the People* (Shanghai: Commercial Press, 1928).

60. E. Friedman, *Backward Toward Revolution* (Berkeley and Los Angeles: University of California Press, 1974).

61. *Ibid.*

62. Andrew Nathan, "Sources of Chinese Rights Thinking," in *Human Rights in Contemporary China,* ed. R. Edwards, L. Henkin and A. Nathan (New York: Columbia University Press, 1986), 125.

63. Karl Marx, "Revolution in China and Europe," *New York Daily Tribune,* June 14, 1953; reprinted in Karl Marx, *On Colonialism* (New York: International Publishers, 1974), 19–26.

64. V. Lenin, "State and Revolution," reprinted in *Essential Works of Marxism,* ed. A. Mendel (New York: Bantam Books, 1965), 103.

65. Zhongguo renmin gongheguo xianfa (People's Republic of China, Preamble to 1982 Constitution). *Reprinted* in both Chinese and English in Commerce Clearing House, *Collection of Laws and Regulations of China Concerning Foreign Economic and Trade Relations* (Melbourne, Australia, 1983), I-2.

66. Fairbank, *supra* note 4, at 277–83.

67. *Ibid.*

68. *Ibid.*

69. For example, relatively successful campaigns to eradicate opium smoking and prostitution were launched.

70. "Text of Deng Xiaoping's Report on the Current Situation," quoted in A. Nathan, *supra* note 62, at 159.

71. A. Nathan, *supra* note 58.

72. J. Cohen, *The Criminal Process in the People's Republic of China, 1949–1963: An Introduction* (Cambridge, Mass.: Harvard University Press, 1968).

73. *See, for example,* the Preamble to the 1982 Constitution, *supra* note 65.

74. I know of no record of a successful constitutional challenge to any issue in the forty-year history of the PRC. Nor are any of the PRC legal scholars I know aware of any such challenges that were successful. For more on constitutions in a Chinese setting, *see* Nathan, *supra* note 58.

75. For a sharp denunciation of the British government's refusal to provide its non-Caucasian subjects resident in Hong Kong with a right of abode, *see* Editorial, "Dialogue with the Deaf Produces No Answers," *South China Morning Post,* July 5, 1989, 22.

76. For a detailed description of the program, *see* P. Kane, *The Second Billion* (New York: Penguin, 1987).

77. Julie Jimmerson, "Female Infanticide in China: An Examination of Cultural and Legal Norms," *UCLA Pacific Basin Law Journal* 8 (1990): 47.

78. Jeffrey Wasserstrom, "Resistance to the One Child Policy," *Modern China* 10 (July 1984): 359.

79. *See* Kane, *supra* note 76.

80. J. Stacy, *Patriarchy and Socialist Revolution in China* (Berkeley and Los Angeles: University of California Press, 1983).

81. *See supra* note 2. In speaking of "dignity," I do not endorse Rhoda E. Howard's suggestion that dignity in traditional culture perforce entails acceptance of hierarchy. See her Chapter 4 in this volume.

82. *See* Kane, *supra* note 76.

83. M. Whyte, *Small Groups and Political Rituals in China* (Berkeley and Los Angeles: University of California Press, 1974).

84. *See* Richard Falk's Chapter 2 in this volume.

85. Toward that end, reference might be made to the example of Taiwan, which appears increasingly to be appreciating the value of openness.

86. For example, one might endeavor to demonstrate the link between economic development and a media not controlled by the state.

87. Alford, *supra* note 40.

88. Ann Joyce, "China: United States Withdrawal of Support from the United Nations Fund for Population Activities," *Harvard Human Rights Yearbook* 1 (1988): 213.

Rhoda E. Howard[1]

4. Dignity, Community, and Human Rights

Introduction

In this chapter I argue that most known human societies did not and do not have conceptions of human rights. Human rights are a moral good that one can accept—on an ethical basis—and that everyone ought to have in the modern state-centric world. To seek an anthropologically based consensus on rights by surveying all known human cultures, however, is to confuse the concepts of rights, dignity, and justice. One can find affinities, analogues, and precedents for the actual content of internationally accepted human rights in many religious and cultural (geographic and national) traditions;[2] but the actual concept of *human* rights, as will be seen, is particular and modern, and representing a radical rupture from the many status-based, nonegalitarian, and hierarchical societies of the past and present. In many cultures, the social order stratifies "individuals" in ways that enhance dignity for some categories of people but leave other categories dishonored, without dignity or respect. Furthermore, most indigenous cultures of the various regions of the world—such as those of North America, Japan, and China—have privileged the community or the collectivity over the individual.[3]

Human rights are a modern concept now universally applicable in principle because of the social evolution of the entire world toward state societies. The concept of human rights springs from modern human thought about the nature of justice; it does not spring from an anthropologically based consensus about the values, needs, or desires of human beings. As Jack Donnelly puts it, the concept of human rights is best interpreted by constructivist theory:

> Human rights aim to establish and guarantee the conditions necessary for the development of the human person envisioned in . . . [one particular]

underlying moral theory of human nature, thereby bringing into being that type of person. . . . The evolution of particular conceptions or lists of human rights is seen in the constructivist theory as the result of the *reciprocal interactions of moral conceptions and material conditions of life,* mediated through social institutions such as rights.[4]

Human rights tend to be particularly characteristic of liberal and/or social democratic societies.[5] These are societies that have undergone changes in the material conditions of life, or, in Marxist terms, in the mode of production, in the direction of various forms of capitalism. These material changes coincided with various changes in ideology or moral conceptions, both in the strictly religious sphere and in conceptions of how society ought to be organized and of what makes a physical human being a social being. Ideologically rights-based societies, then, hold particular conceptions of human dignity and social justice that are in principle universally applicable, although not universal in origin. While ideals of dignity and justice can be located in all societies and can sometimes be used to buttress new ideals of the content of human rights,[6] human rights are a radically new concept in human history, and their acceptance in any given society constitutes a rupture of previous belief systems.

Human Rights, Dignity, and Justice

HUMAN RIGHTS
Human rights adhere to the human being *by virtue of being human, and for no other reason. Every human being ought to have human rights, regardless of status or achievement.* In a rights-based political system, a person's human rights can in principle be removed only under very restricted circumstances adjudicable by law (for example, a convicted criminal loses the right to freedom of movement). Human rights are *claims by the individual against society and the state* that, furthermore, "trump" other considerations such as the legal (but not human) right of a corporation to property. Human rights are private, individual, and autonomous. They are private because they inhere in the human person him- or herself, unmediated by social relations. They are consequently individual; an isolated human being can in principle exercise them. In addition, they are autonomous because again, in principle, no authority other than the individual is required to make human rights claims.

This means that the human being who holds rights holds them not only against the state, but also against "society," that is, against his or her community or even family. This orientation is a radical departure from the way most human societies in the past—and many in the present—have been or are organized. For most human societies, insofar as "rights" might be considered to be applicable at all, collective or communal rights would be preferred to individual human rights. The stress on community as against the individual is reflected in the current debate in international legal circles over whether "human" rights should also include collective rights.[7] But the claim for collective rights is a claim for something very different from human rights; it is a claim that reasserts the value of the traditional community over the individual. Human rights are an egalitarian means of allocating membership in a collectivity to all physical persons, regardless of status. Collective or community rights imply permissible inegalitarian ranking of members in the interests of preservation of "tradition."

DIGNITY

I define human dignity as *the particular cultural understandings of the inner moral worth of the human person and his or her proper political relations with society*.[8] Dignity is not a claim that an individual asserts against a society; it is not, for example, the claim that one is worthy of respect merely because one is a human being. Rather, dignity is something that is granted at birth or on incorporation into the community as a concomitant of one's particular ascribed status, or that accumulates and is earned during the life of an adult who adheres to his or her society's values, customs, and norms: the adult, that is, who accepts normative cultural constraints on his or her particular behavior. In many preliterate societies, individuals who chose not to earn such dignity, who consistently violated instead of obeying the underlying social norms, were cast out through exile or through conversion into slavery. As the sociologist Orlando Patterson explains, as slaves they lost all honor (or dignity) and suffered "natal alienation"; that is, they were literally cast out from their own family group and removed from the networks of privileges and obligations that tied society together.[9]

Many indigenous groups (that is, the remnants of precapitalist societies destroyed—physically, culturally, or both—during the process of European conquest and/or settlement) now make claims for the recognition of their collective or communal rights. When they do so they are not primarily interested in the human rights of the individual members of their collectivities. Rather, they are interested in the recognition of their *collective dignity,* in the acknowledgment of the value of their collective way of life as opposed to the way of life of the dominant society into which they are unequally "integrated." In Canada, this means, among other things, the recognition of the land rights and the fishing, hunting, and trapping rights of collective First Nation or "Native" groups, so that they can maintain an agricultural or hunting and gathering mode of production despite the prevailing capitalism of the dominant European-origin society.

That these collective rights-claims are not synonymous with individual human rights is well illustrated by the recent debate and legislative changes in Canada concerning the right of Native women who married outside the reserves (and their descendants) to return to live on reserves. Some Native women claimed, and all were eventually granted, the right to move back onto reserves; they based their claim on the grounds of equality of women and men. But such grounds stem from the Enlightenment tradition of human rights incorporated in the twentieth century into such documents as the Universal Declaration of Human Rights. Counterposed against the Native women claiming their right of return were some Native leaders who argued for their collective right to determine who would live on a reserve, in such a manner as to preserve the integrity of the Native community even at the possible expense of individual women's rights. The issue was compounded by the fact that the rule expelling intermarried Native women was originally imposed by European-origin Canadians, who used their own patrilineal and patrilocal culture as a means of enforcing assimilation and reducing the number of Indians entitled to treaty rights. Thus Native Canadians, engaged in a continual struggle to preserve their collective dignity, were doubly at the mercy of changes in European ideologies of social membership.[10] The conflict between concepts of individual human rights that require equality of the sexes, and collective rights to a group dignity that might countenance inequality of the sexes, remains.

Thus in most known past or present societies, human dignity is not private, individual, or autonomous. It is public, collective, and prescribed by social norms. The idea that an individual can enhance his or her "dignity" by asserting his or her human rights violates many societies' most fundamental beliefs about the way social life should be ordered. Part of the dignity of a human being consists of the quiet endurance and acceptance of what a human rights approach to the world would consider injustice or inequality. We can see this underlying social belief most clearly in modern North America in the reaction of many men and women to feminists. Women making rights-claims against the state, society, and the family are frequently depicted as "shrill," "strident," or overly emotional. Such depictions emphasize the undignified way in which they are behaving when they refuse to bear injustice as properly socialized women should. This brings us to the question, then, of what exactly "justice" means.

JUSTICE

Different societies have different conceptions of social justice. I define social justice as *the means by which all members of a society are treated in a fashion considered respectful of their (culturally defined) social station*. Justice consists of rules of appropriate social behavior and rules of fairness. Fairness, in most societies, does not imply equality either of wealth or of social status. What is fair varies according to whether one is young or old, male or female, "citizen" or stranger, chief, freeman, or slave; and within these summary categories, there are infinite gradations of status, such as can be seen in the caste system of India.

There are some indications of a cross-cultural, anthropologically based consensus of what fairness ought to entail. Barrington Moore, Jr., for example, suggests that in almost all societies, everyone is expected to work and there is a minimum level of subsistence that a working person can rightfully expect from the society at large. There are, he believes, "indications of a widespread feeling that people, even the most humble members of society, ought to have enough resources or facilities to do their job in the social order."[11] But as his reference to the "most humble" member of society indicates, even if one is treated fairly, one is not necessarily treated equally. Status differences mean differences in dignity, in the respect to which one is entitled, and in the type of justice one can therefore expect.

In modern liberal-democratic societies, the idea of different laws for different categories of persons is anathema. All are subject to the same rules. But in many past societies, laws varied depending on one's social category, and such variation was considered "just" by the majority of citizens socialized into that society. Thus, for example, if a European lord exercised his *droit du seigneur* over a peasant woman (the right to have sexual intercourse with her prior to marriage), that was not considered rape, whereas a sexual advance by a peasant male to a noble's daughter risked a severe penalty. For the same crimes, lords received more humane punishments—for example, simple hangings—than peasants, who might be tortured. Even clothing was regulated by sumptuary laws in order to ensure that everyone's social status was easily apparent.[12] Until the French Revolution, members of the French peasantry were not permitted to wear red; the "traditional" clothing of Breton peasants is in fact a modern adoption of red following the overthrow of Louis XVI.

Thus human rights imply a particular conception of what it means to be human. In the lexicon of human rights, humanity is a mere physical attribute; one is or is not a live human being. In most societies' lexicons of dignity and justice, however, to be human is a social attribute. There are degrees of humanity, the lowest being that of the slave, who is considered "socially dead."[13]

WHAT IS A HUMAN BEING?

What then is a human being? For many societies, the human being is the person who has learned and obeys the community's rules. A nonsocial, atomized individual is not human; he or she is a species of "other"—perhaps equivalent to a (presocialized) child, a stranger, a slave, or even an animal. There is very little room in most societies for Mead's "I"—the individual, self-reflective being—to emerge over the "me," that part of a being that absorbs his or her community's culture and faithfully follows the rules and customs expected of a person of his or her station.[14] The human group takes precedence over the human person.

In Freudian terms, perhaps more familiar to most thinkers about human rights than the sociological analysis of what makes a physical human a social person, many societies suppress the ego. Individualist reflection on the meaning and personal applicability of the rules that the child absorbs into his or her superego is not socially desirable. The type of human being that liberal capitalist society has created—frequently highly individualistic and self-seeking, alienated by choice from family and community—is not valued. Rather, the notion of honor retains its importance, and the honored person is someone integrated into the social group: "honor is a direct expression of status, a source of solidarity among social equals and a demarcation line against social inferiors."[15] But in the modern world the "homeless mind" has displaced the concept of honor. The individual whose egoistic reflection causes him to modify his perceptions of the social order embodied in the superego, and who goes so far as to impose his own desires over that social order, denies honor; and in so doing, he denies society itself.

This does not mean that human rights are not relevant, in the late twentieth century, to those societies in the world that retain precapitalist, nonindividualist notions of human dignity, honor, and the social order. The rise of the centralized state makes human rights relevant the world over. It does mean that to look for universalistic "roots" of human rights in different social areas of the world (often crudely summarized in geographical terms as "Africa" or "Asia") or in different religious traditions, is to abstract those societies and religions from culture and history. One can find, in Judaism and Christianity for example, strong moral analogues to the content—although not the concept—of contemporary human rights. But one can also find moral precepts justifying inequality and denial of what are now considered fundamental human rights. In the words of Arthur Schlesinger, Jr.:

> As a historian, I confess to a certain amusement when I hear the Judeo-Christian tradition praised as the source of our concern for human rights. In fact, the great religious ages were notable for their indifference to human rights in the contemporary sense. They were notorious not only for acquiescence in poverty, inequality, exploitation and oppression but for enthusiastic justifications of slavery, persecution, abandonment of small children, torture, genocide.
> *Religion enshrined and vindicated hierarchy, authority and inequality* . . . .[16]

In many nonliberal societies (and among many members of liberal-democratic polities), now and in the past, there are and have been very deeply rooted, perhaps psychologically inviolable, notions of moral order that obviate a belief in human equality and autonomy. In such societies, religious and community norms frequently entrench social inequalities that are considered immutable and reflective of the natural world. The status inequalities of human beings reflect notions of cosmological rectitude; violations of inequality, therefore, violate not only the human but also the natural order of things.

The Moral Order

ORDER AND CHAOS

In primitive societies the imperative to create social order guards against the possibility of cosmological chaos. Identifications of men with the sun and women with the moon, men with the right hand and women with the

left, men with cleanliness and women with dirt, and a host of other dichotomous interpretations of the obvious biological dichotomy of the human world, ensure that the sun will rise and set as it should, that the gods
will not suddenly destroy all. Anomaly and ambiguity, as Mary Douglas
has informed us, are shunned; in the marginal interstices between orderly
categories danger lies:

> Purity is the enemy of change, of ambiguity and compromise. Most of us . . .
> feel safer if our experience . . . [is] hard-set and fixed in form. . . . [T]he
> yearning for rigidity is in us all. It is part of our human condition to long for
> hard lines and clear concepts.[17]

The easiest and clearest social distinction to make is between men and
women; in many societies, as our own language reflects, the male is the
standard of humanness and the female is the deviation. As Simone de
Beauvoir put it in her classic feminist meditation, to be female is to be the
existential "Other."[18] The female is the threat, in many cultures, to the
orderliness created by males. Her body alone violates order; she bleeds
though she is not wounded. The female possessed of knowledge threatens
the orderly acquisition and delimitation of society's cognitive symbols created—in most cultures—by her male status superiors; thus from Eve to
medieval wise-women[19] and beyond, Judeo-Christian culture has punished the woman who exercises the *human* capacity for self-reflection with
its attendant threat of making claims upon society.

MORALITY AND DEVIANCE

Most societies, then, are rule-bound. Violations not only of law but also
of custom are severely sanctioned. Far from religion's having normally validated what are now considered to be human rights, religious authorities
in the past made it their business to reinforce status inequalities and punish
transgressors of social customs. In early modern Britain, priests could still
sentence social deviants such as adulterers to ostracism and the stocks.[20] In
1785 the Scottish poet Robert Burns did public penance in church for the
sin of fornication (after which he was released from his marriage vows).[21]
Persons not publicly punished for moral transgressions could be shunned,
ostracized, or exiled on the orders of religious or community authorities.

Such punishments seem strange to modern eyes. In modern Western
society, the power of the priest to sentence his parishioners to shunning,
ostracism, and expulsion from the community is difficult to understand.
Most individuals in our society interact simultaneously with a multiplicity

of communities. Family, friends, work associates, and religious cobelievers may have nothing to do with each other and may be completely compartmentalized aspects of an individual's social life; thus a shunning ordered by a priest would not be effective. Only in almost completely closed social groups, such as those of the Amish in the United States or the Hutterites in Canada, can the power of shunning still be effective.[22]

Rule-bounded societies exact punishments for nonconformity that violate fundamental human rights. Torture, a practice universally abhorred by those who favor human rights, is not, as frequently stated, a "cruel, *inhuman* and degrading" treatment.[23] Cruel it certainly is, degrading it is frequently meant to be: inhuman it is not. The human body is a symbol for the entire moral and natural universe. The being who violates the moral universe is corrected by having his or her physical universe violated in turn. Submission of the body to social punishment indicates conformity of the mind: that is, acceptance of the social order and one's place in it.

In such closed traditional societies, maintenance of one's dignity or honor is frequently more important than one's individual "rights," even to life.[24] Dishonor freely sought was severely sanctioned in earlier times. Thus the female rape victim in early Hammaburati society was assumed to have been complicitous in any rape committed within the city walls (where her cries for help should have been heard), and was punished accordingly.[25] "Death before dishonor" was the cry of an earlier world, where a woman's purity was her greatest symbolic attribute; nowadays, the modern North American woman considers such a slogan merely an indication of the degraded status of women. "Dignified" victims of rape are no longer expected to commit suicide or to seclude themselves in shame for the rest of their lives.

Like torture, capital punishment also upholds the moral order. In liberal societies of the present time, the morality of capital punishment is a subject for serious debate, and indeed in Canada and in the European Community it is no longer practiced. Many theorists of criminology deny the moral legitimacy of punishment, advocating that prisons be places of rehabilitation or, at worst, simple deterrence of future crimes. In most societies, however, retribution is the explicit principle that decrees how criminals are to be treated. Executions are public because they thereby demonstrate to those who obey the law the rectitude of their own actions, in comparison to those of the victims of the executioner's sword. The function of punishment is confirmation of social norms. Thus even in France of Revolutionary times capital punishment was explicitly seen as a way of promoting social order. The new, relatively more "humane" guillotine was extolled because "[t]he grandeur and elegance of the spectacle will attract many more people to the place of execution; more people will be impressed, and the rule of law will be more greatly respected."[26] In contemporary times, as the social order breaks down in countries such as Nigeria, public executions have become very popular: when increasing poverty tempts millions to theft, the execution of thieves validates the law-abiding citizen's choice to stay "poor but honest."

Physical punishment, then, is not inhuman. It is a manifestly human way of forcing deviant or recalcitrant individuals to reintegrate into society, to become, again, conforming social being rather than threatening individuals. Torture is used on actual deviants—and execution is displayed to potential deviants—for lack of "better," less physical and more psychological means of enforcing conformity. Personal sadism is not at the root of torture. Even the Nazi Gestapo, undoubtedly one of the cruelest organizations of torturers ever to exist, was interested in Soviet methods of punishment.[27] Presumably this was because the Soviet secret police had devised sophisticated psychological means of extracting confession, conformity, and acknowledgment of the legitimacy of the Stalinist moral order that did not rely on physical torture.[28] While some sadistic Nazis enjoyed torture for its own sake, for others torture was merely a means in an extreme situation to create the new Aryan community to which individualism, privacy, and autonomy were a threat.

CULTURE AND HUMAN RIGHTS

The moral order, then, is a substantial part of the culture that is so frequently extolled by relativists as that which makes societies "unique." Societies are not unique, however, while the particularities of their customs, norms, and beliefs can be fascinating, they are overridden by sociological regularities. The existence of culture itself is one such social regularity.

In all societies, there is a cultural foundation. It consists of the customs, norms, values, and beliefs inculcated by one generation into the next. An important social function of culture is to teach the young the rules of status in a society. Differentiating along status lines, the youngster learns how much deference to pay to different categories of adults and the appropriate demeanor with which to conduct himself or herself in various situations.[29] The young white South African, for example, learns that the deference he shows as a child to his black nanny must be replaced by an arrogant, superior demeanor by the time he reaches adolescence.[30] Culture frequently underpins notions of human dignity radically at odds with the concept of human rights. Most cultures distinguish the degrees of respect owed to different status groups and certainly do not teach their young that all human beings, regardless of social origin or category, deserve equal treatment. The obvious North American example is the segregation practices of the U.S. South, not overturned in law until the 1960s and still constituting powerful social norms, sanctions, and taboos. Such legal segregation also existed in Canada until at least 1965.[31]

A cultural relativist position, then, can easily become a philosophical stance that denies the universality of human rights. All societies do have underlying conceptions of human dignity and social justice. These conceptions can be identified; and certain commonalities of belief, for example, in the social value of work, can also be located on a transcultural basis. But in most known human societies, dignity and justice are not based on any idea of the *inalienable right* of the *physical,* socially *equal* human being against the claims of family, community, or the state. They are based on just the opposite, that is, the *alienable privileges* of *socially unequal* beings, considered to embody gradations of humanness according to socially defined status categories entitled to different degrees of respect.

While all societies have underlying concepts of dignity and justice, few have concepts of rights. Human rights, then, are a particular expression of human dignity. In most societies, dignity does not imply human rights. There is very little cultural—let alone universal—foundation for the concept, as opposed to the content, of human rights. The society that actively protects rights both in law and in practice is a radical departure for most known human societies. Most rights-protective societies are explicitly a product of the liberal tradition that evolved after the eighteenth century in Europe, and they are the products of social change that, both structurally and ideologically, was so disruptive as to create an almost entirely new conception of the human being.

SOCIAL CHANGE AND HUMAN RIGHTS

To discuss all of the various changes that took place, first in Western Europe and the settler colonies, then beyond, to bring about the new social order characterized in principle, if not yet in practice, by human rights, is beyond the scope of this chapter. Briefly, however, the changes in the conception of the human being can be summarized as follows. The key change is the development of a concept of the human being as *private* and individual.

Structural changes in the economy, briefly characterized as capitalism, induced concomitant changes in the way people lived. The change is summarized most succinctly in the sociological dichotomization of all societies into two "ideal types"—"traditional" and "modern." Although this dichotomy is extremely crude and does injustice in the vast array of non-capitalist, non-Western societies that exist, it does nonetheless capture an existential shift in the way human beings (first men, then later and more rarely, women) thought of themselves.

Modernization entails changes in relations of human beings to the natural world. Property, held by communities that used it in accordance with their need, is transformed into an individual possession that can be entirely disconnected from need and from the community's claims upon it. The connection of the community with nature is broken; the communal order no longer represents the natural order. Land and things become commodities to be bought and sold. People also become commoditized; social obligations among unequals give way to a market in labor power in which the purchaser has no obligations to the seller other than to pay an agreed-upon wage.

As the relation of the human to the natural world changes, so also does the relation of the human to the spiritual world. The development of science and technology allows men to control nature directly, without the continued mediation of the gods. A rupture between the individual human soul and the collective spirit occurs; the man in control of a machine no longer relies so clearly on his priest. Both private property and private accumulation of knowledge (as a substitute for religiously based magic) contribute to the emergence of the modern private individual. If he does not become an outright atheist or agnostic, the private man is frequently attracted by a more individualistic type of religion. Protestants communicate directly and silently with God in prayer; the priest no longer mediates for forgiveness of their sins.[32]

The home becomes, for such a private man, his inner sanctum, his castle, over which he rules as the medieval lord ruled his manor. Private property permits the acquisition of wealth, with the consequent accumulation of personal goods. But since it also allows for inheritance by one's own offspring, rather than redistribution to the community, such wealth is often invested in the private domain, inaccessible to the wider society but tangible to and inheritable by one's descendants. The obligation to the group, and to the group's gods, fades: the obligation to self and one's immediate family is strengthened.

Nor is the individual as reliant on the group for knowledge as his forefathers. As literacy spreads, knowledge can be, and is, acquired privately. Methods of socialization are increasingly privatized and increasingly vary by social class and position in the economy. Elite children are educated in their homes or in private academies. Even "public" education systems reflect class and other distinctions that remove individuals from cohesive social groups.

The ideal capitalist, then, is an individualized, private, autonomous creature. He seeks to make his own decisions on the basis of his own judgment: he objects to government "restrictions" on his autonomy even as he expects the government to safeguard his private interests. As his becomes the politically and economically dominant class, his values spread to the entire society. Status-based distinctions give way to a new stress on achievement that allows capitalists, regardless of their social origin, to demand respect for individual accomplishments. Earned money becomes more prestigious than inherited money, and the social order of inherited status disappears. These changes take place all over the world as the capitalist, private-oriented competitive economy spreads.[33] In Ghana, for example, private entrepreneurs increasingly chafe at the restrictions upon the use of their wealth implied by their membership in wider communities of village or ethnic group.[34]

The idea of privacy, then, is not universal; it is little known in precapitalist societies. Without privacy, one cannot develop a sense of the human individual as an intrinsically valuable being, abstracted from his or her social role. Indeed, this is evident in the manner by which different social groups have claimed rights even in the modern era. Women, insofar as they have been considered the embodiments of home and hearth, first had to extricate themselves from this connection and claim their right to privacy and autonomy before they could claim human rights.

Societies that accept the legitimacy of rights claims are modern and atypical. Most known human societies deny privacy, deny autonomy, and especially deny individualism. Socially induced conformity, public living, and collective, stratified decision-making are far more typical of human social existence than the rights-based societies that human rights activists wish were now the universal norm. Such a norm would, in practice, protect individuals in the modern world against the state and against other abusers of rights (such as the patriarch with his control of women and children).[35] But although universally applicable in principle, the human rights norm is not universally locatable in practice or ideology.

Liberalism, Conservatism, and Community

THE CHALLENGE OF HUMAN RIGHTS

The concept of human rights challenges both the ideal of community and, in those societies that are not liberal or individualist in orientation, the ideal of dignity. Dignity frequently means acceptance of social rules and norms; human rights implies challenge to precisely those norms. Dignity is often associated with social constraint, whereas human rights are associated with autonomy and freedom. As Orlando Patterson put it in his analysis of the connection between slavery (dishonor and natal alienation) and freedom, only slaves—those completely removed from society—were able to conceive, originally, of the value of such removal and its possibilities for autonomous freedom (individual rights):

> Before slavery people simply could not have conceived of the thing we call freedom. Men and women in premodern, nonslaveholding societies did not, could not, value the removal of restraint as an ideal. Individuals yearned only for the security of being positively anchored in a network of power and authority. Happiness was membership: being was belonging. . . . [36]

In earlier work I have argued that a liberal—or perhaps better, a social democratic—human rights regime is characterized by the autonomy, equality, and respect accorded to the individual.[37] Human rights challenge the basis on which people in nonliberal societies accord each other *respect*. In such societies, respect was and is frequently a strictly graded matter of degree. One's ascriptively defined natal status influences the degree of respect to which one is entitled; so does one's conformity to one's proper social role. Finally, one's achievements—for example in battle, as a political leader, or as an accumulator and distributor of wealth—can also influence the degree of respect to which one is entitled. But respect merely because one is human, and for no other reason, is usually absent. Witness, for example, the treatment of children as "nonpersons" or merely persons-in-formation in most societies, and the very recent evolution of the idea that children too ought to have specifically defined rights.[38]

The bases on which respect is accorded in nonliberal societies frequently violate the principle of *equality*. In liberal or social democratic political regimes, all citizens must in principle be accorded equal respect; in practice, of course, this principle is frequently violated. Nevertheless, the principle in and of itself challenges not only the organizing principles

of past preliterate or precapitalist societies, but also the organizing principles of other types of communally based societies, such as those communist societies that allocate benefits on the basis of real or perceived class
origin.

Finally, the liberal principle of *autonomy* challenges the organizing
bases of politics in all societies that hold principles of hierarchical authority, whether directed by elders or chiefs in primitive societies, or by party
or dictator in modern ones. The principle of autonomy also challenges
community-based principles of authority, for example, deference to priests
or elders; and finally, it challenges patriarchal control in the family itself,
as younger males, wives, and children claim rights against the father.

CONSERVATISM AND DIGNITY

Nevertheless, the notion of human dignity enshrined in ideological principle in liberal and social democratic societies is rarely practiced in full, if
at all. Canada is a case in point, as a liberal society with social-democratic
(welfarist) leanings. The overriding social division in Canada is stratifica-
tion by wealth and income levels. The respect accorded among Canadians
to each other is in practice largely a function of wealth, and the poor suffer from extreme everyday assaults on their dignity. The formal political
equality of universal suffrage cannot compensate either for economic inequality or for formal inequalities of access to the political process. Finally,
autonomy implies not only the capacity for individual thought, but also a
chance that thought can be realized in action; and such autonomy, for
many of Canada's poor, is completely absent.

Nor is Canada, even as a liberal society, completely innocent even of
one of the most extreme denials of human equality and rights, namely
racism. Rights-based regimes are everywhere extremely fragile, and ethno-
centric exclusions of strangers from the rights bargain are common even
in societies where universal citizenship is supposed to preclude ethnic or
"racial" (phenotypical) discrimination. As is well known, Canada did not
open its doors to refugee Jews—strangers to the dominant Christian society—during World War II.[39] The treatment of both noncitizen and citizen ethnic Japanese in Canada during World War II replicated the early
stage of what Helen Fein identified as the process of European genocide.[40]
Japanese were defined, stripped of property, segregated, and partially isolated; according to Fein, the only other intervening steps before extermination of European Jews were complete isolation and concentration.

Finally, Canada's past and current treatment of First Nation or "Native" peoples could be interpreted as cultural, if not physical, genocide. The Genocide Convention of 1948 defines genocide as

> any of the following acts committed *with intent to destroy*, in whole or in part, a national, ethnical, racial or religious group, as such:
> (a) killing members of the group
> (b) causing serious bodily or mental harm . . .
> (c) deliberately inflicting on the group conditions of life calculated to bring about its physical destruction . . .
> (d) imposing measures intended to prevent births
> (e) forcibly transferring children of the group to another group.[41]

While the issue of intent could be debated in the Canadian context, all of the above measures except possibly (d)—(assuming that the high rates of sterilization of Native women have not been actual policy measures)—have been inflicted upon Canada's Native peoples at various times since contact with European settlers, including the present.

That the liberal principles of human rights continue to be violated in practice in Canada and other liberal societies is not surprising. The conservative values of community and family still motivate many Canadians, as for example, the establishment of the "REAL" (family-oriented) Women of Canada movement, and the Christian Heritage Party in the Hamilton, Ontario, area in the last few years testifies. The stress on community and patriarchal family is easily compatible with ethnocentrism. In most societies, there are strong divisions between insiders and outsiders. In preliterate societies, people not belonging to established ancestrally based or patron-client networks are generally considered to be strangers, and sometimes they are considered natural slaves.

In liberal societies, the only distinction that is supposed to be made is between citizen and alien; hence the continued questions in Canada, for example, of whether alien refugee claimants should be accorded the full legal protections automatically available in principle to any Canadian citizen. Citizenship is a legal category not intuitively recognizable by many Canadians who continue to think in terms of cultural group membership, and to acknowledge as their equals in practice only those who are co-members of their same "racial" (phenotypical), ethnic, linguistic and/or religious group. In 1981, for example, some 31 percent of Canadians said they would support a whites-only Canada.[42] Under such circumstances "self-determination in the sphere of membership"[43] (i.e., the right of a community to decide who shall join it) can easily violate basic human rights provisions for nondiscrimination. The demand for collective rights can become a mask for conservative attempts to retain discriminatory communities that deny equal and individual human rights.

The Potential Incompatibility of Human and Collective Rights

In the following discussion I distinguish between the move for aboriginal rights, which I support as necessary for the preservation of noncapitalist land tenure and productive relations essential to retention of the identity of "Native" groups already subject to several centuries of physical and cultural genocide, and the move for collective or peoples' rights. My remarks concern the latter category insofar as it does not apply to the rights of conquered peoples in settled capitalist societies. My remarks are meant to express doubts, not an absolute rejection of the concept of collective rights.

It is dangerous to assume that collective rights are compatible with, or perhaps even superior to, individual human rights. Collective rights can become exclusivist rights. They establish communities and define—on bases other than universalist citizenship—who is or is not a member of them. The result can be what Michael McDonald calls "tragic choices."[44] For example, the inclusion of peoples' rights in the African Charter of Rights runs the risk of legitimating Sierra Leone's practice of denying citizenship to native-born ethnic non-Africans (usually of Lebanese origin).[45] Many Arab citizens of the state of Israel consider that its ethno-religious basis results in inequalities and indignities; for example, they consider Israel's holidays "irrelevant at best, irritating and insulting at worst," and also hold the view that the Law of Return (allowing Jews from anywhere in the world to become Israeli citizens) discriminates against Arabs born in Palestine, who, in their view, have a stronger ancestral claim to Israeli citizenship than most Jews born outside the Middle East.[46] The assertion of collective, community, or people's right does not simply mean an extra right of individuals to belong to intact communities that embody their own cultural identity. Such assertion also can, and frequently does, mean violation of individual rights.

Not only does the notion of people's rights or collective rights suggest automatic denial of rights to individuals who could be considered noncitizens by virtue of place of origin, it also implies the risk of progressive exclusion of categories of individuals internal to a national society from membership in the community. It must not be forgotten that the most extreme Western example of social exclusion, Nazism, underwent precisely this type of progressive definition of nonmembers of the community. The Nazis adopted pseudoscientific Social Darwinist theories that permitted them to murder "defective" Aryan (German Christian) children and adults even before they began the mass murder of Jews, the Romany people (gypsies), any blacks they could find in conquered Europe, Slavic prisoners of war, homosexuals, and other categories of persons.[47] But Nazism was also deeply rooted in the idea of ascriptively based membership in the localized community as opposed to individualistic egalitarian citizenship. This opposition, in Nazi thought, was exemplified in the dichotomous categorization of *Volk* (people) versus *cosmopolitan*. The cosmopolitan Jew exemplified the stranger at home in and (in Nazi ideology) controlling world civilization but not having any rootedness in the idealized *volkisch* peasant community from which the Aryan race was said to have sprung.[48] Social Darwinism and *volkisch* ideology combined to produce an ever-tightening, exclusivist definition of the collectivity.

Communal or group rights then, are deeply attractive to those aspects even of the modern psyche that are nostalgic for the idealized closed, ordered community of our mythic rural past, that rigidity for which Mary Douglas believes we all yearn.[49] Liberal capitalist societies do contain deeply disintegrative social aspects. Alienation of individuals from established social norms is frequent, and a sense of isolation plagues many modern men and women who no longer belong to established, easily identifiable social groups other than the nation itself.[50] To such alienated people, the cultural (symbolic, normative) integrity of the group is frequently more appealing than the personal (intellectual, spiritual) integrity that they might be able to achieve as individuals.

The late twentieth-century ideology of individualism, embodied in beliefs that people can control their own fate, puts a tremendous strain on many people. One is now expected—in the popular ideology—to take "responsibility" for almost all aspects of one's own life, as if history, politics, economics, and social structure have no meaning. One takes "responsibility" for one's own health through jogging, abstention from physical indulgences, and other such aspects of the fitness movement. One is supposed, moreover, to take charge of one's progress in the competitive economic marketplace through manipulation of the symbolic aspects of success (dress, demeanor) as well as through long hours of hard work. Finally, one's spiritual health is now also one's own responsibility: "self-fulfillment" is an individualized matter, depending on one's recognition and satisfaction of one's own "potential," abstracted from family or community.

Such a culturally individualized society results in extreme strain for many people, a strain that can be overcome by a return to "fundamental" values of home, community, or church.[51] Conservatism has its attractions even in a liberal or social democratic society. Human rights can be compatible with a political conservatism that accepts the fundamental principles of rights even while, in the political marketplace, asking for more attention to be paid to family and community. When conservatism denies the fundamentally individual aspect of human rights, however, then it is positing a radically different notion of human dignity and social justice.

It is in this sense that human (individual) rights and collective rights are incompatible. Human rights is, to repeat, one particular conception of human dignity and social justice. It is not synonymous, despite their joining in the Universal Declaration of Human Rights, with human dignity.[52] All societies and all social and political philosophies have conceptions of human dignity. Some of these—especially those rooted in the view that nation, "people," community, or family must take precedence over the individual—are radically at odds with the idea of human rights. The recent tendency to substitute collective rights for human rights in international debate, or to assume that the two types of rights can exist compatibly, fails to note this crucial difference.

Conclusion

In this chapter I have argued against the enterprise of surveying world cultures and religions in order to establish a consensus on human rights that would answer charges that such rights are a Western creation.

To look for an anthropologically based consensus on the content of human rights is to miss the point. There may be aspects of agreement worth noting among what many societies take to be fundamental to a life of dignity and what the modern notion of human rights includes as its content. The concept of human rights is not universal in origin, however; and it cannot be located in most societies. The human being—free and equal to all others regardless of status or achievement, and permitted to make individualist claims against state, community, and family—is unthinkable in many societies, however much he or she may be in dire need of rights in the modern world.

Notes

1. I am most grateful to Susan Dicklich and Lisa Kowalchuk for their research assistance on this chapter.

2. This point is made by Louis Henkin, "Human Rights and the Judeo-Christian Tradition," a paper presented at a workshop on Cross-Cultural Perspectives on Human Rights in Africa at the Woodrow Wilson International Center for Scholars, Washington, D.C. (June 23–24, 1988), 4.

3. On China and Japan, *see* James D. Seymour, "China," and Lawrence W. Beer, "Japan," in *International Handbook of Human Rights,* ed. Jack Donnelly and Rhoda E. Howard (New York: Greenwood Press, 1987), 75–97 and 209–26. On Canadian Indians, *see* Menno Boldt and J. Anthony Long, "Tribal Philosophies and the Canadian Charter of Rights and Freedoms," *Ethnic and Racial Studies* 7 (1984): 478–93.

4. Jack Donnelly, *The Concept of Human Rights* (London: Croom Helm, 1985), 32, 35 (emphasis added).

5. For an extended discussion of what I mean by the term "liberalism," *see* Rhoda E. Howard and Jack Donnelly, "Human Dignity, Human Rights and Political Regimes," *American Political Science Review* 80 (1986): 805–7; and Neil Mitchell, Rhoda E. Howard, and Jack Donnelly, "Liberalism, Human Rights and Human Dignity" (a debate), *American Political Science Review* 81 (1987): 921–27.

6. *See, for example,* the discussion by Abdullahi A. An-Na'im on how the religious precepts of Islam can buttress modern human rights ideals. "Religious Minorities under Islamic Law and the Limits of Cultural Relativism," *Human Rights Quarterly* 9 (1987): 14–18. *See also* Henkin, *supra* note 2.

7. For example, Koo VanderWal, "Collective Human Rights: A Western View," in *Human Rights in a Pluralist World: Individuals and Collectivities,* ed. Jan Berting *et al.* (Westport, Conn.: Meckler, 1990), 83–98. *See also* Chapter 6, by Michael McDonald, in this volume.

8. This is a revision of the definition I use in Howard and Donnelly, "Human Dignity," *supra* note 5, at 802.

9. Orlando Patterson, *Slavery and Social Death: A Comparative Study* (Cambridge Mass.: Harvard University Press, 1982), part 1.

10. On this issue, *see* Boldt and Long, *supra* note 3, at 482–84.

11. Barrington Moore, Jr., *Injustice: The Social Bases of Obedience and Revolt* (White Plains, N.Y.: M. E. Sharpe, 1978), 47.

12. Michael Walzer, *Spheres of Justice* (New York: Basic Books, 1983), 26. *See also* Susan Brownmiller, *Femininity* (New York: Fawcett Columbine, 1984), 86.

13. Patterson, *supra* note 9.

14. George Herbert Mead, *Mind, Self and Society* (Chicago: University of Chicago Press, 1962), 173–78.

15. Peter Berger, Brigitte Berger, and Hansfried Kellner, *The Homeless Mind: Modernization and Consciousness* (New York: Vintage Books, 1973), 86.

16. Arthur Schlesinger, Jr., "The Opening of the American Mind," *New York Times Book Review,* July 23, 1989, 26 (emphasis added).

17. Mary Douglas, *Purity and Danger: An Analysis of the Concepts of Pollution and Taboo* (London: Routledge and Kegan Paul, 1966), 162.

18. Simone de Beauvoir, *The Second Sex* (New York: Modern Library, 1968), 51.

19. Mary Daly, *Gyn/Ecology: The Metaethics of Radical Feminism* (Boston: Beacon Press, 1978), chap. 6, "European Witch Burnings: Purifying the Body of Christ."

20. On the church and deviance, *see* Peter Laslett, *The World We Have Lost— Further Explored* (London: Methuen, 1983), chap. 7, "Personal Discipline and Social Survival."

21. *Waterstone Literary Diary 1989* (London: Waterstone and Company, 1988), entry for August 6.

22. On shunning among the Amish, *see* the film *Witness.* For a sociological analysis of the practices of shunning and ostracism, *see* Erving Goffman, *Stigma* (Englewood Cliffs, N.J.: Prentice-Hall, 1963).

23. International Covenant on Civil and Political Rights, 1966, Article 7 (emphasis added).

24. For a brilliant fictional depiction of societies in which honor is a matter of major concern, *see* the novel by the Lebanese author Amin Maalouf, *Leo Africanus* (New York: Norton, 1988).

25. Gerda Lerner, *The Creation of Patriarchy* (New York: Oxford University Press, 1986), 116. *See also* Susan Brownmiller, *Against Our Will: Men, Women and Rape* (New York: Simon and Schuster, 1975), 9.

26. From *Voices of the French Revolution,* ed. Richard Cobb and Colin Jones (Topsfield, Mass.: Salem House, 1988), quoted in "Noted with Pleasure," *New York Times Book Review,* July 30, 1989, 31.

27. Robert Jay Lifton, *The Nazi Doctors: Medical Killing and the Psychology of Genocide* (New York: Basic Books, 1986), 290.

28. For the classic fictional account of Stalinist methods of social control, *see* Arthur Koestler, *Darkness at Noon* (Harmondsworth: Penguin Books, 1971 [1st ed., 1940]).

29. Erving Goffman, "The Nature of Deference and Demeanor," in *Three Sociological Traditions: Selected Readings,* ed. Randall Collins (New York: Oxford University Press, 1985), 215–32.

30. Vincent Crapanzano, *Waiting: The Whites of South Africa* (New York: Vintage Books, 1986), 40–41.

31. Morris Davis and Joseph F. Krauter, *The Other Canadians: Profiles of Six Minorities* (Toronto: Methuen, 1971), 45.

32. Max Weber, *The Protestant Ethic and the Spirit of Capitalism* (New York: Charles Scribner's Sons, 1958).

33. Rhoda E. Howard, "Entrepreneurship and Economic Development: A Critique of the Theory" M.A. thesis, Department of Sociology, McGill University, 1972.

34. Paul T. Kennedy, *Ghanaian Businessmen: From Artisan to Capitalist Entrepreneur in a Dependent Economy* (Munich and London: Weltforum Verlag, 1980).

35. Rhoda E. Howard and Jack Donnelly, "Introduction" to Donnelly and Howard, *supra* note 3, at 1–28.

36. Patterson, *supra* note 9, at 340.

37. Howard and Donnelly, *supra* note 5.

38. In 1988 the Economic and Social Council of the United Nations drafted a convention on the rights of the child (United Nations, ECOSOC, Commission on Human Rights, 45th Session, Pre-Sessional Open-Ended Working Group on the Question of a Convention on the Rights of the Child, November 28–December 9, 1988, *Convention on the Rights of the Child: Text of the Draft Convention*, Doc. E/CN.4/1989/29 [December 30, 1988]). A revised *Convention* was passed by the United Nations' General Assembly in November 1989.

39. Irving Abella and Harold Troper, *None is Too Many: Canada and the Jews of Europe 1933–1948* (Toronto: Lester and Orpen Dennys, 1983).

40. Helen Fein, *Accounting for Genocide: National Responses and Jewish Victimization During the Holocaust* (Chicago: University of Chicago Press, 1979), 63.

41. The Genocide Convention is printed in Leo Kuper, *Genocide: Its Political Use in the Twentieth Century* (Harmondsworth: Penguin, 1981), 210–14 (emphasis added).

42. Gallup Omnibus Study conducted for the Minister of State of Multiculturalism (Canada) (November 1981).

43. Walzer, *supra* note 12, at 62.

44. *See* Michael McDonald's Chapter 6 in this volume.

45. On this matter, *see* my *Human Rights in Commonwealth Africa* (Totowa, N.J.: Rowman and Littlefield, 1986), 6 and 101.

46. Raphael Israeli and Rachel Ehrenfeld, "Israel," in Donnelly and Howard, *supra* note 3, at 169 and 171.

47. On "euthanasia" of mentally and physically ill Germans, *see* Lifton, *supra* note 27, at part 1.

48. On Nazi ideology of the *Volk, see* Lucy S. Dawidowicz, *The War against the Jews: 1933–1945* (New York: Bantam Books, 1975), 35–37.

49. Douglas, *supra* note 17.

50. Nevertheless, the trend to anomic individualism is not as strong as critics of individual human rights often maintain. *See* my "Group versus Individual Identity in the African Debate on Human Rights," in *Human Rights in Africa: Cross-Cultural Perspectives,* ed. Abdullahi A. An-Na'im and Francis Deng (Washington, D.C.: Brookings Institution, 1990).

51. *See, for example,* the article in the *Globe and Mail*'s *Toronto* magazine, in which young ethnically Asian women explain why they would rather accept arranged marriages than go on the normal Canadian "meat-market" of individualized mate-selection. Allen Abel, "Scenes from an Arranged Marriage," *Toronto Globe and Mail* (June 1989), 32–35, 63, 70.

52. *Universal Declaration of Human Rights* (1948), Article 1: "All human beings are born free and equal in dignity and rights."

Section *II*

Problems and Prospects of Alternative Cultural Interpretation

Virginia A. Leary

5. Postliberal Strands in Western Human Rights Theory
Personalist-Communitarian Perspectives

> We do not have to become perfectionists when we stop being fatalists.
> —Roberto Unger [1]

Cross-Cultural Implications of Personalist Perspectives

Liberalism has been the predominant philosophical foundation for the concept of human rights in the West. Marxism has provided the main theoretical challenge to the liberal conception of rights. This essay examines a different and less well known discourse on rights within the Western tradition by focusing on the personalist perspectives of three contemporary Western social theorists who have found wanting both liberal and Marxist conceptions. The theorists whose concepts of rights are described here—Emmanuel Mounier, Jacques Maritain, and Roberto Unger—have each independently elaborated a conception of rights based on Western philosophy and social thought which differs radically from traditional liberal conceptions by, inter alia, its inclusion of economic and social rights (and, in the case of Mounier and Maritain, of group rights) in the catalogue of human rights.

Emmanuel Mounier was the editor of the intellectual French journal *Esprit* during the 1930s and 1940s and the leading member of a movement known as "Personalism" in France. He died in 1950. Jacques Maritain was a French philosopher well known in Europe, Latin America, and North America. Serving on the faculty at Princeton for a number of years, he lectured widely at American and Canadian universities during the 1940s and 1950s; he died in 1973. Roberto Unger, a Brazilian social theorist and leading figure in the Critical Legal Studies movement,[2] is presently teaching at Harvard Law School.

Although a number of philosophers and social theorists of the nine-teenth and twentieth centuries could be considered as adopting personalist or communitarian perspectives, I have chosen to limit this essay to the contributions of Mounier, Maritain, and Unger because they have explic-itly formulated detailed catalogues of rights. All three have been critical of the individualist and property-oriented approach of Western liberalism, while also rejecting Marxist collectivism. Each views his conception of rights not as a gloss on liberal or Marxist approaches but as a distinct theoretical approach. I have used the phrase "personalist perspectives" or "personalist-communitarian perspectives" to express the common aspects of their individual approaches to rights. The philosophical and social theo-ries of these three men are certainly not identical, but in their approach to rights there is a striking similarity. The concept of the "person" or "per-sonality" is an essential element of their social and political theory: they distinguish the concept of "person" from the concept of the "individual" by an emphasis on the intrinsic links between persons and community.

A number of contemporary scholars have criticized the limitations of the liberal conception of rights,[3] but few have made constructive contri-butions to a revised theory of rights. Mounier, Maritain, and Unger have attempted to do so. Personalist perspectives on rights are rarely discussed in contemporary literature on the theory of human rights. This essay is an endeavor to bring this alternative approach into public debate, not only the academic and intellectual debate, but the cross-cultural and political debate, since the personalist approach—like the liberal or Marxist—has implications for political choices.

Liberal ideology, based on eighteenth-century Enlightenment phi-losophy, emphasizes the freedom of individuals, civil and political rights, contractually based obligations and, in particular, property rights. Liberal ideology encompasses with difficulty, if at all, economic, social, and group rights. Marxist ideology has been critical of liberal conceptions of rights, considering them to be "bourgeois rights" which sustain power relations in society.[4] Marxists have emphasized economic and social rights. These two ideological approaches have occupied center stage in discussions of human rights in the West. Neither approach is fully in harmony with the perspective on rights contained in the International Bill of Human Rights. Ideological disputes among proponents of the two approaches have also been detrimental to the development of human rights theory and practice.

The problematic of Western philosophical thought on human rights

is whether it is possible within the Western cultural tradition to conceptualize a theory of rights which retains the important concept of individual
rights, but also regards some rights as inhering in groups and some rights
as entailing positive entitlements to a basic level of economic sufficiency.
The inclusion of economic and social rights and group rights in the catalogue of human rights has been forcefully criticized by many in the West
as lacking logical and philosophical coherence. Maurice Cranston, an ardent defender of the individualist conception of rights, has expressed this
objection most forcefully. He argues for a "philosophically respectable
concept of human rights" not "muddied, obscured and debilitated by an
attempt to incorporate rights of a different logical category" such as economic, social, and group rights.[5] Personalist perspectives on rights, which
are becoming increasingly common in the West, demonstrate that a philosophically sound theory of rights may be based on Western cultural traditions and yet not be hidebound by a constrained liberal tradition of rights.
Personalist-communitarian perspectives that emphasize that the person
lives in community with others and not as an isolated individual represent
an evolution within Western culture and provide a more coherent contemporary approach to rights than eighteenth-century liberalism or
nineteenth-century Marxism.[6]

This seemingly theoretical controversy over "rights" has practical consequences. The perception of rights adopted in a particular culture reflects
and influences aspects of social life. Abdullahi A. An-Naʿim points out
elsewhere in this collection that the inadequacy or lack of cultural legitimacy of human rights standards is one of the main underlying causes of
violation of those standards.[7] Advocates for the homeless and for adequate
health care for all in North America have grasped the practical importance
of the conceptualization of rights and refer to the "right to housing" and
a "right to health care." An-Naʿim argues persuasively that internal discourse within particular cultural traditions—including the Western—is a
necessary element in developing cross-cultural legitimacy for human rights
standards. He invites those of us who are human rights scholars and activists to examine our own cultural tradition, to recognize not only its values
but also its limitations and obstacles to a full perception of human dignity.
The Western liberal tradition of rights has made substantial contributions
to the concept of civil and political rights. But one of its limitations is the
inadequate recognition of what economic inequality and deprivation sig-
nify for human dignity.

Western rights theory has been criticized by non-Westerners more fully conscious of the glaring disparity between wealth and poverty in the world. Non-Westerners have also criticized the excessive individualist orientation of Western rights theory, since "community" and the role of groups are perceived as particularly important within many non-Western cultures. In many parts of the world, the most egregious violations of human dignity are the degrading poverty and inhuman conditions of life of millions of individuals, giving rise to a growing conviction that any conception of human rights must encompass economic and social rights. Upendra Baxi, an Indian academic and activist, has expressed this perception well, paraphrasing Ronald Dworkin's work, *Taking Rights Seriously,* by referring to the need to "take suffering seriously."[8]

The preoccupations evident in Mounier, Maritain, and Unger's theories of rights grow out of contemporary historical experiences and resemble the preoccupations expressed by many non-Western commentators on rights. All three view human rights standards as evolving over time and as reflecting particular historical circumstances. Thus, new standards may evolve depending on newly perceived social needs; also, evolution is possible within particular cultural traditions. These basic perceptions indicate an openness to evolution within the Western cultural tradition, an openness that seems requisite to appreciating the approaches of other cultural traditions.

The Personalist Perspectives of Mounier, Maritain, and Unger

The terms "personalism" and "personalist" have been used in a number of philosophical, theological, and political contexts in the twentieth century. An emphasis on the concept of personality can be traced far back in Western philosophical and theological thought, however. Although many differences are apparent among thinkers using these terms, a common thread appears to be conceptualizing the "person" as essentially part of a community, thus distinguishing the "person" from the "individual" regarded as an isolated entity. *The Encyclopedia of Philosophy* defines personalism as

> [A] philosophical perspective or system for which person is the ontological ultimate and for which personality is thus the fundamental explanatory principle. Explicitly developed in the twentieth century, personalism in its historical antecedents and its dominant themes has close affiliations with and affinities to other . . . systems that are not strictly personalist.[9]

In using the plural term "perspectives," I emphasize that there is no single personal perspective but rather that a personalist approach is evident in the social theory of a number of scholars and activists whose thinking is not identical in all respects. It would be impossible in the space available here to do justice to the many movements and theorists who have identified themselves as personalists or have used the terms "personality" or "personalism" extensively in their writings. *The Encyclopedia of Philosophy* refers to two major personalist philosophies: first, American personalism, which it calls "idealistic personalism," and second, "realistic personalism," which is primarily European. *The Encyclopedia* states that "personalism has been decisively influenced by both the Greek metaphysical and Biblical religious motifs of the dominant Western theological tradition." [10] American personalism is closely linked to the schools of philosophy and Protestant theology at Boston University, where it had been a major influence since the early nineteenth century. [11]

Mounier, Maritain, and Unger appear to be representative of realist personalism. All three use the terms "personality," "personalism," and "community" frequently; and I consider that they share a personalist perspective, although their perspectives differ in a number of respects. Sufficient commonalities exist to justify treating them as sharing a common perspective.

Emmanuel Mounier was born in France in 1905 and died in 1950. A philosopher by education, he was best known as the editor of the intellectual French journal *Esprit* and the proponent of a movement called *personalism*. [12] Mounier's personalist movement is little known in the Anglo-American world but is well known in France and certain circles in Latin America. Mounier was a left-wing Catholic who disliked Christian Democracy. He has been called "a serious Christian who wanted to be a social revolutionary." [13] Mounier had an openness to secular social movements unusual in French Catholicism in the early part of the twentieth century. Although he revolted against the bourgeois conservative Catholicism prevalent in his youth, he remained a convinced Christian throughout his life and early became committed to balancing deep religiosity and concern for social justice. To Mounier, Christianity was the most radical of countercultures, yet he found Marxists and atheists exhibiting more charity than Christians in France. By the time of Mounier's death, French Catholicism had become more known for its commitment to social justice through worker-priests and other movements than for its traditional bourgeois conservatism. Mounier and the personalist movement contributed to this extraordinary change in French Catholicism. While embracing a humane socialism, Mounier was not a Marxist, however. He accepted neither the concept of class struggle nor historical determinism.

Jacques Maritain was a French natural law philosopher active in cross-cultural discussions on rights under UNESCO auspices at the time of the drafting of the Universal Declaration of Human Rights. His formulation of rights is outlined in *The Rights of Man and Natural Law,* published in 1944, and in *Man and the State,* published in 1959. Well known in the United States and Canada through his books and for his teaching and lecturing at Princeton University and at the Universities of Chicago and Toronto, he died in 1973 at the age of 91. His extensive philosophical and social writings are influential in natural law circles in Europe and North and South America. Maritain used the terms "political humanism" and "personalism" to refer to his approach to rights theory. He had been involved with Mounier in the initial phases of the development of the journal *Esprit* but at a later period distanced himself from the Mounier personalist movement. Maritain maintained that it is possible for persons holding widely differing beliefs on the justification for human rights to agree on a body of practical human rights standards.

Roberto Unger is a social theorist who divides his time between his appointment on the faculty of Harvard Law School and political participation in his native Brazil. He is primarily identified with the Critical Legal Studies movement in North America. Although Unger does not refer to himself as a "personalist," nor does he refer in his writings to the influence of European or American personalists, I consider him as expressing a personalist-communitarian perspective because of his emphasis on personality and community as essential aspects of his social theory.[14] His formulation of rights theory, like those of Mounier and Maritain, is neither Marxist nor liberal. In elaborating a visionary program of "empowered democracy" he advocates a "personalist program" and a transformed conception of "community" supported by a theory of rights.

The perspectives of these three thinkers are characterized by certain similarities cited here. Focusing only on their commonalities perhaps does an injustice to the development of the individual social and political theories of these three scholars, each of whom has written extensively. Maritain published more than seventy books during his long life. Mounier developed his concept of personalism over many years in the issues of the journal *Esprit*. Unger has thus far published five major volumes on social theory. Mounier's conception of a "personalist and communitarian revolution," Maritain's elaboration of "political humanism," and Unger's visionary program of "empowered democracy" each warrant far more individual consideration than can be given here. The emphasis in this chapter is, however, necessarily on their commonalities rather than their differences. Each of their social theories shares the following perspectives, which have, in turn, influenced their conceptions of rights:

1. an emphasis on the concept of the "person" as distinguished from the concept of the "individual";
2. the view that the term "person" implies relationships with others in a community and a corresponding emphasis on community and the relations between persons and society;
3. a focus on the roles and rights not only of individuals but also of communities, particularly communities smaller than the state: families, groups linked by common cultural ties, local communities, consumer or occupational groups, and so on, and a corresponding view that rights may be claimed against groups as well as against states;
4. the effort to distinguish their social theories from both Marxist collectivism and liberal capitalism;
5. an emphasis on *praxis,* or the practical implications of their social theories.

PERSON AND COMMUNITY

The definition of personalism quoted earlier from *The Encyclopedia of Philosophy* fails to mention an aspect of personalism considered essential by most of those using the term, namely, the communitarian or social implications of the concept of "personality." Max Scheler, a German phenomenologist, philosopher, and personalist who influenced Mounier, considered that "the person as an individual emerges only within a circle of other persons in sociality . . . the person is inseparable from the context of the world and others."[15] Mounier's "first expositions of personalism were notable in their new concern for community, a need to form 'collective persons' and 'persons of persons'." Mounier consistently referred to his movement as "a personalist and *communitarian* revolution."[16] In his view, the "true community was a reality as fundamental as that of the person."[17]

In a fine study on personalism which includes extensive information on the roots of the personalism of a number of European thinkers, Jean Lacroix has written:

> To be a person is to transform the "one" into the "we." The person always lives in a world peopled by other persons . . . the notion of person always entails an elan which carries one beyond one's self.[18]

Lacroix considers personalism not as constituting a philosophy but as providing an inspiration for various philosophies. While emphasizing the concept of the person, he points out that the individualist and the personalist approaches should not be seen as radically opposed but as complementary. Both aspects are important.

Maritain has written that his conception of society is

> *personalist* . . . and *communal,* because it recognizes the fact that the person tends naturally towards society and communion, in particular towards the political community, and because, in the specifically political sphere and to the extent that man is a part of political society, it considers the common good superior to that of individuals.[19]

Unger states that his whole program of "empowered democracy" can "be read as a vision of the forms and conditions of human community."[20] In emphasizing the importance of personal relationship to the development of the institutions of an empowered democracy he writes that "[a]t the center of this revised approach to direct personal relations stands a conception of community as a zone in which the increased acceptance of mutual vulnerability makes it possible to multiply ways of diminishing the conflict between attachment to other people and the claims of self-consciousness and self-possession."[21]

INTERMEDIATE ORGANIZATIONS OR GROUPS: ROLES AND RIGHTS

All three thinkers have emphasized the significance of communities smaller than the state. Maritain speaks of the important role of "autonomous agencies" within the polity and emphasizes "associative forms of industrial ownership" by workers as an example of the role which such agencies should play in economic life. He writes that his conception of a society of free men is

> *pluralist,* because it assumes that the development of the human person normally requires a plurality of autonomous communities which have their own rights, liberties and authority; among these communities there are some of a

rank inferior to the political state, which arise either from the fundamental exigencies of nature (as in the case of the family community) or else from the will of persons freely coming together to form diverse groups. Other communities are of a rank superior to the State, as . . . in the temporal realm, that organized international community towards which we aspire today.[22]

Mounier not only propounded a theory of community but also became the leader of the personalist movement in France that grouped together a small community of like-minded persons linked in one manner or another to the journal *Esprit*. Unger writes of the role of grassroots organizations and the need for decentralization in economic decision making. An emphasis on intermediate groups influenced the conceptions of rights of all three thinkers.

PERSONALISM DISTINGUISHED FROM LIBERAL INDIVIDUALISM AND MARXIST COLLECTIVISM

Maritain, Mounier, and Unger have explicitly distinguished their personalist vision or orientation from both liberal individualism and Communist collectivism. In describing the personalism of Mounier, John Hellman writes:

> [T]he assertion of the 'absolute value of the human person' was not simply an abstract affirmation of human dignity but rather a movement of defence against two antithetical threats. . . . It mirrored the desperate effort of intellectuals in the early nineteen-thirties to navigate a 'third way' between capitalism and communism.[23]

Scheler viewed both Marxism and liberalism as "seeing politics in terms of self-interest and material welfare," rejecting both for a personalist vision.[24] Maritain writes:

> Those whom, for want of a better name, I just called the advocates of a liberal-individualist type of society, see the mark of human dignity first and foremost in the power of each person to appropriate individually the goods of nature in order to do freely whatever he wants; the advocates of a communistic type of society see the mark of human dignity first and foremost in the power to submit these same goods to the collective command of the society body in order to 'free' human labor (by subduing it to the economic community) and to gain the control of history; the advocates of a personalistic type of society see the mark of human dignity first and foremost in the power to make these same goods of nature serve the common conquest of intrinsically human, moral, and spiritual goods and of man's freedom of

autonomy. . . . As far as I am concerned, I know where I stand: with the third of the three schools of thought I just mentioned.[25]

Unger states that the Critical Legal Studies movement, of which he is a leading member, is within the "tradition of leftist tendencies in modern legal thought."[26] He also says, however, that his social theory is liberal, even superliberal. In fact, his social theory and his rights theories cannot be placed squarely within either traditional Marxist or traditional liberal thought.

PERSONALISM AND PRAXIS

As social and political theorists, Maritain, Mounier, and Unger have all been concerned with the practical implications of their theory. None has been solely concerned with speculative philosophical or social systems, although all three have based practice on theory.

The dust jacket of *Passion, An Essay on Personality* reports that Unger is an "active participant in the politics of his native Brazil[;] he has helped develop political programs and party platforms."[27] Unger's professed aim is activist, that is, the "development of practices and institutions that prevent factions, classes or any other specially placed groups from gaining control over the key resources of a society (wealth, power, knowledge)."[28] Although Unger finds social democracy the nearest approach to his social theory, he finds it too constrained by entrenched social roles and hierarchies; he refers to his social theory as a "radical alternative to social democracy." But, he maintains, his theory must be translated into action: "The institutional ideas have to be realized by collective action. They remain unpersuasive and dreamlike until we have complemented them with a view of the social activities that might establish them."[29]

Mounier organized a community of friends at Chatenay-Malabry in France, but his contribution to practical action is also demonstrated in the pages of *Esprit,* where contemporary issues in French political and social life were widely discussed, focusing particularly on issues of labor and education. John Hellman has described Mounier's community as follows:

A great source of consolation and hope for Mounier was the personalist community which he founded at Chatenay-Malabry. . . . Six or seven intellectuals and their families could live comfortably in Les Murs Blancs. At first they all ate meals in common but this was soon abandoned in favour of periodic, optional, common meals. A happy balance was achieved between privacy and community life, intellectual and spiritual collaboration, and the pursuit of individual careers. . . . For several decades, some of France's leading intellectual figures have lived in friendship and harmony at Chatenay-Malabry, living in community according to Mounier's inspiration. Self-conscious avant-garde Christians, they have welcomed visitors from around the world and sought to demonstrate by example that their personalism is more than an intellectual position.[30]

The community continued long after Mounier's death in 1950. Personalism, as developed by Mounier and others linked to *Esprit*, was less a philosophy than "a method for thinking and living."[31] Practical implications were fundamental to the movement.

Jacques Maritain was a philosopher who wrote widely on subjects of political and social theory. His writings were frequently related to current political and social issues, although he took no active part in political life. In one of his best-known books, *True Humanism, A Charter of Social Action,* he expressed the practical orientation of his concerns:

> The questions dealt with here belong to that section of philosophy which Aristotle and St. Thomas called *Practical,* since in a general way it includes the whole philosophy of human action. . . . Practical philosophy is still philosophy and remains a mode of speculative knowledge; but, unlike metaphysics or natural philosophy, it is from the outset directed to action as its object, and however large a part verification of fact may play in it, however much it must needs take historical necessities and conditions into account, it is above all a science of freedom.[32]

Maritain wrote, among other things, on the relation between religious and temporal concerns and between church and state, on the rights of workers, on democracy, and on an international political order. While he did not take an active role in political affairs, he expressed himself on current political issues, protesting the bombing of Madrid and Guernica by the Franco forces at a time when many of his fellow Catholics in France and elsewhere were supporting Franco against the Loyalists, whom they regarded as persecutors of the Church. He became part of the French delegation to the second Conference of UNESCO held in Mexico City and participated actively in early discussions aimed at elaborating a truly international conception of human rights. Particularly in his later books, Maritain evidenced a continuing concern for the political and social implications of his philosophical orientation.

Personalism and Human Rights

Of particular interest for this essay is the detailed formulation of rights elaborated by Mounier, Maritain, and Unger. Emmanuel Mounier drafted a declaration of rights together with other members of the French personalist movement between 1941 and 1944; Maritain described his conception of rights in *The Rights of Man and Natural Law*, published in 1944, and in *Man and the State*, published in 1951; Unger has developed an original conceptualization of rights in his latest book, *False Necessity*, published in 1987. Although these elaborations of rights are not identical, they share a number of elements. Each of them includes economic and social rights, as well as individual rights, in his categorization of rights; all of them maintain that individual rights can be claimed as a protection against group tyranny as well as against state action.

MOUNIER PERSONALISM AND THE 1940S DEBATE OVER REFORMULATION OF THE FRENCH DECLARATION OF RIGHTS

During the Nazi occupation of France, a group of personalists led by Mounier drafted clandestinely a declaration of rights which they believed corrected the rationalism and individualism of the 1789 French Declaration of the Rights of Man and Citizen and which they intended would serve as a model for a treaty to be signed by like-minded states after World War II. This innovative catalogue of rights was one of the model declarations of rights that influenced the drafters of the revised French Declaration of Rights adopted in 1946.[33] In 1989, the two-hundredth anniversary of the drafting of the French Declaration of the Rights of Man and Citizen, we heard much about that 1789 Declaration. We heard little, however, of the revision of the French Declaration that was adopted as the Preamble to the 1946 French Constitution, which established the Fourth Republic. The 1789 Declaration is reprinted in most collections of human rights instruments; the revised formulation is not. The historical importance of the 1789 Declaration is evident, but the state where it originated has determined that it no longer adequately reflects its contemporary conception of rights. Jean Rivero has pointed out that

> In the intervening two centuries between the time the Declaration of the Rights of Man and Citizen was passed in 1789 and now, the Declaration's original conception, both as an ideology and its translation into law, have undergone so many modifications that what prevails today only partially reflects the original document.[34]

The rights recognized in the 1789 Declaration were limited to liberty, property, security, and resistance to oppression. The 1946 Declaration, in contrast, incorporates a recognition of economic and social rights. The intellectual background to the inclusion of these rights in the 1946 French Constitution and the philosophical and social reflections of French thinkers that led to the revision of the 1789 Declaration are of interest in the context of personalism. Certainly, Marxist influence played a part in the revision of the Declaration; other influences were also important, however, including the influence of the declaration of rights prepared by Mounier. The personalist declaration influenced particularly the Mouvement Republicain Populaire (MRP), the Christian Democratic party, and one of the three major political parties that participated in the drafting of the declaration eventually included in the 1946 French Constitution.[35] Their support of the personalist declaration was ironic in view of Mounier's well-known dislike of Christian democratic parties.

The initial draft of the personalist declaration was presented for debate in the pages of *Esprit* in 1944. In subsequent issues a number of perceptive comments were made on the draft by jurists, professors, international lawyers, and other members of the personalist movement. In 1945, the final draft of the declaration appeared in *Esprit*.[36] Entitled "Declaration of the Rights of Persons and Communities," it began:

> The undersigned States recognize the authority over individuals and societies of a certain number of rights attaching to the existence of the human community, not deriving either from the individual or the state, but having double roots:
>
> 1. The good of persons
> 2. The life and normal development of persons within the natural communities where they have been placed: families, nations, geographic and linguistic groups, work communities, affinity groups and groups based on particular beliefs. . . .

> The proper function of the State is to actively assist both the independence of persons and the life of communities: the first, against the menacing tyranny of groups; the second, against the constantly reborn anarchy of individuals. An organism independent of the State should be established to judge the abuses of power by the State.[37]

Part 1 of the declaration relates to the "Rights of Persons." In twenty-six articles it lists most of the traditional civil and political rights, including also under that heading rights to health, to work, to the minimum resources necessary for "a life worthy of man," to necessary leisure, and to social security. Each of the rights is spelled out in some detail. Civil and political rights and economic and social rights are not divided into separate categories.

Part 2 of the personalist declaration is labeled, "Rights of Communities." One of the most divisive issues in contemporary human rights theory and practice is whether groups have rights as well as individuals. The issue has great practical importance for indigenous peoples and ethnic groups. Perceiving the existential need for a concept of group rights, a number of theorists are endeavoring to fit a concept of group rights into liberal ideology. Michael McDonald, for instance, has discussed the difficulty of doing so.[38] Group rights can be made to fit the liberal ideology, which is fundamentally individualistic, only by stretching the concept of liberalism until it snaps and is no longer recognizable as liberalism.[39] A different ideology is required. A concept of group rights is an essential aspect of Mounier's personalist perspective. The personalist declaration also recognizes individual rights and, as is apparent from the excerpt quoted above, the personalist regards rights as a protection against the "tyranny of groups" as well as against the tyranny of the state. In the 1940s in France, the concept of rights for groups was supported not only by personalists. The conviction of the importance of collectivities intermediate between the individual and the state had been "in the air" in Europe for a long time.

Article 27 expresses the basic approach of the section of the declaration on the rights of communities:

> There exist natural communities. Born outside the State, they cannot be subject to it. Their spontaneous powers limit the power of the State. They should be represented as such within the State.

Twelve articles are included under the heading of rights of communities; they relate to the rights of families, the nation, economic and work communities, and the international community. These articles join in a single statement of rights a number of concerns of contemporary international life, concerns that have seldom been joined, even after forty-five years, in a single declaration of rights, either nationally or internationally.[40]

Article 29 relates to self-determination:

> Each nation possesses an absolute right to the independence of its culture, its language, its spiritual life, but not to unconditional political sovereignty.

> Each nation must protect, within the limits of its cohesiveness, its regional communities and ethnic, linguistic or religious groups.

The rejection of both an unconditional free-enterprise system and a Marxist system of production is expressed in Article 30:

> Economic communities and occupational communities are based on the service rendered and not on acquired privileges or the power of money. They should not serve essentially the profit, production or power of the State, but the needs of free consumption in conditions respecting the dignity of the worker and the development of the spirit of enterprise.

Article 33 relates to the use of economic resources and presages the later development of concepts of "the common heritage of mankind" and the "new international economic order":

> The human community is the beneficial owner of the totality of the riches of the universe. Each nation has the right, within the general organization, to receive its just share. Each worker has the right to emigrate, to the limit of possibilities, so that his subsistence might be improved and his work more fruitful.

Article 35 provides that:

> Each person has the right to personal property and the vital space necessary for the human person to constitute a milieu of liberty and autonomy, with the reservation that this possession not be either a means of oppression or a means of spoiling the legitimate results of the work of others.

The right to transmit property to one's heirs is also recognized in the declaration. These provisions are included under the Rights of Communities, however, not in the section on the Rights of Persons, thus emphasizing the social nature of property rights.

Part 3 of the personalist declaration relates to the rights of the state, but refers primarily to limitations on the state. It provides, among other things, that the powers of the state are limited by the powers of the natural societies referred to in part 2 and by fundamental liberties.

While drafting the declaration, Mounier considered the possibility of including a reference to duties in the declaration. Despite his recognition that it is important to link duties to rights from the moral and civic point of view, he concluded that a statement of duties was not acceptable in a legal charter.[41]

In 1789, the drafters of the original French Declaration of the Rights of Man and Citizen, in reaction against orders (clergy, nobility, and commons) in the *ancien régime,* rejected the idea of rights for intermediate groups—only the individual had natural rights. But the rights of groups also did not fare well in the revised declaration adopted by the 1946 Constituent Assembly and incorporated as the Preamble to the French Constitution. Only the rights of the family are mentioned in the Preamble. The personalist division of rights into rights of the individual, of groups, and of the state was discussed at length in the Constituent Assembly but eventually was rejected. In the end, not even the right of association was mentioned in the Preamble to the Declaration.

The concept of economic and social rights included in the personalist declaration fared better in the final draft of the French Declaration. Many influences, including Marxist and socialist as well as personalist ones, played a part in the inclusion of these rights in the Preamble. It refers in some detail to the rights of workers and other social rights, but includes them in a section labeled "economic and social principles," implying a fundamental difference between them and the liberties included in an earlier part of the declaration. The right to property is also included in the section on "economic and social principles" and emphasizes the social function of all property.

The 1946 French Declaration represents a compromise among competing theories of rights. Jean Rivero, professor of law in Paris, has pointed out that, as a result of the inclusion of economic and social rights in the 1946 Preamble to the Constitution, "human rights no longer have a theoretical unity" in France, adding that what they have lost in theoretical purity they have gained in scope.[42]

MARITAIN: NATURAL LAW, PERSONALISM, AND HUMAN RIGHTS

Natural law perspectives have been linked with conceptions of human rights since the eighteenth century. When the French Declaration of Rights, the Virginia Bill of Rights, and the American Declaration of Independence were drafted, references to the sources of the rights enunciated in these Declarations was not to positive law but rather to the "natural and imprescriptible rights of man," "self-evident" truths, "inherent rights"—in short, to natural law concepts. Not all proponents of human rights have been naturalists, but in the absence of a positive law basis for the contention that there are "human rights," an appeal was made to a nonpositive source and that source was called "natural law." Utilitarian, positivist, and Marxist philosophers reject the natural law basis for human rights; as rights have been progressively included in positive law, both at the national and international level, references to "natural law" have diminished.

In his writings on human rights, Maritain has elaborated a natural law approach to rights that does not coincide entirely with eighteenth-century conceptions and not at all with the conservative natural law approaches of the nineteenth- and early twentieth-century judiciary in the United States. Considering that the term has been misused, he, nevertheless, finds no other phrase to replace "natural law":

> The philosophical foundation of the Rights of Man is Natural Law. Sorry that we cannot find another word. During the rationalist era jurists and philosophers have misused the notion of natural law to such a degree, either for conservative or for revolutionary purposes, they have put it forward in so over-simplified and so arbitrary a manner, that it is difficult to use it now without awakening distrust and suspicion in many of our contemporaries.[43]

Maritain's theory of natural law requires explanation since, although it is similar to conceptions of natural law going back to Aristotle, the Stoics, Aquinas, and medieval conceptions, it is not the tradition of natural law best known in the Anglo-Saxon world. Maritain used the terms "personalist" and "humanist" as well as "natural law" to refer to his approach to political organization and rights, and these terms suggest the distinctive elements of his conception of natural law. In distinguishing his approach to rights from that of advocates of a liberal-individualistic approach and of advocates of a communist society, he states that he is an advocate of a personalistic type of society that sees "the mark of human dignity first and foremost in the power to make . . . goods of nature serve the common conquest of intrinsically human, moral and spiritual goods and of man's freedom of autonomy."[44]

Like other naturalists, Maritain bases his conception of natural law on the belief that there is a "human nature" common to all men. The elements of that human nature are simply expressed: man is endowed with intelligence and determines his own ends, which ought to be, but may not be, in accordance with his nature. Further, man's knowledge of his "nature" increases "little by little as man's moral conscience has developed."[45] But there is an "immense field of human things which depend on the variable conditions of social life and on the free initiative of human reason, and which natural law leaves undetermined." Maritain's philosophy, though essentialist, has an existential emphasis that recognizes cultural relativity:

> . . . [A]n immense amount of relativity and variability is to be found in the particular rules, customs, and standards in which, among all peoples of the earth, human reason has expressed its knowledge even of the most basic aspects of natural law.[46]

Man is endowed with intelligence and determines his own ends but those determinations are based on the human situation and "[h]uman situations are something existential."[47] While there may be a fundamental nature of man, there is "progress and relativity" regarding human awareness of it.

Maritain's conception of natural law and rights includes an element of "dynamic development" missing in eighteenth-century natural law philosophy. Although crediting the eighteenth-century Enlightenment philosophers for developing the concept of rights, he criticizes the resulting catalogue of rights for its rationalism, individualism, and rigidity. It led to a static written code and "ended up, after Rousseau and Kant, by treating the individual as a god and making all the rights ascribed to him the absolute and unlimited rights" of a god. It ignored the social nature of the individual, allowing persons to unfold their "cherished possibilities at the expense of all other beings."[48] Maritain divides his own list of rights into those pertaining to the rights of the human person, the civic person, and the social or working person. He also refers to the rights of economic and social groups to freedom and autonomy. Rights pertaining to the human person include most of the traditional liberties and freedoms of the liberal tradition. Within the category of civic rights, he includes the rights to vote, to have political and legal equality before the law, to enjoy freedom of speech and expression, and to have access to professions without racial or social discrimination. His recognition of social rights is the most distinctive because the eighteenth-century natural-law-based conception of rights has not been congenial to such rights.

Maritain makes a particular contribution to the natural law basis of rights theory by his recognition of the evolutionary nature of concepts of human rights. His listing of rights is based on his own period of time and historical situation, as he emphasizes all catalogues of rights are, but it is doubtful that he would have raised ideological objections to such modern conceptions of rights as the "right to development" and "the right to a clean environment." He writes,

We have a tendency to inflate and make absolute, limitless, unrestricted in every respect, the rights of which we are aware, thus blinding ourselves to any other right which would counterbalance them. Thus in human history no "new" right, I mean no right of which common consciousness was becoming newly aware, has been recognized in actual fact without having had to struggle against and overcome the bitter opposition of some "old rights." That was the story of the right to a just wage and similar rights in the face of the right to free mutual agreement and the right to private ownership. The fight of the latter to claim for itself a privilege of divine, limitless absolutism was the unhappy epic of the XIXth Century.[49]

Maritain recognizes that his natural law conception of the source of human rights is contested by many philosophers and theorists. He refers to the paradox implicit in the effort to find agreement on conceptions of human rights. On the one hand, rational justifications for human rights are indispensable because each person wishes to consent to only what he or she recognizes as true and rationally valid. On the other hand, it is precisely in relation to rational justifications for human rights that we find major disagreements among philosophical traditions. Maritain believed that persons of divergent ideological allegiances, philosophical and religious traditions, cultural backgrounds, and historical experiences could not agree on theoretical conceptions but could agree on a common formulation of practical conclusions, a catalogue of rights. He writes:

> During one of the meetings of the French National Commission of UNESCO at which the Rights of Man were being discussed, someone was astonished that certain proponents of violently opposed ideologies had agreed on the draft of a list of rights. Yes, they replied, we agree on these rights, *providing we are not asked why*. With the "why" the dispute begins.[50]

Maritain was convinced that his way of justifying belief in the "rights of man and the ideal of freedom, equality, and fraternity is the only one which is solidly based on truth." His openness to the possibility and even likelihood of agreeing with others on practical action is thus especially striking. In this regard, he underscores the importance of the sociological, rather than the philosophical, point of view:

> [F]rom a sociological point of view, the most important factor in the moral progress of humanity is the experiential development of awareness which takes place outside of systems and on another logical basis—at times facilitated by systems when they awaken consciousness to itself, at other times thwarted by them when they obscure the apperceptions of spontaneous reason.[51]

In focusing on the possibility of agreement on practical action, he states:

> Thus there is a sort of vegetative development and growth, so to speak, of moral knowledge and moral feeling, which is in itself independent of the philosophical systems, although in a secondary way the latter in turn enter into reciprocal action with this spontaneous process. As a result these various systems while disputing about the "why," prescribe in their practical conclusions rules of behavior which appear on the whole as almost the same for any given period or culture.[52]

ROBERTO UNGER'S CONCEPTION OF RIGHTS

Roberto Unger is the best known theorist of the Critical Legal Studies movement (CLS) in North America. That movement has been closely identified with a critique of "rights-talk," the criticism that rights are indeterminate of particular problems and that theories of rights enforce political and social hierarchy.[53]

It may seem surprising, then, that Unger has engaged in "rights-talk" and has elaborated a theory of rights supporting his visionary program of "empowered democracy." As Michael Perry[54] and Unger have both pointed out, however, the criticism of rights by some members of the Critical Legal Studies movement has focused not on the conception of rights as such but on particular versions of rights. A valuable contribution has been made by Unger in calling attention to the importance of a conception of rights in any social theory. By a "system of rights" Unger means

> an institutionalized version of society, which is to say, a form of social life acquiring a relatively stable and delineated form and generating a complicated set of expectations. The stability and the expectations are not merely those of the prison camp: a system of rights defines arrangements that many people . . . treat as the expression of a defensible scheme of human association.[55]

Unger does not draft a declaration of rights in the style of the Mounier personalist declaration. His conception of rights is written in narrative form as an integral aspect of the elaboration of his program of empowered democracy. It is difficult to understand Unger's theory of rights without a detailed understanding of his program of empowered democracy outlined in 653 pages of *False Necessity*. The brief explanation of his conception of rights in this chapter, separated from a lengthy discussion of empowered democracy, risks being inadequate. Even a brief description of Unger's conception of rights, however, will demonstrate how original that conception is, particularly in creating original terminology to refer to various types of rights. His emphasis on concepts of personality and communal life informs his entire conception of rights.[56]

The distinctive elements in Unger's theory of rights are as follows:

First, Unger rejects the conceptualization of rights as relating solely to relations of the individual vis-à-vis the state. In his conceptualization, rights are relevant to all forms of human association, as he expressed in the following excerpt:

> Traditional legal thought has accustomed us to think of communal life as almost beyond the proper scope of legal rights. If the jurists are to be believed, legal regulation appears in the domain of intimate and communal relations as the hand of Midas, threatening to destroy whatever it touches. But this supposed antipathy between rights and community reflects both a rigid view of rights and an impoverished conception of community. Its actual effect is often to leave communal life all the more subject to the forms of self-interested exchange and domination from which the policy of legal abstention is expected to protect it.[57]

Second, in Unger's conception, rights are not necessarily confrontational. They should not be seen as "a loaded gun that the rightholder may shoot at will at his corner of town."[58] Such a concept of rights is incompatible with the give-and-take of a communal vision of society, the necessity of taking other's situations into account.

Third, Unger writes that our traditional concept of rights is incompatible with the communal vision. Under traditional rights theory, obligations derive either from acts of the will such as bilateral contracts or from state-imposed obligations. But most obligations in ordinary life derive from our relationships of interdependence. Reformed varieties of communal experience, advocated by Unger, "need to be thought out in legal categories and protected by legal rights," which are not the traditional categories of rights.[59]

Fourth, a central aspect of Unger's rights theory is a rejection of what he refers to as the "consolidated property right," the relatively unlimited right to private property of free-market economies. He suggests that the criticism of rights theory by members of the CLS movement have been largely criticisms of the consolidated property right. The consolidated property right has been central to traditional rights theory and has influenced the conception of other rights, but, Unger holds, must be rejected from a personalist and communal view.[60]

Fifth, Unger proposes four kinds of rights to support his personalist and communitarian ideal of empowered democracy: market rights, immunity rights, destabilization rights, and solidarity rights. His concept of market rights is best explained in his own words:

> market rights are the rights employed for economic exchange in the trading sector of the society. They come into their own within a fully realized version of the reconstructed economy: the economy that allows teams of workers, technicians, and entrepreneurs to gain conditional and temporary access to portions of social capital and that thereby develops both the absolute degree of economic decentralization and the extent of economic plasticity. . . .

> Such [market] rights would have the basic operational features of contract and property entitlements in current private law. . . . Property, to be sure, would be desegregated, as it has been in so many periods of its history, into a series of distinct powers assigned to different entities or rightholders: central representative bodies of the democracy, the competing investment funds, and the capital takers who have access to the fund on explicitly temporary and limited terms.[61]

Unger's concept of immunity rights relates to security for the individual. And by "security" he means the confidence that an individual's physical security, minimal material welfare, and protection against subjugation by public or private power will not be put at risk. He rejects, however, the necessity for private consolidated property rights, lifelong job guarantees, or a particular caste system as means of providing that security. His concept of immunity rights has much in common with traditional liberal civil and political rights but he also includes in this category certain economic and social rights. He writes:

> Freedom against governmental or private oppression represents only one of two major sets of immunity rights. The other set consists in welfare entitlements: guarantees of access to the material and cultural resources needed to make a life. These include provision for nourishment, housing, health care and education, with absolute standards proportional to the wealth of society.[62]

One of the most unusual aspect of Unger's conception of rights is his category of "destabilization rights." The category is difficult to grasp. He refers to destabilization rights as protecting the citizen's interest in "breaking open the large-scale organizations or the extended areas of social practice that remain closed to the destabilizing effects of ordinary conflict and thereby sustain insulated hierarchies of power and advantage."[63] Unger suggests that these rights may become operational through the arrangements he proposes for empowered democracy; such arrangements have counterparts in the forms of injunctive relief found in contemporary (American) law, as when the courts intervene in institutions like schools or mental asylums or in electoral organization.

Solidarity rights in Unger's conceptualization "give legal form to social relations of reliance and trust." They are intended to support "transformed communal and personal relations" but are not based on altruism or harmony or on a subjective state of mind of the owner of the duty. "Solidarity rights apply to relations within distinct communities and to relations of trust and reliance that take hold outside a well-defined communal setting."[64] Unger points out that the practical legal expression of the view of community underlying the theory of solidarity rights "is the legal protection of claims to abide by implicit obligations to take other people's situations and expectations into account." He cites counterparts in contemporary law supporting his concept of solidarity rights, namely,

> the law of fiduciary relationships, the contractual and delictual protection of reliance, the doctrines of good faith and of abuse of rights, and the many doctrinal devices by which private law supports communal relations while continuing to represent society as a world of strangers.[65]

Unger admits that solidarity rights may be unenforceable. His treatment of the question of unenforceability provides a summary of his concept of a system of rights:

> It may be objected that an unenforceable right is no right at all and that merely to speak of such entitlements is to disinter the illogical language of natural rights with its implicit but halfhearted allusion to a natural, absolute context of social life. But it is a mistake to identify the positivism of governmental enforcement and the idea of innate and eternal entitlements as the only two senses that rights language may bear. . . .

> Not everything in a system of rights need be enforceable, on pain of being treated, if it is unenforceable, as either a natural right or a meaningless gesture. The rights that governmental or other institutions may not enforce remain a public declaration of a public vision, extending, qualifying, and clarifying the ideals embodied in other, enforceable parts of the system of rights.[66]

Sixth, unlike Mounier and Maritain, Unger provides no clear development of group rights. Indeed, in describing market rights, immunity rights, destabilization rights, and solidarity rights, he seems to assume the individual as the right-holder. Nevertheless, his emphasis on the communal nature of society would seem to lead to a conception of the rights of groups as well as individuals. He has not made explicit any such conception of group rights, however.

Similarly to Mounier and Maritain, Unger proposes for our consideration an alternative conceptualization of rights to those we are most familiar with in the West, arguing that some of these alternative views are already implicit in current legal thought and practice.

Conclusion

The central focus of this chapter has been the cross-cultural implications of personalist perspectives on rights. Personalist-communitarian perspectives on rights, which are becoming increasingly common in the West, more closely approach non-Western conceptions of rights and the conception of rights in the International Bill of Rights.

The great contribution of the Enlightenment philosophers was their concept of individual liberty. But the incorporation of that concept in the French Declaration of the Rights of Man and in the American Declaration of Independence was due as much to felt grievances of the time as to philosophical theories. Today, in the West, the South, the North, and the East, felt grievances continue to include deprivations of personal liberty; but the grievances also relate to economic deprivation and deprivation of the rights of cultural groups. Richard Falk has referred to "intolerabilities"—situations that violate elementary principles of humanity and which we cannot accept.[67] The response to such intolerabilities is a conception of rights that relates to them, as the conception of rights of the eighteenth century related to the intolerabilities of that period.

The concept of "rights" is an evolving paradigm. Westerners upholding the traditional liberal concept of "rights" find it conceptually inaccurate to refer to "group rights" or to "economic and social rights." But, as Maritain has pointed out when referring to the term democracy:

> the choice of words in the practical domain is determined, not by the philosophers, but the usage of men and by the common consciousness. And what matters above all is rediscovering the genuine meaning and value of words charged with great human hopes, and the tone given to their utterance by a conviction based on truth.[68]

The term "human rights" is now used in non-Western cultures, and increasingly in the West, with content that is not identical with that of Western liberal rights. The political and practical force of human rights rhetoric is available within a personalist perspective in support of contemporary conceptions of human dignity.

This chapter has focused on Mounier, Maritain, and Unger, three representatives of a personalist-communitarian approach, because they have provided us with detailed explanations of their conception of rights, which retains a strong emphasis on individual freedoms while including economic rights and group rights. I consider them as representative of a trend in Western rights theorizing. The Catholic bishops of the United States, for example, have called for "a new cultural consensus that the basic economic conditions of human welfare are essential to human dignity and are due persons by right."[69] Whether that consensus is referred to as a "personalist-communitarian perspective" or by some other term is not important. But such a new cultural consensus in the West will have significant cross-cultural implications.

Such a perception of rights has much in common with approaches to rights in non-Western countries and the Third World. In addition, it is more fully in harmony with international standards of human rights contained in the Universal Declaration of Human Rights and the two International Covenants on human rights. Mounier, Maritain, and Unger are all contemporary thinkers; as such, they have been influenced by non-Western cultural traditions. Maritain was forced to confront his own tradition of rights with that of other cultural traditions during the drafting of the Universal Declaration of Human Rights, and Unger has recognized the influence of the Third World on his conception of politics and social organization.[70] They may be recognized as harbingers of a new theoretical concept of rights, solidly grounded in Western cultural traditions and guarding the best of that tradition, but open to a concept of rights covering the "intolerabilities" of the present age.

Notes

1. Roberto Mangabeira Unger, *False Necessity* (Cambridge: Cambridge University Press, 1987), 526.
2. For information concerning the Critical Legal Studies movement, *see,* Harvard Law Review Association, "'Round and Round the Bramble Bush': From Legal Realism to Critical Legal Scholarship," *Harvard Law Review* 96 (1982): 1669;

and "Critical Legal Studies Symposium," *Stanford Law Review* 36 (1984): 1. Persons associated with the Critical Legal Studies movement have been particularly critical of the liberal conception of rights and have emphasized communitarian approaches. While Unger is identified with the Critical Legal Studies movement, he must be viewed as a unique scholar within the movement; his reformulated conception of rights and his efforts to formulate a positive social theory distinguish him from many of those writing from a critical perspective.

3. *See* text and bibliographical citations in Ian Shapiro, *The Evolution of Rights in Liberal Theory* (Cambridge: Cambridge University Press, 1986) and literature on the Critical Legal Studies movement, *supra* note 2.

4. Karl Marx, "On the Jewish Question" in *The Marx-Engels Reader,* ed. Robert C. Tucker, 2nd ed. (New York: Norton, 1978).

5. Maurice Cranston, "Human Rights, Real and Supposed" in *Political Theory and the Rights of Man,* ed. D. D. Raphael (Bloomington, Ind.: Indiana University Press, 1967), 43.

6. See the following section of this essay for more detail concerning personalist perspectives.

7. See his Chapter 1 in this volume.

8. Baxi points out that "perhaps in a context like India's one may not take rights seriously if one does not take suffering seriously." Upendra Baxi, "Taking Suffering Seriously, Social Action Litigation in the Indian Supreme Court," *Review of the International Commission of Jurists* 29 (1982): 37, 47, n. 35.

9. "Personalism," *The Encyclopedia of Philosophy,* vol. 6 (New York: Macmillan and Free Press, 1967), 107.

10. *Ibid.* at 108.

11. Martin Luther King studied for his doctorate at Boston University because of his interest in personalist philosophy. He later stated that the personalist idealism which he studied at Boston remained his basic philosophical position. Kenneth L. Smith and Ira G. Zepp, Jr., *Search for the Beloved Community: The Thinking of Martin Luther King, Jr.* (Valley Forge: Judson Press, 1974), 100.

It would be interesting to speculate on the relationship between American personalism and Martin Luther King's conception of human rights, but we have no evidence of explicit links other than King's statement of his basic philosophical position. Smith and Zepp maintain that several themes in King's writings are traceable to personalism: "(1) the inherent worth of personality, (2) the personal God of love and reason, (3) the moral law of the cosmos, and (4) the social nature of human existence," (104). I am indebted to my colleague Stephanie Phillips for informing me of the influence of American personalism on King.

12. The information in this chapter concerning Mounier is taken primarily from the following sources: Eileen Cantin, *Mounier, A Personalist View of History* (New York: Paulist Press, 1973); John Hellman, *Emmanuel Mounier and the New Catholic Left 1930–1950* (Toronto: University of Toronto Press, 1981); R. William Rauch, Jr., *Politics and Belief in Contemporary France, Emmanuel Mounier and Christian Democracy 1932–1950* (The Hague: Martinus Nijhoff, 1972).

13. Hellman, *ibid.* at 251.

14. *See* Roberto Mangabeira Unger, "The Critical Legal Studies Movement," *Harvard Law Review* 96 (1983): 561; *Passion, An Essay on Personality* (New York: Free Press, 1984); and Unger, *supra* note 1.

15. Stephen Frederick Schneck, *Person and Polis, Max Scheler's Personalism as Political Theory* (Albany, N.Y.: State University of New York Press, 1987), ix. For Scheler's influence on Mounier, *see* Hellman, *supra* note 12, at 80.

16. Hellman, *ibid.* at 82.

17. *Ibid.*

18. Jean Lacroix, *Le Personnalisme* (Lyon: Chronique Social, 1981); my translation.

19. Jacques Maritain, *The Rights of Man and Natural Law* (London: Geoffrey Bles, 1958), 14. This book was first published in 1944.

20. Unger, *supra* note 1, at 24.

21. *Ibid.* at 518.

22. Maritain, *supra* note 19, at 15.

23. Hellman, *supra* note 12, at 5.

24. Schneck, *Person and Polis, supra,* note 15, at 153, n. 161.

25. Jacques Maritain, *Man and the State* (Chicago: University of Chicago Press, 1951), 107.

26. Unger, "The Critical Legal Studies Movement," *supra* note 14, at 321.

27. *Ibid.*

28. Unger, *supra* note 1, at 10.

29. *Ibid.* at 395.

30. Hellman, *supra* note 12, at 253.

31. *Ibid.* at 4, quoting Jean-Marie Domenach.

32. Jacques Maritain, *True Humanism* (London: Geoffrey Bles, 1959) [first ed., 1938], vii.

33. *See* Robert Pelloux, "Le Preambule de la Constitution du 27 octobre 1946," in Chronique Constitutionnelle, *Revue du Droit Public* 62, no. 347, 352–53.

34. Jean Rivero, "The French Conception of Human Rights," in *Human Rights, France and the United States of America* (New York: Center for the Study of Human Rights at Columbia University, 1984), 1.

35. *See* Pelloux, "Le Preambule de la Constitution du 27 octobre 1946," 352–53.

36. For the various drafts and discussions concerning the personalist declaration *see Esprit* 13, n.s., nos. 1–6 (December 1944–May 1945), 119–27, 581–90, 696–708, 850–56.

37. *Ibid.* at 852. The translations of the articles of the personalist declaration are mine.

38. See Michael McDonald's Chapter 6 in this volume.

39. *See, for example, ibid.*; and Jack Donnelly, "Human Rights and Western Liberalism," in *Human Rights in Africa: Cross-Cultural Perspectives,* ed. Abdullahi An-Na'im and Francis Deng (Washington, D.C.: Brookings Institution, 1990), 31.

40. It should be recalled in considering these articles that the personalist declaration was drafted in the form of an international treaty.

41. *Esprit, supra* note 36, at 120.

42. Rivero, "The French Conception of Human Rights," *supra* note 34, at 3.

43. Maritain, *supra* note 25, at 80–81.

44. *Ibid.* at 107.

45. *Ibid.* at 90.

46. *Ibid.* at 93.

47. *Ibid.* at 88.

48. *Ibid.* at 83.

49. *Ibid.* at 103.

50. *Ibid.* at 77.

51. *Ibid.* at 80.

52. *Ibid.* at 80.

53. *See* Mark Tushnet, "An Essay on Rights," *Texas Law Review* 62 (1984): 1363; Allan C. Hutchinson and Patrick J. Monahan, "The 'Rights' Stuff: Roberto Unger and Beyond," *Texas Law Review* 62 (1984): 1477.

54. Michael J. Perry, "Taking Neither Rights-Talk nor the 'Critique of Rights' Too Seriously," *Texas Law Review* 62 (1984): 1411–13.

55. Unger, *supra* note 1, at 508–09.

56. Unger develops his concept of rights in *False Necessity*, 508–39, and in "The Critical Legal Studies Movement," *supra* note 14, at 597–600.

57. Unger, *supra* note 1, at 518.

58. Unger, "The Critical Legal Studies Movement," *supra* note 14, at 597.

59. *Ibid.* at 598.

60. Unger, *supra* note 1, at 508–13.

61. *Ibid.* at 520, 523.

62. *Ibid.* at 528.

63. *Ibid.* at 530.

64. *Ibid.* at 536.

65. *Ibid.* at 537.

66. *Ibid.* at 539.

67. *See* Chapter 2, by Richard Falk, in this volume.

68. Maritain, *supra* note 19, at 31.

69. "Economic Justice for All," a pastoral letter approved by the National Conference of Catholic Bishops (November 13, 1986), paragraph 83.

70. Unger, *supra* note 1, at 604.

Michael McDonald

6. Should Communities Have Rights? Reflections on Liberal Individualism

The central question in this chapter is whether communities should have rights. This is a question that I will consider in a certain ideological or normative context, namely, that of liberalism. There are other contexts in which the question could be asked for, in nonliberal ideological settings; there have sometimes been clear positive answers to the question of whether minority communities should have rights. For example, the Ottoman Empire's *millet* system provided a system of group rights.[1] Various other autocratic states such as Czarist Russia have also provided at least some *de facto,* if not *de jure,* protection for various minority groups. One might even argue that various nineteenth- and twentieth-century European colonial regimes protected minority ethnic rights to some extent.[2] On paper and increasingly in reality, Marxist governments in the Soviet Union and Yugoslavia make provision for various sorts of group rights. Indeed, in both the origins and the consequences of the World Wars I and II, group rights played an extensive role.[3] The Canadian context, however, is essentially a liberal democratic one. So, for us, questions of collective rights for French or English minorities, native peoples, religious groups, and even those included under the "multicultural" label are posed in a liberal context. Is the liberal position one that is inherently hostile, sympathetic, or indifferent to group rights? This question can be addressed only by focusing on liberal attitudes to specific types of rights for various kinds of groups. Canadians, for example, would think of rights like those pertaining to language, education, political participation, equality, and ownership for groups identified by language, culture, race or ethnicity, belief, and, perhaps, gender.

It is important at the outset to be clear that I am concerned in this chapter with liberalism as a normative theory; in other words, I am not especially concerned with the beliefs and actions of particular liberals except in a broadly evidential way. I presume that liberals, like Marxists or conservatives, can hold beliefs and perform actions contrary to the deeper ideology they profess. They may do this either because they misunderstand the practical implications of their own deeper commitments or because under the stress of the moment they retreat from those convictions. The nearly unanimous approval of the imposition of the Canadian *War Measures Act* in 1970 is probably attributable to a combination of misunderstanding and backsliding. This means that my chapter is essentially an exploration of theory rather than practice, although I do believe that it has important implications for political and legal practices. In such an exploration, it is crucial to get the starting points right. Here, the potential of this chapter to illuminate depends on my conceptualization of collective rights and liberalism. It is to these starting points that I now turn. Once I have presented, in fairly stark terms, what I take to be the salient features of collective rights and liberalism, I will move on to explore the positions liberals can take on collective rights.

Collective Rights

In the view I take of collective or group rights, I draw a distinction between a group's possession of a right and its members' possession of that right. For example, think of a club having the right to the repayment of a loan in contrast with each of the members of the club individually and severally having that right. It is clear that the existence of similarly situated rights-holders does not automatically make a group which can hold, exercise, and benefit from collective rights. I reject then as a candidate for collective rights what I have described as a *class action concept of collective rights*.[4] In the class action concept, the group as a rights-holder serves as a convenient device for advancing the multiple discrete and severable interests of similarly situated individuals. Thus, all consumers who have been disadvantaged by Bell Canada's exceeding the legal limits set on phone rates might be regarded by the courts as a single litigant, simply because it would be too expensive and inconvenient to have each Bell customer take legal action on his or her own. My comment here is that class action rights are too thin a model for collective rights. A major aim of group rights is to protect interests that are not thus severable into individual interests, for the rights in question benefit the group itself by providing collective benefits. Moreover, group rights paradigmatically involve the collective exercise of rights through the use of group decision-making mechanisms. Collective benefit and collective exercise are not, therefore, captured by the class action conception of collective rights.[5]

For a group to function as a rights-holder, its members must see themselves as normatively bound to each other such that each does not act simply for herself or himself, but rather each plays her or his part in effectuating the shared normative understanding.[6] Shared understandings cover such key aspects of group life as membership and decision-making rules. The existence of a shared understanding is a matter of social fact, not merely a matter of legal assignment or ascription. The law does not, in my view, create groups; collectivities are not legal fictions. To be sure, the law can create opportunities—for example, through secondary rights or powers like marriage, partnership, and incorporation—or incentives, as it does with limited liability and tax advantages in the case of incorporation.[7] A legal system can also betray its deeper principles by falsely ascribing collective status to a group that lacks the relevant understanding. This, as I have argued elsewhere, was the case with the government's internment of Japanese Canadians during World War II.[8]

Similarly, the material or "objective" factors that give rise to the existence of a group must be distinguished from the understanding itself or from "subjective factors."[9] Subjective factors are crucial; what makes diverse individuals into a group is the existence of a shared understanding. This is not to deny the important fact that shared understandings can both be positively correlated with certain objective factors, like a shared heritage, language, belief, or social condition, and be focused on such objective conditions in various ways. Thus, a group-constituting understanding may well be created among individuals who have been selected for oppression because of their ethnicity, race, or language.[10] Since objective factors may provide a focus for a shared understanding in this way, they are often important in correctly interpreting a shared understanding because they help the interpreter to *see the point* of various norms that arise out of a group-constituting understanding. Here, an examination of the history of a group's relationship to other groups—especially in the relation of a minority group to a majority group—is often essential to determining the minority rights in question. That is, one must trace out the story within the context of the other story to comprehend their relationship.

There is a tendency of each group member to see himself or herself as part of an *us* rather just than as a separate *me*.[11] If we distinguish between our shallower and deeper social allegiances, it is plausible to describe the object of the latter as an identifying group. Allegiance to an identifying group structures personal identity; it indicates who one is. At its most profound level, the loss of membership in an identifying group is a loss or shattering of personal identity. This could alternatively be labeled as a *communitarian* feature[12] or an *identifying* one.[13] Even in a highly pluralistic context like our own, it will usually be the case that the most profound sorts of self-identification are nonvoluntary, that is, not a matter of *choosing* to identify with some group or other.[14] Even for voluntary identification, our individual options for identification are often strongly limited by deeply rooted objective and subjective factors, including those set by such processes as socialization and enculturation.

With collective rights, a group is a rights-holder; hence, the group has standing in some larger moral context in which the group acts as a rights-holder in relation to various duty-bearers or obligants. This is to say that for collective rights I picture a shared understanding within another shared understanding. First, there is the understanding that makes disparate individuals into a group or a collective. Second, there is a larger or more encompassing understanding in which that group stands as a rights-holder vis-à-vis others. So with minority rights, a minority, united by its group-constituting understanding, acts or tries to act as a rights-holder in a larger normative, social or legal, context. In particular, the minority wants to have its shared understanding recognized and respected as a distinct part of the larger social understanding in the society of which the minority is a part. To put this in terms of narratives, minority rights involve a story within a story. The stories are related but distinct. One story is not to be eliminated and replaced by the other. The options of assimilation and separation are ruled out as is the option of the substitution of one by the other.[15] Another image here can be drawn from music. Think of a large choir or orchestra with one or more quartets in its midst wanting to sing or play that quartet's music as part of the larger musical offering. Perhaps, for instance, the quartet is a jazz group that wants to improvise during a performance of Ravel's jazz-inspired *Piano Concerto in G*.

The question posed in this chapter concerns the limits set on minority rights and minority shared understandings in a liberal social context. Specifically, in Canada today and in other liberal societies, can various minority stories be told in the setting of the framing liberal story? To answer this question, it is necessary to expand on the key elements of the framing liberal story.

Liberalism

As a political theory, liberalism centers on individuals at three levels: as *political, justificatory,* and *contextual* theses. Conceptual clarification is gained if distinctions are drawn between political and justificatory theses. Political theses may well be justified in a variety of ways. The justification to which appeal is made will likely affect both the interpretation and implementation of a particular political thesis.[16] Clarification is also increased by distinguishing both justificatory frameworks and the political theses in question from their operational or functional contexts. In other words, one can ask what circumstances must be present for a particular political thesis to be realized in practice or for a particular justificatory framework to be relevant. These material conditions I label functional or contextual conditions.

POLITICAL THESES

Here I draw on Allen Buchanan's "Assessing the Communitarian Critique of Liberalism" for his formulation of a basic liberal political thesis: "the thesis that the state is to enforce the basic individual civil and political liberties," including "rights to freedom of religion, expression, thought, association, the right of legal due process."[17] This I label the *individual rights thesis*. The individual rights thesis might be interpreted either as an absolute or as a *prima facie* normative thesis.[18] That is, a liberal could hold that it is always or nearly always the case that individual rights ought to be respected; alternatively, a liberal might well believe that there are some important real-life circumstances in which other values than individual ones should be determinative. With the lexical priority of civil rights over economic and social rights, John Rawls seems to endorse an absolute version of the liberal political thesis. Ronald Dworkin also seems to take this view with his assertion of a seemingly absolute insistence on the obligation to treat all persons with equal concern and respect.[19] On the other side, Joseph Raz presents a version of liberalism that treats individual civil and political rights as important but not as the sole determinants of political action.[20]

There are two aspects to this main thesis of liberalism that will be addressed later on. The first is that this is a thesis about rights—rights that set limits on the actions of others, including the majority or any other *de jure* or *de facto* holder of political power and authority. The second is that such rights are seen as being vested in individuals.

Neutral and Nonvirtuous State Theses

The individual rights thesis is closely tied to the *neutral state* thesis, which is that "the proper role of the state is to protect basic individual liberties," not to make citizens virtuous. The Canadian philosopher Will Kymlicka says:

> Neutrality requires a certain faith in the operation of nonstate forums and processes for individual judgment and cultural development, and a distrust of the operation of state forums and processes for evaluating the good.[21]

I will explore the implications of this neutral state thesis when I consider the possibility that the liberal state might serve as a guarantor of legally recognized collective rights. The *nonvirtuous state* thesis has been put forward by Ronald Dworkin as a primary feature distinguishing liberalism from conservatism.[22] Dworkin takes the conservative's political thesis to be that the state ought to promote virtue and, presumably, punish vice.[23]

Individual Self-Determination Thesis

Both the individual rights and the neutral state theses are closely tied to the thesis that there should be official respect for and protection of a realm of individual choice. This is a thesis that received its classic exposition in John Stuart Mill's *On Liberty*. That is, liberalism recognizes a domain within which the individual is to be sovereign. A necessary condition for justified intervention into this private, protected domain is the prevention or punishment of harm to others. Neither the promotion of public policy nor the protection of the individual's welfare are sufficient to warrant intervention by individuals or by the state. My question concerns the compatibility between collective rights and individual self-determination.

JUSTIFICATIONS

My intention here is to identify *liberal* reasons for promoting and protecting individual rights by means of an essentially neutral and non-virtue-promoting state that protects individual self-determination. A variety of formulations have been prominent. I will focus on the two that have the best historical and conceptual claims to preeminence.

Utility-Centered Justifications

Utilitarian liberals appeal to the ultimate value of the *welfare* of individuals as a ground for the three liberal political theses. Hence, liberal political policies are to be promoted on the basis of their effects on the utility or welfare of individual citizens, each conceived as a separate and self-sufficient evaluator of that welfare.[24] The notion of utility is individualistic in the sense that it is the utility of individual persons and other sentient beings that determines the value of alternatives. The welfare of social groups in which such beings are members is then reducible to the aggregate welfare of the group's members.

Utilitarian justifications of liberal political practices have been robustly individualistic in other, less basic regards as well. While it does not follow from the concept of utility that *sources* of utility are interchangeable and replaceable, utilitarians have tended to use the utilitarian calculus as if this were the case—by moving, for example, from the hypothesis that utility can be mapped in monetary terms to the thesis that redistributive and compensatory justice can be achieved by moving dollars from one person's pocket into another's. It is tempting for the utilitarian to use the claim that a utility is a utility (the good of each person is to be counted equally) as a ground for the conclusion that a good is a good (sources of utility are interchangeable). Thus, it is not a great leap from the utilitarian calculus to Rawls's notion of primary social goods, which he describes as "rights and liberties, opportunities and powers, income and wealth" about "which it is supposed a rational man wants whatever else he wants."[25] It is common then for liberals to believe that the major sources of utility and primary goods are culturally neutral goods in the sense of being transculturally valued.[26]

For my purposes, the most important of these transcultural goods is that of freedom or liberty. Liberal utilitarian justifications of the liberal political theses are designed to present *self-determination* as a key component of individual welfare by arguing that, for extrinsic and intrinsic reasons, either the protection or the enhancement of self-determination, or both, are the primary means of promoting individual welfare. *Extrinsic* reasons for placing a high value on self-determination have to do with both the inefficiency of paternalism and the possible abuses of paternalism by those whose task it is to look after the welfare of others.[27] *Intrinsic* reasons have to do with the value that individuals set upon making decisions for themselves, quite apart from the value they set on securing various outcomes. Thus, I not only want to publish a first-rate chapter in this volume, but I also want the chapter to be my own; publishing a chapter that was ghost-written by Charles Taylor, for example, would not be the same for me as publishing my own thoughts—even though readers might wish otherwise.

Respect-Centered Justifications

Particularly since the publication of John Rawls's *Theory of Justice, autonomy* has been appealed to as a ground for liberal political measures. Following Raz, I will cash out autonomy in terms of *self-authorship.*[28] Thus, one characteristically liberal justification of a position opposed to censorship or in favor of the separation of church and state in public education is that individuals ought to be free to be authors of their own lives. The claim is that it is a good thing, either in itself or given certain background assumptions[29] about the value of the choices being made, that individuals be authors of their own lives. This claim is illustrated by the emphasis placed in contractarian reconstructions of justice on the primacy of free individual *consent.* In these ideal political justifications, consent is often required to be unanimous between choosers in an original position[30] or in a Lockean[31] or Hobbesian[32] state of nature.

I have already suggested that there is not much distance between the utilitarian hypothesis that the sources of utility are interchangeable and the Rawlsian notion of primary goods. This, of course, is important for intercultural as well as intracultural bargaining. The assumption is made that, after securing the physical necessities of existence, every bargainer, regardless of culture, will seek as high a degree of individual freedom as possible. In this regard, there is not as much of a gap between autonomy-based and welfare-based justifications of politics as might first appear to the observer of debates over the past several years in political philosophy. While autonomists complain that utilitarians ignore the separateness of persons, both have generally ignored the distinctness of cultures. Autonomy may represent a more direct way of grounding liberal politics than utilitarianism; both, however, have been strongly supportive of an abstract or acultural individualism.

FUNCTIONAL OR CONTEXTUAL THESES

These political theses and their justifications assume and require a certain context or set of background conditions. Two are central:

1. *Choices:* there must be an array of choices or opportunities open to individuals in the society so that one can meaningfully talk about *marketplaces* of goods, ideas, lifestyles, cultural and political options.[33]
2. *Choosers:* there must be a critical mass of choosers such that most adults can be counted as choosers in a robust sense, namely, as

actually making free and informed choices in both public and private spheres. Here, the most helpful specifications of being a chooser are negative. Thus, choosers are not so hopelessly dependent on drugs, not so dominated by others, not so unaware of the availability or significance of the options before them that it would be a mockery to describe them as free choosers.[34]

In the absence of choices and choosers, liberal political theses could get no footing. A compact way of describing the liberal context is that it is *pluralistic.* This means that liberal political and legal arrangements support an essentially pluralistic society for a variety of cultural, political, economic, and social groups. The liberal must then place a high value on tolerance; indeed, tolerance can be described as the premier civic virtue for liberals in that it is the essential condition for a shared public life. Pluralism can in part be seen as a result of the cumulative impact of acting on the thesis of individual self-determination. There are also close linkages to the neutral state and nonvirtuous state theses in that these can be seen as foundations for pluralism and for the leading social virtue of tolerance.

There is deep disagreement between classical liberals and welfare liberals over the need for redistribution to precede or make possible a pluralistic society. In effect, classical liberal defenses of the minimum state have supposed that there will be choices and choosers under normal market conditions and that state intervention diminishes rather than enhances choices and choosers. Welfare liberals have argued—convincingly in my view—that state intervention, principally through redistributive taxation and social assistance programs, is necessary to assure, insofar as is possible, that nearly everyone has an adequate range of social options and that internal obstacles to autonomy are removed. I shall not enter a discussion of the complex issues—conceptual (over the notion of freedom), factual (over the effectiveness of self-motivation), and moral (over whether there are positive as well as negative obligations)—that divide classical from welfare liberals.[35]

Liberalism and Collective Rights

Now I turn to the main issue: "Can liberals endorse collective rights?" Or, to put this in the terms that I have set: How compatible are the liberal rights and minority rights stories? Can one envisage minority rights in a liberal state?

First of all, liberalism is a theory about rights. These rights essentially establish normative limits on the use of both state and private power for the sake of members of the society in question. Simply as a thesis about the establishment of such normative limits, there is no incompatibility between being a liberal and advocating collective rights. Nevertheless, there is a salient feature of rights that has considerable practical importance for collective and particularly minority rights. In a liberal state, rights-holders must be more than merely passive beneficiaries of rights; rights-holders must be active exercisers of their rights. Now recall here the story-within-a-story metaphor that I used to describe collective and particularly minority rights. Two points need to be made.

The first is that a group may not want to tell its story within the context of what is essentially someone else's story. There just may be too many confining circumstances of that larger story or narrative. A minority may want in particular to break out of a context in which the larger normative context is determined essentially by the majority as a dominant social group. This is how many within Québec and growing numbers elsewhere in Canada would describe their situation within Confederation in the wake of the apparent failure to agree on the *Meech Lake Accord*. [36]

The second point is that to be a rights-holder contextually implies a certain confrontational stance. [37] There is a conflict, and in that conflict one of the parties uses the normative weapon of rights to get its way. One assumes that the parties are essentially possessive and territorial about their rights. But what about groups that are not essentially possessive or territorial, in particular those whose group-constituting understanding is nonpossessive and nonterritorial? Think, for example, of religious groups that are committed to pacifism. Or—in my view a more dramatic case—consider the understandings that are operative with indigenous peoples as they have been confronted by aggressive, possessive, and technologically advanced societies. [38] Can these peoples be true to their own understandings of themselves; will their songs be heard in the cacophonous surroundings of modern societies? It may well be that claiming and then asserting collective rights will destroy the groups that the rights are meant to preserve. [39]

Now I move to the second and crucial part of the liberal political thesis—the attribution of rights to individuals. As has been shown, individualism is apparent in all three parts of liberalism's theoretical structure.

The four political theses basic to liberalism are centered on individuals. The individual rights thesis sets as the state's primary role the protection of the civil and political rights of individuals. According to the neutral and nonvirtuous state theses, this enforcement must be carried out by a state with no ideological axe to grind other than the protection of individual rights. The self-determination thesis vests choices with individuals. At the justificatory level both utilitarian and respect-centered justifications appeal to the value and importance of individuals. Finally, the context of liberalism is pluralistic in a highly individualistic way: individual choosers must have open to them significant options. In the face of this strong individualistic bent, it looks initially as if the liberal must be hostile to collective rights. But I think that it is possible to discern a spectrum of attitudes toward collective rights ranging from outright hostility to all group rights, through moderate scepticism about the need for group rights, to the sympathetic though guarded endorsement of at least some group rights. I now want to scan that spectrum.

OUTRIGHT HOSTILITY

One quote will suffice here. This is from Justice Deschênes' judgment in *Québec Protestant School Boards*:

> The court is, to put it mildly, amazed to hear such an argument from a government which flatters itself that it is keeping alight in America the flame of French civilization, with its promotion of spiritual values and its traditional respect for freedom. The Quebec government in effect puts forward a totalitarian view of society to which the Court cannot subscribe. The human person is the highest value we know and nothing should be allowed to diminish the respect due to him. Other societies place the group above the individual. They use the steamroller of the kolkhoz and see merit only in the collective result, even if individuals are destroyed in the process.
>
> This view of society has not yet taken root here—though close to it—and this Court will not dignify it with its approval. In Canada, in Quebec, each individual must enjoy his rights to the full, whether alone or as a member of a group; and if the group has one hundred members, the hundredth member is as much entitled to benefit from all his privileges as the other ninety-nine. The alleged limitation of a collective right which would prevent the hundredth member of the group from exercising the rights guaranteed by the Charter constitutes a true denial of the rights of that hundredth member. He cannot simply be regarded as the accidental wastage of a collective operation: our concept of the individual cannot be made to embrace this theory.[40]

In part, liberal hostility to collective rights is based on a certain reading of history that identifies collective rights with a totalitarian approach in which the individual is run over by the collective steamroller. Collective rights are seen as having a fascist ancestry—an association with the doctrine of a master race.[41] The liberal's concern is often for the members of minority groups who will suffer at the hands of a majority invoking its alleged collective rights at the minority's expense.

But here it seems to me the liberal simply misunderstands the main reason for advocating collective rights, namely, the protection of minority communities from majorities. A similar misinterpretation—more likely heard from Americans than Canadians—lies in the claim that group rights provide the back door entrance for the introduction into judicial reasoning of such inherently suspect categories as race, gender, and ethnicity.[42] Legally, acceptance of this line of reasoning would run against the group-centered rationale for the selective amelioration clause, section 15(2) of the Canadian *Charter of Rights and Freedoms* (hereinafter the *Charter*).[43]

MODERATE SKEPTICISM

Moving from a liberalism that is hostile to the very concept of collective rights, I now want to consider liberal reasons for being skeptical about the need for collective rights. I shall do this under four closely related headings. Some of these headings may seem to point more to political practice than theory, but I shall concentrate on the theoretical aspects.

One worry is that the attribution of group rights to significant groups *balkanizes* the liberal state. It makes it difficult, if not impossible, to carry out the liberal agenda, whether that agenda is the classical liberal agenda of an open market for material and intellectual goods and services or the welfare liberal agenda of ameliorating the condition of the most disadvantaged. I note here that the balkanization argument has been a central position of those who oppose the *Meech Lake Accord* in Canada. There is in this position, it seems to me, a lingering attraction to the Hobbesian notion of unlimited sovereignty, which I have described elsewhere as involving at the level of normative practice a kind of monotheism of the state—that for each political system there must be one and only one source of legal and political authority.[44] But this position, whatever its other attractions, runs afoul of individual as well as collective rights because all such rights set limits on the state's authority, either directly as rights against the state or indirectly as rights against other persons which the state has an obligation to enforce. To be sure, the liberal skeptic could offer the rejoinder that there is more of a threat to central authority posed by collective rights than by individual rights. But from a moral perspective, this is not in itself a very convincing response.

A more theoretical reason for liberal skepticism is that from a liberal perspective group rights, unlike individual rights, appear to be *nonjusticiable* because they are *inherently political*. Thus, Dworkin assigns to the judiciary the task of adjudicating claims on the basis of rights.[45] The role of judges is to postulate foundational rights, which Dworkin contends will center on individual autonomy. This leaves the care of groups to the legislature, which has the task of advancing the general good in a utilitarian way. Even Oakeshott's notion of the state as a *societas* (as a "nomocracy" that sets "the conditions of conduct") as opposed to a *universitas* (purposeful association) lends itself to this idea.[46] Lon Fuller can, I believe, be cited in the same cause, namely, as providing a liberal conceptual basis for the view that individual rights are apolitical and therefore justiciable in a way in which group rights are not.[47] Individual rights are meant then to be beyond the ordinary give-and-take of everyday legislative politics and confined to judicial determinations of preexisting rights.

As it stands, this claim about the nonjusticiability of collective rights begs the question of whether group rights should also be similarly immune from ordinary political bargaining. Of course, the addition of collective rights to an already existing regime of individual rights creates practical problems. If all political arguments are cast in terms of rights, then the desired effect of setting some situations above or beyond ordinary politics is lost. One should also worry about judicialization of politics, with the attendant loss of democratic self-government. Nonetheless, at the level of normative theory, these practical worries do not determine for Canada or for any other state the appropriate mix of entrenched individual and collective rights.

A third closely related concern centers on the alleged *provincialism* of collective rights in contrast to the *cosmopolitanism* of individual rights.[48] The liberal individualist might want to cite as evidence here the way in which individual but not group rights have been recognized in international codes of human rights.[49] My response here would be that the antipathy of established states to minority rights is easily explainable on grounds of self-interest rather than of principle.[50] As to the more general claim that only individual rights can be cosmopolitan, I would suggest that there is nothing inherent in the notion of group rights that renders them suspect as part of a transnational, normative order. Indeed, the

general recognition of minority rights would do much to improve the situation in various parts of the world, including the Soviet Union, the Middle East, and the Balkans.

A more theoretical response to the moderately skeptical liberal is also in order here. I would suggest that group rights, particularly for minorities, protect both interests and activities that cannot be otherwise protected. The interests that are protected are inherently collective or social interests, in particular the interest that human beings have in belonging to nurturing, identifying cultural groups. There are, in addition, collective activities or ways of doing things that are also inherently social, like speaking a language, making political decisions, or worshipping.[51] This sort of case for collective rights suggests that it may be difficult for the liberal to reject collective rights easily.

But before I look at the positive liberal case that can be made for collective rights, I want to consider yet another variety of liberal skepticism about collective rights, namely, the position that collective rights are at best *redundant*. This skepticism is not based on an essential underestimation of the goods of community, which I think the previous arguments were. Rather, the general claim is that collective rights are unnecessary to protect such goods. Here, I will focus on Buchanan's arguments in favor of the proposition that individual rights provide a better defense of the goods of community than do collective rights.

Buchanan's first argument is that group rights are inflexible in a way that individual liberal political rights are not:

> First, individual rights to freedom of religion, thought, expression, and association facilitate rational, nonviolent change in existing communities as well as the rational, nonviolent formation of new communities. Individual rights do this by allowing individuals who are dissatisfied with current forms of community to advocate and to try to develop alternatives even when the majority of their fellow members (or the official leaders of the community) do not share their views. If rights to freedom of expression, association, thought, and religion accrued to communities, not to individuals, then they would protect existing communities from intrusions by other communities or state agencies. But they would not provide protection for the formation of new communities or for modification of existing communities, so far as either of these two types of changes originate in the beliefs and actions of an individual or a minority.[52]

This argument sets the goods of community clearly within the limits established by the basic liberal right of self-determination. Thus, the liberal self-determination thesis grounds in effect a right to *social mobility* or mobility of the individual among social groups: individuals must be free to leave or to join various social groups.[53] Following Mill, Buchanan claims that "the recognition of these individual rights [does] not threaten limitless change and uncontrolled fragmentation of communities" because of "the tight grip that tradition has on most people." He goes on to argue that in the marketplace of communities only communities which really do meet "the human need for community" will survive and prosper.[54]

I think that Buchanan underestimates the distorting force of individual mobility rights and indeed the way in which such rights can intentionally or unintentionally lead to the destruction of worthwhile groups. Buchanan's position is naive at least as it concerns minority, traditional communities including most aboriginal peoples, and religious groups like the Amish and the Mennonites. Modern mass culture has had a profound effect on such communities. In the case of indigenous peoples or the so-called Fourth World, the effects in most cases have been devastating.[55] For such societies, there is a kind of Humpty Dumpty effect—once such a community is shattered, it cannot be put back together again. To pretend that individual rights without the addition of powerful collective rights and powers would preserve the social goods in question would, I think, be disingenuous. Even for an advanced modern society like Québec, the maintenance of language in a pervasively anglophone environment is extraordinarily difficult. This difficulty has been recognized by the Supreme Court of Canada in the signs case in which it decided that Québec has to have the powers to ensure a "*visage linguistique*."[56] I would hope that in the case of our native peoples, there will eventually be a parallel recognition of collective claims to land and to self-determination as essential to community survival.

I would also contend that the underlying notion of communities that Buchanan assumes is inappropriate. Buchanan pictures communities in a quintessentially liberal way—as if they were products for consumption. One imagines a jaded Californian yuppie shopping for the latest in-group. But this notion of the group as a marketable product does not fit the situation of most identifying groups. I cannot picture a Méti, an Innu, a Mohawk, a Québeçois, an Acadian, a Newfoundlander, a black Canadian, or a Ukrainian Canadian as standardly being able to view their membership in identifying communities in this way. Once a member sees the group as a consumer good, then the group has in fact likely ceased being an identifying group for that person.[57]

I think too that Buchanan fails to appreciate the way in which a community depends on the existence of a shared understanding on the part of that community's members.[58] I would argue that if a minority within the community disagrees deeply with the majority or the community's leaders there exists to all intents and purposes a second community.[59] That is, on the view of collective rights-holders that I have advanced, it is unnecessary to introduce individual rights to allow for the formation of new communities or the alteration of old communities. Instead, one can look to the community-constituting understanding as a necessary condition for the attribution of collective rights. Thus, if one takes seriously the idea of understandings as essential to the attribution of collective rights, one is in a position to provide adequately for new groups or dissident subgroups.[60]

Buchanan also argues that the state's recognition of individual rights is a far more effective way of protecting a community's interests than collective rights would be:

> For if these rights are ascribed to individuals, then all that is needed to trigger official protective action is a violation of the rights of one member of that community. In contrast, a group's right . . . would have to be invoked through an official process involving a collective decision procedure of some kind. The costs of exercising a group right might therefore be considerably higher and the process of doing so more ponderous.[61]

In response, I would suggest that even if Buchanan is correct about costs and procedures, it would still likely be the case that the group would be more efficacious in protecting the community interests in question because it involved action by the community rather than by a single member of the community. This is in part a matter of resources: communities are better able to bear the burdens of litigation than are individuals; and communities can bring the pressure of numbers to bear in order to effect political, as opposed to judicial, recognition of their rights. But the main response I want to give concerns the central thrust of the redundancy argument which is that the interests protected by individual and collective rights are the same. Buchanan's confusion on this point is evident in his subsequent arguments that group rights are hierarchical and paternalistic, while individual rights are not.[62] Just as individual rights focus on an individual's interests, collective rights have as their object collective interests. In short, Buchanan's redundancy arguments fail because each assumes that collective and individual rights have the same focus or intention.

Buchanan also seems to believe that a collective right cannot be individually invoked (and presumably that an individual right could not be collectively invoked). This assumption is false. When a francophone in Alberta invokes rights under section 23 of the *Charter* to ensure that her child can go to a French school governed by French trustees, the right invoked is collective and not individual.[63] The right is crucially dependent in this case on the existence of a critical mass of francophones in the area—a mass that is sufficient to enjoy the good in question.[64] Contrast this with a case in which the litigant's complaint is that the local French school will not admit her child; here, the right is individual.

Nevertheless, there is a good reason to want community interests in general to be protected by the community's rather than an individual member's exercise of a right. For it is the welfare or interests of the community that are at stake and not just the welfare of a given member. The risks to the community's interests are increased if individual members may exercise rights on their own without prior community agreement. The chances of there being either a misconceived or even a mischievous exercise of rights are increased if the power to exercise is not subject to the beneficiary's control.[65] Moreover, there is something perverse about the idea of collective interests being standardly vested in individuals. There is a slide from "ours" to "mine" that should be resisted. In particular, regarding a conservative notion of community as a union of past, present, and future generations, I would argue that the claimant's role in collective rights is one of stewardship, and this role is best played by a present generation that is mindful of its history and its future.

SYMPATHETIC LIBERALISM

I now want to ask if a liberal for liberal reasons could endorse at least some significant collective rights. I will examine in turn a position sympathetic to collective rights that could be taken by classical liberals and one that could be taken by welfare liberals.

Classical liberals would not object in principle to individuals voluntarily pooling their rights. For example, two or more individuals might pool certain of their assets to form a business. In thus pooling their assets, they give up individual control of the assets to some sort of collective decision procedure, say, as specified in articles of partnership or incorporation. In so associating themselves, the individuals in question voluntarily give up certain rights of self-determination with respect to other members of the group (say, with respect to corporate assets). Hence, it can be said the association, partnership, or corporation has collective rights against its members. Also in associating themselves, the individuals in question will be pooling rights they had as individuals against others. Thus, in forming a business partnership, you and I might each bring real estate or other assets to the enterprise. These might well include claims on others in the form of mortgages or other outstanding loans. Our partnership thereby acquires in a meaningful sense certain collective rights against these obligants with respect to payment of the interest and principal due. Hence, in the case of rights the group has against its members and in the case of rights the group has against outsiders, the group's rights are transferred individual rights. Essentially, then, what started as discrete individual rights to self-determination became through the free actions of the individuals in question, rights of the group thus formed.

This transfer is subject to an important *procedural* condition: each of us must give free and informed consent to the association.[66] There are no material conditions or limits on the contents of voluntary agreements. Therefore, in classical liberalism, there is no guarantee that the liberty of the individual will be preserved in agreements made with others. It is unsurprising, then, that the paradigmatic relationship of person to person supported by classical and libertarian liberalism is not the equality characteristic of common citizenship but the inequality of employment—the master-servant relation.

How far does classical liberalism take us toward collective rights as usually understood in the Canadian and international context? I suggest that it does not take us very far. This fact is in part because the central candidates for collective rights in declarations of human rights are "natural" groups—peoples with a language, history, culture, or set of beliefs in common.[67] In all but the case of groups united solely by adherence to a dogma, it is hard to see how such groups meet in a clear and obvious way the free-and-informed consent requirement. In fact, even the majority of dogmatically centered groups acquire the bulk of their new members by birth rather than by adult conversion.

In response, the classical liberal may suggest reinterpretation of the social understanding in question so that it can be determined whether the group is freely and voluntarily composed. Thus, the classical liberal might seek surrogates for consent by proposing that if people continue to speak a certain language and remain in a certain community, then they have freely chosen to remain members of that linguistic community. But maintaining this position may well commit the classical liberal to a number of unrealistic assumptions about available options, particularly that people who want to leave the community have somewhere else to go.[68] It also is not clear that this is how members of the group in question can and do envisage their situation. What if they should see membership in the community not as a matter of choice or its denial—coercion, but rather as simply a fact of existence? Here, the reinterpretation of social practice is unconvincing and normatively irrelevant.

Perhaps, the classical liberal will insist on more than reinterpretation of the relevant social practices; his position may be that for good liberal reasons the state will guarantee, among other things, various rights of association and dissociation. These guaranteed rights may have a distorting and disintegrating effect on the communities in question, depending on how strong the rights are taken to be. Thus, for example, would a classical liberal interpretation of exit rights from a Hutterite community include a significant share of communal assets? Does, for example, a Sandra Lovelace on this view acquire title in a home and does that home then become an island on the reserve exempt from band control?[69]

Finally, it should be noted that if the community in question can meet the voluntariness requirement, then the classical liberal is likely to let the group do as it pleases with regard to its own members. For the classical liberal holds that consent negates claims of unjust treatment. That is, an unsurprising result is that the classical liberal will endorse only negative rights for groups.[70] In this respect, I will argue that the classical liberal may in some circumstance be a better friend of collective rights than his welfare liberal cousin.

Now I want to look at the way in which welfare liberals can and do champion positive collective rights as a means of promoting the redistribution necessary for the achievement of pluralism.[71] The eminent jurist and Scottish nationalist Neil MacCormack links the idea of respect for persons to the idea of respect for cultures:

> The Kantian ideal of respect for persons implies . . . an obligation in each of us to respect that which in others constitutes any part of their sense of their own identity. For many people, though quite probably not for all, a sense of belonging to a nation is an element in this precious fabric of identity. This comprises . . . not merely a consciousness of a continuity with the past, but also a will or hope for continuity into the future; and also consciousness of a form of cultural community which requires protection and expression in appropriate institutional forms.[72]

Similarly, in a recently published article, Kymlicka says:

> The dominant view among contemporary liberals, to which Rawls apparently subscribes, is that liberalism requires the "absence, even prohibition, of racial, religious, language, or [cultural] groups as corporate entities with a standing in the legal or governmental process, and a prohibition of the use of ethnic criteria of any type for discriminatory purposes, or conversely, for special or favored treatment."[73] But this view, which achieved its current prominence during the American struggle against racial segregation, has only limited acceptability. Once we recognize the importance of the cultural structure and accept that there is a positive duty on the state to protect the cultural conditions which allow for autonomous choice, then cultural membership does have political salience. Respect for the autonomy of the members of minority cultures requires respect for their cultural structure, and that in turn may require special linguistic, educational, and even political rights for minority cultures.[74]

Kymlicka goes on to point out that prewar British liberals were able to support minority rights on the basis of respect for autonomy.

As it stands, this welfare liberal argument is powerful and convincing. Briefly, it is that becoming an autonomous person requires a social context—a context in which one acquires an identity not just as an individual but as a member of a community. Language and culture are central to the formation of an autonomous identity. If one's language and culture are penalized or even marginalized, then the barriers to personal autonomy are likely to be high. But language and culture are paradigmatically collective assets; their protection is best vested in the community;[75] hence the need for collective rights to provide linguistic and cultural security of the members of minority cultural, linguistic, religious, and other groups.[76]

Nonetheless, I see a downside to the welfare liberal defense of collective rights that needs to be examined. First, the only groups to which the welfare liberal will extend collective rights are those whose cultures support the formation of autonomous individuals. I would suggest then there is a strong thrust here to support only cultures that meet the liberal individualist paradigm. If your personal identity is rooted in a collectively oriented, nonindividualistic minority, then there is little reason to hope that a liberal welfare state will grant collective rights against society at large to your group. Beyond this, I would argue that the welfare liberal will not only fail to encourage certain nonliberal groups, but will also discourage many of these societies.[77] For insofar as social formation, including socialization and enculturation, is crucial to individual autonomy, the welfare liberal has reasons for interfering in groups that hinder this goal, particularly by altering offending structural and substantive features of the group's practices, including its decision-making strutures and its basic tenets. On this view, it would likely be the case that the liberal would describe the U.S. case of *Yoder* as wrongly decided.[78] The state of Wisconsin had good reason then to insist that Amish children attend high school, for without attending high school their social mobility would be disastrously restricted. This not only threatens the existence of some groups, but it also paradoxically diminishes individual choice while increasing it; for the creation of a new set of options for the child either eliminates the earlier option of remaining within the traditional culture or dramatically raises its costs. This is one of those cases in which it could be said that "You can't go home anymore" or, in the words of the World War I song, "How can you keep them down on the farm after they've seen Paree [Paris]?" What I fear from a welfare liberal endorsement of group rights is the encouragement of an undercurrent movement toward intervention in minority affairs. Collective autonomy for the minority will be diminished in order to advance the autonomy of individual members of the minority. The result may well be that the existence of minority groups faces a greater threat from an activist, welfare liberal state than from a more passive, night watchman state, that of classical liberalism.

A further objection is that the welfare liberal's endorsement of group rights essentially misses the point. The aim of group rights is collective and not individual. Thus, in the case of autonomy, group rights essentially protect group or collective autonomy. To be sure, meaningful participation in autonomous groups can be essential to individual autonomy; and so one might, as Kymlicka does, defend group rights as an effective way of enhancing individual autonomy. This position, however, should not lead one to think that collective autonomy is valuable only as a means of enhancing individual autonomy. In my view, collective autonomy, like individual autonomy, is valuable in its own right; hence one should not be valued simply as a means to the other.

Welfare liberals may suggest this is but a small price to pay for the benefits of individual self-determination, but I wonder; I am haunted by the recollection of missionary schools for Natives, which, it will be recalled, were provided in the name of civilization and for the benefit of the individuals in question. Indeed, they were based on the belief that individual Natives could benefit only if their "Indianness" was eradicated and replaced by "white civilization." I fear the continued destruction of fragile communities, whether it is caused by the classical liberal's indifference to positive rights or the welfare liberal's interventionism. As a communitarian, I feel caught between the advantages offered by welfare liberals to communities, namely that encouragement and support will be provided to important identifying groups in the form of collective rights, and the advantages offered by classical liberals to communities, namely that the state will take a hands-off approach to groups that meet the criterion of free-and-informed consent. In a way I want both and I want neither.

It is then time for a confession—a confession about my lack of faith or at least a deeply felt worry I have about the grounding individualistic values of liberalism. What the liberal takes as basic and unquestionable is the idea that the individual is the measure of everything; hence, the liberal believes that correct normative principles treat the individual as the fundamental unit of value and the ultimate focus of rights. Individuals are regarded as valuable because they are choosers and have interests. But so, too, do communities make choices and have interests. Why not then treat communities as fundamental units of value as well? I am too much attracted by the old faith of liberalism to ignore individual rights, freedoms, and interests; but I am also attracted to a more holistic conception of law, politics, and morality in which communities matter in their own right. I have no algorithm to settle which should be first—the individual or the community. I agree with liberals who are sympathetic to collective rights that in many significant cases this is not an either-or proposition. But I cannot agree with them that when the chips are down the only morally acceptable option is the one that treats the community as either a business partnership or as a glorified Children's Aid Society. I can only say—and this is a statement without comfort—that there are tragic choices. I hope that we Canadians as a nation have the good fortune to avoid having too many tragic choices, but our history and especially our current situation incline me more toward pessimism than optimism in this regard.

Conclusion

I would like to offer a few brief reflections on how my chapter relates to the major theme of this volume. This theme involved a tension between a universal approach to human rights and approaches embedded in particular cultural traditions. This universalist-particularist division has two main dimensions, practical and theoretical. Both revolve around the question of where one anchors oneself in promoting basic human rights: whether within one's own tradition or at the global level? Presumably, human rights should be aimed at avoiding great evils, at what Falk described as "the intolerable,"[79] not at achieving great goods.

Practically, this raises the question of whether it is more effective to appeal to domestic or international standards in denouncing such intolerable practices as torture, slavery, and genocide. Often appeal to local shared understandings has the practical advantage of touching a government or political movement more deeply than an appeal to international standards, for the appeal to international standards can be portrayed as alien and invasive, especially to collective autonomy. Nonetheless, appeals to international standards, imperfect as they are, are ways of reminding violators of human rights that we share a globe and, despite a great many important normative differences, we also share a number of important values, in particular abhorrence of the gratuitous infliction of pain and degradation of human beings.[80]

Theoretically, there is a deep temptation to search for foundations—for the one right answer to normative questions. In part, this is because globally we face, as An-Na'im's chapter demonstrates, conflicts between international and domestic standards, and even within given communities we argue over the appropriate interpretation of shared understandings. Alternatively, the theoretical dispute between universalists and particularists could be phrased in terms of who is the *self* in the human right to self-determination. Different cultures foster different notions of the self. To put the theoretical issue in the terms I have used in this chapter, there is an urge to seek some abstract vantage point—what the great nineteenth-century utilitarian Henry Sidgwick labeled "the point of view of the Universe"—from which one could, say, assess all the different community-constituting understandings in the world today.[81]

I do not think that there is such a vantage point.[82] I share with Tore Lindholm the conviction that we should seek overlapping consensuses to address the differences in perspective we inevitably find on normative issues; that is, the best method is that of Rawlsian reflective equilibrium and not moral foundationalism.[83] But there is something else as well: we can from our different perspectives talk to each other and, as we must, live together in a world that is increasingly fragile. Our community-constituting understandings are not fixed or immutable; they can and do evolve with changed circumstances or they perish. So if we can live together peacefully, and collectively address our increasingly common problems, then we will—we must—come to have a deeply felt, shared global understanding that spans and yet is sensitive to those cultural differences that make us who we are.[84]

Notes

1. Vernon Van Dyke, *Human Rights, Ethnicity, and Discrimination* (Westport, Conn.: Greenwood Press, 1985), 74.

2. *Ibid.* at 351–53.

3. James Fawcett, *The International Protection of Minorities* (London: Minority Rights Group, 1979).

4. Michael McDonald, "Questions About Collective Rights," in *Language and the State: The Law and Politics of Identity,* ed. T. Ducharme (Edmonton: University of Alberta Press, forthcoming).

5. This is not to say that every collective right necessarily both advances a collective interest and is collectively exercised. I will argue below that some collective rights can be individually exercised and that some individual interests can be best advanced by the collective exercise of a right.

6. A. M. Honoré, "Groups, Laws, and Obedience," in *Oxford Essays in Jurisprudence,* ed. A.W.B. Simpson (Oxford: Oxford University Press, 1973), 2; A. M. Honoré, "What is a Group?" *Archiv für Rechts-und Sozialphilosophie* BD.1xi/2 (1975): 168.

7. H.L.A. Hart, *The Concept of Law* (Oxford: Oxford University Press, 1961), 26–48, 94.

8. Michael McDonald, Understandings: Collectivities, Their Rights and Obligations (unpublished manuscript).

9. Francesco Capotorti, *Study on the Rights of Persons Belonging to Ethnic, Religious and Linguistic Minorities* (New York: United Nations, 1979).

10. Ernest Renan says: "Je disais tout à l'heure: «avoir souffert ensemble»; oui, la souffrance en commun unit plus que la joie," ("Ou'est-ce qu'une nation?" in *Oeuvres complètes,* vol. 1 (Paris: Colmann-Levy, 1947–1961), 904.

11. Allen Buchanan, "Assessing the Communitarian Critique of Liberalism," *Ethics* 99 (1989): 856–57. In the view I am outlining, the distinction between myself and my society is itself located in a shared understanding.

12. *Ibid.* at 857.

13. Owen M. Fiss, "Groups and the Equal Protection Clause," *Philosophy and Public Affairs* 5 (1976): 148.

14. In the pluralistic context, personal identity is bound up with the idea of being a chooser or selector of options. Does one choose to be a chooser? *Over time* one does. Thus, I can deliberately improve or degrade my capacities as a chooser up to the point of ceasing to be a chooser, for example, by committing suicide or becoming hopelessly addicted. But at a particular time, the option is not open to me. The old existentialist observation is true: the refusal to choose is itself a choice. But here I want to go beyond these remarks about the concept of being a chooser

to the peculiarly liberal concept of individuals as choosers. Our identity in a liberal society is a construct of the choices we make; we see ourselves as first and foremost *consumers and constructors of options*. Both our natural and social environments are then for us not given but potentially manipulatable elements in our never-ceasing struggle "for power after power" (Thomas Hobbes, *Leviathan* [Harmondsworth: Penguin Books, 1968 (1651)], 161). This is not, I would suggest, how nonliberal individuals such as the Innu or feudal Europeans have seen themselves (Joseph Pestieau, Droits des personnes, des peuples, et des minorités, unpublished manscript).

15. Michael McDonald, *supra* note 8.

16. Allen Buchanan makes this point in his liberal response to communitarian criticisms of liberalism by distinguishing between justificatory frameworks and political theses (Buchanan, *supra* note 11, at 853–56). In effect, he argues that "the most plausible communitarian challenge to the liberal political thesis" is that sometimes the priority given to individual rights can be overridden to "protect the goods of community or community values" (*ibid*. at 855), but that by and large the moderate communitarian, on reflection, will endorse the liberal political thesis.

17. *Ibid*. at 854.

18. *Ibid*. at 855.

19. Will Kymlicka argues that both Rawls and Dworkin can be reinterpreted to take into account communitarian elements in the formation of individual autonomy ("Liberal Individualism, and Liberal Neutrality," *Ethics, supra* note 11, at 899). I discuss Kymlicka's liberal argument for collective rights at the end of this chapter.

20. Joseph Raz, *The Morality of Freedom* (Oxford: Clarendon Press, 1986), 193–216.

21. W. Kymlicka, *supra* note 19, at 899.

22. Ronald Dworkin, *A Matter of Principle* (Cambridge, Mass.: Harvard University Press, 1985), 191–204.

23. Note that as a political thesis the neutral state thesis is compatible with perfectionist justifications of the state. Raz advances such a justification; it is one that is very close to the kind of argument advanced in chapter 3 of John Stuart Mill's *On Liberty* (London: J. M. Dent, 1962 [1st ed., 1859]).

24. Bentham dismissed the notion of the common good and replaced it with the notion of the aggregate good. This schema received its most thoughtful exposition in Henry Sidgwick's *The Method of Ethics* (London: Macmillan, 1907).

25. John Rawls, *Theory of Justice* (Cambridge, Mass.: Harvard University Press, 1971), 92.

26. Many primary goods are perforce social in the sense of requiring a social context. If people lived like hermits, there would be no value in social status.

27. Henry Sigwick, *The Elements of Politics* (London: Macmillan, 1908), 39–43.

28. J. Raz, *supra* note 20, at 369.

29. *Ibid*. at 308.

30. J. Rawls, *supra* note 25, at 139–42.

31. Robert Nozick, *Anarchy, State, and Utopia* (New York: Basic Books, 1974), 9–12.

32. David Gauthier, *Morals by Agreement* (Oxford: Clarendon Press, 1986), 158–60.

33. Joseph Raz, *supra* note 20, at 373.

34. Michael McDonald, "Ideology and Morality in Hard Times," in *Contemporary Moral Issues,* ed. Wes Cragg, 2nd ed. (Toronto: McGraw-Hill-Ryerson, 1987), 590.

35. *See* Jan Narveson, *The Libertarian Idea* (Philadelphia: Temple University Press, 1988), chapters 2–8, for a discussion of these issues from a libertarian perspective.

36. *1987 Constitutional Accord. See* Katherine Swinton and Carol Rogerson, *Competing Constitutional Visions: The Meech Lake Accord* (Toronto: Carswell, 1988), 315.

37. Carl Wellman says, "The very concept of a right presupposes some possible confrontation between the possessor of a right and one or more second parties," C. Wellman, *A Theory of Rights: Persons under Laws, Institutions, and Morals* (Totowa, N.J.: Rowman and Allanheld, 1985), 194. Largely for this reason, Wellman endorses a will-centered rather than an interest-centered concept of rights.

I would add here that one of the sad results of our cultural preoccupation with rights is that there is a general blindness to the questions of when and where it is appropriate to exercise or to press one's rights. Anglophone reactions to Bourassa's invocation of the *notwithstanding* provisions in the *Ford* case struck me as displaying an almost boorish insensitivity to the relatively disadvantaged position of francophones outside Québec compared to the advantaged situation of anglophones within Québec (Ford v. Québec, 54 D.L.R. [4th] 577).

38. Joseph Pestieau, Droits des personnes, des peuples, et des minorités, unpublished manuscript. Presented at the 1989 meeting of the Canadian Philosophical Association.

39. Linda Medcalfe, *Law and Identity: Lawyers, Native Americans, and Legal Practice* (Beverly Hills, Calif.: Sage Publications, 1978).

40. 140 D.L.R. (3rd) 33 at 64. For a detailed discussion of this case, *see* my paper, "Collective Rights and Tyranny," *University of Ottawa Quarterly* 56 (1986): 115–23.

41. Paul Sieghart, *The Lawful Rights of Mankind; An Introduction to the International Legal Code of Human Rights* (Oxford: Oxford University Press, 1986), 164.

42. Kymlicka, *supra* note 19, at 903.

43. I would recall here that my earlier claim that there is more to being a group than being a collection of similarly situated individuals; there must also be a shared understanding. This has, I believe, important implications for selective amelioration under s. 15(2). If a government is genuinely concerned with the welfare of a group, such as a Native band, it must move to meet its collective needs and not just the needs of individual members of the band.

44. Michael McDonald, *supra* note 4.

45. Ronald Dworkin, *Taking Rights Seriously* (London: Duckworth Press, 1977), 84–88, 123–30.

46. Michael Oakeshott, *On Human Conduct* (Oxford: Clarendon Press, 1975), 203.

47. Lon Fuller, "Two Principles of Human Association," in *Voluntary Associations: Nomos XI*, ed. J. Pennock and J. Chapman (New York: Athcuton Press, 1969), 3.

48. Jack Stevenson, "Canadian Philosophy From Cosmopolitan Point of View," *Dialogue* 25 (1986): 17.

49. P. Sieghart, *supra* note 41, at 161–68.

50. Michael McDonald, "Collective Rights in International Relations," in *Challenging the Conventional,* ed. Wesley Cragg, Laurent Larouche, and Gertrude Lewis (Burlington, Ont.: Trinity Press, 1989), 115–17.

51. Leslie Green, "Are Language Rights Fundamental?" *Osgoode Hall Law Journal* 25 (1987): 639–69.

52. Buchanan, *supra* note 11, at 862.

53. This does not preclude groups from having a say by setting limits to entrance and exit conditions, which are compatible with liberal political theses.

54. Buchanan, *supra* note 11, at 863.

55. Ben Whitaker, *The Fourth World, Victims of Group Oppression* (New York: Schocken, 1973).

56. *See* Ford v. Québec, 54 D.L.R. (4th) 577 at 627.

57. Even religious affiliation is pictured by many believers as in the first instance a matter of grace rather than of choice. That is, one does not choose or select a religious affiliation, but one is chosen for it.

58. The same failure is also evident in two other arguments advanced by Buchanan. One is that group rights are likely to involve a hierarchical decision procedure that is open to misuse by leaders. The other is that group rights are likely to encourage paternalism on the part of leaders.

59. The classic 1904 case of *Free Church of Scotland* ([1904] A.C. 515) is interesting in this regard. Roughly speaking, the suit involved a dispute about the ownership of Church property that arose when the Free Church of Scotland decided to form a union with the United Presbyterian Church in 1900. The Free Church had been established in 1843 in the main on the basis of the 1647 Westminster Confession of Faith. A small minority viewed the changes brought about in 1900 to effect union as a heretical deviation from the Westminster Confession and argued that they, as the true guardians of the faith, should keep the Free Church's extensive properties. The House of Lords reversed the earlier decision by holding that the majority had no power to vary the Church's doctrine and awarded the property to the minority. The decision was later reversed by an act of Parliament. Fuller has some interesting comments to offer on similar cases (Fuller, *supra* note 47, at 8–11).

60. Rhoda E. Howard has asked me whether collective rights adequately protect individuals who do not identify with any groups, in particular groupless or stateless persons. (Typically, though, stateless persons are not groupless.) One could also ask the same question about those who deeply identify with more than one group. These are difficult issues, which I can only flag here but not answer. If my argument at this point is correct, I have shown that collective rights can go

much further toward protecting diversity in a particular country or in the international arena than liberal critics of collective rights have allowed.

61. Buchanan, *supra* note 11, at 863.

62. It is worth pointing out the obvious: groups can be nonhierarchical and nonpaternalistic. As I understand it, decision-making procedures among Native groups are far more participatory and inclusive than are the decision procedures typical of Western democracies, political parties, corporations, or even labor unions.

63. Pierre Carignan, "De la notion de droit Collectif et de son application en matière scolaire au Québec," *Thémis* 18 (1984): 91–92.

64. Michael McDonald, *supra* note 40, at 122; D. Réaume, "Individuals, Groups and Rights to Public Goods," *Univeristy of Toronto Law Journal* 38 (1988): 26.

65. As noted earlier, this is one of the central arguments Mill and other nineteenth-century utilitarians brought against paternalism.

66. It is conceivable that this process whereby individual rights-holders transfer their rights to groups could become so extensive that over time the only significant rights-holders remaining would be large groups. Thus, tongue in cheek, one might tell a story that reverses the process Robert Nozick described in his tale about Wilt Chamberlain, whereby individuals freely give up their rights to the state or other powerful types of association (Nozick, *supra* note 31, at 161–63).

67. In *Law's Empire,* Ronald Dworkin offers a liberal characterization of communities in terms of what he labels *associative obligations.* Ronald Dworkin, *Law's Empire* (Cambridge, Mass.: Harvard University Press, 1986), 206–8.

68. VanDyke notes that Rousseau held this view. *See* VanDyke, *supra* note 1, at 347.

69. *See Canadian Native Law Review* 1 (1982): 1 for the 1977 report of the United Nations Human Rights Commission, which investigated Lovelace's complaints.

70. This is hardly surprising, as classical liberalism is defined by its denial of positive rights.

71. Allen Buchanan notes that communitarians have not considered whether groups are entitled to redistribution. He does not consider the claim to "group distributive rights" in his article, although I consider the problems inherent in the liberal approach to this issue.

72. N. MacCormack, *Legal Right and Social Democracy: Essays in Legal and Political Philosophy* (Oxford: Oxford University Press, 1982), 261.

73. From Milton Gordon, "Towards a General Theory of Racial and Ethnic Group Relations," in *Ethnicity: Theory and Experience,* ed. Nathan Glazer and Daniel Moynihan (Cambridge, Mass.: Harvard University Press, 1975), 105.

74. W. Kymlicka, *supra* note 19, at 903.

75. Réaume's identification of language and culture as participatory goods provides an excellent reason for regarding these as essentially shared or collective interests, (D. Réaume, *supra* note 64, at 9–13). Participatory goods are those in which "the good is the participation" (*Ibid.* at 10). In my view, the participatory nature of language and culture makes it appropriate that there be significant

community involvement and direction in their provision, particularly through community-run cultural, linguistic, and educational institutions.

76. L. Green, *supra* note 51, at 658–60. I would set Rhoda E. Howard's Chapter 4 in this volume in the sympathetic liberal camp despite her deep concerns about collective rights becoming "exclusivist rights." I say this because she distinguishes "the move for aboriginal rights" from other moves toward collective or peoples' rights on the grounds that aboriginal rights are "essential to the retention of the identity of 'native' groups already subject to several centuries of physical and cultural genocide." If Howard is to justify this distintion between aboriginal and other collective right movements, the most plausible way I can think of for doing so would be to argue for the sort of sympathetic liberal position I have identified with MacCormack and Kymlicka.

77. The worry I have here centers on nonliberal, as opposed to illiberal, groups. I would suggest that illiberal groups may secure the assent of members in ways that violate both individual and collective rights, for I have argued that collective rights can only be attributed to groups on the basis of their having a group-constituting understanding. M. McDonald, *supra* note 8.

78. Wisconsin v. Yoder, 406 U.S. 205 (1972). Ronald Garet also discusses this case (R. Garet, "Communality and Existence: The Rights of Groups," *Southern California Law Review* 56 (1983): 1001. For a very recent and insightful discussion of collective rights, *see* Darlene M. Johnston, "Native Rights as Collective Rights: A Question of Group Self-Preservation," *The Canadian Journal of Law and Juris prudence* 2 (1988): 19.

79. *See* Richard Falk's Chapter 2 in this volume.

80. I did not find very convincing suggestions that there can be cultural variance in such matters, for example, that Stoics and, allegedly, Buddhists strive to cultivate indifference to pain. None of this shows that they would find morally acceptable another person's acting to cause such pain, especially when, as in political torture, the pain is inflicted to degrade the victim in his own and others' eyes.

81. H. Sidgwick, *supra* note 24, at 382.

82. Holding that there are only different culturally distinct vantage points does not commit me, as an individual observer operating from within one of those perspectives, to accept the equal value of all perspectives on the rights of persons and groups. Thus, theoretical relativism does not commit one to normative tolerance. Moreover, one can move beyond a theoretical relativism to a position that seriously seeks overlapping consensus.

83. *See* Tore Lindholm's Chapter 15 in this volume.

84. A striking instance of the construction of a common cross-cultural perspective is presented by Manuela Carneiro da Cunha, who describes how the land perspective of South American Indians has connected to growing international concern for the global environment. *See* her Chapter 11 in this volume.

7. A Marxian Approach to Human Rights

Introduction

Marx often scorned "rights talk" and other "nonsensical" normative chatter about fairness, freedom, justice, duty, and so forth. Such remarks should not be taken to mean that Marx was opposed in principle to normative evaluation, including the conception of universal human rights. In fact, concern for human rights underlies Marx's whole project, his criticisms of past and present societies and his vision of the future communist society. He condemned the capitalist system for what many would now call gross violations of fundamental human rights, the miserable living conditions of the workers, their subjection to capitalist tyranny in the factory, and brutal state suppression of working-class protests.

The purpose of this chapter is to outline, in broad terms, a Marxian approach to human rights. The focus is on the task of establishing an international standard of human rights and applying this standard to particular societies. For various reasons, Marx did not take up this task himself; his work does not contain a developed theory of human rights. The Marxian position I describe is formulated from principal elements in Marx's philosophy and political and economic sociology. In my interpretation I stress those elements in Marx's complex and not always consistent thought that have the most to offer on questions of human rights.[1] Given these key elements, I asked myself, what would be the Marxian position on the human rights questions discussed herein? The rationale for this essay is to see what can be learned from the Marxian theoretical tradition.

Contrary to what many would contend, I argue that it does make sense from the Marxian perspective to try to construct an international standard of human rights, a standard that can be used to evaluate all societies, and thus societies of very different types. The particular sociohistorical features of a specific society would determine how the universal standard is applied to the society. The concrete human rights for a specific society would have their grounding in abstract universal rights and in the particular features of the society in question. In my discussion of the standard and its application, characteristic features of a Marxian approach to human rights are described—for example, the focus on human needs, the conception of the human as a social being, the importance attached to class and economic factors in the analysis of society, the stress on economic rights, and the belief in collective rights, such as the right to economic development. In the course of the discussion I distinguish between this Marxian approach to human rights and some of the specific answers at which Marx himself arrives regarding certain questions, such as those concerning economic development. One could reject or amend some of these specific answers, for empirical or ethical reasons, and still adhere to the Marxian approach presented in this chapter, thereby ending up with a stronger commitment to immediate human rights.

It is beyond the scope of this chapter to reflect on historical developments since Marx's time, including the experiences of the so-called Marxist states, for their relevance to a Marxian theory of human rights. Instead, this essay is concerned with identifying and clarifying the theoretical elements in Marx's work that could provide the basis for a Marxian theory of human rights. The elaboration of the theory, and the argument for its validity and usefulness, would of course require dealing with historical developments since Marx's time (as well as the history of previous periods). At certain points in this chapter I do indicate examples of empirical work that will be needed for the development of an adequate Marxian theory of human rights.

Marx's Criticism of "Ideological" Commentary

Some discussion of Marx's criticism of "ideological" normative discourse is useful in helping to understand the distinctive Marxian approach to human rights.[2] Marx's often expressed scorn for moral commentary reflected in part what he believed to be the indeterminate and essentially meaningless nature of much of it. Vague and general terms like liberty, freedom, justice, and fair distribution are often bandied about or used as political weapons without a clear indication of what they mean. (The erro-

neous assumption is that the words contain their meaning in themselves.)
In the "Critique of the Gotha Program" Marx criticizes socialists for using
the vague phrase, "a fair distribution of the proceeds of labor."[3] To say
that you are in favor of "fair distribution" is to say very little, Marx
suggests. The bourgeoisie have one conception; socialists, a variety of conceptions. In precapitalist societies there were many other different conceptions. In bourgeois society the predominant view is that fair distribution
includes the right of capitalists to their profits and thereby precludes the
right of the workers to seize capitalist property. In precapitalist European
society, the prevailing view was that fair distribution excluded the right to
usury and thus, in principle, the making of a great deal of money out of
money.

But the intensity of Marx's scorn for moral and politicophilosophical
commentary reflected his view regarding the politicoideological use to
which this commentary is usually put. Once the general terms and formulations are given specific content (as they must, however implicitly,
once the discussion ceases to be mainly rhetorical or highly abstract, and
policies and practices are discussed or referred to), the meaning they take
on usually reflects the nature of the society of the theorist or commentator,
usually in a way which serves the interests of the dominant classes and
elites.[4] For example, the concept of liberty in most of the political and
philosophical discourse in capitalist society (at least in nonrevolutionary
periods) is interpreted, according to Marx, as entailing the specific forms
liberty takes in the capitalist market economy. Thus liberty "entails" the
right to own capitalist property and the right of entrepreneurs to market
commodities wherever they want. Societies that prohibit capitalist property ownership or unduly restrict the free flow of commodities are condemned for violating "liberty." What is really a particular historical
product, the nature that "liberty" takes on in capitalist society, is presented
as something universal.

In class societies, according to Marx, the predominant ideas (and
thus the specific content of those general political concepts and formulations like "liberty" and "fair distribution") lend support to the structures of class exploitation and domination. The view that liberty entails
the right of capitalists to own the means of production helps obscure
the relative "unfreedom" of the proletariat and its economic exploitation.[5] The legal right of individual workers to make contracts with capitalists, and the philosophical defense of this right in terms of the principle
of liberty, help obscure the unequal power relationship between the two

parties. The principle of liberty was even used to help justify the prohibition of trade unions; unions were said to violate the free contractual relationship between employer and the individual employee and thus violate "liberty."

Many of the political and moral philosophers who support these "ruling" political ideas and articulate them in their writings are not, says Marx, aware of the objective class role they play; they are not aware of the class-biased meaning of the ideas with which they work. They have an unjustified belief in the autonomy of the concepts and principles, together with a related unjustified belief in the power of abstract thinking to generate practical conclusions from them. They do not see that the concepts and principles—or, at least, their specific formulations—are tied to a particular social order. They think that they are playing a disinterested role in promoting a free, fair, or just society, that society which is in accord with their general principles.[6]

The Marxian Approach to Human Rights: Preliminary Remarks

In keeping with Marx's critique of ideological commentary, the Marxian human rights theorist is naturally suspicious of what the elites and the intelligentsia (Western, state "socialist," Third World, or Fourth World) say about human rights. She or he focuses on the concrete empirical reality, on the real problems facing men and women in specific situations. The human rights generated by this approach, it is claimed, will not serve the privileged interests of the dominant classes or elites, but will reflect the true needs of the populace. The basic questions the Marxian analyst asks are the following: What are the concrete needs of these men and women? Are the needs being met? If not, why, and what can be done to meet them? To put the matter in other terms, what concrete rights should these people have? To answer such questions, detailed empirical investigation is necessary, with special attention being paid to the economic system, particularly the class relationships. The distinctive nature of the society has to be kept uppermost in mind. The concrete problems and concerns of today's Canadian workers, for example, are quite different from those of fourteenth-century Irish peasants. This focus on concrete human beings and the needs that they have, it is claimed, helps dispel the obfuscating mist produced by the predominant ideas in any class society. It permits us to see things clearly, as they really are. It undermines, for example, the belief that capitalist property ownership is a right derived from the principle of liberty and should be protected despite all the destructive costs to working men and women.

At this stage in the discussion, some brief remarks on Marx's social ontology are necessary.[7] According to Marx, it makes no sense to conceptualize the human being as apart from society, as outside of a given set of social institutions. The individual is a *zoon politikoon*, a social animal. With its complex of institutions and practices, society provides individuals with means to satisfy their economic and social needs, and shapes them (especially important in this regard are the economic institutions) both by the way it provides for these needs, and how well. To a significant extent their social nature, needs, and values will reflect the nature of their society. Though individuals are social beings in this sense, they are at the same time particular individuals with their own distinct characteristics and interests. Furthermore, they are reflective, purposive beings who can act, in concert with others, to change (within limits) the social institutions and practices better to meet their needs. As old needs are met, new ones develop, and thus new activities to satisfy the new needs. History is the accumulated result of the productive/creative activities of purposive individuals (especially the economic activities). In the course of the historical transformation of institutions and practices, humans are themselves changed in their social nature, values, and concrete needs.

Contrary to what many contend, Marx then did believe that there is such a thing as "human nature."[8] Though people differ, often in fundamental ways, from society to society, they do share common features and have common needs. As will be shown, the conception of universal human needs provides the basis on which a Marxian theory of abstract human rights can be constructed, rights to which all humans are entitled. Our Marxian theorist would say that these generalizations and principles are fundamentally different from those of the bourgeois theorists Marx criticizes. They are truly general, not distorted reflections of the features of a particular type of society, bourgeois society. They emerge out of the focus on concrete historical situations and reflection on that historical praxis. Being truly transhistorical and transcultural, they provide part of the necessary theoretical framework for an analysis of particular societies, out of which conclusions can be made regarding what concrete rights there should be in particular societies and judgments regarding whether these human rights have been violated.

The Theory of Needs and Abstract Rights

Implicit in Marx's work is the view that there are three types of fundamental needs that all humans have. Basic *physical life needs*, such as the need for food, shelter, warmth, rest, and fresh air, comprise the first type, and are needs humans share with animals. For humans, though, unlike animals, the satisfaction of these natural needs usually has a specific social form that can vary from society to society. The second type, *autonomy and freedom needs*, and the third type, *community/social needs*, are distinctive to the human species. Humans are by nature actors, creators: it is in their species-nature to reflect on their needs and situation, to formulate goals, and to attempt to realize their goals, especially through productive/creative activity. Accordingly, people have needs for autonomy and freedom. They need autonomy so as to be able to define their own goals and should have meaningful opportunity to realize their goals, including the opportunity to engage in productive/creative activity. Accordingly, forms of servitude, like slavery or serfdom, are illegitimate. The need for personal autonomy is also rooted in the distinctiveness of each individual.[9]

Because humans are social beings by nature, they have community/social needs, needs to belong, to share, to participate, to be recognized. A basic theme running throughout Marx's *oeuvre* is that in a capitalist market society most people have a difficult time in satisfying their social needs. Relationships tend to be "utilitarian," competitive, and adversarial; authoritarian work structures tend to isolate workers from one another and the rich and the powerful get the lion's share of social recognition.[10]

In keeping with contemporary human rights language, one can say that these three types of fundamental needs form the basis for three fundamental abstract rights that all humans have: first, the right to have their basic physical-life needs met (according to the minimal standards agreed upon in the society); second, the right to personal autonomy and freedom; and third, the right to have their community/social needs fulfilled. The abstract right to freedom would include the right for a people to control their own institutions, thus necessitating some form of democracy and the concomitant liberties, such as freedom of discussion.[11] The abstract right to community could conceivably require governments in some societies to help protect local communities from the disintegrating effects of market pressures. All of these rights, of course, are contingent on the availability of the necessary resources.

These rights can be conceptualized as entitlements to "goods" that are required in order for the basic human needs to be met. The society collectively has the obligation to provide these goods or to see that individuals have the opportunity to acquire them (resources permitting). Marx's view of the individual as a *zoon politikoon*, as a being that cannot exist outside of society, would provide the rationale for such an obligation. Since no one can satisfy his or her needs outside of society, so that all benefit from the contributions of others, all would have the obligation to contribute to the society, including help in providing for (directly or indirectly) the welfare of its members. The ties of fraternity that would exist in a nonclass, nonexploitative society would naturally produce strong sentiments that the basic needs of all should be met.

Basic to the Marxian theory of human rights is a principle of equality. Every individual is equally deserving of having his or her basic needs met; thus all are equally entitled to these rights, regardless of sex, race, beliefs, and so on. For Marx, this equality provision means that ideally the society cannot be a class society.[12] Significant socioeconomic inequalities will have to be eliminated so that everyone will have roughly the same opportunity to make use of their formal rights, such as the right to free speech.

This Marxian equality principle does not mean that there should be equal distribution of economic and other benefits, even in ideal conditions. The overarching principle for a just society is that the fundamental needs of the population be satisfied (resources permitting). What people require to meet their needs, however, often differs. A large family requires more resources than a small family. The costs of meeting the basic needs of a disabled person will usually be considerably above average. Because of their special needs, women can justifiably be given special concrete rights, the Marxian theorist can easily argue, such as the right to shorter more flexible working hours for women with babies to nurse. Marx's concern is with benefiting in concrete ways the lives of every individual, not with realizing some abstract principle of equality.[13] Principles and rights are means to this end, not ends in themselves. "Ideological" fixation on the abstract principle of equality can result in blindness to the practical grounds of the principle; such a fixation might well lead to policies not conducive to the equal good of every individual, as would be the case if men and women had exactly the same concrete rights.

According to the Marxian perspective, society's first obligation is to provide for the basic physical-life needs. People first have to have goods like food and shelter before goods like community and personal autonomy can have much meaning. "[I]n general, people cannot be liberated as long as they are unable to obtain food and drink, housing and clothing in adequate quality and quantity."[14] Marx apparently believed that in most past and present societies these basic physical-life needs have not been adequately met for the majority of the population. In the case of most precapitalist societies, insufficient productive capability is in large part the reason. Also important, however, is the grossly unequal distribution of whatever economic goods there are due to the class system.

The productive capability of the society is also an important factor in determining how well a society can provide for nonphysical needs. In most preindustrialized societies, Marx believed, there are only sufficient economic resources to allow a small minority of the population to satisfy most of their nonphysical needs. For example, in ancient Greece, slaves and women did not get to participate in the "good life" of the polis, and thus their freedom and social needs went largely unmet; the society did not have adequate economic resources to permit universal participation.[15] The conclusion that Marx made from such considerations is that economic development, including industrialization, is necessary in order to provide sufficient resources so that everyone's needs can be adequately met.[16] In effect, what Marx was saying is that there is a collective right to economic development.

Rights, according to the Marxian perspective, can be possessed not only by individuals, but also by communities, institutions, and groups. It is the community as a whole that has the collective right to economic development. Also, particular institutions within the society, for example, unions and cooperatives in certain societies, might be given rights so that they can be protected and strengthened and thus better meet the needs of individuals. Such a right might require that adequate resources be directed to the institution, or it might entail restrictions on certain activities that could undermine the institution.

The Sociohistorical Specificity of Needs and Rights

According to the Marxian perspective, the specific nature of these basic universal human needs, how they are or can be realized, and to what extent, will differ from society to society; likewise will the concrete rights to which people are entitled differ. In a highly interdependent industrial society, the abstract right to subsistence goods would require the concrete right to a job, as well as the right to education. In a preindustrial peasant community, the same abstract right would require the concrete right to land; the right to a job would make little sense. In a highly industrialized society where production predominantly takes place in large enterprises, there should also be some form of social ownership of the means of production, including workplace democracy; in other words, there would be no right to private ownership of large enterprises. Collective ownership and control is necessary to ensure that all have access to employment and thus to help ensure that their basic economic needs are met. Workplace democracy is required to help meet the autonomy and freedom needs of the workers within production; with workplace democracy, workers would not be subordinated to the authoritarian dictates of an unaccountable manager. In such a society, institutions of workplace democracy would also be an important means for satisfying community/social needs.

In the preindustrial peasant society the needs of autonomy, freedom, and community would have to be met in other ways. Collective ownership of productive resources would not in most cases be feasible or desirable.[17] But in order to give real meaning to the right of political participation for all, and to the sense of community that would develop out of such participation, there would probably have to be restrictions on how much land any one person may own. Rights of political participation and community would, in other words, preclude a personal right to accumulate large holdings of land.[18]

Note how the Marxian approach to concrete rights is being applied. The theorist does not start out with some abstract principle such as liberty and then see whether or not the right to capitalist property or large tracts of landed property flows from this abstract principle. She or he starts out with the conception of needs and then after empirical investigation sees what kind of liberties promote the good, that is, the satisfaction of the needs, and which do not.

According to Marx, in the highly productive industrial societies individuals have the strong need to express their unique individual personalities; in other words, for these individuals "expressive individualism" is an important part of what freedom entails. Various concrete rights would see to it that these freedom needs could be met, for example, the right to spend part of one's work time engaged in challenging work activity and the right to sufficient time off from work to engage in various activities. In preindustrial society, a much more socially cohesive society, a society in which change usually occurs slowly and in which a great deal of the time has to be spent on meeting subsistence needs, this need to express one's unique talents would not exist to nearly the same degree (and thus the corresponding concrete rights would not be nearly as strong). In this society there would probably be greater concern for managing change so as not to disrupt traditional institutions, institutions which serve, let us assume, important community needs. A collective right to preserve such institutions might result in controls over individuals that would be considered intolerable in the more individualistic industrial society. But Marx would say that opportunities for change and development (especially through productive activities) would still have to be present. It is in the human's "species nature" to try to go beyond what exists in order to realize one's projects. In static societies, Marx suggests, such opportunities have been "unnaturally" blocked by sociopolitical factors, for example, in the case of traditional East Indian society by the caste system and the parasitic state bureaucracy.[19]

The definition of minimal standards for the basic physical-life needs will differ from society to society, and hence conceptions of what one is entitled to. As societies become more economically productive, minimal standards expand (and perhaps even the understanding of what is a basic physical-life need). Marx noted that as societies become wealthier, workers redefine upward what subsistence means;[20] English workers would not tolerate the low level of subsistence that the workers of less-developed Ireland accepted. The right to paid holidays is now considered a right by labor movements in the industrial societies; in a very poor country such a right would likely be considered nonsense. Universal health care is now also being considered a basic right in most of the industrialized countries. In the coming communist society, Marx believed, the definition of economic rights would be expanded even more; the immense productive capability of the society would accommodate such expansion.

As already suggested, there would no doubt be a different priority of needs in different societies. According to the Marxian perspective, in the poorest societies the basic physical-life needs and rights would far outweigh the others in importance; hence in these societies the greatest effort should be spent on trying to satisfy the physical-life needs. As it becomes more easy to satisfy these needs because of economic development, the relative importance attributed to them should decline, even though the minimal standards increase. Autonomy and freedom needs and their concomitant rights should take on more relative importance. Yet the level of economic development is surely not the only important variable in determining the relative priority of goods. Marx notes that much less importance was placed on economic wealth in ancient Greek societies than in the much more economically developed capitalist countries.[21] Concerns of community and what makes a good citizen had higher priority, at least for nonslaves. And in medieval Europe restrictions on certain economic activities in order to preserve the community from disruptive change may have reflected a similar belief in the relative importance of community versus economic wealth, at least for the elite who already had their basic physical-life needs met.

Differing cultural institutions and practices would no doubt provide culturally specific means for satisfying the basic needs; they would even help to shape some needs, particularly community/social needs. These differences would undoubtedly be reflected in different concrete rights. (Some of these rights could conceivably be grounded only in the specific cultural traditions, and not also in the abstract rights; but they would be weaker than those concrete rights also grounded in abstract rights.) A case could perhaps be made that rights concerning religion should be very different in a devout Muslim country from those in the secular West. There is little in Marx that helps us deal with such matters (note that the examples of concrete rights given hitherto were not of rights rooted in cultural traditions). He might in fact be hostile to this part of our intellectual exercise, especially regarding religion. There is a tendency in his work to view cultural factors as largely "superstructural," that is, as "reflections" of more basic socioeconomic factors; they have, he often suggests, little autonomy or importance in their own right. Furthermore, Marx believed that in class societies cultural institutions and practices, especially religious, often serve as means of securing class and elite domination, so that they tend not to be reflections of the genuine needs of the people. Marx's relative neglect of culture reflects, in part, an inadequate philosophical anthropology; Marx underrates the importance of questions of self-identity and the importance that cultural factors play in forming self-identity.[22] This defect, I believe, can be remedied; the Marxian approach to human rights outlined here is compatible with adequate attention to cultural factors.

There would undoubtedly always be conflicts between rights and, in many societies, a need for tradeoffs. Though Marx himself said nothing about such matters, it should be clear from the preceding discussion that the Marxian approach to such conflicts would be to shift the discussion away from an abstract politico-philosophical inquiry into the relative merits of abstract rights, say liberty versus community, toward a discussion of the underlying needs. The key question would be: For this particular society at this time, which needs have priority? Rights, remember, are viewed as instruments for what lies beneath them, goods to satisfy needs. General determination regarding which rights would have priority would be made in a democratic manner,[23] but not the decisions on particular cases (these would be for the "judiciary" to decide on the basis of the general decisions taken by the community). Marxian theory provides little help in dealing with disputes concerning rights between minorities and the majority, conflicts which may carry the risk of majority tyranny, especially in societies with acute scarcities. On this matter, Marxists can learn from the liberal tradition.

The Question of Tradeoffs: The Case of Economic Development

As previously indicated, Marx believed that in order to obtain sufficient economic resources to meet the basic human needs economic development, including industrialization, is required. It would seem to follow that if it could be demonstrated that certain human rights—for example, those concerning democratic freedoms—would hinder the necessary economic development, then these rights could legitimately be suspended or curtailed for the course of the development, but only to the extent necessary.

Marx and Engels did come to this conclusion. According to their theory of economic development, economic exploitation by a property-owning class is required in order to produce the economic surplus that is needed to drive economic development.[24] At a certain stage in history private property is necessary to provide the impetus for economic development. (Communities that did not evolve into societies with private property remained at a low level of economic development.) The more successful private property owners develop into an exploiting class, a class that expropriates surplus from the propertyless producing classes. The democratic practices that were characteristic of the early classless societies are eliminated; authoritarian political structures are required to keep the exploited classes under control. A portion of the expropriated surplus is reinvested, producing economic growth. Eventually, once society's productive capacity is great enough, the capitalist economic system emerges onto the historical scene. This capitalist system is especially effective in promoting economic growth, which in turn creates enormous productive capacity. Marx and Engels contend that this capacity provides the economic foundation on which a society that will provide for all the human rights can be constructed. They also argue that economic exploitation gave the ruling classes the necessary free time and resources to develop and enjoy literature, art, and music. Capitalist economic development has created a sufficient economic base so that after the socialist revolution everyone will be able to enjoy this culture and to contribute to its further development.

Marx's implicit assumption is that ordinary people will not voluntarily limit their consumption, nor submit to work discipline, to the extent necessary to bring about economic development. Class exploitation and authoritarian political structures are excused for the service they provide to economic development. But these developing societies could still be condemned, I believe Marx would say, for having too much exploitation—that is, more exploitation than is required to secure the degree of economic development needed; the exploiting class may be enriching itself too much or treating the producers too harshly.[25] Exploiting classes that do not provide the service of economic development would be unconditionally condemned, such as the "parasitic oriental despotic" state which, according to Marx, exploits while at the same time inhibiting economic development.

Marx did not sufficiently work out and present the explanatory theory and facts, nor the theory of justification, that would support these views of the historical necessity of private property, class society, exploitation, and a repressive state. He does not explain why people will not voluntarily restrict present consumption for future benefits (even if most of those benefits would accrue only to future generations). It might be demonstrated that, given the right conditions, economic development can occur in a democratic way with the minimum of coercion and exploitation, and perhaps without private property, requiring only unjust wage differentials. Also missing in Marx's work is discussion of the crucial question of who has the right to make the decision about such tradeoffs. To have an elite make the decision (particularly, if made mainly for selfish reasons, such as self-enrichment) would be inconsistent with Marx's democracy principle. But what other choice is there, given Marx's assumption that the people would make the wrong decision? Marx might fall back on the "argument" that nobody has "made" the decision; history has just worked out this way. In a certain sense, this may be true for the past. But given today's consciousness, including reflection on past developments, decisions can and are being made about the course of economic development.[26]

In his last years Marx did say that it might be possible for Russia to avoid capitalist development, and to develop in a democratic and nonexploitative way, making use of the still existing protosocialist and democratic institutions of the peasant commune, while at the same time taking advantage of the advanced technology of the developed capitalist countries.[27] He implies that if this advanced technology were not available, Russia would not be able to develop in this relatively humane way.

These rather sketchy comments on Russia were not elaborated on (perhaps because they occurred relatively late in his life); nor was his theory of historical development explicitly amended to accommodate what appears to be a new position. But they do indicate that Marx was open to changing views in light of new empirical findings. His views on the requisites of economic development are severable from the basic elements in his philosophy and social science. The former can be rejected or amended (either for empirical reasons or because of inadequacies in the justificatory theory), while retaining the latter and thus those elements of the Marxian approach to human rights described in the previous sections of this essay. Marxian theorists on human rights have much work to do on questions concerning economic development. The experiences of developing countries since Marx's time, including those of the so-called communist states, are of obvious relevance to this work. What does this experience tell us about the possibility of developing, in a democratic manner, without exploitation and violence? What does it tell us about the desirability of avoiding a capitalist form of economic development?

The Marxian Objective Approach to Evaluation

This Marxian theory of needs and rights provides, our Marxian theorist would say, an objective method for evaluating societies (or at least the beginnings for constructing such a method). One can use the method to determine the extent to which human rights are respected in any society. The use of this method would involve different objective standards for different societies, although all would have the common element, and thus the universal standards, provided by the theory of universal needs. People in the West are thus not in principle, because of social and cultural differences, incapable of making evaluations of the protection of human rights in Third World countries and vice versa. The evaluation is in terms of the concrete needs of the people in the society being evaluated, not in terms of those of the outside observer (some of whose needs might be quite different). As already emphasized, empirical investigation is necessary to determine what these needs are, and whether or not tradeoffs are justified. Because of the class nature of most societies and the legitimating role that the predominant ideas play in such societies, one should not presume that current political, cultural, and religious practices and supporting ideas reflect the true needs of the populace. The priorities of needs proposed by intellectuals in ancient Athens surely did not reflect those of their slaves. And it could probably be argued, our Marxist theorist would say, that many of the restrictions imposed on women in fundamentalist Muslim countries, with the attendant justificatory ideas, do not reflect the needs of these women, but are restrictions imposed because they lend support to the political power of a male religious elite and its secular class allies.

Is it possible that people may not realize what some of their needs are or whether their needs are being met? Marx and contemporary Marxists would say yes. Economic, social, cultural, and ideological factors may make it extremely difficult for people in some circumstances to recognize what some of their true needs are or how to go about meeting them.[28] Such is the case, our Marxian theorist would say, for those women in fundamentalist Muslim countries who willingly accept the restrictions imposed upon them. And in many societies many poor people may be too ground down by poverty to be able to become fully aware of certain of their noneconomic needs. Their access to correct information may be extremely limited. Priests and other ideologists may be able to delude them by false promises and by evoking unjustified fears of the "unknown," such as fear of alien peoples.

In addition, according to Marxists, people may develop "false needs," needs which they think they have but really do not. For example, many people in capitalist society, poor and rich, are enticed into wanting commodities they really do not need. In this acquisitive society, those whose basic physical-life needs are met often continue to strive for more and more money, and more and more "worthless" commodities. These people are acting in a "perverse" manner; they should shift their priorities to developing and exercising their creative capabilities, that is, to satisfying their freedom needs.[29] Perhaps more controversial is Marx's view that the need for religion is a false need. Religion is like opium; it offers believers relief from their suffering and illusions about the exploitative society that is the cause of their suffering.[30] As this last example suggests, the false needs of the underprivileged are, according to Marx, products of a social system in which their real needs are not adequately met. If people cannot adequately meet their basic physical-life needs and/or have little control over their social institutions, so that they have little opportunity to act as purposive beings, they will, as a sort of compensation, develop false needs or, at least, become fertile ground for the implanting of false needs by the dominant class and political elites. These false needs and their "satisfaction" make it more difficult, in turn, for these people to recognize their true needs. Of course, to say that many people have false needs in many, if not most, class societies is not to say that these same people cannot recognize many of their true needs. According to Marx, the workers in nineteenth-century England did recognize that they were ill-housed, undernourished, over-worked, and subject to the unjust discipline of capitalist bosses.

This Marxian method of evaluation would obviously not be easy to use. In coming up with the list of concrete needs and corresponding rights for a particular society, it would often not be easy to separate out the distorting ideological and class elements from what is genuine, especially for the outside observer. An outside evaluator with a Marxian perspective could not simply survey the views of the common people (since many of them might not recognize some of their true needs), nor could he or she simply take as truth what the intelligentsia say. In an effort to apply the Marxian approach, might not the evaluator's views of his or her own concrete needs (which naturally would partly reflect the nature and values of his or her society) create their own distortions, despite determined effort to view the matter from the particular sociohistorical perspective of the society being evaluated? More fundamentally, might not there be biases built right into the observer's Marxian approach and theory, biases that reflect a particular Western intellectual tradition?

Many, of course, would argue along these lines. Some would contend that Marx's view of religion as opium is pure dogma. Religious practices and beliefs, they would say, do serve social needs in genuine ways (as well as reflect the truth about the existence of God); and thus those Muslim women who willingly accept the religiously ordained restrictions on their "freedom" are not acting perversely. Some would make the more serious charge that the freedom needs which Marx views as universal are not really universal, but rather reflect the cultural prejudices of the Western Enlightenment. Some would question whether nearly all people in all, or even most, societies are purposive beings in the strong sense that they are "activist" by nature (and thus would be "activist" given the right social conditions), and accordingly have freedom needs that require personal autonomy, democratic institutions, and opportunity for change and development. According to this view, it is not "unnatural" for women in many traditional societies not to take part in governing their communities. Many Western conservatives have long argued that most humans in all societies are by nature rather passive beings who are not inquisitive, and who find genuine comfort in being directed by their intellectual and moral superiors. Marx, these critics would conclude, is guilty of what he accused the "bourgeois" theorists, presenting as universal what is really a particular historical and cultural product, in this case a product of the Western Enlightenment.

It is not my purpose here to argue for the validity of Marxian premises and interpretations. In partial defense, however, of this Marxian approach to evaluation, and the particular evaluations its application would give, it should be stressed that Marx does not simply make assertions, for instance, about which needs are genuine and which are false. In his work there are arguments and explanatory theories, or at least rudiments of theories, for example, regarding why these and not others are the genuine needs. Moreover, he offers an explanation, however incomplete, for why people have the false needs he notes and not others, and how they come to have these needs. The requirement for such explanations, and the supporting empirical data, would provide some protection from abuse on the part of the evaluator.[31] Contemporary Marxian theorists should be expected to provide a more complete and adequate theoretical defense than can be found in Marx's work; they have, after all, a greater amount of data and many more theories to make use of. The result of this theoretical work might be the rejection of some theories and views Marx held, such as his views on what religion expresses. Such rejection need not necessarily affect the fundamentals of Marxian theory. Furthermore, it should be kept in mind that any approach that makes use of a transhistorical/transcultural standard would face difficulties in applying the standard and in defending it theoretically. Of course, the difficulties concerning the application of the approach would not be as great for those approaches that do not operate with a conception of false needs. Though analysts who do not operate with such a conception may have an easier time in coming up with an answer of what the needs of a particular people are, their answers, however, may not be as good. Because they do not have a conception of "false needs," certain ways by which power can be exercised to control people may be hidden from analysis.

Western Marxian theorists should also recognize that avoiding bias in the analysis of human rights questions will take more than further empirical and theoretical work on their part. Marxian scholars have traditionally understated the difficulties in achieving objective social analysis. It should also be recognized that the difficulties are compounded once some concrete needs are admitted to have, partly or fully, cultural determinants. It is doubtful that outside commentators can comprehend a different cultural tradition well enough on their own to be able to make assured judgments, at least in many cases, regarding which practices reflect class or elite domination and which genuinely reflect the needs of the populace. On the other hand, an outside observer armed with Marxian theory would often, depending on the issue, be more sensitive to the ways political power can be exercised, and thus people manipulated, than many of those within the society; cultural traditions can delude in more than one direction. Furthermore, the democratic principle itself surely requires that the establishment of human rights standards, and how they should be applied, must be an international collaborative effort. Abdullahi An-Naʿim is right in emphasizing, in Chapter 1, that there has to be international dialogue as well as internal discussion. But—and this is what many of those other than An-Naʿim who advocate a multicultural approach to human rights fail to recognize—it makes all the difference who the spokespeople are.

Dominant elites in nearly all societies have a vested interest in maintaining their privileges, and thus in giving their own biased/self-interested interpretations about what the international standards should be and what rights are required for their societies. In order for there to be genuine dialogue, people from all sectors of society, especially those from the less privileged sectors, should be involved in the discussions. Ideally, this dialogue would be theoretically informed, including by Marxian theory. Involvement in such discussion among nations and within particular countries would encourage people to begin discovering for themselves what is genuine and false in their own cultures, thus making them more conscious of what their true needs are and thereby helping them overcome whatever illusions they have. Judgments by Western Marxists regarding what are "false needs" will be vindicated, if correct, in the course of such dialogue.[32]

It is another question, of course, given the class and authoritarian nature of most societies, and the gross economic deprivation present in many, whether there can be such genuine international dialogue and internal discussion on a wide scale; for some countries, radical political change and/or economic development would first be necessary. However imperfect, some international dialogue can take place, and is taking place. Marxian social scientists should participate and try to learn from the discussions. They should continue working on elaborating their own theory of human rights (along the lines I have suggested in this essay), while being as sensitive as they can to differing cultural traditions, and paying particular attention to nonelite ideas and grassroots cultural practices. They should not be timid, however, in criticizing those economic, political, *and* cultural practices that appear to them to involve gross violations of human rights. Such criticism need not entail being closed to dialogue and counter-criticism.

This discussion (and the previous one on economic development) reveals a fundamental tension in Marxian theory, a tension between the stress placed on "objective" social scientific analysis and its democratic principles. Some of its traditional social scientific conclusions result in elitism ("We social scientists know better than you what is good for you") and, if acted on, would result in authoritarian political practice. The early practices of the Soviet Afghanistan government provide a striking example. To reduce the potential for authoritarian practice, Marxists should adopt the principle that an elitist conclusion should not, as a rule, be acted on; the democratic principle would thus, as a rule, have priority. Accordingly, Marxists could (and should) criticize cultural practices which they think violate fundamental human rights even if these practices are supported by those whose rights are said to be violated, but they should not try to "liberate" those people against their will. This general principle would not be possible or desirable to observe in all cases—for example, probably not in the case of a desperately poor and wretched country. Given that economic needs have priority and provided that the country in question cannot develop in a democratic fashion (in an extremely poor country, the requisites for democracy would likely be missing anyway), it might be justified for internal elites (but not foreign powers) to resort to authoritarian means in order to bring about the necessary economic development. There is, of course, the danger that these internal elites will in time transform themselves into a privileged ruling class. On such questions there are no easy answers.

Efforts to Improve Human Rights in Existing Societies: The Need to Go Beyond Marx

Marx did not himself believe that a great deal could be done to improve the state of human rights within the existing structures of most societies. Most societies are class, and thus exploitative, societies, with repressive state apparatuses; still-existing, though disintegrating, "primitive" societies are presumably among the exceptions. For these societies, including liberal capitalist societies, fundamental improvement in human rights requires social revolution and the construction of fundamentally different societies.

According to Marx, as we have seen, significant improvement in human rights for preindustrial societies also necessitates economic development, but this economic development probably cannot take place in a nonexploitative, noncoercive manner. This economic development would presumably take many years. Furthermore, according to Marx, the industrialization process would destroy many of the unique features of these traditional societies and thus, according to the interpretation offered in this essay, the basis for different concrete rights. Industrialization breaks down national barriers and in time "internationalizes" culture.[33] The socialist revolution (which would occur after the societies have industrialized) would further promote this "internationalization" process; workers, Marx said, have no nation.

Marx did suggest that short of the necessary socialist revolution there could be limited improvement in some human rights in capitalist societies. Workers could achieve some improvement in their working and living conditions through unions and political activity.[34] Outright authoritarian regimes, depending on the circumstances, could perhaps be replaced with "liberal" regimes, similar to those in Britain and Holland, regimes that do show some respect for civil liberties (but that still protect the property interests of the exploiters). The focus for Marx, though, was not on reform but on the necessary socialist revolution.

In his discussions of the socialist revolution, Marx stressed that revolutionary success required determined and fierce class struggle on the part of the workers and their supporters; capitalists and their allies will try their utmost to defend their class privileges. Revolutionaries must not be deluded by false sentiments of universal brotherhood; the workers' class interests are antithetical to the capitalists.[35] If forced to by the violent reactions of their class enemies, revolutionaries must even be prepared to violate the human rights of their class enemies. Marx did hope, however, that revolutionary violence could be kept to a minimum; he also said that in some countries the parliamentary road to socialism might be possible.[36]

Several important conclusions follow from these views of Marx. The emphasis on the need for revolution, the stress on antagonistic class interests, and the accompanying "unsentimental" attitude, added to the conviction that this revolution would lead to a society in which the fundamental human rights for everyone will be present—all helped produce a disposition not especially conducive to working for the improvement of human rights within existing capitalist countries.[37] This traditional Marxist orientation helps explain, I believe, why there has been so little work by Western Marxian theorists on human rights questions. The second conclusion is that, for Marx, societies in which human rights are in place to any great extent would be basically all alike—industrialized, socialist, and "cosmopolitan." Efforts to theorize about the particular concrete rights that should be in place in nonindustrial societies, and practical efforts to improve human rights in them, are largely a waste of time.

Marxian theorists interested in human rights obviously cannot accept these "practical" conclusions. Fortunately, the conclusions can be severed from Marxian philosophy and social science. One can adopt the project of constructing concrete rights which are grounded in both the abstract rights and the particular features of a specific society, thus accepting key postulates of Marxian philosophy and social science, while rejecting those particular theories and views held by Marx that would render much of this work largely meaningless.

Marx may have been wrong about the extent of economic deprivation in most nonindustrialized societies and thus about the universal need for industrialization. (Some anthropologists deny that in most "primitive societies" basic economic needs were not well provided for.) Or, as already suggested, he might have been wrong in thinking that the industrialization process necessarily required exploitation and coercion. Alternatively, it might be demonstrated that though exploitation and coercion are necessary, at least in most cases, they can be kept within bounds that would be compatible with strengthened human rights. Further, Marx may have been wrong about the homogenizing effect of industrialization; he did underestimate, after all, the degree of autonomy cultural phenomena possess. Marx also underestimated the extent to which, in most capitalist and precapitalist societies, significant improvements in human rights can be made short of revolution. In advanced capitalist states a gradual extension of human rights—for example, more and improved collective rights for workers—might be the best way of working toward the abolition of capitalism and its attendant human rights abuses. Of course, in some countries (perhaps, for example, El Salvador), armed revolution may be the only option, an option that, the Marxist realist recognizes, probably brings along with it its own human rights abuses.[38]

The development of an adequate Marxian theory of human rights thus necessitates much empirical work, and theoretical working through of the great body of already completed work. Analyzing the experiences of the so-called Marxist states is an important part of this work. The construction of the broad outlines of a Marxian approach to human rights based upon core elements of Marx's theory—which I have attempted in this chapter—is only the first step.

Conclusion

The following list summarizes the major elements of this Marxian approach to human rights:

1. There are abstract rights that all humans have: rights based on universal human needs.
2. The concrete rights are grounded in these abstract rights *and* in the particular features of the society in question. Consequently, the concrete rights, and their priority ratings, may vary greatly from society to society (because concrete needs differ).
3. Rights and concomitant principles, such as the equality principle, should not be "fetishized"; they should be viewed as means to underlying goods—goods to satisfy human needs.
4. Because concrete rights are grounded in concrete needs, there has to be empirical analysis of these societies; a list of concrete rights cannot be deduced from politicophilosophical principles.
5. In this empirical analysis, attention to class and economic factors is crucial.
6. Rights do not entail (as some Marxists have argued) a society of self-centered competitive individualists who live self-enclosed lives. In fact, in such a society certain fundamental needs (community/social needs) would not be met; community/social rights would be largely missing. [39]

7. The basic physical-life needs and the concomitant economic rights are the most important. Human rights advocates should give much more attention to them.

8. Adequate economic resources are prerequisites for human rights.

9. A society with the full complement of human rights cannot be a class society.

10. Fundamental human rights include the right to democratic government and the associated political freedoms (such as freedom of expression).

11. Some human rights are collective rights, such as the right to economic development.

12. People in class societies may not always recognize the needs they have and may have false needs.

13. If circumstances warrant, some human rights can justifiably be curtailed in the short-term for purposes of economic development in order to ensure their fuller realization in the future.

One can accept these fundamental Marxian elements but reject some of Marx's specific theories and views and thus some of his "practical" conclusions concerning human rights. It is also possible to supplement this Marxian approach with elements from other traditions, thereby helping to overcome certain inadequacies, such as Marxism's relative neglect of cultural factors.

Notes

1. In Marx's thought, Hegelian historico-teleological elements are often in tension with the empirically grounded social science elements; the teleological elements tend to undermine a commitment to universal human rights. For the interpretation given here, I largely ignore these teleological elements. This interpretation I contend is much more faithful to Marx's overall mature philosophy and social science than one that emphasizes the historico-teleological elements (such as that presented in Tore Lindholm's Chapter 15 in this volume). It is not my purpose here to provide a detailed exegetical defense of my interpretation, *but see* my "Marx on Moral Commentary: Ideology and Science," *Philosophy of the Social Sciences* 15 (1985): 237–54; "Marx on Evaluating Pre-capitalist Societies," *Studies in Soviet Thought* 31 (1986): 303–19; and "Marx and Utopia: Critique of the 'Orthodox Interpretation,'" *Canadian Journal of Political Science* 20(1987): 755–83. For useful accounts of human rights from a Marxian perspective, *see* William McBride, "Rights and the Marxian Tradition," *Praxis International* 4(1982): 54–74; and Mihailo

Markovic, "Philosophical Foundations of Human Rights," *Praxis International* 4 (1982): 386–400. *And see* Kai Nielsen's excellent *Marxism and the Moral Point of View* (Boulder, Colo.: Westview Press, 1989); Nielsen stresses Marx's "objective approach" to moral evaluation. For a recent example of the common, but mistaken, view that Marx did not believe there were universal human rights (and did not believe that there would be human rights in the communist society), *see* George Brenkert, "Marx and Human Rights," *Journal of the History of Philosophy* 24(1986): 55–77.

2. For a detailed discussion of Marx's criticism of moral commentary, *see* Richard Nordahl, "Marx on Moral Commentary: Ideology and Science," 237–54. *See also* Bhikhu Parekh, *Marx's Theory of Ideology* (Baltimore: Johns Hopkins University Press, 1982).

3. "Critique of the Gotha Program," in *The Marx-Engels Reader*, ed. R. Tucker 2nd ed. (New York: Norton, 1978), 528.

4. *See, for example, The German Ideology*, in Marx-Engels, vol. 5, *Collected Works* (London: Lawrence & Wishart, 1976), 53–55 and 59–62; vol. 1, *Capital* (London: Penguin, 1976), 280; and *The Communist Manifesto*, in vol. 6 *Collected Works*, 501.

5. *Capital* is the best source for Marx's critique of capitalism and critique of its ideological defense.

6. For Marx's relatively early formulation of these ideas, *see The German Ideology, supra* note 4, especially part 1.

7. The most important texts are *The Economic and Philosophic Manuscripts, The German Ideology*, and *Grundrisse. But see also* vol. 1, *Capital*, chap. 7 (on the nature of the labor process).

8. *See* Norman Geras, *Marx & Human Nature* (London: New Left Books, 1983).

9. On the importance of the principle of autonomy for Marx, *see* Nordahl, "Marx and Utopia," *supra* note 1, especially at 765–66. Marx suggests that in the very first societies individuals were not differentiated as distinct individuals; they were like "herd animals," with "sheep-like consciousness." Accordingly, in this "society" there would not be the autonomy needs, and thus also not the freedom needs. Marx is suggesting that in these first societies "humans" were more animal-like than human (*German Ideology, supra* note 4, at 44).

10. Marx's belief that there are these three types of fundamental needs is evident throughout his work, but especially so in *The Economic & Philosophic Manuscripts, supra* note 7 (*see, for example*, the section on "alienated labour"), and *Capital*, vol. 1. Nowhere, to my knowledge, does Marx mention the need for physical security; and for this reason it is not included here as an example of the physical-life needs (nor as the basis for a concomitant right), though obviously it *is* one, indeed, one of the most important, and can easily be incorporated in this Marxian scheme. Marx did recognize some needs other than the three basic ones—for example, sex, recreation, and variety. Because these other needs are of less importance (or so Marx seemed to believe), they are not singled out and would not provide the basis for an abstract right. Useful works on Marx's conception of needs include: Agnes Heller, *The Theory of Need in Marx* (London: Allison & Busby, 1976); Geras, *supra*

note 8; and John McMurtry, *The Structure of Marx's World-View* (Princeton, N. J.: Princeton University Press, 1978), chap. 1.

11. For a discussion of Marx's commitment to democracy and political liberty (in pre-communist and communist society), *see* Richard Hunt, *The Political Ideas of Marx and Engels*, 2 vols. (Pittsburgh: University of Pittsburgh Press, 1974, 1984).

12. *See infra* for exceptions for practical reasons.

13. *See* Marx, "Critique of the Gotha Program," *supra* note 3, at 530–31. For a somewhat different interpretation, *see* Richard Miller, *Analyzing Marx* (Princeton, N.J.: Princeton University Press, 1984), especially 19–26; *see also* Nielsen, *supra* note 1, at chap. 9. In *The German Ideology* (*supra* note 4, at 306) Marx criticizes Max Stirner for substituting abstractions like "freedom of Man" for concrete concern for the "satisfaction of actual needs" of "actual individuals."

14. *Ibid.* at 38.

15. Marx, "Forced Emigration," vol. 11, *Collected Works*, 530–31; and Engels, *Anti-Dühring* (Moscow: Foreign Languages, 1954), 252. But Marx and Engels did note that "primitive societies" were democratic; for this form of democracy there were then apparently sufficient resources, perhaps because needs had not yet begun to expand (*see infra*) and because the "cultural" level of these societies was at a low level. For discussion (with citations), *see* Hunt, *supra* note 11, at chap. 1.

16. *Supra* note 4, at 49.

17. *See* Marx's comments in *ibid.* at 354.

18. As will become evident below, because of his theory of economic development, Marx would not himself have made this Rousseau-like argument.

19. *See* Marx, "The British Rule in India," in *Surveys from Exile*, ed. David Fernbach (Harmondsworth: Penguin, 1974), 301–7.

20. *Capital, supra* note 4, at 275.

21. *See, for example, Grundrisse, supra* note 9, at 487.

22. For critical discussion of this defect by a contemporary Marxist, *see* G. A. Cohen, *History, Labour and Freedom* (Oxford: Clarendon Press, 1988), chap. 8.

23. Marx himself would apparently make an exception in the case of economic development; *see infra*.

24. For a good description (with citations), *see* G. A. Cohen, *Karl Marx's Theory of History* (Oxford: Clarendon Press, 1978), chap. 7.

25. G. A. Cohen, *supra* note 22, at 303–4.

26. On this question of tradeoffs between economic development and human rights, *see* C. B. Macpherson, "Problems of Human Rights in the Late Twentieth Century," in his *The Rise and Fall of Economic Justice* (Oxford: Oxford University Press, 1987).

27. The relevant Marx writings can be found in *Late Marx and the Russian Road*, ed. Theodor Shanin (New York: Monthly Review Press, 1983). For discussion of Marx's views, *see* Hunt, *supra* note 11, at chap. 9.

28. In his *Class Struggles in France* and *The Eighteenth Brumaire*, Marx makes many references to the illusions of the small landholding French peasants. Both can be found in David Fernbach, *supra* note 19.

29. *See* especially *Economic & Philosophic Manuscripts*, in vol. 3, *Collected Works, supra* note 4, at 306–26.

30. "Contribution to the Critique of Hegel's Philosophy of Law. Introduction," *ibid*. at 175–76.

31. *See* Stephen Lukes, *Power* (London: Macmillan, 1974), 41–42.

32. The assumption is that the people involved in the discussion have autonomy and access to needed information. An underlying premise of this Marxian approach is that traditions which deny autonomy to individuals are illegitimate; personal autonomy is considered a fundamental human need. Individuals who do not have autonomy cannot engage in genuine discussion.

33. *See* Marx's discussion of capitalist economic development in *The Communist Manifesto*, part 1, in vol. 6, *Collected Works*, *supra* note 4.

34. *See, for example*, Marx, "Inaugural Address of the Working Men's International Association," in *supra* note 3, at 512–19.

35. *See, for example*, Marx and Engels, "Circular Letter to Bebel, Liebknecht, Bracke, and Others," in *ibid*. at 549–55.

36. *See* Marx's speech to the Amsterdam Congress of the First International, September 8, 1872, in *ibid*. at 522–24. *See* the excellent discussion in Hunt, *supra* note 11, at chap. 10.

37. Stephen Lukes argues that such views have led many Marxist revolutionaries to neglect ethical questions regarding revolutionary means and to act in ways that violate the fundamental human rights of their opponents, before and after the revolution (*Marxism and Morality* [Oxford: Clarendon Press, 1985], chap. 6).

38. Some of these conclusions to which Marx comes, as well as the incompleteness of much of his analysis, can doubtless be explained partly by the often submerged, but still present, Hegelian teleological currents in his thought (*see supra* note 1). In other words, the teleological elements influence the results of Marx's social science, his use of his "historical materialist" methodology. According to this teleology, history works its way forward to the future just society; previous societies are mere way stations to this final destination.

39. The misinterpretation is partly based on a misreading of Marx's critical comments on bourgeois rights in his "On the Jewish Question." *See* Nordahl, "Marx and Utopia: Critique of the 'Orthodox Interpretation,'" *supra* note 1, especially at 776–78.

Section *III*

Regional and Indigenous Cultural Perspectives on Human Rights

James W. Zion[1]

8. North American Indian Perspectives on Human Rights

Introduction: Columbus, Colonialism, and the Cant of Human Rights

Human rights law is an excellent vehicle for a reassessment of relations among Indian and neo-European groups. Following World War II the themes of decolonialization and individual human rights emerged as fundamental concepts, and this is the moment to extend those concepts to Indian groups. The year 1992 marks a half millennium of discovery and settlement by Europeans in the Americas. The initial misnomer "Indian" still denominates and separates the original inhabitants of the Americas and their issue from the dominant culture of the settlers of North America: the Anglo-Europeans.[2]

Indians have never recovered from the initial cultural, racial, and religious onslaught. The sixteenth-century debates about whether Indians are "human" persist in popular thought, modified today to a stereotypical perception of the "dumb Indian."[3] Those debates also persist in the practical relationship of the national governments of Canada, Mexico, and the United States with Indian tribes, bands, and groups. They were colonized but do not have the benefit of decolonization policies. The major policy concession which acknowledges Indians as "human" is a periodic experiment of assimilation of individual Indians and Indian groups in the homogeneous goo of the cultural melting pot.[4]

The written and public views of the relationship are generally one-sided. Aside from a few popular works trying to educate non-Indians about the ways Indians see the relationship, most descriptions are by non-Indian authors who have not had a deep experiential relationship with Indian culture. One good example of the one-sided view is that of "Indian affairs law," as the American Bar Association denominates it as a field of law: Indian affairs law has to do with non-Indian laws designed to regulate Indians, and almost nothing to do with laws of Indians.[5]

The one-sided and imposed view is in human rights law as well. The macrolevel human right of genuine decolonialization through self-determination is not extended to Indian nations, tribes, bands, and groups. This discussion also focuses upon microlevel human rights for Indians, and legal protections in this area are recent and few as well.

National attitudes must change if Indians are to become fully acknowledged as "human" (or as the People).[6] The United States speaks the cant of "human rights" in international arenas without itself observing and implementing them. There are twenty-one global human rights covenants and instruments available for national ratification; the United States has ratified only six, whereas Canada has ratified at least fifteen.[7] Some look to the United States as a model for its rule of law that individuals may invoke international law human rights protections,[8] but an American appellate court has dismissed Indian international human rights claims in a footnote, essentially saying, "You dumb Indians. Don't you know you can't have international law human rights, but only those rights the United States Congress decides to allow you?"[9] While the United States has historically been the home of Enlightenment-era laws enshrining "self-evident truths" that are the basis for international human rights laws, truths are not self-evident to the dominant Anglo culture, which generally rejects international law.[10]

Canada, though better in attitude, is ignorant in application when it comes to human rights. Canada rightly prides itself on its international activities and reputation in the field of human rights. The Canadian government, however, was unable to recognize obvious human rights when it reacted to an embarrassing incident that tarnished Canada's reputation.

In Canada, an "Indian" is a person who fits national statutory qualifications. In 1951 Canada enacted a comprehensive Indian statute in the form of the *Indian Act,* and section 12(1)(b) provided that a woman who married a non-Indian, a non-status Indian, or a Metis would cease to be an "Indian." Indian men who married members of those groups, in contrast, did not lose their status.[11] Unlike the situation in the United States, where Indian tribes, bands, and groups define their own membership, the Canadian system provided national, non-Indian, standards for enrollment, group membership, and Indian status.

In 1973 the Canadian Supreme Court held that the equality provisions of the Canadian Bill of Rights (1960) did not override the discriminatory provision.[12] In 1977 Sandra Lovelace, another Indian woman who had been disenfranchised, complained of sex discrimination in violation of the International Covenant on Civil and Political Rights in a submission to the Human Rights Committee of the United Nations.[13] In 1981 the committee ruled that her disenfranchisement denied her the rights of access to her language and culture in violation of section 27 of the covenant. Canada, recognizing its weak position, told the Human Rights Committee it was in the process of adopting legislation to end the discrimination. It said it was even considering allowing the Indian bands to adopt their own membership standards, but "such by-laws, however, would be required to be non-discriminatory in the areas of sex, religion and family affiliation."[14] The Indian Act amendments of 1985 eliminated the discriminatory membership provision, and section 10 provided for band control of membership through membership rules.[15] However, the national government continues to control entitlement to Indian status.[16]

In the furor over this issue in Canada, what got lost in the debate—which was charged with emotionalism over the rights of women—was the overriding consideration of the fundamental group right of Indians to determine who shall be considered an "Indian." Rather than undertake a revision of the legal relationship between the national government and Indian governments, the amended Indian Act simply continued the old pattern. An embarrassed Canada imposed equality norms upon Indian groups, thus denying those groups the right to fix and enforce their own norms, based upon their own cultural values.

These are the contradictions of human rights law as applied to Indians in this era of post-Enlightenment liberal thought. The premises of modern human rights law are that the individual must be protected against the state in equality with all other individuals. While equality before the law and equality in access to the fundamentals of daily life are essential principles, they are not acceptable for Indians in their external relations with the outside world. Unbending equality is essentially assimilationist; and assimilation is ethnocidal and genocidal in its impact upon Indians, both as individuals and as groups.

Therefore, the formulation of human rights laws and policies that nourish rather than destroy Indian culture depends on the acceptance of Indian views on the matter. This requires a definition of the process of finding Indian norms and values for framing substantive human rights rules, identifying protections required to assure group and individual identity as Indians, and writing substantive rules which enshrine Indian values in law.

Defining Indian Human Rights

To formulate substantive rules to encourage, foster, and protect "human rights," we should have an approach to define their content. The major problem with the existing regime and corpus of human rights law is that it is individualistic and assimilationist.[17] International discrimination law is founded upon "progressive" and "egalitarian" principles that allow special measures for "underprivileged groups" for only a limited transitional period of time.[18] The overall goal of discrimination law as it may apply to Indians is to achieve their assimilation or full integration into the general society.[19] This follows the general pattern that the basis for modern society is ". . . the autonomous individual who possessed a body of rights rooted in natural law, rights that preceded the creation of the state."[20]

The concept of human rights is recent, generally dating from reactions to the atrocities of World War II and the East-West power politics surrounding the birth and growth of the United Nations. We still do not have an understanding of how to approach the content of a corpus of international human rights law. J. R. Brierly has noted the absence of any definition of human rights and freedoms in the United Nations Charter, an omission that weakens the content of its human rights clauses. He discusses the ad hoc process of providing definition in various international and regional instruments.[21] Ian Brownlie, making the same finding, pointed to the 1948 Universal Declaration of Human Rights as an "authoritative guide" to interpret the charter, saying "the concept of human rights has a core of reasonable certainty."[22] Leslie Green approached the question through classification:

> Human rights may be classified into those which are enjoyed by the individual in isolation, such as freedom of conscience, personal freedom and private property; those which are enjoyed by the individual in conjunction with other individuals, such as freedom of speech, discussion, writing and publication; and those which the individual enjoys as a citizen, such as equality before the law, of franchise and in access to public office.

He adopted the concept that the idea of human rights is a combination of liberal and individualistic guarantees of personal freedom and democratic and political rights "of the individual citizen."[23]

These foundations not only have little use for a definition of Indian rights, but they also run contrary to Indian cultural perceptions. The focus on the individual ignores the great importance of the group—of the family (and normally the extended family), of extended relationships of clan and religion, of the band or tribe, and even of "Indian-ness" itself.

A non-Indian analysis of human rights law that appears useful for the formulation of a practical approach to Indian human rights is that of Myres S. McDougal, Harold D. Lasswell, and Lung-Chu Chen.[24] Their method is sociological; and they start with a catalogue of "rising common demands," through "representative value processes." There are eight values, with lists of specific areas of human rights, including positive rights and protections against "nonfulfillments and deprivations." The values are respect, power, enlightenment, well-being, wealth, skill, affection, and rectitude.[25] Future studies of these questions should consider this method.

Another useful analysis is that of Paul Sieghart, who examined the various international human rights instruments and developed a classification of thirteen areas of rights and freedoms. He discusses physical integrity, standard of living, health, family, work, social security, education, property, legal integrity, mental and moral integrity, joint activities, politics and democracy, and collective rights.[26]

The approaches of the last two works are useful in the Indian context because individual Indians need protection of their individual rights. The Indian Law Resource Center, a leading advocate of Indian rights in international arenas, correctly notes, however:

> Many Indians believe that the group rights of Indian peoples are the most important and most endangered of all Indian rights. These rights would include the right to self-government and the right to maintain communal ownership of land and resources. As groups, peoples, communities, tribes and nations—not just as individuals—Indians are asserting the right to self-government, the right to determine their own relations with other nations and other peoples, and the right to preserve their cultures, languages, and religions.[27]

Keeping in mind the importance of group rights as a fundamental human right for Indians, how may one develop a definition of those rights? The first approach, as it has been with others, is content-oriented. One may develop a comprehensive corpus of Indian human rights law by addressing social and economic conditions, acknowledging Indian demands, and by unifying the growing literature of aboriginal international rights law. The second approach is to examine the common base values of the Indians of North America.

SOCIAL CONDITIONS

The Indians of North America fall at the bottom of every indicator of social and economic well-being. A starting point for their human rights law is the census. The 1980 United States Census (which most agree underenumerated Indians) shows there are approximately 1.5 million Native Americans there, about one-half of one percent of the national population.[28] About half of the Indian population lives in the American West, mostly in the states of California, Oklahoma, Arizona, and New Mexico. One-third to one-half of the Indian population lives in cities.[29] The conclusions of the census are grim:

> Native Americans, on a national average, have the shortest life span of any ethnic group; the highest infant mortality rate; the highest suicide rate; the highest unemployment; the highest school dropout rate; the poorest housing; and the most inadequate health care, with extensive diabetes, tuberculosis, high blood pressure, respiratory disease, and alcoholism. Many factors account for these conditions: unproductive land; lack of capital; lack of education; a cycle of poverty difficult to escape; and cultural dislocation and depression caused from an existence as a conquered people within a historically alien culture.[30]

Indian legal issues, which are human rights issues as well, are well documented in the 1977 *Final Report* of the American Indian Policy Review Commission[31] and in the 1981 report of the United States Commission on Civil Rights, *Indian Tribes: A Continuing Quest For Survival*.[32]

There are approximately 300,000 Indians and 25,000 Inuits in Canada, about two percent of the national population.[33] About 30 percent of the Native population lives off-reserve, and there are 573 bands with reserves. Social and economic conditions of Natives in Canada are also poor:

> For Indians in Canada, overall life expectancy is 10 years less than the national average. Perinatal and neonatal Infant mortality is almost twice as high. Suicides occur among Indians at more than six times the national rate. Indians are jailed at more than three times the national rate. Over 50 percent of Indian health problems are alcohol-related. One out of three Indian families lives in crowded conditions. Only 50–60 percent of Indian housing has running water and sewage disposal. Although participation in elementary schools has recently approached the national level, secondary school participation is still

12 percent lower, with a completion rate of about 20 percent, as compared to a national rate of 75 percent. University participation is less than half the national level. Participation in the labor force is less than 40 percent. And with employment at only about 30 percent of the working-age group, and average income well below national levels, about 50 percent of the Indian population has to resort to governmental social assistance. Even for off-reserve Indians who have attempted to enter the economic mainstream, the levels of unemployment and governmental dependency stand at about 25–30 percent.[34]

These conditions are well documented in the 1979 report, *Indian Conditions: A Survey*.[35] The legal and political issues are in the 1982 report of the Canadian Parliament's Special Committee on Indian Self-Government, *Indian Self-Government in Canada*.[36] The governments of both the United States and Canada have an agenda for effective change, as well as national priorities, in these documents if only they would adhere to the fundamental human right of according dignity and true self-government to Native groups.

INDIAN DEMANDS

The Indians of Canada are much more sophisticated in the expression of their demands for human rights than are the Indians of the United States. The literature, reports, briefs, and position papers of Canadian Indians and Indian groups are too plentiful for review here, but there is no shortage of published positions.[37]

In contrast, American Indians have not ventured far into the field of international human rights law, much less the domestic law of discrimination and civil rights. In 1968 Black and Hispanic groups dominated the Poor Peoples Campaign, a dramatic march on Washington, D.C., to demand basic civil and economic rights; and the small Indian contingent there felt ignored, out of place, and voiceless.[38] The American Indian position has been expressed by its Indian lawyers in several excellent works.[39]

Each year more than five hundred books and articles are published on Indian history in the United States.[40] The fact that few such books and articles are by Indian authors or represent the actual positions of Indian groups is of itself evidence of the denial of a fundamental human right— the right to participate in the process of education, persuasion, and change. There are some Indian presses that publish valuable works, but their resources are limited and very few genuinely Indian publications reach the general American audience.

ABORIGINAL INTERNATIONAL RIGHTS LAW

In 1978 Gordon Bennett published a slim work, *Aboriginal Rights in International Law*, which was depressing in its conclusion that there are very few such rights.[41] By 1985, however, the literature in the field grew to a point that advocates of Aboriginal or Native rights felt more optimistic.[42] Recent publications in Canada, [43] Australia,[44] and the United States[45] provide an analysis of Native rights in international law that offers a good starting point.

Article 38.1 of the Statute of the International Court of Justice provides that the "teachings of the most highly qualified publicists of the various nations" are a "subsidiary means for the determination of rules of law." This is a very important consideration for advocates of international Aboriginal rights. The statute follows the civil law scholarship tradition, and Indians must demand recognition for their positions as "highly qualified publicists." Another authority is the findings of the Fourth Russell Tribunal, held in Rotterdam in 1980. That ad hoc international tribunal, staffed and advised by experts in international law, Indian law, and Aboriginal rights, heard complaints of violations of the human rights of Native peoples and issued it judgments in the form of authoritative reports.[46] There was significant Indian participation in the tribunal. The right to be heard is a fundamental human right, and international bodies must acknowledge Indian positions as those of learned publicists in their field.

Indian Base Values

The foregoing discussion of a content methodology for a definition of Indian human rights addresses a prime element of modern industrial culture—you must prove your point by citation to written authority. The printing press completely changed the way modern humankind views reality, and new electronic developments will create further social changes.[47] Indians, the subject of so much printed material, have not written it. Throughout the half millennium of contact in the Americas, the Anglos have done the speaking and writing without significant Indian input. Indians are the victims of stereotyping as "heathen savage," "pagan," or "noble savage." These stereotypes must cease if there are to be any true Indian human rights.

There are hundreds of Indian tribes, bands, and groups with different cultures, languages, and religious beliefs in North America. Despite such great diversity there are some common base values which may be briefly outlined as follows:

FAMILY, CLAN, GROUP, AND PAN-INDIANISM

The individualist thrust of domestic human and civil rights law, as well as international human rights law, is often inappropriate in the Indian context. Indians are highly individualistic, yet that high degree of individualism exists in the context of relationships and groups.[48] Navajos, speaking of a wrongdoer, will say, "He acts as if he had no family."[49]

That family consists of individuals well beyond the Anglo nuclear family, and the Indian family includes individuals who are only distantly related by blood. The Indian family's daily functioning includes relations with parents, grandparents, aunts, uncles, cousins, and other individuals one may call "mother," "father," "brother," "sister," "auntie," "uncle," or "cousin." Some relationships arise from clan kinship systems, such as that of the Navajos, whose relationships are traced in matrilineal lines. Some relationships arise from religious relationships, such as the kivas and moieties of the Pueblo Peoples of New Mexico. They can even arise from customary adoptions, and throughout North America there is a common practice of adopting an individual to create relationship ties.

Non-Indian society is regulated through written laws and coercive bodies such as police and regulatory governmental agencies. Indian society is regulated through familial, religious, and social relationships. Indian relationships are pyramidal, with strong daily ties to the extended family at the base, ties to clan and ceremonial groups, and ties to groups the Anglo world knows as the band or tribe. There are intergroup ties as well.

Indian concepts of humanity go beyond the species, and accord respect to animals and even inanimate beings as part of the human family. This is central to many religious beliefs and practices.

Humanity is essential and starts with the concept that life and its propagation is so important that it must not be impeded. Many Indian cultures have strictures against birth control and contraceptive devices. Humanity extends to the unborn, and many tribes have traditional prohibitions against abortion.[50] What non-Indians see as permissive child-rearing practices, where children are permitted to express themselves as they will and where corporal punishment is absent, are simply expressions of the individual freedom and dignity of children. The child soon knows the world of reciprocal relations with others, however, and has frequent contact with other family members. It is quite common for children to move from one household to another, particularly to that of grandparents, whenever there is family need or stress. The Anglo world sees children as a form of property or the relationship with children as a personal, possessory right, while many Indian cultures believe that a child is a gift of God, and must be respected as such. The child belongs to the family, not the parents. These open relations with children contradict the Anglo norm, while the Anglo practice of placing children outside the family is shocking in the Indian world. A crisis area for the cultures and survival of Native peoples throughout the world is child custody. Social service agencies frequently have little respect for the Indian home, do not provide its members resources to keep families intact, and subject Native children to alien child placements, adoptions, and institutions. This problem is at a crisis level because of values associated with children and the inability of non-Native child protection institutions to understand or respect those values.

Larger group relationships depend upon the size, economy, history, and traditions of the given group. The individual lives in a framework of relationships that regulate life, and he or she associates with the group for survival. Such associations include religious ties. There are relationships to which the non-Indian world refers as the "band," "tribe," or sometimes "nation." The nature and the extent of these relationships vary, depending on the situation of the given group. The Navajos, for example, consider themselves "Dine'," the People. Their cosmology, as it is with many Indian groups, makes them *the* People, created for a given place and with ties to their sacred mountains. The chroniclers of the Navajos make several mistakes about them. Not understanding the survival patterns of the People, who speak a generally similar language, the literature refers to *the* Navajo and assumes that the behavior and customs of a given group are representative of the behavior of all. In fact, there are several Navajo groups, with some variances in dialect, customs, and beliefs. The same is true of governmental relations. The Navajos have been attempting to achieve nationhood in their governmental form, but it is difficult to achieve, given tradition.[51] The *Indian Reorganization Act* of the United States (1934), and the *Indian Act* of Canada (1951, amended 1985) both created artificial bodies called "tribes" and "bands." Those organizations often do not correspond to previous group structures. The Fort Belknap Reservation of Montana and its government include the Gros Ventres (Atsina) and the Assiniboines, traditional enemies whose goals often conflict. Many other tribes and groups were lumped together because of reservation policies designed to contain Indians without regard to their preferences or actual relationships. In some areas there are elder shadow governments with traditional bodies that advise or oversee the operations of the body established by the national government.

Throughout, however, many bands, tribes, and groups simply refer to themselves in their own language as "the People," showing their sense of identity and divine destiny. While Indian governmental forms are not always obvious, and despite imposed governmental forms, that sense of belonging and group identity is strong.

There is another, wider, association from the individual and the family to larger groups. That association is called "pan-Indianism." Indian organizations combine a high degree of individualism with intimate relationships with others. Given facts of geography, distance, and isolation in North America, Indian groups tend to be separate, with a group individualism, yet there are very important intergroup ties. In history those ties come from trade relations. The excavations of Anasazi sites in the American Southwest often turn up macaw or parrot feathers from Mexico, seashells from the California coast, or obsidian from distant points, showing extensive trade relations and group interaction. The horse intensified trade relations; and Anglo explorers noted the presence of horses on the plains of Saskatchewan and Alberta, bearing Spanish brands from Rio Grande Valley ranches in New Mexico.[52] Those relations persist in social and governmental forms.

The national governments of Canada, the United States, and Mexico must recognize the legitimacy of the Native American Church, one of the fastest-growing religions in North America. The sacrament of the Church is Peyote, a cactus from Texas and northern Mexico. The transmission of the sacrament binds adherents and believers throughout Indian North America, and formal associations of the Church involve Indians from the Mexican border to the farthest reaches of Canadian Indian groups. While the national governments of Canada and the United States declare official positions of respect for the Church, ignorance and bigotry, coupled with the international drug scare, manifest as widespread persecution of Church members.[53] The Native American Church is an important pan-Indian institution that provides an international group identity for many Indians.

Another such grouping is social, but it demonstrates both pan-Indianism and the sense of Indian-ness that unites individual Indians. It is the "Pow-Wow Circuit." Many tribes have different accounts for the rise of the pow-wow, some insisting upon religious roots, others saying it is simply a social gathering. There are many variations in the dances, costumes, and practices of the pow-wow. Most tribal and band groups in the United States and Canada begin the season in the late spring, however, and some singers, drummers, and dancers spend the entire summer on the circuit. The pow-wow brings Indians from widely scattered groups together, and it and associated religious ceremonials create very intimate and very binding associations and relationships. The Indian rodeo circuit is another important pan-Indian organization, and large numbers of Indians throughout North America gather at the national Indian rodeo finals in Albuquerque each year, which also has a huge indoor pow-wow. Indian veterans' groups are another example of pan-Indian ties, and a continuation of warrior traditions.

National Indian political patterns differ in the United States and Canada, partly due to history and partly due to governmental funding. In Canada there are strong provincial and national Indian organizations, which come together to develop national agendas, goals, and strategies for use in the political arena. The national organizations of the United States are not so strong as in Canada and lack the unity of purpose that exists there. Perhaps the Indians of the United States reflect a general pattern of American isolationism; in fact, American Indian political strategies are most often put forward by specialized groups.

The Indian concept of humanity, founded in religious belief and group survival, is both highly individualistic and group-oriented. Group bonds are strong on the family level, important in intermediate levels, and have expression in the concept of being of "the People." Trade, religious, and social relations are strong and grow stronger in the pan-Indian movement, and modern sophistication, coupled with communications media, tie many separate groups together.

The human rights perceptions that arise out of these circumstances make child welfare law, religious freedom, international travel, access to communications media, and resources for national and international gatherings very important needs.

THE INDIVIDUAL

It is difficult to avoid stereotyping when speaking of Indian concepts of individualism. Religious beliefs such as the tradition of the vision quest, powers acquired through ceremonials, and the cult of the warrior are important, but sometimes it is difficult to trace them in modern expressions. Many individual Indians do speak of personal achievement and independence in terms of the acquisition of religious power or "knowl-edgeability," but often aspects of individualism are not discussed or appear to be based upon secular considerations.

In whatever varying form individualism may appear, one cannot sepa-rate the individual from the group. Among the Navajos there are people with skills that make them successful in trades, crafts, and business, yet Anglo material success is not a part of Indian business because of family ties and obligations.[54] The individual is responsible to the group even in the sharing of material wealth, as the group is responsible to the individual in time of need. For example, an individual Indian charged with an offense often may rely upon the extended family for bail or fine money. Contri-butions for funerals and funeral feasts are an important obligation, and the extended family is responsible for the welfare of children. The individual may expect financial help in time of need, and there is a corresponding obligation to help others. The implication for human rights law is that in some instances individual rights are important, yet they must be viewed in the context of larger associations.

Another area, which is little understood by non-Indians, is that of gender relations. Many Indian groups have a "men's knowledge" and a "women's knowledge"—separate and distinct bodies of wisdom which ex-press themselves in ceremonial and other obligations. The area of gender relations has been so little explored or understood by non-Indians that it is dangerous to impose non-Indians' concepts of sex equality.

The Navajos, classified as a matrilineal society by anthropologists, are having difficulties sorting out their gender relations in public life. The Bureau of Indian Affairs attempted to disrupt traditional Navajo land use by allocating lands to male heads of household. Women responded by taking warrior names to apply for land.[55] For decades the Navajo tribal court evaded Anglo intestacy law and created unique mechanisms for female-controlled land tenure, using Anglo trust law language.[56] A topic of current controversy in the Navajo nation is whether or not it is against tradition for women to hold public office. Men quote the "River of Sepa-ration" Scripture to the effect that women must not hold public office in command over men, while there is Navajo Scripture to the effect that women are equal.[57] The Navajo Nation adopted the American Equal Rights Amendment in its Navajo Bill of Rights; but many Navajos are not aware of that fact, and the courts are uncertain how to apply it, given culture and tradition.[58] Rape is a common offense now; but it is most likely that, given the equality of relations between men and women in the past, it is an Anglo-induced offense, accompanying male-dominated land use and male-dominated governmental bodies.[59]

Another stereotypical view of Indian social life is that Indian men are wife-beaters and Indian women are passive sufferers. This description is another relic of early, racist accounts of Indian life. Domestic violence is not sanctioned by most Indian traditional laws and, as it is with rape, such violence is more likely the product of Anglo-induced paternalistic values. Personal violence against women violates the strict egalitarian principles of most Indian traditions.

In sum, gender relations as an aspect of the individual in Indian cultures have suffered severely because of Anglo-imposed practices and values. While rights for women are essential to a human rights regime, non-Indians must take great care not to impose Anglo values upon that relationship. Indians of the United States are fortunate in their ability to make their own laws and regulate their own domestic relations, so the corpus of women's rights law may develop along tribal lines.

The Indian as individual will invoke many kinds of right, but he or she will do so within the cultural context of the group. One reason the concepts of sovereignty, self-determination, and autonomy for Indian groups are so important for the protection of Indian culture is that individual rights function in a mileu of group expectations.

RELIGION

The religions of the Indians of North America vary widely, as does religious thought.[60] Indian religious belief is intense, very personal, and part of every aspect of daily life. Many Indians cannot and do not separate religious and secular functions in daily life, as does the Anglo world. An American Cree woman stated it this way: "It is very hard being an Indian because every day is one, long prayer ceremony."[61]

Indian religious belief is also eclectic. Many individuals belong to a Christian sect, practice their traditional beliefs, and may also adhere to emerging beliefs, such as those of the Native American Church.

Animism, the religious classification applied to many Indian religious beliefs, is a very beautiful approach to understanding reality. As a general matter, animism is a belief that accords dignity and meaning to every material thing, living or nonliving. A Canadian Cree educator explained that everything has a soul, and given that fact, one must respect everything. Others explain that you must use everything for good purposes, making offerings for resources such as trees and having a reason for using them.[62]

Through animism one is able to invoke powerful supernatural forces for daily help. The individual and the group are able to call upon resources from a wider community, one of animate, inanimate, and supernatural beings. Those community members act upon and interact with humans as well.

American religious freedom law is destructive of Indian religion, and the American Indian Religious Freedom Act of 1978 is a failure.[63] This is due to a lack of understanding of the intimate relationship between humans and their environment and Anglo ethnocentrism. The Anglo "heathen savage" and "pagan" stereotype persists, and Indian religion is widely persecuted. The Native American Church is a visible target, and persecution of its members is intensifying. The United States Supreme Court exhibits the cultural biases of its members in rulings which accord Indian beliefs less dignity than other faiths.[64]

Nineteenth-century persecution drove Indian religion underground; and while there is greater tolerance for non-Christian belief today, Indian religion largely stays underground. Religious intolerance continues, and while the Thirty Years' War of the seventeenth century was the turning point for the role of religion in Western society, the fact remains that freedom of religion depends upon belonging to a faith that is too strong in numbers to be destroyed.[65]

As it is with the concept of individuals as members of an extended family group, membership or identification with religious groups is very important. Secular, nonreligious North America avoids public expressions of religion owing to the competition of the major religions, while all Navajo public meetings open with a prayer. Given the nature of Indian religion, it is a powerful and important factor that must be acknowledged in many areas of public concern, including resource development and land use.

LAND AND RESOURCE USE

One of the most important and sensitive events in North America in the twentieth century is the extinguishment of aboriginal title. Anglos want the land and its resources at the expense of Indians. The U.S. Indian Claims Commission Act of 1946 was part of a program of assimilationist legislation. Land and resource initiatives in Alaska, the Arctic, and in mineral-rich areas are tied to policies which are either anti-Native or seek to control Natives through imposed policies. But land is an essential part of Indianness. Without a land base there can be no meaningful exercise of group rights, including religion.

A major issue in Canada is the right to hunt and fish off-reserve. Some elders, trying to explain the injustice of restrictive wildlife controls and barriers to land use, say that the Anglos have misinterpreted the treaty process. They say that their Grandparents, believing that no one can "own" the land and understanding the human right of survival, decided to share the land. The Indian understanding was that the sharing process included the Indian right to hunt, fish, gather berries, get firewood, and pray in special places, and such rights could not be surrendered by treaty. No Indian leader could have enough authority. In addition, given the exploitation of mineral rights, some elders explain that the land given to the Anglos was only the surface, perhaps only six inches in depth (or the depth of a plow).

The land use issue is central to Indian thought, and the human rights they invoke are those of a land base for group identity, traditional resource use and access, and respect for religious values and practices tied to the land.

TREATIES

Sometimes it is difficult to understand the emotional value of Indian perceptions of treaties and the treaty-making process. The Anglo world abandoned the original concept of treaty-making, which was a means of securing large portions of Indian land without warfare. At the time many of the Indian treaties were made, the Anglos did not have sufficient military resources with which to take the land by force. North American colonial policy came out of an emerging international law of treaties, and while the original instruments were in fact intended to be arrangements made with sovereign Indian nations, today international law has abandoned and trivialized the original process.[66]

A canon for the construction of treaties in both the United States and Canada is that treaties must be interpreted as the Indians understood them.[67] That canon has not been followed in practice because of ethnocentrism and the inability of the legal system to accommodate Indian concepts of evidence. Some wag has said that during the treaty-making process the United States promised everything and delivered nothing, while the British Crown and Canada promised nothing and kept that promise. Despite the frequent lack of specific content in treaties, Indians regard them highly as fundamental instruments defining relations of Indian nations with the Anglo governments. They are a symbol and a proof of the existence and continuing right of Peoples to be Indians. Therefore, any principle of Indian human rights must acknowledge Indian autonomy and the treaties that prove that autonomy. Treaties are essential to Indian-ness.

Human Beings, the People, and Cultural Rights

Indians accord human rights to all parts of Creation, excluding no one and nothing from the family of reality. They understand human rights as families, groups, and Peoples, neither separating the individual from the group nor separating religion from secular life.

A common complaint about international law is that in its initial development, during the economic expansion which followed the "discovery" of the New World, the commercial powers developed its rules and imposed its values. During the twentieth century the socialist regimes raised similar complaints, using the development of international law as a part of the East-West power struggle. There is a danger that Indian rights may become an issue in that power struggle, as the United States accuses communists of denials of human rights and communists point to the treatment of Indians of the Americas as proof of the hypocrisy of human rights practice there. Emerging Third World nations join the accusation that international law has too long been the tool of the industrial nations.[68]

Hopefully there is a sensitivity and receptiveness to similar accusations by Indians. Human rights laws, which are supposed to be based upon "universal" human values, are presently largely irrelevant to Indians. Indians of the United States seldom use discrimination law, as is reflected in the law reports and human rights agency caseload statistics; and Indian litigation reflects their overwhelming concern about their group rights, rather than individual rights.

Human rights law for Indians must be based upon the values of human dignity. For new initiatives in the field to succeed, the Anglo society must abandon stereotypes and instead "see with a native eye."[69] This is a process which has just begun, and an obvious conclusion of this attempt to outline Indian values and perceptions is that the Anglo world must open up lines of communication and hear Indian views.

Substantive Rights

The growing literature of Indian and Aboriginal rights in international law sufficiently stresses issues such as self-determination, self-government, treaty enforcement, and other such basic rights. These need fine-tuning to flesh out areas such as the meaning of the "right to culture"[70] and the ability of Indian litigants to enforce their international law rights in various bodies.[71]

Given the cultural values discussed above there are several areas of substantive human rights Indians demand. The more important rights are defined below.

THE RIGHT TO BE INDIAN

The right of Indians to be Indians is obvious but seldom discussed as such. It is the group and individual right to persist and to retain the group's values, customs, traditions, usages, religion, language, and overall culture. "Culture" is an elusive term, and one which is the subject of a great deal of anthropological literature.[72] The definition developed by the Canadian Commission of UNESCO is:

> Culture is a dynamic value system of learned elements, with assumptions, conventions, beliefs and rules permitting members of a group to relate to each other and to the world, to communicate and to develop their creative potential.[73]

The denial of this right is a part of the ethnocide and even genocide which an undeveloped human rights law for indigenous population causes.[74] Schusky, in 1965,[75] adds supporting sub elements. One of them is the right not to assimilate[76] or to be subjected to imposed assimilation through tribal termination, assimilationist policies, poor economic conditions which drive Indians from their land base, or even the imposition of assimilationist human rights law.

Family integrity and cultural integrity are important corollaries of the right. Family integrity for Indians is in jeopardy because of imposed domestic relations laws which do not accommodate Indian familial concepts and because of the international child welfare scandal. Cultural integrity is greatly endangered because of religious persecution, land grabs, land use restrictions, language policies, and unresponsive education systems. Indian-controlled education is essential to develop such integrity.

Ethnocide exists not only as a result of the affirmative imposition of Anglo values but because of a refusal to acknowledge the right to be Indian. Genocide exists, and the United States very carefully denied private enforcement in its ratification and implementation of the Genocide Convention.[77] The convention itself does not serve Indian rights because it is a criminal law requiring specific intent to destroy a group. Therefore, Indians must have group protection of their right to be Indian and effective means to enforce it.

THE RIGHT TO RELIGION

The pattern of persecution of Indian religions takes many forms. There is a subtle, yet growing and more active persecution of members of the

Native American Church. The American Indian Religious Freedom Act is a failure, and even American constitutional protections of religion mock Indian religion. International barriers for the free passage of Indians for ceremonials still exist, and there are continuing complaints of the desecration of medicine bundles and confiscation of Peyote.

Religion is one of the most basic values for Indians, and in order to accommodate it, it is time for Anglos to better understand it. Vine Deloria correctly notes that non-Indians can gain a great deal from Indian religion and culture if they will take the time to understand it.[78]

INDIAN LAND

Threats to Indian land bases, in the form of reservations and reserves, continue. Where there are Indian lands, they are inadequate, although the restoration of illegally seized lands would greatly increase that land base. Resource development and the extinction of aboriginal title are continuing threats to Indian cultures, as are restrictions upon Indian land use off-reservation or reserve. The simple point is that Indian groups need their own lands for survival, and the taking or denying of such lands is a policy of ethnocide in its effect.

TREATY RIGHTS

Although the current domestic law of Canada and the United States deals with continuing disputes and claims over Indian treaties, international law has not yet elevated the status of treaties to a protected group human right. Treaty rights are human rights because they are intertwined with the right to be Indian and the right of self-determination.

SELF-DETERMINATION AND SELF-GOVERNMENT

There are two general approaches to support these rights. One is to expand current international doctrines of the law of self-determination to Indian groups,[79] and another is to give liberal construction to the concept of "the right to culture."[80] International status for Indian treaties is also important. Whichever approach is used, the Anglo world must accept the reality of continued Indian existence as separate groups. Five centuries of intentional attempts to destroy Indians have failed, and Indian cultures persist despite such attempts.[81]

The United Nations recognized the need to dismantle colonies for world development, and the same principles apply to Indian colonies. Their decolonization through self-determination will address the shocking demographic data summarized above. While there is a doctrine of sovereignty for Indians in the United States, that does not explain why poor socioeconomic conditions persist. The American self-determination initiative is recent, poorly funded, and hampered by a continuing distrust of the ability of Indians truly to manage their own affairs.

EMPOWERMENT

"Empowerment" is a useful concept for this area, and it is one in accord with Indian beliefs. Many Indian religions speak to the concept of "power," with ceremonials and disciplines to acquire it. Poverty is not simply a lack of material goods, but a lack of access to power and decision-making. The 1987 report of the World Commission on Environment and Development, *Our Common Future* (also called the "Brundtland Report," after Gro Harlem Brundtland, the commission chair), specifically addresses the needs of Aboriginal peoples in conjunction with population and human resource issues.[82] That section of the report, appropriately entitled "Empowering Vulnerable Groups," reinforced the recognition and protection of traditional land and resource rights and found that the disappearance of indigenous or tribal peoples would be a loss to the larger society.[83] Empowerment requires both effective local control by Indians and effective access to decision-making processes.

DISCRIMINATION LAW AND THE EQUALITY PRINCIPLE

Domestic and international discrimination law entrenches the equality principle, which is an assimilationist principle. As international law now stands, special protective measures for Indians would have to be transitory and of short duration. Discrimination law faces an affirmative action crisis. That is, what measures are permissible to cure past patterns of discrimination? And what special measures for special groups—what special privileges—should be allowed? Domestic law deals with such measures in various ways.[84] The United States has dealt with special measures for Indians, recognizing the historical fact that the relations of Indians with the national government are "political," not racial, and that preferences for Indians are permissible.[85]

Discrimination against Indians is widespread and it is special. The group discrimination ignored by discrimination law is that of state and provincial governments that resist Indian self-government rights, impede such rights, and are openly hostile to those rights. Another form of discrimination, which is much more subtle and insidious, is the stereotype of the "dumb Indian." Anglo politicians and bureaucrats, and American

Anglos coming under the control of Indian government, do not state it openly, but restrictions upon Indian-run programs and resistance to tribal government is ultimately founded upon the perception that Indians cannot lead, manage, govern, or "do things right." An associated concept, practiced but not named, is the principle that "the White way is the right way." These malignant views cause conflict and hostility between Indian and Anglo government (particularly at the state and provincial level), and they are a part of growing hate group activity.[86] Discrimination law must be modified to accommodate Indian-ness and Indian group rights.

THE RIGHT TO TRAVEL

Among the treaty rights of Indians are those contained in international documents that ended wars such as the American Revolution, the War of 1812, and the Mexican War. Each peace produced its own treaty, acknowledging the existence of Indians and their rights. Treaty rights have not been given effect in statutes, however, Indian trade, social interaction, and religious travel spreads throughout North America. Many North American tribes had a strange, invisible, "magic line" run through their traditional territories, and it divides them. Some more notable examples are the Makah, the Kootenai, the Cree, the Chippewa, and the Iroquois Confederation groups, split by the U.S.-Canadian border, and the Pimas and Papagos (*Tohono O'odham*), split by the U.S.-Mexican border. Those barriers divide families and destroy communication. Members of the Native American Church want, and should have, free access to the Peyote fields of northern Mexico. A starting point for this human right will be full implementation of treaty rights to cross international boundaries[87] and international recognition of the human right of Indians to freely associate through such crossings.

Conclusion: Seeing With an Indian Eye

Human rights are a product of modern, post-Enlightenment, liberal secular humanism. It is a humanism that seeks to protect the individual against the state and those who have control of access to material goods and wealth. It is a strange humanism because it elevates the individual to the point that the group is forgotten.

Perhaps Octavio Paz is correct in saying, "The great wound of the West has been the separation of morality and history." He continues:

The secret of the resurrection of the democracies—and hence of true civilization—lies in the re-establishment of the dialogue between morality and history. This is the task of our generation and the one to come.[88]

"Morality" is a charged term, alienating many because of its association with religion. International human rights law, however, deals with "self-evident" and "natural law" rights, which have the same vague content. History, on the other hand, provides a measure for the application of a morality. Deprivations of Indian rights and assaults upon their group integrity are sufficiently documented to provide guidance, and the reality of the persistence of Indians and Indian-ness must be acknowledged and protected. Columbus and his Spanish followers had doubts about whether Indians were "human," given their agenda of conquest and settlement. Five hundred years later, it is time to accord full human dignity to Indians through human rights law.

Notes

1. Many ideas and facts outlined in this chapter are the product of fifteen years of practice of Indian affairs law and politics in the United States and Canada. Native teachers from other parts of the world have augmented my education. I hope that this piece says what many of the teachers would like me to say; and it is my way of saying thanks to patient and generous Cree, Navajo, Pima, Maori, and other teachers. Special thanks are due Geneva Stump of the Chippewa Cree Tribe of Montana, who introduced me to Indian affairs law in October 1974.

2. The term "Anglo" is used throughout this chapter to refer to the dominant "Anglo-European" culture of North America. It is preferable to the use of the term "White" to describe the major non-Indian ethnic group because it avoids racial stereotyping and stresses culture. While there clearly have been significant French and Hispanic cultural contributions in North America, the English language and its cultural values still dominate.

There are excellent arguments for use of the term "Native American," but it is best to call people by the term they normally refer to themselves. "Indian" still seems to be the term the Peoples call themselves. *But see*, Robert F. Berkhofer, Jr., *The White Man's Indian: Images of the American Indian from Columbus to the Present* (New York: Vintage Books, 1979), xvi–xvii, 196. "Native American" confuses some because Peoples such as Eskimos and Native Hawaiians have different circumstances (telephone interview with Bureau of Indian Affairs "recognition" regulation author [1977]).

While Mexico is a part of North America, this essay excludes discussion of the special circumstances there. Mexico also has problems integrating European and indigenous cultures. *See* Octavio Paz, *The Labyrinth of Solitude: Life and Thought in Mexico*, trans. Sander Kemp (New York: Grove Press, 1966); and Octavio Paz, *One Earth, Four or Five Worlds: Reflections on Contemporary History*, trans. Helen R. Lane (San Diego: Harcourt Brace Jovanovich, 1985), 100.

3. Lewis Hanke, *Aristotle and the American Indians: A Study in Race Prejudice in the Modern World* (London: Hollis and Carter, 1959); Charles Gibson, "Spanish Indian Policies," in *History of Indian-White Relations, Handbook of North American Indians*, ed. Wilcomb E. Washburn, vol. 4 (Washington, D.C.: Smithsonian Institution, 1988), 96.

Good evidence of the fact that Native peoples were not considered quite "human" in modern times is that, during the 1885 Battle of Batoche in Saskatchewan, a lover of the first machine gun, Lt. Arthur L. Howard of the Connecticut National Guard, happily used a Gatling Gun on Metis and Indian troops (Joseph K. Howard, *Strange Empire: Louis Riel and the Metis People* [Toronto: James Lewis and Samuel, 1952], 450–54). The machine gun was not used on Whites until World War I, but was often used on Native peoples before then (John Ellis, *Social History of the Machine Gun* [New York: Pantheon Books, 1975]). The current "dumb Indian" Anglo cultural perception is not quite so obvious, but it continues the pattern.

4. Cole Duram, Jr., "Indian Law in the Continental United States," *Law and Anthropology* 2 (1987): 93, 94–96; Douglas Sanders, "Aboriginal Rights in Canada," *ibid.* at 181–84, on assimilationist trends.

5. The leading American and Canadian Indian affairs law texts show this quite clearly. D. Getches, D. Rosenfelt, and C. Wilkinson, *Federal Indian Law* (1979); William Canby, *American Indian Law in a Nutshell* (St. Paul, Minn.: West Publishing, 1981); Felix S. Cohen, *Handbook of Federal Indian Law* (Charlottesville, Va.: Mitchie and Bobbs-Merrill, 1982); *Native Rights in Canada*, ed. Peter A. Cumming and Neil H. Mickenberg (Toronto: Indian-Eskimo Association of Canada, in association with General Publishing Co., 1972/1977). These texts discuss Anglo rules of law applicable to Indians and seldom discuss Indian common (customary) law.

6. While discussing things which should appear in this chapter, Lillie Roanhorse (a Navajo professional) advised that it must relate the fact Navajos and most other Indian Peoples refer to themselves in their own languages as "The People." Indians are not simply "humans" but "Peoples" in their own conceptualizations (Vine Deloria, *God is Red* [New York: Dell Publishing Co., 1973], 365–66 [table]). Gary Witherspoon holds a contrary view, stating that the assertion tribal peoples believe they are "the people" is a myth. He also says that the Navajo word "dine'," meaning "Navajo," "includes all people" (Language and Art in the Navajo Universe [Ann Arbor: University of Michigan Press, 1977], 96–97. His linguistic conclusion may be correct, but many Indians translate their tribal name as "The People."

7. The international human rights instruments are global, regional, or subsidiary. *See* Paul Sieghart, *The International Law of Human Rights* (Oxford: Clarendon Press, 1983), xv–xvii, for a listing of forty such documents. The twenty-one multilateral human rights instruments available for ratification as of July 1982, and their treatment by the United States and Canada, are listed in Committee on Foreign Affairs, *Human Rights Documents* (Washington, D.C.: United States Govern-

ment Printing Office, 1983), 609, 624–25, 612–13 (1983). Since then, the United States has finally ratified the Convention on the Prevention and Punishment of the Crime of Genocide in the Genocide Convention Implementation Act of 1987 (the Proxmire Act), Pub. L. No. 100–606, 102 Stat. 3045 (codified at 18 U.S.C. Ch. 50A). While the United States Senate voted (83 to 11) to give consent to the convention on February 19, 1986, actual ratification was conditioned upon the enactment of implementing legislation in the form of the 1987 Act (1988 U.S. Code Cong. & Admin. News [100 Stat.] 4156, 4157).

8. *See* Paquette Habana, 175 U.S. 677, 700 (1900); Kansas v. Colorado, 206 U.S. 46, 79 (1907); United States v. Enger, 472 F. Supp. 490, 504 (D.N.J. 1978); Zenith Radio Corp. v. Matsushita Ele. Indus. Co., 494 F. Supp. 1161, 1179 (E.D. Pa. 1980).

9. The court summarily dismissed international human rights claims that the Secretary of the Interior had erred in refusing to apply the law of the Blackfeet Tribe (of Montana) in the probate matter. The court rejected that claim by saying: "Likewise, the claim that the proceedings violated international law files in the face of overwhelming precedent to the effect that the type of sovereignty afforded to Indians does not diminish Congress' ability to legislate with respect to them even to the extent of abrogating treaty rights." Kicking Women v. Hodel, 878 F. 2d 1203, 1207 n. 10 (9th Cir. 1989) citations omitted.

10. While many nations, other than the United States, freely adopt international human rights conventions, the non-American rule normally is that treaties are not self-executing. (They are to some extent in the United States.) *See* note 7. This denies the human right of access to redress. The popular culture of the United States is essentially xenophobic and isolationist, as international law is viewed as alien.

11. Indian Act, R.S., c. 149, s. 1.

12. Attorney General of Canada v. Lavello, [1974] S.C.R. 1349.

13. Lovelace v. Canada, (R. 6/24) H.R.C. 36, 166; [1982] 1 C.N.L.R. 1.

14. *Ibid.* [1982] 1 C.N.L.R. at 8.

15. R.S., c. I–6, amended by c. 10 (2nd Supp.) 1975–75–76, c. 48, 1978–19; c. 11; 1980–81–82–83, cc. 47, 110; 1984, cc. 40, 41; 1985, c. 27.

16. Bradford W. Morse and Robert K. Groves, "Canada's Forgotten Peoples: The Aboriginal Rights of Metis and Non-Status Indians," *Law and Anthropology* 2(1987): 139, 150–51.

17. *See* "Minorities," *Encyclopedia of Public International Law* (Amsterdam, N. Y.: North-Holland Publishing, 1985), 395, 389, 390.

18. "Discrimination Against Individuals and Groups," *ibid.* at 134, 136, 137.

19. *Ibid.* at 137.

20. J. Sigler, *Minority Rights: A Comparative Analysis* (Westport, Conn.: Greenwood Press, 1983), 59–60.

21. James L. Brierly, *The Law of Nations: An Introduction to the International Law of Peace* (New York: Oxford University Press, 1963), 293–99.

22. Ian Brownlie, *Principles of Public International Law* (Oxford: Clarendon, 1966), 463.

23. Leslie C. Green, *Law and Society* (Dobbs Ferry, N.Y.: Oceana Publications, 1975), 304–05.

24. Myres S. McDougal, Harrold D. Lasswell and Lung-Chu Chen, *Human Rights and World Public Order: The Basic Policies of an International Law of Human Dignity* (New Haven, Conn.: Yale University Press, 1980).

25. *Ibid.* at 7–13.

26. Sieghart, *supra*, note 7, at 123–378.

27. Indian Law Resource Center, *Indian Rights-Human Rights: Handbook for Indians on International Human Rights Complaints Procedures* (Washington, D.C.: Indian Law Resource Center, 1988), 3.

28. Carl Waldman, *Atlas of the North American Indian* (New York: Facts on File Publications, 1985), 201.

29. *Ibid.* at 200.

30. *Ibid.* at 201.

31. *American Indian Policy Review Commission, Final Report* (Washington D.C.: United States Government Printing Office, 1977).

32. *United States Commission on Civil Rights, Indian Tribes* (Washington, D.C.: United States Government Printing Office, 1981).

33. Waldman, *supra* note 28, at 209.

34. *Ibid.* at 209–10.

35. Minister of Indian and Northern Affairs Canada, *Indian Conditions: A Survey* (Ottawa: Department of Indian Affairs and Northern Development, 1980).

36. Special Committee on Indian Self-Government, Indian Self-Government in Canada, House of Commons Issue No. 40 (published under authority of the Speaker of the House of Commons by the Queen's Printer for Canada, 1983).

37. The Federation of Saskatchewan Indian Nations, under the guidance of its barrister and solicitor, Delia Opekokew (Cree), published some particularly helpful Indian views on international law, including Delia Opekokew, *The First Nations: Indian Government and the Canadian Confederation* (Saskatoon, Sask.: Federation of Saskatchewan Indian Nations, 1980); Delia Opekokew, *The First Nations: Indian Governments in the Community of Man* (Regina, Sask.: Federation of Saskatchewan Indian Nations, 1982); and *World Assembly of First Nations, Roundtable on the Politics and Law of First Nations* (Saskatoon, Sask.: Federation of Saskatchewan Indian Nations, 1982), with useful model charters and covenants.

38. Interviews with Indian participants by the author (June–July, 1968).

39. *See* National Lawyers Guild, Committee on Native American Struggles, *Rethinking Indian Law* (New York: National Lawyers Guild, Committee on Native American Struggles, 1982); Rachel S. Kronowitz, Joanne Lichtman, Steven P. McSloy and Matthew G. Olsen, "Toward Consent and Cooperation: Reconsidering the Political Status of Indian Nations," *Harvard Civil Rights-Civil Liberties Law Review* 22(1987):22; Indian Law Resource Center, *supra* note 27.

40. *New Directions in American Indian History*, ed. C. Calloway (Norman, Okla.: University of Oklahoma Press, 1988), ix.

41. Gordon Bennett, *Aboriginal Rights in International Law* (London: Royal Anthropological Institute of Great Britain and Ireland, 1978).

42. Bernadette K. Roy and Dallas K. Miller, *The Rights of Indigenous Peoples in International Law: An Annotated Bibliography* (Saskatoon, Sask.: Native Law Centre, University of Saskatchewan, 1985); Ruth Thompson, *The Rights of Indigenous Peoples in International Law: Workshop Report* (Ottawa: International Conference on Aboriginal Rights and World Public Order, 1986).

43. Maureen Davies, "Aspects of Aboriginal Rights in International Law and Aboriginal Rights in International Law: Human Rights," in *Aboriginal Peoples and the Law: Indian, Metis and Inuit Rights in Canada*, ed. B. Morse (Ottawa: Carleton University Press, 1985), 16, 745.

44. Diane Bell and Pam Ditton, *Law: The Old and the New* (Canberra: Aboriginal History for Central Australian Aboriginal Legal Aid, 1980); P. Hanks and B. Keon-Cohen, eds., *Aborigines & The Law: Essays in Memory of Elizabeth Eggleston* (London: Allen and Unwin, 1984).

45. *See* note 39.

46. *See* Reports of the Fourth Russell Tribunal, *Conclusions; Selected Cases D U.S.A.; Non-Selected Cases A North America* (Amsterdam: Workgroup Indian Project/Projecto Indigena, 1980).

47. Daniel J. Boorstin, *The Discoverors* (New York: Random House, 1983), 480.

48. John F. Bryde, *Modern Indian Psychology* (Vermillion, S.D.:Institute of Indian Studies, University of South Dakota, 1971), 39–51.

49. Clyde Kluckhohn and Dorothea Leighton, *The Navajo* (Cambridge, Mass.: Harvard University Press, 1974), 100.

50. W. Denny, "The Great Words" (a one-page recitation of Cree "commandments," in both English and Cree [syllabuses], published by the Rocky Boy [Montana] High School. Among these are, "Young women should never kill an unborn baby. Babies are the Great Holy's blessing to human beings").

51. Robert K. Thomas, "Pan-Indianism," in *The American Indian Today*, ed. Stuart Levine and Nancy O. Lurie (Baltimore: Penguin Books, 1968), 128.

52. James W. Zion, "Trade as an Aboriginal Indian Right in North America," November 14, 1985, unpublished manuscript.

53. The drug scare increasingly chills the free exercise of religion by Native American Church members. In 1988 the author spoke with an attorney of the Civil Rights Division of the U.S. Justice Department to suggest a test case based upon discrimination against Native American Church members in the state of Montana. The attorney laughed and said, "With Nancy Reagan in the White House we would have to 'just say no' to that kind of case." Many Church members have related their stories of persecution to the author, and coupling these with increasing newspaper articles about arrests of Native American Church members and talks with various lawyers, the author can only conclude that such religious persecution is increasing.

54. K. Gilbreath, *Red Capitalism: An Analysis of the Navajo Economy* (1973), microfiche reprint.

55. Robert W. Young and William Morgan, *The Navajo Language: A Grammar and Colloquial Dictionary* (Albuquerque, N.M.: University of New Mexico Press, 1987), 811.

56. R. Barsh, "Navajo Property and Probate Law, 1940–1972," unpublished manuscript. This is a study of Navajo customary law used in written Navajo court decisions. The study, originally written in 1972 for the use of the Navajo courts, was revised by the author and is forthcoming in *Law and Anthropology*.

57. Berard Haile, O.F.M., *Women Versus Men: A Conflict of Navajo Emergence—The Curly-Tó Aheedlíinii Version*, ed. Karl W. Luckert, Navajo orthography by Irvy W. Goosen (Lincoln, Neb., and London: University of Nebraska Press, 1981); P. Zolbrod, *Din'e Bahane': The Navajo Creation Story* (Albuquerque, N.M.: University of New Mexico Press, 1984), 58–70, 272–75; A. Alfred Yazzie, *Navajo Oral Tradition* (Cortez, Colo.: Mesa Verde Press, 1984), 22–31.

Many individual Indians make statements or take positions with reference to their tribal Creation Scriptures, and Navajos commonly do this. The Navajo "River of Separation" Scripture refers to an incident that took place "at the time of emergence" of the Navajos. First Man and First Woman got into a fight, the details of which differ in various accounts, and the men moved to the other side of the River of Separation. The men prospered, while the women engaged in various depravities and starved. The men finally took pity on the women and took them back. This Scripture is cited to the effect that women should never be leaders. Later in this world, however, Changing Woman gave birth to the Heroes who slayed the Monsters who were destroying the *Dine*, the Navajos, and when the Sun (their father) demanded that Changing Woman join him, She demanded a house in the west, built floating upon shimmering water, gems, plants around the house, and animals. The Sun, wanting to know how She had the right to make such demands, was reminded of the essential equality of women and the need for male-female solidarity for there to be harmony in the universe. The Sun put His arm around Her and promised Her what She wanted.

On May 11, 1989, the author recited the Changing Woman Scripture, for the proposition that women do have a rightful place in Navajo Government, at the retirement luncheon of the first woman Navajo judge. The author suggested that the courts should lead the way and that the Tribal Council should fill upcoming judicial vacancies with women. Male Council members present reacted by disclaiming any view that women should not be tribal leaders, and shortly thereafter the Navajo Judiciary Committee recommended the nominations of two women, who were appointed as district judges. While the author makes no claims to have influenced the decision, the Navajo Courts approach gender equality in their numbers while women delegates are not seen in the council chambers.

58. Navajo Tribal Council Resolution CF–9–80 (February 1980); Help v. Silvers, 4 Navajo Reporter 46, 47–48 (Ct. App. 1983).

59. Paula G. Allen, *The Sacred Hoop: Recovering the Feminine in American Indian Traditions* (Boston: Beacon Press, 1986), 191–92; James Zion and Mary White, "The Use of Navajo Custom in Dealing with Rape," (unpublished manuscript, August 1986).

60. *See* Deloria, *supra* note 6; *Seeing With a Native Eye*, ed. Walter Holden Capps (New York: Harper and Row, 1976); Ake Hultkrantz, *The Religions of the American Indians* (Berkeley: University of California Press, 1979); Joseph E.

Brown, *The Spiritual Legacy of the American Indian* (New York: Crossroad Publishing Co., 1982).

61. Comment of an American Cree woman, 1982.

62. Comments of a Canadian Cree educator and an American Cree leader, 1984.

63. S. Gordon, "Indian Religious Freedom and Government Development of Public Lands," *Yale Law Journal* 94(1985): 1447; R. Michaelson, "The Significance of the American Indian Religious Freedom Act of 1978," *Journal of the American Academy of Religion* 52(1984):104.

64. Bowen v. Roy, 106 S. Ct. 2147 (1986) and Employment Division Department of Human Resources v. Smith, 108 S. Ct. 1444 (1988) particularly demonstrate cultural insensitivity. In *Roy* the Supreme Court dealt with an asserted Indian belief in the evil of using a Social Security number. The court, over a dissent pointing out methods of accommodation and mootness, held the weighty governmental interest in using such numbers outweighed the religious belief. In *Smith* the Court evaded the right of Indians to use Peyote for religious ceremonies in an accommodation of religious beliefs. The overwhelming American precedent to date was to the effect that Indian religious possession of Peyote is a protected right and that the Court had previously accommodated Anglo religious beliefs in a similar situation. The Court's application of the "barbarity principle" demonstrates the inability of Anglos to understand, appreciate, or tolerate Indian cultural beliefs. Canadian and American case law is full of such intolerance.

65. Sigler, *supra* note 20, at 55–56.

66. "Indigenous Populations, Treaties With," *supra* note 17, at 314–316.

67. Cohen, *supra* note 5, at 221–22; Cuming and Mickenberg, *supra* note 5, at 61–62.

68. Green, "Human Rights and the General Principles of Law," *supra* note 23 at 228.

69. Barre Toelken, "Seeing with a Native Eye: How Many Sheep Will It Hold?" in *Seeing With a Native Eye, supra* note 60.

70. F. Capotorti, *Study on the Rights of Persons Belonging to Ethnic, Religious and Linguistic Minorities*, U.N. E CN.4/Sub. 2/384/Rev. 1 (New York: United Nations, 1979). The right to culture, if viewed with a native eye, has great potential.

71. Human rights have little relevance if they are unenforceable in national bodies and the machinery of the state. Most international covenants and bilateral treaties require or envision the enactment of domestic legislation to enforce them. Too often that does not happen, and Indian rights are overlooked, or they are implemented in strictly limited legislation. There should be an individual and group human right to confront national governments in effective ways, including international bodies.

72. *See, for example*, A. Dundes, ed., *Every Man His Way* (Englewood Cliffs, N.J.:Prentice Hall, 1968), 157, for a review of the definitional literature.

73. Canadian Commission for UNESCO, *A Working Definition of Culture for the Canadian Commission for UNESCO* 6 (1977).

74. "Indigenous Populations, Protection," *supra* note 17, at 313.

75. E. Schusky, *The Right to be Indian* (San Francisco: The Indian Historical Press, 1976).

76. Alexander Lesser, "The Right Not to Assimilate: The Case of the American Indian," in *History, Evolution, and the Concept of Culture*, ed. S. Mintz (New York: Cambridge University Press, 1985), 108.

77. Genocide Convention Implementation Act of 1987.

78. Deloria, *supra* note 6.

79. Self-determination requires abandonment of the stereotype of the "dumb Indian" as well as those of the "barbarism principle," "the White way is the right way," and other destructive attitudes. *See* Robert F. Berkhofer, Jr., *supra* note 2. When the United States attempted to implement the concept through the Indian Self-Determination Act of 1975, bureaucratic resistance within the Bureau of Indian Affairs delayed its start. Indian tribal programs under the act are underfunded, and tribes have not been given the resources to meet the need described by the demographics above. One of the worst barriers is institutionalized racism within the United States federal government, and it pervades the "Indian programs" of all federal agencies. *See* "In Search of Pride," *MacLean's* (July 3, 1989), 40–41.

80. *See* Capotorti, *supra* note 70.

81. Anthropologists use the term "persistence of culture" to describe the phenomenon of peoples who continue as groups despite destructive pressures from the outside and even because of those pressures. *Persistent Peoples: Cultural Enclaves in Perspective*, ed. George P. Castile and Gilbert Kushner (Tucson: University of Arizona Press, 1981). The same theory describes the Indian situation. *See* Daniel H. Levine, "The Survival of Indian Identity," in *The American Indian Today, supra* note 51, at 9. The moral is, "If you can't beat them, join them."

82. World Commission on Environment and Development, Our Common Future (New York: Oxford University Press, 1987).

83. *Ibid.*, at 114–16.

84. *See* The Rockefeller Foundation, *International Perspectives on Affirmative Action* (New York: Rockefeller Foundation, 1984), a survey of affirmative action laws in nine countries, both developing and industrialized. Unlike the rubric of international law mentioned, there is a great deal of room for cultural pluralism, and such would strengthen any national body.

85. Morton v. Mancari, 417 U.S. 535 (1974).

86. There are two kinds of anti-Indian "hate groups" in the United States. Some are composed of "Indian fighter" organizations of Anglo landowners who are subject to tribal regulation. In the state of Montana, the groups All Citizens Equal (ACE) and Citizens Rights Organization (CRO, from the Crown Reservation area) are very active and very dangerous. *See* Minutes of the November 18, 1988, meeting of the Committee on Indian affairs, 50th Montana Legislature. The second category of anti-Indian hate groups is more subtle. These are the state governments and governmental subdivisions. While they oppose Indians on intellectual legal grounds, given the fighting of battles long settled in the favor of Indian government, the veneer of legality thinly overlays a core of racism. *See also* Robert F. Berkhofer, Jr., *supra* note 2, at 135 (on imposed White models).

87. Legal Information Service, Native Law Center, University of Saskatchewan, *Customs, Immigration and the Jay Treaty, Report No. 4* (Saskatoon, Sask.: Native Law Centre, 1981). The United States provides for fairly free Indian border crossing by statute, while Canada does not. Even where Indians have the legal right to cross, they complain of a great deal of legal harassment. Some Canadian border guards deny entry on the ground that the Indian applicants do not have sufficient funds for their stay, despite ties to relatives in Canada. There are other problems as well. *See* James W. Zion, *supra* note 52.

88. Paz, *supra* note 2, at 49.

Allan McChesney

9. Aboriginal Communities, Aboriginal Rights, and the Human Rights System in Canada

The peoples who first inhabited the northern part of the North American continent were more concerned with mutual responsibility for the survival and well-being of the group than with concepts akin to individual human rights. After five centuries of pressure from Europeans and their social philosophies, communitarian views are still widely held by descendants of the original peoples of what are now Canada and the United States.[1] Yet, just as some institutions of the now dominant society may have borrowed ideas on democracy and diplomacy from the First Nations,[2] the indigenous residents have not been immune to the political and social ideas surrounding them over the past five hundred years. Just as the diverse tribes, clans, and nations traded and learned from each other before white colonizers arrived, Native peoples have sometimes chosen to adopt and adapt ideas from their oppressors.[3]

Although there is a great diversity of religious, political, and social beliefs and organizations among indigenous peoples, there is a strong and wide current of shared ideals. This point is made by others in this book, notably Patricia Hyndman and James W. Zion. There remain sufficient differences, however, that, given the choices, some groups might opt for the Canadian model of legislated and enforceable human rights, while others would choose more traditional methods of ensuring dignity for all members of their communities. A belief held universally by people who consider themselves to be Aboriginal is that their communities have the right to determine their own destiny, including forms of government and modes of protection for human rights and/or human dignity. While many groups, in Canada and elsewhere, would choose as much political separation as possible from the dominant wider society, others might prefer a high degree of assimilation, hoping that it will lead to a better life. The principles espoused by the World Council of Indigenous Peoples explicitly allow for this broad spectrum of self-determination.[4]

Other authors in this volume explore the essential differences in philosophy between indigenous peoples and those of European origin. The latter are said to place stress on competitive individualism, including striving for individual rights and liberties against the state and against each other. Native peoples are characterized as holding to tenets of solidarity. These are reflected in the idea that dignity is achieved by fulfillment of understood roles, through community sharing, and by espousal of group rights as paramount over individual aspirations.

The first four centuries of contact between whites and First Peoples involved widespread, acquisitory brutality on the part of Europeans that has often been termed genocidal. Canada continues to be, in large measure, assimilationist.[5] Nevertheless, since World War II, there has been social and legal progress in Canada in the field of human rights, including the rights of Aboriginal communities and individuals. This chapter focuses on the interrelations between indigenous persons and groups in Canada and the human rights safeguard systems developed by the dominant society over the past four decades. I shall begin with a look at the mechanisms established in Canada to combat discrimination and to promote equal opportunity within the capitalist system. The implications of Canada's 1982 Constitution will also be considered, as will the relevance of international human rights law. The chapter will conclude with speculation as to what form human rights protective systems might take within self-determined, self-governed aboriginal jurisdictions associated with Canada.

Does Antidiscrimination Legislation in Canada Serve the Interests of Native Individuals and Communities?

Starting in the 1960s, the Canadian provinces consolidated and improved scattered legislation that dealt with prohibition of racial and other discrimination. By the mid-1970s, every province, as well as the federal government, had a comprehensive statute forbidding discrimination, generally in employment, residential and business accommodation, government and commercial services, advertising, and other forms of public communication.[6] Some human rights codes also include certain fundamental freedoms;[7] one includes broad recognition of economic, social, and cultural rights.[8] The grounds on which discrimination is prohibited vary, but most jurisdictions outlaw unfair treatment on grounds of race, national or ethnic origin, ancestry, color, religion, creed, age, sex, marital status, and physical disability.[9] The highest judicial authority in Canada has decided that the law extends to unintentional or "systemic" discrimination as well as to that which is direct or intentional.[10] Generally, complaints of adverse discrimination, if they meet statutory criteria, cause a commission or an equivalent body to attempt settlement between the alleged discriminators and the victims. In a few cases, the dispute is decided by an administrative board or tribunal, or by a court.

Institutions set up in Canada to fight discriminatory practices try to promote equality through public education and special programs that attempt to redress imbalances.[11] The inequities addressed are often in employment. Ameliorative methods include hiring goals and timetables designed to achieve fairer participation by groups perceived to be at a disadvantage because of past unfair practices. These affirmative action measures are sometimes called "employment equity" plans. Though these schemes are sometimes targeted at one group, a number focus on several at once, namely, women, Aboriginal peoples, ethnocultural minorities, and individuals with physical or mental disabilities.

The counterdiscrimination mechanisms in Canada have helped to change perceptions of what constitutes social justice and to remove barriers for large numbers of people. Formal complaints often lead to a settlement. When a hearing is held and the decision-making body finds the grievances to be valid, it is empowered to choose from a variety of remedies. For example, when access to a job or service has been denied, effective access can be ordered, along with financial compensation for costs incurred and for psychological damage caused by discrimination. In employment matters, there might also be an order for reinstatement (or a fair chance to compete for a post) and reimbursement for lost income. In rare cases, orders have required an employer to change practices to rectify discrimination that might continue to hurt people in circumstances similar to that of the complainant. These changes of practice may be termed "systemic" remedies.

From a European-rooted perspective, there may seem many reasons why a Native person would want the help of a human rights commission to clear away barriers to a better life for one's self, one's family, or one's community. There is ample evidence that people of indigenous heritage in Canada are marginalized in terms of livelihood opportunities, health, public services, education, traditional religious practices, and participation in non-Aboriginal governments.[12] Aboriginal peoples have endured pervasive systemic discrimination since the first European settled here. Someone striving for social justice might see human rights codes and their complaint mechanisms to be logical weapons to remove barriers to self-fulfillment for Aboriginal citizens. The bodies which supervise human rights legislation imagine themselves to be accessible to everyone. Great formality is not required in the filing of a complaint; there is no fee for service; and legal assistance, when required, is usually provided by the commission (or equivalent body) itself. Yet, many human rights commission officials, Aboriginal lawyers, community activists, and academics are of the opinion that the federal, provincial, and territorial human rights monitoring organs are not adequate to serve the interests of the indigenous population and are indeed avoided by the majority of those who suffer discrimination.

One can argue that it is in the interests of group survival for Native individuals to avoid calling on the assistance of human rights commissions or courts. Some grievances registered by an Aboriginal person might be contrary to the welfare of his or her community. A complaint against a body controlled by Natives weakens the solidarity of a group that many view as already being vulnerable. Whether the claim of discrimination is made against a Native-controlled or another government, it lends legitimacy to the mores and institutions of the dominant society, by whom human rights norms are imposed.

Based on demography and on the level of discrimination encountered, the caseload of complaints by Native people has usually been inordinately low.[13] My guess, however, is that most people who face adverse treatment because of their Aboriginal-ness do not hold back from contacting human rights enforcement authorities because of a firm philosophical objection or because it would conflict with long-term strategies for achieving a self-determined, Native-governed nation. Many indigenous individuals also seem reluctant to seek aid under employment standards legislation that governs safety, income, and other conditions of work, or to ask provincial Ombudsmen for assistance in attacking government red tape and bureaucratic arbitrariness.[14]

Gathering from my own experience and from advice offered by those consulted for this chapter, I shall speculate as to why Native individuals do not tend to rely on antidiscrimination laws and other instruments devoted to human rights protection in Canada. I shall also offer suggestions as to how Aboriginal people might be encouraged and assisted, if and where appropriate, to make use of these institutions.

For attempting to facilitate interaction between indigenous people and institutions monitoring antidiscrimination statutes, I could be criticized for adding to the encumbrances that prevent First Nations from the true solution to their human rights problems, namely, autonomy through self-determination.[15] Indigenous peoples in North American have undergone a history of domination and attempted assimilation by white-controlled governments and other institutions (commercial, educational, and religious). The optimal future would permit Native communities a full choice as to which traditional and nontraditional forms of rights and responsibilities to uphold in their jurisdictions.[16] Yet self-determination within (or without) Canadian Confederation is not just around the corner. There is also an unknown limit to the quantity of "special" rights which non-Native politicians and other citizens will support for Aboriginal communities in the short term, even though the degree of acceptance of Aboriginal claims by the wider society has shifted favorably in the past twenty years.

Given the uncertainty of achieving self-determination or even limited self-governance soon,[17] it is not surprising that, while struggling for the return of self-determination, many Native leaders have made strategic compromises, making use of existing institutions and laws.[18] Such tactics include constitutional litigation and attempts to influence political parties and governments from the inside. Sometimes Aboriginal groups are compelled to take part, because they are responding to court actions launched by others or because the political process impedes the path toward self-determination.[19]

Individuals who do not consciously confront what others see as philosophical and political inconsistencies, however, still do not turn to human rights laws for help against discrimination. Listed below are reasons which appear to keep Aboriginal persons from taking advantage of available antidiscrimination mechanisms. This list underscores some contrasts between the values of dominant groups in Canada and the belief systems of indigenous peoples.

1. Some Native people undoubtedly have refused to contact a human rights commission because they believe that assertion of their individual rights will damage the collective interests of their band,

tribe, community, or First Nation. Although commissions try to resolve complaints through conciliation and settlements, the ultimate resolution may be through an adversarial hearing. A principle espoused by Aboriginal peoples and still widely practiced is that solutions ought to be arrived at through consensus and compromise.[20] The machinery adopted for enforcement of antidiscrimination laws may thus seem alien.

2. The idea of individual human rights being legislated and enforced through formal structures may be seen as just one more "white" concept to deal with, after years of having to react to unsolicited ideas. It may exist to solve "their" problems, not "ours."

3. Logic suggests that assistance offered by white people's organizations should not be trusted. After all, it has been whites who occupied and misused Native lands, and who have refused to recognize Aboriginal traditions, wildlife harvesting rights, and so forth.

4. History teaches that there is no particular reason to trust institutions provided by the government, whether "white" or "multicultural." As the old joke puts it, one of the three most common lies is, "Hi, we're from the government. We're here to help you."

5. Human rights commissions are provided by the government and are seen as part of government. To a Native person, or to anyone else, it may not make sense that a mechanism provided by the government will or can do a good job of fighting government discrimination. This perception of lack of independence is sometimes shared by government personnel, who have been known to be incensed about having a complaint pursued against them by their "own" human rights commission.

6. Another source of hesitation based in reality is the notion that human rights commissions are slow, bureaucratic, and ineffectual.

7. A high proportion of Native people are partly or heavily dependent on some form of financial or other support from territorial, provincial, or federal governments. Many are fearful that a complaint registered against one part of the bureaucracy will lead to harmful repercussions somewhere down the line.

8. Given the overlap (some say "confusion") in responsibilities among federal, provincial, and Aboriginal community governments, there is difficulty in sorting out who is responsible for what. Consider, for instance, a federal program subcontracted to

a provincial agency carried out on an Indian reserve—not an un-
common situation.

9. Commissions often treat indigenous peoples as being like any
   other "minority," an approach Natives see as wrong.[21]

10. Human rights commissions have sometimes avoided pursuing the
    types of complaints of most concern to Native people, thereby
    damaging credibility. For example, in its early days, the Ontario
    Human Rights Commission, one of the two largest in the coun-
    try, reportedly acted as if complaints by Native people about
    police discrimination were not appropriate matters for the Com-
    mission to handle.

11. In some cases, there has been a conflict between the terms and
    concepts fostered by a human rights commission and those of par-
    ticular Aboriginal communities. Some individual Indian bands, for
    example, have at times expressed profound discomfort with guar-
    antees of gender equality or with the prohibition of discrimination
    on the ground of sexual orientation. From the other side, agencies
    have displayed a lack of knowledge and sensitivity toward Aborigi-
    nal concepts and terms.

12. Other indicia of insensitivity may discourage approaches to hu-
    man rights institutions: lack of native staff; unavailability of
    Native language services; a staff unprepared by cross-cultural
    training.

13. Many Native people, conditioned by experience, are resigned to
    racist slurs and discrimination as being facts of life that have no
    remedy.

14. For a host of reasons, some Aboriginal individuals do not have a
    positive self-image and feel quite vulnerable to external forces. It
    is seen as dangerous to rock the boat. If one is from a group that
    has limited opportunities and very high unemployment, there
    would be a tendency to want to hang on to one's job, for example,
    and suffer whatever forms of discrimination one may endure as a
    result.

There has existed a measure of apathy on the part of human rights
institutions concerning whether Native people made effective use of them.
Nevertheless, there are human rights bodies and experienced personnel
who believe that significant benefit can be obtained by Native peoples
through recourse to antidiscrimination law. They think it is important to

make the current antidiscrimination measures more accessible to indigenous persons. None of the people consulted for this chapter, [22] all of Native origin or/and experienced in working with Aboriginal groups, stated that human rights law should be totally rejected as a method of seeking resolution of disputes affecting indigenous people. Here, then, are some suggested initiatives to help bridge the gap between Aboriginal individuals and communities and institutions intended to promote human rights:

1. While human rights legislation is being developed, there should be consultation with all groups affected, including Native communities. This approach was adopted by the Northwest Territories during the preparation of a draft Human Rights Code, [23] and by the Yukon Territory while its Human Rights Act was being drafted. [24] Some Canadian provinces have held public hearing when contemplating revisions of their human rights statutes. When planning new amendments, as well as the regulations that put specific mechanisms into place, it seems wise to seek input addressed to the needs of Native persons if governments and monitoring bodies genuinely wish to serve Aboriginal interests. Moreover, people are more likely to make use of an institution for which they feel some ownership.

2. During discussions in contemplation of human rights legislation in both the Northwest Territories and the Yukon, Aboriginal organizations and lawyers representing them expressed reservations about human rights codes being used by non-Natives to erode Aboriginal rights and to challenge special programs promoting equality of opportunity in employment and other fields. Both territories chose to allay these fears somewhat by indicating in their respective legislative drafts that the statute would not adversely affect Aboriginal rights. Statements to this effect were in each case proclaimed in the preamble as well as in the main text. [25]

3. An obvious step is to have Native people on the staff and governing body of a commission, to encourage applications from Native complainants and to increase the sensitivity of the supervisory body.

4. Specific staff may be designated as being in charge of complaints from Aboriginal people. It is likely that this tactic will work even better if the designate is of Aboriginal ancestry. This approach was adopted by the Human Rights Commission of New Brunswick, which afterward reported significant caseload increases. [26]

5. When choosing personnel to handle complaints from Native people, relevant Aboriginal communities could take part in the selection process. They might also retain an advisory role to ensure some accountability of the chosen staff. [27]

6. The aura of accessibility can be enhanced through symbols, for example, Native art in and outside the commission's premises, and Native images and faces on commission documents.

7. Innovative approaches need to be undertaken in public outreach and publicity. Like everyone else in Canada, Natives have seen so many government pamphlets that there is a tendency to become inured to them. Few such publications are available in Native languages. Given their tradition of aural learning, it seems appropriate to reach out to Native people through personal visits to their communities by human rights staff and board members (commissioners).

8. Part of the outreach strategy can be regular liaison with Native organizations that funnel complaints and provide policy input. Assuming that a complaint is not against the organization itself, it may be easier for an individual to make contact without having to deal initially with the quasigovernmental bureaucracy.

9. Another stratagem is to give a measure of priority to complaints received from people of Aboriginal ancestry. Cases are normally handled according to the date of application. Since human rights bodies in Canada are notoriously slow, the expediting of a particular group of cases that has been handled badly in the past could generate an improvement in reputation, at least in the communities benefited.

10. The annual report of a human rights commission may be widely discussed. The Yukon publishes its yearly report in the Aboriginal languages used in the territory, as well as in French and English.[28] Commissions elsewhere could translate their reports into the major indigenous languages in their jurisdictions.

11. Using some of the techniques mentioned above, a commission would hopefully build a sufficient volume of cases assisting Native people to attain some continuing credibility among the Native public.

The enumerated suggestions could apply to improvement of service for any group, not just for Aboriginal peoples. Yet, in attempting to carry out these "common sense" steps, one can learn about concepts of human rights and dignity in one culture that do not "compute" in the other. For example, during translation of the 1988 Annual Report of the Yukon Human Rights Commission, it was discovered that the term "equal," in its human rights context, did not have an equivalent in any of the six Aboriginal languages used in the publication.[29]

In keeping with the theme of this book, I would recommend that human rights commissions take account of the tensions between their legislative schemes and the need of Aboriginal communities to protect collective rights. Most of the following approaches have been tried in Canada, with some success. I presume that these kinds of approaches could be used in any country with a framework to combat racial discrimination.

1. While not neglecting efforts to ensure good opportunities for Native individuals in industrialized and government sectors, the human rights authority can push for special programs that foster the traditional livelihoods engaged in by Aboriginal peoples. In Canada, these include hunting, trapping, fishing, the harvesting of wild rice and other edibles, and in some areas farming and lumbering. Given the general disadvantages and barriers faced by members of most Native communities in the "modern" technological and government economies, it makes sense to build on their traditions and expertise in customary lines of endeavor, and to protect their interests from encroachment by non-Aboriginal competitors.[30] We must remember that customary indigenous livelihoods are not merely "economic" in nature, but are also intertwined with cultural and spiritual traditions.

2. Hiring and promotion policies, particularly in the public service, should give proper consideration to the skills, inventiveness, and knowledge learned in traditional livelihoods and assign these due weight in assessing employment qualifications.

3. Commissions can focus on discriminatory practices harmful to the security of Native communities. This might call for concentration on improving police-Aboriginal relations and pursuit of any complaints of discrimination by the police. The education field also requires attention, respecting curriculum and participation of Native staff and administrators.[31]

4. Individual rights claims might weaken the struggle for autonomous group rights. Some discrimination, however, may *itself* undermine collective Aboriginal rights. In Canada there is a long tradition of oppressing Native religious practices. The law has been used to challenge limitations faced by Native inmates desiring to participate more freely in traditional religious ceremonies while in prison.[32] In this same vein, a commission could support the wish of an individual to take a day off work on a day sacred in that person's particular Aboriginal religion.

5. Cross-cultural perceptions ought to be represented on the board which oversees human rights commission work. It is its task to promote public education and to monitor the intake and handling of complaints.

For those few cases resolved through a hearing, in most Canadian jurisdictions a "board of inquiry" or "tribunal" is appointed from a predeter-
mined list of decision-makers. This panel of adjudicators should also
reflect the cultural mosaic. In an area with a high proportion of Aboriginal
people, they should attain more than token representation among the potential and actual adjudicators. They can bring a different evaluation of
what fair conduct means when applying the letter of the antidiscrimination law. Their contribution would be valuable in deciding what redress
might be appropriate for a justified complaint. It is wise to assemble respected members of different communities so that no group senses bias.
In appointing a province-wide commission, one must at least be aware,
however, of elements who think that Natives already receive unfair
advantages.

6. To foster real and perceived fairness, particularly when one party
to a dispute is Aboriginal, it seems astute to follow the example set by the
Yukon in implementing its *Human Rights Act*. Although the option exists
to hold a hearing before a single person acting as a "panel of adjudication,"
this has never been done.[33] By having two to five people joining in a decision, a variety of views, including those of Native people, are represented. This approach also takes some pressure off an adjudicator who
must make a decision while living in a relatively small and close-knit
community.

7. To accommodate Aboriginal ways of resolving disputes, procedures
of a "panel of adjudication," or a body with a similar function, could be
made less formal. The widespread practice of Aboriginal communities, of
trying to reach decisions through consensus rather than through majority
voting practices, can be adopted by the adjudicating organ. Where both
parties have strenuous objections, the process could be modified to be
more legalistic. In essence, though its legislation does not call for deciding
through consensus, that is the practice of boards of adjudication in the
Yukon Territory.[34]

8. Where a complaint of discrimination or unequal treatment does
not fit under local human rights legislation, a commission attuned to
the needs of Aboriginal peoples can assist to have the case dealt with
by the proper authority. This can involve simply referral to another human
rights commission in Canada, but could go further. If the appropriate
recourse appears to be constitutional litigation, the claimant could be
given some guidance about this possibility. Where the laws of Canada
cannot assist, the claimant could be helped to file a petition with the

proper body of the United Nations. The Yukon Human Rights Commission, as an example, has supported reference of two cases of significance to Native people to the Human Rights Committee which oversees the International Covenant on Civil and Political Rights.[35] Thus, while attending to the interests of individuals through the work of a human rights statute, the supervisory body could also be facilitating the protection of the rights of Aboriginal communities through international influence on Canada.

9. Collective rights of communities can be promoted through public statements from the directorship of a commission. For example, the chief commissioner of the Canadian Human Rights Commission, as well as the deputy chief have highlighted the need to protect group rights to help improve the circumstances of Aboriginal peoples in Canada.[36] The commission's 1988 and 1989 Annual Reports underscored the failings of Canadian society in this regard.[37]

One way to reinforce protection of rights for some Native persons is to amend constricting legislation. The *Canadian Human Rights Act* stipulates explicitly that the provisions of the *Indian Act* and actions pursuant to it are not subject to the oversight of the *Human Rights Act*.[38] This is problematic from an individual rights perspective, because sometimes Native leaders are thought to carry out discriminatory practices. The *Human Rights Act* is not available to counteract what some, particularly women, see as discrimination by the governments of Native communities. This problem may arise when individuals are denied the benefits of membership in an Indian band because of membership rules or the way they are applied.[39]

This problem was exacerbated by changes to the *Indian Act* that permitted many women and children to obtain or regain Indian status, without adequate resources being conveyed to Indian communities by the federal government to permit satisfactory absorption of the newcomers (or returners) into education, housing, health, and community development facilities. There have been discussions of possible amendments to the *Canadian Human Rights Act* to permit complaints by individuals against their own Native organizations. The goals of gender equality and of enabling people to participate fully in their cultural community are worthy, but there is a downside. The imposition of rulings from an external source (a human rights commission or adjudicatory tribunal) would weaken the authority of the band and would give priority to individual aspirations over group solidarity objectives. Even if a human rights commission attempts to operate like a council of elders (as in the Yukon),[40] it does not spring from indigenous traditions.

In recent years, there have been efforts in the United States and Canada to set up "tribal courts" or analogous institutions to dispense justice within particular Aboriginal communities. The procedures and allowable sentences or orders of the decision-makers often are different from those applied in similar circumstances in the general Canadian or American court systems. If an internal court were serving an Aboriginal group or region, that organ could assume some of the powers of a human rights supervisory body. Alternatively, the latter function would be available when problems arose between Aboriginal individuals or groups and people from outside the community. A positive experience with the justice dispensed by a distinct "tribal," "band," or "national" court might promote the idea that fair treatment and effective remedies might also be possible from a human rights commission in other circumstances.

Traditional Aboriginal Livelihoods in the Era of Affirmative Action

All Canadian human rights commissions encourage "special programs" to improve economic (or other) opportunities of disadvantaged groups. Such endeavors are protected from legal attack (on the ground of alleged "reverse discrimination") by section 15(2) of the Canadian Constitution.[41] In the employment domain, affirmative action plans are aimed at a number of groups, including women, disabled individuals, and Aboriginal peoples. The economic pursuits of Native people can also be protected through negotiated agreements with different levels of Canadian government and/or through the application of sections 25 and 35 of the Constitution, which safeguard (undefined) "Aboriginal rights."[42]

It is difficult to draw a line between "affirmative action" and protection of "Aboriginal rights." Ordinarily, "affirmative action" refers to measures intended to augment and enrich employment opportunities for members of Native (or other) groups in the governmental, commercial, or "modern" industrial sectors. I perceive "Aboriginal rights" to encompass, among other things, traditional livelihood pursuits (whether or not facilitated by recent technology) such as hunting, trapping, and food-gathering on territories of land, water, or ice.

Some affirmative action schemes strive to be sensitive to the cultural, economic, and social rights of indigenous collectivities. For example, a number of natural resource-based projects in Saskatchewan and Manitoba, as well as in the Northwest Territories, accommodate Native workers in ways that make it easier for them to retain elements of their traditional lifestyles. Employees may be flown to a work site for extended work periods (such as a fortnight of long hours) and then returned to their families and communities for an equal duration. Schedules may be juggled to permit Natives to be home during the main hunting, fishing, or trapping seasons. In areas remote from major population centers, a significant proportion of the Aboriginal residents use age-old methods of obtaining food (albeit with modern tools). The activities associated with these pursuits are central to the retention of Aboriginal culture: teaching of children, close contact with natural surroundings, and the sharing of benefits within the Aboriginal community.[43]

Some special programs in Canada encourage the training and hiring of Native people in job categories wherein they are underrepresented. In some jurisdictions, efforts are made to build upon the expertise acquired over generations by original peoples in livelihoods which they seek to protect through Aboriginal claims negotiations with Canadian governments. In this sphere there are stark contrasts between the way human rights are perceived by white and Aboriginal people. From a legal standpoint, Native leaders see traditional modes of subsistence as being intertwined with Aboriginal rights and also closely connected with concepts of pride, dignity, and collective cultural and physical survival. Some non-Native individuals say that Natives want to "have it both ways." They want affirmative action to gain equal opportunity in "modern" sectors, yet want to keep certain pursuits as their exclusive preserve. This premise may in fact be true, but in my view it is fair for Aboriginals to advocate both policies at the same time. Programs that support continuation of work by Natives in customary employment have sometimes been met with resentment and/or sometimes with lawsuits by whites who feel "cut out of the action" or subjected to "reverse discrimination."[44] Among the regimes attacked by non-Native interests have been priority fishing rights held by Natives in the Northwest Territories and trapping rights of Aboriginal people in the Yukon.[45]

Government support programs to assist Native people are imperfect attempts to redress some of the social devastation linked to centuries of alternating oppression and neglect. There is appeal in the idea of financial assistance to facilitate the continuation of desired but fiscally marginal live-lihoods. The cost-benefit equation of traditional implements and transpor-tation methods used in hunting, fishing, trapping, and so forth, was more favorable than is that of rifles, steel traps, snowmobiles, motorized boats, and the habit of buying some food and supplies from the local cooperative or Hudson's Bay store. Though it makes sense to support work tied to collective Aboriginal rights, sometimes the way in which hunter and trap-per support programs are administered could contribute to the erosion of community bonds. The making of direct payments to individual hunters or trappers may encourage movement toward atomization, that is, small family units within the capitalist economic system.[46] An approach recom-mended by certain authorities as being more sensitive to indigenous com-munitarian traditions involves the payment of aggregate sums (on a per capita or per family basis) to a hunters' or trappers' association or to an Aboriginal government.[47] In either alternative, one presumes that the money received would be more likely to contribute to the solidarity and collective rights of the recipient community.

Just as governments can adopt an inappropriate method of imple-menting a well-meant policy, the judiciary can block positive measures through insensitive interpretation of the law, as was demonstrated in a case dealing with affirmative action in Manitoba.[48] The circumstances involved the type of activity I find difficult to categorize as either "employment justifying affirmative action" or "the exercise of Aboriginal rights," namely, the harvesting of wild rice. Since time immemorial, North Ameri-can indigenous peoples have gathered this crop. Recently, as wild rice has become a fashionable food, agribusiness firms have developed new culti-vation and mechanized harvesting methods and increased their market share. During the 1980s, Manitoba established a licensing scheme for wild rice production, with preference given to Aboriginal applicants. This was seen as affirmative action allowable under provincial human rights legis-lation, because according to economic and social indicators, Natives were a disadvantaged group suffering from systemic discrimination.

Some non-Native wild rice interests challenged the scheme. Their al-legation that the scheme was discriminatory, and not exempted as a pro-gram of affirmative action, was upheld. The trial judge apparently lacked understanding both of Aboriginal collective rights and of "affirmative action." He thought that for an affirmative action plan to be valid, each individual who benefits from it must demonstrate that he or she is "disadvantaged." This misunderstanding ignored the principle that affirmative action attempts to remedy the general disadvantage suffered by a group because of systemic discrimination.[49]

The insensitivity shown by the trial judge in *Apsit* illustrates two dangers faced by Aboriginal communities when the legal concepts of the dominant society in Canada are applied to them. The way the court approached the case allowed for serious debate about whether collective Aboriginal rights deserved to be paramount over the individual economic rights asserted by the non-Native wild rice concerns. The judge also did not heed twentieth-century thinking that holds that for equality to be achieved, it is sometimes necessary to treat different groups differently, and to give assistance to the group that is dominated or "disadvantaged."[50] Judges who do not take a sophisticated approach to human rights laws can harm Aboriginal communities. By reinforcing attitudes of "reverse discrimination," they could leave particular groups worse off than if a human rights statute had never been enacted. Since the Constitution of Canada is our "supreme law" (Constitution Act, section 52), an unthoughtful constitutional decision could do greater damage, since the Constitution "trumps" any other law. That area of potential difficulty will be addressed in the next segment of this chapter.

Collective Aboriginal Rights, Rights of Individuals, and the Canadian Constitution

For First Nations, the ultimate campaign for rights involves the group rights of indigenous peoples, whose governing bodies are not explicitly recognized by the Canadian Constitution. The focus of much recent writing, and the area to be addressed here, is the perceived conflict between the rights of individuals and the collective rights of Aboriginal communities.

While the Canadian Charter of Rights and Freedoms safeguards the rights of individuals against the state, a number of its components are protective of collective rights. There are provisions dealing with linguistic rights for Canada's two major language groups (English and French), minority language education rights, multicultural rights, and equality rights for disadvantaged groups.[51] Most essential to our purposes is section 25, which does not proclaim specific rights but states that the guarantee of rights and freedoms within the Charter "shall not be construed so as to abrogate or derogate from any aboriginal, treaty or other rights or freedoms that pertain to the aboriginal peoples of Canada. . . . " Outside the Charter, in Part II of the *Constitution Act, 1982*, is section 35(1), which states that "existing aboriginal and treaty rights of the aboriginal peoples" are recognized and affirmed.

The principal constitutional statements of individual rights that can conflict with collective indigenous rights are sections 15 and 28. Section 15(1) guarantees equality before and under the law, and the equal benefit and protection of the law. Section 28 stipulates that, notwithstanding anything else in the Charter, "the rights and freedoms referred to in it are guaranteed equally to male and female persons." This precept is reinforced for Aboriginal concerns by section 35(4):

> Notwithstanding any other provision of this Act, the aboriginal and treaty rights referred to [in subsection 35(1)] are guaranteed equally to male and female persons.

Aboriginal societies in North American were organized on a variety of bases before European contact. Many traditions have eroded. Certainly, there is no uniformity among the diverse communities as to the acceptance of liberal-democratic human rights values. One ideal with strong and wide support is that Aboriginal peoples themselves should have the power to determine which customary *and* non-Aboriginal rights and freedoms to embrace for their own circumstances.

A continuing irritant for "Indian" people is the role played by the Canadian state in determining who is an "Indian." Until 1985, a particular problem was a section of the *Indian Act* that deprived Indian women of their official "Indian" status if they married someone who was not part of their community.[52] Indian men, in contrast, did not lose status through marrying out; and their marriage automatically conferred status on their non-Indian spouses and their children. Some people, particularly male members of Indian band governments, felt this form of discrimination was in the interests of group solidarity and the preservation of scarce resources. This chapter cannot do justice to this complex issue, which fortunately has been examined by, among others, Wendy Moss, Douglas Sanders, and Sally Weaver.[53]

Amendments to the *Indian Act* in 1985 remedied many problems stemming from the offending section. These changes result partly from a belief in gender equality, but also because of the likelihood that the equality rights provisions of the Canadian Charter would require such amendments, and publicity generated by the *Lovelace* findings of the Human Rights Committee of the United Nations. The *Lovelace* case involved a woman denied access to her home Indian reserve because she was married to a white man, and thus in the eyes of the reserve's government was no longer an Indian entitled to the housing and other benefits accorded to band members. Because of previous case law in the Supreme Court of Canada, it was futile to litigate her complaint, so Ms. Lovelace referred it to the Human Rights Committee, which supervises implementation of the *International Covenant on Civil and Political Rights* and its *Optional Protocol*. The United Nations body found that Canadian law violated the covenant, because the law operated to deny Ms. Lovelace the opportunity to interact with her own "minority" community. Nevertheless, the Canadian public perceived the case to be about sex discrimination.[54]

Many Indian voices, particularly from certain band governments, opposed changes to the law to allow women and men equal rights to retain Indian status upon marriage. Other tribal communities, as well as women's rights advocates inside and outside indigenous groups, pushed for the 1985 legislative revisions. Progressive as these were, however, they aggravated some existing problems and created new ones.

One element of the 1985 legislation devolved responsibility for determining membership in individual Indian bands to those bands themselves. It is important that self-identification be within the power of affected groups, but it may be objectionable for the source of that authority to be an ordinary law passed by the government of the dominant culture. Nonetheless, the increased (but not total) power to determine membership rules and to apply those rules is a step forward for self-government by Indian nations. It also opens the door for many non-status Indians to obtain the tangible and spiritual benefits of being part of the community they identify with. Recall, however, that the *Indian Act* changes are not directly relevant to the ability of other Aboriginal groups such as the Metis and Inuit to determine their own membership and the entitlements and responsibilities that go with membership status. These are among the myriad questions in Aboriginal claims negotiations between Aboriginal peoples and governments in Canada.

For those indigenous peoples who hold that sexual equality is consistent with their cultural traditions, and for those communities who have no objection to the application of the Canadian Charter of Rights and Freedoms, gender equality poses no philosophical problem as a collective rights issue. In practical terms, however, the 1985 legislative changes led to an immediate and large increase in the numbers of people who can call upon the generally meager resources of Indian communities, and the federal government did not make adequate allowance for this with funding.[55] Some Indian reserves and band communities have found it difficult to bring everyone who wishes to participate into their midst. Women can assert that though they desire to share in and support the Aboriginal collectivity, their individual rights as members of that community must take precedence, and Aboriginal communities oppose having rules of membership imposed by the government. Litigation has been launched on these issues.[56]

Because of the focus on tensions between the rights of women and the right of Aboriginal communities to self-determine, it is sometimes forgotten that other groups might wish to assert rights against an Aboriginal community. Just as concepts of equality and entitlement have evolved concerning women's rights, so has thinking concerning other types of rights. Leaders of Canada's First Peoples are aware of the human rights standards contained in antidiscrimination statutes, the Canadian Charter of Rights and Freedoms, and international human rights agreements. They have sometimes turned to these instruments to defend the interests of their communities, despite objections to the importation of values. As self-government arrangements are put into place, governments of Aboriginal jurisdictions will contemplate which human rights mechanisms are appropriate for them. The next section deals with some issues they will need to confront.

Protection of Human Rights Within Self-Governed Aboriginal Communities

Opinion in multilateral organizations seems to be moving toward support for self-identification by indigenous peoples and attainment of some incidents of self-government, though not as far as full self-determination or secession from the countries in which Aboriginal communities are situated. The tendencies are manifest in International Labour Organization Convention 169 (adopted June 1989) and in recent discussions and working documents of the United Nations with respect to indigenous rights.[57] In general, governments and public opinion in Canada have also stepped away from assimilationist views and toward support for aspects of self-determination.[58] Although Aboriginal communities in Canada wish to retain as much as possible of their governmental and social customs, it seems likely that some human rights guarantees would be demanded by their membership. A number of statements and principles issued by Aboriginal organizations have expressed support for the norms of international human rights, and proclaimed that Aboriginal-controlled governments would honor these ideals.[59]

Although many Native people live on reserves or in remote rural areas, a high proportion live and work in urban settings. They may need to take advantage of existing human rights statutes and of the Charter of Rights regardless of any human rights machinery put into place in self-governed territories. According to the current desk officer, it was demands by some Native people that led to the creation of a designated "Native desk" in the New Brunswick Human Rights Commission, and organizations of Native Friendship Centres in Ontario and elsewhere are seeking better service for Aboriginal citizens in both rural and urban locations from their provincial human rights commissions.

An Aboriginal government designing a human rights protection scheme would need to ponder these questions, among others:

1. Assuming that we can negotiate immunity from imposition of the Canadian Charter of Rights and Freedoms, would we prefer to return to living by our traditional communitarian values and not institute any mechanisms for the protection of individual rights through legal means?

2. If we do want formal rights protections, whom do we plan to benefit?

3. Which human rights standards or antidiscrimination grounds are appropriate for us to proclaim?

4. What procedures and remedies are appropriate for our community?

5. Should any appeal be allowed to an outside authority from any decisions made within our human rights framework?

6. What is the correct mix of individual and collective, political and social, and other rights for our community?

These questions can and should be answered by the affected communities themselves, in consultation with whatever advisors they seek out. There would be nothing strange in having a diversity of mechanisms, just as there is variety in the ways that municipal and Aboriginal governments (for example, band governments) conduct themselves now. There are some matters over which designers of a human rights construct would have little control. Jurisprudence might unfold concluding that semi-autonomous Aboriginal polities are subject to the Charter of Rights. Depending on their degree of independence, these governments might also choose to accept the obligations of international human rights instruments, or Canada may continue to have international obligations with regard to their activities within the Confederation.[60]

In dealing with the questions listed above, the planners would consider precedents. In addition to examples provided by human rights systems of the dominant society in Canada and in international organizations, lessons might be available:

1. The decision-making structures of Native organizations and communities in Canada vary widely. Consensus-based processes can include voluntary withdrawal from discussion by someone who sees that she or he cannot persuade others, or delay of final decisions until agreement can be reached. Regardless of the written rules, that is how many Aboriginal governments and organizations function today. Others choose to operate under procedures that might seem familiar to parliamentarians. In some communities voting on decisions might be used only as a last resort when attempts at conciliated settlements fail.[61]

2. It was noted that 1985 amendments to the *Indian Act* give band and reserve governments freedom to determine who may be a member. Depending on the community, membership decisions may be taken by elders or by an elected organ. Rules for determining membership may some day lead to complaints of discrimination. Some ways of deciding membership might later provide procedural precedents for dealing with claims of discrimination related to definitions or categories that block the participation of particular individuals or groups in employment or in other areas.

3. At present there are a number of experiments in administering justice, particularly in criminal matters, being tried by or in cooperation with Aboriginal communities in Canada.[62] The experiments are sometimes carried out by individual bands (as in the Yukon, in cooperation with the Yukon Human Rights Commission) or by wider groupings of indigenous peoples. The procedures used and the sentences or other remedies arrived at through settlement or binding orders, and the longer-term success of these outcomes, can also provide precedents that could be used by a human rights monitoring body in an Aboriginal-controlled jurisdiction.

In Canada, the accepted norm, at least officially, is for people to have tolerance and appreciation for cultures different from their own. The leadership of a self-governed Aboriginal community would probably wish to incorporate these ideals into their human rights system. When thinking about how to account for the interests of minorities entering their jurisdictions, Aboriginal governments might have to consider section 6 of the Charter of Rights, which proclaims freedom of mobility within Canada to every citizen and permanent resident. These considerations would apply to people of different indigenous origins, to Canada's ethnocultural minorities, and, indeed, to people from the majority groups.

There are other examples of minority interests to be considered when setting up a human rights protective system. An important development is the recent trend by individuals and organizations of physically and mentally handicapped people to assert rights and to have those recognized by the wider society. Disabled Native people would want to benefit from this progressive evolution in thinking and practice.[63]

There are so many diverse heritages among Canada's Aboriginal peoples it is impossible to predict what they might adopt with respect to human rights. Because of the shared tradition of communitarianism, an Aboriginal human rights instrument might stress collective rights more than Canada's Constitution or human rights statutes do. It might proclaim guiding principles of interpretation recognizing the importance of economic and social rights, as is now done in some constitutions.[64]

Another concept which a Native government might consider is a right to a clean and safe environment, including ideals of "sustainable" or perhaps "zero" development. Though respect for nature is a central precept of Aboriginal traditions, there is not, however, a customary right to a healthful environment, just as there has not been one in other cultures. In Aboriginal philosophy, all of nature is important and imbued with spirit, and other parts of nature are no less important than humans. The environment is not seen as a subject for human rights; it is not even perceived as a predominately human preserve. Yet indigenous peoples do share notions of collective *duty* toward nature:

> In the [North American Indian] perspective animals, plants and objects were regarded as having souls or spirits and were dealt with as "persons" who had human qualities of thinking, feeling and understanding. . . . Social interactions occurred between human beings and other-than-human "persons" involving reciprocal relations and mutual obligations.[65]

Though today's worldwide trend of environmentalism is largely a human-centered and self-focused one, indigenous peoples may sometimes choose to use the prevailing language of "rights" in order to further certain goals they may share with the Green movement.

With respect to individual and minority rights, the procedural method I imagine Native-run human rights mechanisms would employ for handling complaints would be to seek negotiated settlements. This is the usual approach of existing human rights commissions, and would accord with Aboriginal traditions of achieving resolution through consensus. Even if a dispute went to a public hearing, the decision-makers (e.g., a board, a group of elders) could reach their conclusions through consensus rather than by voting or by taking majority and minority positions. The remedies chosen, in accordance with custom, may also be ones whose goal is the reconciliation of interests, of making the community whole, rather than of punishment for misdeeds.

It would be possible to devise a mechanism of appeal that protects the interests of individual or minority group complainants at odds with an Aboriginal community and who cannot reach a satisfactory resolution through the efforts of the applicable human rights body. A regional appeal structure could be set up, consisting of people from the homogeneous local community; *or* people from closely similar cultural traditions with shared values; *or* a mix of such individuals with sympathetic experts from outside these communities. The latter mixture would likely be needed in cases of cross-cultural (alleged) discrimination.

Each Aboriginal community is best suited and entitled to choose the "human rights" or other mutual responsibility system appropriate for itself. Some may recoil from the legal mechanisms offered by the overlaying structures in Canada. While searching for their own optimal mechanisms, others may choose to be subject to the *Canadian Human Rights Act*. One reason why some would lean in favor of the primarily individualistic approaches of the act is that traditional consensus methods do not always work. Many customary mores have been eroded, and in some instances in some communities, as in any grouping of people, there are occasions when consensus does not work democratically, when the dominant or most powerful speaker wins, regardless of other majority or minority interests. In some indigenous population centers, distribution of benefits (jobs, housing, and so forth) goes preferentially to the families and friends of those in power. To counter such cases, which involve nepotism more than "discrimination," an ombudsoffice may seem necessary. Such situations may influence some communities not to adopt consensus modes of human rights complaint resolution.[66]

My thoughts concerning self-determined, self-directed human rights monitoring systems for Aboriginal communities are not unique. In 1985, Jeff Richstone, a lawyer advising Inuit organizations, recommended that Nunavut create its own human rights code.[67] It should borrow ideas, where appropriate, from the draft *Northwest Territories Human Rights Code,* but should rely principally on "community justice mechanisms" for administration and enforcement.[68]

A "First Nations human rights and responsibilities law" is being drafted by the Native Women's Association of Canada, partly to discourage Canadian constitutional challenges (by Native people) opposing Aboriginal government actions.[69] The proposed instrument is forecast to include reference to paired groupings of rights and responsibilities based on traditional teachings: "(i) *strength*—cultural rights, (ii) *kindness*—social rights, (iii) *sharing*—economic rights, (iv) *trust*—political and civil rights."[70] Suggested dispute-resolution options to be selected by particular communities would be mediation, a human rights committee, or a council of elders.[71]

Wendy Moss has also put forward ideas to provide a focus for discussion of an Aboriginal human rights system:

> A national human rights panel . . . could be established . . . composed of indigenous and non-indigenous human rights experts as well as leaders from the indigenous community. This . . . panel would [appoint] individuals to [culturally knowledgeable] regional panels . . . responsible for the management or resolution of local human rights disputes.[72]

Where mediation efforts fail, a matter could be heard by an adjudicative panel composed of laypersons and lawyers, who would apply the *Canadian Human Rights Act.* Ultimately, there should be a new and separate human rights act (or acts) "developed in consultation with the national Aboriginal organizations and to be applied to reserve communities expressing their endorsement of it."[73]

Each of the proposals just outlined is more sophisticated than the brief excerpts given here might indicate. These ideas provide ample fuel for discussion of the ways in which an Aboriginal community might choose to deal with tensions among the mix of collective and individual responsibilities and rights. From my perspective, to reflect appropriately the culture(s) and people(s) it hopes to serve during a modern era of (revived) self-determination, an Aboriginal human rights instrument would need to cover both collective and individual rights, and to treat both as fundamental.

Notes

Author's Note: The research and analysis in this chapter are current to the end of May 1990.

The principal sources for this chapter are the individuals listed below. Some advised on earlier drafts. All have contributed valuable insights. Some may disagree with particular statements or approaches in the chapter, though it is inspired by their expertise and their reasoning: Dan Ennis, Darlene Johnston, Roger Kimmerly, Carol Montagnes, Wendy Moss, Graydon Nicholas, William Pentney, Dave Porter, Nancy Recollet, Dan Russell, Joanne St. Lewis, and Marty Schreiter.

1. *See e.g.,* M. Boldt and J. A. Long, eds., *The Quest for Justice: Aboriginal Peoples and Aboriginal Rights* (Toronto: University of Toronto Press, 1985), 166, 169.

2. "The government structure of the Six Nations greatly influenced the thinking of the Founding Fathers of the United States as they sought to develop an independent government prior to the Revolution. There are striking parallels between the Iroquois confederacy and the government of the United States" (R. Gonyea, "Introduction: The Foundation of the Iroquois Confederacy," in *Onondaga-Portrait of a Native People* [Syracuse: Syracuse University Press, 1986], 14–15). *See also* M. Jackson, "Edited Transcript of Proceedings, Consultative Conference on Discrimination Against Natives and Blacks in the Criminal Justice System and the Role of the Attorney General," *Report of the Royal Commission on the Donald Marshall, Jr. Prosecution,* vol. 7 (1988), 7.

3. *See* R. Gonyea, *ibid.* at 13–14. It can also be said that the Metis culture is formed from the fusing of elements of both First Nations and European traditions.

4. Principles 2, 6, and 7, *Declaration of Principles, World Council of Indigenous Peoples* (WCIP IV General Assembly, Panama, 1984).

5. *See, for example,* J. L. Tobias, "Indian Reserves in Western Canada: Indian Homelands or Devices for Assimilation?" in *Native People, Native Lands— Canadian Indians, Inuit and Metis* ed. B. A. Cox, (Ottawa: Carleton University Press, 1988), 148–57.

6. W. S. Tarnopolsky and W. F. Pentney, *Discrimination* (Toronto: De Boo, 1985), chap. 1 and 2; *Canadian Human Rights Reporter,* Volume of *Legislation and Regulations.*

7. *Saskatchewan Human Rights Code* S. S. 1979, sections 4–8; *Quebec Charter of Human Rights and Freedoms* R.S.Q., 1977, sections 1–9; *Yukon Territory Human Rights Act,* S. Y. 1987, sections 3–5.

8. *Quebec Charter of Human Rights and Freedoms,* R.S.Q. 1977, sections 39–48.

9. *See* note 6 and "Prohibited grounds of discrimination in employment," a table compiled by the Canadian Human Rights Commission.

10. Action Travail des Femmes v. C. N. Railway (1987) 8 C.H.R.R. D/4210 (S.C.C.); Ontario Human Rights Commission v. Simpsons-Sears Ltd. [1985] 2 S.C.R. 536; Bhinder v. C.N. Railway [1985] 2 S.C.R. 561.

11. Sources for this and the next two paragraphs are citations at *supra* note 6; R. A. McChesney, "Canada," in *International Handbook on Human Rights* ed. J. Donnelly and R. Howard, (New York: Greenwood Press, 1987), 24–47; and W. W. Black, *Employment Equity: A Systemic Approach* (Ottawa: Human Rights Research and Education and Centre, 1985).

12. *See* Indian and Northern Affairs Canada, *Highlights of Aboriginal Conditions 1981–2001* (Hull, Quebec: INAC, 1989); A. McChesney, "Does the Charter of Rights Guarantee Equality for Everyone?" in *Take Care! Human Rights in the '80s* (Ottawa: Human Rights Research and Education Centre, 1983), 75–81.

13. My sources are individuals listed in the acknowledgments for this chapter and Brian Brophy, Statistician, Ontario Human Rights Commission.

14. *Ibid.*

15. Some Aboriginal spokespersons feel that any participation in or interaction with the institutions of the controlling culture lends legitimacy to it and weakens the position of Native people. On this view, some hold that indigenous persons desirous of full self-determination should not vote in general elections, work for political parties, stand for election, or accept appointments to administrative bodies or organs of the dominant society's governments.

16. Some take a more absolute view of the need to avoid the legal systems of the oppressor society and to focus on attaining full autonomy based on First Nations traditions: M. Boldt and J. A. Long, *supra* note 1, at 165–79; Aki-Kwe/M. E. Turpel, "Aboriginal Peoples and the Canadian Charter of Rights and Freedoms: Contradictions and Challenges," *Canadian Journal of Women Studies* 10 (1989): 149–57; M. Smallface Marule, "Traditional Indian Government: Of the People, by the People, for the People," in *Pathways to Self-Determination—Canadian Indians and the Canadian State* ed. L. Little Bear, M. Boldt and J. A. Long (Toronto: University of Toronto Press, 1984), 36–45.

17. Large budget cuts announced by the federal government on February 20 and 22, 1990, may reduce the ability of Aboriginal organizations to lobby or to litigate on self-determination issues (Canadian Broadcasting Corporation newscasts, February 24, 1990).

18. One Native (Ojibway) commentator asked what should be done for people discriminated against until Aboriginal communities establish independent human rights systems: "It's nice to think about our future, but let's also think about the individual now" (Nancy Recollet, race relations consultant, Ontario Ministry of Citizenship, January 9, 1990).

19. "First Nations are being forced into the courts to protect their rights, quite often because existing levels of government do not have the political will to settle issues through meaningful negotiations," according to Elizabeth Thunder, director, Parliamentary and First Nations liaison, Assembly of First Nations, *Minutes of Proceedings and Evidence of the Standing Committee on Human Rights and the*

Status of Disabled Persons of the House of Commons, Issue No. 11 (October 3, 1989), 11:56.

In the early 1970s, the federal government began to turn away from a pro-assimilation policy. Since 1973 Canada has negotiated with various Aboriginal nations concerning rights claims, with respect to political rights, "property" and "compensation." By 1989 three comprehensive land claims settlements were completed: the 1975 James Bay Agreement with the Cree and Inuit of Quebec; the 1978 accord with the Naskapi of Schefferville, Quebec; and the 1984 COPE (Committee for Original Peoples Entitlement) pact with the Inuvialuit of the Western Arctic. An "Agreement in Principle," expected to lead to formal agreement, was made in 1988 with the Dene and Metis of the MacKenzie River Valley (M. Asch, "Wildlife: Defining the Animals the Dene Hunt and the Settlement of Aboriginal Land Claims," *Canadian Public Policy,* 15 [1989]: 205).

20. Some communities use customary methods (including consensus) to govern most of their affairs. Some use elected governments for certain decisions and traditional institutions for others: F. Cassidy and R. L. Bish, *Indian Government: Its Meaning in Practice* (Montreal: Oolichan Books and Institute for Research in Public Policy, 1989), 74–79. There are localities with strong tensions between power groups adhering to opposing forms of decision-making. This is evident among the Mohawk in the border areas of Ontario, Quebec, and the state of New York. *See, for example,* "Tribe members vote to storm band office," *The Gazette* (Montreal), February 16, 1990.

21. While cross-cultural communication and good race relations are as important to Aboriginal peoples as to other groups, it is inaccurate to equate Native communities to ethnocultural immigrant minorities. This view was affirmed by Nancy Recollet. *See supra* note 18.

22. Those listed in the acknowledgments to this chapter.

23. *Consultation Paper: Proposed Human Rights Code for the Northwest Territories* (Yellowknife: Government of the Northwest Territories, 1984). I was researcher and codrafter of this document.

24. *Yukon Territory Human Rights Act,* S.Y., 1987, c. 3. I was consulted on a few occasions during the legislative development process.

25. *Draft Northwest Territories Human Rights Code* (*see supra* note 23), sections 11(2) and 15(4); *ibid.* at section 1(2).

26. Interviews of Dan Innes, Native complaints officer (1989 and 1990).

27. The involvement of Native communities in the selection and assessment of designated staff must not be so extensive as to cast aspersions on the independence and credibility of the selected personnel.

28. Interview of Marty Schreiter, former director of Yukon Human Rights Commission (December 10, 1989).

29. *Ibid.*

30. Clearly, the Native communities affected will be in the best position to judge what is the best mix of "traditional" and "industrialized society" pursuits for them. For fuller discussions of related issues, *see* Makivik Corporation, "Northern Neglect"; D. Drache and D. Cameron, *The Other MacDonald Report* (Toronto: James Lorimer, 1985), 110–18; B. A. Cox, *supra* note 5, at chap. 14, 16, and 17; M.

Asch, *supra* note 19, at 205–19; F. Wein, *Rebuilding the Economic Base of Indian Communities: The Micmac in Nova Scotia* (Montreal: Institute for Research on Public Policy, 1986), 132–35, 140–61; R. Robertson, "The Right to Food—Canada's Broken Covenant," *Canadian Human Rights Yearbook* 6 (1989): 35–46 of manuscript.

31. Programs to improve learning and teaching opportunities for Native people have been instituted by some human rights commissions, notably in Saskatchewan and Yukon (consultations with Commission personnel, 1984–89). It is important to impart traditional values and skills to Native children, yet prepare them for dealing with the dominant society. Aboriginal teachers provide lessons as instructors and as role models.

32. Funding was provided to an Aboriginal group by Canada's Court Challenges Program (an institution largely independent of government but having federal financing) to consider constitutional litigation against such policies in federal prisons (*Canadian Human Rights Advocate* [1989]:9–10).

33. Schreiter, *supra* note 28; D. Porter, then Director of Yukon Human Rights Commission (consultations, October 12 and 13, 1989, and December 15, 1989); R. Kimmerly, former minister of justice, Yukon Territory (consultations, December 11, 1989).

34. *Ibid.*

35. One concerned education equity for Native pupils; the other related to trapping rights. *Ibid.*

36. *See, for example,* the speech given by M. Yalden, chief commissioner, to the International Conference on Human Rights in Cross-Cultural Perspectives, Saskatoon, October 12, 1989, and the address of Michelle Falardeau-Ramsay, deputy chief commissioner, to the Northwest Territories Bar Association, October 14, 1989, entitled, "Do Human Rights Codes, with their emphasis on individual rights, threaten the collective rights of a people or a community?"

37. *Canadian Human Rights Commission Annual Report* (1988): 19–21; (1989):14–17.

38. *Canadian Human Rights Act,* R.S.C. 1985, c. H-6, section 67: "Nothing in this Act affects any provision of the *Indian Act* or any provision made under or pursuant to that Act."

39. Concerning this problem, see the succeeding paragraph, as well as *infra,* note 52, and accompanying text.

40. *See* text at *supra,* notes 32 and 33.

41. Section 15(1) guarantees equality rights and freedom from discrimination on the basis of race, sex, and so on. Section 15(2) states: "Subsection (1) does not preclude any law, program or activity that has as its object the amelioration of conditions of disadvantaged individuals or groups including those that are disadvantaged because of race, national or ethnic origin, colour, religion, sex, age or mental or physical disability."

42. Section 25 states: "The guarantee in this Charter of certain rights and freedoms shall not be construed so as to abrogate or derogate from any aboriginal, treaty or other rights or freedoms that pertain to the aboriginal peoples of Canada . . . . "

Section 35(1) states: "The existing aboriginal and treaty rights of the aboriginal peoples of Canada are hereby recognized and affirmed."

Section 35(4) states: " . . . the aboriginal and treaty rights referred to in subsection (1) are guaranteed equally to male and female persons."

43. This and the next paragraph are based on my experience as director of legal aid in the Northwest Territories (1981–83), as codrafter of the *Draft Northwest Territories Human Rights Code* (*see supra* note 23) and as coauthor of *Background Research on an Aboriginal Human Rights Instrument* (prepared in 1987 for the Native Women's Association of Canada).

44. *Ibid.*

45. *Ibid.*, and consultations referred to at *supra,* note 33.

46. M. I. Asch, "Capital and Economic Development: A Critical Appraisal of the Recommendations of the MacKenzie Valley Pipeline Commission," in B. A. Cox, *supra* note 5, at 232–40.

47. *Ibid.* The calamities that can arise from insensitivity to communitarian customs were brought home by ill-advised oil exploitation legislation that permitted selling of indigenous land rights by Alaskan Natives, rather than retention for community benefit. Consultations with Alaskan officials, December 1984; and D. Johnston, "Native Rights as Collective Rights: A Question of Group Self-Preservation," *Canadian Journal of Law and Jurisprudence* 2(1989): 34, n. 113, where she says: "The failure of the *Alaska Native Claims Settlement Act, 1971,* which treats native land as a corporate asset susceptible to taxation and alienation, stands as a stark reminder of the hazards of imposing foreign concepts upon the traditional Native life-style." For a discussion of the disintegrative effects of ANCSA Johnston recommends Thomas R. Berger, *Village Journey: The Report of the Alaska Native Review Commission* (New York: Hill and Wang, 1985), at 45.

48. Apsit v. Manitoba Rice Farmers (1986), 7 C.H.R.R. D/3315 (Q.B.).

49. *Ibid.* and consultation, September 21, 1989, with law professor William Black, expert witness at the trial.

50. Andrews v. Law Society of British Columbia (1989), 10 C.H.R.R. D/5719 (S.C.C.); S. Day, "Equality Seekers Troubled by Affirmative Action Rulings," *Canadian Human Rights Advocate* 6, no. 1 (January 1990).

On the other side, the sensitivity shown by the Supreme Court of Canada in two recent decisions on Aboriginal rights demonstrates the merit of seeing litigation as one of the strategies for reinforcement of these rights. In R. v. Sioui, May 24, 1990, the court applied a 1760 treaty in acknowledging the right of Hurons to practice certain customary activities or religious rites, regardless of whether in this instance they conflicted with regulations under the Quebec Parks Act. In R. v. Sparrow, May 31, 1990, the Court gave primacy to Aboriginal fishing rights that were impeded by fishery laws in British Columbia.

51. *See* R. A. McChesney, *supra* note 11, at 36–39.

52. Section 12(1)(b) of the *Indian Act,* R.S.C. 1985, c. 1–5, amended by S.C. 1985, c. 27 (Bill C–31); S.C. 1986, c. 35; S.C. 1988, c. 23; S.C. 1988, c. 52.

53. W. Moss, Indigenous Self-Government in Canada and Sexual Equality Under the Indian Act: Resolving Conflicts Between Collective and Individual Rights (unpublished manuscript, February 21, 1990); D. Sanders, "Indian Status:

A Woman's Issue or An Indian Issue?" *Canadian Native Law Reporter* 3 (1989): 30; S. Weaver, "Judicial Preservation of Ethnic Group Boundaries: The Iroquois Case," *Proceedings of the First Congress, Canadian Ethnology Society,* Paper No. 17 (National Museum of Man Mercury Series, Ottawa, 1974). Broader issues of Aboriginal rights under the Constitution are addressed in, for example, D. Johnston, *supra* note 47; W. Pentney, "The Rights of the Aboriginal Peoples of Canada and the *Constitution Act, 1982.* Part I—The Interpretive Prism of Section 25," *University of British Columbia Law Review* 22 (1988): 22–59; D. Sanders, "The Rights of the Aboriginal Peoples of Canada," *Canadian Bar Review* 61 (1983): 314; B. Wildsmith, *Aboriginal Peoples and Section 25 of the Canadian Charter of Rights and Freedoms* (Saskatoon: University of Saskatchewan Native Law Centre, 1988).

54. Although the committee dwelled on Article 27 (minority rights), a separate opinion by Nejib Bouziri stated "that the *Indian Act* offended Articles 2(1), 3, 23(4) and 26 as it was 'une loi qui fait des discriminations notamment entre l'homme et la femme'" (Lovelace v. Canada 1983, *Canadian Human Rights Yearbook* 1 [1983]: 305–14; W. Pentney, "Lovelace v. Canada: A Case Comment," *Canadian Legal Aid Bulletin* 5 [1982]: 259).

55. *See* authorities in *supra* note 53. A group of women who gained Indian status and Band membership under the 1985 statutory revisions have obtained funding from the Court Challenges Program (*see supra* note 32) to research possible litigation concerning the scarcity of some on-reserve services (especially housing) and benefits for reinstated women and children (*Canadian Human Rights Advocate* 4, no. 1 [1988]: 9).

56. The case of Twinn v. The Queen was launched in the federal court by six bands in Alberta, alleging that Bill C–31, which amended the *Indian Act* in 1985 to remove discrimination against Aboriginal women who married non-Indians, is unconstitutional. Their central argument is that by imposing band membership rules, even in the name of equality, Bill C–31 contravened section 35, which affirms Aboriginal rights, including the right to determine band membership. The federal government argues that no Aboriginal right to determine band membership ever existed, and if it did, it has been extinguished. The New Status Indian Association has obtained funding from the Court Challenges Program (*see supra* note 32) to intervene in the case. They are in favor of preserving the official Indian status gained by some women and children, while seeking a broad interpretation of Aboriginal rights under section 35 (*Canadian Human Rights Advocate* 4, no. 8 [1988]: 10).

57. Some instruments now acknowledge the rights of indigenous peoples to self-identify and to choose their own methods of government and of development. *See* ILO Convention 169 *Concerning Indigenous and Tribal Peoples in Independent Countries,* Articles 1–7; *Draft Universal Declaration on Rights of Indigenous Peoples,* Articles 3–6, 18–27; H. Hannum, "New Developments in Indigenous Rights," *Virginia Journal of International Law* 28(1988): 663–64.

58. There are some elements of self-government in the James Bay and Naskapi agreements, for example. *See supra* note 19.

59. *See, for example, supra* note 4, and "Universal Human Rights: An Ab-

original Dialogue" (Conference Proceedings, Robson Media Centre, Vancouver, 1989).

60. Canada's compliance with "minority rights" protections in the International Covenant on Civil and Political Rights was questioned in the "Views" of the U.N. Human Rights Committee of the United Nations in the case of *Ominayak and the Lubicon Lake Band*, CCPR/C/38/D/167/1984 Annex (28 March 1990): "Historical inequities . . . and certain more recent developments threaten the way of life and culture of the Lubicon Lake Band, and constitute a violation of Article 27 so long as they continue" (*ibid.*, at 29).

61. *See* Moss, *supra* note 53, at 44; Cassidy and Bish, *supra* note 20, at 74 and 78; F. Cassidy, "Aboriginal Governments in Canada: An Emerging Field of Study," *Canadian Journal of Political Science* 23 (1990):73–99.

62. *See* M. Jackson, *supra* note 2, and Report of the Indigenous Bar Association Annual Conference: Indigenous Control of the Justice System: Alternatives to Existing Arrangements (September 30–October 1, 1989).

63. Disabled Natives and the Law, Theme Edition of *Just Cause* 3 (Fall 1985): 1.

64. The Constitutions of India (1950), Ireland (1937), and Spain (1978) provide examples: *Constitutions of the Countries of the World* (looseleaf), ed. A. P. Blaustein and G. H. Flanz (Dobbs Ferry, N.Y.: Oceana Publications). Such a proposal was made for future self-government by Jeff Richstone in *Securing Human Rights in Nunavut: A Study of a Nunavut Bill of Rights* (Ottawa: Nunavut Constitutional Forum, 1985), 25–39, 51.

This approach was recommended for Canada in my "Economic and Social Rights in Canada: The International Bill of Rights and Canadian Human Rights Law," in *supra* note 12, at 61–73, and in R. A. McChesney, "Canada," in *supra* note 11, at 39–42. Kalmen Kaplansky suggests that economic and social rights should have status in the constitution equal to that of other rights (*Rights and Liberties* [December 1988]).

65. M. Boldt and J. A. Long, "Tribal Philosophies and the Canadian Charter of Rights and Freedoms," in Boldt and Long (eds.), *supra* note 16, 165–79 at 166. My understanding of the Aboriginal focus on our *responsibilities* toward nature, contrasted with ideas of a human *right* to a safe environment, was enhanced by advice from Prof. Darlene Johnston, Faculty of Law, University of Ottawa.

66. Specific difficulties that have arisen in some communities in Ontario were described to me by Dan Russell, legal counsel, Ontario Native Council on Justice. An Inuk member of the Northwest Territories Legislative Assembly told me in 1983 that nepotism in Arctic communities was an important "rights" problem to address in any human rights legislation.

67. Jeff Richstone, *supra* note 64, at 62. Nunavut is essentially the Eastern Arctic of Canada, in which the Inuit (sometimes called "Eskimos") strive for self-determination. The *Study* also recommended that the preamble to a bill of rights should refer to the Universal Declaration of Human Rights.

68. *Ibid.* at 51 and 62.

69. Mary Ellen Turpel, "Aboriginal Peoples and the Canadian Charter: In-

terpretive Monopolies, Cultural Differences." *Canadian Human Rights Yearbook* 7 (1989–1990):3–47 at 43. Earlier work on a First Nations human rights law was prepared in M. Austin and A. McChesney, *Background Research, supra* note 43, with advice from M. E. Turpel, W. F. Pentney, and J. U. Bayly.

70. Turpel, *ibid.*
71. *Ibid.* at 58–59.
72. Wendy Moss, *supra* note 53, at 45.
73. *Ibid.* at 45–46.

10. Political Culture and Gross Human Rights Violations in Latin America

Introduction

Human rights violations were on the increase during the 1970s and part of the 1980s in Latin America. Government violence intensified in Latin America, where military regimes ruled Chile, Argentina, Brazil, and Uruguay. During the 1980s Central America took center stage as the focus of political violence in the Western hemisphere.

Political violence has always played a key role in the evolution of Latin American societies. Some authors have interpreted the recurrence of human rights violations as the by-product of a prevailing cultural tradition antagonistic to democracy.[1] They perceive human rights violations as expressing some form of monism, that is, "support for the unification of groups at all levels of society: an attempt to eliminate competition among groups in their pursuit of wealth, power, prestige. . . ."[2] This, in turn, is said to reflect the influence of an Ibero-American cultural tradition.

This interpretation of Latin America's social evolution is not the only one that has been used in analyses of the recurrence of authoritarianism and repression. Research on Latin America has also criticized the universality of some assumptions on political change in attempts to specify the characteristics of the situation. Examples of this type of analysis can be found in some explanations for the rise of bureaucratic authoritarianism in Brazil, Argentina, Uruguay, and Chile during the sixties and seventies. Guillermo O'Donnell's theory on the rise of authoritarianism in the most advanced Latin American countries stresses the impact of socioeconomic modernization on the relations among social classes. He argues that once the initial phase of industrialization was over, the coalitions in power had to accelerate that process by manufacturing intermediate and capital goods domestically. This approach, however, meant adopting orthodox economic policies that were challenged by increasingly powerful popular sectors. To subdue their resistance, a coalition between the military and civilian technocrats installed authoritarian rule with support from dominant classes.[3] According to this view, it is possible to identify different types of political systems in Latin America in accordance with varying regime-coalition-policy patterns. Some of them, populist in some cases and bureaucratic-authoritarian in others, cannot be considered democratic and in fact tend to be fairly repressive. Nevertheless, they are neither a product of the same factors nor a mechanical expression of one cultural tradition, regardless of different historical contexts.

An alternative explanation for political instability and the breakdown of democratic regimes in the region—that eventually might lead to gross human rights violations—is basically political. A good example of this line of analysis is Arturo Valenzuela's book on the crisis of Chilean democracy.[4] He focuses on the Chilean political system's shortcomings in dealing with a crisis situation. He also stresses that the Chilean political bargaining system became too rigid as a result of an attempt to modernize society.

All these explanations do not necessarily contradict one another. It is true that the prevailing authoritarian culture is deeply rooted in Latin America.[5] It does not have the same influence in all countries of the region, however, nor is it capable of provoking gross and systematic violations of human rights in itself. It is manifested differently in different historical contexts. On the other hand, despite their weaknesses, democratic institutions have enjoyed considerable stability in a few countries. Larry Diamond and Juan J. Linz state that there is a reciprocal relationship between political culture and political systems; democratic culture clearly presses for the maintenance of democracy but, historically, the choice of democracy by the elites preceded the presence of democratic values among the general population.[6]

The general thesis of this chapter is that violence is a particular way of managing conflicts in Latin America and gross human rights violations evolve from a lack of consensus among contending political forces. Gross human rights violations, then, are the outcome of the state's inability to assert its authority over society by other means. The systematic violation of fundamental rights depends upon an alliance among existing repressive institutions and requires an ideological justification capable of overcoming any moral barriers to such violent actions.[7] Once violence is instituted as a permanent instrument of power, it is extremely likely that further violence will occur.

Why has reaching a consensus on fundamental freedoms been such a difficult feat in recent years? The variety of factors involved make the answer to this question very complex. Moreover, the differences among national realities are too great to allow only one answer for Latin America as a whole. The recent history of Latin American societies, however, suggests a few hypotheses:

1. The modernization of Latin American societies has intensified social and political cleavages in societies which lack the institutional and symbolic mechanisms to integrate new demands by the state. In contrast to what happened in developed societies, industrialization through import substitution and national control of natural resources failed to deliver in terms of sustained economic growth, income equality, and the social incorporation of subordinate classes and social groups.[8]

2. This process led to a radicalization of those in power and of opposition intellectual elites in Chile, Argentina, Peru, Uruguay, Brazil, and Colombia at different stages during the 1960s, 1970s, and in the case of Peru, the early 1980s. The upsurge of radical politics also was nourished by external ideological influences. The success of the Cuban and the Nicaraguan revolutions influenced perceptions of the left. The concepts of the cold war and the anti-subversion issuing from the United States strengthened the resolve of the civilian elite and prepared the military to assume an autonomous institutional role.[9]

3. The process of political polarization led in some cases to the installation of extremely repressive military regimes (Brazil in 1964, Uruguay and Chile in 1973, Argentina in 1976) and in others to the maintenance of civilian heads of state while the military waged its own ruthless war against guerrilla groups (Colombia and Peru).

4. Gross and systematic violations of human rights indicated, on the one hand, a determination to resist socialist change and to reimpose the old hierarchical social order shaken by popular mobilization. But, on the other hand, especially in the case of the Southern Cone, these violations became an instrument for disciplining the masses and introducing new value orientations that emphasized private capital accumulation over income redistribution and social reform.

The process that I have sketched out further polarized the perceptions of the contending forces. Political compromise and negotiation were aban-

doned as conflict management methods and replaced by war. Nevertheless, there is still some hope for democracy and a strengthening of human
rights protection. In the struggle against the state, respect for human
rights became the banner of the opposition. New social movements
emerged that defended human rights and advocated the solidification of
civil society and the ending of abuses by the state.[10] They were supported
in their struggle by North Atlantic governments, political parties, and
churches. Encouraged by the saliency of the concept of human rights,
both social scientists and political elites rediscovered the values imbued in
the democratic system.[11] This chapter will discuss the impact that these
changes might have on the human rights situation in the future.

The first part of this chapter analyzes the impact that authoritarian
political culture has had on the observance of human rights in Latin
America. The second focuses on the social process that has provoked massive violations of human rights in recent years. The final part considers the
reactions that emerged within society against human rights violations and
their effect on the situation.

The Legacy of an Authoritarian Political Culture

According to a number of specialists, Latin American culture embodies a
tradition whose ingredients are all antagonistic to a process of democratic
modernization. In the words of Howard Wiarda:

> Latin America, we shall see, remains hierarchical, authoritarian, paternalistic,
> Catholic (in the broad political-cultural sense as used here), elitist, corpora-
> tist, and patrimonialist to its core. These ingredients have been and remain at
> the heart of its development tradition and are what help make it distinctive.[12]

In Claudio Veliz's historical analysis explaining Latin America's inability to establish ideological models similar to those prevailing in Western Europe, he suggests that the centralism of the Latin American
tradition is one of the main differences from that of Europe.[13] According
to Veliz, certain factors explain why it is so difficult to apply democratic
European models in Latin America.

First, Latin America's cultural tradition lacks a feudalist experience.
America was colonized at a period when feudalism had already disappeared, and the institutional structure devised for the Indies reflected

strong centralism. [14] When the colonial system collapsed, its centralist and authoritarian tradition was passed on to the newborn republics. Thus, the institutional custom of compromise between alternative centers of political power never became part of the Latin American tradition. Political centralism was reinforced by the lack of religious dissent. The religious authority of the Catholic Church has never been challenged from within. [15] Finally, in Latin America political and religious centralism were coupled with economic centralism.

Although Glenn Dealy approaches the Latin American tradition from quite a different angle, he reaches coincident conclusions. His basic premise is that for more than a century and a half the Latin American ideal of government has not been that of liberal democracy. [16] Latin Americans did not simply borrow a constitutional and political tradition from the United States and continental Europe and then fail to implant it for an assortment of reasons. Rather, there is a Spanish American tradition that is reflected in the political practice of Latin American societies. [17]

Spanish American constitutions did not make a distinction between external conduct and internal morality. The internal morality of the citizens was prerequisite for the achievement of the common good. The common good was identified with the Spanish American natural law tradition. Thus, it is understandable that most early nineteenth-century constitutions established Roman Catholicism as the state religion. Even today, Dealy asserts, constitutional rights are subject to several limitations that legitimize undemocratic processes and propagate the authoritarian tradition. [18]

The conclusions of these authors are certainly pessimistic regarding the prospects of improved human rights conditions in Latin America. If the authoritarian tradition equally pervades all societies of the region and has lasted for so long, then changing the current human rights situation would seem to be extremely difficult.

Authoritarian Political Culture and Gross Human Rights Violations

The argument that I have just outlined requires a series of qualifications. I will begin by looking at Veliz's argument that centralism as part of the Latin American culture has become a real obstacle for political pluralism and democracy. Any observer of the scene would feel that the centralization of state power is indeed a feature of Latin American life. The reasons provided by Veliz, however, are not very persuasive in themselves.

It is true that feudalism never existed in Latin America, but this was also the case for North America. The lack of a tradition of compromise between alternative power centers might be a consequence of this fact. This probably played a major role in the factional civil wars that took place after independence, and which ended up putting strong men and repressive governments in power.[19] Liberalization, however, has indeed taken place for long periods of time in some countries that have experienced the same tradition already depicted. Besides, could centralism be blamed for such different episodes as the mid-nineteenth-century civil wars or the present Central American situation, in which so many other factors are at play?

According to Veliz, the fact that Catholicism has continued to be the official religion of Latin America has reinforced political centralism. The weight of Catholic influence has supported existing social and political arrangements, but this is neither a necessary nor a permanent relationship. To begin with, the Church's influence is not very great in Mexico or Uruguay. Secondly, since Vatican Council II, the Church has redefined its relationship with political ideologies. This redefinition has inspired growing concern for social change, popular participation, and human rights. While these changes have had no impact on the Church's political stance in Colombia or Argentina, they have certainly reversed more traditional attitudes in Central and South America.[20] Furthermore, the opposition to the military and to human rights violations has been strongly backed by the Church in Chile, Brazil, and El Salvador. While Catholicism continues to be the most influential religion of the region, its weight in political events varies from one country to the next. It becomes difficult to say that gross human rights violations are the consequences of a Catholic-inspired authoritarian tradition. Finally, Veliz asserts that Latin America has remained economically centralized. The state's role in promoting industrialization has not been altogether undemocratic, however. On the contrary, it has often reflected the concern of the elites for the prevailing social situation, and in some countries meant the fostering of the welfare state. In fact, military regimes have been the ones to promote free market policies that have cut into the state's economic role.

Glenn Dealy's approach puts utmost emphasis on the argument that there is only one distinct tradition in Latin America. One of his main contentions is that the natural law concepts of the elite who fought the wars of independence were radically different from the concepts of natural law prevailing at that time in Europe and the United States. Thus, he dismisses the argument that the new republics borrowed the principles of Western constitutionalism from Europe and the United States, but lacked the preparation to implement them. According to Dealy, the new republics merely put into practice the principles that they believed in, which are antagonistic to pluralism. This position seems to me to exaggerate the influence of one distinct tradition over a period of two centuries and to create a misleading impression that no other competing ideologies have expounded and defended—sometimes with success—opposing ideological claims. In considering the influence of the Spanish authoritarian tradition, one should not forget that wars of independence and subsequent civil and international wars destroyed what was left of Spanish colonial institutions. [21]

The Chilean case clearly shows that, despite obvious sociological differences, by the end of the nineteenth century the legal system in many aspects resembled the legal systems of Western Europe. [22] It is true that during the first half of the nineteenth century liberal constitutional provisions were contradicted by the hegemony of authoritarian governments that held complete political control. By 1874, however, constitutional amendments enlarged the catalogue of fundamental freedoms to be protected, presidential power was limited, and political parties gained in organization and leverage. The Chilean institutional evolution, which could be very favorably compared in democratic terms with that of some European countries, proves at least the following proposition: whatever the initial influence of medieval natural law concepts may have been, they were no obstacle to the liberalization of the institutional system in the case of Chile.

Uruguay is another case in point. Its first seven decades of independent life were chaotic and violent. However, by the end of the nineteenth century, it was developing an institutionalized political mechanism for limiting political conflict. The 1903 civil war won by Jose Battle y Ordonez put an end to armed civil strife for six decades. [23] Although the constitutional government system suffered two interruptions during this period, the full enjoyment of civil liberties by Uruguayan citizens reaffirmed Uruguay's claim that it was the most democratic country in Latin America. It might very well be that the judicial system was not as efficient or assertive as those existing in Europe or North America. There is no question, however, that the ideology of constitutional liberalism was hegemonic in Uruguay for at least several decades during this century.

These two examples demonstrate quite clearly that the historical evolution of Latin America has not been shaped by merely one set of beliefs. Competing ideologies have had social consequences, but their end result has depended on the particular social context within which they were worked out. The Chilean and Uruguayan constitutional systems evolved very differently from those of Argentina and Peru. Yet there is no reason to believe that the Chilean and Uruguayan cultural heritage was distinctly different from that of Argentina and Peru.

Competing Ideologies and Authoritarian Political Culture

Latin America's history shows not so much the prevalence of only one cultural tradition, but rather the coexistence of different ideological patterns that have evolved outside the region and are assumed in accordance with local realities. Therefore, modern ideological conceptions are "reinterpreted" by societies whose cleavages, class divisions, and national problems are unlike those of the most developed countries of the world. [24]

Modernizing ideologies were, in fact, assumed in Latin America by intellectual elites immediately before, during, and after the wars of independence. Their impact and application, however, varied in relation to the particular social context. The concept of republicanism, the rule of law, and the independence of the judiciary could hardly be applied in societies like Peru that lack a national identity. The absence of a national state capable of gaining the loyalty of the masses there made a gradual evolution toward political pluralism impossible. However, democratic liberalism continued—even in Peru—to set the standards of legitimacy against which any state could be judged. This fact explains why authoritarianism, personalism, and unequal application of the law have survived together with republican constitutional forms. It also explains the tendency to oscillate between limited democracy and authoritarian regimes that is reflected in most Latin American countries. When tensions arise within the coalition in power, the question of democracy usually surfaces, bringing with it an improvement of the human rights situation. [25] When political and social domination is threatened by social mobilization or by other factors, however, some form of authoritarian rule is imposed again.

In the Chilean case, the evolution toward more liberal forms of government took place in part because the ruling elite was able to consolidate a legitimate central authority. The consolidation facilitated a gradual acceptance of a political opposition. This liberalism, however, was developed in a social context that differed radically from the one present in Europe and the United States. The economic system was much weaker, industrialism came much later than in Europe, and very large segments of the population remained isolated from the political and social system. Nevertheless, by 1945, Chileans could claim that their democratic political tradition was older than that of Italy and Germany.

Marxism has also had an important influence in Latin America; it shaped the actions of leftist parties, trade unions, intellectuals, and guerrilla movements. Yet, as Zapata points out, Marxism has faced the reality that capitalism has developed in Latin America in quite specific ways.[26] What are the differences between this and European capitalist evolution?

1. Many Latin American countries did not follow the European model by which the penetration of capitalism created a strongly autonomous working class that could play a revolutionary role. The penetration of capitalism in some countries was too uneven, creating modern as well as traditional sectors whose interests did not coincide. In countries such as Peru, where the majority of the population was ethnically different from the dominant coalition, their demands took on indigenous and messianic connotations.[27]
2. In many societies, the working class was unable to establish autonomous organizations because they were co-opted by the state, which forged populist alliances depriving the working class of its revolutionary aims. This was the case in Argentina, Mexico, and Brazil.
3. In most cases, the middle classes are not progressive and cannot be counted upon as permanent supporters of revolutionary policies.

     Differences such as the ones already described explain why only two Marxist revolutions succeeded in taking power: the Cuban and the Nicaraguan. In both instances, the revolutionary coalition was very broad and heterogeneous and not based on the industrial working class. Moreover, the two movements were directed against a violent dictatorship and were able to gather support from different repressed social groups. Finally, in both cases, reaction to U.S. influence in the country activated nationalistic feelings against the government in power. [28]

The preceding analysis suggests at least the following hypotheses:

1. The Latin American republics inherited an authoritarian tradition from Spain and Portugal.
2. This tradition has not been the only one that has had an effect upon social actors and intellectuals. Liberalism and Marxism have had an important influence during different historical periods.
3. These foreign intellectual influences have had to adapt to the complex milieu within which they have been worked out. The net result of this adaptation is due not only to the nature of the ideas themselves, since they have social consequences, but also to the complexities of the social context within which these ideas are received.

A brief sketch of events that have taken place in South America in recent years will illustrate the consequences of this interplay between ideology and context for the human rights situation.

Human Rights Violations as a Social Process in South America

Gross and systematic human rights violations have taken place in Brazil, Chile, Argentina, Uruguay, Peru, and Colombia in recent years. In the case of the Southern Cone countries, this occurred after military rule took over. In Peru and Colombia, human rights abuses have taken place despite the existence of democratic political systems. As has already been noted, prior to these violations, Chile and Uruguay had become stable political democracies in which the use of political violence was unusual, but Argentina and Peru had been characterized by political instability. Colombia had returned to civilian rule after the massive *Violencia* of the forties and the resulting military government of General Rojas Pinilla. [29] Colombia had already experienced long periods of political violence during the nineteenth and mid-twentieth centuries. Thus, political violence and human rights abuses were not alien to the political culture of some of these countries and the likelihood of further violence was high.

A careful look at the socioeconomic context of these countries prior to the outbreak of the crisis that led to massive human rights violations reveals a number of problems. All of them experienced an important process of industrialization and modernization. At the same time, however, the income distribution was not significantly altered. Those countries where the distribution of income became more egalitarian were simultaneously the ones that experienced the slowest growth rate. Moreover, redistributionist policies usually ended up provoking high inflation rates that dissolved their impact on income equality. Although not rendering a comparison between countries, the following statistics illustrate the points I have made.

In Uruguay, for instance, the gross domestic product (GDP) fell 5.4 percent in 1967, while inflation ran 89.3 percent. Consumer prices rose by an average of 25 percent annually between 1969 and 1971.[30] The economy stagnated. Argentina, another country where the poor sectors of the population had increased their share in the national income, also experienced a stagnating economy. According to Sabato and Schwarzer, between 1970 and 1982 the GDP almost did not grow at all, and the industrial product declined.[31]

In the case of Chile, the reformist administration of Eduardo Frei and the socialist government of Salvador Allende made concerted efforts to improve income distribution. Organized labor and, after 1964, the peasantry voiced their interests through representative institutions. GDP growth was sluggish, however. Between 1955 and 1977 the growth rate of Chile's per capita income was only 1.1 percent.[32]

Inequality of income distribution increased in Peru between 1962 and 1972, despite the rise to power of a reformist military government in 1968. While in 1962 the poorest one-fifth of the population received 3.0 percent of the national income, in 1972 it received 2.5 percent. In 1962, the richest 5 percent of the Peruvian population received 26 percent of the national income, while in 1972 its share rose to 33 percent.[33]

In the case of Brazil, the rate of growth of the GDP slowed down, and the inflation rate was over 80 percent in 1964, the year of the coup d'état.

I am not trying to make a deterministic economic argument. What I am saying is simply that the economic situation in the context of a modernizing process was unfavorable for political and social stability. Here a clear distinction must be made between what happened in the Southern Cone countries and Brazil and what happened in Peru and Colombia. The following refers only to Chile, Argentina, Brazil, and Uruguay. The socio-economic context created conditions for social mobilization in a poorly performing economic system. The upper middle classes felt that income distribution and social reform did not secure sustained economic growth, but rather threatened the subsistence of the capitalist system. Moreover, social reform, far from preempting mobilization, accelerated it. During the 1960s, revolution became the central theme of the political intellectual debate in South America.[34] The influence of the Cuban revolution on Latin American intellectuals radicalized their views on the social situation and meant the emergence of newly radicalized leftist groups. In Uruguay and Argentina urban guerrilla groups were formed that utilized terrorist tactics against their enemies, whether military officers, rival union leaders, or representatives of "imperialist powers."[35] The common feature of all these situations is that political negotiations between government and opposition political forces were unsuccessful and that violence in the streets escalated.

It is hard to judge whether the breakdown of these democratic systems could have been avoided. What is clear, though, is that the installation of these authoritarian systems was preceded by strife and competition over state power among ideologically opposing forces. Conservative and revolutionary forces were, in fact, involved in a power struggle to replace the socioeconomic system. Ideological influences also shaped the thinking of conservative forces who felt that the only way to restore order was by imposing military rule in the country. The influence of orthodox economic thought on technocrats working for the new authoritarian administration meant a strong emphasis on economic stabilization programs and on the demobilization of leftist parties and unions.[36]

Military rule and subsequent repression were justified by the "national security doctrine," which, as Margaret E. Crahan puts it, "is a systematization of concepts of the state, war, national power, and national goals that places national security above personal security, the needs of the state before individual rights, and the judgment of a governing elite over the rule of law."[37] This national security doctrine justifies the elimination of dissent, the dissolution of political parties and labor unions. It is not the cause of the repressive process, however. The reasons for gross human rights violations can be found in the social crisis and political polarization process just described.

These were not traditional military coups engineered to put a new leader in power. The military participated as institutions; only in the case of Chile was power personalized in just one general. Moreover, even the aims of these new rulers were revolutionary. Their goals entailed a transformation of economic and social structures in an effort to smother any potential threat to economic and social systems.

The intensity of the repression, as well as the tactics it utilized, depended on a number of factors: first, belief that the very nature of the threat itself (suppression of guerrilla groups) required particular brutality; second, belief that implementing the desired socioeconomic changes need repressive measures; and third, the variety of political and social influences having an impact on the government coalition. External pressures to moderate security policies, as well as internal calls for reconciliation emanating from the Church, also had an important effect in some cases. In addition, repression sometimes led to infighting within the military and to disputes between the security establishment and more professionally oriented officers.[38] Thus, the evolution of the human rights situation in each of the countries was a result of a variety of forces affecting repressive policies.

Most assuredly, authoritarian policies gained legitimacy through authoritarian concepts. National security notions gave shape to a set of values that inspired the social exclusion of the left, as well as a tremendous distrust for democratic politics. A market ideology supported the criticism of governmental economic intervention and the welfare state.[39] Thus, a new authoritarian concept of the world emerged, one that bore little resemblance to the Ibero-American culture and the Catholic concept depicted by some of the authors mentioned earlier. This new vision advocated economic competition, consumerism, and a limited role for the state in the protection of weaker sectors of the population. In terms of economic values, nothing was absolute and the "common good" did not exist.

As we are aware today, all of these countries began a process of transition to a democratic system. In fact, authoritarian regimes were never fully able to create an air of legitimacy around themselves, and as tension within the governing coalitions mounted, the calls for a return to democracy multiplied. A closer look at this process of redemocratization shows that it faces impending dangers. Civilian authorities have not been able to completely assert their authority over the military. Human rights violations have gone unpunished, and the economy requires drastic changes that would demand a high social cost and provoke further turmoil. However, the struggle against authoritarian domination has expressed cultural traits that are beneficial to the stabilization of democracy. But, since no trend is fatal and unchangeable, it becomes difficult to predict what will happen next. An examination of this issue will be undertaken in the next section. I will turn for the moment to the cases of Peru and Colombia, where the process underlying gross human rights violations differed from that of the Southern Cone and Brazil.

In neither Colombia nor Peru have the perpetrators of human rights violations been military regimes. Both countries are governed by duly elected civilians. Human rights abuses have been a response to armed resistance. Yet, the nature of the political system differed from that of the Southern Cone countries. Colombia and Peru can be characterized by the state's inability to integrate the polity. The state seems unable to control and assimilate social and political pressures to a much larger extent than in the Southern Cone societies. Citizens become alienated from the state, not just from the political regime in power. This has meant that in both Peru and Colombia a continued thinness in the formal-legal integration goes well beyond what is known to exist in the other countries analyzed earlier.[40]

In both countries, also, the integration of emerging social classes into the political and social system occurred later than in the Southern Cone. In the case of Colombia, the legitimacy of the political system was eroded by the permanence of the ruling elite and the exclusionary nature of the party system controlled by liberals and conservatives.[41] In the case of Peru, the roots of recent violence can be found in social and regional inequalities, as well as in an explosive process of urbanization and rising expectations among young migrants from rural areas, whose views become radicalized by the lack of opportunities.[42]

In Peru and Colombia the issue of political violence and human rights abuses is connected with a sort of structural reality. Social and regional differences, together with social dislocation created by processes of modernization, have virtually established a situation of political "normlessness." This explains the reason why the nature of the political regime—whether democratic or authoritarian—has been irrelevant in terms of the occurrence of human rights violations. Another difference from the countries of the Southern Cone is that the guerrilla movements that are threatening state stability and being repressed by the state have become stronger during the 1980s. They do not respond to the transitory influence of the Cuban revolution on Latin American elites.

It is true that in the case of Colombia the emergence and consolidation of the guerrilla movement took place in the mid-1960s. Although the rise of leftist movements working within the legal system pushed it to the sidelines during the 1970s, by the end of that decade the movement revived, partially due to the repression unleashed by President Turbay Ayala, and new groups were formed.[43] Today, Colombia is experiencing a wave of terror in which state institutions (police and armed forces) seem to be deeply involved, at least in terms of abdicating the responsibility to investigate and punish the perpetrators of politically inspired crimes.[44]

In the case of Peru, guerrilla groups were also created during the 1960s, but were finally defeated. Today the major threat to social peace is the "Communist Party of Peru—Sendero Luminoso" (Shining Path). Its origins can be found in a Maoist splinter group of the Communist Party that emerged in Ayacucho, possibly the poorest administrative district of Peru. In this region the state exercised extremely little control, and a dominant class capable of preserving existing social structures did not exist. In 1980, Sendero Luminoso began its offensive against the state with a series of terrorist actions. Up to now, though, it has been unable to gather enough support in urban areas.[45] In their struggle against Sendero Luminoso, which to date has been unsuccessful, the armed forces and the police have committed countless human rights violations; hundreds of people have disappeared. While at the very beginning of his term President Carcia seemed willing to restrain illegal repression, he later found himself acquiescing to it in the face of a situation that was out of control.[46]

The comparison just made between the Southern Cone countries and Peru and Colombia proves that, beyond general characteristics such as authoritarian political culture, major differences remain. To begin with, in the case of Southern Cone, human rights violations were associated with the rise of an authoritarian regime. While it is difficult to predict the evolution of the present democratic structures, the human rights situation has improved considerably. The situation of Colombia and Peru is much more difficult since the state is generally unable to assert its authority over different social actors.

Second, in the case of the Southern Cone countries, human rights violations were curtailed as a result of the economic and political failures of military regimes and because the political elites slightly moderated their views, thereby reducing political polarization. Thus, conflict management was more effective in easing political and social conflicts.

The cases of Peru and Colombia are much less manageable. Political violence has become a part of social life in Colombian society and past peace initiatives have failed. Moreover, the authority of the civilian government over the armed forces remains weak. In the Peruvian case, Sendero Luminoso ideology cannot be tamed by any peace initiative. Moreover, any reduction of political violence requires a social investment in depressed regions and in the cities at a time when Peru faces a tremendous economic crisis.

Despite the grim outlook faced by Colombia and Peru, Latin America is turning to democracy. This is partly the result of a human rights struggle that took place during the harshest repressive period. I will now consider the impact that this struggle might have on the political culture.

The Human Rights Struggle and Beyond

In reaction to the rise of repressive regimes in the Southern Cone and some other Latin American countries, a network of horizontal links among human rights organizations, church institutions, and private research centers was developed. They are dedicated to denouncing human rights violations, providing social services to the poor, and conducting research on prevailing social conditions.

The development of this network of nongovernmental organizations (NGOs) was made possible by the international support that they were able to gather; the involvement of the Catholic Church in human rights in Chile, Brazil, and to a lesser extent, Peru; and the economic and political support that they received from North Atlantic governments. The emergence and development of these nongovernmental groups is encouraging for the human rights cause. First of all, they play a major role in checking government violence.[47] Also, the concept of human rights itself has gained a new saliency and importance among policymakers, judges, and lawyers. This is a positive and reassuring development which certainly strengthens the forces fighting for peaceful solutions to the problems facing the countries of the region. New initiatives that these groups are launching in the field of human rights education, conferences, and proposals for judicial reform are most helpful in terms of creating a better climate for the observance of human rights.

In recent years the Inter-American System for Protection of Human Rights has been strengthened and began playing an important role in supervising compliance with human rights standards. The political weight of the Inter-American Commission on Human Rights grew substantially during the 1970s as some of its country reports produced an important impact upon public opinion.[48] With the enforcement of the American Convention on Human Rights, the commission and the state parties thereto had the opportunity to bring cases decided by the commission to the Inter-American Court on Human Rights. Just recently, the Inter-American Court handed down its decisions on its first contentious cases.[49] Thus, new actors have surfaced that are concerned with respect for human rights in the Latin American scene and can play a key role in denouncing cases of gross human rights violations.

These developments seem to be connected to a shifting international political climate. Recent events in Eastern Europe have strengthened the cultural weight of concepts such as human rights, freedom of expression, and the legitimacy of representative institutions. These political changes will have an impact on the perceptions of the Latin American left, which might feel more inclined to pursue peaceful social change. On the other hand, the end of the confrontation between the superpowers will leave the Latin American dominant classes and the military with little room to justify repression by invoking a foreign communist threat. This new international climate will certainly help to further advance the democratization process as the new ideological influences to be assumed by the Latin American context will be more receptive to human issues.

The return to electoral competition in most Latin American countries is certainly a positive development. The suffering inflicted by authoritarian regimes has instilled a new awareness about the relevance of fundamental liberties among civilian leaders. While violence has coexisted with democratic politics on several occasions, it becomes easier to denounce abuses once certain fundamental freedoms are restored.

The long-term implications of these developments for the future of the region is unpredictable at this moment. Cycles of transition to democracy in most of Latin America are not new, and some of these processes have been short-lived. The new attitudes of the elite are certainly an important element for the consolidation of an improved human rights situation. It is too early, however, to know how deep these changes in attitudes run. Moreover, it is clear that some of the structural socioeconomic dilemmas faced by Latin American nations cannot be solved by cultural changes alone, as Latin America is facing the burden of the foreign debt, soaring inflation rates, and poor growth.

New nongovernmental human rights organizations do not usually have much power to alter the course of events. Their role is educational and symbolic, and they can do little to change the policies of a government that views repression as serving its best interest. The regional system alone cannot effectively handle situations in which gross human rights violations take place, for OAS political organs have been reluctant to consider sanctions or other measures against states that violate human rights.[50] Moreover, situations in which gross human rights violations occur create a dynamic of their own. The armed forces develop corporatist autonomy and refuse to simply go back to the barracks. The security apparatus that served the repressive aims of previous authorities so well is rarely disbanded as transitions to democracy usually demand cautious negotiations between the civilian opposition and senior army officers.

Latin America is facing the tremendous challenge of building up a democratic culture. Social, cultural, and even ethnic heterogeneity are to be integrated into a common democratic culture. Yet here the process of unequal development takes place in mass societies that cannot wait a long time to see a solution to their social problems. The gradual process by which the masses acquired the full rights of citizenship in Europe is more difficult to follow here. Social mobilization will usually be accompanied by additional conflicts.

As Jose Joaquin Brunner notes, the dilemma is to create a political culture capable of integrating all these traits of cultural, economic, and social heterogeneity despite high levels of social conflict.[51] A consensus on shared values will be more difficult to attain in Latin America than has been the case in Europe and North America. Therefore, emphasis should be placed on establishing institutions and mechanisms capable of settling these conflicts and gaining legitimacy in Latin America despite the weaknesses inherent in the prevalent civic culture and the lack of fundamental shared beliefs. Only the acceptance of social conflicts by all political actors involved and a shared willingness to solve them peacefully will be capable of reducing present levels of political violence.

Conclusions

Political violence, in the form of gross human rights abuses, has become part of the historical evolution of Latin American societies. Yet, it has been more prevalent in some countries in contrast to others that have enjoyed long periods of democratic stability. The conflicts that preceded these periods in which extensive human rights abuses took place have had different connotations. Thus, their roots cannot be traced back to the hegemony of a particular authoritarian tradition that can be blamed for these processes. What is clear, though, is that the recurrence of these violent episodes creates a dynamic of its own so that it becomes likely that further violence will again take place.

Latin American societies are the recipients of ideological traditions that have been developed in the more affluent cultural centers of the world. Their impact and application have changed in accordance with the context. Thus liberal legalism and democratic values have remained a part of the culture, but their application has not been successful. Yet the fact that they continue to set standards of legitimacy for the governments is important. For if they were a mere facade with no normative value, it would have been easy to replace these principles altogether.

A fruitful path to exploring the divergence between principles and reality seems to me to be the analysis of the tensions aroused by late modernization in mass societies which face great economic constraints. These tensions appear to have been too much for political systems that lack the capability required to manage such conflicts. Still, recent events in the region seem hopeful as the most repressive dictatorships installed during the 1960s and 1970s have come to an end. Besides, the new social actors emerging during the last decade have concentrated on promoting and defending human rights. What will happen next depends in part on the elites' ability to moderate their ideological views, and to build up a tradition of compromise and cooperation. The odds against such a goal are enormous, as financial imbalances erect tremendous obstacles for improving the social welfare of the masses through redistributionist policies. Yet it is precisely the sad historical experiences of the recent past that could become the strongest incentive for trying hard to rebuild democratic institutions.

Notes

1. Glen Dealy, "Prolegomena on the Spanish American Political Tradition," in *Politics and Social Change in Latin America: The Distinct Tradition*, ed. Howard J. Wiarda (Amherst, Mass.: University of Massachusetts Press, 1982), 163–83. On the differences between American and Latin American conceptions of human rights, *see* Howard J. Wiarda, "La Lucha por la Democracia y los Derechos Humanos en America Latina," *Estudios Sociales* 18 (1978): 43–66.

2. Glen Dealy, "The Tradition of Monistic Democracy in Latin America," in Howard J. Wiarda, *ibid.* at 77.

3. These issues are addressed in Guillermo O'Donnell, *Modernization and Bureaucratic Authoritarianism: Studies in South American Politics* (Berkeley: Institute of International Studies, University of California, 1973); and in "Reflections on the Patterns of Change in the Bureaucratic-Authoritarian State," *Latin American Research Review* 12 (1978): 3–38. For an exhaustive discussion of O'Donnell's thesis, *see The New Authoritarianism in Latin America*, ed. David Collier (Princeton, N.J.: Princeton University Press, 1979).

4. Arturo Valenzuela, *The Breakdown of Democratic Regimes: Chile* (Baltimore: Johns Hopkins University Press, 1978).

5. José Joaquin Brunner, "America Latina entre la Cultura Democratica y la Cultura Autoritaria: Legados y Desafios," in *Revista Paraguaya de Sociologia*, 24 (1987): 7–15.

6. Larry Diamond and Juan J. Linz, "Introduction: Politics, Society, and Democracy in Latin America," in *Democracy in Developing Countries: Latin America*, ed. Larry Diamond, Juan J. Linz, and Seymour Martin Lipset (Boulder, Colo. and London: Lynne Rienner Publishers, Adamantine Press Limited, 1989), 10–11.

7. Jorge Nef, "Violence and Ideology in Latin American Politics: An Overview," unpublished manuscript, 1988. *See also* Alex P. Schmid, *Research on Gross Human Rights Violations: A Programme*, 2nd ed. (Leiden: Center for the Study of Social Conflicts, 1989), 93–95.

8. Francisco Zapata, "Revolutionary Movements in Latin America and the Development of Marxist Theory," in *Developments in Marxist Sociological Theory: Modern Social Problems and Theory*, ed. A. G. Zdravomyslov (Beverly Hills, Calif.: Sage, 1986).

9. The "new professionalism" oriented the military toward active participation in political and economic life. The National Security Doctrine justified the methods they used to wage internal war. *See* Alfred Stepan, "The New Professionalism of Internal Warfare and Military Role Expansion," in *Authoritarian Brazil: Origins, Policies, and Future*, ed. Alfred Stepan (New Haven: Yale University Press, 1973), 46–63; Margaret E. Crahan, "The Evolution of the Military in Brazil, Chile, Peru, Venezuela and Mexico: Implications for Human Rights," in *Human Rights and Basic Needs in the Americas*, ed. Margaret E. Crahan (Washington, D.C.: Georgetown University Press, 1982), 46–99.

10. Hugo Fruhling, "Nonprofit Organizations as Opposition to Authoritarian Rule: The Case of Human Rights Organizations in Chile," in *The Nonprofit Sector in International Perspective*, ed. Estelle James (New York: Oxford University Press, 1989), 358–76; Patricia T. de Valdez, "Las Organizaciones Nogubernamentales de Derechos Humanos en Peru," in *Derechos Humanos y Democracia: La Contribución de las Organizaciones do Gubernamentales* (ed. Hugo Fruhling (Santiago: Instituto Interamericano de Derechos Humanos, 1991), 219; Elizabeth Quay Hutchinson, "The Politics of Human Rights in Chile Under Authoritarian Rule, 1973–1988," M.A. thesis, Latin American Studies, University of California, Berkeley, 1989.

11. Norbert Lechner, "De la Revolucion a la Democracia. El Debate Intelectual en America del Sur," *Opciones* 6 (1985): 57–72.

12. Howard J. Wiarda, "Social Change, Political Development and the Latin American Tradition," in Howard J. Wiarda, *supra* note 1, at 23.

13. Claudio Veliz, "Centralism and Nationalism in Latin America," in *ibid.* at 211–25.

14. *Ibid.* at 212–15.

15. *Ibid.* at 214.

16. Glen Dealy, *supra* note 1, at 163.

17. *Ibid.* at 165.

18. *Ibid.* at 172–73.

19. A sample of books dealing with the violence that preceded the formation of modern states in Latin America is James R. Scobie, *Argentina: A City and a Nation* (New York: Oxford University Press, 1971); and Frederick B. Pike, *The Modern History of Peru* (New York: Frederick A. Praeger, 1967), 56–90.

20. Emilio F. Mignone, *Iglesia y Dictadura* (Buenos Aires: Ediciones del Pensamiento Nacional, 1986); Brian H. Smith, *The Church and Politics in Chile* (Princeton: Princeton University Press, 1982); Enrique Correa y José António Viera-Gallo, *Iglesia y Dictadura* (Santiago: CESOC-Ediciones Chile y America, 1986); Daniel H. Levine, "Continuities in Colombia," in *Journal of Latin American Studies* 17 (1985):295–317; Margaret E. Crahan, "A Multitude of Voices. Religion and the Central American Crisis," mimeo on file at the Program on Human Rights of the Academy of Christian Humanism, 1987.

21. Martin Weinstein, *Uruguay, Democracy at the Crossroads* (Boulder: Westview Press, 1988); Charles Gillespie et al., eds., *Uruguay y la Democracia*, 3 vols. (Montevideo: The Wilson Center Latin American Program/Ediciones de la Banda Oriental, 1985); Milton I. Vanger, *Jose Battle y Ordonez of Uruguay. The Creator of His Times* (Cambridge, Mass.: Harvard University Press, 1963).

22. Hugo Fruhling, "Liberalismo y Derecho en Chile," in *Ensayes* (Santiago: Editorial Debates, 1978), 746.

23. Martin Weinstein, *supra* note 21; Charles Gillespie, in *ibid.*; Milton I. Vanger, in *ibid.* (Cambridge, Mass.: Harvard University Press, 1963).

24. José Joaquin Brunner, "Los Debates Sobre la Modernidad y el Futuro de America Latina," *Documento de Trabajo* FLACSO No. 293 (April 1986).

25. Guillermo O'Donnell, "Tensions in the Bureaucratic-Authoritarian State and the Question of Democracy," in David Collier, *supra* note 3, at 285–318.

26. Francisco Zapata, *supra* note 8.

27. Julio Cotler, "State and Regime: Comparative Notes on the Southern Cone and the 'Enclave Societies,'" in David Collier, *supra* note 3, at 265.

28. Francisco Zapata, *supra* note 8, at 88–91.

29. Mauricio Solaun, "Colombian Politics: Historical Characteristics and Problems," in Albert Berry, Ronald G. Hellman, and Mauricio Solaun, eds., *Politics of Compromise Coalition Government in Colombia* (New Brunswick, N.J.: Transaction Books, 1980), 1–57.

30. Martin Weinstein, *supra* note 21, at 36–38.

31. Jorge F. Sabato and Jorge Schwarzer, "Funcionamento da Economia e Poder Politico na Argentina: Empecilhos Para a Democracia," in *Como Renascem*

as Democracias, ed. Alain Rouqiue, Bolivar Lamounier, Jorge Schwarzer (São Paulo: Editora Brasiliense, 1985), 166–67.

32. Elizabeth Dore and John F. Weeks, "Economic Performance and Basic Needs: The examples of Brazil, Chile, Mexico, Nicaragua, Peru and Venezuela," in Margaret E. Crahan, *supra* note 9, at 152–53.

33. *Ibid.* at 155.

34. Norbert Lechner, *supra,* note 11, at 57.

35. Kenneth F. Johnson, "Guerrilla Politics in Argentina," *Conflict Studies* 63 (1975):1–15; Richard Gillespie, *Soldados de Peron: Los Montoneros* (Buenos Aires: Grijalbo, 1982); Maria Esther Gilio, *The Tupamaro Guerrillas: The Structure and Strategy of the Urban Guerrilla Movement* (New York: Saturday Review Press, 1972).

36. For an analysis of the relationships between orthodox economic policies and state's coercion, *see* David Pion-Berlin, "The Political Economy of State Repression in Argentina," in *The State as Terrorist, The Dynamics of Governmental Violence and Repression,* ed. Michael Stohl and George A. Lopez (Westport: Conn.: Greenwood Press, 1984), 99–122.

37. Margaret E. Crahan, "National Security Ideology and Human Rights," in Margaret E. Crahan, *supra* note 9, at 101.

38. Hugo Fruhling, "Modalidades de la Represion Politica en el Cono Sur de America Latina," RIAL Conference Paper, 1987, mimeographed. Hugh Fruhling, "Repressive Policies and Legal Dissent in Authoritarian Regimes: Chile 1973–1981," *International Journal of the Sociology of Law* 12 (1984):351–74. Alfred Stepan, *Os Militares: Da Abertura a "Nova Republica"* (São Paulo: Paz e Terra, 1986), 67–71.

39. José Joaquin Brunner, "La Concepcion Autoritaria del Mundo," *Documento de Trabajo* FLACSO (1979).

40. For an excellent analysis of the inefficiency of the Colombian legal system regarding human rights violations, *see* Jean-Denis Archambault, *La Violacion de los Derechos Fundamentales y la Responsabilidad Civil de la Nacion Colombiana: La Estatizacion de la Violencia* (Colombia: Copycolor Editores, 1988).

41. Mauricio Salaun, *supra* note 29, at 1–57.

42. Julio Cotler, "La Cultura politica de la Juventud Popular del Peru," in *Cultura Politica y Democratizacion,* ed. Norbert Lechner (Buenos Aires: CLACSO, 1987), 127–45.

43. *Colombia: Violencia y Democracia. Informe Presentas al Ministerio de Colombia* (Bogotá: Universidad Nacional de Colombia—Centro Editorial, 1987), 46–47.

44. Americas Watch Committee, *The Killings in Colombia, An Americas Watch Report* (New York: Americas Watch Committee, 1989), 39–73.

45. Comision Especial del Senado sobre las Causas de la Violencia y Alternativas de Pacificacion en el Peru, *Violencia y Pacificacion* (Lima: DESCO y la Comision Andina de Juristas, 1989), 269–86.

46. *Ibid.* at 312–29. Americas Watch, *Human Rights in Peru after President Garcia's First Year* (New York: Americas Watch Committee, 1986). *See also,* Americas Watch, *Tolerating Abuses: Violations of Human Rights in Peru* (New York: Americas Watch Report, 1988).

47. *See* Hugo Fruhling, *supra* note 38.

48. Some of these have been reports on Argentina, OEA/Ser.L/V/II.49, doc. 19 (April 11, 1980) [original in Spanish]; Chile (3 reports), OEA/Ser.L/V/II.34, doc. 21, corr. 1 (October 25, 1974) [original in Spanish]; OEA/Ser.L/V/II.37, doc. 19, corr. 1 (June 28, 1976) [original in Spanish]; OEA/Ser.L/V/II.40, doc. 10 (February 11, 1987) [original in Spanish]. *See* Edmundo Vargas Carreno, "Las Observaciones in Loco Practicadas por la Comision Interamericana de Derechos Humanos," in *Inter-American Commission on Human Rights* (IACHR), *Human Rights in the Americas* (Washington, D.C.: Inter-American Commission of Human Rights, 1984), 290–305; Cecilia Medina Quiroga, *The Battle of Human Rights. Gross, Systematic Violations and the Inter-American System* (The Hague: Martinus Nijhoff Publishers, 1988).

49. *I/A Court H.R.*, Velasquez Rodriguez Case, Series C No. 4 (Judgment of July 20, 1988). I/A Court H.R., Godinez Cruz Case, Series C No. 5 (Judgment of January 20, 1989).

50. Cecilia Medina Quiroga, *supra* note 48, at 326–29.

51. José Joaquin Brunner, *supra* note 5, at 14–15.

11. Custom Is Not a Thing, It Is a Path
Reflections on the Brazilian Indian Case

For five hundred years, from the very beginning, Indian rights have been considered in Hispanic and Portuguese legal thought both as collective rights and as individual human rights. Two broad questions were considered: the first was whether Indians had any collective titles to their lands; the second was whether or under what conditions Indians would be subject to enslavement. The question of customary law also arose, since discussions went along on the topic of the right of the Indians to remain heathen, to retain polygamy, and even to practice cannibalism.

The issue of enslavement is now forgone, yet what is called nowadays "the right to difference" is very much alive. Such rights, as well as rights to land and to its natural resources, constitute the core of Indian rights discussion in Brazil. It has been claimed by native Brazilian leaders that both issues are fundamental human rights, a status that entails a collective as well as an individual dimension to these rights.

This position is consistent with sociological thought, at least since Emile Durkheim: the concept of the individual is historically Western; it gained hegemony around the eighteenth century and was enshrined two hundred years ago by the French Revolution. Yet such an equality of individuals is a highly abstract idea. No concrete individual can be thought of outside his or her context, which encompasses modes of perceiving the world, social values, and institutions, since to be human is also to have what is commonly called culture. Hence, in order to ensure the protection of fundamental individual rights, one must also protect its social conditions. And therefore, equality in rights as is claimed by Article 1 of the Universal Declaration of Human Rights of 1948 rates recognition not only for individuals but for societies as a whole.

Clearly, land rights stand foremost among the preconditions of social life in the case of indigenous societies. There have been gross violations of rights in that connection in Brazil, for which the state must bear a heavy responsibility.[1]

The Indian Issue Today

To understand the situation, at least a sketchy idea is needed of the actors involved in Indian issues in Brazil. These could be grouped as follows:

1. A heterogeneous state, which includes national and local government, the Congress, the judiciary, the public ministry, and, last but not least, the military, with specific and transient alliances in each of its subdomains.
2. Local and national organizations of Indians (UNI).
3. Other nongovernmental organizations or NGOs, both national and international, such as Indian, ecological, and general human rights support groups, as well as Brazilian professional associations of lawyers, geologists, anthropologists, scientists, journalists, and the Catholic church (sometimes, as recently, acting in cooperative efforts).
4. Local elites, national and international capital, lumber magnates, gold prospectors, mining companies, their workforce and possibly their own NGOs or trade unions.
5. International loci of power (moral or pecuniary) such as the Organization of American States (OAS), the United Nations, and above all, multilateral banks.

Although I have listed certain types of actors together, there is a great amount of heterogeneity in every one of these categories, which means they cannot be expected to act in any uniform or corporate way. The congress, the Public Ministry, and the judiciary (as their roles mandate) have challenged the executive branch, as will be seen in the example of the Yanomami case discussed below. Local elites and national and international capital may clash internally (for example, mining companies consistently try to dislodge gold prospectors, but they might encourage these same prospectors to break into Indian land). Grassroot movements and national organizations may occasionally be at odds regarding strategies and goals, not to mention competition among the NGOs in general.

An understanding of the role of the federal government and the implementation of military policies is crucial to understanding what goes on in the Amazon, where most of the Indian population is concentrated. Since at least the early seventies, the federal government was active in providing the region with an infrastructure that includes highways, hydroelectrics, and a railroad with a seaport at its terminal. It has also been engaged in establishing programs of "colonization" and providing fiscal incentives to investors, particularly for cattle-raising. The general plan was to utilize the energy and mineral resources of the Amazon, favor cattle-raising in the area, and start colonization projects that would alleviate the tensions posed by the landless peasantry in the south. The Amazonians—both the upper classes and the forest dwellers—were not much of a concern. The policy was instead geared toward Brazilian and transnational companies' interests.

Such a policy directly as well as indirectly affects Indian survival, and the direct effects are by no means insignificant: just as an example, in the southeast state of Para, public projects already occupy 72,000 hectares of Indian land, and 408,000 hectares are earmarked for flooding by plans for damming the Xingu River.[2] Indirect effects range from increases in land value, to epidemics, and to deforestation for pastureland, encroachment by lumberers, gold prospectors, mining companies, and so forth.

Another major component of Amazonian policies is represented by the military. Their view of the Amazon is a strategic one. When news of the program called "Calha Norte" leaked in 1987, it became clear that the program's design was to occupy the northern borders of the Amazonian area with a "human frontier." This "human frontier" was conceived as a colonization plan carried out by "real Brazilians," preferably as agriculturalists or ranchers.

Major assumptions were implied by such a conception; for one thing, that the Amazon was a demographically empty space, with no human occupation, a wholly natural space to be taken possession of; and for another, that the Indians, since they were not Brazilians who could be depended on, counted neither as occupants nor as persons eligible for providing a human frontier.

This dismissal of the Indians as an appropriate human frontier was both historically unfair and unconstitutional. For one thing, up to the end of the eighteenth century, Indian groups in borderline regions had been called by various officials the "walls of the hinterland" (*as muralhas do sertão*), or "the guardians of the frontier," and were used accordingly. In the early twentieth century, Brazilian and British litigation over a disputed area between the state of Roraima and then British Guiana was fought on the grounds of establishing the presence of certain Indian groups in the area and their alliance to one of the two parties or their predecessors in the region—the Portuguese and the Dutch, respectively.

Dismissing Indians as occupants of borderline regions is also unconstitutional. Indians have exclusive rights of possession (though not of dominion) and topsoil exploitation of their lands, and the federal government is obliged to have their lands demarcated. Such demarcation, initiated long ago, was to have been completed, by law, in 1978; but it was not. Although the new constitution, promulgated in 1988, contains provisions for a new five-year period during which to achieve demarcation, this plan has yet to be carried out.

What seems to be under suspicion is the actual "Brazilianness" of the Indians, on the one hand, and their ability to resist or avoid manipulation by foreign interests, on the other. Actually, in the introductory document to the Calha Norte Program, there is an explicit reference to the potential threat of Yanomami separatism under the manipulation of unspecified foreign interests, as these Indians span the border of Brazil and Venezuela.

The invasion of Yanomami land by gold prospectors is but a symptom of more extensive strategies. In 1986, the Air Force dislodged a group of gold prospectors who forcibly invaded Yanomami land disguised as army troops, but failed to take any action against subsequent encroachments. The very first landing strips were built by the Air Force allegedly to support the government Indian Agency (the ill-famed FUNAI, or Fundacão Nacional do Indio) to give medical and other assistance to the Yanomami. But FUNAI lacks any sort of airplanes in Roraima, where gold prospectors rely on a fleet of small airplanes which, in 1989, had turned Boa Vista airport into the second busiest airport in the country. I visited the area in June 1989, as part of a team from the "Action for Citizenship" movement, an association of major Brazilian professional organizations, the National Council of Bishops, and some members of congress. Gold prospectors had not only occupied Air Force—built air strips but also opened more than a hundred new clandestine airstrips themselves. These are euphemistically described by the military as "non-homologated." All these airstrips could be located through satellite photos, and one of them was just five minutes away by plane from a border military post. They could hardly have gone unnoticed by the authorities.

As to the role of FUNAI, this agency's post at Paapiu, which we visited, had been abandoned for at least five months; drugs and syringes were lying on the floor and the radio device had been ripped apart. Those Yanomami who still lived in a beautiful round communal house at one end of the airstrip were mostly ill, and subsequent visits by medical teams showed alarming malaria and mortality rates. The official report of a medical team that returned from the area in February 1990 indicated that in Paapiu 91 percent of the members of some communities were affected by malaria. Surucucus, a region that until 1987 had been totally free of malaria, registered a malaria rate of 78 percent of its population. Sixty-eight percent of the members of one community, and 53 percent of another, died in 1989. On the whole, it is estimated that 13 percent of the Yanomami have died in the last two years.

It became clear to our team that the invasion could not have occurred without the knowledge, and therefore acquiescence, of the Brazilian army and the air force. Why did they choose to allow it? As the Air Force commander who was our host explained, gold prospectors were bold but rather unruly people, desperadoes unsuited for relocation to the cities. Yet, and rather inconsistently, he added that they could perfectly well mix with the Yanomami, with whom they were on very friendly terms. Many of these prospectors seemed to be originally northeastern peasants, but a great number had previously held small jobs in southeastern towns. A lot of gold smuggling was known to be going on, and therefore national revenue had little profit coming out of this business. Although it is difficult to know with certainty why the military favored this invasion of Indian land, one can speculate as to the reasons.

My own guess is as follows: I do not think the military held the gold prospectors in great esteem as those best-suited to be a buffer at the frontier, but they were the ones who could and would penetrate the forest and face the Indian threat. Also, they caused irreversible destruction of the forest and of the Indians themselves. It is entirely possible that the military hoped to replace the prospectors by mining companies. In previous years, there had been a close alliance between Brazilian-owned mining companies and the military, resulting, among other things, in barring foreign-owned mining companies from the Amazon under the new Constitution. Moreover, for a number of years the military has been trying to persuade public opinion that mining companies, in Indian lands or elsewhere, were better than individual gold prospectors since they were more organized and more disciplined, so that they can control their workers. In 1987, the mining companies were actually able to secure contracts in Tukano Indian lands (in the state of Amazonas, near the Colombian border) with the help of the then National Security Council (CSN). That deal provided for the company's control and expulsion of the encroaching prospectors.

Another clue is the military's attempt to divide Yanomami territory (at the very moment when the issue of Indian land was being decided in the Constituent Assembly) into an archipelago of isolated subunits with intervening National Forests. According to this plan, the Indians would not retain exclusive but solely preferential rights of use, and mining would be permitted, in these isolated subunits. From all these facts, it is at least reasonable to suppose that the military was not unhappy to see the Yanomami area being invaded because that could prove helpful in disputing Yanomami occupation of the territory or in supporting the claims of Brazilian mining companies to exploit the underground resources. An orderly colonization would also come in handy. This was explicitly expected to happen around military borderline posts, notwithstanding the fact that they were in Indian land. Such an outcome would at last provide a "proper" human frontier in the area.

One might muse as to why the military seems to back local elites rather than worry about them, since local elites are clearly resentful of the use of their region to provide energy or iron to southern-owned companies. In fact, there seems to be a growing chauvinism among dominant classes in the Amazon that are trying to establish "horizontal links" among themselves. There are strong attempts by the ruling class to establish Amazonian identity and even pan-Amazonian cooperation treaties reaching other South American countries.

What is interesting is that at the dominant class level, a strong regionalism has evolved. Regional elites claim exclusive local competence on what has been otherwise a universal concern, while at the bottom level, rubber-tappers and Indians have shown a tendency to universalize local claims.

The National Security Council (CSN), later renamed as Strategic Affairs Bureau (Secretaria de Assuntos Estratégicos, SAE) a kind of military intelligentsia, expanded its influence on federal policies not only during the military regime but particularly during the rule of President José Sarney, who came to rely on the CSN to a great extent as his civilian support diminished. Thus since the early 1980s, Amazonian affairs, which encompassed Indian affairs, have fallen into the ever-broadening category of National Security Issues. Indian issues, even outside the Amazon, have become subject to military scrutiny and interference.

On the other hand, radical jargon such as the insistence on the term "nations" to designate the Indian ethnic units, used primarily by the Indigenist Missionary Council (CIMI), a sector of the very powerful Catholic Church, alarmed the military who interpreted it as evidence of forthcoming claims of independence. Here again one remains doubtful of the extent to which the military actually rather than rhetorically believed in threats of separatism by microethnic groups such as the lowland South-American groups. It should be noted in this connection that in Brazil today, there are only two hundred thousand (200,000) Indians dispersed in 180 ethnic groups in a total population of roughly 120 million inhabitants of the country. The largest Indian groups, such as the Tikuna and the Yanomami, number around 8,000 to 10,000 people.

But Indians do not matter as much as their lands and riches. There seem to be two major reasons for this being the case: First, Indians have held constitutional rights to land which, although widely scattered, amounts to something like 8.5 percent of Brazilian territory. Not surprisingly, Indians have been able to maintain control of large portions of their traditional land at the fringes of the internal economic frontier, which means that some of it stands next to international boundaries. The military, for strategic reasons and because of its strong suspicions regarding the extent of the Indians' Brazilian patriotism, have consistently resisted the demarcation of significant Indian land close to the frontier.

The second reason seems literally to lie underground. Since RADAM Brasil, an aerial photography program carried out over the Amazon in the seventies, many have come to believe that the area contains abundant mineral resources. Thus remote areas where, in the past, no one would think of disputing Indian land claims, became the core of the disputes of the last ten years.

Indian Rights in the New Brazilian Constitution

Brazil has a strong tradition of extensive Indian rights, but likewise an at least equally strong tradition of violation of these rights. It is true that the balance of power relations is and has always been strongly against the Indians, and that practice does not conform with the provisions of the law. Nevertheless, the discourse of rights is powerful in itself; hence fierce battles have been fought over legal texts.

Brazil has had a long series of constitutions, beginning with the 1824 Charter granted by the emperor, which was followed by a Republican

Constitution in 1891. More recently, it has had a string of constitutions closely following coups and democratic periods in 1934, 1937, 1946, 1967, 1969, and finally 1988. The drafting of this latest Brazilian constitution started in March 1987, and the constitution itself was promulgated in October 1988.

Since the third Brazilian Constitution of 1934, Indians have had constitutional rights to their lands. These rights were progressively specified in subsequent constitutions until, ultimately, dominion over this land was imparted to the Union (federal government), while Indians retained exclusive and inalienable possession of it and the exclusive usufruct of all of its natural resources. Since 1967, however, it has remained unclear who had rights to subsoil resources since, as a general rule, a distinction was made between rights to the topsoil and rights to the subsoil. When the very important *Indian Statute* was adopted by Congress in 1973, its author opted for the interpretation that subsoil resources were not to be included in the constitutional formula. In the late 1970s, after the program of aerial photography of the Amazon referred to earlier had raised high expectations for finding mineral resources, this issue became crucial.

By the time of the drafting and adoption of the new Constitution of 1988, the Indian issue stood as one of the five most controversial issues in the Constitutional Assembly because of the importance of mineral resources believed to lie underneath Indian land. Discussions about conditions to establish and control research and mining in Indian areas became one of the most hotly debated issues in the National Constituent Assembly from 1986 to 1988. The position taken by UNI (Indian Nations' Union) and by NGOs including the Brazilian Anthropological Association (ABA) and the Association of Professional Geologists (ONAGE) proposed that concessions to subsoil resources under Indian land should be sanctioned by Congress on a case-by-case basis, that they should be limited to Brazilian state-owned mining companies, and pursued only in the case of strategic minerals that could not be obtained elsewhere in the country. As this proposal began to win support in Congress in early September 1987, five major newspapers around the country launched a violent campaign (covering half of their front pages for more than a week) against defenders of Indian rights, accusing them of a conspiracy against Brazilian sovereignty. In support of these accusations, this campaign produced fabricated "proofs" of such a conspiracy, which was allegedly backed by tin companies around the world in order to keep Brazilian tin out of the market. By the time these charges had been disproved in a series of congressional hearings, the safeguards on mining in Indian land had been reduced to congressional case-by-case approval.

Another attempt to militate against Indian rights in the constitution was the distinction between "real Indians" and "acculturated Indians." The idea was simple, actually, and had already been tried on various occasions by successive governments from 1978 on. Since Indians had broad constitutional rights, an easy ploy to avoid honoring these rights was to diminish the number of legal Indians by arguing that so-called acculturated Indians should have no land rights. Ultimately, then, there would be virtually no holders of Indian rights and coveted land would become available. The idea was crude but also powerful because it appealed to common sense, including judicial common sense, through the notion that traditional culture should be the touchstone of ethnic identity. Instead of being recognized for what they are, namely, as historical rights, Indian land rights were presented to the Brazilian public as minority rights that had been bestowed on underprivileged people. According to common sense, then, there seemed to be nothing wrong in denying these special rights to people who looked just like everyone else. It took a great deal of mobilization (in which anthropological understanding of ethnic identity was crucial to the debate) to defeat these proposals.

Following extensive debate over amendments, the final outcome was a broad victory for Indian rights, although some major issues were postponed. Thus, the specific conditions under which the search for and exploitation of mineral resources in Indian land, as well as the building of hydroelectric facilities affecting such land, could be carried on were to be set by ordinary law. On the whole, however, some highly significant progress was achieved, such as the introduction of a separate chapter (Title VIII—Of the Social Order, chapter 8—On Indians) on Indian rights in the text of the constitution, the dropping of the previous assimilation program, the recognition of Indian cultural rights, and the transfer of all legislative and judicial matters relating to Indians to the federal sphere. Moreover, the responsibilities imparted to the congress in Indian affairs were all new and important.[3] I would like to stress here three other points in which substantial progress was achieved.

The first such point was the definition of Indian rights in land as originary rights. This means that such rights existed prior to the state itself: they were recognized rather than granted by the state. As such, they are therefore historical rights. The importance of this is not merely rhetorical. As indicated above, the common understanding in Brazil has it that Indians are entitled to special rights only as long as they are vulnerable to and not cognizant of other people's malice. This perspective fails to acknowledge Indian rights to their land as rights of primary occupancy of the land, even though this had been the Portuguese and Brazilian tradition prior to the early twentieth century.[4] When the Civil Code was drafted in 1916, the Indians were included, for their protection, among the "relatively capable," and were thus lumped together with people from sixteen to twenty-one years of age and married women. They became wards of the federal government, which in turn delegated its duties to a special bureau (the Service of Indian Protection [SPI] from 1910 to 1967, FUNAI from 1967 to 1991, and the recently renamed Instituto Nacional do Indio [INI] in a very special case of tutelage over which no control was exercised. The SPI was abolished on serious charges of corruption; and FUNAI has been subject to ongoing criticism.

Although wardship has not been a very good solution, Indians and their supporters cling to it because it seems nowadays to provide the only basis for special rights. The recognition of Indian rights as historical rather than as special protection rights might open the way to an alternative legal basis for Indian rights.

The second major progress relates to the definition of Indian land. There has been much litigation in recent years about the subject, with judges ruling alternatively in favor of a restricted interpretation of Indian land as inhabited and cultivated land or upholding its broad definition as a territory. The definition provided in the new constitution (article 231, paragraph 1) is the broadest possible.

The last achievement I would like to stress is the recognition of Indian judicial capacity. This again was something judges did not necessarily recognize. Since FUNAI, for the reasons stated earlier, did not necessarily take judicial initiatives, there were serious limitations to Indian enforcement of the law. In the new constitution, not only is such judicial capacity explicitly stated but the Public Ministry is now also obliged to provide mandatory judiciary assistance in these matters. In less than two years' time, this has proven to be a most powerful change. The Public Ministry, which previously acted as the defender of the federal government, now has the functions of a collective ombudsman, as a defender of diffused rights. Its action in the case of the Yanomami, for example, has set new standards for the legal handling of Indian affairs.

On the initiative of the Public Ministry in December 1989, Justice Reis and Justice Aguiar ruled for the interdiction of airstrips and the removal of the gold prospectors from the Yanomami area. The Air Force protested that the task was not feasible. The Minister for Justice himself and the Federal Police Chief went to the area but, instead of enforcing the judicial order, they drafted an agreement relocating the gold prospectors in another part of Yanomami territory. For the first time in Brazilian history, officials of such high rank were threatened with imprisonment. Then, in February 1990, the Public Ministry issued an unprecedented accusation against President Sarney and four of his ministers for noncompliance with judicial orders and "crimes of responsibility," that is, criminal failure to comply with their responsibility to enforce the law.

New Actors: Are Indians Worthy of Support?

Since the early 1980s, multilateral development agencies started imposing clauses on loans for development projects calling for protection of the environment and indigenous peoples. They also started to require an impact assessment of the project. These measures are supposed to be safeguards. The very idea of impact, however, carried the assumption that the agent was the state, and that there was some natural environment out there which would be subject to impact. Indigenous peoples were thus seen as passive recipients of impacts, if not part of the natural scenery.[5] There was by then a sort of transparency and naturalization of local groups by which they were not recognized as agents with their own specific projects. Parallel to their long-standing demographic invisibility, traditional peoples had become politically invisible as well.

In the last five years, this process has been challenged, and new political actors emerged, or rather were recognized as such. How this was achieved is quite an interesting story. Multilateral banks had been under pressure, mainly in the United States, from environmental groups, who were ultimately responsible for the abovementioned environmental and human-rights clauses becoming part of routine bank contracts in the first place. Since about 1982, Brazilian indigenous organizations and support groups have been able to exert some degree of pressure on the Brazilian state and influence its policies by carrying out and publicizing independent analyses of the social and ecological effects of some big projects in Brazil. On the basis of such analysis, multilateral banks would sometimes temporarily withhold money for developmental projects if it could be shown that companies were not complying with certain clauses, thus linking what Abdullahi An-Na'im calls "internal cultural discourse" to cross-cultural dialogue.[6] The most effective way of exerting this international pressure was the linking accomplished by the World Bank and the Interamerican Development Bank of new loans to the Brazilian government with internationally accepted standards of protection for environmental and indigenous land rights.

It is worth observing that, to a great extent, even among environmentalists, human rights and environmental issues were dissociated. Human rights dealt with victims, whereas environmental issues dealt with centrally designed preservation programs. Local populations were victims of human rights violations, but they were not supposed to formulate programs. The old environmentalist world was no more human than the military's: both perceived the environment as a no-man's land, to be preserved or to be conquered. Recent developments, however, indicate a growing awareness that "only man's presence can save nature."[7]

One consequence of these developments, namely, the obligations prescribed in the new Brazilian constitution and by multilateral banks, is an attempt to change public opinion in respect to Indians in Brazil. Until now, one of the major tactics employed in dismissing Indian rights was to disqualify *ethnically* the holders of such rights. To this strategy might now be added a still embryonic attempt to disqualify Indian groups *ethically* as unworthy of the support they get. The idea is to reverse the normal flow of accusations and let Indians stand as the accused instead of as the victims. This reversal can be achieved by accusing Indian culture of being inconsistent with internationally recognized human rights.

The issue of the "right to difference" is somewhat more complicated than this sort of accusation might suggest. It may be true that cultural norms specific to a group—and here I am speaking of any cultural minority within a state, not merely indigenous groups—collide with generally accepted human rights. Some groups, for instance, might practice infanticide of malformed children or of consecutive children spaced too close together. Or, for that matter, the Catholic church might bar access to priesthood for women as against generally accepted standards of equal opportunity for all. Cannibalism might have been a central institution among the Aztec and some Melanesian and lowland South American societies. Now, in such cases, which should prevail: respect for local culture and customary law or enforcement of "truly universal standards of human rights"?

If I were to judge an issue bluntly put in such terms, I sincerely would not know how to solve it. But I think that this is not the way the issue presents itself. One *important* reason for that is, I suspect, a prevailing misconception about what exactly "culture" and "customary law" are.

Problems with the Concepts of Culture and Customary Law

What I see as the fundamental problem is the tendency to reify the notions of "culture" and "customary law," and to deprive them of all their political content. This tendency is identifiable in the very use of these expressions. Thus one hears, for instance, about the incorporation of customary law through reference or replication.[8] Implicit in such terms is the assumption that one is speaking of an identifiable set of categories and legal norms with three characteristics:

- they are supposed to constitute a circumscribed and limited "corpus" of traditional norms.
- they are supposed to be previous and autonomous in relation to States.
- they are supposed to be similar in nature to positive law, thereby enabling States to incorporate them explicitly, given the necessary political conditions.

These assumptions can hardly stand, however, when confronted with the facts. What is commonly called customary law is what anthropologists have traditionally called social structure, a concept that in turn is directly derived, as made clear by A. R. Radcliffe-Brown, from legal studies.[9] It might help to remember that most of the founders of anthropology in the nineteenth century were originally jurists who were trying to find categories analogous to Western political and juridical institutions in what was then called primitive society.

Social structure had, for such anthropologists as Radcliffe-Brown and Meyer Fortes, for instance, a substantive content, permanent in time.[10] Yet, a great part of the generation which followed Radcliffe-Brown and Fortes concentrated on the ambiguity of rules, their multiplicity, and their contextual validity. In contrast to Radcliffe-Brown, who described a universe of mechanical and imperative rules, with no ambiguities or contradictions, and whose distance from reality was solved through juridical fictions, his successors began to perceive a field of strategies based on norms not necessarily unequivocal or convergent.

Radcliffe-Brown, for whom societies could be understood by analogy to living organisms, thought that changes did not alter a society's structural form (an aging rabbit does not cease to be a rabbit). To him, this was also true with societies, which could be recognized without hesitation through the application of substantive criteria. But by the end of the sixties, anthropology started to question whether the very units with which it worked, namely societies, were recognizable by any criteria at all. It discovered the failure of substantive criteria and the importance not of homeostatic reproduction but of autopoietic production of society. Society was no longer, as it had been for Emile Durkheim, the autoregenerative point of departure that ensured its own permanence, but rather a process of continuous elaboration. Forging this process for the recognition of an identity is what Eric Hobsbawm would later call "the invention of tradition." As will be shown, this means that *change* in society (concealed and) conceived of itself as *tradition*.

With such a perspective, the idea that each society has a *corpus* of traditional rules which can be simply transposed into positive law without further ambiguities does not hold. *Since such rules are social products continuously elaborated, what has to be granted to minorities whose customary law one wishes to respect is not specific norms but rather the authority to elaborate them.*

Another observation to which anthropology paid attention in the late 1960s, following the decolonization of Africa, was that, contrary to all expectations, there was an exacerbation of ethnic identities in the newly formed African states. Within a few years, it became clear to political scientists and to anthropologists alike that ethnicity, which at first sight appeared to be concerned with the maintenance of culture and tradition, was in fact propelled by and concerned with unequal distribution of power. Culture, or rather selected items of traditional culture, served important but nevertheless *new* ends, namely, the establishment of a contrasting identity vis-à-vis other groups. Thus, cultural items were selected that could be used as diacritical signs within a shared language of cultural difference among competing groups: ways of dressing, languages, religions, or sects within religions were commonly used to establish such distinctions. The apparent paradox was, of course, that such selected cultural items were detached from the original system to which they belonged in order to enter a new multiethnic symbolic system: their status was enhanced, the result being that it appeared as if traditions were stronger than ever when in exile. In short, cultural traits of ethnic groups did not derive solely from an autonomous elaboration. Rather, they were also externally manipulated to form systems of contrast with cultural traits of other ethnic groups,[11] or of the dominant nation within the state.[12]

These perceptions reinforce what was mentioned above, namely the conditions in which the cultural production of a society takes place, and which assume other societies or social groups' existence and interaction. It is as if the emphasis had passed from the analogy of societies with living organisms, considered in their irreducible singularity, to the analogy with communication systems. Thus the anthropological classical fiction that societies could be observed in perfect isolation and untouched by time— for many years a sort of private anthropological poetic license—was repudiated.

This being so, neither the priority nor the autonomy from the state of customary law can be held anymore. The former only exists in relation to the latter and requires its presence in a double fashion: First, because one can speak of customary law only in opposition to positive law which assumes the existence of a state; second, because the very content of customary law, as has been shown, is partially and by contrast determined by the existence of the state. *Thus, both the notion and the specific content of customary law are tributaries to the existence of a state which it confronts.*

Finally, writing is a difference betwen positive law and customary law which should not be underestimated. The importance of writing in this context has been emphasized since Max Weber. More recently, anthropologist Jack Goody has called our attention to the implications of writing and its diffusion in the transformation of societies of oral tradition.[13] Without entering into the considerations Goody makes on the impact of this new means of communication on cognitive processes, it seems certain that written and oral law lend themselves to different logical operations and social use. I have attempted to show elsewhere the significance of nineteenth-century Brazilian positive law having deliberately omitted largely practiced rules of customary law on slave manumission.[14] Such silence was a key element in the building up of personal links of dependency necessary to the system.

I would only emphasize here that positive and customary law, though they may easily coexist, are of a different nature and social use, and cannot be reduced to a single system. As a consequence it is absurd to replicate, in an explicit and substantive way, a system of customary law into positive law, and *a fortiori* some of its fragments, which can only make sense within the system.

Human Rights in Process

The implications of this discussion for our debate about how to adjust generally recognized human rights to customary law are clear: the content of customary law—and for that matter, the content of what are considered "universal human rights" as well—are continually being modified. Therefore, what has to be acknowledged for other people is not *a substantive set of norms* that might be incompatible with our present standards of human rights. Rather, what has to be acknowledged is other people's *authority* over the ever-changing content of customary law. Ethnicity, which defines one's relationship to proximate neighbors, constitutes one of the factors affecting the content of customary law. Another factor that modifies the content of customary law is the relationship of a minority to the rest of the world. It is probable that there will be a tendency toward an internally conducted adjustment to current international human rights standards. For one thing, most minorities are largely dependent for political support on public opinion, be it national or international, and they have proved highly capable of translating their claims into general issues. In Brazil, for instance, the rubber-tappers' (*seringueiros*) movement in the state of Acre started in the 1970s as a labor movement. It was organized into labor unions and phrased its claims mainly in terms of the injustice characterizing labor relations on rubber estates. Also, to defend rubber-tappers' access to hevea trees that produce latex, they opposed, through sit-ins, the deforestation promoted by cattle-ranchers in the Amazon. The interesting thing to observe is that it was not the Greens who first recognized the ecological dimension of the *seringueiros* movement, but rather *seringueiros* leaders, among them Chico Mendes (winner of the United Nations Global Prize for ecology in 1987), who was murdered in December 1988. Kaiapo Indian leaders of the southern state of Para were able to make a similar connection in early 1989, in which their struggle for land matched a more widely ranging campaign against the building of dams on the Xingu River; in addition to flooding their lands, these dams had far-reaching negative effects on the ecology. What is amazing (for Brazil at least) is that Kaiapo Indians became the leaders of a very general movement: they gained support not merely because they were struggling for land but also because they were championing a general ecological issue. In short, they managed to establish the link between their particular interests and universal interests. In the same vein, Davi Yanomami was awarded the 1989 United Nations Global Prize because of his struggle against golddiggers encroaching on Yanomami territory. It is significant that the National Council of Rubber-Tappers and the Indigenous Nations Union in the state of Acre united in 1985 to constitute the Alliance of the Forest People. Ten years ago, rubber-tappers and Indians were still enemies. Today, the alliance is consulted by the World Bank on issues regarding policies for the Amazon.

One might remember at this point Gyorgy Lukacs' thesis about the coincidence—in a given historical period—of the interests of a particular social class with universal interests.[15] Thus, the bourgeoisie carried such universals in the late eighteenth century; one century later, the working class was its successor. It does appear that indigenous people and workers of the forest such as *seringueiros* would present themselves, after another century, as the heirs of the working-class, for their specific interests merge with a universal concern for the future of the planet and of humankind. Yet they should not be valued only as defenders of the forest. The diversity of societies, that is, the different forms of sociability, are to be treasured as much as the diversity of biological species. Such merging requires a connection with equally general standards.

The Yanomami, mentioned above, are a case in point. They have been differently described by different anthropologists. One has depicted the Yanomami as especially aggressive warriors, as "fierce people." I will not discuss here whether such a description is appropriate or whether the reactions of the press to such description were well founded. It is significant, however, to note that some of the reactions of the press and the general public seem to indicate a feeling of being tricked in some devious way into supporting the land rights of these fierce Indians.

One position, to which some anthropologists adhere, would be extreme cultural relativism, entailing statements about the right of people to have their own values and standards. Another would be the general public reprobation of such standards. But Indian leaders seem to have a much more balanced position: they perceive the conflict and they try to adjust. The point is that their authority to do so must be recognized.

The very same Yanomami have entered cross-cultural dialogue, stating the global significance of their own specific history. At a press conference and congressional hearing on March 9, 1990, at which the medical team reported the apalling morbidity and mortality rates I have already mentioned, political and shamanic leader Davi Yanomami explained that should the Yanomami *shabori* (shamans) die as they are indeed dying, their attendant spirits would, in anger, cut the ropes which sustain the present-day heaven. Since there would be no more living shamans left to stop them, which is one of their tasks, heaven would fall on earth, pushing the trees and the mountains into the subterranean world, "theeee!" People would fall in fear, "aaaaaa." The sun and the spirits of the night would fall as well.[16] Thus, the death of the Yanomami literally entails the end of the world. "You have to tell those who do not look ahead, who do not dream," said Davi, "that the earth is one. You have to teach your children to look ahead, and they have in turn to teach their children. This is important not just for us Indians, but also for whites, blacks, yellows, reds. You say that the earth is a ball. It is. The earth is one, the moon is one, the sun is one alone. This is why all of us need the shabori [*shaman*]. It is he who sustains the world. We are the people of Omam, this is why we are called yanomami."

I wish to conclude with a historical example which I particularly like because it points out how relative and historically based our own values are. In the sixteenth century, Portuguese colonial authorities blamed the Tupi Indians along the Brazilian coast for ceremonially killing and eating their enemies instead of killing them on the battlefield or enslaving them "*as all civilized countries do.*" Consequently, they enforced a rule that all Indian wars should not be conducted without the prior authorization of the governor, and that captives should be killed on the spot or, better, sold as slaves to the colonists. Since the colonists badly needed slaves, they encouraged wars for their own ends, and wars raged as never before. Ritual killing and cannibalism had been central to the Tupi social system: a prerequisite for a youth who wanted to marry and, for adults, for gaining political prestige and even immortality. Yet eventually the Tupi abandoned ritual killing and cannibalism for attenuated forms of it (for instance, breaking skulls of already dead enemies) which were more palatable to the Portuguese. Such is *Realpolitik*.

Notes

1. M. C. da Cunha, "Native Realpolitik," *NACLA Report On The Americas* 23 (1989): 19–22.
2. L. Santos and L. Andrade, eds., *As hidrelétricas do Xingu e os Povos Indígenas* (São Paulo: Comissão Pró-Indio de São Paulo, 1988).

3. For these and other significant gains for Indians, *see* Articles 20, 22, 26, 49, 115, 135, 182, 210, 215, 231, and 232 of the Brazilian Constitution of 1988.

4. *See*, for instance, João Mendes, Jr., *Os indígenas do Brasil, seus direitos individuaes e políticos* (São Paulo: Comissão Pró-Indio, 1912).

5. *See* E. Viveiros de Castro and L. Andrade, "Hidrelétricas do Xingu: o Estado Contra as Sociedades Indígenas," in L. Santos and L. Andrade, eds., *As hidrelétricas do Xingu e os Povos Indígenas* (São Paulo: Comissão Pró-Indio de São Paulo, 1988).

6. *See* Abdullahi A. An-Na'im's Chapter 1 in this volume.

7. This is the conclusion of a recent forum on ecology. *See Harper's Magazine* (April 1990).

8. B. R. Morse and G. R. Woodman, "Introductory Essay: The State's Options," in *Indigenous Law and the State*, ed. B. R. Morse and G. R. Woodman (Dordrecht and Providence, R.I.: Foris Publications, 1988), 5–23.

9. *See* A. R. Radcliffe-Brown, "Patrilineal and Matrilineal Succession," in *Structure and Function in Primitive Society* (New York: Free Press, 1952), 32–48; A. R. Radcliffe-Brown, "On Social Structure," in *ibid*. at 188–204.

10. Thus, Radcliffe-Brown was able to describe, in 1930, the Australian hord as a local patrilineal group, with collective rights over a territory and its products. In other words, a political unit with rules of citizenship and of rights over persons and things (A. R. Radcliffe-Brown, "The Social Organization of Australian Tribes," *Oceania*, 1 [1930]:34–63).

11. *See* F. Barth, "Introduction," in *Ethnic Groups and Boundaries*, ed. F. Barth (Bergen/Oslo: Universitets Forlaget, 1969); A. Cohen, *Custom and Politics in Urban Africa* (London: Routledge and Kegan Paul, 1969); Manuela Carneiro da Cunha, "Ethnicidade: da cultura, residual mas irredutível," in *Antropologia do Brasil: Mito, Historia, Etnicidade* (São Paulo: Brasiliense, 1986), 97–108; Manuela Carneiro da Cunha, *Negros, Estrangeiros: Os Escravos Libertos e sua Volta à Africa* (São Paulo: Brasiliense, 1985), 231.

12. This being so, one can hardly think of the possibility of a culture being untrue to itself, as Michael McDonald has suggested. (*See* Chapter 6 in this volume.) Since cultures respond to each other in a multiethnic situation, they have to speak a common language.

13. *See Literacy in Traditional Societies*, ed. J. Goody (Cambridge: Cambridge University Press, 1968); J. Goody, *The Domestication of the Savage Mind* (Cambridge: Cambridge University Press, 1977).

14. *See* M. Carneiro da Cunha, "Silences of the Law: Customary Law and Positive Law on the Manumission of Slaves in Nineteenth-Century Brazil," *The Discourse of Law, History and Anthropology* 1, no. 2 (1985): 427–44.

15. *See* Gyorgy Lukacs, "Class Consciousness" and "Reification and the Consciousness of the Proletariat," in *History and Class Consciousness: Studies in Marxist Dialectics* (Cambridge, Mass.: MIT Press, 1973), 46–82 and 83–222, respectively.

16. Bruce Albert, "Mitos ianomami explican leis do cosmo," *Folha de São Paulo,* 5 de Maio (1990), letras F-5.

Patricia Hyndman

12. Cultural Legitimacy in the Formulation and Implementation of Human Rights Law and Policy in Australia

Introduction

In a unitary and essentially monocultural society, the problem of cultural legitimacy in the formulation and implementation of human rights law and policies (whether these take the form of constitutional provisions, legislation, administrative or executive action) is relatively simple. If the human rights law and policies are generated from within the society, they can be assumed to be culturally legitimate, or at least as legitimate as any other legislation or governmental policy generated within that society.

If human rights law and policy is taken from outside, however—for instance by the adoption, through legislation or otherwise, of international human rights standards, there may well be a problem of legitimacy. Ordinary members of the community may not understand, know of, agree with, or accept the standards in question. Some of the standards may be seen as conflicting with local traditions and mores. It is common to hear it said that the major international human rights instruments reflect the value systems of Western liberal democracies and are inappropriate to countries at a different stage of development, with different traditions, political systems, and needs.[1] Still, no country is forced to accept international human rights treaties. Moreover, the process of domestic implementation through judicial interpretation and through the establishment of domestic procedures and other domestic implementation measures is likely to give its own slant to the international standards, which may over time—to a degree at least—become assimilated into, and become more widely accepted as a part of, the local legal fabric.

In a multicultural society, especially one that consists both of indigenous peoples and of a large number of immigrant groups, and in which these are diverse ethnic communities with widely differing traditions, mores, and social expectations, the difficulties with cultural legitimation in respect to human rights norms and domestic human rights law and policy become more varied and complex. Australia is one such society. Although it still has a dominant monoculture, it is now a multicultural society, and it has an indigenous population. In consequence, problems of cultural legitimacy are experienced in full measure.

In this chapter I will discuss, first, some aspects of the problem of cultural legitimacy in relation to the majority, the Anglo-Celtic English-speaking population of Australia—those people who, from shortly after the time of the first white settlement of the country in the late 1700s until the end of World War II, comprised almost the entire population; second, I will outline some of the acute problems of cultural legitimacy in the human rights field which the relations between Aboriginal and white Australia have created; and third, I will refer briefly to the (as yet tentative and embryonic) attempts to deal with human rights issues involving immigrant communities.

A Demographic Outline

There are two indigenous populations of Australia, the Torres Strait Islanders (from the Torres Strait Islands, a part of Queensland) and the larger group of indigenous peoples (from the rest of Australia) known as the Aboriginal people. In the 1981 census, the first group was numbered at 15,232 and the second at 144,665—making an indigenous population of 159,897—or 1.1 percent of the total population of Australia.[2] The Aboriginal proportion of the overall population in Australia's States and Territories is distributed as follows: in New South Wales (NSW) and the Australian Capital Territory (ACT), 0.68 percent; in Victoria, 0.16 percent; in Queensland, 1.95 percent; in South Australia, 0.76 percent; in Western Australia, 2.46 percent; in Tasmania, 0.64 percent; and in the Northern Territory, 23.59 percent.[3] Both the lifestyle and the geographic distribution of the indigenous population vary considerably in different parts of the country.[4]

From the outset of British settlement of Australia two hundred years ago, the aim of the Imperial government was to populate the continent with British subjects. As is well known, originally many immigrants to Australia arrived involuntarily, being sent by ship from England, Ireland, Scotland, and Wales under the penal transportation scheme. It was not long, however, before organized migration and settlement programs began—and over the years, until the 1970s, first Imperial[5] and colonial legislation, and later bilateral treaties and Australian legislation[6] contained terms governing the provision of assisted passage for migrants.

Australian immigration policy was restrictive from the outset. In the 1850s a rush to the gold fields attracted, among others, immigrants from China. Shortly afterward, the Victorian State parliament, followed by the other five Australian state parliaments, enacted laws restricting Asian immigration. The desire to control immigration was one of the most significant reasons for the Australian States joining together in a federation in 1901. Indeed, one of the first statutes to be enacted by the newly established Commonwealth (federal) parliament was the *Immigration Restriction Act 1901*. This legislation, passed with the almost complete agreement of all parties, provided, among other things, for the administration, at the discretion of a customs officer, of a dictation test of not less than fifty words "in any European language." Any person who failed this test was prohibited from immigration. Although the words of the statute were general in application, the dictation test was used to exclude nonwhite immigrants. The implementation of this test came to be known as the White Australia Policy.[7] Proponents of this policy shared not only the wish to restrict immigration to members of the white race, but also within that restriction, the desire to encourage British and Irish immigration in preference to immigration from some of the continental European countries.[8] After the fall of Singapore during World War II, however, and the threat of Japanese invasion that followed, Australian immigration policies changed. No longer limited to attracting migrants of British and Irish origin, immigration was sought from the whole of the European continent. In addition, in the late 1940s and early 1950s, some of the tight restrictions on non-European settlement were relaxed slightly.[9] Between 1947 and 1989, approximately 4.5 million people arrived to settle in Australia from some 140 different countries and localities around the world.

The total population of Australia is currently 17 million people. Australia presently has the highest rate of population growth of any developed country in the world (from 1980–86, 1.4 percent as compared with 1.1 percent for Canada and 1.0 percent for the United States); during 1986 Australia's population growth was 1.5 percent and in 1987 1.6 percent.[10]

During 1987, 130,000 migrants arrived in Australia; and during 1988, the figure was 143,200. In these two periods immigration accounted for more than half of the country's increase in population. The rate of immigration per head of population is two or three times higher than that for Canada or the United States—the only two other developed nations still maintaining a significant level of immigration.[11] Australia has a higher percentage of people born overseas in its population (21 percent) than does either Canada (16 percent) or the United States (6.0 percent).[12] As a consequence of all these factors, cultural legitimacy in the formulation of the country's law and policies assumes a particular significance.

Human Rights and Cultural Legitimacy: The Majoritarian Perspective—The Absence of a Culture of Legal Rights

In Australia, little protection is provided for individual or group rights by the Commonwealth or any of the state constitutions.[13] This state of affairs has flowed from the derivation of the Australian legal system from the legal system of the homeland of its settler majority: the United Kingdom. In the United Kingdom, the dominant constitutional theory bases practically the whole Constitution on the single premise of the sovereignty of the United Kingdom Parliament, composed of the Queen, the House of Commons, and the House of Lords. Rules that would be found in the constitutions of states with rigid constitutions are, in the United Kingdom, either rules of practice (as in the case of the separation of powers) or rules of statute law subject to change by Parliament at any time (for example, the rules relating to the independence of the judiciary).

It follows from this basic premise—or has been thought to follow—that there are and perhaps can be no fundamental constitutional rights in the United Kingdom. The only rights that exist are those created by legislation and those developed under the common law, and the legislature is always competent to repeal or amend any legislation and to override judicially created law. Of course, there are a number of fundamental rights stated in legislative form, some in statutes of great ancestry,[14] but all such laws are subject to this basic premise.

Thus there is a strong sense in which all rights in the United Kingdom are legislative or protected by common law only and not by the Constitution. Undoubtedly it is partly for this reason that the various suggestions for some form of entrenched bill of rights have made no headway. Of course, "absolute sovereignty" is in practice subject to many limitations, so much so that a recent constitutional text described the sovereignty of Parliament as a "noble lie."[15] British involvement in the European Community has had an impact on parliamentary sovereignty, but that impact should not be exaggerated.[16]

The approach to legal rights in Australia (or, more accurately, the lack of any perceived need for legal rights) reflects much from the constitutional and legal theory of the United Kingdom. Although Australia does have a rigid federal constitution that directly and indirectly seeks to protect rights to some degree, there is no constitutional bill of rights, nor any coherent scheme for the protection of rights at the constitutional level. Most of the protection of rights at the constitutional level is the protection of rights that are essentially federal in character—those thought by the Founding Fathers to be required by the dictates of federation—rather than a guarantee of individual rights. Besides, the individual rights that do receive protection are essentially guaranteed only against the Commonwealth (that is, the federal body) leaving the states free to act inconsistently with those rights. There are virtually no rights provisions at all in the state constitutions.[17] Hence Australia also does not have a culture of legal rights, and recent developments suggest that this situation is likely to remain unchanged for a considerable period of time.

The federal rights that do receive protection are principally rights to be treated equally in particular respects. There is no general right of equality or of equal protection before the law. Apart from these (so far rather erratically interpreted)[18] federal guarantees of equality and nondiscrimination, the Constitution provides only a limited number of federal rights to representation or participation in government.[19] More significantly the Constitution can only be amended with the approval of a majority of the electors in Australia, and, in addition, a majority of the electors in a majority of the states (four out of six states). This has been a major impediment to constitutional change. Outside the area of federal guarantees, there are only a few individual rights, and these are of a distinctly miscellaneous character.[20]

Thus it cannot be said that the federal Constitution adopts a coherent approach to questions of individual rights. The notion that individual rights ought to be protected is conceded in certain areas, but there is no rationale to the selection of those areas. The attempt to establish even a legislative bill of rights has failed repeatedly;[21] and a recent proposed constitutional amendment that would have made the three most significant individual rights in the Constitution—trial by jury (section 80), freedom of religion (section 116), and acquisition on just terms (section 51[31]—both more coherent and more rigorous, in particular by binding the states and territories to the observance of those rights, failed by a very large majority to be adopted.[22]

One consequence of this situation has been that in Australia questions of human rights are debated more and more with reference to international human rights standards.[23] This situation holds true in relation not only to issues of concern to the dominant cultural majority, but also in relation to issues of particular relevance to Aboriginal or immigrant groups. Aboriginal groups recently have become increasingly interested in the use of international arenas as vehicles for gaining attention for, and furthering, their cause, and a corresponding and continuing interest in their situation has been evident in the discussions of different international bodies.[24]

Australian Law and Policy and the Aboriginal People

THE DEFINITION OF "ABORIGINE" AND OF ABORIGINAL CUSTOMARY LAWS.[25]

In some early statutes, the term "Aborigine" was defined by reference to blood (for example, there is some early use of terms such as "half-caste," "full blood,"[26] or "octoroon"; and in some 700 pieces of Australian legislation there can be found "no less than 67 identifiable classifications, descriptions or definitions [which] have been used from the time of white settlement to the present."[27] Nonetheless, today the definition is not dominated by an accretion of technicalities or restrictions. Unlike the situation in both Canada and the United States—where the question of criteria for membership of indigenous minorities has occasioned considerable difficulty—in Australia the present accepted definition of "Aborigine" and "Aboriginal race" is flexible and broad, both for the purposes of constitutional law and in relation to the use of the terms by governments (federal, state, and territory) for administrative matters. The accepted definition for administrative purposes is that Aborigines are people of Aboriginal descent identifying, and accepted by others, as Aborigines; this definition is also the one to be found in many legislative enactments.[28]

With regard to the ambit of the definition for the purposes of constitutional law Deane J. (a judge of the Australian High Court) has stated:

[B]y "Australian Aborigine" I mean, in accordance with what I understand to be the conventional meaning of that term, a person of Aboriginal descent albeit mixed, who identifies himself as such and who is recognized by the aboriginal community as an Aboriginal.[29]

The definition of "Aboriginal customary laws" on the other hand, has been, and remains, somewhat more complicated. There is no agreement on one all-purpose definition of the term. The absence of such a definition does not seem to have resulted in any real problems. Still, partly because Aboriginal laws form a part of an oral tradition and are not contained in written codes, there has been until recently a marked failure to recognize that any system of Aboriginal laws exists. Today this approach is changing. Considerable discussion has taken place among anthropologists concerning the content of these laws,[30] and in recent years there have been clear instances of judicial acceptance that early Aboriginal communities did possess a system of laws. In 1971, in the *Gove Land Rights Case*[31] Blackburn J. stated that it was not a necessary prerequisite to such a system that there be either a well-defined territorial area with clear boundaries or a specific sovereign. He said:

> I do not think that the solution . . . is to be found in postulating a meaning for the word "law." . . . What is shown by the evidence is, in my opinion, that the system of law was recognized as obligatory upon them by the members of the community which, in principle, is definable in that it is the community of Aboriginals which made ritual and economic use of the subject land. In my opinion it does not matter that the precise edges as it were, of this community were left in a penumbra of partial obscurity.[32]

In the same case Blackburn J. described the legal system of the Aboriginal people whose land was the subject of the matter before him in the following terms:

> A subtle and elaborate system highly adapted to the country in which the people led their lives, which provided a stable order of society, and was remarkably free from the vagaries of personal whim or influence. If ever a system could be called "a government of laws, and not of men" it is that shown in the evidence [here]. . . .[33]

THE BASIS OF LEGISLATIVE POWER RELATING TO ABORIGINAL ISSUES

In Australia the legislative power of state parliaments is much broader than that which is given to the Commonwealth body. This is because the grant of power to state parliaments is couched in terms such as the power to make laws for the "peace, order and good government" of the state—whereas the grant to the Commonwealth parliament is comprised in specific enumerated heads of power. To be valid, Commonwealth legislation must fall within one, or within a combination, of these heads of power. Where the constitution gives legislative power to the Commonwealth parliament, generally speaking, the state parliaments remain competent to pass legislation in the same field[34] and any state legislation which is enacted will be valid, notwithstanding the existence of a federal head of legislative power on that topic, unless or until conflicting Commonwealth legislation is enacted. Where legislative conflict occurs, section 109 of the Constitution provides that the Commonwealth legislation is to prevail.

The main basis of the power of the Commonwealth parliament to legislate in relation to Aboriginal matters is found now in section 51(26) of the federal Constitution. In its original form, section 51(26) prohibited the Commonwealth parliament from enacting special laws for the Aboriginal people in any state. In a referendum held in 1967, a vast majority of the population approved a constitutional amendment that empowered the Commonwealth parliament to enact special legislation for Aboriginal people in the states.[35] In addition, the Commonwealth parliament is able to pass legislation concerning Aboriginal issues whenever the subject matter falls within one of the other federal legislative heads of power contained in the Constitution (for example, the power to legislate for Aborigines in relation to social security matters).

THE FIRST PHASE (1788–1967): THE DENIAL OF RIGHTS

> It might be presumed that the native inhabitants of any land have an incontrovertible right to their own soil: a plain and sacred right, which seems not to have been understood. Europeans have entered their borders uninvited, and when there, have not only acted as if they were undoubted lords of the soil, but have punished the natives as aggressors if they evinced a disposition to live in their own country. . . . If they have been found upon their own property they have been treated as thieves and robbers. They are driven back into the interior as if they were dogs and kangaroos.[36]

This is an account, by a Select Committee of the House of Commons in 1837, of the treatment received by Aboriginal people at the hands of the settlers from the time of first British settlement in 1788.[37] At that date, Australia was divided into hundreds of tribal areas, and there may have been as many as six hundred different dialects or languages. The numbers of indigenous people in the country at the date of settlement are not known, the earliest estimates (of approximately 300,000) were made some time after initial settlement and may have reflected the numbers only after the population had been decimated by introduced diseases.

During the first hundred years after initial British settlement, the impact of the settlers on Aboriginal culture, traditions, and way of life, and on the people themselves, was disastrous. Introduced diseases took a tremendous toll; there were, for example, epidemics of smallpox in 1789 and 1829, and of influenza in 1820 and 1838. Aboriginal communities were displaced from the more fertile lands and lost access to their traditional food sources. Many were killed in conflicts with the settlers.[38]

It has been estimated that between 1824 and 1908 at least 10,000 Aborigines died violently in Queensland.[39] Throughout the first half of the nineteenth century, with the increase in settlement and continuing clashes between the settlers and the indigenous people, reprisals and punitive expeditions were common. Martial law was sometimes declared (for example, in Tasmania from 1828 to 1832 and in New South Wales in 1824), and a number of massacres took place. It is estimated that the indigenous population was reduced to one-fifth perhaps even less—of its original numbers. Indeed, in the state of Tasmania, at one stage the Aboriginal population was thought to have been exterminated entirely.[40] Those who survived physically frequently saw their way of life changed completely. By the early 1930s, the number of Aboriginal people in Australia had decreased to approximately 70,000. At that time it was generally expected that these people would either become absorbed within the majority population or die out completely.

Aboriginal people are thought to have occupied Australia for 40,000 to 50,000 years.[41] Sites of Aboriginal habitation dated more than 40,000 years ago have been found in both Western and Eastern Australia.[42] Although the indigenous people had their own laws, languages, customs, traditions, and social structures, none of these received any recognition under early British rule.

The decision as to whose law—that of the settlers (or conquerors) or the original inhabitants—would form the basis of the legal system of any British possession after its acquisition was determined according to whether the colony was categorized as "settled" or "conquered or ceded."[43] Colonies were said to be "settled" if, prior to the arrival of the British, they were "desert and uninhabited" or had no settled inhabitants with a recognizable system of laws of their own. If this were the case the British settlers upon arrival notionally brought with them, along with their other possessions, all the English law, common and statutory, in existence at the time, leaving behind them only that law that would be inapplicable to the circumstances of the colony.[44] Such English law was then immediately in force, and was said to apply by reception. It, not the law of the earlier inhabitants, formed the basis of the colony's legal system.

Colonies were said to be "conquered or ceded," on the other hand, when acquired from people "that have already laws of their own."[45] In this case, the established legal system did continue in existence and it, rather than English law, formed the basis of the new possession's laws, although of course the local legal system might be subjected to considerable amendment by the Imperial parliament as time went on.[46]

Once a colony had been attributed to one of the two categories, the classification became settled as a matter of law, even though subsequent research may show that, on the historical facts, the colony should have been attributed to the other class (because, for example, it could be shown that at the date of acquisition of the territory there had been a legal system in existence, whereas this proposition had earlier been denied). It has been said that this discovery will not serve to reopen the question of the colony's correct classification.[47] It was decided early on that the Australian colonies were settled;[48] hence the basis of their legal system became English and not Aboriginal law.

The question of the correctness of this categorization of the Australian colonies as settled territories has been raised recently, however. In *Coe v. The Commonwealth*[49] (a case of a claim on behalf of an Aboriginal community alleging, among other things, wrongful proclamation of sovereignty by Captains Cook and Phillip over the eastern part of Australia) it was argued that Australia had been acquired by conquest, not by settlement. Mason J. at first instance dismissed this claim, holding that the accepted legal foundation was that Australia was settled,[50] and this judgment was upheld on appeal to the Full Court of the High Court.[51] Of the four judges who heard the appeal, however, two disagreed. Jacobs J. said that although the view has generally been taken that the Australian colonies were settled there is no actual decision of the High Court or the Privy Council to that effect.[52] Murphy J. observed that there is a wealth of historical material to support the claim that the Aboriginal people had occupied Australia for many thousands of years, and that they did not give up their lands peacefully but were killed or removed forcibly in what amounted to attempted genocide.[53] He went on to state that the question whether Australia was settled was still open to argument. The views of the two judges, Jacobs and Murphy, suggest that the question is more open than had been thought previously, but the case was nevertheless decided on the basis that Australia was settled. As the High Court was evenly divided, the view of the trial judge prevailed.[54]

Consequent upon this approach, Aboriginal institutions, traditions, and customs were ignored and no place was made for them in the legal system of the dominant majority. Nonrecognition applied both in the civil and in the criminal law sphere and resulted, among other things, in the denial of land rights,[55] the failure to accord legitimacy to traditional marriages,[56] and the failure to acknowledge customary Aboriginal laws and defenses to English law crimes.[57]

In contrast to the position in Canada, the United States, and New Zealand, in Australia no treaties were concluded with any of the Aboriginal groups. The Aboriginal people were not regarded by British law as sovereign peoples, as nations, or as identifiable communities. Instead, Aborigines were regarded as individual British subjects governed by British law. Although it was recognized in some quarters that this was unjust (for example, in a House of Commons Parliamentary Paper of 1837),[58] and also unrealistic (since the Aboriginal people continued to act in accordance with their own laws and customs and had no knowledge or understanding of the imposed legal system), this remained the prevailing policy;[59] and it totally failed to provide equality before the law. Such equality can occur only where all people share a similar knowledge and comprehension of the law and have equal access to its protection. This was certainly not the position of the Aboriginal people. Further, since Aborigines were not Christians, they were unable to testify when they were involved in proceedings before the courts. Although in 1843 the Imperial parliament passed "An Act to authorize the legislatures of certain of Her Majesty's Colonies to pass laws for the admission in certain cases, of unsworn Testimony in Civil and Criminal Proceedings"[60] (allowing for unsworn evidence to be given by members of "Tribes of barbarous and uncivilized peoples, destitute of the knowledge of God and religious belief"), the Australian colonies were slow to utilize their new power and to enact appropriate amendments to their legislation.[61] At the time of federation in 1901, no agreement to the new Constitution was sought from the indigenous populations. Further, sections 24 and 127 provided that Aborigines could not be counted in reckoning the size of electorates for the House of Representatives. It was assumed they would not vote, and most were ineligible to do so anyway.

Throughout this early period the failure to give recognition to Aboriginal laws, customs, and traditions was leavened to some degree by the practice, by law-enforcement agencies, of nonintervention in Aboriginal disputes, of nonprosecution of Aborigines for certain criminal offenses, and of mitigation in matters of sentencing. In Western Australia a special court was set up to hear cases involving Aborigines, and in several jurisdictions proposals were made (though not always carried through) for the establishment of special tribunals to deal with criminal cases involving Aboriginal people.[62] In some circumstances, specific legislative provisions were made in relation to trial procedures, magistrates' discretionary powers, the admission (or nonadmissibility) of evidence of confessions of guilt, and in regard to the maximum sentences permissible for Aboriginal offenders.[63]

After the initial period of nonrecognition a growing awareness of the injustices being perpetrated against the Aboriginal people led to the introduction, in the 1840s, of an era of protectionism. Aboriginal protectors were appointed in New South Wales, South Australia, and Western Australia with the mandate to protect Aborigines from abuse and to give basic provisions (blankets, rations, and so on) to those living near to towns. The protectors were given few powers and achieved very little. By the middle of the nineteenth century, this office virtually ceased to exist. A few years later, a more formal system of protectionism followed, coupled with a policy of segregation.

To take one example, in 1858 the government of the state of Victoria established a select committee to enquire into the situation of Aborigines. This committee reported that Aborigines were in need of protection and should be confined to reserves. A Central Board for Aborigines was set up, reserves were selected, and in 1869 legislation—"An Act to provide for the Protection and Management for Aboriginal Natives in Victoria"—was enacted. It conferred wide powers on a newly constituted Board for the Protection of Aborigines.[64] Behind these moves lay certain assumptions, such as that the Aborigines were dying out, that they were incapable of looking after themselves, and that any hope of civilizing them lay with educating the young—if possible, in isolation.[65]

There were systematic attempts to take "part-Aboriginal children" from their parents so that they could be educated as white Australians. For full-blooded Aborigines there was some tolerance for their traditional way of life; but not infrequently those entrusted with the management of the reserves established for these people were unsympathetic or even hostile to customary ways.

In the early 1940s these approaches were superseded by a new policy of assimilation. The aim now was to assimilate the Aboriginal people entirely into the dominant white Australian culture. The policy was defined at the 1961 Native Welfare Conference of Federal and State Ministers in these terms:

> The policy of assimilation means that all Aborigines and part-Aborigines are expected to attain the same manner of living as other Australians and to live as members of a single Australian community, enjoying the same rights and privileges, accepting the same customs and influenced by the same beliefs as other Australians.[66]

Programs of education, health, and housing were developed with the purpose of ensuring that Aboriginal Australians achieved a standard (and hopefully a mode) of living identical to that of their white Australian counterparts.[67]

In the 1960s and 1970s this aim of assimilation was replaced in turn. It came to be regarded as paternalistic and arrogant, and in its stead a new aim was developed, that of integration—a term used by the critics of the assimilation policy to denote a policy that recognized the value of the preservation of Aboriginal culture and identity.[68] Provision began to be made for the granting of land rights to the indigenous population, measures were adopted to increase funding for Aboriginal community projects, and emphasis was placed on improved programs whose aim was to ensure that formal equality was in reality accompanied by definite social and economic advances. The right to vote was conferred on all indigenous people. This period—the extension of rights—is considered in the next section. More recently, Commonwealth government policy has been founded on "the fundamental right of Aboriginals to retain their racial identity and traditional lifestyle or, where desired, to adopt wholly or partially a European lifestyle."[69] Under this policy Aboriginal participation in local or community government has been encouraged. Government-supported programs, managed by Aboriginal organizations, have been introduced. The policy is described as one of self-government or self-management. It will be discussed as "the Third Phase" in a later subsection.

THE SECOND PHASE (SINCE 1967): THE EXTENSION OF RIGHTS
In this section, particular attention will be paid to land rights[70] since these are so inextricably bound to all other issues of Aboriginal identity, law, culture, and religion. In 1966, no Aboriginal Australian owned land by

virtue of his or her Aboriginality.[71] By January 1986, freehold title to 643,079 square kilometers (8.37 percent of the land mass) was held in Aboriginal ownership.[72]

As noted earlier, since 1967, section 51(26) of the Constitution has provided a specific Commonwealth legislative power in relation to Aboriginal issues; and, to an extent, the Commonwealth government has used this power to bring about the change from the policy of assimilation to one of some recognition of Aboriginal cultural identity: for instance in the *Aboriginal and Torres Strait Islander Heritage Protection Act, 1984*. There seems, however, to be a federal reluctance to rely on this mandate of 1967;[73] and most of the laws that affect Australian indigenous people today originate at the state and territorial levels.

In the mid-1970s the Commonwealth government established a new system of Aboriginal land rights in the Northern Territory providing, under the *Aboriginal Land Rights (Northern Territory) Act 1976*, for the direct transfer of existing reserves into the ownership of local Aboriginal land trusts, and setting up a claims procedure in relation to "unalienated Crown land" whereby an Aboriginal Land Commission, if satisfied that Aboriginal claimants are the traditional owners of land, may recommend to the minister that they receive inalienable freehold title to that land.[74]

The act establishes three bodies: the Northern Land Council, the Central Land Council, and the Town Land Council. These bodies represent Aboriginal owners in relation to resource development (for example, mining) agreements and in the preparation and presentation of land claims. Under the Northern Territory legislation, pastoral and other leasehold lands cannot be made the subject of claims by Aboriginal people; but excisions from these lands to provide living areas for resident Aboriginal communities have been negotiated. Under separate legislation, an Aboriginal Land Fund Commission (later the Aboriginal Development Commission) was set up by the Commonwealth to purchase land for Aboriginal people on the open market anywhere in Australia. Several non-claimable areas of land, such as pastoral leaseholds, have been purchased by the commission and later converted to inalienable freehold title. In addition, both the Northern Territory legislature and the Commonwealth government have transferred national park land to Aboriginal ownership (for example, land in the Coburg peninsula and the Kakadu and Ulura National Parks).

Substantial grants of rural land, on the basis of traditional association with that land, have been made in South Australia. The *Pitjantjatjara*

Land Rights Act 1981 and the *Maralinga Tjarutja Land Rights Act 1984* followed a similar pattern to that of the Northern Territory legislation. The acts transferred inalienable freehold title (to 102,630 and 50,000 square kilometers, respectively) to corporate bodies. These bodies also represented the traditional owners in negotiations concerning matters such as resource development agreements. To a lesser extent, legislative provision has been made for land rights in New South Wales, Victoria, and Queensland. Western Australia and Tasmania still have no legislation recognizing land rights. In the case of Western Australia, this is a particularly serious omission in view of the large number of Aboriginal groups with potential claims on the basis of traditional affiliation with the land.[75] All state parliaments, as well as the federal parliament, have enacted legislation dealing with sacred sites;[76] and in the legislation of several states exemptions have been made from conservation, fishing, and wildlife laws in order that Aboriginal people might continue to pursue their traditional hunting and fishing rights.[77]

In relation to other issues, in some matters recognition has been granted to Aboriginal laws, customs, and traditions without any support from legislative provisions. As noted above, law-enforcement agencies, judges, and magistrates, over a long period, have quite often taken this approach in matters of sentencing[78] whether or not supported by legislation; and courts have been willing to consider customary laws when determining the intent of the accused in criminal cases and when considering the availability of specific defenses.[79] In several instances courts have held that loss of traditional status, which may result from brain damage or other incapacity, can be taken into account in the assessment of damages in road accident cases.[80] Judicial recognition has been granted in a Northern Territory case in which a traditional Aboriginal marriage was recognized in relation to an adoption.[81]

In a number of other areas federal, state, and territory legislation now gives recognition to aspects of Aboriginal customary laws and traditions—for instance: in recent initiatives recognizing Aboriginal child-care practices (for example, the *Community Welfare Act 1983* [Northern Territory], section 69); in allowing a distribution of property on death which is more in accordance with Aboriginal family and kin relationships (for example, *Aboriginal Affairs Planning Authority Act 1972* [Western Australia], section 35), and in establishing local courts or other implementation mechanisms staffed by Aboriginal personnel. The purpose of this last measure is to set up bodies with an awareness of local circumstances and hence better equipped to take issues of Aboriginal tradition and custom into account during the decision-making and implementation process. Examples are the office of the South Australian Tribunal Assessor, established under the *Pitjantjatjara Land Rights Act 1981* (Southern Australia), sections 35 and 36, and the system of Aboriginal courts introduced by the *Aboriginal Communities Act 1979* (Western Australia).[82]

Where special legislative provisions are made for Aboriginal people, these provisions are not infrequently challenged. Challenges have been mounted both through the legal and the political processes. An example of a challenge attempted through the political process was the stated intention of the present New South Wales government to repeal the New South Wales *Aboriginal Land Rights Act*[83] enacted by its predecessor. The government has proved incapable of fulfilling this intention, however, as it does not command the necessary numbers in the Upper House. Attempts have been made at the administrative level to avoid the effects of the act's provisions. These, too, have been unsuccessful, having been held to be *ultra vires*,[84] (i.e., beyond the powers of the administrators in question).

An example of a challenge mounted through the legal process was that made in relation to the validity of section 19 of the *Pitjantjatjara Land Rights Act*[85] in *Gerhardy v. Brown*.[86] Section 19 of the act provides that a person, not being a Pitjantjatjara, may not enter Pitjantjatjara land except with the permission of the body established to administer that land.

The challenge was to the effect that section 19 contravenes provisions of the Commonwealth *Racial Discrimination Act 1975*.[87] This last act was enacted to bring into force, in the domestic legal system, the aims of the *Convention for the Elimination of All Forms of Racial Discrimination 1966*, which Australia ratified in 1975.[88] The convention, in Articles 1, 2, and 5, prohibits distinction on the basis of race, color, descent, or national or ethnic origin. In *Gerhardy* the High Court held that although section 19 of the Commonwealth act did make such a distinction, in this case the distinction was a special measure within the terms of section 8(1)—section 8(1) directly incorporates Article 1(4) of the Convention—and hence was justifiable.[89] It was accepted by the court that, provided there is no denial of basic rights to Aboriginal communities, and provided there is an intention to further culture and cultural identity, it is permissible to legislate for reasonable measures in relation to the recognition of particular Aboriginal claims or needs. The court held further that Article 1(4) deals not only with matters such as economic or educational advancement, but also legitimately covers provisions for the recognition of matters such as the culture and identity of minority communities.[90]

In 1988 the High Court handed down its decision in *Mabo v. State of Queensland*[91] and there built on the position reached in *Gerhardy v. Brown*. In *Mabo* the legislation was a special measure of a detrimental, not of a benevolent, kind. Briefly, the facts of the case were that the plaintiffs, descendants of the indigenous inhabitants of an island in the Torres Strait and residents of that island, sought, among other things, a declaration as to their rights concerning the land, its seas, seabeds, and reefs. After commencement of the proceedings, but before the action was heard, the Queensland Parliament enacted legislation[92] with the purpose of extinguishing, retrospectively, any traditional right to the island and its surrounds which the claimants may have possessed. (For the purposes of the judgment it was assumed that the Islanders did possess traditional rights and claims to the land that were recognized by the common law.) The court held that legislation that singled out Torres Strait Islander people specifically in order to abrogate land rights claimed by them was discriminatory, inconsistent with section 10 of the *Racial Discrimination Act 1975*, and invalid.[93]

Mabo has significant potential for Aboriginal rights in the future. It may have the effect that henceforth retrogressive legislation affecting Aborigines or Islanders can be validly enacted only by the Commonwealth parliament and not by the states.[94]

To summarize: in Australia today the recognition of Aboriginal laws and customs is in no way either systematic and consistent, or comprehensive. Any recognition that does exist is piecemeal and spasmodic, remaining largely an ad hoc exercise of discretion which is particular rather than general. Although this approach has some advantages and can achieve flexibility and the potential for ready adaptability to differing circumstances, it also carries with it accompanying disadvantages: too much discretion in the hands of officials and judicial officers can produce a confusing inconsistency; also, not infrequently, it leads both to disappointments and to impermissible distortions of legal principle.

When provisions to benefit Aboriginal groups are challenged and justification is provided, that justification tends to be in terms that indicate that the special provisions are intended to be of merely temporary duration, to be phased out when no longer necessary. Such an approach suggests no acknowledgment of the necessity for a real settlement of grievances. Australian government Aboriginal policy has been based on a premise that what is required is a series of short-term provisions, provisions that are necessary so that people who have been disadvantaged in the past might be given an opportunity for betterment now, hence the design of programs to bring about Aboriginal advancement and to secure Aboriginal welfare. Until very recently there has been no sense of a necessity either to give serious consideration to questions of local Aboriginal autonomy and/or self-determination[95] or to take steps to a real reconciliation and settlement of Aboriginal grievances.

Accordingly, the Aboriginal Land Trusts (and other like bodies) that exist in some states and in the Northern Territory are not agencies of self-government but rather agencies of proprietorship; even then, they are subject to strict governmental controls.[96] So also are the Aboriginal and Islander councils developed on reserves in Queensland. Aboriginal control of land, Aboriginal self-government, and Aboriginal control of natural resources are all regarded as dependent on legislation. Where Aboriginal forms of government have been instituted, the Aboriginal organs have been incorporated within the wider Australian public service in a manner that has allowed no autonomy and that has left those organs subject to direction and control by the minister and department in question. So far such attempts have not worked satisfactorily.[97]

The National Aboriginal Council (for which the Commonwealth government ceased to provide funding in 1985) had important advisory and political, but no direct governmental, functions.[98] In 1979, the council began urging that a treaty (*Makarratta*) be negotiated between Aboriginal Australia and the Commonwealth government. This move was supported by an Aboriginal Treaty Committee (now no longer in existence); it received consideration in consultations with the then Liberal federal government, which responded favorably,[99] and its constitutional and legal feasibility was examined by the Senate Standing Committee on Constitutional and Legal Affairs, which, in a unanimous report in 1983, recommended ways of proceeding.[100] The proposals, prepared by the council and discussed with Aboriginal communities in different parts of Australia, have not had any concrete outcome, however. The Liberal party, now in opposition, no longer supports the idea of negotiation and agreement with the Aboriginal people.[101]

Nonetheless, some indications of a recognition that more is required have begun to manifest, at least tentatively, and this recognition has received clearer articulation in international opinion. A 1988 report of a mission to Australia of the United Nations Working Group on Indigenous Peoples recommended among other things "that the Aboriginal and Islander peoples be given self-government over their local and internal affairs . . . [with] powers sufficient for the protection of the groups' collective right to existence and for the preservation of their identities" and with "a secure financial basis."[102]

A THIRD PHASE: BEYOND THE GRANTING OF RIGHTS TO SELF-DETERMINATION?

Although, as indicated by the title of the preceding section, greater recognition is now given to Aboriginal rights, the initial situation—that Aborigines remain Australian citizens and subject to Australian law in the same manner as all other citizens—has not changed.[103] M. Mansell, a solicitor for the Tasmanian Aboriginal Centre, is critical of the assumption behind this—that Aborigines and other Australians are all one and the same people—that, given the opportunity Aboriginal people will make their own future as citizens of the Australian nation.[104] Mansell rejects this view. He prefers the term "Australian Aborigines" to "Aboriginal Australians," saying:

> If we are in fact *Aboriginal Australians*, then our whole aim is to get the best deal we can for our people within the Australian society. If we are in fact *Australian Aborigines*, what we are really aiming for is to get the best deal possible from the world which includes the nation of Australia to which we are not subordinate.[105]

He argues that there is an option available to Australian Aborigines that has not thus far received any detailed consideration: for Aboriginal people to reach a status of statehood—to become a separate state. Whatever the likely success of arguments such as these, they should alert negotiators to the fact that if future agreements are to achieve real reconciliation, a greater reformulation of ideas may be required than has yet been realized.

Steps toward a reconciliation have not gone very far at all, at least to date. The events of the bicentennial year, 1988, are instructive and are briefly outlined here. On August 23, 1988, a joint resolution of both Houses of the Commonwealth Parliament stated that it was considered "desirable that the Commonwealth further promote reconciliation with Aboriginal and Torres Strait Islander citizens providing recognition of their special place in the Commonwealth of Australia."[106]

References to similar effect can be found in some legislative enactments, for instance in the Preamble to *The Aboriginal and Torres Strait Islander Bill* (the lynchpin of current federal government policy on Aboriginal issues). Despite these references the bill goes on to establish precisely the kind of institutional arrangement that has proved inadequate in the past and that, in light of the words quoted above, is manifestly inappropriate today. The elected body established—the Aboriginal and Torres Strait Islander Commission (ATSIC)—if it retains its presently projected form, will be chaired by a nominee of the minister and thus be subject to his or her general direction.[107] Again, autonomy and the possibility for self-management are denied. The Minister for Aboriginal Affairs, on the introduction of the bill into Parliament in December 1987, said that the government must be satisfied that the proposals have been endorsed by the people they will directly affect.[108] As a consequence, there was consultation:

> The Committee asked virtually every witness who appeared before it in the latter part of 1988 whether they wished the Bill to proceed given their current level of knowledge. With very few exceptions their answer was "no." Support for the immediate passage of the Bill tended to come from well funded organizations which had supported A.T.S.I.C. from the outset, for example the Northern and Central Land Councils.[109]

Despite these findings, the government members recommended immediate enactment of the bill.[110] Other inconsistencies of approach have been exhibited in relation to different paragraphs of the preamble to this same act.[111] Twice in the House of Representatives the Minister for Aboriginal Affairs has insisted that the preamble is not intended to have any legal significance.[112]

Conflicting statements and actions relating to the recognition of Aboriginal claims occur also with respect to state legislation. In *The Aboriginal Land (Lake Condah and Framlingham Forest) Act*[113] the preamble states that the government of Victoria "acknowledges that . . . Aboriginals residing on [the land in question] and other Aboriginals are considered to be the inheritors in title from Aboriginals who owned, occupied, used and enjoyed the land from time immemorial," but adds, "the Commonwealth of Australia does not acknowledge the matters acknowledged by the Government of Victoria." Despite the disclaimer of acknowledgment by the Commonwealth government, however, the statute was nonetheless passed by the Commonwealth parliament as requested by the parliament of the state of Victoria (with the result that only the Commonwealth parliament has the power to repeal or amend the enactment).[114] In other areas progress remains disappointing—the legislation recommended by the Australian Law Reform Commission which would give recognition to Aboriginal customary law has not been introduced,[115] and the proposal of the Hawke government to enact national land rights legislation has been abandoned.[116]

The clearest statement so far made by an Australian government indicating an intention to come to terms with Aboriginal demands is contained in the Barunga Statement, made on June 12, 1988, after discussions held with Aboriginal representatives at Barunga in the Northern Territory. (This statement, however, marked the dropping of a consultation process to lead to an "agreement, treaty or *Makarratta*" which had been announced by the Minister for Aboriginal Affairs in December 1987 when introducing the Aboriginal and Torres Strait Islander Commission proposal.)[117] The Barunga statement consists of two separate documents: one, a statement of a number of Aboriginal leaders;[118] and the second, a statement signed by the prime minister and three Aboriginal leaders.

As yet no "treaty" has been agreed, and many questions arising in relation to any such agreement remain unresolved. It has been suggested that this will continue to be the position as long as the matter remains in the hands of the government, given that bipartisan support, so essential to any long-term solution, may be impossible to achieve while the government has carriage of the matter. F. Brennan and J. Crawford, in a paper presented to the twenty-sixth Australian Legal Convention (Sydney, August 1989) suggest that the negotiations should be removed from the party political forum and entrusted for the time being to some independent body that can carry forward a process of consultation and negotiation on which at least the major parties may be able to agree. Their view is that this will require the establishment of an independent statutory commission, with power to convene an annual meeting of federal and state governments, major political parties, and Aboriginal groups.[119]

At the moment, the attempts toward a reconciliation and an agreement or treaty seem to be deadlocked. It may be well to recall that at the time of the making of the treaties in Canada, the United States, and New Zealand there was no suggestion that one national agreement could simply bind individual bands, tribes, or communities. In Canada and the United States, agreements were made at local or regional levels. The treaty in New Zealand was agreed upon with representatives of many groups, then ratified separately by individual groups. Perhaps what this means for Australia is that any form for the proposed treaty envisaged thus far may not be the final preferred solution. What is vital is that the government make adequate provision to ensure that Aboriginal and non-Aboriginal consultations are held that canvass a broad spectrum of opinions, and particularly that the solutions desired by the indigenous populations be clarified. In Mansell's words: "[w]e . . . have to determine for ourselves in which direction we move. Then it makes it easier for non-Aboriginal people to be able to respond appropriately from their side."[120]

If a total impasse is to be avoided, attempts at solutions need to be addressed thoroughly, negotiations and consultations need to be designed carefully, and adequate financial support for this process needs to be provided. It is imperative that the discussion be conducted with a flexibility and open-mindedness that will permit the development of some completely innovative approach, if, after thorough consideration and consultation, this is what appears to be appropriate.

Cultural Legitimacy and Immigrant Communities

THE DIFFERENCE BETWEEN CLAIMS OF INDIGENOUS PEOPLE AND THOSE OF IMMIGRANT COMMUNITIES

An argument not infrequently put forward[121] against the recognition of Aboriginal customary law, and against special legislation directed toward the Aboriginal people, is that such measures could be seen as discriminatory to the extent that the cultural practices, traditions, and laws of some of Australia's distinct immigrant groups do not receive recognition, and that special legislative provisions are not made for them. Valid distinctions can be made, however, between the two situations.

First, in many cases (although, of course, not in all) the customs, laws, traditions, and practices of immigrant groups are not so dissimilar to those of the dominant Australian culture as to result in any real difficulties other than those of language and interpretation.

Second, migrants coming to Australia since its colonization by Britain have come to a country that has established laws and traditions and have done so, not as communities, but as individuals or families. Although on arrival these people have a right to express their views, of course, and to participate in the formulation and alteration of law and practice, their position is very different from that of Australia's Aboriginal communities. For the latter, Australia is their country of origin. Later settlement has taken place without their invitation and without their consent and has impacted on their way of life, their culture, and their traditions in a devastating manner.[122]

> Aboriginal unemployment is six times the national average, 90 per cent of Aborigines live in poverty, their rate of preventable diseases such as leprosy, trachoma and syphilis is among the highest in the world and life expectancy is 20 years lower than for whites. Infant mortality is four times the national average. Aborigines are 22 times more likely to die from infectious diseases, 13 times more likely to die violently and eight times more likely to die from respiratory diseases. In desert areas, 25 per cent of children up to the age of four are susceptible to serious illness and retarded development due to malnutrition. Only 14 per cent of Aborigines complete secondary school compared to 41 per cent of whites.[123]

It can hardly be a source of surprise that Aboriginal people see no cultural legitimacy in a system of the dominant group that produces such effects.

In other jurisdictions in Australia's geographic region (for example, in some of the small Pacific island entities,[124] in some Asian countries,[125] and in New Zealand) it has been accepted that a distinction may be made between indigenous and migrant groups when it comes to special legislation directed to the indigenous groups, recognizing their customary laws and traditions. In both Canada and the United States the Supreme courts have arrived at the position, albeit by different routes, that the established federal constitutional responsibility for indigenous Indians makes legislation specifically directed to these groups acceptable when legislation singling out other groups on racial or ethnic lines would not be.[126] While the constitutional position, the history, and the nature of the dealings with their Native peoples by these other governments has been different from those that have been the pattern in Australia, their approach is nonetheless instructive, given the not dissimilar problems faced in many of the jurisdictions at the present time.

In Australia, the numbers and the diversity of the immigrant groups make the question of legal pluralism as it impacts on migrant and on indigenous communities both difficult and delicate.[127] Nonetheless, both the need and the justification for making a distinction and allowing special legislation for indigenous communities have received some recognition.[128]

The Australian Council on Population and Ethnic Affairs in its report on multiculturalism (a report that on the whole takes a restrictive approach and favors assimilation) acknowledges the impact settlement has had on the Aboriginal people and the need for some adaptation of Aboriginal tribal law.[129] Regarding migrant groups, however, the report concludes: "multi-culturalism does not involve separate and parallel development of the major institutions—such as education, law and government—for minority groups. These institutions are common to all Australians." Some writers feel that, far from being an undesirable phenomenon, legal pluralism in the sense of the recognition of indigenous customary law is a definite advantage.[130]

Nonetheless, despite support such as that cited above for the idea that recognition of difference is appropriate where indigenous populations are concerned, on the whole Australian government policy has remained limited by the notion of "equality," and thus susceptible to arguments that legislative or even administrative recognition of Aboriginal rights and customs would run counter to the principle that everyone in a democratic society should be subject to "one law" and that all should be treated "equally." On the other hand, recognition of the need to draw such a distinction can be found in Australia's activities in the international sphere. Australia supported the establishment of the United Nations Working Group on Indigenous Populations, a body that has a mandate distinct from that of the United Nations Subcommission on the Prevention of Discrimination and the Protection of Minorities. The latter considers issues relating to cultural, ethnic, and religious minorities generally; the mandate of the Working Group, on the other hand, is to draw up international standards for the protection of the rights of indigenous peoples.

Thus it is argued that, despite the presence of many distinct ethnic and cultural migrant groups within the Australian community, a strong case can be presented for special and distinctive provision to be made in Australian law for the Aboriginal people. It is not denied, however, that problems with cultural legitimacy in relation to domestic law and policy do arise for some of these different immigrant groups. A brief examination of their situation is in order.

The Idea of Multiculturalism

In recent years it has become popular to speak of Australia as a multicultural society. In terms of actual composition, the population is clearly multicultural. The people living in the country come from many and diverse backgrounds. Apart from the very small numbers of indigenous peoples, the population is composed entirely of immigrants and the descendants of imigrants who have arrived in the country during the last two hundred years.

Nonetheless, Australia remains dominated by a monoculture—the Anglo-Celtic culture of the predominant groups of the early settlers. Very little has been written in Australia on issues of multiculturalism and the law,[131] although there are a large number of studies on the social impact of multiculturalism. Perhaps this lack of written material reflects a lack of attention to, and provision within, the current legal system for the legitimate interests and needs of those with cultural backgrounds different from that of the dominant majority.[132]

In recent years both the Commonwealth and the state governments have taken a variety of measures to counter injustices arising from differences in background and race, and from other particular differences such as a person's sex, age, or physical and mental handicap. In 1975, the Commonwealth government ratified the *Convention for the Elimination of All Forms of Racial Discrimination*; consequent thereto, the *Racial Discrimination Act*[133] was enacted. This act provides that it is unlawful to discriminate against a person on the ground of race, color, or national or ethnic origin in relation to access to public places and facilities, the provision of land, housing, and accommodation, the provision of goods and services, or joining a trade union and employment. The act also provides for equal treatment under the law regardless of race, color, and national or ethnic origin. In December 1986, the Commonwealth parliament passed legislation[134] that established the Human Rights and Equal Opportunity Commission (to take over from the earlier Human Rights Commission).[135] The new commission has undertaken various inquiries and activities in relation to issues of racial discrimination; unresolved complaints of racial discrimination are referred to it under its nonbinding complaints procedure. Under its statute the commission hears complaints about discrimination in employment on grounds of race, color, sex, religion, political opinion, national extraction, or social origin. The commission also has advisory, research, and educative powers. Partly for constitutional reasons, both the *Racial Discrimination Act* and the *Human Rights and Equal Opportunity Commission Act* are based on the relevant international conventions.

At the state level other measures have been taken. Each of the states, except Queensland and Tasmania, has enacted antidiscrimination legislation and has established agencies to implement this legislation. All the acts make discrimination unlawful on various prohibited grounds. In 1966 South Australia enacted a *Prohibition of Discrimination Act,* which was replaced in 1976 by a *Racial Discrimination Act.* In addition, in 1984 South Australia enacted an *Equal Opportunities Act.* In 1977 New South Wales enacted an *Anti-Discrimination Act* and Victoria enacted an *Equal Opportu-*

nity Act. In 1984 the Victorian legislation was amended to deal with discrimination on the grounds of race as well as other grounds. In 1985 Western Australia enacted an *Equal Opportunities Act*. Under arrangements made between the Commonwealth and some states, the antidiscrimination agencies of those states have been given power to administer the federal legislation. Unfortunately, federal and state antidiscrimination legislation has proved a fertile field for important constitutional cases, a factor that, in many cases, has impeded the effectiveness of the protection that the legislation should have provided.[136]

Equal opportunity legislation is "complaint-oriented"; that is, generally, in order for an act of discrimination to come to the attention of the relevant antidiscriminatory body, a specific complaint must be made. Usually the complaint will be made either by, or on behalf of, the victim of the alleged discrimination. The experience of the antidiscrimination bodies suggests that people from non-English-speaking backgrounds who are likely to be suffering the most from discriminatory practices and policies are not coming forward to lodge complaints. Female migrant blue-collar workers, for example, are substantially underrepresented in complaints.[137] Nonetheless, since the coming into force of these provisions, and consequent upon the activities of the bodies set up to administer them (for example, in New South Wales the Anti-Discrimination Board and the Equal Opportunity Tribunal), there is evidence that the Australian community has become more sensitive to issues of discrimination as issues of general law, particularly in relation to racial discrimination and discrimination against women.[138]

Other, general, legislative steps have been taken with the aim of providing better protection for the rights and interests of all residents of Australia: since the mid-1970s there has been considerable statutory reform in the field of Australian administrative law. The changes have been designed to ensure the right of the individual to obtain fairness at the hands of administrative authorities, government departments, and public bodies. The changes include the establishment, at both state and federal level, of an Office of Ombudsman.[139] The ombudsman is given power to investigate, report, and make recommendations concerning maladministration by government departments, but has no coercive powers to ensure that these recommendations will be implemented. At the federal level (and in the state of Victoria) the Administrative Appeals Tribunal has been set up to bring consistency and efficiency to the matter of appeals concerning administrative decisions affecting citizens and residents. This body has determinative powers in most instances of its jurisdiction.[140] Resorting to it is quicker and cheaper than taking a case to court. Also in the federal sphere, the *Administrative Decisions (Judicial Review) Act,* enacted in 1977, has simplified, extended, and codified the common law system of judicial review of administrative action.[141] A federal Administrative Review Council has been established to monitor the current system and procedures of administrative law and, where necessary, to make recommendations for its improvement. In addition, freedom of information legislation, both federal and state, has been enacted with the professed aim of providing Australians with access to information held by government departments.

This "new administrative law" is intended to operate for the benefit of all residents in Australia and to provide all those aggrieved by decisions of government departments, public authorities, and so on, with avenues of redress. Migrants not infrequently are more in need of this kind of assistance than others. Often the very reasons causing them to have these needs in the first place, however (lack of language skills, failure to understand their rights, inadequate information concerning the social security system—in fact, the way the system works generally) militate against the likelihood that they will have the knowledge or resources (the access to information or advice), or perhaps the confidence, to use the avenues provided in this or in other spheres.

There is a culture of poverty, and within Australia certain migrant groups tend to fall within this culture.[142] They tend (here reference is made mainly to immigrants from non-English-speaking backgrounds)[143] to be disadvantaged in all the major social parameters when compared to the dominant Australian community.[144] This state of affairs is often not confined to the initial settlement period but continues into succeeding generations.[145] Because people in disadvantaged groups lack power, they lack access to the very avenues available to others, which would provide opportunities to transform their situation, so that their choices tend to be restricted.[146]

Migrants often become caught up with legal problems. This situation may occur both in the civil and in the criminal sphere; and the problems are made more complex by migrants' particular differences, which translate, given the circumstances, into difficulties. The results are frustrating, time-consuming, and expensive, yet no comprehensive strategy has been devised whereby the effects of language and cultural difficulties might be offset somewhat. Migrants seek legal advice less frequently than do members of the dominant social group because of problems of language and expense and lack of information about the availability of legal aid. A clear correlation can be shown to exist between those who have legal representation and those who secure lesser penalties or other successes in court.[147]

Different societies and circumstances produce very different attitudes to the law, to the police, and to government authorities. A refugee fleeing from a history of persecution is unlikely to view these bodies as organs to be trusted. The adversarial system of Australian court procedure is not easy for someone from a system of inquisitorial investigation to understand.[148] Different cultural standards of behavior can also lead to problems. One clear example of such problems was provided by those early Turkish immigrants to Australia who continued their practice of slaughtering their own meat at home, a practice that created difficulties both with neighbors and with local authorities.[149] There are many other areas where conflict with the legal system is likely as a result of the difference in the beliefs and practices of migrant families or communities, and those of prevailing social policies embodied in the law. Examples here would be the legal requirement of compulsory attendance at school, a requirement not always in line with migrant communities' attitudes toward family responsibilities and roles,[150] and the requirement of licenses for some activities (such as fishing), when there may have been no such requirement in the migrant's country of origin. The latter difference has caused problems in the case, among others, of Vietnamese people now settled in Australia.

In the dominant Australian culture there has tended to be a lack of perception of problems such as these, and this lack of awareness has been reflected in the absence of suitable legislative or administrative provision to deal with the resultant difficulties. To take one example, the stage has not yet been reached when the role, function, and necessity for interpreter services in court has been fully assimilated by judges, yet the decision as to the provision of these services is left to judicial discretion.[151] The Australian judiciary historically has been, and overwhelmingly continues to be, monocultural and monolingual (as well as predominantly male). As yet, generally, its members are not sensitive to the adjustments that linguistic and cultural differences require if the system of institutional justice is to become responsive to the different needs and perceptions of a multicultural society. Similar differences in background often mean that lawyers also fail to understand fully the problems of poor clients.[152]

> It is a fundamental tenet of the Australian legal system that all people should be equal before the law. . . . At the heart of much of our law are concepts about "reasonable" and "normal" behaviour. They require judgments which of their nature cannot be absolute and fixed, but relate to an ever-changing social context. The application of these concepts in multi-cultural Australia is a particularly complex and difficult matter, demanding considerable social awareness and sensitivity on the part of the legal system.[153]

The requisite social awareness on the part of those administering the system remains, for the most part, something still to be developed.

Nonetheless, awareness is growing and, concomitantly, attitudes are changing. As a consequence, some appropriate legislative and administrative changes have been made. In some situations provisions are now available to deal with language difficulties: for instance, language instruction for migrants and interpreter services are available in a variety of situations; in some circumstances notices are now exhibited in different languages and provision is made for translations of documents. Educational programs are broadcast on radio and television, and some programs in either medium are designed specifically for ethnic communities. Community education programs have also been designed to assist migrants in comprehending the legal system: for example, in Victoria the Ethnic Affairs Commission, the Equal Opportunity Commission, the Victoria Law Institute, and community legal services now incorporate community education into their programs, while the Police Department has appointed ethnic liaison officers with the task, among others, of educating the community about the role of the police force.[154]

The provision of equality of opportunity and fair dealing for all is necessarily a complex task. The disadvantages and inequalities which some of Australia's migrant groups have suffered have existed over a long period, and attitudes change slowly—even when appropriate legislative and administrative amendments are made. The disadvantages cannot be removed overnight. Over the last decade the process has begun. There is, however, still a long way to go.

A Regional Perspective: The Draft Pacific Charter of Human Rights

For several years now, a nongovernmental organization, the Law Association for Asia and the Pacific (LAWASIA), has been taking initiatives to encourage the idea both of a Charter of Human Rights for the Pacific region and the establishment of regional mechanisms there for the promotion and protection of these rights. In April 1985, LAWASIA convened a meeting in Fiji at which these ideas were given consideration. All sixty-three delegates were keenly interested in human rights; they included lawyers, nongovernmental representatives, social workers, church and community leaders, academics, representatives of minority ethnic groups (including indigenous ones), and government representatives. Another regional human rights body, the European Human Rights Commission, also furnished representation and input.[155]

Having received a mandate from this initial meeting to pursue the idea, LAWASIA established and organized meetings of first, a Drafting Committee and, later, a Working Party comprised of representatives from the region. These bodies collaborated to draw up a Draft Charter of Human Rights for the Pacific region. Then in May 1989, in Apia, Western Samoa, LAWASIA convened a further meeting, this time primarily of representatives of governments of different island entities, to consider this Draft.

One matter that has emerged clearly from the discussions held so far is that, in order for a charter to be acceptable in this part of the word, it is essential that the customs and traditions of the peoples of the Pacific islands be accorded significance in the charter's terms, both in its interpretation and in its implementation. During his keynote address to the most recent Apia meeting, the minister of justice of Western Samoa observed:

> . . . in many Pacific cultures our human rights still rest on collective assets—our title, our dignities, our land, and our security—and every one of them must still be matched by obligations. If we are led to think of individual rights and freedoms as due us by some wealthy government, we may unthinkingly tear our culture apart. How will we feel when it lets us down? Very lonely and deprived, at the bottom of someone else's world. . . . [156]

In some of the constitutions of Pacific island states, provisions to allow for local traditional values already have a place. For instance, section 15(1) of the 1986 Tuvaluan Constitution (which contains a bill of rights) requires that "all laws, and all acts done under a law, must be reasonably justifiable in a democratic society that has a proper respect for human rights and dignity." In determining this standard, factors which the Courts may take into account include the "traditional standards, values and practices . . . of Tuvalu" (section 15(4)).

At the Apia meeting the delegates agreed that the Preamble to the Draft Charter should state, among other things:

> . . . the need to promote and to protect those rights and characteristics which stem from Pacific peoples' history, philosophy of life, traditions and social structures, especially those tied to those territories of the earth which these peoples have traditionally occupied . . .

> Acknowledging the need for minimum acceptable standards taking into account the diverse relations of peoples in all parts of the Pacific . . .

> Concerned that persons, having duties to their families and communities, and to other persons, are under an obligation to observe the rights and duties in the present Charter, have agreed . . .

Later articles in the charter give effect to these ideas. For instance, Article 29(3) includes the words "to preserve and strengthen positive Pacific cultural values," and Article 61A states:

> The Parties recognize the customs and traditions of the diverse communities of this region. The rights freedoms and duties recognized in this Charter shall be interpreted and understood by the Parties and the Commission in the light of these customs and traditions.[157]

Hence, here is an instance where there has been, from the outset, a clear determination to ensure cultural legitimacy in the formulation of a proposed human rights instrument.

Conclusion

An essay such as this inevitably leaves out much that could be said on each of the issues considered. Moreover, each of these areas tends to intersect with, and even to impede progress in, other areas. Nonetheless, some progress, however hesitant, halting, and inadequate, has been achieved over the last few years. Australia has ratified several relevant international instruments;[158] and important consequent legislative changes have been made—for example, the enactment of the *Racial Discrimination Act* and of land rights legislation. The federal government has adopted a policy of multiculturalism and fairness for all and has committed itself publicly to the need for a real reconciliation to be made between the Aboriginal people and the dominant community. Institutions (such as the federal Human Rights and Equal Opportunity Commission and the State Anti-Discrimination Boards) have been established—designed to tackle problems of inequality arising from, among other things, cultural differences. Perhaps more significant, however, has been the increase (even though at times frustratingly slow) in the community awareness of the dominant cultural group toward the increasingly multifaceted nature of Australian society, and the necessity for change if real equality is to be made available for its different sectors.

Greater recognition of and concern about the injustices that have been perpetrated consistently, since white settlement, on the indigenous peoples of Australia is developing not only at the government level but also in the wider community. There is increasingly an acknowledgment that reparation must be made for these injustices, insofar as this is at all possible. The form that this should take, however, is as yet unclear.

In regard to minority immigrant groups there is, among the general population, a gradually increasing appreciation of the contributions these communities are making to the Australian way of life. Recognition is growing that special steps need to be taken to eliminate the injustices and inequalities which have their roots in cultural, linguistic, and other differences—differences that form an inevitable (and rich) part of the varied pattern of Australian society.

Clearly, much still needs to be done. Nonetheless, it is fair to say that today Australia has progressed a long way from the times when its prevailing laws and attitudes resulted in practices such as the "White Australia Policy" and the failure to accord voting rights to all of its indigenous peoples.

Notes

1. It is instructive to note, however, that at the time (1966) of the adoption of the texts of the two major international human rights instruments, the *International Covenant on Civil and Political Rights* and the *International Covenant on Economic Social and Cultural Rights,* the majority of the member states of the United Nations were not Western liberal democracies but Third World countries.

This is even more true of the international human rights instruments drawn up and adopted since that date.

2. Some consider these figures to have been underestimated by as much as 16,500. *See, for example,* A. Gray and L. Smith, "The Size of the Aboriginal Population," *Australian Aboriginal Studies* 1 (1983):2; D. Jordan, "Census Categories," *Australian Aboriginal Studies* 1 (1985): 28.

3. 1981 Census.

4. G. Nettheim, "Australian Aborigines and the Law," *Law and Anthropology* 2 (1987): 372.

5. *See, for example, Empire Settlement Act,* 1922 (Imp.).

6. *See* M. J. Salter, *Studies in the Immigration of the Highly Skilled* (Canberra: Australian National University Press, 1978), 15–61, for a useful historical outline of assigned passage policies throughout Australian history.

7. For a comprehensive discussion of the White Australia Policy, *see* M. Willard, *History of the White Australia Policy to 1920,* 2nd ed. (Melbourne: Melbourne University Press, 1967). The assumption underlying the White Australia policy was articulated by one Member of Parliament as follows: "We are here upon a continent set apart by the Creator exclusively for a Southern Empire—for a Southern nation—and it is our duty to preserve this island continent for all eternity to the white race . . . " (K. O'Malley, Commonwealth of Australia, Senate and House of Reps. [1901], *Parl. Debates,* Session 1901–02, vol. 4 at 4639 [6 September 1901]). Although this rationale totally ignored the fact that the original inhabitants of Australia are nonwhite Aboriginal people, it was nevertheless a widely accepted view.

8. *See* the debates at the time on the proposed *Immigration Restriction Bill,* Senate and House of Representatives, *Parl. Debates,* Session 1901–02, vol. 4 at 4265–4666 (6 September 1901) (2nd Reading), Session 1901–02, vol. 5 at 5801–5828 (9 October 1901) (3rd Reading).

9. For example, in 1952 it was decided to admit Japanese wives of Australian servicemen under permits initially valid for five years.

10. C. Young, "Australia's Population: A Long-Term View," *Current Affairs Bulletin* (Sydney), 65 (1989): 4.

11. *Ibid.*

12. *Ibid.*

13. Of course, the legal protection of rights, whether by ordinary legislation or under a constitution is, in itself, not necessarily a guarantee that those rights will be implemented. Within Australia's immediate geographical region, fundamental rights are incorporated in the constitutional documents of many states. (This situation holds in all independent island states of the Pacific except Australia and New Zealand and in many Asian states. New Zealand, however, now has a legislative bill of rights.) In Asia, two particular ways of detracting from the effectiveness of constitutional human rights guarantees have been very evident in recent years: first, the excessive use (and abuse) of the concept of states of emergency and of the arrogation of powers to the executive body and/or military forces thereunder; and second, a not infrequent tendency to interfere with the independence

of the judiciary. The reality is that guarantees of fundamental rights, however impressive their appearance, will be only as effective as those wielding real power allow them to be.

14. *For example,* the basic rule in the *Bill of Rights 1688* that the Crown may not dispense with laws or the execution of laws without parliamentary authority.

15. I. Harden and N. Lewis, *The Noble Lie: The British Constitution and the Rule of Law* (London: Hutchinson, 1986). It is certainly a myth, in the sense of a value that both is axiomatic and that may bear no particular relationship to reality; but then law often depends on myths, especially in its ultimate foundations.

16. In a relatively large number of cases, the European Court has found the United Kingdom to be in breach of its obligations under the European Convention. Some of these decisions, particularly the *Northern Ireland Case* Ser. A vol. 24 (1977), and the *Sunday Times Case* 1 E.H.R.R. (1979), have had a particular impact, resulting in some instances in both legislative amendment and in the enactment of some legal provisions that protect rights.

17. *See generally* Constitutional Commission, Committee on Individual and Democratic Rights, *Report* (Canberra: Australian Government Publishing Service, 1987).

18. *See, for example,* the summary of interpretation of s. 92 in PH Lane, *A Manual of Australian Constitutional Law,* 4th ed. (Sydney: Law Book Co., 1987), 375–409; Clark King & Co. Pty. Ltd. v. Australian Wheat Board (1978) 140 C.L.R. 120; Uebergang v. Australian Wheat Board (1980) 145 C.L.R. 266; Cole v. Whitfield (1988) 78 O.L.R. 42; Bath v. Alstin Holdings Pty. Ltd. (1988) 78 A.L.R. 669; Henry v. Boehm (1973) 128 C.L.R. 482.

19. Ss. 7 and 24.

20. *Australian Constitution* s. 51 (23A); s. 51 (31); s. 80; s. 116; s. 74; s. 103.

21. Most recently, the Australian Bill of Rights Bill, 1985 (Cth), which was withdrawn after passing through the House of Representatives.

22. There is legislation at federal and state levels protecting some specific individual rights, especially in the area of antidiscrimination. This is outlined in section 5. *See further* I. Moss and M. Newton, "The Anti-Discrimination Board of NSW: Eight Years of Achievement," *Australian Law Journal* 60 (1986): 162; J. Mathews, "Protection of Minorities and Equal Opportunities," *University of New South Wales Law Journal* 11 (1988): 1. At the federal level *see, for example,* Racial Discrimination Act 1975, Sex Discrimination Act 1984; Committee on Individual and Democratic Rights, *Report* (1987), 4–6. There is also a nonbinding human rights complaints procedure under the Human Rights and Equal Opportunity Commission Act 1986 (Cth). Partly for constitutional reasons and partly because of the absence of a domestic bill of rights, all three acts are based on the relevant international human rights treaties.

23. *See, for example,* G. Nettheim, "The Relevance of International Law," in *Aborigines and the Law,* ed. P. Hanks and B. Keon-Cohen (Sydney: George Allen and Unwin, 1984), 50.

24. *For example,* in discussions in the United Nations Human Rights Commission and in the United Nations Working Group on Indigenous Peoples.

25. Parts of this subsection are taken from a paper presented by the author

for a Seminar on Comparative Constitutionalism organized by the American Council of Learned Societies in conjunction with the Centro de Informaciones y Estudios del Uruguay and held in Uruguay in November 1988.

26. For example, in 1901 when Attorney General Deakin had to consider the meaning of "aboriginal native" for the purpose of section 127 of the Constitution (repealed in 1967), he said: "Section 127 of the Constitution makes a particular exception that in reckoning the numbers of the people of the Commonwealth or a State, 'Aboriginal natives shall not be counted.' The rule as to the construction of such exceptions, where, as in this case, they are not remedial, is that they should be construed strictly. I am of the opinion that half-castes are not 'Aboriginal natives' within the meaning of this section, and should be included in reckoning the population" (cited in *Opinions of Attorney-General of the Commonwealth of Australia*, ed. P. Brazil and B. Mitchell, vol. 1 [Canberra: Australian Government Publishing Service, 1981], 24).

27. J. McCorquodale, "Aborigines: A History of Law and Injustice, 1929–1985" (chap. 1, doctoral thesis, University of New England [Armidale]), cited in G. Nettheim, *supra* note 4, at 373.

28. *See, for example,* Aboriginal Land Act 1978 (N.T.); Aboriginal Land Rights Act 1983 (N.S.W.); Aboriginal Affairs Planning Authority Act 1972 (W.A.); Fisheries Act Amendment Act 1979 (W.A.). The definition of the term in legislation is still, however, not uniform, and is sometimes circular, *see, for example,* Aboriginal Land Rights (Northern Territory) Act 1976 (Cth.) s. 3(1): "'Aboriginal' means a person who is a member of the Aboriginal race of Australia."

29. Commonwealth v. Tasmania (1983) 46 A.L.R. 625, 817.

30. Discussions relating to matters such as Aboriginal relationships to land, to hunting and fishing traditions, to kinship, marriages and matters of dispute resolution.

31. (1971) 17 F.L.R. 141.

32. *Ibid.* at 266–7.

33. Milirrpum and others v. Nabalco Pty. Ltd. (1971) 17 F.L.R. 141, per Blackburn J., 267.

34. In some specific instances (*for example,* Constitution s. 52) the legislative power given to the Commonwealth parliament is given exclusively to that parliament; in other instances, again very few, earlier legislative power was specifically removed from state parliaments (*see* Constitution ss. 114, 115).

35. At the same time, s. 127 of the Constitution—"In reckoning the numbers of the people of the Commonwealth, or of a State or other part of the Commonwealth, Aboriginal natives shall not be counted" [referred to in s. 4(3)]—was removed completely. In Koowarta v. Bjelke-Petersen (1982) 39 A.L.R. 417, two members of the High Court were of the opinion that any legislation enacted under s. 51(26) must necessarily be discriminatory; three said only that discriminatory legislation *could,* not must, be passed under the power, while one judge said the power authorized the enactment of beneficial, but not of adverse, discriminatory legislation.

36. House of Commons, Select Committee on Aborigines (British Settlements), *Report,* Parl. Paper, no. 425, 1837, 5–6, cited in Australian Law Reform

Commission, Report 31, *The Recognition of Aboriginal Customary Laws,* vol. 1 (Canberra, 1986), para. 109 (hereafter A.L.R.C. 31).

37. *See further* on this point N. G. Butlin, *Our Original Aggression: Aboriginal Populations of South-Eastern Australia 1788–1850* (Sydney: Allen and Unwin, 1983). Today it is not infrequently argued that special measures must now be taken to redress these wrongs. *See, for example,* D. Partlett, "Benign Racial Discrimination: Equality and Aborigines," *F.L.R.* 10 (1979): 254–56.

38. R.H.W. Reece, *Aborigines and Colonists: Aborigines and Colonial Society in New South Wales in the 1830s and 1940s* (Sydney: Sydney University Press, 1974), 3.

39. R. Evans, K. Sanders, and K. Cronin, *Exclusion, Exploitation, and Extermination: Race Relations in Colonial Queensland* (Sydney: A.N.Z. Book Co., 1973), 128.

40. In recent years Aborigines in Tasmania have come forward and identified themselves. The 1986 Census figures record 6,500 Aborigines in Tasmania.

41. D. J. Mulvaney, *The Prehistory of Australia,* rev. ed. (Ringwood: Penguin, 1975), 52.

42. For example, on the Upper Swan River in Western Australia and in the Willandra lakes region in New South Wales. For further information *see* D. J. Mulvaney, *The Prehistory of Australia, supra* note 41.

43. International law also drew a distinction between land acquired by settlement and land taken by conquest or settlement, but its purpose was different. For English law, the purpose was to decide which system of law (that of the earlier inhabitants or English law) would prevail in the territory. In international law, the purpose of the distinction was either to allocate state responsibility for territory where there were claims for damage done to foreigners (*see further* J. Crawford, *The Creation of States in International Law* [Oxford: Clarendon Press, 1979], 182–83) or to resolve disputed claims between states for the control of territory. Because of this difference in focus, territory classified as settled for the purposes of English law could be classified as acquired by conquest or cession for the purposes of international law. This happened, for example, in the case of New Zealand. *See further,* A.L.R.C., *supra* note 36, at chap. 5.

44. W. Blackstone, *Commentaries on the Laws of England,* Tucker, ed. (Philadelphia: Par, Birch and Small, 1803), 108; W. Forsythe, *Cases and Opinions on Constitutional Law* (London: Stevens and Haynes, 1869), 1.

45. W. Blackstone, *Commentaries on the Laws of England,* vol. 1 (Oxford: Clarendon Press, 1966), 105.

46. *Ibid.*

47. Milirrpum and others v. Nabalco Pty. Ltd. (1971) 17 F.L.R. 141, 242.

48. As far as New South Wales is concerned, the Privy Council stated in Cooper v. Stuart (1889) 14 App. Cas. 286 that acquisition had been by settlement. Opinions to the contrary had been expressed earlier, but in any case, the Australia Courts Act 1828 provides that all the laws of England in force on July 25, 1828, apply in New South Wales and Van Dieman's Land (Tasmania), as long as they were applicable to the circumstances of those colonies at that date. New South Wales at that stage included Queensland and Victoria. The other two colonies were also considered to be settled. Statutes fix the date of reception

of English laws for South Australia and for Western Australia at December 28, 1836 (s. 48 Acts Interpretation Act 1915 [S.A.] for the former), and at June 1, 1829 (S. 43 Interpretation Act 1918 [W.A.] for the latter). *See further*, P. Hyndman, *Constitutional Law and Government* (Canberra: Canberra Series of Administrative Studies, 1987), 9–13.

49. (1979) 53 A.L.J.R. 403.

50. (1978) 52 A.L.J.R. 334.

51. By Gibbs and Aickin JJ. (1979) 53 A.L.J.R. 408, 412. Both held that the Australian colonies were settled.

52. *Ibid.* at 411.

53. *Ibid.* at 412.

54. Judiciary Act 1903 (Cth) s. 23. In South Australia an early attempt had been made to adopt a different policy, but it had failed in the face of Colonial Office treatment of the colony as previously uninhabited. *See further* H. Reynolds, *The Law of the Land* (Ringwood: Penguin, 1987), chaps. 5–6.

55. Milirrpum v. Nabalco Pty. Ltd. (1971) 17 F.L.R. 141.

56. *For example*, R. v. Cobby (1883) 4 L.R. (N.S.W.) 355, 356.

57. *See* B. Bridges, *The Extension of English Law to the Aborigines for Offences Committed Inter Se, 1829–1842*, J.R.A.H.S., vol. 59 (1973), 264.

58. Paper No. 425, 1837, 84.

59. *See, for example*, the report by Captain George Grey, "The Method for Promoting the Civilization of Aborigines, Enclosure, Lord John Russell to Sir George Gripps, 8 October 1840," *Historical Records of Australia*, vol. 21 (Series 1), 35.

60. 6 and 7 Vict. No. xxii.

61. Changes were enacted in 1848 in South Australia, in 1854 in Victoria, in 1876 in New South Wales, and in 1884 in Queensland. (In Western Australia, a similar law had been in force since 1841.)

62. A.L.R.C., *supra* note 36, at paras. 52, 56.

63. *Ibid.* at paras. 52, 53, 55. Today most of these provisions no longer exist. Recognition tends to depend on the exercise of discretion and continues to be ad hoc and spasmodic. *See* J. Crawford, *Legal Pluralism and the Indigenous People of Australia* (1989), 5 (mimeo).

64. Similar legislation was enacted in Western Australia in 1886, Queensland in 1897, New South Wales in 1909, South Australia and the Northern Territory in 1910–11.

65. M. Christie, *Aborigines in Colonial Victoria 1835–1886* (Sydney: Sydney University Press, 1979), 164–65, 172, *see* A.L.R.C., *supra* note 36, at para. 25.

66. Cited in H. Reynolds, *Aborigines and Settlers: The Australian Experience 1788–1939* (Sydney: Cassell Australia, 1972), 175.

67. *See further* A.L.R.C., *supra* note 36, at para. 26.

68. *See* A.L.R.C., *ibid.* at para. 26.

69. Hon. R. I. Viner M.H.R., Minister for Aboriginal Affairs, Commonwealth of Australia 112 *Parl. Debates* (H of R) (24 November 1978) 3442.

70. *See generally Aboriginal Tenure and Land Population* (Canberra: Department of Aboriginal Affairs, 1986).

71. Australian courts have not recognized continuity of Aboriginal title. In

Gerhardy v. Brown (1985) 57 A.L.R. 472 at 532, Deane J. said: "If that view of the law be correct, and I do not suggest that it is not, the common law of this land has still not reached the stage of retreat from injustice which the law of Illinois and Virginia had reached in 1823 when Marshall C.J. in Johnson v. McIntosh (1823) 8 Wheaton 543 at 574 . . . accepted that, subject to the assertion of ultimate dominion (including the power to convey title by grant) by the State, the 'original inhabitants' should be recognized as having 'a legal as well as just claim' to retain the occupancy of their traditional lands."

72. "As at January 1986, 458,100 sq. kms constituting 34.02% of the Northern Territory were held by Aboriginal people in freehold title. Much of this land is poor quality in non-Aboriginal terms, which is why it has remained unalienated. It should also be noted that Aboriginal people represent some 64% of the Territory's non-urban population" (G. Nettheim, *supra* note 4, at 378).

73. F. Brennan and J. Crawford, "Aboriginality, Recognition and Australian Law: Where to go from Here?" Paper presented at Twenty-Sixth Australian Legal Convention, Sydney (August 1989), 12, 13 (mimeo).

74. By February 1986, it was 27,056 hectares. G. Nettheim, *supra* note 4.

75. *See* the *Aboriginal Land Bill* (1985) (W.A.) and (1985) 12 A.L.B. 6.

76. For example, *Aboriginal and Torres Strait Islanders Heritage Act* (1985) (Cth). *See further* A.L.R.C., *supra* note 36, at para 78.

77. *See, for example, Fisheries Act* 1905 (W.A.) s. 56(3), *Aboriginal Land Rights Act* 1983 (N.S.W.) s. 4(1). *See further* A.L.R.C., *ibid.* at para. 79, 9060–69.

78. For example, R. v. Sydney Williams (1976) 14 S.A.S.R. 1; R. v. Moses *Mamarika* (1982) 42 A.L.R. 94. *See also* E. Eggleston, *Fear, Favour or Affection* (Canberra: Australia National University Press, 1976), 287–88.

79. *See* on provocation R. v. Muddarubba [1956] N.T.J. 317.

80. For example, Napaluma v. Baker (1982) 29 S.A.S.R. 192.

81. R. v. Pilimapitjimiri, ex parte Gananggu (1965) N.T.J. 776, 785 (Bridge J.). *See* A.L.R.C., *supra* note 36, at para. 276. Some recognition has been granted by legislation: *for example,* statutes of the Commonwealth, of South Australia, and of the Northern Territory recognize traditional marriages for some limited purposes. *See further* A.L.R.C., *ibid.* at para. 80, 237–40.

Aboriginal traditional marriages are given little recognition in Australian law. This can lead to both social and legal problems. Accurate statistics are not available, but it has been estimated that at least 90 percent of the marriages of Aborigines who live a traditional lifestyle are not contracted in accordance with the requirements of the *Marriage Act 1961* (Cth). H. Dagmar, *Aborigines and Poverty: A Study of Inter-ethnic Relations and Culture Conflict in a W.A. Town* (Nijmegen: Katholicke Universiteit, 1978), 101, cited in A.L.R.C., *ibid.* at para. 233.

82. For elaboration *see* A.L.R.C., *ibid.* at chap. 6.

83. 1983 (N.S.W.).

84. *See* N.S.W. Land Council v. Minister Administering the Land Rights Act, N.S.W. Sup. Ct. (Bryson J., unreported, 13 May 1988).

85. 1981 (S.A.).

86. (1985) 57 A.L.R. 472.

87. This act has been significantly amended by the *Human Rights and Equal*

Opportunity Commission (Traditional Provisions and Consequential Amendments) Act 1986, partly in response to criticisms of its efficacy.

88. The act is of particular relevance for both Aboriginal and certain migrant communities; and consistently for the first few years 30–35 percent of complaints brought under it were brought by, or on behalf of, people of indigenous descent.

89. Art. 1(4) of the *UN Convention Against All Forms of Racial Discrimination* provides special measures "shall not be continued after the objectives for which they have been taken have been achieved." Art. 1(4) receives domestic implementation within Australia by virtue of s. 8(1) of the Racial Discrimination Act 1975 (Cth). These provisions can be interpreted as implying that special measures made pursuant to them shall be temporary only and although valid arguments can be mounted against this interpretation it is the one accorded by the Australian public to land rights legislation (although not the one accorded by recent High Court decisions). *See* Gerhardy v. Brown (1985) 57 A.L.R. 472 at 504, 527, 541–42 and comments of the Australian Law Reform Commission thereon in A.L.R.C., *supra* note 36, at para. 153–57.

90. (1985) 57 A.L.R. 472, 516–57. Mason and Deane JJ. were in agreement, at 497–98 and 532 respectively. Art. 1(4) states that special measures taken for the sole purpose of securing the advancement of racial or ethnic groups to ensure them equal exercise of human rights shall not be deemed racial discrimination "provided however that such measures do not, as a consequence, lead to the maintenance of separate rights for different racial groups and that they shall not be continued after the objectives for which they were taken have been achieved."

91. (1988) 82 A.L.R. 14.

92. *The Queensland Coast Island Declaratory Act 1985* (Qld).

93. (1988) 83 A.L.R. 14, 33–34.

94. *See further* F. Brennan and J. Crawford, *supra* note 73, at 16.

95. This is in contrast to the experience in Canada, where there is active discussion about the right of Indian bands to self-government and indigenous claims are couched in terms requiring recognition that they are seeking forms of self-government, not simply government provisions of services or financial assistance with projects. And *see, for example,* the Report of the House of Commons Committee on Indian Self-Government, and *The Indian Self-Government Bill* (Bill 52 of 1984).

96. *See, for example,* particularly the situation in Western Australia, where the Trust acted only as an advisory body with some management functions and did not even hold title to the lands.

97. For an account of the disappointing results of this system, *see* R. Wetenhall, "Aboriginal Administration: Should We Bend the Rules?" *Current Affairs Bulletin* 65 (1989): 4.

98. Consultation is under way on the appropriate form of a successor body. The proposed Aboriginal and Torres Strait Islander Commission is discussed in the next section.

99. *For example,* F. M. Chaney, then Liberal Minister for Aboriginal Affairs, Press Statement, 13 November 1979; Senate (1981) *Parl. Debates,* 25 March 1981, 713.

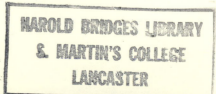

100. Senate Committee on Constitutional and Legal Affairs, *Two Hundred Years Later* (Canberra: Australian Government Publishing Services, 1983).

101. J. Howard, "Treaty is a Recipe for Separation," in *A Treaty with the Aborigines?* (Melbourne: Institute of Public Affairs, *Policy Issues,* no. 7, 1988), 4.

102. E.I.A. Daes, Rapporteur, *United Nations Working Group on Indigenous Populations, Report on Visit to Australia* (12 December–2 January to 7–22 January 1988), (mimeo, April 1988), 12, 26.

103. Interestingly the first motion debated in the new federal parliament building (opened in mid-1988) resulted in a roll call as a consequence of disagreement regarding the effects of considering Aborigines subject to the law in the same manner as all other citizens. The government motion, which affirmed "the entitlement of Aborigines and Torres Strait Islanders to self-management and self-determination subject to the Constitution and the laws of the Commonwealth of Australia" was passed in both Houses, an amendment by the Opposition to add, after "self-determination," "in common with all other Australians" having been rejected, House of Reps. (1988) *Parl. Debates,* 23 August 1988, 137–52; Senate (1988) *Parl. Debates,* 23 August 1988, 56–72. Owing to the failure of the Opposition amendment, the resolution was passed without Opposition support, thus detracting from even its symbolic effect.

104. C. Holding (then Minister for Aboriginal Affairs), *United Nations Working Group on Indigenous Populations,* 3rd session (Geneva, 1984).

105. M. Mansell, Options, Seminar Report, *Aboriginal Peoples and Treaties* (Sydney: CCI, 1989), 102, 103.

106. Senate (1988) *Parl. Debates,* 23 August 1988, 137; *ibid.* at 56.

107. *Aboriginal and Torres Strait Islander Commission Bill 1988* (Cth), ss. 8, 11, 21(2), 223, 230.

108. House of Reps. (1987), *Parl. Debates,* 10 December 1987, 2.

109. Description by government members of the Senate Select Committee, *The Administration of Aboriginal Affairs* (Canberra: Australian Government Publishing Service, 1989), 85.

110. *Ibid.* at 89–90.

111. *See* paras. 2–4.

112. House of Reps. (1988), *Parl. Debates* 24 August 1988, 251, repeated in April 11, 1989. Earlier versions of the Bill would have stated that the Aboriginal and Torres Strait Islander peoples "have no recognized rights over [their land] other than those granted by the Crown." For further discussion and critical comment, *see* G. Nettheim and J. Crawford, "Preamble Perils," *Aboriginal Law Bulletin* 30 (1988): 15.

113. (1987) Cth. *See also* the preamble to *The Aboriginal and Torres Strait Islander Heritage Protection Act 1987* (Cth) for similarly conflicting statements by the state of Victoria and the Commonwealth.

114. Federal legislation cannot be repealed or amended by state legislation.

115. It should be noted, however, that in some areas the commission's proposals (particularly those regarding the adoption and welfare of children) have been adopted at state and territory level. *See* R. Chisholm, "Aboriginal Children and the Placement Principle," A.L.B., 31 (1988): 4.

116. *See further* G. Nettheim, *supra* note 4, at 383, 384.

117. *Foundations for the Future* (December 10, 1987), 4. *See further* F. Brennan and J. Crawford, *supra* note 73, at 17, 18.

118. Already misunderstandings seem inevitable. For example, to one Aboriginal leader the treaty has ramifications unlikely to be attractive to the Australian government. For this leader the treaty will be one "which is recognized by International Convention . . . [it] must lead to full legal recognition of our rights in the Australian Constitution," Yunupingu, *Aboriginal Peoples and Treaties*, in *supra* note 105, at 26. For a comprehensive discussion of these and other difficulties, *see* J. Crawford, "Legal Pluralism and the Indigenous Peoples of Australia" (mimeo, 1989).

119. F. Brennan and J. Crawford, *supra* note 73, at 17, 18.

120. M. Mansell, Opinions, Seminar Report, *supra* note 105, at 110. This seminar report contains an interesting collection of speeches by Aboriginal leaders on this whole issue.

121. *See, for example,* submissions made to the Australian Law Reform Commission during its consideration of the recognition of Aboriginal customary law: Human Rights Commission (P. H. Bailey), Submission 346 (20 September 1982); Attorney-General's Department, Victoria (G. Golden), Submission 277 (11 May 1981), 1; B. M. McIntyre, Submission 242 (23 April 1981) (but accepting the distinction between immigrants and indigenes); Law Society of N.S.W. (D. E. McLachlan), Submission 358 (16 November 1982); Justice H. E. Zelling C.B.E., Submission 369 (26 January 1983), 1 (though only with respect to separate systems of law), A.L.R.C., *supra* note 36, at para. 163, no. 149.

122. *See further* A.L.R.C., *supra* note 36, at paras. 21–23, 39, 64–68. They are severely disadvantaged according to all the social indicators.

123. K. D. Suter, "Australian Aborigines: The Struggle Continues," *Contemporary Review* 253 (1988): 177. In the words of the Anti-Slavery Society, "In some interior towns the atmosphere is closer to that of the U.S.A.'s Deep South with its history of slavery than to the Canberra-promoted image of multi-cultural society" (*Land and Justice: Aborigines Today* [London: Anti-Slavery Society, 1987], 26).

124. In some Pacific island jurisdictions, the validity of special legislation for indigenous groups is recognized. *See, for example,* Clarke v. Karika, a decision of the Cook Islands Court of Appeal, (unreported, February 25, 1983) (Cooke P., Speight C.J., Keith J.); A–G of Western Samoa v. Saipa'ai Olomalu (unreported, August 26, 1982 [Cooke P., Mills, Keith JJ.), both cited in A.L.R.C., *supra* note 36, at paras. 145, 146, respectively.

125. For accounts of decisions allowing that differences in treatment may be legitimate when accorded to indigenous populations for which the government has a special responsibility, *see, for example,* in relation to India, A. M. Katz, "Benign Preference: An Indian Decision and the Bakke Case," *A.J.C.L.,* 25 (1977): 611. In relation to Singapore, *see* Ong Ah Chuan v. Public Prosecutor [1981] A.C. 648, 673–74 (P.C.).

126. *See, for example,* Morton v. Mancari 417 U.S. 535 (1974) where the U.S. Supreme Court concluded, at 555: "On numerous occasions this Court specifically has upheld legislation that singles out Indians for particular and special treatment.

As long as the special treatment can be tied rationally to the fulfillment of Congress' unique obligation toward the Indians, such legislative judgments will not be distributed. Here, where the preference is reasonable and rationally designed to further Indian self-government, we cannot say that Congress' classification violates due process." For similar statements by judges of the Canadian Supreme Court, *see, for example,* Attorney General for Canada v. Canard (1975) 52 D.L.R. (3rd) 548, Maitland J. at 560–61, Beetz J. at 575, 578.

127. *See, for example,* Yildiz v. R. (1983) 11 A. Crim. Rep. 115 on the question of the admissibility of expert evidence concerning Turkish approaches and customs; Re Qazaz (1984) S.S.R. 219; Moffra v. R. (1977) 13, A.L.R. 225.

128. *See, for example,* Australian Law Reform Commission, para. 164. Nonetheless, the commission in making its recommendations applied guidelines intended to ensure that any proposals made would not be discriminatory or unequal as between Aboriginal and non-Aboriginal Australians generally, or in relation to specific groups, including immigrant groups. *See also* D. Partlet, *supra* note 37, at 238; J. Crawford, "International Law and the Recognition of Aboriginal Customary Laws," in B. Hocking, *International Law and Aboriginal Human Rights* (Sydney: Law Book, 1988), 43.

129. Australian Institute of Multicultural Affairs, *Multiculturalism for All Australians* (Canberra: Australian Government Publishing Service, 1982), 4, 15, 21, 24, 30–31.

130. *See, for example,* T. Rowse, "Liberalising the Frontier: Aborigines and Australian Pluralism," *Meanjin* 42 (1983): 71, 83; M. B. Hooker, *Legal Pluralism: An Introduction to Colonial and Neo-Colonial Laws* (Oxford: Clarendon Press, 1975), vi–viii.

131. Some of the writings include: *Migrants and the Legal System* (Canberra: Australian Government Publishing Service, 1978); and more generally *supra* note 129; G. Bird, *The Process of Law in Australia: Intercultural Perspectives* (Sydney: Butterworths, 1988).

132. Of course much of this section has application also to the indigenous people of Australia—they are not specifically mentioned here since they have been the subject of discussions elsewhere in the paper.

133. 1975 (Cth).

134. *The Human Rights and Equal Opportunity Commission Act 1986* (Cth).

135. The first federal Human Rights Commission had been set up for a five-year period beginning in December 1981.

136. *See, for example,* Viskauskas v. Niland (1983) 153 C.L.R. 280; University of Wollongong v. Metwally (1984) 158 C.L.R. 447.

137. J. Mathews, "Protection of Minorities and Equal Opportunities," *University of New South Wales Law Journal* 11 (1988): 23.

138. I. Moss and M. Newton, "The Anti-Discrimination Board of NSW: Eight Years of Achievement in a New Area of Law," A.L.J. 60 (1986): 162, 168, 169.

139. *See, for example,* Ombudsman Act 1976 (Cth).

140. The tribunal may hear such appeals as are prescribed—either in the Schedule of its Act or as set out in legislation concerning other administrative decision-makers.

141. One state, Victoria, has enacted similar legislation.

142. *See, for example, The Culture of Poverty: A Critique*, ed. E. Leacock (New York: Simon and Schuster, 1971); R. Henderson, A. Harcourt, and F. Harper, *People in Poverty: A Melbourne Survey* (Melbourne: Cheshire, 1970), 123.

143. English-speaking migrants do, of course, experience problems of adjustment to the Australian way of life. Most of them, however, particularly those from Britain, have the advantage (relative to migrants from other places) of a similar legal and political system making the society, its culture, expectations, and requirements very much easier to comprehend. In addition, many migrants to Australia from non-English-speaking countries come from small rural communities and on arrival must deal with a country that, despite its huge land mass, is an exceptionally urbanized society.

144. For surveys of the situations of these groups *see, for example,* "Migrants and the Legal System, Australian Government Commission of Enquiry into Poverty," *Law and Poverty Series,* ed. A. Jakubowicz and B. Buckley (Canberra: Australian Government Publishing Service, 1975).

145. P. O'Malley, "Australian Immigration Policies and the Migrant Dirty Worker Syndrome," in *The Immigration Issue in Australia: A Sociological Symposium,* ed. R. Birrell and C. Hay (Melbourne: La Trobe University, 1978), 47–50.

146. Van Moorst, The Fitzroy Legal Service—An Evaluation (B.A. Honours thesis, Melbourne University, October 1973), cited in *supra* note 144, at 65.

147. *See, for example,* T. Vinson, *Legal Representation and Outcome,* New South Wales Bureau of Statistics and Research, 1973 (language skills, class, access to resources such as lawyers—all affect the types of justice received in the courts), 2.

148. For a discussion of some of the problems this system poses, see P. D. Connolly, "The Adversary System—Is It Any Longer Appropriate?" A.L.J. 49 (1975): 439–42; A. Crouch, "The Way, The Truth and the Right to Interpreters in Court," *Law Institute Journal* 59 (1985): 687, 689–90.

149. *Supra* note 144, at 24.

150. In relation to education, although the policy of multiculturalism represents an advance on the earlier policies of assimilation and integration, the developments nonetheless remain piecemeal and inadequate.

151. *See further,* A. Crouch, *supra* note 148, at 690–91; R. Dixon, A. Hogan, and A. Wierzbicka, "Interpreters: Some Basic Problems," *Legal Service Bulletin* 5 (1980): 162, 163, 166; *Evolution of Post-Arrival Programmes and Services* (Australian Institute of Multicultural Affairs), 152, 266–67.

152. *See, for example,* P. O'Malley, *Law, Capitalism and Democracy* (Sydney: George Allen and Unwin, 1983), 85–86, 101–102; M. Morrissey and J. Jakubowicz, *Migrants and Occupational Health Report* (University of New South Wales, Social Welfare Research Centre, 1980), 34–36.

153. Evolution of Post-Arrival Programmes and Services, *supra* note 129, at 264.

154. G. Bird, *The Process of Law in Australia: Multicultural Perspectives* (Sydney: Butterworths, 1988), 427.

155. The proceedings and recommendations and conclusions of the meeting

are recorded in *Conference on Prospects for the Establishment of an Inter-govern-mental Human Rights Commission in the South Pacific*, ed. P. Hyndman (Sydney: LAWASIA, 1985), 506–10.

156. To be published later in 1989 in the LAWASIA report of the Apia Seminar.

157. Seminar Papers, LAWASIA Apia Seminar.

158. In addition to the *Convention on the Elimination of All Forms of Racial Discrimination*, Australia has ratified the *International Covenant on Civil and Political Rights*, the *International Covenant on Economic Social and Cultural Rights*, the *International Covenant on the Elimination of All Forms of Discrimination Against Women*, and the *Convention on the Political Rights of Women*, the various slavery conventions, those relating to stateless persons and refugees, and the *Convention on the Prevention and Punishment of the Crime of Genocide*.

Diane Bell[1]

13. Considering Gender
Are Human Rights for Women, Too?
An Australian Case

Universal Human Rights?

In commemorating the fortieth anniversary of the Universal Declaration of Human Rights, there is cause for celebration, but there is also a pressing need for critique. How are we to understand the discrepancies between the theory and practice of human rights? By what means may the credibility of national and international standards be enhanced? What strategies of promotion and implementation might deliver human rights more effectively?[2] To these questions, posed by those who, on the one hand, yearn for a world order in which all persons may enjoy human dignity, justice, and peace but, on the other, recognize the pervasive and seemingly intractable nature of the obstacles to its realization, I would add several questions concerning gender. If human rights are to apply universally, why has there been a persistent and continuing need to qualify them with respect to race, religion, and gender? How do these characteristics of the persons who are to be the beneficiaries of human rights instruments intersect, interact, and get prioritized? How can the state, as the body responsible for ratifying and reporting on human rights issues, be expected to be blind to the conflicts within it that give rise to the need for the specification of human rights?

In addressing these questions, I am drawing on my work as a feminist anthropologist with a special interest in the plight of indigenous peoples. Central to my analysis are the ways in which concepts of woman, culture, and the state are encoded and evoked in the appeals to law, both domestic and international, to protect the vulnerable. By focusing on texts rather than contexts, much of the literature dealing with human rights instruments fails to offer a systematic analysis of the power relations in which the law, and attempts to use it to restructure relations within societies, are embedded. In looking to history and ethnography to provide a context for my exploration of human rights, I think it is possible to begin to map the terrain on which we might gainfully explore the gaps between theory and practice.

While the conventions, subcommissions, working groups, transnational voluntary associations, and nongovernmental organizations (NGOs) refine, review, and recast the instruments and machinery of human rights, there continue to be significant abuses and avoidances. These are not confined to the Third World or to the stereotypically repressive political regimes, but also include developed Western democracies. In 1988, as Australia celebrated its bicentenary, two major international authorities cited Australia for failing to meet its obligations under human rights conventions. For the first time, Australia was included by Amnesty International in its report on human rights abuses,[3] and Professor Erica Deas, chair of the United Nations Working Group on Indigenous Populations, in a diplomatically worded report on her visit to Australia, found progress in the area of human rights to be less than sufficient.[4] Drawing attention to the gap between the domestic practices and the international pronouncements of the Australian government is a common means by which Aborigines have kept their causes in the public arena. Australia does not wish to be shamed in the eyes of the world. Not all nations are as sensitive, however. Indeed, many powerful nations manifest a marked ambivalence toward conventions they were instrumental in drafting. The U.S. government, for instance, has not ratified the Convention on the Elimination of All Forms of Discrimination Against Women; if it did, the Congress would almost certainly have to ratify the Equal Rights Amendment (ERA).

The Australian Agenda

Unlike the United States, Australia is a signatory to the Convention on the Elimination of All Forms of Discrimination Against Women (United Nations, 1980, ratified by Australia, 1983): its policies can thus be subject to scrutiny by the international community. In addition to this convention, Australia is a party to the International Conventions on the Elimination of All Forms of Racial Discrimination (1966/1975). When the other two major Covenants on Civil and Political Rights (1966/1980) and on Economic, Social and Cultural Rights (1966/1975), are added to the Universal Declaration of Human Rights, the broad framework and specifications that underpin Australia's obligations in the area of human rights are established.

These conventions intersect in a myriad of ways and, in themselves, might be considered competent to protect the rights of indigenous persons and women, and therefore of Aboriginal women. In the absence of an Australian Bill of Rights,[5] the provisions of human rights conventions are particularly important in protecting individuals against abuses of state power. Article 1 of both the Civil and Political Rights and the Economic, Social and Cultural Rights Covenants declares: "All persons have the right of self-determination." Under Article 27 of the Civil and Political Rights Covenant,[6] which addresses the needs of ethnic groups, it could be argued that the rights of Aborigines to enjoy their own culture are protected. This may not be acceptable, however, as Aborigines have often resisted being included under the rubric "ethnic." Erica Deas, looking for ways to increase the protection Aborigines could enjoy under these conventions, urged Australia to ratify the Optional Protocol to the Covenant on Civil and Political Rights, and to make a declaration under Article 14 of the Racial Discrimination Convention so as, among other things, "to recognize the rights of Aboriginal and non-Aboriginal individuals to bring their communications to the respective treaty-bodies for international review."[7]

With respect to the provisions concerning women, we find that the ground is less secure. Articles 27 and 23(3) of the Civil and Political Rights Covenant[8] appear to be in tension with one another, as do Articles 10(1) and 15(1)(a) of the other covenant.[9] On the one hand, the culture is supposed to be preserved but, on the other, "arranged marriages," for example, are considered a violation. Further, the Western assumption of the universality of the family as the "natural and fundamental group unit of society" with an entitlement to protection "by society and the State," puts Aboriginal social structure under threat and denies ways in which women maneuver within plural and arranged marriages.[10] For Aboriginal women, the most fundamental and "natural" configuration may be a grouping of other women. This is so for the women with whom I have worked in Central Australia. In terms of residence, ritual, economic, social, and political life, women spend most of their time and energy in all-women camps.[11] To expect that a husband, wife, and children constitute the basic unit is to severely limit the political, economic, and civic responsibilities of Aboriginal women. It is also to promote a unit that may itself be the locus of violence and oppression for many women and that is a normative, rather than actual, patterning of residential units in Australia. The nuclear family is not the experience of the majority of white Australians, let alone Aboriginal peoples.

As kin networks are fractured and transformed by the intrusion of the state in ways that redefine their place in their own society and limit the spaces they may occupy in the broader Australian society, Aboriginal women have become increasingly vulnerable.[12] The ratification of international instruments does not mean that the content of the conventions, or the reporting procedures or censures of the nation-state in the United Nations are common knowledge for those groups the conventions purport to protect, nor does it mean that persons, believing themselves to be injured by a transgression of one of these international instruments, have standing in the United Nations.

Indigenes and International Conventions

Indigenous peoples have looked beyond deficient procedures and challenged the very basis on which nation-states negotiate their interests within the United Nations. They have argued that, as Fourth-World peoples—peoples encapsulated within the nation-state—they cannot, by definition, speak for themselves in the United Nations and therefore are in a particularly vulnerable position.[13] Australian Aborigines have made representations to the United Nations through the working group on indigenous populations, have consistently challenged the self-congratulatory reports of the Australian government regarding its policy of self-determination, and have had a measure of success in shaping procedures within the United Nations.[14] The government, for its part, has supported some Aborigines to speak and work with members of the subcommission on the rights of indigenous peoples, has acknowledged that the doctrine of settlement is false, has contributed to the Voluntary Fund for Indigenous Populations, and has promised a treaty with the Aborigines by 1990.[15]

Within Australia, Aboriginal groups have long sought ratification of ILO Convention No. 107 as the only instrument that deals exclusively with the rights of indigenous persons.[16] Australia has consistently procrastinated on ratifying ILO No. 107 (the Protection and Integration of Indigenous and other Tribal Populations in Independent Countries), and its language of assimilation is now quite out of kilter with the philosophy of self-determination.[17] It was, after all, originally concluded in 1957 and is very much a product of that era. In Geneva in June 1989, however, the Conference of the ILO agreed on a revised text. No doubt there will now be renewed, frustrating, and inconclusive debate regarding the need for this convention.[18] It is interesting here to note that the United States, Canada, New Zealand, and the Union of Soviet Socialist Republics, like Australia, all developed states with Fourth World populations, have also failed to ratify ILO No. 107.

Aboriginal Women and Human Rights

In the Aboriginal struggles to achieve a measure of self-determination, the rights of Aboriginal women have been submerged. Let me here present an observation for which as yet I have no disconfirming evidence, but that I think warrants serious attention for those concerned with human rights. Regardless of the particularities of constitutional arrangements, legal provisions, and histories of contact with European settlers, in the self-determination movements of Fourth World peoples, women's traditional bases of power, authority, and legitimacy have been eroded. The shift in productive relations and economic interdependence of women and men occasioned by settling seminomadic, hunter-gatherer people, the transformation of governance practices from face-to-face, kin-based negotiations to representative decision-making bodies, and cultural stereotypes of women's role and status render women vulnerable, create intermediate "representative" bodies through which their interests may be "balanced" and "brokered," and mystify the basis on which this transfer of power occurs.[19]

An anecdote will illustrate my point. A woman working for an international organization wrote to an indigenous organization in Australia asking that it nominate an Aboriginal woman to attend a gathering of indigenous women in Europe.[20] All expenses would be covered. She was informed by the spokesman for the organization, which purported to speak for all Aborigines, that it was not proper for one of their women to attend. Although she doubted this, she had no other way of locating a suitable candidate. Then in July 1989 she was able to attend the First International Indigenous Women's Conference in Adelaide, Australia. Through this conference the woman learned that there were many competent, vocal spokeswomen, and that they did not consider themselves to be restrained by tradition. Rather, it was the absence of an institutionalized structure through which they could be contacted that was the constraint. The Adelaide conference was for many their first opportunity to forge links with other indigenous women on the basis of their shared concerns as women, to extend invitations to visit, and to build networks.[21] Men have enjoyed state and organizational support in establishing, maintaining, and institutionalizing similar links at the local, national, and international level for several decades.

Here I am suggesting that we ground our critique of human rights in an understanding of ways in which the colonization of indigenous peoples has created a niche for the consolidation of male power in the emerging political structures established by the state to "represent" the interests of the colonized. In framing their analysis of the impact of changes on indigenous peoples, historians and anthropologists have developed more and more sophisticated models of colonial relations. But in writing of "internal colonization," "welfare colonization," and "the nation within" they have, for the most part, paid scant attention to the different impact of colonial practices on men and women. The work of Eleanor Leacock is a significant and insightful exception.[22] Drawing on the work of Friedrich Engels, Leacock argued that it was the emergence of private property that transformed the egalitarian relations between women and men in band society to the hierarchies of class society. In the process women move from being autonomous, independent producers to dependents within patriarchal structures and a new sexual division of labor was born. Women constitute a different colonial "subject" from men; and despite their cozy integration in certain domestic regimes, they are located at the margins of the new political order. The most consistent outcome appears to be that while men assume the political spokesperson role, the women run the welfare structures. From this I am inclined to conclude that self-determination movements serve the political interests of men but do little to assist and, in fact, do much to undermine women's power.

One counter to my analysis is to argue that foregrounding gender is divisive, irrelevant, a middle-class feminist plot to divide and demean indigenes—in fact, a form of gender imperialism. Racism, such analysts and activists argue, is more fundamental than sexism. These arguments, raised in the name of self-determination, serve to mask the power that the new elites enjoy in decision-making, in negotiations, and in their interactions with the instruments of the state. Not surprisingly, a feminist analysis is threatening both to the colonizer and the colonized. But, I would suggest, it is helpful in explicating the failure of universal notions of human rights to protect women's interests.

Let me be clear regarding my stance. I do not claim to speak for, or on behalf of, Aboriginal women, nor do I mean to imply that all women are or need to be the same, but I assert that the commonalities and differences which a focus on gender reveals are important in understanding the impact of human rights conventions on women, and the use women may make of the machinery of human rights. In agreement with Henrietta Moore, I am urging that our analyses of women in society "spell out the intersections of social, economic, political, ideological spheres" and thus build pictures of women as "historically and culturally specific individuals within certain types of social formations."[23] Only then will we be in a position to analyze the success or failure of human rights for women. The fact that some women are able to exercise their rights as citizens more fully than others does not alter the relative inequalities between men and women. Following Moore, I contend that race, class, gender, history, and culture are experienced, constructed, and mediated in interrelation with each other.[24] Thus a first step is not to assume that women share similar difficulties and experiences worldwide, but that these must be demonstrated and specified in each case, and that it is important to do so within a framework allowing for gender as a critical variable. In this I am close to Alison Jagger's conclusion of her book *Feminist Politics and Human Nature*,[25] in stressing that the use of the concept of "woman's standpoint" to expose the way in which overinclusive and abstract categories "conceal the special nature of women's oppression" is itself in need of specification.

Human Rights, the Person and Gender

The United Nations faces a tall order in trying to give form to such diverse and often contradictory notions of what it is to be human and what it is to enjoy rights. We all have dearly held common-sense notions of abstract concepts such as justice, human rights, and equality that build on our understanding of what it is to be human and to have rights. For Anglo-Australians, this would include notions of fair dealings, dignity, health, happiness, noninterference by the state in certain domains and regulation in others. There is no requirement that these be consistent; indeed, we often hold contradictory beliefs without ever confronting the conflict. To create further diversity in the pool of common-sense notions of human rights, we need to acknowledge that Australia is not a homogeneous society; it is made up of many different cultures. One in five Australians was born overseas; many of these people have brought to their adopted country notions of just and reasonable ways of interacting with each other as persons that deeply influence the way in which they would conceptualize "human rights." The 1.4 percent of the population that is Aboriginal draws on dramatically different historical and cultural considerations in framing notions of person and human rights.

Women constitute 51 percent of the population but, despite equal pay provisions, still earn less than 80 percent of the average male wage. It would be unrealistic to imagine that women endorse the notion of the "fair wage" free of the historical and cultural baggage that notion carries. A quick backward glance at the intertwining of law, cultural expectations of women's economic position within the family, and conditions in the workplace reveals that the fair wage was not set with women's right to self-determination in mind. Rather, the Harvester decision in 1907 drew on a model of a society prosperous enough for a man to be able to support his wife.[26] The fact that not all women married, that not all men supported their wives, that women might wish to pursue a career and marriage was background noise. Under this division of labor, women and men occupied different social, economic, and political spaces, one of which was dependent on the other. They were different kinds of persons. Although the law has changed, the value system in which it is enmeshed has been more recalcitrant in accepting women as wage earners with the same human rights as men. The most apparent and accessible source of discrimination may be law and, as such, reformable. More often, though, it is "customary practice" presented as "the natural order of things" in the unexamined cultural codes that underpin and inform the law.

Thus the Universal Declaration of Human Rights represents a bold and brave attempt to specify the universals, and to provide a global enunciation of the person. Now this codification has a history and a cultural context that, like the common-sense notions, shape content and form of expression. Most immediately, the commitment to universalize human rights strengthened in the aftermath of World War II with the Nuremberg trials and the development of a determination that such crimes against humanity must never happen again. In this sense, it was reactive rather than exploratory. Like the Nuremberg Code, to which so many ethical codes look for guidance, and in the shadow of which so many have been drafted or have simply evolved, the urgency and the specificity of its conception constitute both a strength and a weakness. The moment ensured that there would be a document and that there was the will to sustain the parties through the process of negotiation in drafting the declaration. But the impetus to universalize glossed over differences in a way that, it could be argued, has been an impediment to its realization, and that partly explains the reluctance of certain states to implement it or, once they have adopted it, explains the lack of success in achieving its goals.

Informing the concept of person enshrined in the Universal Declaration is the post-Enlightenment rights-holder, exquisitely individuated from fellow persons. One piece of cultural baggage this individual carries, however, is gender; "man" designates not the generic member of the human race but the male. Furthermore, he is the rational man differentiated from woman, who constitutes the Other in this scheme. His canvas is the world of political rights; hers, the moral domain of family. Although Article 2 speaks of the entitlements of "everyone, without distinction . . . race, colour, sex, language, religion . . . ," and so forth, by Article 10 the declaration reads "his rights," and Article 13, "his country." Now those who have a copy of the Interpretation Act by their bedside as a constant and intimate reminder, can read that "he" embraces/incorporates/subsumes "she," and should be read to mean "he and she": in short, they may recognize or interpret this as the generic use of the pronoun. But what are we to make of Article 12, which speaks of "his privacy, family, home or correspondence . . . his honour and reputation"; Article 17, which speaks of "his property"; and Article 23, which appears to secure equal, just wages for "everyone" and then bestows the remuneration on "himself and his family"? When we can observe that women customarily do not occupy certain positions, own less land, and work longer hours, we could be forgiven for thinking that this person to be endowed with rights is gender-specific "man." Since Article 16(3) establishes the family as the basic unit, we could well conclude that is where women should be located, in "his home." The declaration, which was drafted before the days of inclusive language guidelines, provides a clear example of why those reforms were necessary. There is a significant slippage between the apparent inclusiveness of the use of "everyone" and the characteristics which "person" possesses.

The context within which the Convention on the Elimination of all Forms of Discrimination Against Women was forged in the late 1970s was shaped dramatically by the International Women's Year and the World

Plan of Action adopted in Mexico City. These provided a very different philosophical milieu from that which yielded the Universal Declaration of Human Rights. But this encoding also had a cultural context, the so-called second wave of the women's movement, wherein the gender of the human rights-holder had been starkly revealed. Like the Universal Declaration, this convention, for the most part, concentrates on Western practices and preoccupations. It sets out to guarantee the principle of equality of and nondiscrimination against women. Article 2 enjoins states to take "all appropriate measures . . . to abolish existing laws, customs, regulations, and practices which are discriminatory against women." Initially, feminists had concentrated on understanding the nature of discriminatory practices and on proposing strategies that would equalize opportunities. At the time that the convention was being drafted, feminists, sustained by the inclusiveness of a global sisterhood, sought to improve the lot of women by appeals to equality of rights. By the 1980s, it was apparent that the pursuit of equality was problematic, open to abuse and appropriation; there were significant differences between women and their ability to enjoy and access the newly articulated rights. The rolling back of civil liberties, together with the erosion of women's reproductive rights, currently being accomplished by the United States Supreme Court, indicates how fragile the reliance on affirmative action to achieve social restructuring can be in a culture where the rights of the individual are held to be sacrosanct.

By the mid-1980s, feminists had looked more seriously at the gendered self and at the politics of difference. Added to this proliferation of feminisms, to the radical, socialist, and liberal feminist framings of questions of gender, were critiques by "Third World" women and women of color. They have pointed out that the right to work is a mixed blessing when a woman was undereducated, and that the extended family is a locus of support, not of oppression. They spoke of double and triple oppression. Anthropologists pointed to different authority structures, to the nonrecognition of the power women exert through what are classified as "informal" and "personal" channels, which, in non-Western terms, may make negotiation possible but, in Western nuclear familial contexts, make woman a lesser party. It was, they pointed out, a misreading of politics to dismiss women as dependents and leave it at that. As citizens, women often have political power; yet their ability to exercise it is limited in terms of authority, legitimacy, access to decision-making, force, and sanctions. Women pursue strategies designed to protect their interests, but the or-

ganizational structure may not be immediately recognizable or even consciously articulated.

Gender and Culture

What is important to women in the region and under a particular regime
may not be critical to others in different circumstances. It is a delicate
line we walk between cultural sensitivity and protecting women from exploitation. What is the standard of universality against which women's
rights are to be tested? At first glance, Aboriginal customary marriages are
in conflict with human rights provisions, for they involve "promised marriage" and "infant bestowal." The cultural context within which such
marriages were contracted, however, binds kin in a web of reciprocal obligations, rights, and responsibilities that have implications for land ownership and ceremonial duties: in short, they were part and parcel of the
survival of the culture.

By focusing on the individual rights of one woman, the nature of the
system of Aboriginal marriage arrangements is obscured. Marriage was
not an event but a process, which established and maintained alliances
between families. Within this framework, the interests of young girls were
protected by mothers, aunts, and male kin. Many of these checks and balances, however, no longer operate to protect women;[27] dramatic changes
in women's life cycles have further confused the issue. For Aboriginal
women in Central Australia, the indication that they were ready to take up
residence with their husbands was that they were postpubescent, that is,
they were sixteen to eighteen years old. With changes in lifestyle, however, especially diet, the age of first menstruation has dropped to twelve or
thirteen. At this age, especially if she has spent time at school away from
the socializing forces of her family, a girl is ill-equipped for marriage. Furthermore, with the decline of polygamous marriage, it is now possible that
the young girl will find herself to be the only wife. Traditionally she would
have had an older woman, often a sister, as a co-wife and ally. The way in
which the Law Reform Commission proposed dealing with this enigma
was to recommend "functional recognition" of marriage, that is, recognition for the purposes of legitimacy of children, social security benefits, and
so on. This, they observed, left culture negotiable: Aborigines should decide for themselves what constitutes marriage. They did little, however, to

address the unequal position from which women might attempt to establish their interpretation of marriage as binding.

In struggling to come to terms with "tradition," "marriage," "group rights," and "individual rights," the Law Reform Commission confronted this tangle of individual, cultural, and human rights. The discussion has tended to focus on human rights for minority groups versus individual rights, and the meaning of "discrimination" in respect of special laws. This is much more agreeable terrain than the power plays of men and women to privilege one interpretation of culture over another. Unlike Article 4 of the Racial Discrimination Convention, which permits "special measures," if women wish to have "special privileges," they must look to the specific provisions and seek exemptions. It was in this way that Aboriginal women who wished to restrict attendance at a dance performance at the Adelaide Arts Festival were able to exclude men, without acting in a discriminatory fashion. The company had received Commonwealth monies and therefore came under the jurisdiction of the legislation.[28]

Currently several moves to enfranchise Aboriginal women, to ensure they have a place in certain decision-making fora, have been contested on the basis of tradition. If Aboriginal women were to be made aware of the provisions of the Convention on the Elimination of All Forms of Discrimination Against Women and of the position adopted by Australia in its first report under this convention, the onus of proof that under customary law they enjoyed rights in land and responsibilities for the protection of sacred sites would not weigh so heavily on their shoulders.

> The role and status of women and men in traditional Aboriginal society were well defined and complementary. They had clear roles and duties which, although defined by sex, were equally important. . . . The exclusion of women from decision-making has been reinforced by governments' self-management policies and programs. . . . One effect of lack of consultation with women has been that women's role as traditional owners and custodians of land and sacred sites has not always been taken into account in the preparation of land claims under States' land rights legislation.[29]

The report reads as good anthropology, which no doubt was its source. But because the drafters of such documents do not appear bound by the same rules of citation as research scholars, no references are supplied. Unfortunately, the argument presented in the report informs the behavior of the few who are in positions of power in local organizations, or those who shape policy. The report was written by the Office for the

Status of Women, which is located within the Department of the Prime Minister and must constantly maneuver in order to imprint its agenda on budgetary decisions. While I am delighted to find a feminist analysis in a document of state, I am aware that without an economic base, it will be dismissed as rhetoric.

The report from Australia was due August 1984, but was over two years late coming to the Committee on Elimination of Discrimination Against Women (CEDAW), the body that considers the progress made in implementing the convention.[30] How to deal with recalcitrant states is but one of the problems facing CEDAW. Justice Elizabeth Evatt, the Australian member of the committee of twenty-three experts, mentions the scheduling of meetings, slow reporting procedures, general lack of procedural rules, specification of the required content of reports, communication between committee members, and the need to develop an ethos and an ethic.[31] Of all problematic aspects of CEDAW, none is as emblematic of unresolved tensions between what it is to be human and what it is to be woman than its location. CEDAW meets in Vienna, while other bodies addressing "human" rights meet in Geneva. Different explanations have been offered for the separation of the secretariats, one being that neither director wanted the other to be seen as senior.

Gender and Race

The most visible consequence of Australia's having ratified the convention concerning women is the enactment of sex discrimination legislation but, as a recent decision by Human Rights Commissioner Justice Marcus Einfeld illustrates, the expectations of what women may encounter by way of behaviors from men in the workplace inform decisions in ways that do little to encourage women in general to use the legislation to protect their rights. Justice Einfeld, in his decision not to award damages in a case in which the women demonstrated that they had been the subject of unwanted physical advances, including tampering with clothing and fondling, said that "women with normal experiences . . . know very well the ways in which some men occasionally behave."[32] From what then was the legislation supposed to protect women?

Those legal provisions which protect the rights of Aborigines have enjoyed greater understanding from the same commissioner, who awarded damages of $6,000 to an Aboriginal man who was refused a drink. There insult to human dignity was recognizable as discriminatory! Particular notions of what are appropriate behaviors for men and women, for men and women of color, for men and women of various religions, intimately affect the access to and experience of state law. Aboriginal women, stereotyped as promiscuous in the towns and as drudges within their own society, face a burden of prejudice that is hard to dislodge.[33] Superficially there is a certain symmetry between the convention dealing with the elimination of discrimination against women and that concerning race; but the repetition indicating that the articles of the International Bill of Human Rights covers all races is given greater force than the specification that "human" encompasses men and women.

It is, I think, true to say that there is little to celebrate on this fortieth anniversary of the Universal Declaration of Human Rights if you are an indigene or a woman, and even less if you are both. Examining the successes and failures helps explain this. In Australia there have been successes at certain levels, but they have been hard won and are quickly dissipated. When the Law Reform Commission, charged with the reference on the recognition of human rights, began its work, it was an all-male team of lawyers. After much lobbying, including a research project jointly undertaken with a woman lawyer and publication of a book on women's interests in law, certain changes occurred. Aboriginal women were consulted, and not just on matters commonly assumed to interest women (babies and food), but also on land and protection of sacred sites; in addition, women were appointed to the commission. Here it is important to note that the initial critique of the proceedings came from a feminist lawyer and anthropologist.[34] Without this presence, it is doubtful that the work of the Law Reform Commission would have been accessible to Aboriginal women as quickly and as forcefully as it was. It would have been deemed "men's business." It was the cross-cultural communication and intervention that prized open a space within which Aboriginal women could begin to press their rights in the political domain.

There were many obstacles to overcome, and some of them were cultural. Aboriginal women socialize with women, men with men. Male lawyers therefore had easy access to male culture and assumed that, as in their own social order, that was where decisions were made. To hear the voices of women, it was necessary to bend the edges of the law. For women to give evidence in land claim cases meant taking group evidence, scaling down the court, and arguing for submissions restricted to female eyes only.[35] The converse, for "male eyes only," had presented no problem. It was "woman" who was the anomaly, who had to make submissions requesting that she be heard. It was a problem to be solved by a special provision, while the experience of the male was normative.

But the gains of all the hard work of myself and others in giving expert testimony in the courts, of sensitizing learned men (and women) on the law reform commission of issues of gender, were quickly shuffled into an academic backwater. The bureaucrats charged with implementation of nondiscriminatory policies, together with the all-male organizations put in place to represent Aboriginal interests, constituted an almost insurmountable barrier. Thus, in common with other women, Aboriginal women may have political rights (they can vote), but they do not enjoy the same access to arenas of power—they are a different sort of citizen. What they experience is considered personal, and thus removed from the political agenda. Reforms concerning women have come to be identified or associated with the "personal," whereas the ones concerning men are perceived as addressing grander questions of criminal justice and civil rights.

While the impact of international conventions per se may have been minimal, the existence of an arena wherein the conduct of the nation-state toward its indigenous people may be publicized has been extremely important for the Aboriginal campaigns to secure land rights. Aboriginal spokespersons continue to look to the international court of justice, the World Council of Indigenous Peoples (WCIP), and the subcommission on indigenous peoples for support in their local campaigns. The politics of embarrassment, which Aborigines have used so effectively to bring their claims before the international community, grant indigenes a different sort of leverage from that which women may exploit. In respect to the attention their claims of mistreatment will attract, Aborigines fare better than women. It is a racist slur to call an Aborigine a "coon" and refuse him service in a hotel, yet it is not as deeply offensive at law for an Aboriginal woman to be called a "black slut."[36] By focusing on women, and more specifically on Aboriginal women, it becomes patent that the characteristics of race and gender occupy different space in the hierarchy of sympathy, and that there is a greater quotient of shame available to be exploited by indigenes than there is for women. If Aborigines are neglected in a First World country, that is a crime against humanity: if women are denied access to all important decision-making fora, that is culture.

Gender and the State

I realize, in looking back on my own writings on classical anthropological concerns—religion, kinship, marriage, social and local organization, social change—and on my more applied work in the courts, that I have been worrying away at this cluster of issues for some time. I have explored the differential impact on women and men of Christian missionaries,[37] the assimilation policy,[38] law reform,[39] legal aid,[40] and land rights.[41] In each context I have suggested that women experience the power of the state differently from men and have unequal access to its machinery. Here, then, I am moving toward drawing together some of the threads of earlier analyses to provide a more sustained feminist critique of the state that makes explicit that men and women are differently constituted by it as citizens.

In addressing this complex, a more sophisticated theory of the state is needed than that embodied in the position adopted by many prominent politicians, both Aboriginal and Anglo. The Australian prime minister, on January 1, 1988, for example, spoke of the injustices committed by the state and the responsibility of the government to make amends. Spokespersons for various Aboriginal interests insist that the state took the land, impoverished indigenous people, and should now compensate them. In both of these arguments the state is monolithic, and its act of dispossession should be undone by an act of restitution, be that by way of land, economic compensation, or recognition of sovereignty. Those who would see the state adjudicate in the interests of development see a similarly coherent state: one which balances competing interests in terms of the common good, here defined in economic terms. None of these models of the state allow that it is itself a site of conflict. It may act in the interests of the powerful, but it does so at one step removed in order to ensure its own survival. The role of bureaucrats, of the police, and of the courts in providing its continuity is critical. The elected representatives and their activities cannot be the sole focus. Any analysis of the working of the state must include all who exercise power on behalf of government or as a result of government policy. It must include the full state apparatus, from local government to the Senate, the bureaucracy, the judiciary and law-enforcement agencies.

Moore identifies four main areas on which a feminist analysis of the state has focused.[42] Initially, the emphasis was the welfare function of the state and how it provides for and controls women. Given that the only income many Aboriginal women ever receive is through the welfare system, this is an important dimension.[43] The second approach is to examine the "ideological state apparatuses," to use Louis Althusser's term, such as schools, media, church, family, and political parties, which work together to reinforce and reproduce dominant ideologies. As I have suggested, assumptions about family structure undermine women's bases of power in other groupings. The role of the church in constructing "woman" through its promotion of a particular model of marriage has created "shame" and submissiveness, where there was defiant independence.[44]

The third area of interest identified by Moore is the way in which the "state responds to women organizing—with ways in which it manages to disorganize, control and institutionalize women's activities." Marian Sawer has written extensively on this topic and has traced the "long march" women have undertaken through the bureaucracy, the institutionalization of the femocrats, and the capture of women's budgets.[45] In 1984–85, a government-sponsored task force set out to consult with Aboriginal women across Australia on their needs and to report to the federal government. The agenda was one of interest to the government; and, not surprisingly, the findings were directed at the government and required government support to succeed.[46] The Office of Status of Women, which provided the necessary bureaucratic support, did a remarkable job in coordinating the research phase and in bringing the report to publication. The budget for such an endeavor, the policy and program initiatives, would have to be generated in other parts of the bureaucracy, but in other departments Aboriginal women are not a priority.

Lastly, Moore explores the unequal influence men and women have on state action and their unequal access to state resources. For this aspect I have been suggesting that a historical dimension is necessary to the analysis so that the transformations generated by colonization of Aboriginal land can be understood. Moore quotes approvingly from Catharine MacKinnon:

> Is the state to some degree autonomous of the interests of men or an integral expression of them? Does the state embody and serve male interests in its form, dynamics, relation to society, and specific policies? Is the state constructed upon the subordination of women? If so, how does male power become state power? Can such a state be made to serve the interests of those upon whose powerlessness its power is erected [sic].[47]

On the basis of case material from Kenya, Iran, India, and socialist societies, Moore argues that women and men do not have the same relationship to the state.[48] "The modern state is predicated upon gender difference, and this difference is inscribed into the political process."[49]

I have explored certain dimensions of the processes of incorporation of Aboriginal practices within the ambit of the state, and demonstrated that this has the consequence of consolidating power in the hands of men. A common criticism of anthropology is its neglect of larger structures and contexts within which people operate. I have suggested that a study of kinship and marriage need not only address traditional practices, but can also inform our models of colonial relations. Moreover, a study of gender relations will inform our understanding of the working of the state.

Anthropologists in the 1970s struggled with their relationship to colonialism and pondered whether they were the "handmaidens of imperialism." This critique has been further elaborated by James Clifford; but unfortunately, gender is not a salient category for him.[50] His is, in fact, a very old-fashioned reworking of a set of questions which feminist anthropologists have approached with greater subtlety in their analyses of the intersections of gender, race, class, age, and so on. None of this has been easy.[51] Anthropologists have been dismissed as "bleeding hearts"—advocates, not experts, sentimental traditionalists, not rigorous scientists. But, in trying to make explicit the position from which they speak, they have begun an analysis of their own power in the construction of culture and persons.[52]

Gender, Law, and Power

Similarly, I am suggesting that lawyers have played a critical role in the construction of the subject of human rights. In 1986, at a conference of the International Commission on Folk Law and Legal Pluralism in Sydney, Australia, I asked: How is it that lawyers have become the new paternalists? Why is it that the limits of the rights to be enjoyed by any one group is what white male lawyers find reasonable? Why is it that the very instruments that legitimized the dispossession are specifying the conditions under which those disadvantaged by the previous actions may now be enfranchised? I suggested that we needed to interrogate moments in the legal arena that had as their purpose the empowerment of Aborigines (referenda, land rights, law reform). The political nature of appealing to the law to solve what is a political question will always be flawed, I observed.

I was not universally cheered for this critique of law as implicated in the ordering of power relations. Still, it was no less than I would ask of my own discipline, and no less than I demand of myself in making plain the conditions of my practice. It may make us more susceptible to challenges of subjectivity if we begin to scrutinize our own power as actors in the situations we analyze, but it also allows us to begin to account for the failure of law alone to restructure the relations between indigenes and the colonizer, and to reorder relations within the patriarchy.

Law, in my mind, remains opaque to its own source of instrumentation. In so doing, the power of the state, of the law, and of ideological components of the constructs of the person, of women, of culture are not scrutinized. Without recognizing the power of the law and the state as constitutive of the person, of women, of the indigene, there can be no systematic analysis: there are texts, but no context. In such a framework, law cannot have a theory of power. Power will always be oblique to itself and represented in other ways, such as the specification of equality at law. The exercise of power is too raw to be disclosed in legal discourse, and needs to be mediated for the law, the nation-state, and the international community to operate.

It is well to remember that it was international law that legitimated the original disposession of Aborigines, and that it was the legal fiction of *terra nullius* that for almost two hundred years remained unchallenged by lawyers. Law also operates in concert with imperialism. It could be suggested that human rights have become an area of colonization for the law, a means by which the First World can impose its standards on Third World countries, and contain decolonization movements by Fourth World peoples within the nation-state. Since a number of Third World countries have begun to look to the United Nations for support in framing their own resolutions, the United States has been notable for not paying its bills there. A deflection of purpose is evident; instead of pursuing human rights, for example, women's rights are being curtailed by a focus on the rights of the unborn.

The institutional framework for the international promotion and protection of human rights for some is an impressive and extensive infrastructure. To me, it is a labyrinth with much pretension, few sanctions, and many obstacles. I find it interesting that when lawyers and diplomats, normally pragmatists, speak of human rights, they speak of possibilities, of how standards might be set; they look forward, not backward. They rarely analyze why there has been a need for more and more fine-grained specifications of what constitutes human and what is a right.[53]

The human rights instruments to which Australia is a party appear to constitute a triumph of good will, good sense, and a commitment to extend dignity, equality, and opportunity to all, regardless of creed or color, gender, or generation. But the beneficiaries have little access to, or knowledge of, the machinery. At the most cynical level, it could be suggested that the conventions provide a screen through which those nations that might interfere in "domestic affairs" must now peer. In short, one consideration in signing a human rights convention is the creation of a protective mechanism for the nation-state. Given that it is those nations most in need of standing in the international community that have signed most prolifically, this cynical thesis appears to have some merit. While it may inform the initial impulse to sign, however, the process is more complex.

Beginning with conditions under which human rights documents are drafted, it is necessary to note that in order to achieve a consensus the convention moves as close to the lowest common denominator as is possible without entirely compromising its purpose. This process of negotiation continues through the ratification process; as the convention passes into domestic law, it must accommodate and balance diverse, often contradictory interests of the nation-state. Australia reserves on certain articles of conventions, if these are considered to come into conflict with the constitution, or with federalism. Then, as the machinery for implementation evolves locally, the convention must once again be rendered amenable to local conditions. As the laws and policies are tested, interpreted, and amended, a further accommodation to customary practice occurs. It is, I suggest, this series of funnels and filters through which the language and intent of the international conventions must pass that constitutes a formidable constraint on the capacity of conventions to succeed, and that accounts for the gap between theory and practice, between the ideals of world justice, and the reality of local law.

Are the efforts to secure human rights through promulgation of conventions at the international level misguided? I think not. They are a necessary but insufficient step in the attainment of human rights. It is only those who believe that law is applied in a cultural vacuum who harbor expectations that the law may restructure relations between the state and the individual. In a sense, if lawyers were to recognize law as an instrument of state control or of male privilege in any wholesale fashion, their practice would be severely jeopardized. They rely on the person as the rights-holder and seek to specify these rights as exhaustively as possible, but cannot acknowledge that some rights-holders are in a better position to enjoy those rights than others, and that those with power are unlikely to relinquish it for the greater enjoyment of the less powerful.

Notes

1. I am grateful for the invitation to participate in this conference, for the tolerance of Prof. Abdullahi A. An-Naʿim when it became apparent that I could not attend, and to Rhoda Howard for presenting the paper in Canada. I thank also Martha Crunkleton for her comments on this paper.

2. *See* the Introduction to this volume.

3. *Canberra Times*, October 15, 1988.

4. Erica I. A. Deas (Chairperson-Rapporteur of the United Nations Working Group on Indigenous Populations, 1988), Confidential Report on Visit to Australia (December 12, 1987-January 2, 1988, and January 7–22, 1988), para. 99.

5. *See* N.F.K. O'Neill, "A Never-Ending Journey? A History of Human Rights in Australia," in *Human Rights: The Australian Debate*, ed. Lynne Spender (Redfern: Redfern Legal Centre Publishing, 1987), 7–23, for an excellent account of the complicated history of the attempts to pass a Bill of Rights in Australia.

6. Article 27 reads as follows: "In those states in which ethnic, religious or linguistic minorities exist, persons belonging to such minorities shall not be denied the right, in community with other members of their group, to enjoy their own culture, to profess and practice their own religion, or to use their own language."

7. Erica I.A. Deas, *supra* note 4, at para. 6.

8. *See supra* note 6 for Article 27. Article 23(3) states: "No marriage shall be entered into without the free and full consent of the intending spouses."

9. Article 10(1) states: " . . . Marriage must be entered into with the free consent of the intending spouses." Article 15(1) states: "The States Parties to the present Covenant recognize the right of everyone: (a) To take part in cultural life."

10. Diane Bell, "Desert Politics: Choices in the 'Marriage Market,'" in *Women and Colonization*, ed. Mona Etienne and Eleanor Leacock (New York: Praeger, 1980), 239–69. *See also* Helen Bequaert Holmes, "A Feminist Analysis of the Universal Declaration of Human Rights," in *Beyond Domination: New Perspectives on Women and Philosophy*, ed. Carol C. Gould (Totowa, N.J.: Roman and Allanheld, 1983), 250–64, for a crituqie of the problematic nature of the concept of family.

11. Diane Bell, *Daughters of the Dreaming* (Sydney: Allen and Unwin, 1983), 2–4.

12. Diane Bell, "Aboriginal Women and Customary Law," in *Indigenous Law and the State*, ed. B. W. Morse and G. R. Woodman (Holland: Foris, 1987), 297–314.

13. Noel Dyck, "Aboriginal Peoples and the Nation-States: An Introduction

to the Analytical Issues," in *Indigenous Peoples and the Nation State: Fourth World Politics in Canada, Australia and Norway*, ed. Noel Dyck (Saint John's, Nfld.: Institute of Social and Economic Research, 1985), 1–26 and 236–241, argues that by taking their claims to the international community, Fourth World peoples create a point of leverage at the local level but that their lives constantly hang in the balance.

14. *See* in particular the positions presented to the Working Group on Indigenous Populations by the National Federation of Land Councils, "Australian Government is merely perpetuating past colonial practices," in *Land Rights Now: The Aboriginal Fight for Land in Australia* (Copenhagen: IWGIA Document 54, 1985), 120–34; and Charles Perkins, head of the Department of Aboriginal Affairs, regarding the negotiations over the proposals for national land rights in 1985, "The Australian Government has done much to recognize and meet the needs of its Aboriginal citizens," in *ibid.* at 107–19.

15. *See* Gerry Hand, "Foreword," in *International Law and Aboriginal Human Rights*, ed. Barbara Hocking (Sydney: Law Book Company, 1988), v; Marcia Langton, "The United Nations and Indigenous Minorities: A Report on the United Nations Working Group on Indigenous Populations," *ibid.* at 90–91; Erica I.A. Deas, *supra* note 4, at para. 6; T. Simpson, "Geneva-Indigenous Rights in International Forums," *Aboriginal Law Bulletin* 2, no. 34 (1988): 10.

16. Australian Law Reform Commission, *The Recognition of Aboriginal Customary Laws*, vol. 1 (Canberra: Australian Government Publishing Service, 1986), 128–30.

17. Gough Whitlam, "Australia's International Obligations," in *Human Rights for Aboriginal People in the '80s*, ed. Grath Nettheim (Sydney: Legal Books, 1983), 12–22.

18. *See* Geoff Clark, "Statement During the ILO Conference 1988," *Aboriginal Law Bulletin* 2 (1988): 13; Garth Nettheim, "Geneva: Revision of ILO Convention No. 107, 1988," *Aboriginal Law Bulletin* 2 (1988): 12–13; T. Simpson, *supra* note 15, at 10–11.

19. Diane Bell, *supra* note 11, at 94–106.

20. I have been asked not to disclose the identities of the parties involved in this incident.

21. *See* Jackie Huggins, "International Indigenous Women's Conference," *Australian Feminist Studies*, no. 11 (1990): 113–14.

22. Mona Etienne and Eleanor Leacock, *supra* note 10, at 12–16.

23. Henrietta Moore, *Feminism and Anthropology* (Minneapolis: University of Minnesota Press, 1988), 134.

24. *Ibid.* at 196.

25. Alison Jagger, *Feminist Politics and Human Nature* (Sussex: Harvester Press, 1988), 385–89.

26. The decision of H. B. Higgins, president of the Australian Court of Conciliation and Arbitration set the parameters of a "fair and reasonable wage." It was set at a level that allowed the working man to support himself and dependents. Women's wages were set for the needs of a single woman. This ignored the number of women "breadwinners," and the judgment was a considerable obstacle to wom-

en's gaining equal wages. *See* Edna Ryan and Anne Conlon, *Gender Invaders: Australian Women at Work 1788–1974* (Melbourne: Nelson, 1974).

27. *See* Diane Bell, *supra* note 10.

28. Law Reform Commission, *supra* note 16, at 490.

29. Commonwealth of Australia, *1986 Report of Australia under the Convention on the Elimination of Discrimination Against Women* (Canberra: Australian Government Publishing Service, 1986), 6–7.

30. *See* Elizabeth Evatt, "Discrimination Against Women: The United Nations and CEDAW," in *Human Rights: The Australian Debate*, ed. Lynne Spender, *supra* note 5, at 27–38.

31. *Ibid.*, at 32–36.

32. Marian Sawer, "Human Rights: Women Need Not Apply," *Australian Society* (September 1988), 9.

33. Diane Bell with Topsy Napurrala Nelson, "Speaking About Rape is Everyone's Business," *Women's Studies International Forum* 12 (1989): 411–14.

34. Diane Bell and Pam Ditton, *Law: the Old and the New* (Canberra: Aboriginal History, 1980).

35. Diane Bell, "Aboriginal Women and Land: Learning From the Northern Territory Experience," *Anthropological Forum* 5, no. 2 (1984): 357–58.

36. Diane Bell, "Exercising Discretion: Sentencing and Customary Law in the Northern Territory," in B. W. Morse and G. R. Woodman, eds., *supra* note 12, at 372.

37. Diane Bell, "Choose Your Mission Wisely: Christian Colonials and Aboriginal Marital Arrangements on the Northern Frontier," in *Aboriginal Australians and Christianity*, ed. D. B. Rose and T. Swain (Adelaide: Australian Association for the Study of Religions, 1988), 338–52.

38. Diane Bell, *supra* note 35.

39. Diane Bell and Pam Ditton, *supra* note 34.

40. Diane Bell, *supra* note 33.

41. Diane Bell, *supra* note 35.

42. Henrietta Moore, *supra* note 23, at 129.

43. *See* Diane Bell and Pam Ditton, *supra* note 34, at 94–96.

44. Diane Bell, *supra* note 37, at 348–50.

45. Marian Sawer, *Sisters in Suits: Women and Public Policy in Australia* (Sydney: Allen and Unwin, 1990), 22–23, 227ff.

46. Phyllis Daylight and Mary Johnstone, *Women's Business: Report of the Aboriginal Women's Task Force* (Canberra: Australian Government Publishing Service, 1986), 11–19.

47. As quoted in Henrietta Moore, *supra* note 23, at 183. *See also* Catharine A. MacKinnon, *Toward A Feminist Theory of the State* (Cambridge, Mass.: Harvard University Press, 1989).

48. *Ibid.* at 136–78.

49. *Ibid.* at 183.

50. James Clifford, *The Predicament of Culture: Twentieth-Century Ethnography, Literature and Art* (Cambridge, Mass.: Harvard University Press, 1988).

51. Francis E. Mascia-Less, Patricia Sharpe, and Colleen Ballerino Cohen,

"The Postmodernist Turn in Anthropology: Caution from a Feminist Perspective," *Signs* 15 (1989): 7–33.

52. Grace G. Harris, "Concepts of Individual, Self and Person in Description and Analysis," *American Anthropologist* 91 (1989): 599–612.

53. *See, for example*, Lynne Spender, *supra* note 5; and Barbara Hocking, *supra* note 15.

Tom G. Svensson

14. Right to Self-Determination: A Basic Human Right Concerning Cultural Survival. The Case of the Sami and the Scandinavian State

Introduction

The question of cultural survival has become a growing concern for encapsulated minorities in ethnically plural situations. In the relationship between relatively powerless indigenous minorities and the nation-state, cultural survival is not only a matter of culture per se. It can also be regarded as a human rights issue based on political rights and land rights, the two predominant elements contained in what is referred to as "Aboriginal rights." Political rights refer to self-determination, whereas land rights can be either territorial rights to land and water, or rights and ability to develop traditional natural resources, such as sovereignty over a land base sufficient to maintain a particular way of life.

How then can a particular culture survive? It can be sustained only by the common action of many people whose main concern is to maintain and develop their basic and culturally defined characteristics. These people share fundamental interests and values, as well as a distinct identity, which make them readily recognizable and different vis-à-vis the outside world. Cultural survival, therefore, is primarily a collective objective and should be viewed in contrast to individual physical survival.

If one assumes this connection between culture and human rights to be a significant legal property according to international law and uses it as a fruitful point of departure in attempts at clarification of human rights in general terms, the somewhat unnecessary debate between liberal and nonliberal positions and the controversy as to whether human rights are individual or collective might be settled.[1]

In my view, it is a human right to be part of a culture, but to have full *meaning* this right must be shared with other people. It is foremost a question of social rights: rights to a distinct way of life, rights to a system of beliefs and values, the meaning of which emerges when they are shared. These rights are collectively exercised, although their strength and importance are individually experienced as well. No doubt this is true for indigenous minorities viewed internationally in a global Fourth World perspective; however, human rights cover a far broader field, and in many instances individual human rights must predominate. For that reason, it may be an impossible task to try to specify some kinds of general human rights, that is, rights that are applicable to all mankind. If we pursue such a goal, we may be left with very little, whereas if we allow the meaning of the concept of human rights to expand situationally without losing its fundamental support, it will continue to evolve as a powerful asset that can be used strategically by actors in various arenas, national or international, where confrontation between different cultures is called for. The primary concern must be that general human rights are equal in weight and significance, for individuals as well as collectivities, without being identical in content. With such a simple clarification we may come to terms with the difficulties generated by extreme cultural relativism.

Let me sum up this introductory statement by quoting a Native person belonging to the Plains Cree whom I met after the Human Rights conference in Saskatoon, Canada:

> To us Indians human rights is a matter of daily survival; it is the right to food, to firewood and to fresh water, but above all it is the right to our customs. If we are denied these rights we are denied human rights, the way we see it.

Obviously, he is emphasizing the collectiveness of human dignity, so strongly accentuated by human rights advocates.

In this chapter I intend to explore the ethnopolitical goal of cultural survival, linking the discussion to ideas of human rights wherever appropriate. The case material in support of the argument derives from the Sami in Northern Fennoscandia, a indigenous minority in a European context with long Western democratic traditions.

The Concept of Human Rights in Cultural Terms

According to Richard Falk, a leading contemporary expert on broadening the perspectives of human rights, human rights discourse must include the dimension of culture to counteract, or balance, the unidimensional acknowledgment of sameness promoted legally by international law through its human rights instruments.[2] Bringing in, and making explicit use of, the perspective of culture makes the realization of human rights accountable for difference as well as sameness or equality, for the right of people to be culturally distinct from any other people in the world.

Indigenous people have already challenged the internationally held contention that human rights mean only individual civil rights; instead they insist firmly on the need for these fundamental rights to be collective. In Latin America, for example, indigenous poeple have made definite advances when it comes to articulating and promoting this shift of emphasis, for instance in the United Nations seminar on recourse procedures in Nicaragua in 1981.[3] For a long time the same ethnopolitical ideas have been placed on the agenda of Pan-Sami politics (Nordic Sami Political Platform, 1971 and 1980) and are frequently spelled out and articulated in various arenas of interethnic confrontations, especially those related to legal and legislative processes. The most recent example is the separate statement made by the Sami participating in the Sami Rights Committee, appointed by the Swedish government with explicit instructions to inquire in the broadest possible manner into the status of Sami rights, presenting the government and the parliament with proposals for subsequent legislative changes.

In this statement the Sami argue for the importance of collective rights and that it is crucial to them to have these rights constitutionally protected. The non-Sami members of the committee, on the other hand, refused to consider this possibility in the proposals they submitted, referring to the official Swedish opinion that human rights are individual rights and consequently cannot be subject to constitutional protection in the sense required by the Sami as a distinct people. This controversy will certainly cause thorough debate preceding final legislation.[4]

In this same report one of the advances made by the Sami refers to the concept *people*. A new "Sami Act" is suggested that for the first time would meet Sami demands to be firmly and unequivocally recognized as a distinct people in the constitution. Once constitutionally ratified, the immediate impliction of this legally valid statment is the opening of a full reconsideration of rights issues. Owing to ongoing parliamentary inquiries, this change is presently about to take place in both Norway and Sweden; eventually it will probably also occur in Finland.

The idea of cultural survival for people with Aboriginal status such as the Sami is an ethnopolitical goal, defined collectively and sought to be realized through means and activities collectively agreed upon. No strategy or effort to attain this ultimate goal can be singled out as individually based. On the contrary, each reflects the mobilization of groups of varying size in order to oppose assimilation pressure inevitably exerted by the dominant society, while at the same time securing and maintaining their cultural peculiarity. Cultural survival for an individual becomes more or less meaningless unless it is paired with cultural survival for the group. No culture or lifestyle can be maintained without having a viable number of individuals taking part in the same way of life, sharing values, beliefs, and aesthetic manifestations included therein. The struggle for cultural survival reflects communal belongingness at the same time that it reactivates and reconfirms ethnic identity for each individual taking part. Thus, in a sense, there does not have to be a sharp, irreconcilable contradiction between the two dimensions of human rights, individual versus collective, especially in reference to cultural survival. Instead of viewing these sets of rights in either/or terms, I submit that they should be viewed as equally valid and not mutually exclusive, though emphasis may be placed on one or the other, depending on context.

In the Fourth World context, dealing mainly with indigenous minorities, the position seems clear enough, but I do not believe that advocacy for collective rights should be restricted to this particular context. When discussing human rights problems where structural properties and culture constitute the significant framework, however, it is important to define and specify the context in question.

Following Michael McDonald, an ardent advocate of collective human rights, I wish to maintain that community survival depends on powerful collective rights held by individuals in common, and that cultural survival is based on several local communities proving successful in this endeavor.[5] The importance of community survival has been stressed many times by the Sami; the National Assembly of Sami, for instance, cannot allow even one community to be extinguished from the group of Sami communities as a result of external encroachments. It is believed that such extinction, no matter how small the community might be, would cause a severe blow to the Sami and undermine their ability to survive culturally. The sense of collectiveness is strongly felt among most indigenous people out of mere instinct for self-preservation because these people are constantly subject to encroachments circumscribing their land base as well as to assimilation pressure.

The achievement of cultural survival, despite the tensions caused by rapidly changing external circumstances and conditions, helps to reinforce rights among individuals, which in turn reconfirms and strengthens collective rights as the legal foundation on which community survival is based. The right to be different, referring to the use of both language and culture as a means of expressing distinct, autonomous identity, is invariably actualized in this ongoing process which aims at a reaffirmation of cultural survival. Cultural survival for indigenous minorities cannot be considered an end in itself; it is more a question of a perpetual activity having a most positive impact on cultural revitalization. It is primarily in interethnic encounters between an all-powerful nation-state and a relatively powerless minority that diverse features connected to cultural distinctiveness become salient and are emphasized in actual social life. It must be remembered that culture is not an observable entity but essentially an analytical construct; in order to comprehend culture more readily, one must look for situations in which a whole range of culturally defined features become evident in interaction. The focus on ethnicity, as developed in anthropology, offers a theoretical perspective pointing to this end.[6] I am convinced that such ethnicity theories are most adequate in the interdisciplinary effort to broaden the understanding of human rights in this collective sense.[7]

Being part of a viable culture implies, moreover, a realization of *self*; it has to do with *qualities of life* that are deeply rooted in people's minds as well as their patterns of behavior. To a great extent, such qualities of life are culturally linked and form an essential part of what we consider human dignity. According to international law each individual should be entitled to human dignity; it is a basic human right. When that right is shared by many individuals, however, the quality of human dignity is strengthened; it then becomes an individual right that can be exercised and expressed collectively.

Aiming toward cultural survival is a political action as well as a legal matter with certain definite cultural constituents. Cultural survival is closely connected to rights to *self-determination,* that is, political rights; and the crucial question is the quality of that right. In other words, how far can an indigenous minority group be allowed to go in terms of developing self-determination without violating the idea of self-determination for the nation-state, not least in reference to national security regarding external, foreign relations? Once again, there is no single blueprint for coping with this dilemma. On the other hand, the question of national security as such should in no way be permissible grounds for any denial of the most decisive human rights for indigenous people and their cultural continuity.

Self-determination refers to autonomy when it comes to decision-making. In other words, an ethnically defined group will have obtained self-determination when it is fully authorized to run its own affairs and determine its own destiny without interference from various authorities of the dominant society. Most, if not all, indigenous ethnic minorities have not reached that level of autonomy yet; for this reason, the issue of self-determination is highly urgent, especially in regard to cultural survival. The question who is the *self* in this term, sometimes raised in discussion of this principle and right, is not a very difficult one to answer. The term *self* may refer to anything from a single individual to a nation-state, depending on diverse contexts. When the ethnic minority situation prevailing among indigenous people is examined, self encompasses all members of a given group who wish to define themselves in ethnic terms. It is to them, and them only, that self-determination in a specific case has meaning. Consequently, the answer to the question as to who the self is has to be determined empirically in each particular case. On the other hand, if we are too uncomfortable with the concept of self-determination due to conceivable ambiguity, *political and cultural autonomy* in a real sense embraced and exercised by a distinct group of people may help us out of this predicament.

The crucial factors affecting the capacity for cultural maintenance are first, *environmental conditions,* and second, *social circumstances,* which are primarily perceived as the structural framework for action. The latter factor is, by and large, defined by the majority society; it involves conditions imposed by political and bureaucratic authorities on all levels of administration—national, regional, and municipal—and laws and regulations especially designed for the indigenous minority. As these factors are not consistent but tend to vary continuously over time, goal-oriented action toward cultural survival should be viewed as an adaptive response to these changes; it constitutes an essential part of the comprehensive ecological reality for the group in question.

Such continuous adaptation is a necessary force, without which no indigenous ethnic minority can persist as a distinct cultural unit; the viability of such groups depends on how well this dynamic is managed. What I am stating here corresponds in part to the useful point made by Manuela Carneiro da Cunha concerning elaboration of customary law.[8] Or put differently, what matters for indigenous ethnic minorities is that they have authority to elaborate their own customs. Of course, all adaptation aimed at cultural maintenance is a question of selective elaboration of customs, varying from case to case and determined by strategic considerations.

As regards environmental conditions, the issue of *land* needs to be investigated. Certainly land does not mean the same to all indigenous people; the meaning varies according to ecological adaptation and to livelihood. People whose economy is based on reindeer pastoralism, or hunting and trapping, such as the Sami and the James Bay Cree, respectively, are characterized by an extensive land-use pattern. This means that they have to have access to a much larger area of land to carry on their traditional mode of production, whereas people who use the land more intensely usually require far less territory for their cultural maintenance. For example, there is a noticeable contrast between Indians who live in small-scale reserves, as is often the case in Canada, and nonreserve, more freely adapting, indigenous groups. In the latter case, competition for absolute control of and authority over the land base, but not for the same natural resources, generates a constant problem which has to be resolved. Confrontations concerning rights to land and water become more absolute and consequential in situations where kinds of resource development differ appreciably, for example, development of renewable resources on the one hand and exploitation of nonrenewable resources, which is typical of the dominant industrial society, on the other.

The land itself is also a crucial factor for practically all indigenous ethnic minorities; it represents the core issue concerning cultural survival. All cultures, small and large, are anchored in a territorial base to which they belong; land, then, has definite meaning both in a real, material sense and in a symbolic one. Accordingly, Native claims to land and water are the primary issue at present for many indigenous people in the Fourth World.

The question of land rights has to be determined in both legal and political terms; without clarification of these rights, the indigenous minority will not acquire real *negotiation power*. Rights can never be obtained, however, unless a party with opposing interests is confronted with the issue. The ongoing struggle for improved land rights, therefore, reflects a stage of profound confrontation between the majority society and various indigenous minorities encapsulated therein. And the outcome of these efforts will to a large extent determine the capability indigenous minorities will have to sustain viable and distinct cultural units in the future. Following my previous argument, it is primarily for this reason that the land rights struggle, so commonly engaged in by Native peoples, can be regarded as a legal contest with a clear human rights perspective, although it relates more specifically to property law.

The Strategic Use of the Human Rights Issue

Pressure on land originally used by the Sami has increased markedly in more recent years, especially in the era following World War II. In order to meet this challenge the Sami have initiated an ethnopolitical process, very broad in scope, in which the legal arena and the legislative process appear equally significant. The Sami are consistently trying to improve their land rights while, at the same time, strengthening their political position in terms of self-determination. In the following, I want to illustrate this ongoing process of change by discussing two current court cases and their gradual implications for new legislative measures.

Before doing so, however, a brief description of the Sami as people and their cultural background is in order. The Sami number approximately 60,000 persons living in four different North European countries: 35,000 in Norway; 18,000 in Sweden; 5,000 in Finland; and 2,000 on the Kola peninsula in the Soviet Union. Ethnically, they are one people speaking three distinct branches of the Sami language, with dialect divisions within each one. Originally, the Sami were hunters and gatherers who gradually differentiated into various subcultures varying according to means of livelihood and specialized ecological adaptation. Since at least the sixteenth century it has been possible to distinguish four major subgroups of Sami: 1) coastal and river Sami, who are sedentary and subsist on inshore or freshwater fishing, in some cases combined with dairy farming; 2) mountain Sami, who are pure, seminomadic reindeer pastoralists, migrating long distances between the tundra and the taiga; whereas 3) forest Sami, and 4) east Sami are seminomadic, migrating within the same ecological zone, the taiga, all year round.

In modern times many Sami fall outside this division, being engaged in all kinds of occupations and in many instances living permanently quite far from Sami core areas of habitation. This further occupational separation has in no way weakened Sami ethnopolitical activity and degree of mobilization for common political goals, however. The entire post-World War II era reflects this state of affairs. The two court cases discussed in this chapter and their respective aftermaths give additional proof of this necessary development in cultural-political terms. Cultural survival is a concern for all the Sami, who define themselves as Sami regardless of occupation and place of residence. In Oslo, for example, there are as many as 5,000 Sami, whose Sami Association has for years taken an active part in the general political life of the Sami in Norway, as illustrated by the Alta

case. Similar levels of engagement are found in Stockholm and other big
urban areas.

THE ALTA CASE

This case involves a confrontation between the Sami and the Norwegian
state regarding the legality of a state-managed hydropower development
that affects a vital section of the core area of Sami habitation in Northern
Norway. In addition to both organized and spontaneous demonstrations
and public protests concerning the decision to execute the project, the
Sami also brought the contest to court for a legal examination. The more
specific objective of the suit was to prevent the hydropower project from
being carried out. Equally significant, however, was the symbolic issue.
For the Sami, Alta represented the critical limit of encroachments. For a
very long time the Sami had experienced a great number of land losses for
which they were compelled to accept only limited compensation. They
considered it urgent to be able to control the state's process of successively
circumscribing their ecological niche. The Sami were no longer prepared
to accept that each case be viewed separately, resulting in losses they could
not control. Consequently, it was not the scale of the Alta exploitation as
such that caused the Sami to react differently this time compared to earlier
similar cases. Rather, in the Alta case the Sami for the first time said a
straight no to development instead of entering a more or less lenient negotiation with the authorities concerning compensation. The Alta case
was thereby converted into an ethnopolitical conflict with far-reaching implications, soon becoming a news item in various media both in Norway
and internationally. Through this extensive news coverage the Sami were
placed on the social map as never before.

The strategy in court evolved from this conversion, and international
law was emphatically stressed. This was the first time the issue of international law, including its human rights principles, was forcefully presented
in a Norwegian court focusing on the Sami minority. Even this emphasis
can be explained in terms of ethnopolitics; the two interventional parties
NSR (Norske Samers Riksforbund, or the Assembly of Norwegian Sami)
and NRL (Norske Reindriftssamers Landsforbund, or the Union of Norwegian Reindeer Sami) gave their general support to the Sami group
which actually suffered losses in the district in question because it was in
their interest to test legally whether international law had any relevance
for Norwegian courts. Two goals justified such strategy at the trial: first,
to have the issue of international law tested in a Norwegian court; and

second, to impose the human rights perspective upon the working Sami Rights Committee.

In other words, the Sami chose to define the contest in their own way, laying extra emphasis on a holistic perspective. The Alta case gave them an opportunity to broaden the legal argument, thus transforming the trial into an Aboriginal rights contest in which sociocultural implications of the ecological change were joined with fundamental human rights principles embedded in international law. To argue their cause, the Sami were allowed to include the human rights perspective; unfortunately, however, they were not given sufficient time to prepare their plea regarding this complicated matter. The Norwegian authorities wanted to have the controversy settled as soon as possible in order not to delay the process of development; accordingly, they took certain measures to speed up the legal procedure. Consequently, it was decided that the case should go directly from the District Court to the Supreme Court for final decision, thus omitting the Court of Appeal, which plays a significant role as the intermediary that scrutinizes new evidence. This ruling of procedure, which reflects the uneven distribution of relative power between the two contesting parties, was a noticeable drawback for the Sami, a state of affairs they could only protest in vain.

Important to note is the fact that the lawyer acting on behalf of the Sami is a Sami himself with background in reindeer pastoralism. This gave him particular authority to argue the case, especially as the link between legal intricacies and culture came to predominate in his plea. In this respect Article 27 of the United Nations Covenant on Civil and Political Rights (1966) formed a leading theme. As Article 27 is considered the breakthrough for *collective rights,* it was important on this opportunity to point to the general international development regarding a broadening of the interpretation of its content and system of ideas. And in this respect *protection of culture* seems to be a critical point, mainly because culture is not a juridical concept. To support this connection of ideas, expert insight from the field of anthropology supplemented evidence given by experts of human rights and international law.[9]

The work of the Human Rights Committee in Geneva was also brought forth, mainly because Norwegian delegates had recently been so active in the forefront advocating improvements and clarifications of the legal concepts. One issue worth noting in this respect was that regarding material preconditions for cultural protection; here the question of land rights prevails. The elucidation of certain ambiguities of the 1966 Covenant with reference to its protective power was considered absolutely relevant in a contest like the Alta case, the primary controversy of which dealt with rights to land and water.

In addition, the Sami pointed to the fact that Norwegian authorities had acquired an outstanding international reputation and respect for their activities and explicit dedication to the continuous process of making human rights principles more precise in the international arena. The Sami in Norway, therefore, could readily expect a sincere understanding for their claims as presented at the trial.

How, then, did the Supreme Court respond to this legal strategy? In their argumentation the Sami party spelled out very strongly how crucial it is for them to distinguish between individual and collective rights and that collective rights by far predominate over individual rights. The Supreme Court had no difficulty in approving this contention. Another legally valid clarification was made in the verdict. According to the Supreme Court, it is undeniable that the Sami represent an ethnic minority within the Norwegian state and, consequently, it is protected by Article 27 of the covenant, that is, on the bases of human rights principles.[10] This is the first time that the highest court in Norway acknowledged the Sami as a distinct people entitled to special rights. The Sami's introduction of the ideas contained in international law aimed at such authoritative statements upon which future confrontations can be built.

As to the particular conflict, however, the Sami lost the case. The previous decision by the Norwegian authorities to proceed with the hydropower development of the Alta River was approved. The decisive reason for this conclusion was the size and scale of the encroachment. In the court's view the implications and detrimental consequences to the local Sami were not large enough to implement Article 27 and to justify preventing the proposed exploitation. In its decision the Supreme Court maintained that

> A pre-condition for art. 27 to be appropriate for questioning is that a case of dam regulation must cause the Sami powerful and very damaging encroachments, e.g. their reindeer economy must be undermined to such degree that their culture would be threatened. The encroachment in question is, however, of no such serious nature.[11]

By this choice of wording, the Supreme Court affirmed that international law as a protective instrument is not irrelevant in cases of conflicting interest between the Sami and the Norwegian state. Its adequacy must be carefully estimated and judged in each specific case. And this is exactly what the Sami asked for when they decided to argue their case from the perspective of international law. This approval by the Supreme Court was considered by the Sami to be a partial victory; at last they had succeeded in making international law legitimate for decisions in Norwegian national law. From now on, there are no restrictions on Norwegian courts in examining and testing the validity of administrative decisions concerning, for example, hydropower development projects and the extent to which they may violate prescriptions and rules embedded in international law.[12]

As the Norwegian expert on international law, Professor Carsten Smith, former chairman of the Sami Rights Committee has said, the verdict is not precedent for the proposition that international law is superior to national law in cases of conflict in which cultural difference is the issue.[13] It is primarily a declaration of principle that opens up new vistas in legal practice, that is to say, from now on international law is considered relevant; furthermore, the authority of this declaration is strengthened considerably by the fact that the entire Supreme Court in full assembly (eighteen justices) reached this conclusion. This proves that it was absolutely worthwhile and expedient to introduce international law and its human rights principles in court, and that the Supreme Court responded in a rather constructive way to this meta-argument as an essential part of the legal strategy of the Sami.

In order to meet the Sami demands articulated during the Alta controversy, the Norwegian government in 1980 appointed a broadly composed Sami Rights Committee, which included Sami participation and had as its main purpose an inquiry into the extensive issue of Sami rights. As the terms of reference for this inquiry involved a thorough examination of Sami rights in relation to international law, especially in regard to whatever significance such legal principles might have for any proposals advanced by the committee, the committee followed the Alta court case and its outcome very closely. The guiding ideas on this point echoed the general debate about Sami rights that emanated from the Alta conflict and, in particular, the emphasis the Sami laid on this perspective in the court case. The Sami Rights Committee chose to take this part of its inquiry quite seriously, urging the Department of Justice to appoint a separate group of experts on international law to prepare a statement for its final report. The report of this expert group constitutes one third of the entire text (192 pages) of the first report from the committee to the government in 1984,[14] and it is probably one of the most comprehensive reports ever to be published in this legal field.

The ideas of international law are thus not restricted only to the judicial arena but, owing to Sami initiation, they have also made a marked breakthrough in terms of legislative processes. Parliamentary inquiries and their proposals form the basis on which new legislation is founded. Referring to the verdict of the Supreme Court, the Sami Rights Committee maintains that the premises of the verdict show explicitly that rules derived from international law may have significance for Norwegian Sami in Norwegian courts. In support of Sami demands a very strong statement was made by the Sami Rights Committee; indeed, for the Sami minority it is extremely important that such a statement on matters of principle was made by a parliamentary committee. The statement is unique in Sami history and was expressed in a forum of the highest possible legitimacy:

> Protection of minorities is not primarily a question of assuring the minority a living standard comparable to that of the majority population. *Crucial for the protection of a minority is the protection of its culture* [italics added]. The minority must get necessary means to maintain and transfer to new generations its own culture. It is not enough that the members of a minority as individuals are given a fair living standard from an economic point of view. If their unique culture is extinguished they will cease to exist as a people.[15]

In this way new ideas and legally valid reasoning break into new arenas. The intent and purpose of Article 27, giving extra weight to protection of culture, should, in the views of the Sami Rights Committee, guide any legal interpretation in future conflicts of interest. The Sami Rights Committee goes one step further in its conclusion that the Norwegian state is obligated to work for positive discrimination (or affirmative action) toward the Sami to the degree this may be required for maintaining their culture. This means not only diverse expressions of ideal culture in a narrow sense, such as, for example, language, aesthetics, folklore, belief systems, and so on, but—far more important—also its *material base*. The foundation for such active policy rests heavily on Article 27.

After a hearing process, the proposals of a parliamentary inquiry were eventually worked out into formal legislation. The proposition of the government built on both the verdict of the Supreme Court and the report of the Sami Rights Committee. First of all, the Department of Justice agreed that legal principles that are contained in international law and that had already been endorsed and ratified by the Norwegian government clearly bind the state in its activities toward the Sami.[16] As to the interpretation of Article 27, the department concluded, moreover, that the state must assume the responsibility of contributing positively so that the Sami minority will be able to secure sufficient means to cultivate their culture and language. For this purpose, a special *Sami Act* was instituted, the purpose of which is to facilitate for the Sami people in Norway the securing and development of their language, their culture and their social life.[17] The Department of Justice explicitly concludes that the Sami are a characteristic ethnic group—a distinct people—who existed long before the Norwegian state was formed. This is a formal affirmation of the Sami idea that they consider themselves as indigenous people claiming Aboriginal rights. In the proposition the government goes so far as to vindicate a people's right to practice and express its own culture as a *fundamental human right*. In its concise formulation the proposition also suggests that special positive discrimination will be required in order to grant the Sami minority this human right. For the Sami, who have been subject to constant assimilation pressure for so long, such wording in new legislation represents an appreciable advance in their persistent endeavor to improve their capability to survive culturally.

In summing up this case, the constitutional recognition of the Sami as a distinct people emerges very much from the process that started with the Alta case and was later carried over into the inquiry undertaken by the Sami Rights Committe, spelling out in clear terms both the extensive background to and the contemporary legal status of principles related to international law. Had it not been for the Sami initiative power and their willingness to push for new positions, it is doubtful that human rights principles would have had such impact on new legislation concerning the Sami. One should not forget that in this process of development all initiatives rest entirely with the Sami. The authorities representing the majority remain the passive party, which is only responding to Sami leads.

THE TAXED MOUNTAINS CASE

Already in the early 1960s the Sami in Sweden had felt apprehension similar to that of the Sami in Norway concerning the escalation of encroachments. The Swedish Sami, having experienced very little understanding from the political authorities concerning their attempt to bring about improvements by means of new legislation, decided in 1966 to go to court and test their fundamental rights to land and water. The Taxed Mountains

Case did not refer to a particular case of industrial development but to rights in principle concerning ownership of land and water. This was a total confrontation between the Sami and the Swedish state, a most important legal test. The case, which lasted for fifteen years, was the most comprehensive ever to be decided by the Supreme Court (*Högsta Domstolen,* or HD).

In specific matters the verdict turned out to be disadvantageous to the Sami; in its wording, however, several important legal specifications were made that should have a positive impact on future relations between the Sami and the authorities. First, the Sami's usufructuary land rights are confirmed as being equally as strong as real ownership rights, both in terms of protection against expropriation and in regard to compensation. Second, it is stated firmly that these usufructuary rights are based on immemorial usage and occupation and should in no way be viewed as a privilege of the state, thus finally eliminating a previous false assumption. The Sami considered such legal clarification by the Supreme Court as a crucial landmark that acknowledged their Aboriginal status, even if they emerged as losers in the actual dispute.[18]

The Sami legal argument was very broad in perspective and emphasized legal history, customary law, and international law, as well as introducing additional nonlegal support for their plea. The latter incorporated such unconventional perspectives as those of anthropology, history, culture-history, and ecology, as well as history of ideas and historical linguistics. In the trial the Sami did not spare any effort to elucidate as fully as possible the issue at stake; on the other hand, everything presented in court had to relate to appropriate sections of Swedish national law, that is, primarily to property law.

From the very start, the Sami wanted to internationalize the issue, referring to the Taxed Mountains Case as part of a general ethnopolitical process occurring in many Fourth World areas. Hence principles contained in international law, combined with penetrating insights in customary law, played a decisive role in the case. These tactics did not help the Sami to obtain their ultimate goal—land ownership rights—but it certainly contributed to a revision of important legal views concerning the only indigenous ethnic minority in Sweden.

This long-lasting case brought about meager results in concrete terms; in general, the Sami were utterly disappointed and demanded immediately that the government should appoint a Sami Rights Committee with a mandate similar in scope to that of the Norwegian Sami Rights

Committee. Approximately two years after the HD verdict, in the fall of 1982, such a committee was indeed appointed.[19]

So far the Sami Rights Committee in Sweden has delivered two extensive reports: first, a separate report devoted entirely to the perspective of international law,[20] and second, a principal report on Sami rights and a Sami parliament, *sameting*.[21] A third and final report dealing with general cultural questions, including language and education, is expected in the early 1990s. To a large extent, the first report forms the foundation on which all the suggestions for improvement concerning Sami rights are based. In other words, international law, not only in a broad sense but also in specific reference to Article 27, impressed the Swedish Sami Rights Committee in a decisive manner. Three previous events influenced the views adopted by the Sami Rights Committee on this perspective, a perspective which certainly is new in the Swedish legislative process: 1) the HD verdict in the Taxed Mountains Case (1981); 2) the HR verdict in the Alta Case (1982); and 3) the conclusions in NOU 1984: 18. In its conclusion the committee establishes that Sweden has various obligations vis-à-vis the Sami based on international law. Therefore, the Swedish majority must refrain from such encroachments in the natural environment as may jeopardize the preconditions for the continuity of a viable reindeer economy. Furthermore, the Sami must be assured necessary resources for their cultural survival and development. The authorities have to observe these prescriptions through their legislation, administration, and legal practice.[22]

The direction for legal improvements is thus laid down; for the first time such change rests on a thorough and highly competent appraisal and analysis of international law and its implications for indigenous people and their legal status in national law. Article 27 as an instrument for the protection of indigenous minorities and their way of life will serve as the basis for a protective regime for the Sami. In order to meet the special needs the Sami have as indigenous people, such a protective regime should include the following:

1. support for the Sami culture and language;
2. secured access to land and water required to maintain Sami-specific modes of production;
3. participation in the decision-making process concerning the Sami and their social life, that is, limited self-determination.[23]

The listed improvements are based in part on a special Sami Act and in part on a constitutional enactment that firmly recognizes the Sami as an

ethnic minority and an indigenous people in Sweden, codified in the Constitution Act.[24]

Three major gains can be derived from the report of the Swedish
Sami Rights Committee:

1. A *Sami Act* and a constitutional enactment. This progress in constitutional terms, offering an entirely new framework for legislative and administrative measures and considerations, is a political
   goal the Sami have aimed at for the last fifty years or more. It
   represents a cornerstone in the development of ethnopolitics
   among the Sami.
2. A Sami Parliament, *sameting,* a representative assembly of Sami
   with limited authority and self-determination. In range and delegated power, it is very similar to its Norwegian counterpart. The
   authority base is, however, reasonably elastic; this allows for expansion in the range of actual power, depending on what initiatives the Sami take and in what activities they engage themselves,
   that is, how they choose to define the situation.
3. The *Reindeer Management Act* of 1971 (RNL 1979) has to be revised considerably to reinforce the Sami right to reindeer pastoralism and to specify a protective regime for Sami land use
   patterns.

The changes suggested will necessarily contribute to increased cultural autonomy and to a new framework for action, which, to a large extent, is presupposed by the HD verdict in the Taxed Mountains Case and
leading principles embedded in international law.

Three constraining factors can be identified in the comprehensive
proposal for change. First, as far as real power is concerned, even in the
future the Sami will not be granted *veto* rights in critical conflict situations.
The closest they come to such an ideal position, one which has been given
highest priority by the Sami for quite some time, is the following assertion: "Permission to expropriate will not be granted if the conditions to
continue exercising the right to reindeer pastoralism will be jeopardized."
The question remains, however, who is to decide in such crucial matters?
If limited Sami influence is accepted in the final proposition for legislation,
the question as to the extent of that influence will most likely dominate
Sami political activities in the years to come. Limits to Sami influence must
be tested; its validity, as well as its applicability in various situations, must
also be proven.

Second, when it comes to confirmation of land rights, the unacceptable distinction between pasture based on year-round use, on the one hand, and winter pasture, on the other, still prevails. This means that the Sami must continue to exercise rights to pasture that are of different quality; unfortunately, the ecologically most vulnerable part, the winter pasture so necessary for the reindeer herding annual cycle, will remain the poorest one. In this respect Sami demands have not been met. This refusal to understand Sami needs will affect the forest Sami the most; these are the reindeer pastoralists who migrate within the same ecological zone, the taiga, year-round.

Third, there is a total neglect of the rights of the Sami who base their subsistence on freshwater fishing or who are engaged in diverse forms of handicraft production, both considered traditional means of livelihood. Since the Sami Rights Committee claimed to adopt a holistic perspective in their inquiry, there is reason to question this remarkable omission.

Otherwise, the establishment of a new practice of permanent joint deliberation between 1) the forest industry and reindeer pastoralists, and 2) municipal councils and Sami local communities, may remedy some of the deficiencies in the interethnic relations so far prevalent. Because to an increasing degree forest development also occurs in the region for year-round pasturing, this imposed consultation will definitely be beneficial for the Sami minority. In the future it will be considerably more difficult to exploit forest resources. Two possible means for preventing such exploitation are conferred upon the Sami: the Sami local community and the Sami Parliament. The Sami Parliament, as a compulsory hearing authority, must hear arguments for and consent to proposed development before formal approval can be issued by the National Forestry Board. In this way forest development is finally placed on the same level as other kinds of encroachments, giving the Sami necessary joint influence in a vital area of resource management.

As the process of change discussed in this section of the chapter is still going on, its definitive outcome is somewhat uncertain. In Norway the principal report on Sami rights is still in progress, and in Sweden the government has not yet presented a proposition for new legislation. The directions of change are clearly mapped out, however, and there is no reason to believe that in the end the Sami will experience major impairments compared to the proposals outlined. The process of change, though gradual, certainly points in the right direction. This limited remodeling of relative distribution of power between the Sami and the majority, offering the Sami a definite say in their own affairs, evidently reflects an official approval of the signification and implications of international law.

Conclusion

In this chapter I have tried to demonstrate the close connection between *self-determination* and *cultural survival*. In particular, the human rights perspective of self-determination has been emphasized. In any Fourth World context, cultural survival is a predominant issue, growing in importance every year because, for many of the hard-pressed indigenous ethnic minorities, cultural survival can no longer be taken for granted. Rather, it is a constant struggle in which Fourth World peoples must get involved. Cultural survival relates to ethnic boundary maintenance,[25] or holding the line vis-à-vis the outside world. Consequently, it is mainly a social concern. In specific terms, the viability of such minority cultures depends on firm *environmental protection,* authority over their *education* in a broad sense, affirmation of the official status of the *native language,* and means to counteract *tutelage.* For example, the recently proposed language law which recognizes Sami as an official language on an equal footing with Norwegian or Swedish, definitely represents a strengthening of Sami human rights, both for the individual Sami and for the Sami as a collectivity. The Sami can now insist upon using Sami in diverse communications with the authorities, an advance which adds to Sami self-respect.

For indigenous minorities, land rights claims are particularly significant, and to break new ground and make advances in the legal arena the issue of land rights must be internationalized to supplement the legitimacy of the specific claim. This process of internationalizing relates intimately to the principles of human rights; and, as has been shown, the opinions given by national courts are gradually changing to the advantage of Native peoples. This process of change, however, appears to be extremely slow. The process for which Native peoples themselves are primarily responsible aims at what could be called *development law.* That is, the legal premises applying to the surpressed indigenous ethnic minorities must be changed and developed to such a degree that economic development and progress, as well as sufficiently strong protective measures in cultural terms, are conceivable.[26]

To obtain this ultimate goal, the Sami have used special legal tactics. Each issue chosen must refer to a definite section of the codified national law, in the Alta Case that of *administrative law*, in the Taxed Mountains Case that of *property law*. In both cases the strategy for the Sami acting in the legal arena was based on a clever combination of several legal properties which are referred to in their legitimate argumentation and used effectively to plead their cause. International law, with its particular focus on human rights, and customary law were skillfully woven into a strictly legal argument, a strategy that usually forces the courts to respond unconventionally, possibly laying new grounds for precedential assertions. The two court cases presented illustrate this point. In later years it has become a common strategy among Native peoples to complicate essentially narrow legal issues, such as those dealing with land rights, thus broadening the foundation on which decisions are made. International law and customary law appear as legal cornerstones in Native claims for improved land rights, Aboriginal rights, and so on. National law will thereby be revised and adjusted to better suit Native demands and needs in order to secure cultural continuity. This legal strategy has become part of Native culture in many areas of the Fourth World and aims at legally appropriated gains which can readily be transferred to political gains.

The two court cases discussed above also support an argument for the predominance of collective human rights in Fourth World situations. The strong focus on the cultural dimension of human rights makes such an emphasis obvious. I do not take a stand against the importance of individual human rights in cross-cultural perspectives, however, and, as I have maintained, such controversy of fictitious polarization is not very fruitful. In this respect, my general thesis should be viewed as support for very accurately determining the *context* in which human rights are to be discussed. Rights within their context are what one should be concerned with and the link between anthropology and human rights helps to achieve such methodological clarification.[27]

The *meaning* of human rights may vary considerably; all cases in which a reinforcement of human rights contributes to cultural survival rights are loaded with meaning. The right to cultural diversity is sanctioned by means of increasing acknowledgment of the relevance of human rights. From my anthropological horizon, I am convinced that the connection between anthropology and various legal disciplines in observing human rights in cross-cultural perspectives will grow in importance. From a methodological point of view, actual fieldwork in the courtrooms, incorporating thorough observations of behavior and views expressed outside of, but in connection to, courtroom activities concerning a specific case, is one way of attaining proper insights in a most complex field of inquiry.

Notes

1. *See for example,* chapters 4–6 in this volume, by Rhoda Howard, Virginia Leary, and Michael McDonald.

2. *See* the chapter by Richard Falk in this volume.

3. As discussed by Roxanne Dunbar Ortiz in her paper, "Cultural Legitimacy of Human Rights in Latin American Indigenous Perspectives," given at the International Conference on Human Rights in Cross-Cultural Perspectives, Saskatoon, Canada, October 12–14, 1989.

4. SOU: 41, *Samerätt och Sameting* (Stockholm: Justitiedepartementet, 1989).

5. *See* Chapter 6 by Michael McDonald in this volume.

6. *See, for example, Ethnic Groups and Boundaries,* ed. F. Barth (Bergen: Universitesforlaget, 1969; London: Allen, 1969); Abner G. Cohen, *Customs and Politics in Urban Africa* (London: Routledge and Kegan Paul, 1969); *Ethnicity and Resource Competition in Plural Societies,* ed. L. Despres (The Hague: Mouton, 1975).

7. *See* Chapter 11 by Manuela Carneiro da Cunha in this volume.

8. *Ibid.*

9. R. Paine, *Dam a River, Damn a People?* (Copenhagen: IWGIA Document 45, 1982); D. Sanders, "Indigenous Rights and the Alta-Kautokeino Project," in *Samene-Urbefolkning og Minoritet,* ed. Trond Thuen (Tromso: Universitesforlaget, 1980), 175–86.

10. H. R. 1982, 103.

11. *Ibid.* at 119.

12. *Ibid.* at 35–36.

13. C. Smith, "Altadomen og Prøvelseretten," in *Norsk Rett og Folkeretten,* ed. C. and L. Smith (Oslo: Universitesforlaget, 1982), 229.

14. NOU: 18, *Om Samenes Rettslige Stilling* (Oslo: Universitesforlaget, 1984).

15. *Ibid.* at 243.

16. Ot., prop. no. 33 (1987): 37.

17. *Ibid.* at 123.

18. HD-verdict DT 2 (Stockholm, 29 January, 1981).

19. For further information, *see* T. Svensson, "Local Communities in the South Sami Region," in *The Sami National Minority in Sweden,* ed. B. Jahreskog, (Stockholm: Almqvist & Wiksell, 1982), 102–16; Svensson, "The Land Claims Issue and the Sami—Reflections on Contemporary Legal Struggle," *Geographica Helvetia* 4 (1988): 184–93. (A monograph concerning the entire case is forthcoming shortly.)

20. SOU: 36, *Samernas Folkrättsliga Ställning* (Stockholm: Justitiedepartementet, 1986).

21. SOU: 41, *Samerätt och Sameting* (Stockholm: Justitiedepartementet, 1989).

22. *See supra* note 20, at 16.

23. *See supra* note 21, at 65.

24. *Ibid.* at 66.

25. *See* F. Barth, ed., *supra* note 6, at 15.

26. T. Svensson, The Sami and Development Law, paper presented to International Bar Association Conference, Buenos Aires, 1988.

27. *Human Rights and Anthropology*, ed. T. Downing and G. Kushner (Cambridge, Mass.: Cultural Survival Report 24, 1988).

Section *IV*

Prospects for a Cross-Cultural Approach to Human Rights

Tore Lindholm

15. Prospects for Research on the Cultural Legitimacy of Human Rights
The Cases of Liberalism and Marxism

Introduction

Constructive and critical concern with the cross-cultural foundations and legitimacy of universal human rights standards is no novelty. When in 1946 the Universal Declaration of Human Rights (UDHR) was first prepared by the United Nations Division of Human Rights, serious efforts were made by its director, John Humphrey, and his staff to provide the United Nations Commission on Human Rights with culturally and historically diverse background materials.[1]

In 1947 UNESCO carried out a theoretical inquiry into the foundations of an international declaration of human rights, drawing on a large number of individual philosophers, social scientists, jurists, and writers from UNESCO member states. Late in the summer of 1947, the resulting report[2] was forwarded to the Human Rights Commission in the hope that it "would help to clarify its discussion and to explore the ground for a constructive agreement."[3] The report included a thirteen-page statement of "UNESCO's conclusions," drawn from answers to its long and detailed questionnaire, distributed to respondents in March 1947. This statement, "The Grounds of an International Declaration of Human Rights," was prepared in Paris in July 1947. "All rights derive," it says, "on the one hand, from the nature of man as such and, on the other, since man depends on man, from the stage of development achieved by the social and political groups in which he participates." Furthermore, a modern declaration of human rights must recognize that civil and political, as well as economic and social, rights "belong to all men everywhere without discrimination of race, sex, language or religion . . . not only because there are no fundamental differences among men, but also because the great society and community of all men has become a real and effective power, and the interdependent nature of that community is beginning at last to be recognized."[4]

Also in 1947, the American Anthropological Association issued its well-known words of warning, authored by Melville Herskovits:

> Standards and values are relative to the culture from which they derive so that any attempt to formulate postulates that grow out of the beliefs or moral codes of one culture must to that extent detract from the applicability of any Declaration of Human Rights to mankind as a whole. . . . The rights of Man in the Twentieth Century cannot be circumscribed by the standards of any single culture, or be dictated by the aspirations of any single people. Such a document will lead to frustration, not realization of the personalities of vast numbers of human beings.[5]

The preceding questions and concerns about cross-cultural foundations have been addressed repeatedly during the ensuing four decades by politicians, jurists, social scientists, philosophers, and others engaged in creating, implementing, or evaluating evolving international human rights standards and procedures.

Although much work has been done in this field, definitive intellectual progress has been hard to come by. Meanwhile the practical problems of making universal human rights norms to be understood and accepted worldwide are more pressing than ever. I therefore welcome the fresh start recently undertaken by Abdullahi An-Naʿim in several papers of his, most thoroughly in "Problems and Prospects of Universal Cultural Legitimacy for Human Rights."[6] With An-Naʿim (and most human rights observers), I share the view that in order to be able to remedy the widespread and alarming discrepancies worldwide between the theory and the practice of human rights, we need to understand the underlying factors and forces that contribute to the persistence of such discrepancies. Furthermore, I share with An-Naʿim the perhaps more controversial assumption that a significant portion of these factors and forces springs from a deficient legitimacy of human rights in cultures, traditions, and doctrines that are practiced and accepted as a matter of fact, explicitly or implicitly, by people in the contemporary world.[7]

This, then, is the task at hand: how to go about elucidating culturally based support, indifference, and rejection of the full range of human rights standards, or parts thereof, in a cross-cultural, and potentially world-encompassing, perspective? For the purpose of this paper, the task is not to contribute to the study of the specifically *juridical* strengths and frailties of international human rights, nor to focus on *structural* explanations of human rights violations or compliance. The idea of delineating a research strategy for the study of cross-cultural foundations does not of course belittle the importance of other approaches to the study of societal conditions for human rights; it is, rather, a much-needed complement to other approaches.[8]

Part 1 of this chapter is programmatic and methodological; it discusses various conceptual and procedural aspects of research on the cultural legitimacy of human rights. Part 2 is substantive; it discusses, though only by way of illustration, the legitimacy of human rights in two influential traditions of political doctrine, both of Western origin: liberalism (of the political, egalitarian variety) and Marxism (as propounded in "really existing socialism"[9]). I have chosen to deal with liberalism and Marxism because, first, they are two formative political traditions close to my Western home, and one's critical inquiries into the cultural basis of human rights ought to start at home. Second, both of these political doctrines were inextricably involved in the construction of modern internationally recognized human rights.

Part 1: Programmatic and Methodological Issues

Inquiring into the Cultural Legitimacy of Human Rights

Let me first explain how I conceive of the study of the "cultural legitimacy" of human rights. It is, perhaps obviously, to inquire into the kinds and degrees of support for human rights standards and for their implementation in "culture(s)"—be they "microcultures" of villages or tribes, or "subcultures" of professions and social classes, or "national cultures," or "regional cultures," or globally shared "macrocultures." In such inquiries there are two principal ways to proceed:

1. We may study a particular empirically given culture and ask what difference that culture makes to its carriers regarding their recognition and promotion of human rights.
2. Or we may, by way of abstraction, select some doctrinal component or manifestation of culture(s): an articulated belief-system,

Weltanschauung, or political theory (as in Part 2 below), in order to elicit its role and potential, whether as a resource or a barrier, in the fulfillment of human rights.

Typically, the first kind of studies are pursued by social scientists, while the latter come naturally to philosophers and perhaps to students of intellectual history. No sharp division of labor should be required, however; both kinds of studies must be informed by a modicum of juridical knowledge; and interdisciplinary cooperation may often be highly desirable.[10] A practical aim of such inquiries, particularly when conducted along the lines proposed by An-Na'im, is to facilitate ways of enhancing the legitimacy of the full range of contemporary human rights standards in the culture or doctrine being studied, and preferably in ways congenial to it.

The questions to be asked when conducting research on the cultural legitimacy of human rights will vary, of course, depending on the subject matter and the kind of study undertaken. I shall now indicate three broad categories of questions: empirical, exegetical, and practical questions about the specific "cultural objects" being studied; theoretical and more general questions about the project of establishing a global human rights regime; and self-critical questions about currently recognized human rights standards. Within the first category there are three subgroups of questions.

When one studies the human rights proficiency of a specific culture, a tradition, or a doctrine, it is natural (again following An-Na'im) to ask:

1. Which principles and conceptions, norms, and values of the given culture or tradition or doctrine are more conducive to which features of modern human rights, and which are antagonistic or resistant?
2. What elements may have to be modified, further developed, replaced or rejected in order to facilitate and enhance the intellectual and moral legitimacy of human rights within the tradition?
3. To what extent, and how, can indifference or resistance to aspects of human rights be overcome in ways that are legitimate, and not ad hoc, within the given tradition?

A reasonable general working assumption (a "zero" hypothesis, as it were) would be that any culture or doctrine that impinges significantly on contemporary politics has shortcomings as well as undeveloped potentials when considered as a candidate for the honorific title of cultural basis, or foundational doctrine, of human rights. To spell out specific answers for specific cases, it is necessary to elucidate the extent to which and for what reasons this assumption applies, if at all, to the culture in question.

Before proceeding to the two remaining types of questions, I wish to briefly address the question: Could the actual or potential legitimacy of human rights in a given culture or doctrine really matter? I need not here elaborate the extent of human rights violation and neglect in the world, east, west, north, and south, nor argue that the gap between principle and practice needs to be explained—and to be narrowed by raising the level of compliance to globally acceptable norms. Also, it hardly needs saying that in this field structural explanations, and structural remedies, are often indispensable; human rights violations in the wake of the international debt crisis are just one extreme case in point.[11] Yet it is certainly true that cultural determinants shape and constrain people's understanding and value commitments, and in particular their reasons for action and inaction, even when structural explanations apply and people are trapped by unintended consequences and impersonal social forces. The study of the cultural legitimacy of human rights is one major concern, because human rights violations and compliance spring from human action informed by cultural determinants. If properly conducted, such studies might indirectly help eliminate violations by enhancing or preparing the way conceptually for the cultural legitimacy of human rights in specific sociocultural and ideological contexts.

The second category includes the more theoretical questions that address, directly or indirectly, the political project of setting up a world-encompassing human rights regime and its ramifications: To what extent, by what policies and strategies, through what historical and social processes, and at what moral and other "costs" is it possible to establish cross-cultural intelligibility, recognition, and support for a human rights regime, ultimately on a world-encompassing scale? The nature of the relations of legitimacy between cultural items and human rights, will, obviously, not be the same for all kinds of studies. When dealing with normative political theories, and more generally with explicitly formulated doctrines, a major concern will be with various conceptual and epistemological relations, such as implication and contradiction, compatibility, coherence, and more or less well-founded or ad hoc relations of support between, on the one hand, the doctrines in question and, on the other hand, human rights standards. Dealing with the social practice of a given culture, empirical relations of compatibility, mutual reinforcement, and stabilizing or destabilizing effects will be more prominent.

The third category of questions to be raised by research on the cultural legitimacy of human rights is self-critical; these focus, critically and constructively, on the existing standards and procedures of human rights: What modifications, further developments, or revisions, of presently acknowledged human rights standards (procedures for adoption and for implementation included) are required to facilitate a deeper, more well-founded, and more stable global consensus on human rights?

What Conception of Human Rights?

If we try to elaborate an adequate and comprehensive conception of modern human rights, we are soon faced with theoretical uncertainty as well as with political controversy.[12] Nevertheless, it is imperative, if we want to investigate their cultural legitimacy, that we proceed from some definite (though not definitive!) conception of human rights, against which cultural items may prove—and hopefully improve—their human rights proficiency. To this end I shall now make three interconnected proposals: Taking the International Bill of Rights for our "paradigm," I present some salient points about human rights, from which an important corollary follows; I submit a ten-point list of core features of human rights; and I advance a justificatory prototheory of human rights.

The methodological consideration behind these three proposals is that without this (or some other, and perhaps more suitable) explicit elaboration of our working conception of human rights, research on their cultural legitimacy may all too easily become inaccessible to objective assessment and to step-by-step progress. Such studies are also liable to be of little use for practical purposes, beyond edification and self-congratulatory exercises. In other words, we must make our working human rights conception accessible to public advocacy and public criticism in order to minimize arbitrary cultural subjectivism at the very outset of research on cultural legitimacy of human rights. For instance, neither semi-educated North American or Western European common sense about human rights (say, that taken for granted in the 1980s by the Reagan administrations or by the Thatcher cabinets), nor such rhetorically useful but analytically ambiguous formulas as "human rights are entitlements that people have simply by virtue of being humans" suffice for the purpose of cross-cultural studies.[13]

A Paradigmatic Starting Point: The International Bill of Human Rights

By "human rights" I refer (over and above anything else) to the system of internationally negotiated and accepted human rights norms as developed after 1945, mainly under the auspices of the United Nations Charter. The core of this system is the International Bill of Human Rights, comprising the Universal Declaration of 1948 (UDHR) and the two International Covenants of 1966 (CCPR and CESCR). Many specialized international instruments have been adopted later or are presently in process. Some salient points concerning human rights (in this preferred sense) are:

- They include, but they are not exhausted by, an evolving system of positive norms in international law that is legally binding on states, though to various degrees, depending on the accession of individual states to international human rights instruments.
- To some degree, this system informs and is bolstered (and at times questioned) by what at present appears to be a growing and deepening global human rights culture—to which the U.N., ILO and a growing number of international organizations, many governments, a variety of activist nongovernmental organizations (NGOs), and a multitude of minority, opposition, and mass movements all contribute, in various ways and degrees. One baseline of this incipient global human rights culture is, I think, that it is now taken for granted that people, individuals as well as groups, are entitled to deference by the state to their human rights, whenever circumstances permit.
- As a matter of abstract presumption, the system of human rights in international law (or at least its core) is widely supposed to have adequate theoretical backing normatively (in justifiable moral or political principles) and descriptively (in tenable diagnoses of global societal circumstances).
- But it is contestable in what specific way modern human rights should be provided with adequate theoretical foundations, so as to make them—one would hope—intelligible and reasonably defensible from within the differing, and often rival, political and juridical perspectives intrinsic to major contemporary cultural traditions.

From the preceding points, one important corollary seems to follow: that the modern, internationally acknowledged system of human rights is becoming a touchstone for the moral and political legitimacy of any culture, tradition, or doctrine which has political import in the contemporary world. This makes questions about the grounds, interpretation, and implementation of human rights a crucial matter for the carriers and adherents of any of them.

A Checklist: Ten Features of the Internationally Acknowledged System of Human Rights Standards

Human rights, as conceived in the International Bill, I now submit, among other things,

1. are strictly universal: they apply to all human beings;[14]
2. are globally binding:[15] they are grounded in considerations of global societal relations and are morally and legally[16] binding on states as well as on other pertinent actors everywhere in the world;
3. are inherent: they should be seen as inherent, inalienable, and inviolable entitlements;
4. are a system of normative trumps: they should normally be accorded priority when they conflict with other norms or values;[17]
5. imply state obligations: governments are the main depositories of the obligations to respect, protect, or fulfill people's human rights;
6. are subjective rights under international as well as under domestic law;
7. protect a wide range of interdependent and equally important categories of claims: from civil and political to economic, social, and cultural, to certain "third-generation" goods or advantages;
8. serve not only individuals: among rights-holders are also collectivities such as nations (peoples) and ethnic and religious minorities;
9. authorize both strong and weak norms: human rights comprise norms which for conceptual reasons are enforceable and justiciable as well as nonenforceable and nonjusticiable; and
10. are compatible with soft international implementation procedures (such as reporting and monitoring), including for rights that conceptually would permit of standard court adjudication and enforcement.

The point of culling these ten features is to provide us with a schedule for the appraisal of cultures and doctrines. In the section on "The Legitimacy of Human Rights in Liberalism and in Marxism," I shall only begin to make use of the above checklist concerning human rights. My assumption of these features, of course, cannot claim to be exhaustive, and my preceding claims about human rights are certainly not beyond question. But the ten features are, I would argue, relatively modest for the purpose of studying the cultural legitimacy of human rights, because they are plausible interpretations of the International Bill itself and its preparatory works, including the crucially important prototheory of human rights that may be drawn from these sources.[18] They also fit in with the subsequent mainstream practice of international human rights bodies.

The Justificatory Prototheory of Human Rights
Informing the Universal Declaration

But why elevate the International Bill to the status of paradigm for human rights? In a cross-cultural perspective, such a choice is in need of some justification.[19] As noted, we must proceed without the benefit of a comprehensive and uncontroversial theory of human rights. On the other hand, when inquiring into the human rights proficiency of normative traditions and doctrines, we cannot do without some fixed points in the justificatory theory of human rights. I now want to argue that a justificatory prototheory[20] of human rights may be drawn from the International Bill and especially from the Universal Declaration of Human Rights (UDHR), including the discussions in the competent United Nations bodies that preceded its adoption. Over and above being sanctioned by as politically authoritative international bodies and procedures as could be had at the time, this prototheory sketches an intrinsically reasonable strategy for the justification of globally binding and universally applicable rights. In particular, this strategy of justification seems promising with a view to cross-cultural legitimacy for human rights.[21]

Limiting my analysis in this subsection to the much debated question of the foundations of human rights according to the Universal Declaration,[22] I reach the following conclusions: Article 1 of UDHR establishes that the proximate normative premise in justifying universal human rights is the moral principle that every human being is entitled to freedom and to equal dignity, where "entitled" indicates what human beings are due as a question of reciprocal moral recognition. It further settles that heeding freedom and equal dignity is an overriding concern, perhaps always and everywhere, but certainly universally among human beings now and in the foreseeable future. The universal reciprocal moral recognition among human beings in terms of inherent freedom and equal dignity is, on this reading of the Universal Declaration, the minimal common normative grounds for universal human rights. But, since the concepts of freedom and dignity are largely left unexplicated, as are the characteristics of human beings by virtue of which they owe each other such moral recognition, the more fundamental questions are left open to various interpretations and specifications, which may conflict among themselves, without affront to the Universal Declaration. The leeway of interpretation is nevertheless constrained, not least by the system of human rights provisions that is contained in the declaration as a whole. Thus "all human beings are born free and equal in dignity" cannot be interpreted so that it is not, in some way, an essential normative premise for this system. But Article 1 does not, by itself, answer the further questions as to how and why such a mandatory commitment to freedom and to equal dignity helps prescribe a system of inalienable human rights—as spelled out in the rest of the declaration. Nevertheless, the declaration as a whole clearly indicates a preferred answer to this further question.

To begin with, if we consult the discussion, and voting, of the Third Committee of the General Assembly in the Fall of 1948, it becomes clear what the "official" United Nations answer to this further question is *not:* the answer is not assumptions about God, or about Nature, or about Human Nature, or about Reason—although none of these answers were outlawed, and each of them welcomed, as it were, as optional rationales of human rights (along with other admissible rationales).

In a more positive vein, the second sentence of Article 1 ("Endowed with reason and conscience . . . ") posits human reason and human conscience as foundations of certain duties on all humans endowed with reason and conscience: such duties are implied by the phrase "they should act toward one another in a spirit of brotherhood," and these duties are made explicit in Article 29 of the declaration. From Article 1, however, it is not clear what job, if any, "reason" and "conscience" are meant to accomplish in justifying human rights. I think that, strictly, they are not intended to justify rights at all, but perhaps to indicate that it takes reason and conscience to respect and to justify rights (but not to hold rights). And even if they should be intended as characteristics in virtue of which human beings are entitled to rights,[23] this is arguably not the main thrust of the doctrine of justification for human rights in UDHR.

Drawing now also on the text of and the discussions devoted by the Third Committee to the UDHR Preamble, the "official" positive justificatory strategy for the projected system of international human rights may be reconstructed thus: Article 1 provides the crucial, but open-ended, normative justificatory principle, to wit: all human beings are born free and equal in dignity. The second essential piece of "official" justificatory premise is a condensed description of the pertinent situation: in several preambular paragraphs the Universal Declaration spells out a political, sociological, and historical interpretation of historical circumstances of world society in the aftermath of World War II. Only from the normative principle of inherent freedom and equal dignity in conjunction with the interpretation of the contemporary and prospective world situation does a binding commitment to a global human rights system follow. Briefly it runs: recent events (Hitler's "democratic" rise to power, Auschwitz, Hiroshima . . .) as well as challenges, threats, and prospects harbored by the world situation are seen to be such that a globally binding consensus, and a negotiated implementation program, on universally applicable human rights are (now and in the foreseeable future) mandatory in order to secure freedom and equal dignity for "all members of the human family."[24]

One interesting thing about the justificatory prototheory of human rights in the Universal Declaration, on the above reading of it, is that it is not a traditional Western natural rights theory, it is neither theological nor metaphysical but rather an exercise in "situated" geopolitical moral rationality (to use somewhat fashionable language).

To summarize: Compared to its classical Western predecessors, the "official" United Nations foundation of the internationally acknowledged system of human rights is a more complex, more realistic, and more "open-ended" scheme of justification, at least if we accord pride of place to the Universal Declaration of Human Rights. This justificatory scheme relies on a commitment to inherent freedom and equal dignity for its proximate normative premises (leaving the deeper premises out of the official doctrine) and on an interpretation of historically evolving global societal circumstances for its descriptive premises.[25]

Criticism of Some Recent Natural Rights Interpretations of the Universal Declaration

If the interpretation offered above, of the foundations of human rights according to Article 1 and Preamble of the Universal Declaration, were mistaken, I could not rightly claim to proceed from a human rights conception that informs the International Bill. Since the above interpretation does challenge what has become a standard view of the philosophy behind the UDHR, recently spelled out by Jack Donnelly and by Johannes Morsink,[26] I shall briefly explain why I hold such a natural rights interpretation of the declaration to be wrongheaded.

Donnelly and Morsink are doubtless correct in claiming that, according to the international founding fathers and mothers of human rights, human rights are "logically antecedent to the rights spelled out in various systems of positive law" and "are seen as inherent and inalienable, and thus as held independent of the state."[27] Thus the philosophy of the Universal Declaration contradicts the view that only positive rights are binding and the view that human rights derive solely from man's legal and political status in society: straightforward "positivism" in legal philosophy is out, as is, apparently, the "Marxist" position voiced to the Third Committee by Soviet delegate Bogomolov, who made it clear that "[t]he USSR delegation . . . did not recognize the principle that a man possessed individual rights independently of his status as a citizen of a given State."[28]

But, as we have seen, the international founders also excluded from the instrument the specifically natural law doctrines that humans have human rights by virtue of their human nature or their natural, or divinely given, endowment.

Defenders of a natural rights intepretation of UDHR might claim that any moral or legal doctrine which advocates pre-state, or pre-positively valid, human rights is a natural rights doctrine, *by (their) definition*. But, I will now argue, this would be an excessively watered-down version of a genuine natural rights doctrine. On a natural rights doctrine, I submit, the binding character of basic rights must be shown to be conclusions of an argument, the premises of which propound pertinent aspects of God, nature, reason or human nature, and whose cogency does not depend essentially on interpretations of sociohistorically evolving circumstances.[29]

Other arguments pertaining to a natural rights interpretation of UDHR must be set aside for now.[30] I shall round off my methodological exercise by marshaling the virtues of the justificatory strategy I have imputed to the Universal Declaration, virtues at least as regards the cross-cultural legitimacy of human rights.

Cross-Cultural Legitimacy for Human Rights and
the Philosophy Behind the Universal Declaration
The practical relevance and potential of Article 1 and the Preamble of the Universal Declaration for the global implementation of human rights may

not appear striking to the hardheaded legal specialists.[31] Yet skepticism may be premature, for this reason: In the years to come some of the most crucial intellectual, moral, and ideological battles about human rights issues may well turn on their cross-cultural intelligibility and justifiability. The open-ended mix of moral and sociohistorical rationales for human rights commitments prefigured by Article 1 and the Preamble may be employed, I would argue, to enhance the cross-cultural legitimacy of human rights. The reason is that it exhibits a dynamic justificatory approach which, from the outset, is prone to be sensitive to differing and even conflicting cultural, religious, and political traditions. It epitomizes a pluralism as to justification which is minimally exclusive and yet not spineless. On this approach to justification, any normative tradition could be brought to support universal human rights, as long as it honors inherent freedom and equal human dignity (on some human rights-conducive reading) and facilitates an (empirically monitored) appreciation of the pertinent aspects of the modern world system and its dynamics.

Here are my concluding points on the prototheory behind the Universal Declaration and its relevance to cross-cultural legitimacy for human rights:

1. The justificatory prototheory of human rights which informs the Universal Declaration is not metaphysical, not theological, not a natural rights doctrine, not based on any specific philosophical anthropology, not founded on an authoritative theory of human history and human destiny. What is unsound about Western justificatory traditions falling under these labels is certainly not their Western origin, and not that they are all safely known to be false. It is rather that they commit, or are conducive to, the mistake of monopolizing answers to questions about justification in a novel global problem situation which for strategic as well as moral reasons requires a pluralist, and overlapping, global consensus on universal human rights. (But see point 4 below, and the discussion of liberalism in part 2.)

2. The UDHR prototheory makes the justification of a global human rights regime depend on interpretations and analyses of sociohistorical global circumstances, and these are open to empirical control and revision.

3. The UDHR prototheory sketches a minimal justificatory strategy, which invites and (in order to carry rational conviction and/or to facilitate stable consensus among various groups of people) perhaps also requires that it be filled out with both supplementary normative principles and analyses of pertinent "global circumstances of rights." While the *additional descriptive premises* must command a substantial degree of consensus across

the board, different sets of *supplementary normative premises* may be at odds among themselves: Christians, Muslims, atheists, Buddhists, Marxists, liberals and so on, may from their own normative heartland come up with full-fledged justificatory doctrines of globally binding human rights, none of which need be compatible with any of the others, if only each of them provides the proper kind of support to the principle of inherent freedom and equal dignity for every human being, and accords priority to that principle over other principles, as regards the political and other societal issues covered by human rights. What these issues are is partly a question to be answered by empirical investigations and geopolitical judgment, which in turn will be influenced by historical changes in public human self-definitions.

4. On the interpretation offered here, the Universal Declaration is a proposal for an overlapping moral and political consensus on human rights, worldwide, much in the sense intended for the question of social justice, at the domestic level, by John Rawls.[32] Obviously, the project of overlapping consensus on a global human rights regime differs from Rawls, both in subject matter (a system of basic rights, and not only a basic social structure) and in scale (the relations within world society, and not only within single national societies). It further differs substantially in the way it deals with the respective situational constraints: The Preamble of the Declaration, and the procedural legitimation it helps establish, is utterly different from Rawls's "original position" argument. I think Rawls is historically correct in holding that the idea of an overlapping consensus is of liberal pedigree. It is a sophisticated, liberal moral response to recalcitrant facts of irreconcilable religious and philosophical conflict among consociates.[33] To this origin we return below.[34] The project of establishing an overlapping global consensus between cooperating parties in deep and perhaps even irreparable disagreement on fundamentals does inform the deliberations of the authors of the Universal Declaration. I fail to see how a free and reasonable recognition of globally binding human rights could be viable in a cross-cultural perspective and gain a worldwide foothold without some such approach. Nor do I know of any serious alternative.

5. An essential feature of the prototheory of human rights I impute to the Universal Declaration is that it relies on a structural explanation of the societal circumstances that make human rights morally mandatory. The modern project of a global regime of universal human rights does not arise from any single political tradition or legal system or combination of traditions and legal systems, as such, but from structurally imposed changes

and challenges to which human rights are discovered, in part through painful collective experiences, to be strategically and morally required "answers."

6. None of the above contradicts that we at present must do without a comprehensive and non-controversial theory of human rights. The UDHR prototheory reconstructed here is not even an approximation— but it points in the right direction and hopefully it helps us to avoid some pitfalls. And it does provide us with some necessary theoretical fixed points in the study of the human rights proficiency of contemporary political doctrines. The prototheory reconstructed above recommends itself, then, on the following interrelated counts: (a) its justificatory approach to global human rights standards is more promising than that of rivaling approaches, such as natural rights doctrines, Marxism, any of the great world religions—partly because it may accommodate them all; (b) it does in fact inform—and therefore receives added authority from—the Universal Declaration; (c) it may facilitate a worldwide cross-cultural acceptance and absorption of internationally recognized human rights standards; and (d) it is useful for the purpose of objective and critical research on the cultural legitimacy of human rights. Or so I would like us to think.

Part 2: The Legitimacy of Human Rights in Liberalism and in Marxism

INTRODUCTION

In this part I single out Ronald Dworkin and Hermann Klenner as representatives, respectively, of a liberal and a Marxist doctrine about human rights. I also turn to John Locke and Karl Marx for guidance, since these founding fathers nourished ideas about "the rights of man" that in part eclipse the conceptions of these latter-day heirs. (Recall that we have adopted the maxim to seek to overcome resistance and indifference to human rights in ways that are congenial to the traditions under scrutiny.) Dealing with the works of individual writers enables me to quote chapter and verse as evidence for my interpretation. Thus it helps ward off self-tailored constructs on my part.

Why select Dworkin and Klenner? My reasons are not quite symmetrical: As for Dworkin, it implies dealing only with the egalitarian variety of political liberalism. Among prominent liberal theorists of law, Dworkin appears promising, owing to his egalitarianism and his incorporation of welfare rights. Unfortunately, he elaborates his ideal system of basic rights comfortably detached from the political realities of the United States and the United Kingdom. Klenner, on the other hand, represents a clear-cut "pre-*glasnost*" specimen of Marxism. His theory of rights is situated squarely within the *staatsphilosophische* confines of (what in October 1989 was still) "really existing socialism" in the German Democratic Republic. He seems to be an uncompromising spokesman of a Leninist tradition and is an expert on international human rights. I could not say that Klenner's contributions are promising with a view to enhancing legitimacy for human rights in Marxism. Nevertheless, his unquestionable competence and the clarity of his reasoning help identify the problems of legitimacy at hand.

In the discussion below I assume that Dworkin as well as Klenner, if asked, would affirm that questions about the grounds, interpretation, and implementation of human rights are a crucial matter to the liberal and to the Marxist political tradition, such that a demonstration of full or partial failure to provide properly for human rights would jeopardize the political legitimacy of their respective traditions.[35] I can only provide a brief and partial illustration of the approach proposed in part 2, mainly by discussing the grounding of human rights norms in liberal and in Marxist doctrines and by intimating modifications or replacements, when it seems required.

LIBERALISM AND HUMAN RIGHTS

John Locke on the Idea of a Morally Binding Modus Vivendi for the Political Domain

John Locke, says Karl Marx, provided "the classical expression of bourgeois society's ideas of right as against feudal society."[36] Perhaps. I now want to present an idea, stemming from Locke's *A Letter Concerning Toleration,*[37] which is equally pertinent to capitalist and socialist politics today. What has aptly been termed Locke's *modus vivendi idea of religious toleration*[38] may, when suitably generalized and secularized, still be a crucial component of a reasonable liberal theory of international human rights (which Locke, of course, had no occasion to contemplate). Locke's idea is this: people may have deep, even constitutive ties to different and incompatible ideals of personal salvation and yet sustain a morally binding political *modus vivendi* with one another.[39] How? By abstracting from the religious principles in dispute, however deep one's commitment to them, in order to reach for reasonable agreement on binding terms of political intercourse and social cooperation. In other and more secularized terms:

what to each of us, an individual or group, is of the highest importance as regards our own conception of the ends of life, this commitment of ours need not and ought not—on Locke's liberal reasoning—function as the paramount value of our domestic political order:

> the business of laws is not to provide for the truth of opinions, but for the safety and security of the commonwealth, and of every particular man's goods and person. And so it ought to be.[40]

This Lockean moral "ought" springs not from pluralism as a political ideal but from the recognition of a pluralist political predicament. Later I shall suggest that Locke's reasons for using the public/private distinction to separate the political from the religious spheres of human action and commitment may be generalized and transferred to the contemporary international level of political and moral reconciliation, between rivaling religions and ideologies, cultures and states. In particular we shall make constructive use of the Lockean idea of a moral *modus vivendi* when dealing with certain objections to Dworkin.

Of course, Locke's theology and his metaphysical theory of natural rights, long since "principles in dispute," cannot provide a globally binding normative justification for human rights.[41] Contemporary liberalism must rely on specifically "modern" answers, and below I discuss how far Dworkin's justification for rights squares with the justificatory scheme for international human rights outlined in part I.

The Constitutive Morality of Liberal Politics

We now turn to contemporary liberal political doctrine as expounded by Ronald Dworkin, beginning with the constitutive political position of liberalism, moving on to a liberal view of what rights are, then to a liberal derivation of what basic rights there are, and ending with the crux of a liberal justification for a modern system of human rights. In his magisterial essay on "Liberalism" Dworkin says:

> "A constitutive position" is a political position valued for its own sake: . . . such that any failure fully to secure that position, or any decline in the degree to which it is secured, is *pro tanto* a loss in the value of the overall political arrangement.[42]

According to Dworkin, "there is broad agreement within modern politics that the government must treat all its citizens with equal concern and respect." This obligation can, however, be interpreted in two fundamentally different ways:

> The *first* supposes that government must be neutral in what might be called the question of the good life. The *second* supposes that government cannot be neutral on that question, because it cannot treat its citizens as equal human beings without a theory of what human beings ought to be. . . . This distinction is very abstract, but it is also very important. *I shall now argue that liberalism takes, as its constitutive political morality, the first conception of equality.*[43]

From this constitutive morality of liberal politics, it follows that people have moral rights, and hence that a domestic system of basic rights ought to be legally institutionalized and implemented. It also settles what rights are, within a political theory, "when taken seriously":

> Individuals have rights when, for some reason, a collective goal is not a sufficient justification for denying them what they wish, as individuals, to have or to do, or not a sufficient justification for imposing some loss or injury upon them.[44]

To the liberal a right is a "political trump," a species of political aim such that it "cannot be defeated by appeal to any of the ordinary goals of political administration, but only by a goal of special urgency."[45]

But what basic rights are there? Dworkin's derives, by means of a counterfactual exercise proceeding from the constitutive political morality of liberalism, a system of particular basic rights to be secured by the state. It encompasses, in order of exposition:[46]

1. the pertinent rights of civil and criminal laws of universal application,
2. rights required by the economic market and by representative democracy,
3. a scheme of welfare rights financed through redistributive income tax and inheritance tax . . . which redistributes to the Rawlsian point . . . at which the worst-off group would be harmed rather than benefited by further transfers, and finally
4. a scheme of civil rights whose effect will be to determine those political decisions that are antecedently likely to reflect strong ex-

ternal preferences[47] and to remove those decisions from majoritarian political institutions altogether.

In his deduction Dworkin relies, as liberals almost unfailingly do, on a *Gedankenexperiment*. Starting from the assumption that all citizens are exactly equal in talents, in inherited wealth, in their conception of the good life and therefore in preferences, he is able, by way of a four-stage reintroduction of things as they really are (that is, in societies considered by Dworkin), to derive a system of basic rights on an unflinching egalitarian and ends-of-life-neutral rationale. I cannot here discuss in any detail how Dworkin elaborates a domestic system of basic rights which is a fair proxy of left-liberal political ideals. From the vantage point of the above-stated ten-point checklist of features of the system of internationally recognized human rights, only four are unproblematically provided for: that human rights are inherent (3), are normative trumps (4), protect a wide range of interdependent goods (7), and imply state obligations (5). On another three features of human rights, stated above, Dworkin is silent, for the trivial reason that he only addresses domestic systems: universal applicability (1), globally binding character (2), and subjective rights under international as well as domestic law (6). The remaining three features—incorporation of collective rights-holders (8), inclusion of weak rights (9), and of soft implementation procedures (10)—are not easily accommodated by Dworkin's conception of rights.[48]

But this observation is only in passing; my main concern is with Dworkin's liberal-egalitarian justification for a comprehensive system of rights to be implemented in domestic legislation.

A Liberal-Egalitarian Justification of Rights

What establishes, in the first place, the moral obligation of government to treat its citizens as equals *and* in an ends-of-life-neutral manner? Dworkin claims his "favorite form of argument for political rights . . . is the derivation of particular rights from the abstract right to [equal] concern and respect taken to be fundamental and axiomatic."[49] His elaboration is more enlightening:

> Anyone who professes to take rights seriously . . . must accept, at the minimum, one or both of two important ideas. The first is the vague but powerful idea of human dignity . . . associated with Kant . . . [which] supposes that there are ways of treating a man that are inconsistent with recognizing him as a full member of the human community, and holds that such treatment is

profoundly unjust. The second is the more familiar idea of political equality. This supposes that the weaker members of a political community are entitled to the same concern and respect of their government as the more powerful members have secured for themselves . . . I do not want to defend or elaborate these ideas here, but only to insist that anyone who claims that citizens have rights must accept ideas very close to these.[50]

The justificatory function of this passage matches the commitment to equal human dignity and inherent freedom that constitute what I have previously called the "proximate normative" basis for human rights according to Article 1 of the UDHR. Dworkin, in a footnote, adds that to take rights seriously a person "need not consider these ideas to be axiomatic. He may, that is, have his reasons for insisting that dignity or equality are important values, and these reasons may be utilitarian."[51] Thus, to ground human rights a moral doctrine need not be deontological[52] in basic character, it may be teleological and even basically heteronomic, if it only includes a commitment to human dignity or to political equality, such that this commitment is not offset by other values, goals, or interests. Furthermore, such a commitment must require not only that a regime of human rights be set up but that violations of basic rights be seen as "special moral crimes, beyond the reach of ordinary utilitarian [or teleological or heteronomic] justification."[53] In other words, in order to justify human rights a moral doctrine must simulate deontology for the political domain. But that is a moral minimum, as regards the form of justification for the system of rights.

This is as deep as Dworkin cares to take us. I now turn to some of the difficulties facing his liberal theory, with a view toward grounding international human rights. I shall deal with three points, the first and second of which I seek to resolve by stretching the liberal idea, originating with Locke, of a morally binding political *modus vivendi*.

First Difficulty: Is Personal Autonomy an Obligatory Political Ideal?
Dworkin's liberal platform requires "the government" to heed human rights and, indirectly, each citizen to respect such rights. Does it also make mandatory some specifically liberal ideal of the person? To find out, we may speculate about how Dworkin could respond to an individual, or a group, or an entire cultural community, who for (to them worthy[54]) moral reasons reject dignity and equality interpreted as binding ideals of personal autonomy. This challenge intimates that the liberal indulges in squaring a moral circle: legislating rights in virtue of (some controversial interpreta-

tion of) dignity and equality and yet claiming moral neutrality for the resulting system.

A liberal's own ideals of the person may of course be inspired by Kantian autonomy, or by the experimental lifestyle advocated by Mill, or by moral skepticism, or by seeing people as choosers and constructors of options (to mention some familiar alternatives).[55] No such ideal of the person is prescribed by a regime of human rights, but is it prescribed by its minimal liberal rationale? Is, accordingly, "uncritical" acceptance of the system of basic rights, by people in the hold of tradition, convention, or authority, necessarily suspect to liberals?

Such a basis for accepting rights cannot be reconciled with a Kantian conception of the grounds for human dignity (individual rational self-determination, or autonomy, in a strong, individualist sense), nor with Mill, nor with moral skepticism. My hunch is that it is therefore suspect to Dworkin as to many other latter-day liberals. Limitations of space prohibit further discussion. But liberals, I now submit, could draw on Locke for relief from excess foundational burdens, as I will here outline. A minimal moral substance, from which a liberal political defense for rights might proceed, is the practice of taking seriously as a moral person, the other fellow, who disagrees with us on fundamental ideals of the person or the good life, in line with the principle of reciprocity implicit in Article 1 of UDHR. Of course we take our own moral commitments seriously, and we expect the same from him. When confronted with deep moral conflict a liberal—provided she is informed, that is, by a Lockean conception of moral *modus vivendi*—calls neither for moral warfare nor for relativist surrender, but for serious dialogue and negotiation about the terms of political intercourse. I leave aside the question why such discourse would terminate in the joint construction of a system of rights.

The Lockean move here is to abstract from, but not abandon, principles in dispute between us, in order to reach for common grounds for the limited, but important, societal domain of human rights. This train of thought suggests that it doesn't require a commitment to Kantian dignity-as-individual-autonomy "to take rights seriously." Perhaps the liberal need not even legislate what it takes, beyond a willingness to serious talk among political adversaries?

The issue at stake is how to decide what constitutes the proper kind of support for a global system of human rights. Not any lip service will do; the danger of delusive apologetism, on behalf of various religions and ideologies, is not to be belittled. Neither is it a solution, however, to make the liberal's cherished ideal of the person mandatory for all. The issue cannot presently be decided—and need not be—by a global consensus on moral principles. Part of what it takes is to distinguish the sphere of human rights from other moral concerns and then to reach for globally shared practices and institutions to safeguard a progressively widening circle of globally recognized human rights. The criterion of "the proper kind of support" for human rights is in the end not purely theoretical; in the end it depends on social practice, to which religious, moral, and political doctrines are nevertheless crucial inputs.

A Lockean liberal, as interpreted above, is not squaring a moral circle. But she is engaged in social multiplication of moral circles. To her the moral sphere of rights does not encompass all of morality; far from it: her personal friendships and familial life, her business endeavors and professional pursuits, her life in the congregation of believers, and so on, may be tied up with specific sets of values and norms, sources of justification and scope for the exercise of moral judgment. By embracing such a functionally specialized morality and the moral complexities it heralds the liberal is likely, however, to offend those who remain committed to the idea that any good society must be some kind of organic whole, animated by a single overarching purpose in virtue of which it is a good society. But what if it has become a sociological fact about the modern world that no such society can prevail and safeguard human freedom and equal dignity (even on a minimal interpretation)? That brings up the second difficulty with Dworkin's liberal mode of thought.

Second Difficulty: Specifying the Circumstances of Rights
Dworkin's justification for a system of basic rights is insufficiently specific about what social and historical conditions make such a system morally mandatory. He never elaborates on the sociological reasons that make the system of rights required in order to safeguard freedom and equal dignity. Under what specific societal circumstances are what configurations of market and democracy most fitted to the liberal's constitutive political morality? Is that morality transhistorically and transsocially valid?

The rationale behind the Lockean response to the predicament of religious antagonists could profitably be carried further. When threatened politically by imprisonment in, or by, monolithic moralities we are admonished, as it were, to reach for sociological exits. Here are two sociological considerations in this vein: First, in contemporary societies, as a matter of recalcitrant fact, there exist deep disagreements about the proper purpose and meaning of individual and collective life. Such disagreements are very unlikely to disappear soon; no party can reasonably demand that they be dissolved by the global adoption of one master conception; and every party must come to terms with them morally. Second, what is more, in modern societies—and in contemporary world society at large—there exist a multiplicity of functionally separate channels of communication that may allow for more or less untrampled social pursuit of nonpolitical ends in the spheres of economy, science, arts, religion, familial life, professions, and so on.

If we acknowledge that there is no reasonable escape from this doubly pluralist character of our social orders, we are further absolved, I believe, from the dilemma of having either to contradict ourselves morally (phony liberal tolerance) or to subjugate others politically (liberal intolerance): we are brought to see further pertinent rationales for Lockean moral *modus vivendi* for the domains of civil rights, democratic politics, minority protection, basic welfare for all, and so on.

In order to work out a system of basic rights that facilitates a suitable *modus vivendi* between adherents of competing conceptions of the good life, and that simultaneously safeguards social channels for reasonably independent nonpolitical pursuits, we cannot do without empirical analyses of those historically specific circumstances that make specific human rights arrangements morally mandatory or preferable. Moral principles, whether in isolation or in tandem with tacit sociological common sense, are not enough.

Recognizing the importance of sociological input into the foundations of rights theory is, I would think, not foreign to Dworkin; Marxist criticisms for eternalist and transhistorical illusions about the foundations of rights would be off-target. Yet, there are few explicit historical and sociological considerations in his argument. That is a major area of neglect, if it takes analyses of historically shifting societal circumstances not only to delineate a system of rights but also to establish its foundations. I shall proceed to discuss one such neglect.

Third Difficulty: Neglect of International Relations

Dworkin's theory of rights is erected, to put it bluntly, upon the policy of leaving foreigners out of the picture: in his theoretical universe the terms are "government" (always one), "its citizens," and "their law." Law's empire has, as it were, no foreign affairs. Domestic law is handled without the benefit of concerns with the world market, international terms of trade, debt crisis and hunger, refugees and asylum-seekers, people's control over resources, the production and affliction of transnational pollution, or war and peace. Dworkin's theoretical isolationism, with respect to the moral problem of grounding a domestic system of basic human rights, parallels John Foster Dulles's consequential policy of keeping the United States aloof from internationally binding human rights instruments from the 1950s onward. (The United States has never reversed this policy.)

This objection to Dworkin's liberal doctrine hinges on his claim that, to take rights seriously, we must accept Kantian human dignity or political equality or both. Of course, Dworkin would not argue that non-U.S., or non-U.K. citizens, or stateless persons, are not fully human. As for the idea of political equality, he may hold that it pertains to the citizenry of single national states taken in isolation, that for his part he studies (say) the United States and the United Kingdom, and that similar principles would be applicable, when differences in legal traditions and so forth are provided for, to questions of law and basic rights in any modern state.

I do not here question Dworkin's choice of subject matter, nor do I say that he ought to work out a justificatory and critical theory for international human rights (though that would be fine, and in the end perhaps required for his own purpose). My complaint is different: Dworkin proceeds as if it were feasible to erect a morally adequate theory of basic rights for domestic systems, while ignoring, morally and intellectually, the impact of international relations. How can he claim to contemplate basic human rights from a universalistic moral point of view in the contemporary world and yet close his eyes to the global order (and the global disorder) of interdependent, interpenetrating, externality-inflicting and externality-ridden societies?

Dworkin's liberalism does not face the problem of the proper scope and scale of morally pertinent societal relations among human beings in contemporary world society. By omission it inflicts upon itself a measure of parochial, self-congratulatory rich man's ideology.

Liberal Society = Implementation of Human Rights? A Note on a Thesis Proposed by Donnelly and Howard

There is a significant overlap between egalitarian liberalism as elaborated by Dworkin and the project of universal human rights as conceived by the International Bill of Human Rights: some of the intellectual sources are the same and, more importantly, both may reasonably be interpreted as attempted "answers" to arising, and mainly socially engendered, threats to human freedom and equal dignity, respectively in the form of theory construction at the domestic level and institution building at the global level. But, for reasons such as those advanced above, I cannot accept the thesis advanced by Jack Donnelly and Rhoda Howard that there is a seamless continuity between internationally accepted human rights and egalitarian liberalism. Among their claims are that "the full list of human rights in the Universal Declaration . . . demand—and if implemented would play a crucial role in creating—a liberal society, and the ideal person envisaged by liberalism."[56] I particularly object in the name of a more "liberal" and globally acknowledgeable liberalism, to making a liberal ideal of the person a mandatory part of what human rights are for. Other rationales are equally legitimate, and equally nonmandatory.

MARXISM AND HUMAN RIGHTS

Human Rights and Total Emancipation

To my knowledge, Hermann Klenner's book, *Marxism and Human Rights*,[57] is the intellectually most ambitious effort to furnish the post-Stalinist East-European Marxist conception of human rights with theoretical foundations.[58] Of its five chapters, the first three deal with historical topics, chapter 4 discusses basic rights and human rights in socialism, and chapter 5 deals with "Human Rights as a Standard for Intervention and Cooperation." Appended are nearly two hundred pages of historical and contemporary source materials, ranging from Magna Carta Libertatum (1215) to the recent convention on discrimination against women (1979), all in German.

Klenner writes: "Without [Marx's] *Capital* [there would be] no Marxist conception of human rights."[59] Historically this is no doubt correct, but the way Klenner handles this dependence of a Marxist conception of human rights on Marx's *Capital* is nevertheless regrettable. Let me explain.

In *Capital* Marx proceeds from a penetrating analysis of modern socioeconomic structures, and in particular from the "contradiction" between surface nonexploitative and in-depth exploitative worker-capitalist relations.[60] This critical Marxian legacy ought not be fortified by also sticking to Marxian mistakes, such as his badly argued analysis of bourgeois rights set forth in a review article at age 24.[61] Klenner, however, claims that Marx, in *Capital*, elaborates and above all provides "proof" for the thesis, proposed in "On the Jewish Question," of an impending total emancipation of humanity in which the partial and purely political emancipation achieved by the bourgeoisie will be transcended and the ("prehistorical") circumstances of rights be left behind.[62]

Klenner accepts an orthodox Marxist doctrine about the historical necessity of Communism. And (paraphrasing Marx) he even claims scientific status for the following thesis of Total Emancipation ("TE" for short):

> TE Capitalist production begets, with the Inexorability of a natural process, its own negation. The Historical Calling of the modern Proletariat arising from the economic contradictions of capitalism, is to Lead Humanity into a Totally New Mode of production, appropriation and life, in which all members of society are guaranteed a Perfectly Free development and active discharge of their physical and spiritual talents.[63]

For the sake of economy I capitalized those terms which, to my mind, signal claims far beyond scientific credentials on any known philosophy of science.[64]

The trouble with Klenner's thesis about inevitable total emancipation, his TE, is that he, as of 1982, still essentially relies on it for argumentative support in developing a Marxist doctrine of contemporary human rights. He admits as much himself, with commendable honesty. After having quoted and paraphrased Marx on capitalism, revolution, and Communism he writes:

> No marxist conception of human rights that moves beyond purely negative points can be developed without the detailed proofs provided by Marx and Engels . . . of the epoch of world-historical transition from capitalism to communism.[65]

In other words, Klenner straps the human rights conception of Marxism to the Marxian vision of, and prognosis of, impending world Communism. The implication is that human rights are conceived not only as historically conditioned and changing (certainly a valid and important point), and as ideologically suspect (again pertinent in a purely capitalist context), but also as something to be transcended and made superfluous in principle, by the ineluctable advent of full Communism, for the realization of which a Communist is morally required to struggle with uncompromising commitment. As Steven Lukes has convincingly argued, this paramount moral commitment, which is founded on TE, cannot be squared with taking human rights seriously.[66] Thus conceived human rights must appear to be but instruments, and not for the protection of people's freedom and diginity in any modern social order—in particular against those who claim to act in the name of the emancipatory "historical calling of the modern proletariat."[67] The objection to relying on TE for construing a Marxist conception of human rights is, to put it simply, that it bars that conception from being a conception of a system of rights as opposed to a system of policy.[68] Perhaps acceptance of, and propagation of, TE as true can be squared with belief in and respect for human rights. But then the presumed "historical calling of the modern proletariat . . . to lead humanity" must yield, within the relevant societal domain, to a morally and legally binding system of (genuine) human rights: heed of people's human rights must never be outweighed by stratagems for the "total new mode of production, appropriation and life."

Perhaps not so surprisingly, Klenner makes no attempt to argue for his TE. Neither are there references to such arguments produced by others, beyond invoking Marx (and Engels and Lenin). And if we study the most promising source among these classics of Marxism, *Capital,* we shall look in vain for the requisite sociological, economic, and historical (or other varieties of reasonable) "proofs" for anything approaching the Marxian conception and prediction of Communism.[69]

In his polemics against those who propound bourgeois human rights doctrines, Klenner repeatedly invokes "social science" and "scientific analysis," he calls for "verification" and "falsification." Such calls are hardly convincing, considering that he bases his own conception of human rights on a *Gesellschaftswissenschaft* predicated upon the unquestioned acceptance of Historical Necessity, the Calling of the Proletariat and impending Total Emancipation in Communism. It is hard to think of a doctrine more fit for Marxian critique of power-holder ideology than the one called upon by Klenner to certify his conception of human rights.

One disturbing aspect of Klenner's theory of international human rights is that in relying essentially on TE he is asking us to take seriously a doctrine which he, on his own standards of scientificness, could not take seriously himself. He must be well aware that TE (when not simply laughed at or joked about) is extremely controversial, that it is held, by the appropriate scholarly communities, to be intellectually suspect. Yet Klenner claims to stand up to scientific standards—and ridicules others who admit they do not (such as Martin Kriele, who concedes that his commitment to human dignity is metaphysical).

The Implications of "Total Emancipation" for Human Rights
Klenner's major premise when arguing for his Marxist positions on human rights is TE. Several of these positions are clearly unacceptable from the point of view of our provisional human rights conception, set forth in the first part of this paper on "Programmatic and Methodological Issues." Thus they backfire on TE itself. Among these controversial Marxist positions on human rights, propounded by Klenner, I shall mention the following six:

1. "All communist parties under capitalist regimes rightly claim that they, and not the rulers, are the authentic defenders of constitutional rights in their countries."[70]

2. "[A]s inevitably as the proletarian revolution, and the proletarian dictatorship it brings, intervenes in the basic structure of bourgeois society, as inevitably it must violate ('verstossen') the basic rights of this society, that pass for human rights."[71]

3. The historical laws of social progress towards communism is, Klenner claims, the objective measure of legitimacy *de lege lata* and *de lege ferenda* in socialist regimes; "the foundation, evaluation, justification, criticism, and adjustment, the demands for the further development [of socialist legal systems] must therefore be established by means and methods of social science." Similarly: "Our law is . . . legitimate (that is: historically justified), when it corresponds to the objective laws of societal development and is instrumental to their optimal realization."[72]

4. The separation of powers, essential for safeguarding the independence of the judiciary and hence for the implementation of a system of basic rights, is not binding for Klenner: "also for juridical guarantees the principle of democratic centralism applies (Art. 47 of the GDR constitution), which means that the elected representation of the people is always the superior organ of state power." Klenner, incidentally, thinks the separation of powers doctrine was refuted by Rousseau no later than 1762![73]

5. In the service of human emancipation, human rights against the state must be complemented with human duties to the state; in socialism both exist independently of government recognition and legislative intent.[74]

6. In the contemporary world system there can be no universally shared conception of universal human rights, nor any globally

binding catalogue of such rights, Klenner argues. But, he holds, there are some binding human rights norms in international law: Supreme among these is the right to national sovereignty, or the right of peoples to self-determination, which outlaws any international humanitarian intervention(except brotherly interventions by socialist states?) and leaves each people, in practice each state, in unbridled control of its domestic system of law and of human rights, the sole proviso being that those holding state power cannot totally negate the right to self-determination of its own people or of other peoples and organizes violations of human rights to a degree that threatens international peace, "such as in Palestine, Chile and South Africa."[75]

Limitations of time, space, and perhaps patience, prevent me from further discussion of Klenner's positions on human rights that stem from his thesis of Total Emancipation. One may also wonder to what extent they should be taken seriously as attempts at theoretical discourse, since it is hard to believe that Klenner is intellectually serious concerning his basic argument. As I see it, Klenner's mistake is to start from maximally controversial principles, from a Marxist metaphysics of history, rather than from internal criticism of capitalism in conjunction with those tenets that might be shared with ideological opponents and become common grounds for a morally binding international and domestic agreement on human rights norms, institutions, and procedures.

Marxist Human Rights Backing That Is Independent of TE

Finally, I want to object that Klenner's deployment of TE tends to emasculate Marx's critical theory of capitalism. But, fortunately, an important core of Marx's contribution, in *Capital,* to the theory of bourgeois human rights can be upheld on grounds that are independent of TE. It is now incumbent on me to explain why and how.

Accepting Marx's theory of capitalist reproduction in *Capital* we may summarize, much simplified, Marx's *Internal Criticism of the "Rights of Man"* ("IC" for short) as follows:

IC The rights of man are *characteristic social forms* of a capitalist mode of production in so far as legally instituted civil rights are required to facilitate economic exploitation of workers by capitalist, by (a) making exploitation invisible to social actors, (b) legitimating class relations in the eyes of the actors, (c) thus, stabilizing the economic structure as a basis of a self-reproductive exploitative economic system.[76]

"Exploitation" may be interpreted commonsensically to mean: "A exploits B whenever A and B are engaged in freely chosen exchange and A thereby gains through harming B."[77] The IC thesis strikes core bourgeois social arrangements on internal grounds, that is on descriptive and normative suppositions that come "natural" to a bourgeois mind. As indicated, it can be interpreted without drawing on Marx's labor theory of value.

No doubt Marx's genuine discoveries in *Capital* are inspired by something like his Communist expectation and hope (TE). And though Marx never succeeded in establishing a stringent argument for his conception and prognosis of (full) Communism, neither did he ever reject it. Marx's major intellectual and moral contribution, the critical economic diagnosis of pure capitalism, remained unfinished, I believe, because it turned out that the political and history-theoretical components of his research program could not be redeemed by analyses at the intellectual level of *Capital*. What is pitiful is that Marx's followers after 120 years have not been able to discard the Master's reckless pseudoproofs for historically inevitable total emancipation, since it tends to undermine the Marxist contribution to a badly needed critical theory of modern capitalist economies. Hence, for our purpose we must insist that when Marx in *Capital* did establish his potent IC, it neither relies on, nor lends argumentative support to, his historical metaphysics or his (rather vague) political recommendations.

My discussion of Klenner's contribution to a Marxist theory of human rights has focused on foundations and, consequently, turned out rather negative. I cannot leave the subject of Marxism and human rights without briefly indicating what I hold to be potential building stones for a revised Marxist theory of human rights—over and above reinterpreting or, better, abandoning TE:

1. Informed by IC, it becomes clear that the implementation of civil and political rights in a modern society does not by itself secure a good society: rights may be heeded and be socially protected, and yet social life may be miserable. Marxism may provide a healthy antidote to excessive enthusiasm about rights, and to class biases in the implementation of rights.

2. The basic moral commitment implicit in the Marxist protest

against capitalist exploitation and mutual instrumentalization, and against any socially avoidable human degradation and suffering, is congenial to the fundamental human rights values of freedom, equal dignity, and nondiscrimination. But traditional Marxist doctrines of modern society and of Communism must be rewritten to establish that human freedom, equality, and solidarity require a state-protected system of rights in order to be safeguarded.[78]

3. Unorthodox Marxist social and historical analyses might improve our current poor understanding of the relations between shifting "circumstances of justice" (or, in Marxian parlance, "modes of production") and the optimal construction, and the proper development and limitations, of a system of basic rights.

4. Marxist theory of modern history and society is from the outset wedded to a global moral and political conception: When the move to take rights seriously is undertaken, modern world society remains the fundamental object of analysis. This is a welcome corrective to most liberal discussions.

5. One obvious Marxist move—which has already been implemented politically in the wake of *glasnost* and *perestroika*—is to recur to historical materialism for a reappraisal of the social conditions required for further growth of the forces of production in existing socialism: a deeper and more thoroughgoing protection of peoples' basic rights seems to be one essential requisite.

6. Materialism, in the ontological sense, should make Marxists sensitive to the formidable idealist illusions harbored by the project of overcoming the social circumstances of rights. And the epistemological implications of materialism makes mandatory some version of fallibilism, which again is conducive to respecting peoples' rights.

7. Revision and rejection of untenable parts of the Marxian intellectual legacy that is detrimental to respect for human rights should, considering the Marxist profession of allegiance to science and the scientific spirit, be congenial to, and not held to be a forfeiture of, the Marxist tradition.

8. At the level of international political deliberations and negotiations the Marxist preoccupation with questions of human rights to peace, to people's self-determination, and to development might acquire a new lease of legitimacy and urgency—once the

Marxist conception of human rights is liberated from the "Heads I win, tails you lose" logic that comes with the orthodox employment of the thesis of total emancipation.

Somewhat Inconclusive Conclusions

In my discussion of "Programmatic and Methodological Issues," I have presented a set of conceptual and methodological proposals for research on the legitimacy of modern, internationally acknowledged human rights in cultures and traditions, doctrines and ideologies. More specifically, I have first distinguished between a more sociological and empirical approach, on the one hand, and a more philosophical and reconstructive approach on the other, while emphasizing the need for interdisciplinary cooperation in this field of study. Second, I have proposed three broad categories of questions to be pursued: the substantive questions that address particular cultural units, those that deal with the global cross-cultural conditions for setting up a world-encompassing human rights regime, and those that focus on the system of human rights itself: the contemporary standards, institutions, and procedures of human rights. Third, and most importantly, I have elaborated and defended a definite conception of human rights which is based on the International Bill of Human Rights, against which cultural items as well as further developments and elaborations of the existing system of human rights may be tested.

In my discussion of "The Legitimacy of Human Rights in Liberalism and in Marxism," I treated questions of a less abstract nature, partly in order to illustrate, and partly to further elaborate, the largely conceptual and methodological analysis of the part on programmatic issues. I have investigated the potential legitimacy of human rights norms in two Western traditions of political theory, considering them as potential foundations of the modern system of human rights. Here the chapter is only a takeoff, and hardly ready for a landing. Of the unfinished business, the most urgent task is now to parallel the conceptual and reconstructive study of doctrines, attempted earlier, with empirical studies of political cultures.

Liberalism comes in many varieties. I have chosen one that is promising vis-à-vis human rights, for its egalitarianism and its incorporation of welfare rights. Dworkinian liberalism, which is the point of departure for Donnelly and Howard as well, does, in my interpretation, have its share of problems when measured by internationally negotiated and accepted human rights. I have suggested how some difficulties might be amended by drawing on inspiration from Locke. Yet the questions of international morality and solidarity and, by implication, the problems of collective rights, of weak norms, and of soft implementation mechanisms are left unprovided for. Dworkin's justificatory departure may seem to be similar to the normative principles incorporated in the International Bill of Rights. But Dworkin's interpretation of freedom and equality—enthusiastically endorsed by Donnelly and Howard—is perhaps infested with a peculiarly Western, and unnecessarily contestable, ideal of the person. From the constitutive morality of liberalism Dworkin proceeds without the benefit of explicit considerations of variable socioeconomic conditions, historical contexts, and the global scope of moral relations pertinent to systems of basic rights.

Of course, Dworkin is not all there is of liberal rights theory. Others in the tradition like Rawls, Beitz, and Walzer, have begun facing international relations in novel ways. But it remains to be seen what a liberal system of human rights and corresponding government obligations would be if Dworkin's framework was brought to bear on international relations and the network of global, regional, and domestic human rights regimes. On this score liberal theory could benefit from Marxist approaches to the analysis of the global economic system, international labor relations, and international terms of trade.

According to Marx's critique of bourgeois human rights, the commodity-owning rights-holders to equality and freedom routinely use one another purely as means to egocentric ends; exploitation is endemic, as is the reproduction of illusions about society and self. Marx, fascinated by his genuine discoveries about the process of capitalist reproduction and expansion, certainly does minimize or overlook the casual weight and cultural significance of the many other social spheres of intercourse developing in any modern Western-type society. Marx is quiet about the long list of bourgeois rights which cannot plausibly be reduced to vehicles of capital and class rule. Marx's own theory of rights is vitiated by his belief in, and tacit moral commitment to, impending Communism. In consequence, all rival moral concerns must yield: To contribute optimally to the total emancipation of mankind is the overriding calling of the class-conscious revolutionary who is acting on behalf of the modern proletariat. In this perspective, rights are but instruments of policy.

But Marx's reckless dialectical "proof" of historically necessitated total liberation should be discarded, or at least domesticated. From a human rights perspective the doctrine, as such, is not the problem; the trouble is the weight and paramount status accorded to it by Klenner, as compared with more reasonable approaches open to Marxists who take a serious interest in cross-ideological dialogue and negotiations about human rights. Here the unreformed Marxist still can learn from liberalism and Lockean *modus vivendi:* we do not have to agree on the good society to agree on the system of rights, without which any modern society is destructive of equal dignity and freedom.

Liberated from the straightjacket of monolithic moral futurism, Marxism might still contribute to the cross-cultural dialogue about a globally binding conception of human rights. It may also bring itself to defend human rights in unexpected ways. Hopefully, Marxists will find good Marxist reasons for reconsidering the case for human rights.[79] I should like to add that, whereas traditional Marxist political regimes are collapsing in Eastern Europe and are losing ground worldwide, the Marxian legacy of critical social theory is too powerful, and too valuable, to be discarded.

Reading An-Na'im's fine study on "Religious Minorities under Islamic Law and the Limits of Cultural Relativism"[80] aroused my interest in the general problematics of inquiring into the legitimacy—the support, rejection, indifference, and so forth—for human rights in various cultures and traditions. And, soon, it set me off on the project of investigating the human rights proficiency of two hegemonic political traditions close to (my Western) home: liberalism and Marxism. The main focus in the present chapter has been on methodological and agenda-setting issues. Hopefully it will motivate or provoke others to contribute to the study of the cross-cultural, and global, legitimacy of human rights.[81]

Notes

1. E/CN.4/30 (Nov 12/47). Albert Verdoodt, *Naissance et signification de la Declaration Universelle des droits de l'homme* (Paris and Louvain: Nauwelaerts, 1964). Chapters 1 and 2 survey the background materials provided to the Commission on Human Rights.

2. When submitted the report was entitled: "The Bases of an International Bill of Human Rights. Report submitted by the UNESCO Committee on the Philosophical Principles of Human Rights to the Human Rights Commission of the United Nations." It was finally published as: *Human Rights. Comments and Interpretations,* ed. UNESCO (London and New York: Auan Wingate 1949). Introd. by Jacques Maritain.

3. *Ibid.* at 8.

4. *Ibid.* at 268 and 287.

5. *American Anthropologist* 49, no. 4 (1947): 539–43.

6. In *Human Rights in Africa: Cross-Cultural Perspectives,* ed. A. An-Naʿim and F. Deng (Washington D.C.: Brookings Institution, 1990). *See also* his "Religious Minorities under Islamic Law and the Limits of Cultural Relativism," *Human Rights Quarterly* 9 (1987): 1 and "Islamic Law, International Relations and Human Rights: Challenge and Response," *Cornell International Law Journal* 20 (1987): 317.

7. This assumption does not, of course, imply that other types of causes of human rights violations are not important, among these structural impediments and sheer ignorance. Note also that this assumption leaves open the question of the relative weight of cultural, as opposed to structural and other, factors. And there is of course no denying here the obvious and important fact that a variety of different cultural factors are supportive of human rights to various, and shifting, degrees.

8. For instance, Alex P. Schmid, *Research on Gross Human Rights Violations: A Programme,* 2nd enlarged ed. (Leiden: Center for the Study of Social Conflicts, 1989), proposes a pertinent and promising research agenda for identifying and explaining human rights violations by state-actors and state-supported actors.

9. The *real existierende Sozialismus* of the German Democratic Republic, which is the backdrop of my specimen of Marxism, seems, at the time of revising this paper (February 1990), to be a doomed enterprise; my object of diagnosis may well vanish before I publish!

10. Colleagues have suggested that research on the cultural legitimacy of human rights require that we elaborate very precise conceptions of culture and of legitimacy. I tend to think we are best served by a commonsensical approach, at the programmatic level. I see no serious obstacle arising from rival theories of culture (for which I have consulted Roger M. Keesing, "Theories of Culture," *Annual Review of Anthropology* (1974): 73–97). The term "legitimacy" I shall employ, depending on the context, in the descriptive anthropological sense, indicating factual support, or in the critical philosophical sense, indicating normative validity.

11. *See also supra* note 8.

12. The somber appraisals, quoted by Shestack, of the state of affairs in the theory of human rights are still apposite. *See* his "The Jurisprudence of Human Rights" in Theodor Meron, ed., *Human Rights in International Law: Legal and Policy Issues* (Oxford: Clarendon Press 1983), 69.

13. I do not question the truth of the formula in quotes, only its analytical pertinence for the purpose of cross-cultural studies. *See infra* section on Donnelly and Morsink.

14. This is a simplification, since some human rights are due only to certain "human rights-acceptable" subcategories of all human beings, such as children and citizens.

15. I here use "universal" to denote universal applicability, and "global" to denote universality of recognition and obligation.

16. Among human rights principles that are binding *de lege lata* are those that are found valid as customary law, binding resolutions of international organs, and general principles of law.

17. The system of human rights contains norms that may conflict with each other. For such cases it requires, internal principles of priority, which it provides via jurisprudence. By the same token, very few human rights can be absolute, that is, without legitimate limitations, exceptions, and derogations. This does no violence to the point that human rights are inviolable as a normative system.

18. On UDHR, its Article 1 and Preamble, *see* my "Article One: A New Beginning" in Asbjorn Eide and Göran Melander, eds., *The Universal Declaration of Human Rights, A Commentary Article by Article* (Oslo: The Norwegian Institute of Human Rights, 1991).

19. *See* text to *supra* note 5.

20. By justificatory prototheory, I mean a sketch of a justificatory argument that points the way toward a fully elaborated theory without itself being one. Incidentally, I do not think that the authors of the Universal Declaration conceived of their project as theory construction. The eminently political character of their project, in this case, may be part of the explanation of why they succeeded even at producing interesting contributions to theory.

21. The following reconstruction and appraisal is borrowed, in part, from Lindholm, *supra* note 18.

22. *See* Philip Alston, "Making Space for New Rights: The Case of the Right to Development," *Harvard Human Rights Yearbook* 1 (1988): 24–38.

23. *See*, recently, Jon Wetlesen, "Inherent Dignity as a Ground for Human Rights, A Dialogical Approach," *Archiv für Rechts- und Sozialphilosophie,* Beiheft 41 (Stuttgart: Franz Steiner Verlag, 1990). I am happy to be able to divorce the Universal Declaration from the justificatory doctrine referred to in the text. In opposition to Wetlesen I find this doctrine unpalatable, as it either involves one in the muddy waters of essential potentiality, or jeopardizes the human rights of foetuses, infants, the demented, the mentally handicapped, or other humans who cannot safely be said to be capable of reason or conscience.

24. For more on the justificatory prototheory of human rights imputed to UDHR *see* Lindholm, *supra* note 18.

25. *See also* the justificatory reasoning indicated in the UNESCO statement quoted in *supra* note 4.

26. *See* Jack Donnelly, "Human Rights and Human Dignity: An Analytic Critique of Non-Western Conceptions of Human Rights," *The American Political Science Review* 76 (1982): 303–16; his "Human Rights as Natural Rights," *Human Rights Quarterly* 4 (1982): 391–405; and Johannes Morsink, "The Philosophy of the Universal Declaration," *Human Rights Quarterly* 6 (1984): 309–34.

27. Morsink, *ibid.* at 333–34.

28. *Third Committee Records for 1948, 775.* "Marxist" here is in scare quotes, since on this point Klenner is the better Marxist; *see* part 2, below.

29. In particular, I hold Donnelly's view to be a diluted natural rights doctrine. Maybe Donnelly wants to have it both ways, as it were: "A natural rights

theory attributes human rights solely on the basis of one's humanity, that is human nature," he asserts (Donnelly, "Human Rights as Natural Rights," *supra* note 26, at 398). On the other hand, he recommends "the idea of human rights . . . to be an approach particularly suited to contemporary social, political, and economic circumstances" (Donnelly, "Human Rights and Human Dignity," *supra* note 26, at 303). Our disagreement might boil down to whether such circumstances are held, and rightly, by the authors of the Universal Declaration to be an essential part of the justification of human rights. For further discussion of these matters, I refer to Lindholm, *supra* note 18.

30. I have much sympathy with Philip Alston's discussion of these questions in *supra* note 22, at 24–38.

31. *See* John Humphrey, *Human Rights and the United Nations: A Great Adventure* (Dobbs Ferry: Transnational Publishers, 1984), 44. Humphrey holds that Article 1 of the UDHR contains "philosophical assertions which [do] not enunciate justiciable rights" and thus "weakens the case for saying that . . . the Declaration . . . is now part of positive customary law and therefore binding on all states."

32. John Rawls, "The Idea of an Overlapping Consensus," *Oxford Journal of Legal Studies* 7, no 1 (1987): 1–25.

33. The analysis of overlapping consensus is informed, I believe, by discoveries in the philosophy of science originating with Raymond Poincare and Pierre Duhem and further developed by Arne Naess and W. V. Quine. I am referring to the thesis of "theory pluralism," which says, simply, that many rivaling scientific theories may explain the same set of data equally well, although, for logical reasons, at the most one of these theories could be true, and the one reasonable persons would want to accept. The last point does not carry over into the political domain, for moral and epistemological reasons. Epistemological reasons would include the following: In the global human rights-predicament outlined above, the conflicting basic principles are by general knowledge much harder to defend by generally convincing arguments than is the overlapping consensus on human rights that can be erected upon such principles; heed of universal human rights is also a practical precondition for getting nearer to a reasonable global consensus on controversial basic principles.

34. See my discussion of Lockean moral *modus vivendi* in part 2 following. Here I only want to add that in the deliberations of the Third Committee as well as in the Report by UNESCO (referred to in *supra* note 2), similar ideas were advanced.

35. *See* the corollary from part 1.

36. Karl Marx, vol. 1, *Theories of Surplus Value* (Moscow: Progress Publishers, 1956), 367.

37. John Locke, *A Letter Concerning Toleration* (Indianapolis: Bobbs-Merrill, 1955.)

38. By Charles Larmore, *Patterns of Moral Complexity* (Cambridge: Cambridge University Press, 1987), 76.

39. *Ibid.* at 130.

40. Locke, *supra* note 37, at 45.

41. *See also* part I, *supra*.

42. Ronald Dworkin, *A Matter of Principle* (Cambridge, Mass.: Harvard University Press, 1985), 408.

43. *Ibid.* at 191–92 (emphasis added).

44. Ronald Dworkin, *Taking Rights Seriously* (London: Duckworth, 1977), xi. The full, and cumbersome, characterization of what a right is, is spelled out in *ibid.* at 91.

45. Dworkin, *ibid.* at 92. His celebrated theory of rights as political trumps is promising, with a view to a system of human rights, and I have alluded to it above; *see* text to *supra* note 17.

46. Dworkin, *supra* note 42, at 193–98.

47. External preferences are "preferences people have about what others shall do or have." Democratic majority decisions that reflect such preferences would "invade rather than enforce the rights of citizens to be treated as equals," in the sense prescribed by the constitutive morality of liberalism. *Ibid.* at 196.

48. *Cf.* Chapter 6 by Michael McDonald in this volume.

49. Dworkin, *supra* note 44, at xi.

50. Dworkin, *supra* note 44, at 199; *see also* at 272–73.

51. Ibid. at 199.

52. A deontological moral doctrine *cannot* base all moral evaluations of actions, norms and institutions solely on their differential contribution to the realization of some ultimate value, such as utility, happiness, or perfection.

53. Dworkin, *supra* note 44, at 199.

54. *Cf.* the case of Islam, discussed by An-Naʿim in this volume and in his *Toward an Islamic Reformation. Civil Liberties, Human Rights, and International Law* (Syracuse: Syracuse University Press, 1990).

55. *See also* Michael McDonald's Chapter 6 in this volume.

56. Rhoda E. Howard and Jack Donnelly, "Human Dignity, Human Rights, and Political Regimes," *American Political Science Review* 80 (1986): 806.

57. Hermann Klenner, *Marxismus und Menschenrechte: Studien zur Rechtsphilosophie* (Berlin: Akademie-Verlag, 1982). Page references in this section are to this German edition; translations are mine.

58. My knowledge of Klenner's work is limited. Beyond his book on *Marxism and Human Rights* from 1982 I have consulted a number of his articles on human rights and his numerous contributions to the *Bulletin of the GDR Committee for Human Rights* from 1975 onward. His position can be gleaned from the more accessible paper "Marx gegen/für Menschenrechte," in *Nederlands Tijdschrift voor Rechtsfilosofie en Rechtstheorie* 12 (1983): 107–12. Klenner is honorary president of the International Association for Philosophy of Law and Social Philosophy and member of the German Democratic Republic Academy of Sciences in Berlin. He has published extensively on human rights and related issues during several decades. His command of the history and the social contex of intellectual and political struggles about human rights over the last three hundred years is impressive. His philosophical position is Leninist, with Hegelian affinities; his literary style is that of a polemical, and at times verbose, Brecht-Liebhaber.

59. *See* Klenner, *supra* note 57, at 101.

60. *Ibid.* at 102–3 and the discussion of Marx's internal criticism of bourgeois rights *infra.*

61. Elsewhere I have shown that Marx's analysis of the rights of man in his "On the Jewish Question" is deficient and much inferior to the economic analysis of rights in *Capital; see* my *Why Marx Scorns Civil and Political Rights* (Bergen: Chr. Michelsens Institutt. Publikasjoner, 1989 [in Norwegian]).

62. *Ibid.* at 61 and 101ff.

63. *Ibid.* at 104.

64. The above passage might, more profitably, be read to reflect the basic (but mostly nonexplicit) Marxist commitment to the value of human freedom interpreted as solitary self-realization of all members of global human society.

65. *Ibid.* at 105.

66. Steven Lukes, *Marxism and Morality* (Oxford: Oxford University Press, 1985), 61–70.

67. *See* Lindholm, *supra,* note 61, at chaps. 3 and 4.

68. In Dworkin's sense; *see* text to *supra* notes 44 and 45.

69. I do not expect Klenner or any orthodox Marxist to agree with my rejection of the Marxian "negation of the negation." But as far as I can see this is empty verbiage, from the beginning. I hold the intellectual undermining of the Marxian theory of Communism to be finished business. *See* Alec Nove, *The Economics of Feasible Socialism* (London: Allen & Unwin 1983), Leszek Kolakowski, *Main Currents of Marxism,* 3 vols. (Oxford: Clarendon Press, 1978), and *supra* note 57. Marx himself never developed his political theories to anything near the level of his economic diagnosis of capitalism.

70. Klenner, *supra* note 57 at 146.

71. *Ibid.* at 109.

72. *Ibid.* at 126 and 157.

73. *Ibid.* at 91.

74. *Ibid.* at 136 and 138. Klenner invokes the "Statuten und Reglement des Internationalen Arbeiterassoziation," ["Statutes and Rules of the International Association of Workers"] written by Marx, as indicating Marx's support for the "socialist" both-rights-and-duty doctrine, (at 145, his note 386). Klenner knows better. In his note 210 (at 84) he, correctly, uses the same reference to Marx (in volume 16 at 15 of Marx-Engels Werke; Berlin: Dietz Verlag, 1970) to clinch the point that Marx, who to his dismay had to write laudatory of "justice," "morality," "duty," and "rights" in the said statute, was himself allergic to such a "Ruckfall in die vorwissenschaftliche Zeit des Sozialismus."

75. Klenner *supra* note 57, at 2D, 179, 183 and 199.

76. For an excellent reconstruction of Marx's analysis of "social forms" (in contrast to their "material carriers"), *see* A. G. Cohen, *Karl Marx's Theory of History: A Defense* (Oxford: Oxford University Press, 1978), chap. 4. Marx's development of the *phusis/nomos* distinction for social critique is fertile.

77. In line with Marx in *The German Ideology* (Marx-Engels Werke, vol. 3, 1970), 394.

78. *See* Lindholm, *supra* note 61, at chap. 3. The main sociological points are addressed in part 2, *supra.*

79. The section on Marxist doctrines on human rights in this chapter, written well before the revolutionary upheavals in GDR in Fall 1989, was inspired by the following comment made by a GDR professor of international law (not Klenner!) when asked, in December 1988, about the novel theoretical departures in this area in the U.S.S.R., Poland, and Hungary: "Wir haben kein Grund gefunden, umzudenken." ["We have found no reason to rethink."] Subsequently such reasons—knock-down arguments, as it were—seem to have found their way to the non-rethinking.

80. *See supra* note 6.

81. Thanks are due to those who generously contributed comments and suggestions on an earlier draft: Bård-Anders Andreassen, Krzysztof Drzewicki, Stener Ekern, Donna Gomien, Rhoda Howard, Kjell Madsen, Ines Vargas, Jon Wetlesen, and above all, Abdullahi An-Naʿim.

Abdullahi Ahmed An-Naʿim

Conclusion

In this brief conclusion, I do not propose to offer a systematic summary of the conclusions of the various contributors to this book, or engage in a substantive discussion of their views. Instead, I wish to present somewhat personal reflections and tentatively suggest some issues for further examination. I believe that this approach to a concluding chapter is advisable to avoid misrepresentation or distortion of the view of the other contributors, as well as unnecessary repetition. Time constraints prevent me from consulting them on the appropriateness of the approach I am adopting here, but I expect that the other contributors will not object since I am not claiming that the following remarks represent anyone's views but my own.

My scholarly interest in questions of the cultural legitimacy for international standards of human rights emanates from my personal situation as a Muslim advocate of human rights. This personal situation forced me to focus on the obvious conflicts and tensions between international standards of human rights, on the one hand, and principles of Islamic Shariʿa (the comprehensive religious, ethical, and legal norms which purport to regulate the private and public lives of all Muslims), on the other. I started my inquiry about ten years ago, in an attempt to identify these conflicts and tensions clearly and candidly, and to seek ways of resolving them from an Islamic theoretical point of view. I undertook that effort in the belief that it is necessary to establish the Islamic legitimacy of international human rights standards, in order for Muslims to accept and implement them effectively. In due course, I came to describe my project as an attempt to promote the "cultural legitimacy of human rights" within the Muslim context. As my work progressed, however, I began to appreciate three factors that indicated to me that I need to revise and broaden my approach.

First, I found that I was taking too simplistic and formalistic a view of the current international standards of human rights. As I began to examine the rationale and content of these standards more closely, from a cross-cultural point of view, I became more appreciative of their bias. Like all normative principles, they are necessarily based on specific cultural and philosophical assumptions. Given the historical context within which the present standards have been formulated, it was unavoidable that they were initially based on Western cultural and philosophical assumptions. Although this orientation was somewhat modified during the international negotiation processes through which those standards were subsequently elaborated, the formative Western impact continues to influence the conception and implementation of human rights throughout the world.

In this connection, I became more sensitive to the fact that Western hegemony (in the economic, technological, intellectual, and other fields) profoundly influences ruling elites, as well as scholars and activists in the South or the Third World. Even in trying to resist this hegemony, we are reacting to its philosophical premises, rather than seeking to articulate our own indigenous ideas and concepts. Since we are just emerging from centuries of colonization by the West, and continue to suffer various types of dependencies on it, we have not yet had the opportunity to develop our own thinking on many fundamental philosophical and practical issues. Some Third World scholars have addressed some of the issues arising from this situation, and will probably continue to do so in their respective disciplines or fields of interest.

I am more greatly concerned with the specific implications of this situation for human rights scholarship. For example, I believe that it is important to note the impact or influence of the facts of international power relations when evaluating contributions of Third World delegates at international fora, including those where human rights instruments are negotiated and adopted. In view of what might be called a "human rights dependency," it is misleading to assume genuine representation of popular perceptions and attitudes toward human rights in our countries from the formal participation of "our delegates" to international fora. From the point of view of universal cultural legitimacy of international human rights standards, we should not assume from the fact that governmental delegates "participated" in their formulation and adoption that there is necessarily sufficiently broad popular acceptance of these standards, and commitment to their implementation, in our respective countries.

Second, upon taking the full range of the present international human rights standards, I find that all major cultural traditions of the world reject, or are at least hostile to, some of these rights and/or their implications. For example, Third World countries have insisted on, and achieved in collaboration with socialist countries at the time, recognition of individual economic and social rights and collective rights, such as the "right to self-determination," as human rights. Yet proponents of the Western liberal tradition(s) continue to resist granting human rights status to these rights and refuse to cooperate in their implementation. This liberal (cultural) position indicates to me that there is a strong need to promote the cultural legitimacy of human rights throughout the world, and not only within a Muslim context, which was the subject of my initial inquiry.

Third, I also began to appreciate the need to relate this approach to the concrete social, political, and economic circumstances of each society. I have never claimed that cultural factors are the sole determinants of human behavior. On the contrary, I have always assumed, albeit somewhat implicitly, that human rights performance is affected by structural economic, political, and other factors. In due course, however, I realized that even in relation to what might be called the cultural factor, the situation is much more complex than I had originally perceived. As I came to understand the concept of culture better and to work with it in its dynamic and interactive nature, I became more concerned with the political struggle for control of cultural resources and symbols. Achieving this control calls for concerted action within each culture to claim and maintain the moral and political high ground for human rights. From the scholarly point of view, this state of affairs indicates the need to develop an integrated, interdisciplinary methodology of internal and cross-cultural analysis of human rights issues in order to apply it to specific case studies.

In light of these factors and their implications, I am now convinced that the concept and practice of human rights is much more problematic than I had originally contemplated. In relation to my concern with the practical efficacy of international human rights standards in particular, I am now more sensitive to the existence of a serious tension between two basic perspectives. On the one hand, much of the authority of the concept is derived from its presumed or alleged universality—that is, the notion that human rights are the entitlements of all human beings throughout the world with no distinction as to race, gender, religion, and so on. It is generally conceded that the practical realization of some of these rights (especially those commonly known as economic, social, or cultural rights) is largely contingent on circumstances of wealth and economic infrastructure. But it is also generally assumed that such factors relate only to implementation of these particular rights, and not to the concept of human rights itself, and its content. On the other hand, it can be argued that universality may be, at best, more potential than actual, in view of the obvious conflicts and tensions between the current standards and specific cultural traditions. To the extent that culture significantly influences individual and institutional or collective behavior, such cultural antagonisms will hamper the practical implementation of those human rights not presently accepted by the particular culture.

Yet to note this discrepancy and to argue for the need to promote the cultural legitimacy of human rights in relation to specific cultural traditions is commonly taken by universalists to be an effort to undermine the efficacy of human rights. Apparently, universalists tend to assume that whoever speaks of actual or potential conflict between the presumed (or desirable) universality of human rights and the relativity of the concept and its content, in relation to specific culture(s), is either deliberately seeking to justify violation of human rights, or naively undermining their global efficacy. Cultural relativists, on the other hand, seem to interpret efforts which point out this discrepancy, and to argue for the need for the cultural legitimacy of human rights as a total repudiation of the universality of the present international standards. It seems to me, however, that either characterization of the issues is too simplistic and absolutist. I suggest a balanced, or middle-ground, position between these two extremes: the reality of relativity does not mean, in my view, that an acceptable degree of genuine universality cannot be achieved.

Universality and Relativity of the Concept of Human Rights

To my mind, the idea of human rights is one of the most characteristic phenomena of our time. Despite its very recent and limited origin, this concept has quickly gained global significance, penetrating into the consciousness of millions of people in every corner of the world. It is commonly claimed to be embodied in the ideologies of political and social movements; and there is a wide demand for it to be integrated into the foreign policy of nations and the decision-making processes of international donors or lending institutions. The mass media now routinely report on human rights issues; and scholars discuss them from various disciplinary perspectives. Some might even claim that this is an independent discipline, or will soon become one.

Yet the currency, the moral authority, and the great political force of this idea in fact conceal serious disagreements about its concept, rationale, and content. The almost mystical appeal of the idea of human rights may even be partly due to its ambiguity, in that it lends itself effectively to support different, sometimes even diametrically opposed, positions. While each person or group assumes that the concept denotes only what its proponents respectively understand or wish it to mean, they can use it to support their specific claims or demands; and governments can utilize it to legitimize their powers and policies, without serious fear of contradiction. No one needs to risk incurring the adverse consequences of rejecting the concept or openly refusing to comply with its dictates as long as its ambiguity allows them to retain their own views or objectives while appearing to comply with shared standards.

Ironically, the same ambiguity that makes the idea so useful and effective now is bound to reduce its moral authority and political force, hence diminishing its practical utility, in the long run. In fact, this may already be happening as the target constituencies become increasingly skeptical, because of the contradictions and double-standards exhibited by those who employ the term in national and international political discourse. It is therefore in the best interest of all those who take human rights seriously to clarify the concept and its content in order to improve practical implementation.

As I have briefly stated in my Introduction and have also argued in the first chapter, I believe that universal cultural legitimacy is essential for international standards of human rights. If international standards of human rights are to be implemented in a manner consistent with their own rationale, the people (who are to implement these standards) must perceive the concept of human rights and its content as their own. To be committed to carrying out human rights standards, people must hold these standards as emanating from their worldview and values, not imposed on them by outsiders. It would therefore necessarily follow that if, or to the extent that, the present concept and its content are not universally valid, we must try to make them so. Otherwise, those standards that are not accepted as culturally legitimate will remain ineffective unless we are prepared to contemplate attempts to impose these standards on people against their will!

It can be argued that there are two possible approaches to defining a universal concept of human rights that will be accepted and respected by all the peoples of the world. One approach is to extrapolate a universal concept through the interpretative reading of the existing international standards, on the assumption that these standards have already been accepted by the people of the world, through governmental ratification of the various human rights treaties. In its strict form, this approach is similar to exegesis of religious or constitutional texts seeking to discover the "original intent" of the author(s) of the text whose authority cannot be questioned at the stage of interpretation. The second approach is to derive a universal concept from globally shared norms and values, or from an understanding of notions such as human nature or dignity. The concept thereby developed will then be upheld irrespective of its consistency or inconsistency with any "original intent" that may be discovered from the interpretive reading of the existing international standards.

I suggest, however, that it is both possible and desirable to mix these two approaches by working on two fronts: one is that of the present international standards; the other, what might be called the cultural side of the equation. First, we must try to extrapolate, *as much as possible,* a universal concept through the interpretive reading of existing international standards, while being open to the possibility of revising these standards if necessary. This possibility of revision can then allow for the use of globally shared norms, values, and understandings to influence and refine the definition of the universal concept, which need not conform fully to preconceived notions of what it can or cannot be. Such a hybrid approach is based on the premise that it is neither advisable to discard the existing standards nor appropriate to uphold them in absolute terms. As explained in the Introduction, it is not advisable to discard the existing international human rights standards for three reasons: we may never recover the gains so far achieved through these standards; they are needed as a framework for discourse; and they provide necessary protection to activists and scholars. Nevertheless, as I have already explained, it is inappropriate to uphold these standards in absolute terms, irrespective of their problems with universal cultural legitimacy.

On the cultural side, each of us must work from within his or her culture to bridge the gap, *as much as possible,* between the present international standards, on the one hand, and the norms and values of the culture, on the other. Much can be achieved in this way because, as I indicated earlier and as has been emphasized by other contributors to this book, cultures are dynamic and changing, both internally and in response to external forces and influences. I believe that there are always alternative resources and positions within the culture that are closer to the present international standards than those perceived to be problematic from the point of view of those standards. For example, what is presented as the "official" or dominant cultural position, say, on the status and rights of women in the Islamic context, can probably be challenged in an internally legitimate and authentic manner from within the Islamic tradition itself.

The question remains, however, as to what is to be done when both these processes are exhausted without bringing about total agreement between the positions of the present international standards and a particular cultural tradition on a given issue. In Chapter 1, I attempted to deal with this ultimate challenge to my approach, but I wish to explore whether or not there may be a better answer to this question. This is therefore one of the issues I would suggest for further consideration.

Suggested Proposals for Research

In Chapter 15, Tore Lindholm discusses conceptual and procedural aspects of research on the cultural legitimacy of human rights, which provides an excellent framework and agenda for further work in this field. There is little point in reiterating or trying to summarize Lindholm's analysis and suggestions, but I wish to refer the reader to that chapter's formulation of agenda for research on the primary theme of this book. I wish to add for consideration, however, some issues arising out of my personal reflections presented above.

First, there is the question of the validity of my basic premises or assumptions. Inquiry into these premises could deal with questions such as the validity of the assumption that cultural legitimacy is essential for the implementation of international standards of human rights. Do people in fact behave, individually and collectively or institutionally, out of a cultural frame of reference, or is their behavior prompted by other considerations? Assuming that there are cultural as well as other determinants of, or contributors to, human behavior, what is the relative importance or significance of the cultural factor?

Second, assuming that my basic thesis is accepted as plausible, or at least as a working hypothesis, what *empirical evidence* is there in support of the three factors I mentioned at the beginning of this chapter? By empirical evidence I refer to hard empirical data on actual attitudes, perceptions, and practice rather than purely academic or theoretical analysis. Questions raised by this item of the agenda for research include the following: Is it true that there is a cultural bias in the present international human rights standards, and if so, what are its likely consequences? That is to say, is this bias, if it exists, purely theoretical, or does it have some practical consequences with regard to the implementation of human rights standards? Is it true that all major cultural traditions reject or resist some of the present international standards of human rights or their implications? Which standards are in fact rejected or resisted by which cultural traditions(s), in a practical rather than a theoretical sense? Finally, under this heading, how does cultural analysis relate to the concrete social, political, and economic circumstances of each society? For example, what is the nature and dynamics of the political struggle for control of cultural resources and symbols within the society? What factors influence the outcome of these struggles and how do they do so?

Third, and again assuming the utility of cultural analysis, what is the appropriate methodology for internal and cross-cultural analysis of human rights issues? For example, what methodological issues are raised by the two-tier approach I have suggested above? One set of methodological issues relates to the extrapolation of a universal concept of human rights from the present international standards: for instance, should this be based exclusively on the text of the final documents as ratified by governments or take into account the negotiation process leading to the final text? If the negotiation process is to be taken into account, what weight should be given to governmental positions, and what implications follow from those positions? Should governmental positions be taken at face value, or examined further to discover bargaining or other motives? Is it true, as I have suggested earlier, that international power relations in fact influence the bargaining and final voting positions of various governments, especially those of Third World countries? What is the significance, if any, of the nature of the political regime in power in a country like the Sudan, for example, at the time of various stages of the negotiation process? In other words, do delegates at these negotiations actually receive specific instructions from their governments reflecting the ideological orientation of the regime or government in power at the time? If so, does that vary with the nature and implications of the human rights treaty being negotiated, and how?

Another set of methodological issues relates to the cultural side of the equation. Are the processes of cultural dynamics and change in relation to human rights issues governed or regulated by some common general principles? If so, do these principles vary with political and economic circumstances of each society, and how? What is the role of internal and external factors and influences in this cultural change process? For example, in relation to the question of the status and rights of women in the Muslim context, how do internal and external factors influence the internal struggle in favor of an authentically Islamic position that will be at the same time more consistent with the present international standards of human rights?

Finally, there is the question of what is to be done when both processes of extrapolation from the international standards and internal cultural change fail to produce total agreement on a given issue, such as the matter of cruel, inhuman, or degrading treatment or punishment discussed in Chapter 1. Assuming that international agreement on the meaning of this human right is achieved among all except Muslim nations, should Muslims accept that meaning or insist on their irreducible cultural position? Should this choice vary from one issue to another; that is, should a society concede to international consensus on more or on less fundamental issues? What criteria should be applied to determine what is more or less fundamental?

Many further questions can be drawn from, or added to, the agenda I have set forth. My final recommendation is that, in view of the unacceptable discrepancy between the theory and practice of human rights today, every effort should be made to understand and redress the underlying reasons for the discrepancy. I believe that the proposed approach to promoting the cultural legitimacy of human rights has sufficient plausibility to warrant further investigation and consideration by scholars and activists throughout the world.

Bibliography

Abella, Irving, and Troper, Harold. *None Is Too Many: Canada and the Jews of Europe 1933–1948*. Toronto: Lester and Orfen Dennys, 1983.

Aki-Kew/Turpel, M. E. "Aboriginal Peoples and the Canadian Charter of Rights and Freedoms: Contradictions and Challenges," *Canadian Journal of Women's Studies* 10 (1989): 149–57.

Alford, William. "The Inscrutable Occidental: Roberto Unger's Uses and Abuses of the Chinese Past." *Texas Law Review* 64 (1986): 915.

———. "On the Limits of 'Grand Theory' in Comparative Law." *Washington Law Review* 61 (1986): 945.

———. "Seek Truth from Facts—Especially When They Are Unpleasant: America's Understanding of China's Efforts at Law Reform." *UCLA Pacific Basin Law Journal* 8 (1990): 177.

———. "Women Hold up Half the Sky, but Which Half? The Impact of China's Reforms on the Status of Women." Unpublished manuscript.

Allen, Paula G. *The Sacred Hoop: Recovering the Feminine in American Indian Traditions*. Boston: Beacon Press, 1986.

Alston, Philip. "Making Space for New Rights: The Case of the Right to Development." *Harvard Human Rights Yearbook* 1 (1988): 3–40.

American Indian Policy Review Commission, Final Report. Washington, D.C.: U.S. Government Printing Office, 1977.

Americas Watch Committee. *Human Rights in Peru after President Garcia's First Year*. New York: Americas Watch Committee, 1986.

———. *The Killings in Colombia: An Americas Watch Report*, 39–73. New York: Americas Watch Committee, 1989.

———. *Tolerating Abuses: Violations of Human Rights in Peru*. New York: Americas Watch Report, 1988.

Amnesty International. *Violations of Human Rights: Prisoners of Conscience and the Death Penalty in the People's Republic of China*, 24–27. London: Amnesty International, 1984.

An-Na'im, Abdullahi A. "Islamic Law, International Relations and Human Rights: Challenge and Response." *Cornell International Law Journal* 20 (1987): 317.

———. "Religious Minorities under Islamic Law and the Limits of Cultural Relativism." *Human Rights Quarterly* 9 (1987): 1–18.

———. *Toward an Islamic Reformation: Civil Liberties, Human Rights and International Law*. Syracuse: Syracuse University Press, 1990.

An-Na'im, Abdullahi A., and F. Deng, eds. *Human Rights in Africa: Cross-Cultural Perspectives*. Washington, D.C.: Brookings Institution, 1990.

Anti-Slavery Society. *Land and Justice: Aborigines Today.* London: Anti-Slavery Society, 1987.

Archambault, Jeane-Denis. *La Violacion de los Derechos Fundamentales y la Responsabilidad Civil de la Nacion Colombiana: La Estatizacion de la Violencia.* Colombia: Copycolor Editores Ltda., 1988.

Asch, M. I. "Capital and Economic Development: A Critical Appraisal of the Recommendations of the MacKenzie Valley Pipeline Commission." In *Native People, Native Lands,* ed. Bruce Alden Cox, 232–40. Ottawa: Carleton University Press, 1987.

Asch, M. "Wildlife: Defining the Animals the Dene Hunt and the Settlement of Aboriginal Land Claims." *Canadian Public Policy* 15 (1989) : 205.

Australian Institute of Multicultural Affairs. *Multiculturalism for All Australians,* 4, 15, 21, 24, 30–31. Canberra: Australian Government Publishing Service, 1982.

Australian Law Reform Commission. *The Recognition of Aboriginal Customary Laws.* Vol. 1. Canberra: Australian Government Publishing Service, 1986.

Barme, G., and J. Minford, eds. *Seeds of Fire, Chinese Voices of Conscience.* Hong Kong: Far Eastern Economic Review, 1986.

Barsh, R. "Navajo Property and Probate Law, 1940–1972." Unpublished manuscript. Forthcoming in *Law and Anthropology.*

Barth, F., ed. *Ethnic Groups and Boundaries.* Bergen: Universitesforlaget, 1969; London: Allen, 1969.

Baxi, Upendra. "Taking Suffering Seriously: Social Action Litigation in the Indian Supreme Court." *Review of the International Commission of Jurists* 29 (1982) : 37, 47, n. 35.

Beer, Lawrence W. "Japan." In *International Handbook of Human Rights,* ed. Jack Donnelly and Rhoda E. Howard, 209–26. New York: Greenwood Press, 1987.

Bell, Diane. "Aboriginal Women and Land: Learning From the Northern Territory Experience." *Anthropological Forum* 5, no. 2 (1984) : 357–58.

———. "Choose Your Mission Wisely: Christian Colonials and Aboriginal Marital Arrangements on the Northern Frontier." In *Aboriginal Australians and Christianity,* ed. D.B. Rose and T. Swain, 338–52. Adelaide: AASR, 1988.

———. "Exercising Discretion: Sentencing and Customary Law in the Northern Territory." In *Indigenous Law and the State,* ed. B. W. Morse and G. R. Woodman, 297–314. Providence, R.I.: Foris Publications, 1988.

Bell, Diane, and Pam Ditton. *Law: The Old and the New.* Canberra: Aboriginal History for Central Australian Aboriginal Legal Aid, 1980.

Bell, Diane, with Topsy Napurrala Nelson. "Speaking About Rape Is Everyone's Business." *Women's Studies International Forum* 12 (1989) : 411–14.

Benedict, Ruth. *Patterns of Culture.* Boston: Houghton Mifflin Co., 1959.

Berger, Peter, Brigitte Berger, and Hansfried Kellner. *The Homeless Mind: Modernization and Consciousness.* New York: Vintage Books, 1973.

Berkhofer, Robert F., Jr. *The White Man's Indian: Images of the American Indian from Columbus to the Present.* New York: Vintage Books, 1979.

Bird, G. *The Process of Law in Australia: Multicultural Perspectives*. Sydney: Butterworths, 1988.

———. *The Process of Law in Australia: Intercultural Perspectives*. Sydney: Butterworths, 1988.

Black, W. W. *Employment Equity: A Systemic Approach*. Ottawa: Human Rights Research and Education Centre, 1985.

Blackstone, W. *Commentaries on the Laws of England*, ed. St. George Tucker. Vol. 1. Philadelphia: Par, Birch and Small, 1803; rpt. Oxford: Clarendon Press, 1765–1769.

Blaustein, A. P., and G. H. Flanz, eds. *Constitutions of the Countries of the World*. Dobbs Ferry, N. Y.: Oceana Publications, updated periodically. Looseleaf.

Boldt, Menno, and J. Anthony Long. "Tribal Philosophies and the Canadian Charter of Rights and Freedoms." *Ethnic and Racial Studies* 7 (1984): 478–93.

Boldt, M., and J. A. Long, eds. *The Quest for Justice: Aboriginal Peoples and Aboriginal Rights*. Toronto: University of Toronto Press, 1985.

Bossuyt, M. J. *Guide to the "Travaux Preparatoires" of the International Covenant on Civil and Political Rights*. Dordrecht: Martinus Nijhoff, 1987.

Brazil, P., and B. Mitchell, eds. *Opinions of Attorney-General of the Commonwealth of Australia*. Vol. 1, 24. Canberra: Australian Government Publishing Service, 1981.

Brenkert, George. "Marx and Human Rights." *Journal of the History of Philosophy* 24 (1986): 55–77.

Brennan, F., and J. Crawford. *Aboriginality, Recognition and Australian Law: Where to Go from Here*. Twenty-sixth Australian Legal Convention paper, mimeo, 1989.

Bridges, B. *The Extension of English Law to the Aborigines for Offences Committed Inter Se, 1829–1842, J.R.A.H.S.* 59 (1973): 264.

Brierly, James L. *The Law of Nations: An Introduction to the International Law of Peace*. New York: Oxford University Press, 1963.

Brown, Joseph Epes. *The Spiritual Legacy of the American Indian*. New York: Crossroad, 1982.

Brownlie, Ian, ed. *Basic Documents on Human Rights*. 2nd ed. Oxford: Clarendon Press, 1981.

———. *Principles of Public International Law*. Oxford: Clarendon Press, 1966.

Brownmiller, Susan. *Against Our Will: Men, Women and Rape*. New York: Simon and Schuster, 1975.

———. *Femininity*. New York: Fawcett Columbine, 1984.

Brunner, José Joaquin. "America Latina entre la Cultura Democratica y la Cultura Autoritaria: Legados y Desafios." *Revista Paraguaya de Sociologia* 24 (1987): 7–15.

———. "La Concepcion Autoritaria del Mundo." *Documento de Trabajo* FLACSO (1979).

———. "Los Debates Sobre la Modernidad y el Futarode America Latino." *Documento de Trabajo* FLACSO, No. 293 (April 1986).

Bryde, John F. *Modern Indian Psychology*. Vermillion, S.D.: Institute of Indian Studies, University of South Dakota, 1971.

Buchanan, Allen. "Assessing the Communitarian Critique of Liberalism." *Ethics* 99 (1989): 856–57.
Butlin, N. G. *Our Original Aggression: Aboriginal Populations of South-Eastern Australia 1788–1850.* Sydney: Allen and Unwin, 1983.

Calloway, C. G., ed. *New Directions in American Indian History.* Norman: University of Oklahoma Press, 1988.
Canadian Commission for UNESCO. *A Working Definition of Culture for the Canadian Commission for UNESCO*, 6 (1977).
Canby, William. *American Indian Law in a Nutshell.* Saint Paul, Minn.: West Publishing Co., 1981.
Cantin, Eileen. *Mounier, A Personalist View of History.* New York: Paulist Press, 1973.
Capotorti, Francesco. *Study on the Rights of Persons Belonging to Ethnic, Religious and Linguistic Minorities.* New York: United Nations, 1979.
Capps, Walter Holden, ed. *Seeing With a Native Eye.* New York: Harper and Row, 1976.
Carignan, Pierre. "De la notion de droit Collectif et de son application en matière scolaire au Quebec," *Thimis* 18 (1984): 91–92.
Carreno, Edmundo Vargas. "Las Observaciones in Loco Practicadas por la Comision Interamericana de Derechos Humanos." In *Inter-American Commission on Human Rights* (IACHR), *Human Rights in the Americas*, 290–305. Washington, D.C.: Organización de los Estados Americanos, 1984.
Cassidy, F., and R. L. Bish. "Aboriginal Governments in Canada: An Emerging Field of Study." *Canadian Journal of Political Science*, 23 (1990): 73–99.
———. *Indian Government: Its Meaning in Practice.* Montreal: Oolichan Books and Institute for Research in Public Policy, 1989.
Chisholm, R. "Aboriginal Children and the Placement Principle." *A.L.B.* 31 (1988): 4.
Christie, M. *Aborigines in Colonial Victoria 1835–1886.* Sydney: Sydney University Press, 1979.
Clark, Geoff. "Statement During the ILO Conference 1988." *Aboriginal Law Bulletin* 2 (1988): 13.
Clifford, James. *The Predicament of Culture: Twentieth-Century Ethnography, Literature and Art.* Cambridge, Mass.: Harvard University Press, 1988.
Cobb, Richard, and Colin Jones, eds. *Voices of the French Revolution.* Topsfield, Mass.: Salem House, 1988.
Cohen, A. *Custom and Politics in Urban Africa.* (London: Routledge and Kegan Paul, 1969.
Cohen, Felix S. *Handbook of Federal Indian Law* (Charlottesville, Va.: Mitchie and Bobbs-Merrill, 1982).
Cohen, G. A. *History, Labour and Freedom.* Oxford: Clarendon Press, 1988.
Cohen, G. A. *Karl Marx's Theory of History.* Oxford: Clarendon Press, 1978.
Cohen, J. *The Criminal Process in the People's Republic of China, 1949–1963: An Introduction.* Cambridge, Mass.: Harvard University Press, 1968.

Collier, David, ed. *The New Authoritarianism in Latin America.* Princeton, N.J.: Princeton University Press, 1979.

Comision Especial del Senado sobre las Causas de la Violencia y Alternativas de Pacificacion en el Peru. *Violencia y Pacificacion,* 269–86. Lima: DESCO y la Comision Andina de Juristas, 1989.

Committee on Foreign Affairs. *Human Rights Documents.* Washington, D.C.: United States Government Printing Office, 1983.

Commonwealth of Australia. *1986 Report of Australia under the Convention on the Elimination of Discrimination Against Women.* Canberra: Australian Government Publishing Service, 1986.

Connolly, P. D. "The Adversary System—Is It Any Longer Appropriate?" *Australian Law Journal* 49 (1975): 439–42.

Constitutional Commission, Committee on Individual and Democratic Rights. *Report.* Canberra: Australian Government Publishing Service, 1987.

Convention on the Rights of the Child: Text of the Draft Convention. Doc E/CN.4/1989/29, 30 December 1988.

Correa, Enrique, and Viera Gallo, Jose Antonio. *Iglesia y Dictadura.* Santiago: CESOC-Ediciones Chile y America, 1986.

Cotler, Julio. "State and Regime: Comparative Notes on the Southern Cone and the 'Enclave Societies.'" In *The New Authoritarianism in Latin America,* ed. David Collier, 265. Princeton, N.J.: Princeton University Press, 1979.

Cotler, Julio. "La Cultura politica de la Juventud Popular del Peru." In *Cultura Politica y Democratizacion,* ed. Norbert Lechner, 127–45. Buenos Aires: CLACSO, 1987.

Cox, Bruce Alden. "Changing Perceptions of Industrial Development in the North." In *Native People, Native Lands: Canadian Indians, Inuit and Metis,* ed. Bruce Alden Cox, 223–31. Ottawa: Carleton University Press, 1988.

Crahan, Margaret E. "The Evolution of the Military in Brazil, Chile, Peru, Venezuela and Mexico: Implications for Human Rights." In *Human Rights and Basic Needs in the Americas,* ed. Margaret E. Crahan, 46–99. Washington, D.C.: Georgetown University Press, 1982.

———. "A Multitude of Voices: Religion and the Central American Crisis." Mimeo on file at the Program on Human Rights of the Academy of Christian Humanism, 1987.

———. "National Security Ideology and Human Rights." In *Human Rights and Basic Needs in the Americas,* ed. Margaret E. Crahan, 101–27. Washington, D.C.: Georgetown University Press, 1982.

Cranston, Maurice. "Human Rights, Real and Supposed." In *Political Theory and the Rights of Man,* ed. D. D. Raphael. Bloomington, Ind.: Indiana University Press, 1967.

Crapanzano, Vincent. *Waiting: The Whites of South Africa.* New York: Vintage Books, 1986.

Crawford, J. *The Creation of States in International Law.* Oxford: Clarendon Press, 1979.

———. "International Law and the Recognition of Aboriginal Customary Laws."

In *International Law and Aboriginal Human Rights,* ed. B. Hocking, 43. Sydney: Law Book, 1988.

———. *Legal Pluralism and The Indigenous People of Australia.* Mimeo, 1989.

Crouch, A. "The Way, The Truth and The Right to Interpreters in Court." *Law Institute Journal* 59 (1985) : 687, 689–90.

Cumming, Peter A., and Neil H. Mickenberg, eds. *Native Rights in Canada.* Toronto: Indian-Eskimo Association of Canada in association with General Publishing Co., 1972/1977.

da Cunha, M. C. "Ethicidade: da cultura, residual mas irredutível." In *Antropologia do Brasil: Mito, Historia, Etnicidade.* São Paulo: Brasiliense, 1986.

———. "Native Realpolitik." *NACLA Report On The Americas* 23 (1989) : 19–22.

———. *Negros, Estrangeiros: Os escravos libertos e sua volta à Africa.* São Paulo: Brasiliense, 1985.

———. "Silences of the Law: Customary Law and Positive Law on the Manumission of Slaves in Nineteenth Century Brazil." *The Discourse of Law, History and Anthropology* 1, no. 2 (1985): 427–44.

Dagmar, H. *Aborigines and Poverty: A Study of Inter-ethnic Relations and Culture Conflict in W.A. Town.* Nijmegen: Katholicke Universiteit, 1978.

Dahrendorf, Ralf. *The Modern Social Conflict.* London: Weidenfeld and Nicolson, 1988.

Daly, Mary. *Gyn/Ecology: The Metaethics of Radical Feminism.* Boston: Beacon Press, 1978.

Dassa, Shiraz. "What Rushdie Knew." *Cross Currents* 39 (1989) : 204–12.

Davies, Maureen. "Aspects of Aboriginal Rights in International Law," and "Aboriginal Rights in International Law: Human Rights." In *Aboriginal Peoples and the Law: Indian, Metis and Inuit Rights in Canada,* ed. B. Morse, 16–47 and 745–94, respectively. Ottawa: Carleton University Press, 1985.

Davis, Morris, and Krauter, Joseph F. *The Other Canadians: Profiles of Six Minorities.* Toronto: Methuen, 1971.

Dawidowicz, Lucy S. *The War against the Jews: 1933–1945.* New York: Bantam Books, 1975.

Day, S. "Equality Seekers Troubled by Affirmative Action Rulings." *Canadian Human Rights Advocate* 6, no. 1 (January 1990).

Daylight, Phyllis, and Mary, Johnstone. *Women's Business: Report of the Aboriginal Women's Task Force.* Canberra: Australian Government Publishing Service, 1986.

Dealy, Glen. "Prolegomena on the Spanish American Political Tradition." In *Politics and Social Change in Latin America: The Distinct Tradition,* ed. Howard J. Wiarda, 163–83. Amherst, Mass.: University of Massachusetts Press, 1982.

———. "The Tradition of Monistic Democracy in Latin America." In *Politics and Social Change in Latin America. The Distinct Tradition,* ed. Howard J. Wiarda, 75–107. Amherst, Mass.: University of Massachusetts Press, 1982.

Deas, Erica I. A. Confidential Report on Visit to Australia, 12 December 1987–2 January 1988, and 7–22 January 1988. Chairperson-Rapporteur of the United Nations Working Group on Indigenous Populations, 1988; para. 99.

————. Rapporteur UN Working Group on Indigenous Populations, Report on Visit to Australia, 12 December–2 January and 7–22 January 1988. Mimeo, April 1988; 12, 26.

de Beauvoir, Simone. *The Second Sex.* New York: Modern Library, 1968.

Deloria, Vine. *God is Red.* New York: Dell, 1973.

Department of Aboriginal Affairs. *Aboriginal Tenure and Land Population.* Canberra: Department of Aboriginal Affairs, 1986.

Despres, L., ed. *Ethnicity and Resource Competition in Plural Societies.* The Hague: Mouton, 1975.

de Valdez, Patricia T. "Las Organizaciones Nogubernamentales de Derechos Humanos en Peru." Unpublished manuscript.

Diamond, Larry, and Juan J. Linz. "Introduction: Politics, Society, and Democracy in Latin America." In *Democracy in Developing Countries.* Larry Diamond and Juan J. Linz, eds. Boulder, CO: L. Rienner; London: Adamantine Press, 1988.

Disabled Natives and the Law, March 10/90, Special issue, *Just Cause* 3, no. 1 (Fall 1985).

Dixon, R. Hogan, and A. Wierzbicka. "Interpreters: Some Basic Problems." *Legal Service Bulletin* 5 (1980) : 162.

Donnelly, Jack. *The Concept of Human Rights.* London: Croom Helm, 1985.

————. "Cultural Relativism and Universal Human Rights." *Human Rights Quarterly* 6 (1984) : 400.

————. "Human Rights and Human Dignity: An Analytic Critique of Non-Western Conceptions of Human Rights." *American Political Science Review* 76 (1982) : 303.

————. "Human Rights and Western Liberalism." In *Human Rights in Africa: Cross-Cultural Perspectives,* ed. Abdullahi A. An-Na'im and F. Deng. Washington D.C.: Brookings Institution, 1990.

————. "Human Rights as Natural Rights." *Human Rights Quarterly* 4 (1982) : 391–405.

Dore, Elizabeth, and John F. Weeks. "Economic Performance and Basic Needs: The Examples of Brazil, Chile, Mexico, Nicaragua, Peru and Venezuela." In *Human Rights and Basic Needs in the Americas,* ed. Margaret E. Crahan, 152–53. Washington, D.C.: Georgetown University Press, 1982.

Douglas, Mary. *Purity and Danger: An Analysis of the Concepts of Pollution and Taboo.* London: Routledge and Kegan Paul, 1966.

Downing, T., and G. Kushner, eds. *Human Rights and Anthropology.* Cambridge, Mass.: Cultural Survival Report 24, 1988.

Drache, D., and D. Cameron. *The Other MacDonald Report.* Toronto: James Lorimer, 1985.

Duram, W. Cole, Jr. "Indian Law in the Continental United States: An Overview" *Law and Anthropology* 2 (1987) : 93–112.

Dworkin, Ronald. *Law's Empire.* Cambridge, Mass.: Harvard University Press, 1986.

————. *A Matter of Principle.* Cambridge, Mass.: Harvard University Press, 1985.

————. *Taking Rights Seriously.* London: Duckworth Press, 1977.

Dyck, Noel. "Aboriginal Peoples and the Nation-States: An Introduction to the Analytical Issues." In *Indigenous Peoples and the Nation State: Fourth World Politics in Canada, Australia and Norway,* ed. Noel Dyck, 1–26 and 236–41. St. John's, Nfld.: Institute of Social and Economic Research, 1985.

Edwards, R. "Ch'ing Legal Jurisdiction Over Foreigners." In *Essays on China's Legal Tradition,* ed. J. Cohen, R. Edwards, and F. Chang Chen, 222. Princeton, N.J.: Princeton University Press, 1980.

Eggleston, E. *Fear, Favour or Affection.* Canberra: Australia National University Press, 1976.

El-Awa, Mohamed S. *Punishment in Islamic Law.* Indianapolis, Ind.: American Trust Publications, 1982.

Elias, Robert T. *The Politics of Victimization.* New York: Oxford University Press, 1986.

Ellis, John. *Social History of the Machine Gun.* New York: Pantheon Books, 1975.

Encyclopedia Judaica. Vol. 5, 142–47; and vol. 6, 991–93. Jerusalem: Keter Publishing House, 1971.

Encyclopedia of Public International Law. Amsterdam, New York, Oxford: North-Holland Publishing, 1985.

Engels, Friedrich. *Anti-Dühring.* Moscow: Foreign Languages, 1954.

Esprit, vol. 13, n.s., nos. 1–6 (December 1944–May 1945): 119–27, 581–90, 696–708, 850–56.

Evans, R., K. Sanders, and K. Cronin. *Exclusion, Exploitation and Extermination: Race Relations in Colonial Queensland.* Sydney: A.N.Z. Book Co., 1973.

Evatt, Elizabeth. "Discrimination Against Women: The United Nations and CEDAW." In *Human Rights: The Australian Debate,* ed. Lynne Spender, 27–38. Redfern: Redfern Legal Centre Publications, published with the assistance of the Law Faculty of the University of New South Wales, 1987.

Executive Board of the American Anthropological Association, "Statement on Human Rights." *American Anthropologist* 49 (1947): 539.

Fairbank, John King. *The Great Chinese Revolution: 1800–1985.* New York: Harper and Row, 1986.

Fawcett, James. *The International Protection of Minorities.* London: Minority Rights Group, 1979.

Fein, Helen. *Accounting for Genocide: National Responses and Jewish Victimization during the Holocaust.* Chicago: University of Chicago Press, 1979.

Fernbach, David, ed. *Surveys from Exile.* Harmondsworth: Penguin, 1974.

Fischel, W. *The End of Extraterritoriality in China.* Berkeley and Los Angeles: University of California Press, 1952.

Fiske, Jo-Ann. "Fishing Is Women's Business: Changing Economic Roles of Women and Men." In *Native People, Native Lands: Canadian Indians, Inuit and Metis,* ed. Bruce Alden Cox, 186–98. Ottawa: Carleton University Press, 1988.

Fiss, Owen M. "Groups and the Equal Protection Clause." *Philosophy and Public Affairs* 5 (1976): 148.

Forsythe, W. *Cases and Opinions on Constitutional Law.* London: Stevens and Haymes, 1869.

Fox, Matthew. *The Cosmic Christ.* New York: Harper and Row, 1988.

———. "Is the Catholic Church Today a Dysfunctional Family? A Pastoral Letter to Cardinal Ratzinger and the Whole Church." *Creation* 4 (1988): 23–28.

Friedman, E. *Backward Toward Revolution.* Berkeley and Los Angeles: University of California Press, 1974.

Fruhling, Hugo. "Liberalismo y Derecho en Chile." In *Ensayes.* Santiago: Editorial Debates, 1978.

———. "Modalidades de la Represion Politica en el Cono Sur de America Latina." RIAL Conference Paper, 1987, mimeographed.

———. "Nonprofit Organizations as Opposition to Authoritarian Rule: The Case of Human Rights Organizations in Chile." In *The Nonprofit Sector in International Perspective,* ed. Estelle James, 358–76. New York: Oxford University Press, 1989.

———. "Repressive Policies and Legal Dissent in Authoritarian Regimes: Chile 1973–1981," *International Journal of the Sociology of Law* 12 (1984): 351–74.

Fuller, Lon. "Two Principles of Human Association." In *Voluntary Associations: Nomos XI,* ed. J. Pennock and J. Chapman. New York: Athcuton Press, 1969.

Garet, R. "Communality and Existence: The Rights of Groups." *Southern California Law Review* 56 (1983): 1001.

Gastile, George P., and Gilbert Kushner, eds. *Persistent Peoples: Cultural Enclaves in Perspective.* Tucson, Ariz.: University of Arizona Press, 1981.

Geertz, Clifford. "Distinguished Lecture: Anti Anti-Relativism." *American Anthropologist* 86 (1984): 263–65.

———. *Interpretation of Culture.* New York: Basic Books, 1973.

Geras, Norman. *Marx & Human Nature.* London: New Left Books, 1983.

Getches, D., D. Rosenfelt, and C. Wilkinson. *Cases and Materials on Federal Indian Law.* St. Paul, Minn.: West Publishing Co., 1986.

Gibson, Charles. "Spanish Indian Policies." In *History of Indian-White Relations,* vol. 4, ed. Wilcomb E. Washburn. *Handbook of North American Indians,* gen. ed. William C. Sturtevant, 96–102. Washington, D.C.: Smithsonian Institution, 1988.

Gilbreath, K. *Red Capitalism: An Analysis of the Navajo Economy.* Microfiche reprint, 1973.

Gilio, Maria Esther. *The Tupamaro Guerrillas: The Structure and Strategy of the Urban Guerrilla Movement.* New York: Saturday Review Press, 1972.

Gillespie, Charles, et al., eds. *Uruguay y la Democracia.* 3 vols. Montevideo: Wilson Center Latin American Program/Ediciones de la Banda Oriental, 1985.

Gillespie, Richard. *Soldados de Peron: Los Montoneros.* Buenos Aires: Grijalbo, 1982.

Goffman, Erving. "The Nature of Deference and Demeanor." In *Three Sociological Traditions: Selected Readings,* ed. Randall Collins, 215–32. New York: Oxford University Press, 1985.

———. *Stigma.* Englewood Cliffs, N.J.: Prentice-Hall, 1963.

Gonyea, R. "Introduction" In *Onondaga-Portrait of a Native People,* ed. Fred Ry-
ther Wolcott, 11–32. Syracuse: Syracuse University Press, 1986.

Goody, J. *The Domestication of the Savage Mind.* Cambridge: Cambridge University
Press, 1977.

Goody, J., ed. *Literacy in Traditional Societies.* Cambridge: Cambridge University
Press, 1968.

Gordon, Bennett. *Aboriginal Rights in International Law.* London: Royal Anthropological Institute of Great Britain and Ireland, 1978.

Gordon, Milton M. "Towards a General Theory of Racial and Ethnic Group Relations." In *Ethnicity: Theory and Experience,* ed. Nathan Glazer and Daniel
Moynihan, 84–110. Cambridge, Mass.: Harvard University Press, 1975.

Gordon, S. "Indian Religious Freedom and Government Development of Public
Lands." *Yale Law Journal* 94 (1985):1447.

Gough, Whitlam. "Australia's International Obligations." In *Human Rights for
Aboriginal People in the '80s,* ed. G. Nettheim, 12–22. Sydney: Legal Books,
1983.

Government of North-West Territories. *Consultation Paper: Proposed Human Rights
Code for the Northwest Territories.* Yellowknife: Government of the North-West
Territories, 1984.

Gray, A., and L. Smith. "The Size of the Aboriginal Population," *Australian Aboriginal Studies* 1 (1983):2.

Green, Leslie. "Are Language Rights Fundamental?" *Osgoode Hall Law Journal* 25
(1987):639–69.

Habermas, Jürgen. *The Theory of Communicative Action: Lifeworld and System.* Boston: Beacon Press, 1989.

Haile, Father Berard, O.F.M. *Women Versus Men: A Conflict of Navajo Emergence—The Curly Tó Aheedlíinii Version,* ed. Karl W. Luckert. Navajo orthography by Irvy W. Goossen. Lincoln and London: University of Nebraska
Press, 1981.

Hand, Gerry. "Foreword." In *International Law and Aboriginal Human Rights,* ed.
Barbara Hocking. Sydney: Law Book Company, 1988.

Hanke, Lewis. *Aristotle and the American Indians: A Study in Race Prejudice in the
Modern World.* Chicago: Henry Regnery, 1959.

Hanks, P., and B. Keon-Cohen, eds., *Aborigines & The Law: Essays in Memory of
Elizabeth Eggleston.* London: Allen and Unwin, 1984.

Hannum, H. "New Developments in Indigenous Rights." *Virginia Journal of International Law* 28 (1988):663–64.

Harden, I., and N. Lewis. *The Noble Lie: The British Constitution and the Rule of
Law.* London: Hutchinson, 1986.

Harris, Grace G. "Concepts of Individual, Self and Person in Description and
Analysis," *American Anthropologist* 91 (1989):599–612.

Hart, H.L.A. *The Concept of Law.* Oxford: Oxford University Press, 1961.

Harvard Law Review Association. *Essays on Critical Legal Studies.* Cambridge,
Mass.: Harvard Law Review Association, 1986.

Hatch, Elvin. *Culture and Morality: The Relativity of Values in Anthropology.* New York: Columbia University Press, 1983.

Heller, Agnes. *The Theory of Need in Marx.* London: Allison & Busby, 1976.

Hellman, John. *Emmanuel Mounier and the New Catholic Left 1930–1950.* Toronto, University of Toronto Press, 1981.

Henderson, R., A. Harcourt, and F. Harper. *People in Poverty: A Melbourne Survey.* Melbourne: Cheshire, 1970.

Herskovits, Melville J. *Cultural Dynamics.* New York: Alfred A. Knopf, 1964.

Hobbes, Thomas. *Leviathan.* Edited with an introduction by C. B. Macpherson. Harmondsworth: Penguin Books, 1968.

Holmes, Helen Bequaert. "A Feminist Analysis of the Universal Declaration of Human Rights." In *Beyond Domination: New Perspectives on Women and Philosophy,* ed. Carol C. Gould, 250–64. Totowa, N.J.: Roman and Allanheld, 1983.

Honig, E., and G. Hershatter. *Personal Voices: Chinese Women in the 1980's,* 323–25. Stanford, Calif.: Stanford University Press, 1988.

Honor, A. M. "Groups, Laws, and Obedience." In *Oxford Essays in Jurisprudence,* ed. A.W.B. Simpson. Oxford: University Press, 1973.

———. "What is a Group?" *Archiv für Rechts-und Sozialphilosophie* 61, no. 2 (1975):168.

Hooker, M. B. *Legal Puralism: An Introduction to Colonial and Neo-Colonial Laws.* Oxford: Clarendon Press, 1975.

House of Commons. Select Committee on Aborigines (British Settlements), *Report,* Parliamentary Paper, no. 425, 1837; 5–6. Cited in Australian Law Reform Commission, Report 31, *The Recognition of Aboriginal Customary Laws.* Canberra, 1986. Vol. 1, para. 109.

Howard, J. "Treaty is a Recipe for Separation." In *A Treaty with the Aborigines?* Institute of Public Affairs, *Policy Issues* no. 7 (1988).

Howard, Joseph K. *Strange Empire: Louis Riel and the Metis People.* Toronto: James Lewis and Samuel, 1952.

Howard, Rhoda. *Human Rights in Commonwealth Africa.* Totowa, N.J.: Rowman and Littlefield, 1986.

———. "Entrepreneurship and Economic Development: A Critique of the Theory." M.A. thesis, Department of Sociology, McGill University, 1972.

———. "Is There an African Concept of Human Rights?" In *Foreign Policy and Human Rights,* ed. R. J. Vincent. Cambridge: Cambridge University Press, 1986.

Howard, Rhoda E., and Jack Donnelly. "Human Dignity, Human Rights and Political Regimes." *American Political Science Review* 80 (1986):801.

———. "Introduction." In *International Handbook of Human Rights,* ed. J. Donnelly and R. E. Howard. New York: Greenwood Press, 1988.

Huggins, Jackie. "International Indigenous Women's Conference." *Australian Feminist Studies* 11 (1990):113–14.

Hultkrantz, Ake. *The Religions of the American Indians.* Trans. Monica Selterwall. Berkeley: University of California Press, 1979.

Laslett, Peter. *The World We Have Lost—Further Explored.* London: Methuen, 1983.

Leacock, E., ed. *The Culture of Poverty: A Critique.* New York: Simon and Schuster, 1971.

Lechner, Norbert. "De la Revolucion a la Democracia: El Debate Intelectual en America del Sur." *Opciones* 6 (1985): 57–72.

Legal Information Service, Native Law Centre, University of Saskatchewan. *Customs, Immigration and the Jay Treaty, Report No. 4.* Saskatoon: Native Law Centre, 1981.

Lenin, V. "State and Revolution." Reprinted in *Essential Works of Marxism,* ed. A. Mendel. New York: Bantam Books, 1961.

Lerner, Gerda. *The Creation of Patriarchy.* New York: Oxford University Press, 1986.

Lesser, Alexander. "The Right Not to Assimilate: The Case of the American Indian." In *History, Evolution, and the Concept of Culture,* ed. S. Mintz, 108. New York: Cambridge University Press, 1985.

Levine, Daniel H. "Continuities in Colombia." *Journal of Latin American Studies* 17 (1985): 295–317.

Levine, Stuart. "The Survival of Indian Identity." In *The American Indian Today,* Stuart Levin and Nancy O. Lurie, eds. Baltimore, MD: Penguin Books, 1970.

Lifton, Robert Jay. *The Nazi Doctors: Medical Killing and the Psychology of Genocide.* New York: Basic Books, 1986.

Lindholm, Tore. "Article One: A New Beginning." In *The Universal Declaration of Human Rights, A Commentary Article by Article,* ed. Asbjorn Eide and Göran Melander. Oslo: The Norwegian Institute of Human Rights, 1991.

———. *Why Marx Scorns Civil and Political Rights.* Bergen: Chr. Michelsens Institutt. Publikasjoner, 1989 (in Norwegian).

Lipset, Seymour Martin Lipset. *Democracy in Developing Countries: Latin America.* Boulder, Colo., and London: Lynne Rienner Publishers, Adamantine Press Limited, 1989.

Lizhi, Fang. *Women zhengzai xieli shi* [My Collected Speeches and Writings]. Taipei: Reprint, 1987.

Locke, John. *A Letter Concerning Toleration.* Introduction by P. Romanell. Indianapolis: Bobbs-Merrill, 1955.

Lukács, G. *History and Class Consciousness: Studies in Marxist Dialectics.* Cambridge, Mass.: MIT Press, 1971.

Lukes, Steven. *Marxism and Morality.* Oxford: Oxford University Press, 1985.

———. *Power.* London: Macmillan, 1974.

Maalouf, Amin. *Leo Africanus.* New York: Norton.

MacCormack, N. *Legal Right and Social Democracy: Essays in Legal and Political Philosophy,* 261. Oxford: Oxford University Press, 1982.

MacKinnon, Catherine A. *Toward A Feminist Theory of the State.* Cambridge, Mass.: Harvard University Press, 1989.

Macpherson, C. B. "Problems of Human Rights in the Late Twentieth Century." In *The Rise and Fall of Economic Justice.* Oxford: Oxford University Press, 1987.

Mansell, M. Options, Seminar Report, *Aboriginal Peoples and Treaties.* Sydney: CCI, 1989.

Maritain, Jacques. *Man and the State*. Chicago: University of Chicago Press, 1951.

————. *The Rights of Man and Natural Law*. London: Geoffrey Bles, 1958.

————. *True Humanism*. London: Geoffrey Bles, 1959.

Marule, M. Smallface. "Traditional Indian Government: Of the People, by the People, for the People." In *Pathways to Self-Determination-Canadian Indians and the Canadian State*, ed. L. Little Bear, M. Boldt, and J. A. Long, 36–45. Toronto: University of Toronto Press, 1984.

Marx, Karl. "The British Rule in India." In *Surveys from Exile*, ed. David Fernbach, 301–07. Harmondsworth: Penguin, 1974.

————. *Capital*. Vol. 1. London: Penguin, 1976.

————. *The Communist Manifesto*, part 1. In *Collected Works*, ed. Karl Marx and Friedrich Engels. London: Lawrence & Wishart, 1976.

————. "Contribution to the Critique of Hegel's Philosophy of Law. Introduction." Vol. 3, *Collected Works*, 175–76.

————. *Economic & Philosophic Manuscripts*. In Karl Marx and Friedrich Engels, *Collected Works*, vol. 3, 306–26.

————. "Forced Emigration." In *Collected Works*, vol. 11, 530–31.

————. *The German Ideology*. In Marx and Engels, *Collected Works*, vol. 3, 1970.

————. "Inaugural Address of the Working Men's International Association." In *The Marx-Engels Reader*, ed. Robert C. Tucker. 2nd ed., 512–19. New York: Norton, 1978

————. *On Colonialism*. New York: International Publishers, 1974.

————. "On the Jewish Question." In *The Marx-Engels Reader*, ed. Robert C. Tucker. 2nd ed., 26–52. New York: Norton, 1978.

————. *Theories of Surplus Value*, vol. 1, 367. Moscow: Progress Publishers, 1956.

Mascia-Less, Francis E., Patricia Sharpe, and Colleen Ballerino Cohen. "The Postmodernist Turn in Anthropology: Caution from a Feminist Perspective." *Signs* 15 (1989): 7–33.

Mathews, J. "Protection of Minorities and Equal Opportunities." *University of New South Wales Law Journal* 11 (1988): 23.

————. "Protection of Minorities and Equal Opportunities." *University of New South Wales Law Journal* 11 (1988): 1.

McBride, William. "Rights and the Marxian Tradition." *Praxis International* 4 (1982): 54–74.

McChesney, Allan. "Canada." In *International Handbook on Human Rights*, ed. J. Donnelly and R. Howard. New York: Greenwood Press, 1987.

————. "Does the Charter of Rights Guarantee Equality for Everyone?" In *Take Care! Human Rights in the '80's*, 75–81. Ottawa: Human Rights Research and Education Centre, 1983.

McDonald, Michael. "Collective Rights and Tyranny." *University of Ottawa Quarterly* 56 (1986): 2.

————. "Collective Rights in International Relations." In *Challenging the Conventional*, ed. Wesley Cragg, Laurent Larouche, and Gertrude Lewis, 115–23. Burlington, Ont.: Trinity Press, 1989.

————. "Ideology and Morality in Hard Times." In *Contemporary Moral Issues*, ed. Wes Cragg. 2nd ed. Toronto: McGraw-Hill-Ryerson, 1987.

————. "Questions About Collective Rights." In *Language and the State: The Law*

and Politics of Identity, ed. T. Ducharme. Edmonton: University of Alberta
Press, forthcoming.

———. "Understandings: Collectivities, Their Rights and Obligations." Unpublished manuscript.

McDougal, Myres S., Harrold D. Lasswell, and Lung-Chu Chen. *Human Rights
and World Public Order: The Basic Policies of an International Law of Human
Dignity.* New Haven, Conn.: Yale University Press, 1980.

McMurtry, John. *The Structure of Marx's World-View.* Princeton: Princeton University Press, 1978.

Mead, George H. *Mind, Self and Society.* Chicago: University of Chicago Press,
1962.

Medcalfe, Linda. *Law and Identity: Lawyers, Native Americans, and Legal Practice.*
Beverly Hills, Calif.: Sage Publications, 1978.

Mendes, Jr., João. *Os indigenas do Brasil, seus direitos individuães e politicos.* São
Paulo: Comissão Pró-Indio, 1912.

Michaelson, R. "The Significance of the American Indian Religious Freedom Act
of 1978." *Journal of the American Academy of Religion* 52 (1984):104.

Michnik, Adam. *Letters from Prison.* Berkeley, Calif.: University of California
Press, 1985.

Mignone, Emilio F. *Iglesia y Dictadura.* Buenos Aires: Ediciones del Pensamiento
Nacional, 1986.

Mill, John Stuart. *On Liberty.* London: J. M. Dent, 1962.

Miller, Richard. *Analyzing Marx.* Princeton: Princeton University Press, 1984.

Morrissey, M., and J. Jakubowicz. *Migrants and Occupational Health Report.* University of New South Wales (Australia): Social Welfare Research Centre,
1980.

Milne, A.J.M. *Human Rights and Human Diversity: An Essay in the Philosophy of
Human Rights.* Albany, N.Y.: State University of New York Press, 1986.

Minister of Indian and Northern Affairs Canada. *Indian Conditions: A Survey.*
Ottawa: Department of Indian Affairs and Northern Development, 1980.

Minzhu, Han, ed. *Cries for Democracy.* Princeton, N.J.: Princeton University Press,
1990.

Mitchell, Neil, Rhoda E. Howard, and Jack Donnelly. "Liberalism, Human Rights
and Human Dignity" [a debate]. *American Political Science Review* 81 (1987):
921–27.

Moore, Barrington, Jr. *Injustice: The Social Bases of Obedience and Revolt.* White
Plains, N.Y.: M. E. Sharpe, 1978.

Moore, Henrietta. *Feminism and Anthropology.* Minneapolis: University of Minnesota Press, 1988.

Morse, B. R., and Woodman, G. R. "Introductory Essay: The State's Options."
In *Indigenous Law and the State,* ed. B. R. Morse and G. R. Woodman, 5–23.
Providence, R.I.: Foris Publications, 1988.

Morse, Bradford W., and Robert K. Groves. "Canada's Forgotten Peoples: The
Aboriginal Rights of Metis and Non-Status Indians." *Law and Anthropology*
2 (1987):139–67.

Morsink, Johannes. "The Philosophy of the Universal Declaration." *Human Rights
Quarterly* 6 (1984):309–34.

Moss, W. "Indigenous Self-Government in Canada and Sexual Equality Under the Indian Act: Resolving Conflicts Between Collective and Individual Rights." Unpublished manuscript, February 21, 1990.

Moss, I., and Newton, M. "The Anti-Discrimination Board of NSW: Eight Years of Achievement." *Australian Law Journal* 60 (1986):162.

Mulvaney, D. J. *The Prehistory of Australia.* Rev. ed. Ringwood: Penguin, 1975.

Narveson, Jan. *The Libertarian Idea.* Philadelphia: Temple University Press, 1988.

Nathan, A. *Chinese Democracy.* Berkeley and Los Angeles: University of California Press, 1985.

———. "Sources of Chinese Rights Thinking." In *Human Rights in Contemporary China,* ed. R. Edwards, L. Henkin, and A. Nathan, New York: Columbia University Press, 1986.

National Conference of Catholic Bishops. *Economic Justice for All.* A pastoral letter approved by the National Conference of Catholic Bishops, November 13, 1986, para. 83.

National Federation of Land Councils. "Australian Government Is Merely Perpetuating Past Colonial Practices." Presentation to the Working Group on Indigenous Populations. In *Land Rights Now: The Aboriginal Fight for Land in Australia,* 120–34. Copenhagen: IWGIA Document 54, 1985.

National Lawyers Guild, Committee on Native American Struggles, comp. and ed. *Rethinking Indian Law.* New York: National Lawyers Guild, Committee on Native American Struggles, 1982.

Nef, Jorge. "Violence and Ideology in Latin American Politics: An Overview." Unpublished manuscript, 1988.

Nettheim, Garth. "Australian Aborigines and the Law." *Law and Anthropology* 2 (1987):372.

———. "Geneva: Revision of ILO Convention No. 107, 1988." *Aboriginal Law Bulletin* 2 (1988):12–13.

———. "The Relevance of International Law." In *Aborigines and the Law,* ed. P. Hanks and B. Keon-Cohen, 50. Sydney: George Allen and Unwin, 1984.

Nettheim, Garth, and J. Crawford. "Preamble Perils." *Aboriginal Law Bulletin* 30 (1988):15.

Nickel, James W. "Cultural Diversity and Human Rights." In *International Human Rights: Contemporary Issues,* ed. Jack L. Nelson and Vera M. Green, 43–56. Stanfordville, N.Y.: Human Rights Publishing Group, 1980.

Nielsen, Kai. *Marxism and the Moral Point of View.* Boulder, Colo.: Westview Press, 1989.

Nordahl, Ricard. "Marx and Utopia: Critique of the 'Orthodox Interpretation.'" *Canadian Journal of Political Science* 20 (1987):755–83.

———. "Marx on Evaluating Pre-capitalist Societies." *Studies in Soviet Thought* 31 (1986):303–19.

———. "Marx on Moral Commentary: Ideology and Science." *Philosophy of the Social Sciences* 15 (1985):237–54.

NOU:18. *Om Samenes Rettslige Stilling.* Oslo: Universitetsforlaget, 1984.

Nove, Alec. *The Economics of Feasible Socialism.* London: Allan and Unwin, 1983.

Nozick, Robert. *Anarchy, State, and Utopia.* New York: Basic Books, 1974.

Oakeshott, Michael. *On Human Conduct*. Oxford: Clarendon Press, 1975.

O'Donnell, Guillermo. *Modernization and Bureaucratic Authoritarianism: Studies in South American Politics*. Berkeley: Institute of International Studies, University of California, 1973.

———. "Tensions in the Bureaucratic-Authoritarian State and the Question of Democracy." In *The New Authoritarianism in Latin America*, ed. David Collier, 285–318. Princeton, N.J.: Princeton University Press, 1979.

———. "Reflections on the Patterns of Change in the Bureaucratic-Authoritarian State." *Latin American Research Review* 12 (1978) : 3–38.

O'Malley, K. Commonwealth of Australia, Senate and House of Representatives, *Parliamentary Debates*, Session 1901–2, (6 September 1901) vol. 4 at 4639.

O'Malley, P. "Australian Immigration Policies and the Migrant Dirty Worker Syndrome." In *The Immigration Issue in Australia: A Sociological Symposium*, ed. R. Birrell and C. Hay, 47–50. Melbourne: La Trobe University, 1978.

———. *Law, Capitalism and Democracy*. Sydney: George Allen and Unwin, 1983.

O'Neill, N.F.K. "A Never-Ending Journey? A History of Human Rights in Australia." In *Human Rights: The Australian Debate* ed. Lynne Spender. Redfern: Redfern Legal Aid Centre, 1987.

Opekokew, Delia. *The First Nations: Indian Governments in the Community of Man*. Regina, Sask.: Federation of Saskatchewan Indian Nations, 1982.

Ortiz, R. D. *Indians of the Americas: Human Rights and Self-Determination*. London: Zed Press, 1984.

Paine, R. *Dam a River, Damn a People?* Copenhagen: IWGIA Document 45, 1982.

Parekh, Bhikhur. *Marx's Theory of Ideology*. Baltimore: Johns Hopkins University Press, 1982.

Partlett, D. "Benign Racial Discrimination: Equality and Aborigines" *Federal Law Review* 10 (1979) : 254–56.

Patterson, Orlando. *Slavery and Social Death: A Comparative Study*. Cambridge: Harvard University Press, 1982.

Paz, Octavio. *The Labyrinth of Solitude: Life and Thought in Mexico*. Trans. Sander Kemp. New York: Grove Press, 1966.

———. *One Earth, Four or Five Worlds: Reflections on Contemporary History*. Trans. Helen R. Lane. San Diego: Harcourt Brace Jovanovich, 1985.

Pelloux, Robert. "Le Preambule de la Constitution du 27 octobre 1946." In Chronique Constitutionnelle, *Revue du Droit Public*, vol. 62, no. 347 : 352–53.

Pentney, W. "Lovelace v. Canada: A Case Comment." *Canadian Legal Aid Bulletin* 5 (1982) : 259.

———. "The Rights of the Aboriginal Peoples of Canada and the *Constitution Act, 1982*. Part I—The Interpretive Prism of Section 25." *University of British Columbia Law Review* 22 (1988) : 22–59.

Perry, Michael J. "Taking Neither Rights—Talk nor the 'Critique of Rights' Too Seriously." *Texas Law Review* 62 (1984) : 1411–13.

Pestieu, Joseph. "Droits des personnes, des peuples, et des minorités." Unpublished manuscript. Presented at the 1989 meeting of the Canadian Philosophical Association.

Pike, Fredrick B. *The Modern History of Peru*. New York: Frederick A. Praeger, 1967.

Pion-Berlin, David. "The Political Economy of State Repression in Argentina." In *The State as Terrorist, The Dynamics of Governmental Violence and Repression*, ed. Michael Stohl and George A. Lopez, 99–122. Westport, Conn.: Greenwood Press, 1984.

Po-ling, Cheung. "Clandestine Hit Squads Reportedly Forming." *Hong Kong Standard*, July 19, 1989, p. 6.

Preiswerk, Roy. "The Place of Intercultural Relations in the Study of International Relations." *The Year Book of World Affairs* 32 (1978): 251.

Quiroga, Cecilia Medina. *The Battle of Human Rights: Gross, Systematic Violations and the Inter-American System*. The Hague: Martinus Nijhoff, 1988.

Radcliffe-Brown, A. R. "Partilineal and Matrilineal Succession." In *Structure and Function in Primitive Society*, 32–48. New York: The Free Press, 1952.

———. "The Social Organization of Australian Tribes." *Oceania* 1 (1930): 34–63.

Ramos-Horta, Jose. *FUNU: The Unfinished Saga of East Timor*. Trenton, N.J.: Red Sea Press, 1987.

Rauch, William, Jr. *Politics and Belief in Contemporary France: Emmanuel Mounier and Christian Democracy 1932–1950*. The Hague: Martinus Nijhoff, 1972.

Rawls, John. "The Idea of an Overlapping Consensus." *Oxford Journal of Legal Studies* 7, no. 1 (1987): 1–25.

———. *Theory of Justice*. Cambridge, Mass.: Harvard University Press, 1971.

Raz, Joseph. *The Morality of Freedom*. Oxford: Clarendon Press, 1986.

Reece, R.H.W. *Aborigines and Colonists: Aborigines and Colonial Society in New South Wales in the 1830s and 1940s*. Sydney: Sydney University Press, 1974.

Renan, E. "Ou'est-ce qu'une nation?" In *Oeuvres completes*. Vol. 1, 904. Paris: Colmann-Levy, 1947–1961.

Renteln, Alison. "A Cross-Cultural Approach to Validating International Human Rights: The Case of Retribution Tied to Proportionality." In *Human Rights: Theory and Measurement*, ed. David L. Cingranelli, 7–40. Basingstoke, Hampshire, and London: Macmillan Press, 1988.

———. "International Human Rights: The Case of Retribution Tied to Proportionality." *Human Rights Theory and Measurements*. Basingstoke, Hampshire and London: The Macmillan Press, 1988.

———. *International Human Rights: Universalism Versus Relativism*. Newbury Park, Calif.: Sage Publications, 1990.

———. "Relativism and the Search for Human Rights." *American Anthropologist* 90 (1988): 64.

———. "The Unanswered Challenge of Relativism and the Consequences for Human Rights." *Human Rights Quarterly* 7 (1985): 514–40.

Report of the Indigenous Bar Association Annual Conference: "Indigenous Control of the Justice System: Alternatives to Existing Arrangements." September 30 to October 1, 1989.

Reports of the Fourth Russell Tribunal. *Conclusions; Selected Cases D U.S.A.; Non-Selected Cases A North America.* 1980.

Reynolds, H. *The Law of the Land.* Ringwood: Penguin, 1987.

Richstone, Jeff. *Securing Human Rights in Nunavut: A Study of a Nunavut Bill of Rights.* Ottawa: Nunavut Constitutional Forum, 1985.

Rivero, Jean. "The French Conception of Human Rights." In *Human Rights, France and the United States of America.* New York: Center for the Study of Human Rights at Columbia University, 1984.

Robertson, R. "The Right to Food—Canada's Broken Covenant." *Canadian Human Rights Yearbook* (1989–90): 185–216.

"'Round and Round the Bramble Bush': From Legal Realism to Critical Legal Scholarship." *Harvard Law Review* 95 (1982): 1669–90.

Rowse, T. "Liberalising the Frontier: Aborigines and Australian Pluralism." *Meanjin* 42 (1983): 71.

Roy, Bernadette K., and Miller, Dallas K. *The Rights of Indigenous Peoples in International Law: An Annotated Bibliography.* Saskatoon, Sask.: Native Law Centre, University of Saskatchewan, 1985.

Ruiz, Lester Edwin J. "Towards a Theology of Politics." *Tugon* 6 (1986): 1–44.

Rushdie, Salman. "An End to the Nightmare." *Seminar* (Delhi, India), 351 (1988): 14–15.

Ryan, Edna, and Anne Conlon. *Gender Invaders: Australian Women at Work 1788–1974.* Melbourne: Nelson, 1974.

Sabato, Jorge F., and Jorge Schvarzer. "Funcionamento da Economia e Póder Politico na Argentina: Empecilhos Para a Democracia." In *Como Renascem as Democracias,* ed. Alain Rouqiue, Bolivar Lamounier, Jorge Schwarzer, 166–67. São Paulo: Editora Brasiliense, 1985.

Safwat, Safia M. "Offenses and Penalties in Islamic Law." *The Islamic Quarterly* 26 (1982): 149.

Said, Edward. *Orientalism.* New York: Pantheon, 1978.

Saksena, K. P. Foreword to *Human Rights and Development: International Views,* ed. David P. Forsythe. London: Macmillan, 1989.

Salaun, Mauricio. "Colombian Politics: Historical Characteristics and Problems." In *Politics of Compromise Coalition Government in Colombia,* ed. Albert Berry, Ronald G. Hellman, and Mauricio Solaun, 1–57. New Jersey: Transaction Books, 1980.

Salter, M. J. *Studies in the Immigration of the Highly Skilled.* Canberra: Australian National University Press, 1978.

Sanders, Douglas. "Aboriginal Rights in Canada: An Overview. *Law and Anthropology* 2 (1987): 177–93.

———. "Indian Status: A Woman's Issue or An Indian Issue?" *Canadian Native Law Reporter* 3 (1989): 30.

———. "Indigenous Rights and the Alta-Kautokeino Project." In *Samene-Urbefolkning og Minoritet,* ed. Trond Thuen. Tromso: Universitesforlaget, 1980.

———. "The Rights of the Aboriginal Peoples of Canada," *Canadian Bar Review* 61 (1983): 314–38.

Sawer, Marian. *Sisters in Suits: Women and Public Policy in Australia.* Sydney: Allen and Unwin, 1990.

———. "Human Rights: Women Need Not Apply." *Australian Society* (September 1988): 9.

Schell, O. *Discoes and Democracy: China in the Throes of Reform.* New York: Pantheon, 1988.

Schlesinger, Arthur, Jr. "The Opening of the American Mind." *New York Times Book Review.* July 23, 1989, p. 26.

Schmid, Alex P. *Research on Gross Human Rights Violations: A Programme.* 2nd, enlarged ed. Leiden: Center for the Study of Social Conflicts, 1989.

Schneck, Stephen Frederick. *Person and Polis: Max Scheler's Personalism as Political Theory.* Albany, N.Y.: State University of New York Press, 1987.

Schusky, Ernest Lester. *The Right to be Indian.* San Francisco: Indian Historian Press, 1970.

Scobie, James R. *Argentina. A City and a Nation.* New York: Oxford University Press, 1971.

Senate Committee on Constitutional and Legal Affairs. *Two Hundred Years Later.* Canberra: Australian Government Publishing Service, 1983.

Seymour, James D. "China." In *International Handbook of Human Rights,* ed. Jack Donnelly and Rhoda E. Howard, 75–97. New York: Greenwood Press, 1987.

Shanin, Theodor, ed. *Late Marx and the Russian Road.* New York: Monthly Review Press, 1983.

Shapiro, Ian. *The Evolution of Rights in Liberal Theory.* Cambridge: Cambridge University Press, 1986.

Shestack, Jerome. "The Jurisprudence of Human Rights." In *Human Rights in International Law: Legal and Policy Issues,* ed. Theodor Meron, 69. Oxford: Clarendon Press, 1984.

Sidgwick, Henry. *The Elements of Politics.* London: Macmillan, 1908.

———. *The Method of Ethics.* London: Macmillan, 1907.

Sieghart, Paul. *The International Law of Human Rights.* Oxford: Clarendon Press, 1983.

———. *The Lawful Rights of Mankind: An Introduction to the International Legal Code of Human Rights.* Oxford: Oxford University Press, 1986.

Sigler, J. *Minority Rights: A Comparative Analysis.* Westport, Conn.: Greenwood Press, 1983.

Simpson, T. "Geneva—Indigenous Rights in International Forums." *Aboriginal Law Bulletin* 2, no. 34 (1988): 10.

Smith, Brian H. *The Church and Politics in Chile.* Princeton: Princeton University Press, 1982.

Smith, C., ed. *Norsk Rett og Folkeretten.* Oslo: Universitesforlaget, 1982.

Smith, Kenneth L., and Ira G. Zepp, Jr. *Search for the Beloved Community: The Thinking of Martin Luther King, Jr.* Valley Forge: Judson Press, 1974.

Special Committee on Indian Self-Government, Indian Self-Government in Canada, House of Commons Issue No. 40. Published under authority of the Speaker of the House of Commons by the Queen's Printer for Canada, 1983.

Spender, Lynne. *Human Rights: The Australian Debate*. Redfern: Redfern Legal Centre Publishing, 1987.

Stacy, J. *Patriarchy and Socialist Revolution in China*. Berkeley and Los Angeles: University of California Press, 1983.

Stepan, Alfred. "The New Professionalism of Internal Warfare and Military Role Expansion." In *Authoritarian Brazil: Origins, Policies, and Future*, ed. Alfred Stepan, 46–63. New Haven: Yale University Press, 1973.

———. *Os Militares: Da Abertura à "Nova Republica."* São Paulo: Paz e Terra, 1986.

Stevenson, Jack. "Canadian Philosophy From Cosmopolitan Point of View," *Dialogue* 25 (1986): 17.

Suess, Paulo. "Brazil's Aboriginal Peoples." "Evangelization and the Tribal Cultures of Brazil." *Cross Currents* 39 (1989): 161–80.

Suter, K. D. "Australian Aborigines: The Struggle Continues." *Contemporary Review* 253 (1988): 177.

Svensson, Tom. "The Land Claims Issue and the Sami—Reflections on Contemporary Legal Struggle." *Geographica Helvetia* 4 (1988): 184–93.

———. "Local Communities in the South Sami Region." In *The Sami National Minority in Sweden*, ed. B. Jahreskog, 102–16. Stockholm: Almquist & Wiskell, 1982.

———. "The Sami and Development Law." Paper presented to International Bar Association Conference, Buenos Aires, 1988.

Swinton, Katherine, and Carol Rogerson. *Competing Constitutional Visions: The Meech Lake Accord*. Toronto: Carswell, 1988.

Taha, Mahmoud Mohamed. *The Second Message of Islam*. Trans. Abdullahi A. An-Na'im. Syracuse: Syracuse University Press, 1987.

Tarnopolsky, W. S., and W. F. Pentney. *Discrimination and the Law: Including Equality Rights under the Charter*. Don Mills, Ont.: De Boo, 1985.

Thomas, Robert K. "Pan-Indianism." In *The American Indian Today*, ed. S. Levine and N. Lurie. Baltimore, MD: Penguin Books, 1968.

Thompson, Ruth. *The Rights of Indigenous Peoples in International Law: Workshop Report*. Ottawa: International Conference on Aboriginal Rights and World Public Order, 1986.

Thunder, Elizabeth. *Minutes of Proceedings and Evidence of the Standing Committee on Human Rights and the Status of Disabled Persons* (House of Commons). Issue No. 11, October 3, 1989, 11:56.

Thurston, A. *Enemies of the People: The Ordeal of the Intellectuals in China's Great Cultural Revolution*. Cambridge, Mass.: Harvard University Press, 1988.

Tobias, J. L. "Indian Reserves in Western Canada: Indian Homelands or Devices for Assimilation?" In *Native People, Native Lands—Canadian Indians, Inuit and Metis*, ed. B. A. Cox, 148–57. Ottawa: Carleton University Press, 1988.

Tucker, R., ed. "Critique of the Gotha Program." In *The Marx-Engels Reader*. 2nd ed., 528. New York: Norton, 1978.

Turpel, Mary Ellen. "Aboriginal Peoples and the Canadian Charter: Interpretive Monopolies, Cultural Differences." *Canadian Human Rights Yearbook* (1989–1990): 3–45.

Tushnet, Mark. "An Essay on Rights." *Texas Law Review* 62 (1984): 1363.

UNESCO, *Human Rights: Comments and Interpretations*. London: Allan Wingate, 1949. Appendix I.
UNESCO, ed., *Human Rights, Comments and Interpretations*. London: Allan Wingate, 1949.
Unger, Roberto Mangabeira. "The Critical Legal Studies Movement." *Harvard Law Review* 96 (1983): 563–675.
———. *False Necessity*. Cambridge: Cambridge University Press, 1987.
———. *Passion, An Essay on Personality*. New York: Free Press, 1984.
United Nations. *International Covenant on Civil and Political Rights: Human Rights Committee, Selected Decisions under the Optional Protocol (Second to Sixteenth Sessions)*. New York: United Nations (CCPR./C/OP/1), 1985.
———. *Religious and Linguistic Minorities*, U.N. E CN.4/Sub. 2/384/Rev. 1. New York: United Nations, 1979.
United Nations General Assembly Resolution 469 (1979). Cited in Amnesty International, *Human Rights: Selected International Standards*. London: Amnesty International Publications, 1985.
United Nations General Assembly Resolution 3452 (XXX), 30 U.N. GAOR, Supp. (No. 34) 91, U.N. Doc. A/100 (1975).
United States Commission on Civil Rights, *Indian Tribes: A Continuing Quest for Survival*. Washington, D.C.: United States Government Printing Office, 1981.
"Universal Human Rights: An Aboriginal Dialogue." Conference proceedings, Robson Media Centre, Vancouver, B.C., 1989.
"Universal Declaration on Indigenous Rights: A Set of Draft Perambular Paragraphs and Principles." Report of the Subcommission, 40th Session (August 8–September 2, 1988), E/CN.4/1989/3, E/CN.4/Sub. 2/1988/45, 25 October 1988.

Van Dyke, Vernon. *Human Rights, Ethnicity, and Discrimination*. Westport, Conn.: Greenwood Press, 1985.
Valenzuela, Arturo. *The Breakdown of Democratic Regimes: Chile*. Baltimore: Johns Hopkins University Press, 1978.
VanderWal, Koo. "Collective Human Rights: A Western View." In *Human Rights in a Pluralist World: Individuals and Collectivities*, ed. Jan Berting et al., 83–98. Westport, Conn.: Meckler, 1990.
Vanger, Milton I. *Jose Battle y Ordonez of Uruguay: The Creator of His Times*. Cambridge: Harvard University Press, 1963.
Verdoodt, Albert. *Naissance et signification de la Declaration Universelle des droits de l'homme*. Louvain: Nanwelaerts, 1964.
Vincent, R. J. "The Factor of Culture in the Global International Order." *Year Book of World Affairs* 34 (1980): 256.
Vinson, T. *Legal Representation and Outcome*. New South Wales Bureau of Statistics and Research, 1973.

Waldman, Carl. *Atlas of the North American Indian*, 201. New York: Facts on File Publications, 1985.

Walker, R. B. "Ethics, Modernity, and the Theory of IR." Unpublished manuscript.

Walzer, Michael. *Spheres of Justice.* New York: Basic Books, 1983.

Wasserstrom, Jeffrey. "Resistance to the One Child Policy." *Modern China* 10 (July 1984): 359.

Weaver, S. "Judicial Preservation of Ethnic Group Boundaries: The Iroquois Case." *Proceedings of the First Congress, Canadian Ethnology Society,* Paper No. 17, National Museum of Man Mercury Series, Ottawa, 1974.

Weber, Max. *The Protestant Ethic and the Spirit of Capitalism.* New York: Charles Scribner's Sons, 1958.

Wein, F. *Rebuilding the Economic Base of Indian Communities: The Micmac in Nova Scotia.* Montreal: Institute for Research on Public Policy, 1986.

Weinstein, Martin. *Uruguay, Democracy at the Crossroads.* Boulder, Colo.: Westview Press, 1988.

Wellman, C. *A Theory of Rights: Persons under Laws, Institutions, and Morals.* Totawa, N.J.: Rowman and Allanheld, 1985.

Wetenhall, R. "Aboriginal Administration: Should We Bend the Rules?" *Current Affairs Bulletin* 65 (1989): 4.

Wetlesen, Jon. "Inherent Dignity as a Ground for Human Rights." *Archiv für Rechts- und Sozialphilosophie.* Beiheft 41. Stuttgart: Franz Steiner Verlag, 1990.

Whitaker, Ben. *The Fourth World, Victims of Group Oppression.* New York: Schocken, 1973.

Whyte, M. *Small Groups and Political Rituals in China.* Berkeley and Los Angeles: University of California Press, 1974.

Wiarda, Howard J. "La Lucha por la Democracia y los Derechos Humanos en America Latina." *Estudios Sociales* 18 (1978): 43–66.

———. "Social Change, Political Development and the Latin American Tradition." In *Politics and Social Change in Latin America: The Distinct Tradition,* ed. Howard J. Wiarda, 163–83. Amherst, Mass.: University of Massachusetts Press, 1982.

Wildsmith, B. *Aboriginal Peoples and Section 25 of the Canadian Charter of Rights and Freedoms.* Saskatoon: University of Saskatchewan Native Law Centre, 1988.

Willard, M. *History of the White Australia Policy to 1920.* 2nd ed. Melbourne: Melbourne University Press, 1967.

Williams, Raymond. *Keywords: A Vocabulary of Culture and Society.* New York: Oxford University Press, 1976.

Wu, Y. L., et al. *Human Rights in the People's Republic of China.* Boulder, Colo.: Westview Press, 1988.

Yat-sen, Sun. *San Min Chu I: The Three Principles of the People,* ed. L.T. Chen. Trans. F. Price. Shanghai: Commercial Press, 1928.

Yazzie, A. *Navajo Oral Tradition.* Cortez, Co.: Mesa Verde Press, 1984.

Young, C. "Australia's Population: A Long Term View." *Current Affairs Bulletin* (Sydney), 65 (1989): 4.

Young, Robert W., and William Morgan. *The Navajo Language: A Grammar and*

Colloquial Dictionary. Albuquerque, N.M.: University of New Mexico Press, 1980.

Zapata, Francisco. "Revolutionary Movements in Latin America and the Development of Marxist Theory." In *Developments in Marxist Sociological Theory: Modern Social Problems and Theory,* ed. A. G. Zdravomyslov. Beverly Hills, Calif.: Sage, 1986.

Zion, James. "Trade as an Aboriginal Indian Right in North America." Unpublished manuscript, November 14, 1985.

Zion, J., and M. White. "The Use of Navajo Custom in Dealing with Rape." Unpublished manuscript, August 1986.

Zolbrod, Paul G., trans. *Diné bahaneᶜ: The Navajo Creation Story*. Albuquerque, N.M.: University of New Mexico Press, 1984.

Contributors

William P. Alford is professor of law and director of the East Asian Legal Studies Program at Harvard Law School. He holds a Master's degree in Chinese studies and another Master's in Chinese history, both from Yale University, together with law degrees from the universities of Cambridge and Harvard. Professor Alford is a specialist in Chinese and East Asian law, on which he has published extensively in legal journals. He served for several years as executive director of the China Center for American Law Study in Beijing, and serves as consultant to several bodies, including the World Bank's International Advisory Board, the Ford Foundation, and Asia Watch.

Abdullahi Ahmed An-Na'im is associate professor of law, University of Khartoum, the Sudan, and was the Ariel F. Sallows Professor of Human Rights, College of Law, University of Saskatchewan, Canada, from 1988 to 1991. He holds law degrees from the universities of Khartoum and Cambridge, England, and a Ph.D. in law from the University of Edinburgh, Scotland. His research interests are in human rights and Islam and human rights in cross-cultural perspectives. He is the author of *Toward an Islamic Reformation: Civil Liberties, Human Rights and International Law* (1990) and coeditor of *Human Rights in Africa: Cross-Cultural Perspectives* (1990).

Diane Bell is professor of Religion, Economic Development and Social Justice, College of the Holy Cross, Worcester, Massachusetts. Prior to taking up this position, she was professor of Australian studies and director, Center for Australian Studies, Deakin University, Victoria, Australia. She received her B.A. in anthropology from Monash University, and a Ph.D. in anthropology from Australia National University. Professor Bell is author of *Daughters of the Dreaming* (1983), *Generations: Grandmothers, Mothers & Daughters* (1987), and co-author of *Law: The Old and the New* (1980/4). She has also coedited several books and published numerous articles and chapters on women's issues, religion, and Aboriginal rights and problems. She has written many papers and reports and participated in commissions and committees in Australia.

Manuela Carneiro da Cunha is professor of anthropology, Universidade de São Paulo, Brazil. She was visiting professor at the École des Hautes Études, Paris, and the University of Chicago. She is a graduate of the Faculté des Sciences, Paris, and holds a Ph.D. in anthropology from the Universidade de Campiás, Brazil. Professor da Cunha has worked on issues relating to Brazilian Indian rights and on ethnicity since 1978, and was first president of Comissão Pro-Indio and president of the Brazilian Anthropological Association, 1986–1988. She is the author of four books, including *Direitos dos Indios* [Indian Rights] (1987).

Richard Falk has been professor of international law and practice, Princeton University, since 1961. He holds degrees in economics from the University of Pennsylvania and in law from Yale University. His doctorate in law is from Harvard University. He is the author of eighteen books and editor or coeditor of another thirteen books. His books include the edited four-volume collection, *The Vietnam War and International Law* (1968–1976), and *Human Rights and State Sovereignty* (1981). Since 1959, Professor Falk has published many chapters and articles in edited volumes and in scholarly journals, in addition to countless contributions to other publications. His publications range from international law and international relations to environmental and peace issues.

Hugo Fruhling is professor of law, Diego Portales University, and Human Rights Researcher, Academia Humanismo Cristiano, Chile. He holds a first degree in law from the University of Chile, and a Master's and doctorate in law from Harvard Law School. Professor Fruhling held the Human Rights Chair, Human Rights Research and Education Center at the University of Ottawa, in 1987. He is the editor of *Political Repression and the Defense of Human Rights* (1987) and author of several articles on human rights and political repression in South America. His most recent publication in English is "Human Rights Organizations as Opposition to Authoritarian Rule in Chile," in *Nonprofit Organizations in International Perspectives* (1988), ed. E. James.

Rhoda E. Howard is professor of sociology, McMaster University, Canada. She holds a B.A. in political science, and Master's and Ph.D. degrees in sociology from McGill University. Professor Howard is the author of

Human Rights in Commonwealth Africa (1986), another book and eighteen articles, coeditor of *International Handbook of Human Rights* (1987), and current editor of the *Canadian Journal of African Studies*. Her most recent relevant publication (with Jack Donnelly) is "Assessing National Human Rights Performance: A Theoretical Analysis," *Human Rights Quarterly* (1988).

Patricia Hyndman is associate professor of law and director of The Human Rights Center, University of New South Wales, Australia, barrister-at-law, Gray's Inn, and barrister, Supreme Court of New South Wales. Her LL.B. and Master's in law are from the University of London. She is a specialist in international human rights law and law relating to refugees. Professor Hyndman has been the Secretary of the Human Rights Committee of the Law Association for Asia and the Pacific (LAWASIA) since 1982. Professor Hyndman is the editor of several human rights and LAWASIA publications and author of numerous articles, chapters, and reports on human rights and refugees. Her most recent publications include "Australian Immigration Law and Procedures pertaining to the Admission of Refugees," *McGill Law Journal* (1988), "The Exploitation of Child Workers in South and South East Asia," *Nordic Journal of International Law* (1989), and "Refugees in South and South East Asia," to be published as the inaugural paper in a new series of occasional papers by the Human Rights Center of the State University of New York at Buffalo.

Virginia A. Leary is professor of law, State University of New York at Buffalo. She obtained her doctorate from the Graduate Institute of International Studies, University of Geneva, Switzerland. She is the author of *International Labour Conventions and National Law* (1982) and coeditor of *Asian Perspectives on Human Rights* (1990). Professor Leary has also published several articles and chapters on various aspects of international human rights law and practice and authored reports for the International Commission of Jurists on the Philippines and Sri Lanka. Her teaching experience includes teaching a seminar course on law and cultural pluralism. She is also active in a number of human rights organizations, including the Lawyers' Committee for International Human Rights and the Helsinki and Asia Watch Committees.

Tore Lindholm is a researcher at the Norwegian Institute of Human Rights, Oslo, Norway. He studied philosophy of science and hermeneutics in Oslo, Norway, and Heidelberg, Germany. He taught philosophy in the doctoral program of the Faculty of Social Science, University of Oslo, until 1986 and was director of the Center for the Study of Science at that university from 1981 to 1985. Dr. Lindholm has published several articles on Marx's theory of modern society, tradition and rationality, and human rights. The title of his latest publication in Norwegian may be translated as *Why Marx Scorns Civil and Political Rights* (1990).

Michael McDonald was professor of philosophy, University of Waterloo, Canada. He holds a B.A. in philosophy from the University of Toronto, and M.A. and Ph.D. degrees in philosophy from the University of Pittsburgh. He has published work in ethics, political philosophy, and the philosophy of law. He was the English-language editor of *Dialogue,* and past president of the Canadian section of the International Association for Law and Social Philosophy. His current research is on collective rights; and he has just completed a major commissioned study entitled "Towards a Canadian Research Strategy for Applied Ethics," which has led to the establishment by Canadian Social Science and Humanities Research Council of a new strategic theme in applied ethics. He has just been appointed as the first Maurice Gouas Chair in Applied Ethics at the University of British Columbia.

Allan McChesney taught international human rights law at the Faculty of Law, University of Ottawa, in 1990 and teaches at Carleton University. He is research consultant to Canada's Parliamentary Sub-Committee on International Human Rights. Formerly, he was executive director of the Legal Services Board (Legal Aid) of the Northwest Territories, Canada. His publications on human rights include works on Canada's Charter of Rights, aboriginal rights, foreign policy, democracy, and development. He is coauthor of *Human Rights Training for Public Officials* (1990), published by the Commonwealth Secretariat.

Richard Nordahl holds a Ph.D. in political science from Princeton University. He is professor of political studies, University of Saskatchewan, Canada. Professor Nordahl has published several articles and chapters on Marx, including "Marx and Utopia: A Critique of the 'Orthodox' View," *Canadian Journal of Political Science* (1987) and "Marx on Moral Commentary: Ideology and Science," *Philosophy of the Social Sciences* (1985). His research interests are in political theory and Marxian thought.

Tom G. Svensson holds a Fil. Dr. degree in social anthropology from the University of Stockholm. He is associate professor at the Department of Anthropology (Ethnographic Museum), University of Oslo, Norway. His special interest is devoted to the Sami indigenous minority in northern Fenno-Scandia and other northern Fourth World peoples, focusing on ethnicity, political movements as well as esthetic manifestations. Dr. Svensson has published numerous articles in this field in addition to the monograph: *Ethnicity and Mobilization in Sami Politics* (1976). He has lectured extensively on Sami issues in Norway and Sweden, and participated in work of official committees and international conferences dealing with northern indigenous peoples. From 1983 to 1984, Dr. Svensson was research associate at McGill University, Montreal.

James W. Zion, attorney, is general counsel of the Navajo Housing Authority, a public agency of the Navajo Nation. He has been active in the field of Indian affairs since 1974 and acted as legal counsel for several Indian tribes in the United States. He has published nine recent articles and chapters relevant to this field, including "Searching for Indian Common Law," in *Indigenous Law and the State* (1987), ed. B. W. Morse and G. R. Woodman, and "A Question of Sovereignty: Tribal, State and Federal Law," in *Law and Anthropology* (1988).

Index

Aboriginal Affairs Planning Authority Act 1972 (Australia), 309

The Aboriginal and Torres Strait Islander Bill (Australia), 314

Aboriginal and Torres Strait Islander Commission (ATSIC), 314, 315

Aboriginal and Torres Strait Islander Heritage Protection Act, 1984, 308

Aboriginal Communities Act 1979 (Australia), 310

Aboriginal Development Commission (Australia), 308

Aboriginal Land Fund Commission (Australia), 308

The Aboriginal Land (Lake Condah and Framlingham Forest) Act (Australia), 314

Aboriginal Land Rights Act (1983, Australia), 310

Aboriginal Land Rights (Northern Territory) Act 1976 (Australia), 308

Aboriginal Land Trusts (Australia), 312

Aboriginal peoples (Canada); and affirmative action, 233–36; autonomy of, 225, 230; culture of, 225–26, 230, 234, 238; decision-making structures of, 241, 243; discrimination against, 222–27, 230–33; economic status of, 223, 226, 227, 230, 233–36, 242; mistrust of government, 226–27, 234–35; rights of, 221, 222, 224, 228, 229, 230–45; and self-determination, 222, 225, 239; and self-government, 225, 233, 238, 239–45; and self-identification, 237–38. *See also* Indigenous peoples; North American Indians

Aboriginal Rights in International Law, 198

Abuse of artistic freedom, 59

Action for Citizenship movement (Brazil), 279

Administrative Appeals Tribunal (Australia), 320–21

Administrative Decisions (Judicial Review) Act (Australia), 321

Administrative Review Council (Australia), 321

Affirmative action, 348, 375, 376; in Canada, 210, 223, 233–36

Africa, 289

African Charter of Rights, 97

Alaska, 205

Alford, William, 9

Allende, Salvador, 263

Alta Case, the (Norway), 371–76, 378, 382

Althusser, Louis, 355

Amazon, the, 278, 280, 281

American Anthropological Association, 388

American Bar Association, 191

American Convention on Human Rights, 269

American Declaration of Independence, 120, 128

American Indian Policy Review Commission *Final Report* (1977), 196

American Indian Religious Freedom Act (1978), 205, 209

Amish, the, 89, 147, 153

Amnesty International, 340

An-Naʿim, Abdullahi A., 49, 51, 53, 69, 107, 155, 179, 287, 388–89, 390, 418

Anthropology, and human rights theory, 339, 348, 350, 354, 356, 367, 372, 377, 382–83

Anti-Discrimination Act (1977, Australia), 320

Anti-Discrimination Boards (Australia), 326

Antidiscrimination law, 194, 210, 211; in Australia, 299, 308, 310–11, 319–21, 325, 326, 340, 341, 347–48, 350–52; in Canada, 222–33

Arctic, the, 205

Argentina: authoritarianism and opposition to, 253, 255, 258, 260, 261; and human rights violations as social process, 262, 263, 264

"Assessing the Communitarian Critique of Liberalism," 137

Assimilation, 136, 194, 342, 366; attitudes toward, 221, 222, 239; of Australian Aboriginals, 307, 308, 317, 354; of Brazilian Indians, 284; of North American indigenous peoples, 84, 191, 193, 208, 225, 247 n.19; of the Sami, 376

Australia: approach to legal rights, 298–300, 301–2, 303–6; constitutional change in, 299, 302, 305, 308, 312, 320; domestic human rights legislation, 299, 307–23, 347–53; historical development of, 296–98, 302, 303–5; and international human rights standards, 198, 295, 300, 313, 318, 325, 340–41, 358; multiculturalism of, 296, 297–98, 316–23, 326, 346; ratification of human rights covenants, 310, 319, 324–25, 338 n.158; status of women in, 341, 342, 346, 348–49. See also Australian Aboriginals

Australian Aboriginals: assimilation of, 307, 308, 317, 354; and Australian law, 302, 303–6, 308, 309–11, 313, 351–52; culture of, 303, 305, 307, 317; customary laws of, 301, 304–5, 306, 307, 309–10, 311, 315, 316, 318; definition of, 300–301; government policy toward, 311–12, 314–16; population, 296, 302–3, 318, 346; rights of, 300, 302–17, 326; and self-government, 307, 312, 313, 314; status of women, 341–45, 348–59

Australian Capital Territory, 296

Australian Council on Population and Ethnic Affairs, 317–18

Australian Law Reform Commission, 315, 349, 350, 352, 353

Authoritarianism, 60, 173, 174, 180, 181, 340; in Latin America, 253–54, 255, 256–62, 264–68, 269–70, 271

Autonomy, 93, 94; and indigenous peoples, 204, 206, 225, 312, 314, 333 n.95, 367–68, 381; in liberalism, 95, 140, 141, 152–53, 406–8; in Marxism, 167, 168, 170, 171, 178, 182, 187 n.32

Ayala, Turbay, 267

Balkans, the, 146

Battle y Ordonez, Jose, 259

Baxi, Upendra, 108

de Beauvoir, Simone, 88

Beijing Spring, 65, 68

Bell, Diane, 13

Bennett, Gordon, 198

Boston University, 109

Brazil, 110, 114; authoritarianism in and opposition to, 253, 255, 258, 261, 268; constitution(s) of, 280, 282–83, 284, 285, 287; government Amazonian policies, 278–82; human rights violations as social process in, 262, 263, 264; and Indian issues, 277–86, 287; role of multilateral banks in, 277, 286–87. See also Indians of Brazil

Brazilian Anthropological Association (ABA), 283

Brazilian Association of Professional Geologists (ONAGE), 283

Brennan, F., 315

Brierly, J. R., 194

Brownlie, Ian, 194

Brundtland, Gro Harlem, 210

Brunner, José Joaquin, 270

Buchanan, Allen, 137, 146, 147, 148–49

Burke, Edmund, 26

Canada, 89, 191, 196–97, 198, 202, 221; and Aboriginal self-determination, 239–45, 300; affirmative action policy, 210, 223, 233–36; antidiscrimination law in, 222–33, as-similationist policies of, 222; constitution and Aboriginal rights, 236–39, 315, 317; human rights record of, 95–97, 192, 343; minority rights in, 84, 95, 133, 142. See also Aboriginal peoples (Canada); Indigenous peoples; North American Indians

Canadian Bill of Rights (1960), 192–93

Canadian Charter of Rights and Freedoms, 144, 149, 236–37, 238, 239, 240, 241, 242

Canadian Human Rights Act, 232, 243, 244

Canadian Human Rights Commission, 232; Annual Report: (1988), 232; (1989), 232

Capital (Marx), 411, 412, 413, 415, 416

Capitalism, 92, 93, 261; in Marxist theory, 173–74, 175, 183, 412, 413–14; and personalism, 119, 120

Capital punishment, 89–90

Catholicism, 59, 60, 109, 110, 129; in Latin America, 257, 258, 265, 268, 277, 282, 287

Central America, 253, 258

Charter of Human Rights for the Pacific (Draft), 324–25

Children, rights of, 199–200

Chile, 415; authoritarianism in, 253, 254, 255, 264, 265; evolution toward liberalism in,

261, 262, 263, 268; human rights violations in, 258, 259, 260

China, People's Republic of (PRC), 81; and cultural relativity of human rights standards, 73–76; and human rights in historical context, 69–73; pro-democracy movement in, 65, 66–69

Christian Heritage Party of Canada, 96

Christianity, 51, 57, 109

Civil and political rights, 7, 394, 404–5, 406; and liberalism, 137, 157; and Marxism, 170, 173, 184, 415–16; and personalism, 106, 118, 122

Class action rights, 134, 135

Clifford, James, 356

Coe v. The Commonwealth (Australia), 304

Collective rights, 120, 152–53, 313, 372, 393, 429; and Brazilian Indians, 276, 284–85; and Chinese Communism, 72–73, 75, 76; definition of, 134–36; and liberalism, 106, 107, 138, 141–54, 403–9, 419; of North American indigenous peoples, 193, 195–96, 199, 208, 221–45, 324–25, 363–64, 365–67, 373, 381; personalist perspective of, 107, 111, 112, 116–28; versus individual rights, 83, 86–87, 92–93, 97–99, 141–54, 172–73, 403–9. See also Minorities

Collectivities. See Collective rights

Columbia, 255, 258, 262, 263, 266–68

Communism, 72, 73, 121, 412, 413, 414, 416, 417, 419. See also Marxism

Communitarianism, 136, 154, 157 n.16, 157 n.19; and indigenous peoples, 221, 225, 235, 240, 242. See also Personalism

Communities, notion of, 147–48, 149

Community Welfare Act 1983 (Australia), 309

Confucianism, 70, 71, 72, 73

Conservatism, 95–97, 99, 121, 134, 138

Constitution Act (Canada), 236

Constitution Act (Sweden), 379

Constructivist theory, 81–82

Crahan, Margaret E., 264

Cranston, Maurice, 107

Crawford, J., 315

Critical Legal Studies (CLS) movement, 105, 110, 114, 124, 125

Critique of the Gotha Program, 164

Cruel, inhuman, or degrading treatment, 29–38, 89

Cuba, 255, 261, 264, 266

Cult of modernization. See Modernization

Cultural hermeneutics, 46

Cultural relativists, 44, 45, 90, 91, 430

Culture: and cross-cultural dialogue on human rights standards, 3–7, 15, 21–23, 27, 29, 36, 37, 46, 287, 292, 420; and cross-cultural legitimacy of human rights standards, 4–5, 21, 23, 27, 28, 107, 178; and cross-cultural perspectives on human rights, 2–6, 20–29, 38–40, 49–51, 123, 155–56, 161 n.84, 183, 230, 428, 429, 434; definitions of, 2–3, 23, 208, 288–91; diversity of, 21, 22, 27, 177, 242, 382; and ethnicity, 284, 287, 289, 291; foundations of, 75, 90–91; and human rights, 7, 53, 90–91, 152, 363, 376, 382; and human rights protection, 27, 45–60; influence of, 23, 44, 49, 81; and legitimacy of human rights standards, 1–6, 19–20, 22–23, 28, 37–38, 52–53, 107, 287, 295, 296, 298, 317, 318, 323, 326, 387, 389–401, 420, 427–35; in Marxist theory, 172, 179, 181; protection of, 152, 372; reinterpretation of, 27–28, 49–60, 69, 129; relativity of, 3, 23–26, 41 n.25, 45, 65, 69, 90–91, 122, 292, 293, 322, 346, 364; and research on human rights standards, 389–93, 395–401; and social order, 87–91; and survival of indigenous minorities, 363, 365–83; traditions of, 3, 81, 180, 182, 289–90; traditions of in Latin America, 253, 254, 256–62, 265–66, 270

da Cunha, Manuela Carneiro, 12–13, 69, 368

Customary law, 368, 377; of Australian Aboriginals, 301–18 passim, 350; concept of, 288–91

Customary practice, 346, 358

Dealy, Glenn, 257, 258–59

Deas, Erica, 340, 341

Deloria, Vine, 209

Democracy, 52, 76, 178, 409; and culture, 54, 59; and human rights, 48, 56–57, 59–60, 128, 145, 179, 212; in Latin America, 253–57, 259, 260, 262, 264, 265–68, 269, 270; and Marxist theory, 167, 170, 173, 174–75, 180, 184. See also Pro-democracy movement (China)

Deng Xiaoping, 65, 72

Development agencies, 286

Development law, 381

Diamond, Larry, 254

Discrimination, 234, 243, 346, 350, 388, 417; against indigenous peoples, 210, 219 n.86, 224, 227, 241; in Australia, 316, 319, 320, 326; countering of, 230–33; systemic, 223, 224, 226, 227, 235, 236. *See also* Antidiscrimination law; Racism; various indigenous groups

Domestic law, 346, 358, 394, 404, 409–10, 415; and international law, 374, 375–76, 378, 380–81, 382

Donnelly, Jack, 41 n.25, 81, 396, 411, 418, 419

Douglas, Mary, 88, 98

Dulles, John Foster, 408

Durkheim, Emile, 276, 289

Dworkin, Ronald, 108, 137, 138, 145; and liberal theory, 401–10, 418, 419

Economic and social rights, 7, 388, 394; from a liberal perspective, 137, 404; from a Marxist perspective, 163, 166, 169, 170, 171, 172, 173, 174, 183, 184; from a personalist perspective, 105, 107, 108, 120, 122, 126, 129

Economic development, and Marxist theory, 173–75, 180, 181, 184, 417. *See also* Economic and social rights

Einfield, Justice Marcus, 351

El Salvador, 258

Empowered democracy. *See* Unger, Roberto

Empowerment, of indigenous peoples, 210, 356

The Encyclopedia of Philosophy, 108, 109, 111

Engels, Friedrich, 173, 174, 344, 411

Enlightenment, philosophy of: as basis for human rights standards, 45, 57, 58, 84, 192, 193, 211; as basis of liberalism, 106, 122, 128; and Western cultural prejudices, 177–78

Environmentalism, 122, 243, 286, 287, 291, 292, 410

Equality, principle of, 94–95, 168, 183, 193, 210–11, 345; in Australia, 299, 305, 318, 319, 323, 326; and liberalism, 404, 405, 406, 407, 410, 419; and Marxism, 419. *See also* Gender equality

Equal Opportunities Act (1985, Western Australia), 320

Equal Opportunity Act (1977, Victoria, Australia), 320

Equal Opportunity Act (1984, South Australia), 319

Equal Rights Amendment (United States), 203, 340

Esprit, 105, 109, 110, 113, 114, 115, 117

Ethnic minorities, 68, 96–97, 296, 297, 318–23, 326, 363, 367. *See also* Minorities

Ethnocentrism, 38; and cultural relativism, 24, 25; definition of, 23–24; and indigenous peoples, 205, 206; influence of, 24, 39, 75, 95, 96

Ethnocide, 193, 208, 209

Europe, 89, 269

European Convention on the Protection of Human Rights and Fundamental Freedoms, 30

European Human Rights Commission, 324

Evatt, Justice Elizabeth, 351

Falk, Richard, 9, 75, 128, 364–65; and "intolerabilities," 128, 129, 155

False Necessity, 124

Fang Lizhi, 66, 67

Fein, Helen, 95

Feminist Politics and Human Nature, 345

Fennoscandia, 364

Finland, 365, 370

First International Indigenous Women's Conference (1989), 343–44

First Nations. *See* Aboriginal peoples (Canada); Indigenous peoples; North American Indians

First Peoples. *See* Aboriginal peoples (Canada); Indigenous peoples; North American Indians

Fortes, Meyer, 288

Fourth Russell Tribunal (1980, Rotterdam), 198

Fox, Matthew, 56

France, 105, 109, 114–15

Freedom, concept of: in human rights theory, 396, 397, 399, 400; in liberalism, 139, 406, 408, 411; in Marxism, 167, 170, 171, 173, 177–78, 184, 413, 417, 419, 420

Frei, Eduardo, 263

French Declaration of Rights (1946), 116, 117, 120

French Declaration of the Rights of Man and Citizen (1789), 116, 117, 120, 128

Fruhling, Hugo, 12

Fuller, Lon, 145

Fundamentalism, 45, 58, 59. *See also* Islamic law

Ghandi, Mahatma, 56
Geertz, Clifford, 24–26
Gender equality, 354–56; and indigenous peoples, 84, 203–4, 227, 232, 237–38. *See also* Status of women
Genocide, 95, 96, 97, 155, 193; and indigenous peoples, 208, 222, 303, 304
Genocide Conventions: (1948) 96; (1987) 208
Gerhardy v. Brown (Australia), 310, 311
German Democratic Republic, 402
Ghana, 93
Goody, Jack, 290
Green, Leslie, 194
Greens, the, 56, 57, 243, 291
Guerilla movements. *See* Resistance movements

Harvard Law School, 110
Hellman, John, 113, 114
Herskovits, Melville J., 25, 27, 388
Hinduism, 49, 52
Hobsbawm, Eric, 289
Howard, Rhoda E., 10, 50, 69, 411, 418, 419
Human being, concept of. *See* Humanity
Human dignity, concept of, 81, 82, 107, 129; in China, 73, 74, 76; and conservatism, 95–97, 99; definition of, 83–85; as an expression of human rights, 91, 207, 364, 367; and human rights theory, 396, 397, 399, 400; and liberalism, 406, 407, 408, 410, 411; and Marxism, 413, 417; violations of, 48, 89, 108
Humanism, 211
Humanity, 92–93, 347, 358, 396, 419; according to Marx, 167–68; definitions of, 69–73, 74, 86–87, 91–93, 99, 276, 345, 351, 352; indigenous concepts of, 191, 192, 199–200, 202, 365; and *self*; 367–68
Human nature, 121, 166, 171
Human rights: codes, 222–23, 224, 228, 346–47; concepts of, 81–82, 128–29, 194, 195, 269, 382, 392–401; consensus on, 3, 81, 85, 99; cross-cultural foundations of, 388–89; cross-cultural perspectives on, 4, 20–29, 38–40, 45–46, 51, 123, 155–56, 183, 234, 287, 365, 428, 429, 430, 434; cultural legitimacy of, 54, 363, 364–70, 375–76, 378–82, 389–401; definitions of, 46, 82–83, 194–95, 363–64; development, evolution, and reinterpretation of, 48, 51, 52, 53–54, 122–23, 128–29, 346–47, 358–59;

development of through internal cultural discourse, 3–4, 5, 7, 21, 26, 27, 28, 29, 37–38, 51, 129, 240, 287, 316, 380; discrepancy between theory and practice, 1, 2, 54, 340, 347, 358, 388–89, 391, 435; foundations of, 21, 44, 51–53, 94, 99–100, 345, 387–88, 391, 395–401; implementation of, 1, 3, 21–23, 46, 51, 339, 340, 357–59; justification of, 7, 29, 50–51, 395–98, 399–401, 405–6; in non-Western societies, 22, 30, 39, 45, 47, 58, 59, 87, 94–95, 129; and politics, 52, 56, 430–31; protection of, 45, 48, 54–56, 56–57, 60, 268–69; relevance of, 75, 87; study of, 389–401, 428, 433–35; theory of, 105, 106, 107, 108, 118, 120–24, 126–28, 179, 392–98, 399–401; theory of, according to Maritain, 105, 106, 108–24, 127–28, 129; theory of, according to Mounier, 105, 106, 108–20, 127–28, 129; theory of, according to Unger, 105, 106, 108–16, 124–28, 129; and the Universal Declaration of Human Rights, 393–401; Western influence on, 8, 22, 39, 45, 50, 60 n.2, 75, 99, 106, 107–8, 177, 295, 341, 348, 428, 429. *See also* International standards of human rights; Liberalism; Marxism; Universality of human rights; Violations of human rights; individual indigenous groups; individual countries
Human Rights and Equal Opportunity Commission (Australia), 319, 326
Human Rights and Equal Opportunity Commission Act (1986, Australia), 319
Human Rights Commissions, 223, 224, 226, 227, 229–31, 233, 240, 243; Australian, 319, 326; Canadian, 232; European, 324; Inter-American, 268–69; New Brunswick, 228, 240; Ontario, 227; United Nations, 387–88; Yukon, 232. *See also* Anti-Discrimination Boards
Human Rights in Africa: Cross-Cultural Perspectives, 8
Human rights law, 1, 66; analysis of, 66 n.12, 195, 433, 435; cross-cultural perspectives on, 229, 235, 236, 365; and culture, 46–60; and domestic law, 374, 375–76, 378, 380–81, 382; and indigenous peoples, 191–93, 198, 206–7, 209–10, 212, 228, 357, 371–76, 377, 378, 382; and individualism, 194, 199, 203; as protection for human rights, 48, 58, 207, 373–74; theory,

Human rights law (*continued*)
44–45, 46, 393–94. *See also* Antidiscrimination law; Customary law; Domestic law; Islamic law
Humphrey, John, 387
Hutterites, the, 89, 151
Hyndman, Patricia, 13, 221

Idealistic personalism. *See* Personalism
ILO (International Labor Organization), 391; Convention No. 107, 342–43; Convention 169, 239
Immigration Restriction Act 1901 (Australia), 297
India, 53, 54, 57, 85, 171, 355
Indian Act (1951, Canada; amended, 1985), 192–93, 200, 232, 237, 238, 241
Indian affairs law, 191–92
Indian Claims Commission Act (1946, United States), 205
Indian Conditions: A Survey, 197
Indian Law Resource Center (Washington, D.C.), 195
Indian Nations Union (Brazil), 277, 283
Indian Reorganization Act (1934, United States), 200
Indians. *See* North American Indians
Indian Self-Government in Canada, 197
Indian Statute (1973, Brazil), 283
Indians of Brazil: discrimination against, 276–77, 278, 282, 284; government colonization policy toward, 278–82; rights of, 276, 279, 280–86; and relationship with military, 278–82; Yanomami, 277, 279–82, 285, 286, 292–93
Indian Tribes: A Continuing Quest For Survival, 196
Indigenous peoples, 48, 221; cultural survival of, 57, 286, 363, 365–69, 375, 377, 378, 381; and international standards of human rights, 47–48, 292, 342–43, 345, 353, 372–76; rights of, 81, 83–84, 97, 118, 324, 364, 366, 369, 371–81; rights of in a multicultural society, 296, 316, 317. *See also* Aboriginal peoples (Canada); Australian Aboriginals; Indians of Brazil; North American Indians; the Sami
Individualism, 93, 106, 183, 366; concepts of, 98–99, 222, 276; indigenous concepts of, 199, 202–4, 276; Marxist theory of, 170–71

Individual rights, 107, 126, 145; as basis of human rights, 82, 89, 94–95, 364, 365, 367, 393; in China, 70, 72, 75; cross-cultural perspectives on, 382, 428–29; liberal theory of, 137–55, 404–5; from a personalist perspective, 116–28; versus collective rights, 83, 99, 122, 143–54, 171, 349–50, 366, 373, 404, 405. *See also* Aboriginal peoples (Canada); Australian Aboriginals; Indians of Brazil; Indigenous peoples; North American Indians; the Sami
Inter-American Commission on Human Rights, 268–69
Inter-American Court on Human Rights, 269
Inter-American Development Bank, 287
Inter-American System for Protection of Human Rights, 268
International Bill of Human Rights, 106, 128, 352, 411, 418, 419; as foundation of international human rights standards, 392–401
International Commission on Folk Law and Legal Pluralism (1986), 356–57
International Conventions on the Elimination of All Forms of Racial Discrimination (1966/1975), 310–11, 319, 340, 341, 350
International Covenants on Civil and Political Rights, 7, 30, 31, 193, 232, 238, 340, 341; Article 27 of, 372, 373, 375, 376, 378
International Covenants on Economic, Social and Cultural Rights (1966/1975), 7, 340, 341
International human rights movement, 5, 6, 22–23, 38
International standards of human rights: in China, 74–76; cross-cultural approach to, 5–6, 15, 38–40, 179–80, 352–53; cultural legitimacy of, 2–6, 22–23, 75, 295, 385, 389–93, 395–401, 427–31, 433, 435; and democracy, 46–47, 179; implementation of, 1, 55–56, 59–60, 155, 295, 300, 395; improvement of, 1, 108, 181–83; interpretations of, 110, 129, 394–95, 404–5, 414–15; and Marxism, 162–63, 165–73, 179–80; and rights of ethnic minorities, 300, 341; and rights of indigenous peoples, 207, 232, 239, 240–45, 287, 341, 342–43, 345; and rights of women, 341. *See also* Culture

Intifada, 56
Inuit, the, 196, 238, 244
Iran, 34, 60, 61 n.7, 355
Islamic culture, 33–38, 54, 57–58, 172
Islamic law (Shari°a), 33–38, 39, 40, 51, 427
Israel, 97

Jagger, Alison, 345
Japan, 81
Japanese Canadians, 95, 135
Jews, 95, 97–98
Judeo-Christian traditions, 87, 88

Kaiapo Indians (Brazil), 291–92
Kant, Immanuel, 406, 407, 410
Kenya, 355
Khomeini, Imam, 57, 58, 59
King, Martin Luther, Jr., 130 n.11
Klenner, Herman, 401, 402, 411–12, 413, 420
Kothari, Smitu, 52, 53–54
Kriele, Martin, 413
Kymlicka, Will, 138, 152, 153

Lacroix, Jean, 112
Ladd, John, 24
Land rights, 363, 366, 369, 381; of Australian Aboriginals, 307–13, 314–15, 352–53, 354; of Brazilian Indians, 276–85; of North American Indians, 205–6, 209; of the Sami, 369, 370, 371–81. See also Treaty rights
Lasswell, Harold D., 44, 195
The Last Temptation of Christ, 59
Latin America, 109; Catholic church in, 257, 258, 265, 268, 277, 282, 287; evolution of society, 253–62, 263–68, 270–71; and human rights, 253–60, 262–71; liberalization of, 258, 259, 260, 261, 271. See also individual countries
Law Association for Asia and the Pacific (LAWASIA), 323–24
Law of return (Israel), 97
Law reform. See Antidiscrimination law; Australian Law Reform Commission
Leacock, Eleanor, 344
Leary, Virginia, 10
Lenin, V., 402, 413
A Letter Concerning Toleration, 402–403
Liberalism, 8, 105, 154, 389, 400; and collective rights, 97–99, 106, 118, 125, 133, 134–

36, 141–54; and human rights doctrine, 401, 402–411, 418–20; and individual rights, 106, 121, 138–40; and personalism, 107, 113–14, 118, 121; and self-determination, 146–47; theories of, 137–41, 142–43
Liberals, types of, 133–34, 141, 144, 149–51, 151–54
Liberal societies, and human rights, 82, 85–86, 87, 91, 93, 94–97, 98
Liberation theology, 52
Liberty, concept of, 164, 165, 166, 170
Lindholm, Tore, 14, 75, 155, 433
Linz, Juan J., 254
Locke, John, 401, 402–403, 406, 407, 408, 409, 419, 420
Lovelace, Sandra, 151, 193, 238
Lukacs, Gyorgy, 292
Lukes, Steven, 410
Lung-chu Chen, 44, 195

Mabo v. State of Queensland, 311
McChesney, Allan, 12
MacCormack, Neil, 151
McDonald, Michael, 10–11, 97, 118, 366
McDougal, Myres S., 44, 195
MacKinnon, Catharine, 355
Man and the State, 110
Manitoba, 234, 235
Mansell, M., 313, 316
Maralinga Tjarutja Land Rights Act 1984 (Australia), 309
Marcos, Ferdinand, 56
Maritain, Jacques, 35; and natural law, 120–24; and personalism, 105–16, 127–28, 129
Marx, Karl, 162, 166, 184, 401, 402; and critique of human rights ideology, 163–65, 182; and cultural traditions, 172–73; economic theory of, 173–75, 181, 182; and human needs, 167–73, 175–77, 178; Marxist doctrine of human rights, 411, 412, 413, 419, 420
Marxism, 8, 105, 107, 121, 134, 389, 402, 413; approach to human rights of, 162–84; human rights doctrine of, 401, 409, 411–18, 419–20; in Latin America, 261–62; and personalism, 106, 109, 113–14, 117, 119, 120
Marxism and Human Rights, 411
Mead, George Herbert, 86
Meech Lake Accord (Canada), 142, 144
Mendes, Chico, 291

Mennonites, the, 147

Metis, the, 238

Mexico, 191, 201, 258, 261

Middle East, 97, 146

Mill, John Stuart, 138, 147, 407

Minorities, 135, 242, 322–23; protection of, 144, 407; rights of, 133, 135, 173, 239, 287, 291, 350, 406; rights of in Australia, 306, 309, 310–11, 314; rights of in Brazil, 284, 287; rights of in Canada, 84, 133, 136, 142, 193, 225, 236–37; rights of and liberalism, 142, 145–46, 147, 152–53. *See also* Collective rights; Ethnic minorities; various indigenous peoples

Modernization, 63 n.33, 92, 93; and China, 66, 75; negative effects of, 45, 49, 50, 57, 61 n.10; repudiation of, 48, 56, 61 n.10

Moore, Barrington, Jr., 50, 85

Moore, Henrietta, 345, 354, 355–56

Morality, 87–90, 211–12

Morsink, Johannes, 398

Moss, Wendy, 237, 244

Mounier, Emmanuel: and the 1946 French Declaration of Rights, 116–20; and personalism, 105–15, 124, 127–28, 129

Multiculturalism: in Australia, 296, 317, 318–23, 326; in Canada, 133, 142, 236

National Aboriginal Council (Australia), 312

Native American Church, 201, 204, 205, 209, 211

Native peoples. *See* Aboriginal peoples (Canada); Indigenous peoples; North American Indians

Native Women's Association of Canada, 244

Natural law, 44, 110, 212, 257, 259; and natural rights doctrine, 397, 398–99, 401; and personalism, 120–24

Natural resources. *See* Land rights

Navajo, the, 199, 200, 203, 205

Nazism, 90, 98, 116

Neutral state thesis (of liberalism), 138, 141, 143

New Brunswick Human Rights Commission, 228, 240

New South Wales, 296, 306, 309, 310, 319–20

New Zealand, 315, 317, 343

NGOs (Non-governmental organizations), 55–56, 268–70, 277, 283, 323–24, 340, 393

Nicaragua, 255, 261, 365

Nihilism, 24

Nonliberal societies, and human rights, 87, 94–95

Nonvirtuous state thesis (of liberalism), 138, 141, 143

Non-Western perspectives, on human rights, 22, 30, 39, 45, 47, 58, 59, 129

Nordahl, Richard, 11

North American Indians: definition of, 192–93; definition of Indian human rights, 194–96; human rights demands of, 197–98, 208–11; history of, 191–94; and religion, 201, 204, 205, 208–9, 211; social conditions of, 196–97, 204; values of, 198–207. *See also* Aboriginal peoples (Canada); Indigenous peoples; the Inuit

Northern Territory (Australia), 296, 308, 309, 312

Northwest Territories (Canada), 228, 234, 244; Human Rights Code (Draft), 244

Norway, 365, 370, 371–76, 380

Nuremberg Code, 346–47

Oakeshott, Michael, 145

O'Donnell, Guillermo, 253

Ombudsmen, 224, 320. *See also* Affirmative Action; Human Rights Commissions

One-child policy (China), 74, 75

On Liberty, 138

Ontario Human Rights Commission, 227

Organization of American States (OAS), 270, 277

Our Common Future (World Commission on Environment and Development), 210

Pakistan, 34, 58

Palestine, 415

Pan-Indianism, 201–2

Particularists, 154–55

Passion, An Essay on Personality, 114

Patterson, Orlando, 83, 94

Paz, Octavio, 211–12

People, The, 192, 199, 200, 201, 202, 206, 207

Perry, Michael, 124

Personalism, 105, 129; communitarian implications of, 111–13; definition of, 108–9, 111; and human rights, 116–28; influence on French law, 117–20; and natural law, 120–24; and personalist movement, 114–15; personalist perspectives, 105–8, 111,

128; versus liberalism and Marxism, 113–14, 119

Personalist and communitarian revolution. *See* Mounier, Emmanuel

Peru: and authoritarianism, 255, 260, 261; and human rights violations as social process, 262, 263, 266–68

Pinilla, General Rojas, 262

Pitjantjajara Land Rights Act 1981 (Australia), 308–9, 310

Pluralism, 397; in Latin America, 257, 259; and liberalism, 141, 143, 151, 403, 409

Poland, 54, 57, 60

Political humanism. *See* Maritain, Jacques

Political violence, in Latin America, 253, 254, 255, 259, 262, 264, 266–68, 270–71

Positive law, 44, 120–21, 288, 289, 290–91, 398

Private property, 125, 173, 174

Pro-democracy movement (China), 65, 66–69

Prohibition of Discrimination Act (1966, South Australia), 319

Property rights: in Marxism, 164, 170, 173, 174; in personalism, 106, 119, 120, 125, 126

Quebec, 142, 143, 147

Quebec Protestant School Boards, 143

Queensland, 296, 303, 309, 311, 312, 319

Racial Discrimination Act 1975 (Australia), 310, 319, 325

Racial Discrimination Act (1976, South Australia), 319

Racism, 95–97, 320. *See also* Discrimination

Radcliffe-Brown, A. R., 288–89

Ratzinger, Cardinal Joseph, 57

Rawls, John, and liberal theory, 137, 139, 140, 152, 155, 400, 405, 419

Raz, Joseph, 137, 140

Realistic personalism. *See* Personalism

REAL Women of Canada, 96

Reciprocity, principle of, 28, 396, 407

Reindeer Management Act (1971, Sweden; revised 1979), 379

Religion, 177, 178, 212, 324, 355; and indigenous peoples, 204–5, 208–9, 230. *See also* Catholicism; Native American Church

Renteln, Alison, 22

Ren Wending, 66

Repression. *See* Authoritarianism

Resistance movements, 54, 56, 264, 265, 266–67. *See also* Pro-democracy movement (China)

Rethinking Human Rights, 52

Richstone, Jeff, 244

The Rights of Man and Natural Law, 110

Rivero, Jean, 116, 120

"The Road to Damascus: Kairos and Conversion," 51–52, 53

Rushdie, Salman, 57–58

Sabato, Jorge F., 263

Said, Edward, 59

Sami, the (Norway), 364, 365, 369, 376; and the Alta Case, 371–76; culture of, 365–66, 370–71; land and resource development, 369, 370, 371–76; rights of, 365, 369, 370, 371–76; and the Sami Association, 370–71; and the Sami Rights Committee, 365, 372, 374, 375, 376, 377–78

Sami, the (Sweden): cultural survival of, 378; land and resource claims, 376–77, 380; rights of, 377, 378, 379, 380, 381; and the Sami Rights Committee, 377–78, 379, 380; and the Taxed Mountains Case, 376–81

Sami Act (Norway), 376

Sami Act (Sweden), 378–79

Sanders, Douglas, 237

Sarney, Jose, 281, 286

Saskatchewan, 234

Saudi Arabia, 34

Sawer, Marian, 355

Scheler, Max, 111, 113

Schlesinger, Arthur, Jr., 87

Schusky, E., 208

Schwarzer, Jorge, 263

Scorsese, Martin, 59

Secularism, 44–45

Self-determination, 415, 417; of Australian Aboriginals, 312, 343–45, 351–54; and cultural survival of indigenous peoples, 222, 225, 245, 363–82; liberal thesis of, 138–55; of North American Indians, 192, 204, 207, 209–10. *See also* Self-government

Self-government: for Australian aboriginals, 312, 313, 314, 354; for North American Indians, 195, 204, 207, 209–10; for indigenous peoples, 225, 238, 239–45

Self-identification, 136; for indigenous peoples, 237–38, 300

Sendero Luminoso, 267, 268
Sethi, Harsh, 52, 53–54
Shariʿa. See Islamic law
Shining Path. See Sendero Luminoso
Sidgwick, Henry, 155
Sieghart, Paul, 195
Sierra Leone, 97
Smith, Carsten, 374
Social change, and human rights, 91–93
Social Darwinism, 98
Social justice, 81, 82, 84–86, 87, 91, 99, 223, 224
Social order, 86, 87, 88–90, 93; and human rights, 87–90
South Africa, 90, 415
South Australia, 296, 306, 308, 310, 319
Soviet Union, 56, 90, 133, 175, 343, 398; minorities in, 146, 370
Status of women, 88, 89, 168; and affirmative action, 223, 233; cross-cultural perspectives on, 4, 23, 49, 74, 343, 345; and human rights, 68, 72, 85, 93, 204, 344, 349–50; and human rights law, 48, 339, 341, 345–49, 351; of indigenous women in Australia, 320, 341, 342, 343–45, 346, 348–59; of indigenous women in Canada, 84, 193, 203, 204, 217 n.57; of indigenous women, 232, 237–38, 239; in Islamic cultures, 176, 177, 178, 431, 435; Office for, in Australia, 350–51, 355. See also Gender equality
Statute of the International Court of Justice, 198
Sudan, the, 34, 434
Sun Yat-sen, 71, 72, 73
Supreme Court: of Australia, 304–5, 310–11; of Canada, 147, 238; of Norway, 372, 373, 374, 375; of Sweden, 377, 378, 379; of the United States, 205, 348
Svensson, Tom, 14
Sweden, 63 n.31, 365, 370, 376–81

Taha, Ustadh Mahmoud Mohammed, 51
Taking Rights Seriously, 108
Tasmania, 296, 303, 309, 319
Taxed Mountains Case (Sweden), 376–81, 382
Taylor, Charles, 139
Theory of Justice, 140
Third World, 47, 348, 434; and human rights, 51, 52, 53, 60 n.2, 129, 176, 340, 357, 428

Tiananmen Square, 56, 69
Tolerance, 61 n.7, 141, 242
Torres Strait Islands, 296, 311, 313
Torture, 29, 32, 50, 89, 90, 155
"Total Emancipation" thesis, 412–18
Transnational voluntary associations. See NGOs
Treaty rights, 206, 209–10, 211, 305, 315–16. See also Land rights
True Humanism, A Charter of Social Action, 115
Tuvaluan Constitution, 324–25

UNESCO, 22, 110, 115, 123, 208, 387–88
Unger, Roberto: "empowered democracy" concept of, 110, 112, 124–28; and personalism, 105–16; 129
United Kingdom, 298–99, 402, 410
United Nations, 194, 209, 345, 357, 393; and the development of the Universal Declaration of Human Rights, 395–98; and indigenous rights, 193, 232, 238, 239, 277, 342
United Nations Code of Conduct for Law Enforcement Officials (1979), 31
United Nations Commission on Human Rights, 387–88
United Nations Committee on the Elimination of Discrimination Against Women (CEDAW), 351
United Nations Convention Against Torture and Other Cruel, Inhuman, or Degrading Treatment or Punishment (1984), 32–33
United Nations Convention for the Elimination of All Forms of Discrimination Against Women (1980), 340, 347–48
United Nations Convention for the Elimination of All Forms of Racial Discrimination (1966), 310–11, 319, 340, 341, 350
United Nations Covenants on Civil and Political Rights (1966/1980), 7, 30, 31, 193, 232, 238, 340, 341; Article 27 of, 372, 373, 375, 376, 378
United Nations Covenants on Economic, Social, and Cultural Rights (1966/1975), 7, 340, 341
United Nations Human Rights Committee, 31–32, 372
United Nations Subcommission on the Prevention of Discrimination and the Protection of Minorities, 318

United Nations Working Group on Indigenous Peoples, 312–13
United Nations Working Group on Indigenous Populations, 318, 340, 342
United States, 198, 348, 357, 402; and international human rights covenants, 192, 340, 343, 410; and relationship with indigenous peoples, 3, 191, 196, 197, 201, 202, 205, 300, 315, 317
Universal Declaration of Human Rights, 1948 (UDHR), 1, 7, 74, 194, 339, 340, 348, 352; Article 1 of, 276, 395–97, 398, 399, 406, 407; and cultural diversity, 22, 110, 387, 395, 399–401; as embodiment of fundamental human rights, 67, 75, 84, 99, 346, 347, 393, 396, 399–401; 411; Preamble of, 398, 399
Universalists, 44, 154–55, 436
Universality of human rights, 1, 6, 81, 207; concept of, 5, 8, 44, 69, 87, 99–100, 431–32; cross-cultural perspectives on, 3, 7, 20–23, 25–26, 65, 73–76, 91, 93, 163, 169, 364, 432–34; and human rights theory, 399–401; and liberalism, 155, 407–8, 409–11; and Marxism, 162–63, 166, 167–73, 175–81, 182, 183, 414–15, 420; and pro-democracy movement (China), 66–69; revision of, 6, 291, 432–33
Universal suffrage, 95
Utilitarianism, 120–21, 138–39, 140, 143, 155
Uruguay, and authoritarianism, 253, 255, 258, 259–60; and human rights violations as social process, 262, 263, 264

Valenzuela, Arturo, 254
Vatican Council II, 258
Veliz, Claudio, 256, 257–58
Victoria (Australia), 296, 306, 309, 314, 320
Violations of human rights, 1, 55–56, 89–90, 155, 391, 415; in Canada, 95–97; and cultural relativity, 3, 49, 180, 430; of indigenous peoples, 96–97, 198, 207; and "intolerable practices," 49–51; in Latin America, 253, 254, 255, 258, 262–68, 270–71; and Marxist theory, 162, 166, 181–82,

184; underlying causes of, 19–20. See also Discrimination; Social justice
Virginia Bill of Rights, 120
Volkisch ideology, 98
Voluntary Fund for Indigenous Populations, 342

Walker, R. B. J., 49, 50
War Measures Act (1970, Canada), 134
Weaver, Sally, 237
Weber, Max, 290
Wei Jinsheng, 66, 77 n.8
Welfare, of the individual, 138–39
Western Australia, 296, 306, 309, 310, 320
Western constitutionalism, 259
Western democracy, 70, 340
Western influence: on China, 70–72, 73–74; on human rights theory, 39, 45, 50, 60 n.2, 75, 99, 106, 107–8, 177, 428, 429; on international human rights covenants, 348; on international human rights standards, 8, 22, 75, 295, 341; on non-Western cultures, 47, 175–76. See also Liberalism; Modernization
Western theological tradition, 108, 109
White Australia policy, 297, 326
Wiarda, Howard, 256
Women. See Gender equality; Status of women
World Bank, 287, 292
World Council of Indigenous Peoples, 222
World War II, 397

Yanomami, Davi, 292, 293
Yanomami Indians (Brazil), 277, 279–82, 285, 286, 292–93
Yugoslavia, 133
Yukon, the, 228, 229, 231, 232, 233, 234, 241
Yukon Human Rights Act, 228, 231
Yukon Human Rights Commission, 232; Annual Report of (1988), 229

Zapata, Francisco, 261
Zion, James W., 11, 221

This book has been set in Linotron Galliard. Galliard was designed for Mergenthaler in 1978 by Matthew Carter. Galliard retains many of the features of a sixteenth century typeface cut by Robert Granjon but has some modifications which gives it a more contemporary look.

Printed on acid-free paper.